KB082112

특례영어

실전문제 총정리

특례영어 실전문제 총정리

하지석 지음

초판 1쇄 | 2012년 05월 20일
개정 1쇄 | 2015년 02월 20일
개정 2쇄 | 2018년 08월 20일

지은이 | 하지석
펴낸이 | 신현운
펴는곳 | 연인M&B
기   획 | 여인화
디자인 | 이승신 이희정
마케팅 | 박한동
등   록 | 2000년 3월 7일 제2-3037호
주   소 | 143-874 서울특별시 광진구 자양로 56(자양동 680-25) 2층
전   화 | (02)455-3987   팩스 | (02)3437-5975
홈주소 | www.yeoninmb.co.kr
이메일 | yeonin7@hanmail.net

값 39,000원

ⓒ 하지석 2012 Printed in Korea

ISBN 978-89-6253-115-2 03740

이 책은 연인M&B가 저작권자와의 계약에 따라 발행한 것이므로 본사의 허락 없이는
어떠한 형태나 수단으로도 이 책의 내용을 이용하지 못합니다.
잘못된 책은 바꾸어 드립니다.

재외국민특례입학
일반 편입학 및 학사 편입학, 공무원 시험, 토익·토플

최고의
적중률

개정판

특례 영어

실전문제 총정리

하지석 지음

METRO

cafe

연인M&B

훈민정음에도 나와 있듯이 언어란 많은 사람들이 가장 쉽게 배워 쓸 수 있도록 만들어졌습니다. 그럼에도 불구하고 어린 시절부터 성인이 되어서까지 치열한 경쟁 구도 속에 우리는 평생 영어 시험이라는 장벽을 넘어서기 위해 여전히 많은 시간과 경제적인 투자를 합니다.

이 '종합 문제집' 『특례영어 실전문제 총정리』는 한국에서 치러지는 모든 영어 시험의 유형들을 파트별로 나누어 〈재외국민특례입학, 일반 편입학 및 학사 편입학, 공무원 시험, 토익·토플〉 등에서 나올 수 있는 모든 시험의 유형을 총망라했음에도 불구하고 문제를 풀면서 영어를 이해할 수 있으며, 영어 시험에 자신감을 가질 수 있도록 문제들을 수록했을 뿐만 아니라 문제에 대한 상세한 해설로 누구나 혼자서도 충분히 공부할 수 있으며, 여러분들이 치르는 어떤 시험이라도 '최고의 적중률'을 보여 줄 수 있는 완벽한 종합 문제집이라 자신합니다.

이 '종합 문제집' 『특례영어 실전문제 총정리』와 함께 여러분은 영어 시험이라는 장벽이 그리 높지 않음을 스스로 깨닫고, 평생 영어로부터 해방되시길 진심으로 바랍니다.

2012년 5월
하지석

특례영어 실전문제 총정리

CONTENTS

정답 및 해설

ENGLISH

PART I

English Structure

1. 동사의 종류

※ 다음 빈칸에 알맞은 것은?

1. The patient wanted to know how the drug would _____ her body.

   ① effect   ② harmful   ③ affect   ④ sick

2. He died _____ that his friend had to pay for his funeral.

   ① too poorly   ② so poorly   ③ too poor   ④ so poor

3. Even if no violation of law is discovered, it _____ troubling questions of political ethics.

   ① rises   ② raises   ③ has risen   ④ arises

4. "Which one would you like, this one or that one?"
   "It _____."

   ① is not matter to me   ② doesn't matter to me
   ③ matters not me   ④ matters me not

5. The child in the full health of his mind will put his hand flat on the summer turf, feel it, and give a little shiver of private glee at the elastic firmness of the globe. He is not thinking how well it will _____ for some game or to feed sheep upon.

   ① do   ② give   ③ make   ④ pay

6. It is polite not to speak at the dinner table until you are _____ .

   ① spoken to   ② of speaking
   ③ speaking   ④ in speaking

7. Do not _____ a trick on innocent people.

    ① give   ② do   ③ play   ④ take

8. Experts set themselves up as authorities on any matter-technical, social, or political. They seem to have all the answers and enjoy giving advice and making suggestions. They are very happy to give advice on any problem and do not mind _____ their vast knowledge with their co-workers. Their motto is; "Ask me anything; I'll give you the answer."

    ① providing   ② giving   ③ offering   ④ sharing

9. "Have you anything to _____ ?" The custom officer generally asks.

    ① reveal   ② declare   ③ expose   ④ mention

10. _____ on my back on the tiled floor, I was full of worried questions.

    ① Laying   ② Lying   ③ Lay   ④ Lie

11. Noam Chomsky, a professor at MIT, _____ as one of America's greatest linguists.

    ① has acknowledgement   ② is acknowledged
    ③ acknowledges   ④ acknowledged

12. We _____ an apartment when we lived in San Francisco, but it was very expensive.

    ① borrowed   ② were using
    ③ loaned   ④ rented

13. "I _____ your present very much."
    "You're quite welcome."

    ① appreciate   ② thank   ③ welcome   ④ grudge

14. It is not what you have but what you are that _____.

    ① believes   ② counts   ③ hands in   ④ gives in

15. If we hurry we can _____ there in time for the opening speech.

    ① go to   ② get to   ③ go   ④ get

16. I always _____ asleep as soon as I get into bed.

    ① fall   ② go   ③ get   ④ turn

17. It is generally believed that men are created _____.

    ① to be equal   ② equally   ③ as equal   ④ equal

18. "All the people in this village have black hair."
   "Yes, they all _____ each other."

    ① resemble as   ② resemble with
    ③ resemble   ④ resemble to

19. We might still catch the train if we _____.

    ① make hurry   ② haste   ③ make haste   ④ hastily

20. It will do you _____ to have a holiday.

    ① well   ② better   ③ good   ④ fine

21. It was also a way of _____ our teacher for his forty years of faithful service, and of _____ our respects to the fatherland which was vanishing.

    ① thinking - playing   ② thanking - paying
    ③ showing - sending   ④ waving - bowing

22. An electrical motor _____ electrical energy into mechanical energy.

    ① converting   ② converts

    ③ is converted   ④ which converts

23. "Yesterday was my birthday. My mother _____."

    ① made a cake to me   ② made a cake me

    ③ made for me a cake   ④ made me a cake

24. X-rays are able to pass through objects and thus make _____ details that are otherwise impossible to observe.

    ① they are visible   ② it visible

    ③ visible   ④ visibly

25. A : As a result of his failure in business he became penniless.

   =B : His failure in business _____ him penniless.

    ① became   ② left   ③ allowed   ④ got

2. 동사의 시제

※ 다음 빈칸에 알맞은 것은?

1. I will go home for a vacation as soon as I _____ my exams.

   ① am finishing   ② will finish

   ③ finish   ④ finished

2. By the time we got to the airport, our plane _____.

   ① has already left   ② had already left

   ③ left   ④ had already been left

3. I try to live by old say that goes "time and tied _____ for no man."

   ① waiting   ② wait   ③ have wait   ④ was waiting

4. If it _____ rain tomorrow, we'll have a picnic.

   ① wouldn't   ② doesn't   ③ didn't   ④ won't

5. "Did you take your medicine ?"

   "Yes, I took it just before I _____ home."

   ① leaving   ② have left   ③ left   ④ leave

6. Before becoming president in 1928, Herbert Hoover _____ as Secretary of Commerce.

   ① has served   ② was served

   ③ had served   ④ serving

7. "What will happen?"

"By next June we _____ a million refrigerators."

① will have sold ② sell ③ shall sell ④ will sell

8. This is the first time I _____ a car.

① drive ② drove ③ have driven ④ had driven

9. She has been here _____.

① after 1983 ② in 1983 ③ for 1983 ④ since 1983

10. Tom called me last night because I _____ him earlier.

① have visited ② paid a visit to
③ would pay a visit to ④ had visited

11. We can go when the ground _____.

① is drying ② has dried ③ dried ④ dry

12. She _____ a nurse for over three years when she decided to qualify as a doctor.

① is ② is being ③ had been ④ has been

13. "Does he believe in God ?"

"No, he _____ in God."

① don't believe ② isn't believing
③ doesn't believe ④ wasn't believing

14. The shoes _____ you well.

① fit ② is fitting ③ fits ④ not fit

15. "Are you going to stay at the lake?"

    "If I _____, I'll let you know."

    ① stay   ② will stay   ③ would stay   ④ staying

16. What did you do when _____?

    ① he's making a noise   ② he makes a noise

    ③ he made noise   ④ he made a noise

17. "Is this the last examination we have to take?"

    "Yes, but there _____ another test three months from now."

    ① will have been   ② will be

    ③ is   ④ was

18. "Anne works very hard." "In fact, I think she _____ right now."

    ① studying   ② is studied

    ③ is studying   ④ studies

19. "Where is George going this afternoon?"

    "He is being _____ to see the Statue of Liberty."

    ① take   ② to take   ③ taking   ④ taken

20. We _____ to read all of Chapter Eight.

    ① suppose   ② are supposing

    ③ are to suppose   ④ are supposed

21. This is _____ such a thing.

    ① my first time of seeing   ② my first time to see

    ③ the first time I have ever seen   ④ my first time I have ever seen

22. I have lived in Busan _____.

    ① for six years   ② sis years before

    ③ since six years   ④ six years ago

23. Have you ever _____ in an airplane?

    ① gone to   ② up there

    ③ been up   ④ gone flying

24. The clock _____ three and they left.

    ① hit   ② sounded   ③ struck   ④ set

25. When she got home she found that they _____ searching for her for three days.

    ① are   ② were   ③ have been   ④ had been

26. It _____ all week up until last night.

    ① have rained   ② rained

    ③ was raining   ④ been raining

27. A : "Have you visited the new library yet?"

    B : _____.

    ① It closes early   ② I was there just yesterday

    ③ It's a really nice one   ④ I like the new design

※ 다음 빈칸에 알맞은 것은?

1. You _____ me because I never said that I would meet you there.

   ① must be misunderstanding　　② had to misunderstand

   ③ must misunderstand　　④ must have misunderstood

2. "Which rug did your wife buy?"

   "The blue one, but I _____ bought the brown one."

   ① should rather have　　② would rather have

   ③ rather had　　④ would have rather

3. Bill didn't come to his nine o'clock class yesterday.

   He _____ himself.

   ① must overslept　　② must be oversleeping

   ③ must have overslept　　④ must had overslept

4. "You ought to have done it last night."

   "Yes, I _____."

   ① ought to　　② should　　③ must　　④ should have

5. I _____ play baseball at school.

   ① am used to　　② get used to　　③ use to　　④ used to

6. _____ you like a cup of coffee?

   ① Would　　② Could　　③ Shall　　④ May

7. Susan and I can go to the lecture, _____.

   ① but neither can Charles   ② but Charles can't

   ③ and so Charles can   ④ and Charles also can

8. The distance from the earth to the moon _____ measured today by radar or by laser.

   ① is easy to   ② easily being   ③ can be easy to ④ can easily be

9. We can no more explain a passion to a person who has never experienced it than we _____ explain light to the blind.

   ① can   ② cannot   ③ don't   ④ must

10. Since the road is wet this morning, _____ last night.

   ① it must rain   ② it must raining

   ③ it must have rained   ④ it must have been rain

11. It's the first time that she has been to the United States, _____?

   ① isn't she   ② isn't it   ③ hasn't she   ④ hasn't it

12. Whales go under water, _____ ?

   ① shall they   ② do they   ③ aren' t they   ④ don' t they

13. "You'd better stay, _____ you ?"

   ① wouldn't   ② hadn't   ③ won't   ④ didn't

14. Since your roommate is visiting her family this weekend, _____ you like to have dinner with us tonight?

   ① will   ② won't   ③ do   ④ wouldn't

15. We _____ the letter yesterday, but it didn't arrive.

   ① must receive   ② must have received

   ③ ought to receive   ④ ought to have received

4. 태

※ 다음 빈칸에 알맞은 것은?

1. The music at the party was very loud and could _____ from far away.

   ① hear   ② heard   ③ be heard   ④ have heard

2. Jim was married _____ Audrey on October 5.

   ① with   ② at   ③ between   ④ to

3. "If someone falls into deep water and can't swim, what will become of him?"
   "He will probably be _____."

   ① drowning   ② drown   ③ drowned   ④ the drowning

4. We _____ to hear the news.

   ① were all surprise   ② were all surprised
   ③ were all surprising   ④ were all to surprise

5. "When did the lecture begin?"
   "When all the students _____, the professor began his lecture."

   ① seated   ② sit
   ③ were seated   ④ seat

5. 가정법

※ 다음 빈칸에 알맞은 것은?

1. His doctor suggested that he _____ a short leave of absence.

   ① will take   ② would take   ③ take   ④ took

2. Sarah demanded that she _____ given a refund.

   ① is   ② be   ③ will be   ④ was

3. "What did the policeman say to you?"
   "He demanded that I _____ him my driver's license."

   ① show   ② showed   ③ would show   ④ will show

4. _____ today, he would get there by Friday.

   ① Would he leave   ② Were he to leave
   ③ Was he leaving   ④ If he leaves

5. A : Miss Park supervises three hundred employees.
   B : _____.

   ① Come to think of it, I don't have any idea
   ② If I did that, I'd have a nervous breakdown
   ③ I can't get along without you
   ④ I'm worried about my stress

6. If your hair _____, you'd look almost exactly like my sister.

   ① was little darker   ② was a little darker
   ③ were little darker   ④ were a little darker

7. I'd rather you _____ anything about it for the time being.

   ① do   ② didn't do   ③ don't   ④ didn't

8. "Poor Brian, he lost the contest."
   "If he had been luckier he might _____."

   ① won   ② have won   ③ win   ④ have win

9. I could have gone better if I _____ more time.

   ① have had   ② had
   ③ will have had   ④ had had

10. "I am very tired."
   "You would be less tired if you _____ to bed earlier."

   ① go   ② went   ③ have gone   ④ had gone

11. I am sure that something has gone wrong with their car ; _____ our guests would have arrived long ago.

   ① otherwise   ② yet   ③ then   ④ therefore

12. "What can I do for you?"
   "If you _____ see Mr. Allen, give him my regards."

   ① should   ② would   ③ shall   ④ will

13. If I had time _____ see that new movie at the University Theater.

   ① I'll   ② I shall   ③ I may   ④ I'd

14. It is time that we _____ home.

   ① go   ② shall go   ③ went   ④ have gone

15. "He would go to see you."

"_____ he did not come?"

① What if   ② What come   ③ Where for   ④ Whether for

16. "How are you feeling now?"

"I feel as if I _____ tired."

① were   ② am   ③ is   ④ be

17. "Were you at the concert last night?"

"No, but _____, I would have enjoyed the music."

① I went   ② did I   ③ had I gone   ④ I had gone

18. "It is too bad you didn't win the prize."

"It sure is. I _____ a new car if I had."

① bought   ② would buy

③ would have bought   ④ had bought

19. I wouldn't have called her unless _____.

① you have told me to   ② you haven't told me to

③ you had told me to   ④ you hadn't told me to

20. If the United States had built more homes for poor people in 1955, the housing problems now in some parts of this country _____ so serious.

① wouldn't be   ② will not have been

③ wouldn't have been   ④ would have not been

21. "May I have the loan?" "_____ you offer good security."

① But   ② Unless   ③ Provided   ④ But for

※ 다음 빈칸에 알맞은 것은?

1. A : Shall we go?

   B : No, _____.

   ① not allowed   ② let's not   ③ shall not   ④ it's not

2. We had no choice _____ his strict conditions.

   ① to accept   ② over accepting   ③ but to accept   ④ about accepting

3. I must remember _____ Jone that the garden needs watering.

   ① reminded   ② to remind
   ③ reminding   ④ to be reminded of

4. Jone F. Kennedy was the first Catholic _____ elected President of the United States.

   ① having been   ② who   ③ he was   ④ to be

5. He was never _____ his wife and children again.

   ① to see   ② see   ③ seen   ④ have seen

6. I wanted to discuss the matter with my uncle, but he was not an easy man _____.

   ① to be talked to ② for talking   ③ to talk   ④ to talk to

7. She _____ very kind-hearted.

   ① believes to be   ② believes in to be
   ③ is believed to be   ④ is believed in being

8. "How do you know these shoes are handmade?"

   "I saw _____ myself."

   ① them to make   ② them made

   ③ made them   ④ make them

9. "I asked my mother to _____ me go to the end-of-year party."

   ① allow   ② leave   ③ enable   ④ let

10. The doctor was very surprised that his patient had let his condition _____ so much before calling him.

    ① deteriorate   ② to deteriorate

    ③ to deteriorating   ④ deteriorating

11. I could not make him _____ the meaning of the word.

    ① being understood   ② understanding

    ③ understood   ④ understand

12. You _____ your visa extended before it expires.

    ① had better to get   ② had to get better

    ③ had better get   ④ had better got

13. "What did Prof. Park say to his students?"

    "He wanted them _____ late for the examination."

    ① not be   ② be not   ③ not to be   ④ to be not

14. Bill told me that _____ live with his roommate again next year.

    ① he'd rather not   ② he'll rather not

    ③ he won't rather   ④ he'd rather didn't

15. "Are you going to the football game?"

"No, the tickets are _____ expensive for me."

① very much   ② so much   ③ far too   ④ highly

16. _____ us a letter.

① Don't forget to write   ② Forget not to write

③ Forget to not write   ④ Don't forget to writing

17. "Tom's father wants to send him to medical school."

"Yes, He wants _____ him."

① making a doctor   ② to make a doctor by

③ a doctor made from   ④ to make a doctor of

18. A student must learn _____.

① to make wise use of his time

② that his time need a wise use

③ how to use his time in a way which is wise

④ wise ways in his time's use

19. Jill is very interesting _____.

① to talk to   ② to talk to her

③ to talk   ④ to be talked

20. A good man is difficult _____.

① at finding   ② to be found   ③ with finding   ④ to find

21. He doesn't want _____.

① that the doctor come   ② that the doctor comes

③ the doctor to come   ④ the doctor comes

22. "Is Maggie coming with you?"

"I'll get her _____ on the next trip."

① coming along with me   ② to come to with me

③ to come along with me   ④ with me to come along

23. You have an examination tomorrow.

So, I cannot permit you _____ to the movie tonight.

① will go   ② going   ③ go   ④ to go

24. I would like the exercise _____ by everybody before tomorrow.

① to finish   ② be finished   ③ to be finished   ④ finish

25. The principal wants _____ to come to his office at once.

① for you   ② to you   ③ of you   ④ you

26. For the clothes _____ properly, they must be hung out in the sun.

① to dry   ② dried   ③ dry   ④ drying

27. Let your reactions to the things and persons that interest you _____ as far as possible friendly rather than hostile.

① are   ② make   ③ do   ④ be

28. He didn't pass the test but he still _____.

① hopes so   ② hopes it   ③ hopes to   ④ hopes that

29. She asked me _____ anyone what happened.

① to not tell   ② not to tell

③ to tell not   ④ not tell to

※ 다음 빈칸에 알맞은 것은?

1. I am certainly looking forward to _____.

   ① watch the champion play   ② watching the champion to play
   ③ watch the champion to play   ④ watching the champion play

2. In many ways, riding a bicycle is similar to _____.

   ① driving a car   ② the driving of a car
   ③ when driving a car   ④ when you drive a car

3. The Thompson's party next Friday should be fun.
   I'm looking forward _____ it.

   ① to attend   ② to attending
   ③ attend   ④ when you drive a car

4. I have not seen my old classmates since I graduated and look forward to _____ again.

   ① met them   ② meeting them   ③ meet them   ④ meet with them

5. Mary's father approved of _____ in the United States for another year in order to work toward her M.A.

   ① her to stay   ② she staying   ③ she to say   ④ her saying

6. _____ the money without authorization will be criticized.

   ① If we spend   ② Our spend of   ③ When we spent   ④ Our spending

7. She is _____ forward to _____ to Europe after she finishes her studies at the university.

   ① seeing-going   ② looking-go
   ③ seeing-go   ④ looking-going

8. They never meet _____ quarreling.

   ① but   ② always   ③ without   ④ except

9. "What did they struggle for?"
   "The two men resisted _____ it."

   ① to examine   ② by examine
   ③ examining   ④ examine

10. "Why don't you try to do that kind of work?"
    "I can't risk _____ something new right now."

    ① do   ② of doing
    ③ to do   ④ doing

11. I am considering _____ your offer.

    ① to accept   ② accepted   ③ accept   ④ accepting

12. We went _____ with Charles last Saturday.

    ① to swim   ② swimming   ③ swam   ④ swim

13. "Is Mrs. Brown happy now?"
    "Jack's _____ the book pleased her very much."

    ① to return   ② returning
    ③ returned   ④ return

14. I really appreciate _____ to help me, but I am sure that I will be able to manage by myself.

    ① you to offer   ② you offer

    ③ your offering   ④ that you are offering

15. A : Why didn't he come to the party?

    B : He was too busy _____ his wife.

    ① to help   ② for helping   ③ helping   ④ helped

16. I have difficulty _____ a place to live.

    ① find   ② finding   ③ found   ④ to find

※ 다음 빈칸에 알맞은 것은?

1. She found the window open and something _____ when she came back to her office.

   ① stolen   ② steal   ③ to steal   ④ steals

2. He got somehow _____ in the scandal.

   ① involved   ② to involve   ③ involving   ④ involve

3. One's first day in a new country is often _____.

   ① strangely felt   ② a bewildered feeling

   ③ a confusing experience   ④ a baffled event

4. The hibernation takes place even among _____ animals.

   ① blood warm   ② whose blood is warm

   ③ warm-blooded   ④ they have warm blood

5. Are you going to keep me _____ all day long?

   ① to wait   ② wait   ③ waiting   ④ waited

6. "How do yo like your new job?"
   "_____."

   ① I find it very interesting   ② That sounds like a lot of fun

   ③ I made an important appointment   ④ Because I am very much interested

7. I want the work _____ by tomorrow.

   ① doing   ② to do   ③ do   ④ done

8. George had his nose _____ in a fight.

   ① break   ② broke   ③ breaking   ④ broken

9. I got my baggages _____ by the porter.

   ① carry   ② to carry   ③ carried   ④ carrying

10. "Did you like that restaurant?"
    "Not really ; the food was _____."

    ① disappointment   ② disappointed
    ③ disappointing   ④ disappoint

11. After two hours, I began to _____ with my professor's lecture.

    ① bored   ② was bored   ③ boring   ④ grow bored

12. _____ an ardent admirer of Tolstoy, Chapman was overwhelmed when he
    found himself standing face to face with the great author at the station.

    ① To be   ② As
    ③ Having been   ④ For being

13. _____ these characteristics, one has the outline of an educated man.

    ① Give   ② Given   ③ To give   ④ Giving

14. The most common form of candle is a hard cylinder of paraffin with a wick _____ through
    its center.

    ① and run   ② running   ③ runs   ④ run

15._____, we were ready to begin our task.

   ① For all the plans being laid out   ② When all the plans laid out

   ③ On all the plans laying out   ④ With all the plans laid out

16. One day, when she was sitting on a _____ tree, she _____ a voice from behind a bush.

   ① falling, hears   ② fallen, heard   ③ fell, heard   ④ fall, has heard

17. There was nothing _____ of his library.

   ① left   ② to be left   ③ leaving   ④ to leave

18. The pen _____ on the table belongs to me.

   ① lying   ② which it is   ③ is   ④ which set

19. "I met John _____ some books in the store yesterday."
"Why didn't you greet him?"

   ① buy   ② bought   ③ buying   ④ to be buying

20. The gates remained _____ for years.

   ① to close   ② closed   ③ to be closed   ④ closing

21. In my mind I could see my classmates _____.

   ① to stand on the shore   ② standing on the shore

   ③ stand on the shore   ④ being stood on the shore

22. You had better have that teeth _____.

   ① pulled out   ② to pull out

   ③ pulling out   ④ pull out

23. I'll just get these dishes _____ and then I'll come.

    ① wash   ② to wash   ③ washed   ④ being washed

24. Mary gets her work _____ quickly.

    ① do   ② doing   ③ done   ④ to do

25. There was so much noise that the speaker couldn't make himself _____.

    ① to hear   ② heard   ③ hearing   ④ being heard

26. I won't be _____ until I become a millionaire.

    ① satisfaction   ② satisfied   ③ satisfactory   ④ satisfying

27. Upon returning from class, _____.

    ① he found a letter in the mailbox
    ② a letter was in the mailbox
    ③ a letter was found in the mailbox
    ④ the mailbox had a letter in it

28. Standing on a busy street corner and peering into the darkness,_____.

    ① no place was available for the stranger to go
    ② the stranger realized that he had no place to go
    ③ and the stranger realized that he had no place to go
    ④ a shot sounded and the vicious hunter appeared presently

29. Born and educated in New York, _____.

    ① he practiced medicine until his death
    ② medicine was practiced by him until his death
    ③ until his death he practiced medicine there
    ④ there he took part in practicing medicine until dying

30. _____ for her anthropological research, Margaret Mead also was involved with the World Federation for Mental Health.

① She primarily noted   ② She is primarily noted

③ Noted primarily   ④ Primarily is noted

31. "Why are they talking all the equipment away?"

"The job _____, they are packing up to leave."

① was done   ② done   ③ is to done   ④ having done

32. Whether _____, the picnic will be held as scheduled.

① permits   ② should permit   ③ will permit   ④ permitting

33. "What are those two people doing?"

"The day's work _____, Mary and Jane are playing cards."

① is done   ② done   ③ doing   ④ did

34. His health failing, _____ in 1782.

① so Henry Lee went on leave from the army

② the army gave Henry Lee leave

③ when the army gave Henry Lee leave

④ Henry Lee went on leave from the army

※ 다음 빈칸에 알맞은 것은?

1. All of the people at the meeting are _____.

   ① mathematics teachers   ② mathematic teachers

   ③ mathematics teacher   ④ mathematic's teachers

2. Dr. Jones ordered _____ for the laboratory.

   ① two equipments   ② two pieces of equipment

   ③ two pieces of equipments   ④ two equipment pieces

3. Rarely _____ clover is considered a lucky sign.

   ① find four-leaf   ② found four-leaf

   ③ find four-leaves   ④ found four-leaves

4. "Would you like to hear classical music or contemporary music?"
"Classical music is my _____."

   ① one preferring   ② one prefer

   ③ preferring   ④ preference

5. To our great relief we learned that the child was safe.
= We were greatly _____ to learn hat the child was safe.

6. They shook _____ with each other and made up.

   ① hand   ② hands   ③ the hand   ④ a hand

7. _____ of caffeine can result in restlessness, insomnia, and even delirium.

   ① Consuming in excess   ② An excessive consumption

   ③ To consume excessively   ④ The consumption excessive

8. "How is the work?"

   "Two-thirds of the work _____ finished."

   ① are   ② is   ③ to be   ④ will

9. A : What do you have?

   B : I've got a _____ bill.

   ① five-dollar's   ② five-dollar   ③ fives-dollar   ④ five-dollars

10. "What did you get?"

   "I got a _____ bill."

   ① five-dollars   ② fifth-dollars   ③ five-dollar   ④ five-dollars'

11. Spanish claim to California began in 1542 _____ discovery by Cabrillo.

   ① with its   ② with their   ③ when its   ④ when their

12. You look best in _____ of that color.

   ① dress   ② a dress   ③ that dress   ④ the dress

10. 관사

※ 다음 빈칸에 알맞은 것은?

1. I bought the stocking _____.

   ① at the half price   ② half at the price
   ③ at half the price   ④ the half at price

2. "What do you want?"
   "I want _____ that is on the table."

   ① the loaf of bread   ② some bread
   ③ a loaf of bread   ④ a bread

3. Mrs. Lindon has _____ that she is unable to get a job.

   ① such small education   ② a such little education
   ③ so little education   ④ a so small education

4. Mr. Kim will get in touch with you _____ phone.

   ① with   ② using   ③ by   ④ in

5. James Joyce _____ of many books.

   ① has written   ② was the author
   ③ author writing   ④ was written

6. I felt foolish after making _____.

   ① a such mistake   ② such mistake
   ③ such a mistake   ④ such a mistakes

11. 대명사 I

※ 다음 빈칸에 알맞은 것은?

1. The man who is only interested in himself is not admirable, and _____.

   ① does not feel to be so   ② is not felt to be so
   ③ does not feel to be such   ④ is not felt to be such

2. He has six children, so _____ is a large family.

   ① he   ② his   ③ him   ④ himself

3. Mary can borrow a pencil if she needs _____.

   ① one   ② any   ③ that   ④ some

4. "The cake is delicious, John."

   "Then, do you want _____ more?"

   ① a little   ② some   ③ little   ④ much

5. The creature may breathe _____.

   ① only once every five minute   ② once five only every minute
   ③ only once every five minutes   ④ only once every fifth minutes

6. A : I wish you a happy new year.

   B :_____.

   ① Many happy returns   ② The same to you
   ③ Congratulations   ④ Thanks to you

7. Today's typewriter keyboard is _____ Shole's 1867 keyboard.

   ① as same as   ② the same as

   ③ the same than   ④ a same one as

8. What kind of hat did you buy last week?"

   "Oh, I bought the same kind of hat _____ yours."

   ① with   ② as   ③ to   ④ like

9. Corn depends on human cultivation for survival because it _____ reliable method of seed dispersal.

   ① has no   ② has not

   ③ does not have   ④ is not having

10. Canada does not require that U.S. citizens obtain passports to enter the country, and _____.

   ① Mexico doesn't either   ② Mexico does neither

   ③ neither Mexico does   ④ either does Mexico

11. They found _____ impossible to live with her in the same house.

   ① so   ② that   ③ it   ④ also

12. Sit down and _____ yourself at home.

   ① comfortable   ② make   ③ comfort   ④ be

13. Rather than _____ ourselves with the whole man, we plug into a module of his personality.

   ① entangling   ② being entangled

   ③ entangle   ④ to entangle

14. "Is there any milk in the bottle?" "_____."

① No, I'm afraid there's any left   ② No, I'm afraid there's some left

③ No, I'm afraid there's none left   ④ No, I'm afraid there's nothing left

15. They were here, but they've gone back to _____ apartment.

① his   ② its   ③ their   ④ theirs

16. It was between 1830 and 1835 _____ the modern newspaper was born.

① when   ② that   ③ which   ④ because

17. "Were all three people in the car injured in the accident?"

"No, _____ only the two passengers who got hurt."

① there is   ② there were   ③ it was   ④ it were

18. A : Are you ready to order, sir?

B : Yes, Can I have _____ coffee?

① some   ② any   ③ a few   ④ many

19. "Will you go by boat?"

"If John does, _____."

① I'll do so ② so I'll go   ③ so will I   ④ so I do

20. A : I went to see the football game yesterday.

B :_____. It was quite exciting.

① All right   ② So went I   ③ I'd like to   ④ So did I

21. It is a message of importance for every man and woman who _____.

① votes   ② vote   ③ voting   ④ are vote

22. _____ of the three boys got a prize.

    ① Both   ② Each   ③ A few   ④ Every

23. In the United States Senate, _____, regardless of population, is equally represented.

    ① where each state   ② for each state

    ③ each state   ④ which each state

24. The current economic crisis caught _____ by surprise.

    ① almost everyone   ② the most everyone

    ③ most anyone   ④ each one and everyone

25. You should not rely on such a dishonest man _____.

    ① like him   ② as he   ③ as him   ④ like he

26. Many modern novels have _____ recognizable plot.

    ① never   ② none   ③ not   ④ no

27. A : Mr. Kim is not interested in geography.

    B : Mr. Lee _____.

    ① isn't either   ② isn't neither

    ③ doesn't either   ④ isn't too

28. _____ should be planted in the shade.

    ① This kind of flowers   ② These kind of flowers

    ③ This kinds of flowers   ④ This kind flower

29. The volume of Hawaii's Mauna Loa is fifty times _____ Mount Everest.

    ① of   ② more of   ③ that of   ④ than of

30. Today's libraries differ greatly from _____.

    ① that are past   ② those of the past

    ③ those past   ④ the past

31. I can't give you any because there's _____ left.

    ① some   ② no   ③ none   ④ any

12. 대명사 II

※ 다음 빈칸에 알맞은 것은?

1. Dams can be beneficial to the areas _____.

   ① in which they are built   ② building them where

   ③ which they are built   ④ where are they built

2. _____ do you call this in Korean?

   ① When   ② How   ③ Which   ④ What

3. "How did you come here?"

   "_____."

   ① on business   ② on foot

   ③ to see you   ④ Because I missed you

4. "Will I have time to change my clothes before we go out?"

   "That depends on how soon _____."

   ① we finish eating   ② do we finish eating

   ③ do we eat   ④ we finish to eat

5. This is the poem of a poet _____ I believe is greater than Keats.

   ① that   ② who   ③ whose   ④ whom

6. He arrived half an hour late, _____ annoyed us very much.

   ① that   ② as   ③ which   ④ what

7. Gold and silver have no function _____ we cannot easily dispense with.

    ① it   ② when   ③ that   ④ of

8. With a small needle, he was making a line of stitches _____ tiny and even _____ could be done on any machine.

    ① very - that   ② as - so   ③ as - as   ④ very - only

9. Soldiers are obligated to obey their superior _____ he happens to be.

    ① whomever   ② whatever   ③ whom   ④ whoever

10. The man _____ lives next door is very friendly.

    ① where   ② which   ③ when   ④ who

11. "It seems we have just finished buying summer clothes."
   "I never know _____ when I go on a trip."

    ① what clothes should take   ② what clothes to take
    ③ what clothes will I take   ④ I take what clothes

12. I wonder _____.

    ① how much are these shoes cost ② how much cost these shoes
    ③ how much do these shoes cost ④ how much these shoes cost

13. I could imagine _____ as they waited there.

    ① how did they look   ② how they looked
    ③ how they look   ④ did how they look

14. _____ will make the best class president.

    ① Whom do you think   ② Do you think who
    ③ Do you think whom   ④ Who do you think

15. The farmer builds a house _____ to store grains.

① with which   ② where   ③ which   ④ in which

16. All _____ is a continuous supply of fuel oil.

① what is needed   ② that is needed
③ the thing needed   ④ for their needs

17. You are the only foreigner _____ I saw this year.

① whom   ② that   ③ who   ④ which

18. _____ is perhaps even more important for the anthropologist's work is the fact that he is all alone.

① Which   ② That   ③ What   ④ As

19. What we say and _____ somehow seem out of joint.

① the things to   ② things that we do
③ what we do   ④ our deed

20. Bread is to baker as clothes are to _____.

① cloth   ② jacket   ③ tailor   ④ people

21. When manners are superficial, artificial, and forces, no matter _____ their form, they are bad manners.

① how   ② why   ③ when   ④ what

13. 형용사 Ⅰ

※ 다음 빈칸에 알맞은 것은?

1. "Do you like the Chinese food served in American restaurants?"
   "It's not bad but I prefer _____."

   ① Chinese food authentically   ② Chinese authentic food
   ③ food Chinese authentically   ④ authentic Chinese food

2. Scientists are searching for the oldest _____ because it can teach them a great deal about many matters.

   ① tree alive   ② tree lively
   ③ alive tree   ④ tree living

3. "Which shoes belong to his father?"
   "The _____."

   ① blue large five ones   ② five blue large ones
   ③ five large blue ones   ④ large five blue ones

4. Staying in a hotel costs _____ renting a room in a dormitory.

   ① twice as much as   ② twice as many as
   ③ as much twice as   ④ as many twice as

5. Travelers checks are useful when one is travelling because _____ people refuse to accept them.

   ① quite a few   ② a few   ③ few   ④ many

6. The guerrillas' intention is to capture her _____.

   ① living   ② alive   ③ to live   ④ to be alive

7. There is a great _____ of population on the beaches this summer.

   ① deal   ② lot   ③ number   quality

8. Most of the students seemed _____ to the entrance examination.

   ① indifferent   ② concerned   ③ happy   ④ enthusiastic

9. "Bill's idea is ridiculous."
   "Is Professor Baker _____ the idea?"

   ① concern with   ② pleased with
   ③ happy about   ④ critical of

10. "What gate should I go through?"   "You should go to _____."

    ① Three Gate   ② Third Gate   ③ Gate Three   ④ Gate Third

11. This work will come _____ for him after he has had more practice.

    ① easily   ② easy   ③ easiness   ④ for easiness

12. "The exam will be on the first half of the book."
    "That means we'll have to finish _____."

    ① fifteenth chapter   ② fifteen chapter
    ③ chapter fifteenth   ④ chapter fifteen

13. A tropical tree that grows in _____, the mangrove is utilized in coastal land building.

    ① salty ocean water   ② ocean salty water
    ③ ocean water is salty   ④ water of the ocean is salty

14. Ulysses Simpson Kay is known as a _____ and the creator of eloquent symphonic music.

    ① trained traditionally classical composer

    ② trained composer traditionally classical

    ③ traditionally trained composer of classical

    ④ traditionally trained classical composer

15. _____ apples are delicious and juicy.

    ① Those dark red   ② Dark those red

    ③ Those red dark   ④ Red dark those

16. She doesn't think that your coat is _____.

    ① worthy the price   ② worth the price

    ③ worthy to buy   ④ worth of the price

17. We often forget to be _____ to the plight of others around us.

    ① sensible   ② sense   ③ sensual   ④ sensitive

18. My appointment with the doctor is on Friday, _____.

    ① the five of March   ② fifth March

    ③ five March   ④ the fifth of March

19. "That trumpet player was certainly loud."

    "I wasn't bothered by his loudness _____ by his lack of talent."

    ① so much as   ② rather than

    ③ as   ④ than

※ 다음 빈칸에 알맞은 것은?

1. Few people who live on the cooperatives _____ than they were as laborers.

① is well off financial   ② financially well off
③ are better off financially   ④ financial better off

2. Poetry is as universal as language, and almost _____ ancient.

① so   ② as   ③ like   ④ such

3. A : Is Mike's son well-behaved?
   B : _____.

① Yes, he is crazy about you   ② Yes, he is adequate
③ Yes, he is a sort of a boy   ④ Yes, as far as two years old

4. Steve is as good as his word.
   If he said he'd help you, then he _____.

① will   ② is   ③ won't   ④ did

5. A : Why do you treat me like that?
   B : _____.

① As you treat me, like will I treat you
② As you treat me, thus will I treat you
③ As you treat me, so will I treat you
④ As you treat me, and will I treat you

6. "The exam was very stiff."

   "Now don't begin making excuses. Other boys _____ have passed."

   ① as clever not like you　　　② clever not than you

   ③ not cleverer like you　　　④ no cleverer than you

7. Those students do not like to read novels _____ text books.

   ① much less　　　② leaving out of the question

   ③ forgetting about　　　④ in any case

8. _____, William Shakespeare is the most widely known.

   ① With all writers in English　　　② All writers in English

   ③ All of the writers in English　　　④ Of all writers in English

9. This girl is _____ of all the girls I have ever met.

   ① less charming　　　② the most charming

   ③ less charmed　　　④ most charmed

10. He looks at us sadly with his eyes _____ as her grandmother's.

   ① a size as large　　　② of large size

   ③ so large　　　④ as large

11. Mr. Robert is a noted chemist _____.

   ① and too a very efficient teacher

   ② as well as an efficient teacher

   ③ but he teaches very good in addition

   ④ however he teaches very good also

12. I don't know about the matter _____ than you do.

   ① not more　　　② no more　　　③ any more　　　④ not less

13. "Did the medicine make you feel better?"

   "No, _____ the worse I feel."

   ① taking more medicine   ② to take more medicine

   ③ more medicine taken   ④ the more medicine I take

14. The questions seem to the world to be scarcely worth asking, <u>let alone</u> answering.

   ① not to mention   ② frankly speaking

   ③ in a word   ④ taking care of

15. It was the worst hurricane _____ recorded.

   ① which   ② that   ③ ever   ④ as

15. 부사

※ 다음 빈칸에 알맞은 것은?

1. _____ the simple monument, dedicated to the memory of unknown soldiers, was erected at the foot of the hill is still a mystery even to the villagers.

   ① As   ② Though   ③ When   ④ Since

2. They _____ forbid a husband to beat his wife.

   ① absolute   ② absolutely   ③ are absolute   ④ are absolutely

3. He will not be _____ to vote in this year's election.

   ① old enough   ② as old enough
   ③ enough old   ④ enough old as

4. _____ volcanoes exist in North America at the present time.

   ① Thirty-three only active   ② Thirty-three active only
   ③ Only thirty-three active   ④ Only active thirty-three

5. "What should we do if it rains tomorrow?"
   "I guess we should _____."

   ① call it off   ② cancel it off
   ③ call off it   ④ cancel off it

6. "Are you going to the football game?"
   "No, the ticket is _____ expensive for me."

   ① far too   ② a lot of   ③ so much   ④ very much

7. Never _____ fallen in love before I met my wife.

① have I   ② I had   ③ had I   ④ I have

8. George _____ he could improve his test scores, but he did not have enough time to study.

① knew how to   ② knew how

③ knew how that   ④ knew to

9. _____, the monument was erected, is still a mystery to everyone.

① Though   ② When   ③ Since   ④ For

10. There are those to whom a meal is merely a bore.

_____, they feel that it is uninteresting.

① How excellent the food is

② However excellent the food may be

③ What an excellent food it is

④ As far as the food is excellent

11. I was born in September, and love it _____ of all the months.

① well   ② best   ③ hard   ④ good

12. "Your dress is marvelous, Helen."

"Yes, but it doesn't fit me around the neck _____ right."

① almost   ② quite   ③ rather   ④ nearly

13. He thinks _____ me.

① different with   ② differently

③ differently from   ④ different from

14. "I slipped on the stairs. I think my arm is broken."
"Oh! I _____."

① do not hope so   ② do not hope

③ hope not so   ④ hope not

15. _____ an increasing international exchange of educational films.

① It is   ② There is

③ Though there is   ④ Although it is

16. "Can you tell me where my niece is?"
"Yes, of course!" "_____."

① come your niece   ② Your niece here comes

③ Here your niece comes   ④ Here comes your niece

17. I first met Mr. Brown two years _____.

① ago   ② before   ③ then   ④ last

18. A : Have you finished your homework?
B : _____.

① As yet   ② Not yet   ③ Not now   ④ so far

19. Are you leaving for London _____?

① soon   ② lately   ③ late   ④ sooner

16. 전치사

※ 다음 빈칸에 알맞은 것은?

1. I congratulate you _____ your success.

　① with　　　② at　　　③ for　　　④ on

2. "Are you walking there with Phil?"
　 "Yes, if he gets here _____ 6:00 o'clock."

　① until　　② as far as　　③ for　　④ by

3. We arrived _____ the village at night.

　① in　　② on　　③ at　　④ with

4. Forget those things which are _____, and reach for what lies ahead.

　① ago　　② behind　　③ for　　④ to

5. The destruction of the bridge _____ the retreating army gave them time to flee to safety.

　① with　　② due to　　③ by　　④ prior to

6. He had no information as ___ whether the workers organized the labor union or not.

　① of　　② to　　③ in　　④ about

7. Many embarrassing situations occur _____ a misunderstanding.

　① for　　② because of　　③ of　　④ because

8. My supervisor _____ my talking two week's leave without pay.

   ① consented to   ② consented for
   ③ consented of   ④ consented about

9. "Do you ever dance like that in public?"

   "Certainly not! That would be _____ my dignity."

   ① beneath   ② under   ③ beyond   ④ above

10. "I'm sorry. I don't think he will be back _____ time for dinner."

    ① within   ② during   ③ in   ④ on

11. Nobody in the office had completed his share of the project _____ then.

    ① at   ② by   ③ on   ④ in

12. I have to sing _____ a crowd of 5000 people.

    ① with   ② on   ③ before   ④ across

13. This conclusion has created a major controversy _____.

    ① to the professors   ② among the professors
    ③ between the professors   ④ with the professors

14. He earns a hundred dollars _____ the week.

    ① in   ② by   ③ for   ④ at

15. "Is John your relative?"

    "Yes, he's a cousin _____ me."

    ① for   ② of   ③ to   ④ in

16. He is very proud _____ his promotion.

    ① of   ② for   ③ with   ④ at

17. The flight from New York to Los Angeles was delayed _____ the heavy fog.

    ① as result   ② owing of   ③ on account   ④ because of

18. She is _____ a doubt the best teacher I have had.

    ① without   ② with   ③ through   ④ on

19. His actions at the party yesterday was _____ contempt.

    ① at   ② on   ③ beneath   ④ over

20. I should like to congratulate you _____ success.

    ① with   ② on   ③ at   ④ to

21. I spend a lot of time _____ my stamps.

    ① with   ② on   ③ at   ④ to

22. _____ his earlier study, Dr. Melon's new study indicates a general warming trend in global weather.

    ① In contrast of   ② In contrast as

    ③ In contrast by   ④ In contrast to

23. "He helps you quite a lot."

    "We feel grateful _____ his help."

    ① to   ② for   ③ in   ④ with

17. 일치와 화법

※ 다음 빈칸에 알맞은 것은?

1. The number of cars _____ remarkably increasing.

   ① has been   ② have been   ③ has   ④ have

2. One of the best indicators of past living standards that present-day investigators can point to _____.

   ① was being height   ② is height
   ③ being height   ④ was height

3. Wool processing _____ arts to be developed by man.

   ① was the first one   ② it was the first
   ③ as one of the first   ④ was one of the first

4. It is one _____ best sellers.

   ① of them   ② of those   ③ of this   ④ of their

18. 접속사

※ 다음 빈칸에 알맞은 것은?

1. She will never get there in time _____ she leaves immediately.

   ① unless   ② because   ③ for   ④ if

2. The farm workers dig the soil, cut wood, _____ raise cattle.

   ① and   ② but   ③ as   ④ so

3. Greenpeace believes that we must all learn to live in peace, not just with other humans, but with all the beautiful animals on earth. We must work now to protect the future of the earth, _____ it may be too late.

   ① but   ② and   ③ or   ④ hence

4. The book is at once interesting _____ instructive.

   ① or   ② but   ③ both   ④ and

5. Professor Jones is both creative _____.

   ① or intelligent   ② as well as intelligent
   ③ and has intelligent   ④ and intelligent

6. We arrived _____ late that there were no seats left.

   ① much   ② too   ③ so   ④ very

7. The test of a great book is _____ we want to read it only once or more than once.

   ① whether   ② who   ③ which   ④ what

8. "Why are you mad at Mary?"

   "Because although I wrote to her three times _____ has not written back."

   ① she   ② but she   ③ and she   ④ yet she

9. _____ Rhode Island is much smaller than Taxas, it has the same number of senators.

   ① Although   ② Because   ③ Unless   ④ If

10. He works hard _____ he may succeed.

    ① that   ② lest   ③ though   ④ unless

11. You must study diligently _____ you can succeed in life.

    ① in order to ② so that   ③ if not   ④ otherwise

12. _____ small specimen of the embryonic fluid is removed from a fetus, it will be possible to determine whether the baby will be born with birth defects.

    ① When a   ② That a   ③ If a   ④ When it is a

13. Not a flower _____ even a blade of grass will grow in this desert.

    ① neither   ② either   ③ or   ④ nor

14. "Youngsoo, how are you today?"

    "I am _____ that I can meet you."

    ① too glad   ② so glad   ③ such glad   ④ fine

15. He buys presents for his relatives _____.

    ① if he can afford it or not   ② when he can afford it or not
    ③ whether he can afford it or not   ④ for he can afford it or not

16. When a bacterium becomes too large, it splits in half and forms two new bacteria, _____ its own cell and wall and protoplasm.

　① each has　　② each with　　③ has each　　④ with each

17. _____ we are not perfect ourselves, we cannot make perfect institutions.

　① Although　　② Since　　③ For　　④ If

18. He's difficult to understand _____ he speaks so quickly.

　① but　　② how　　③ because　　④ why

19. _____ Indiana is in a rich farming and dairy area, it is primarily a diversified industrial center.

　① Fort Wayne　　　　　　② Although Fort Wayne
　③ Fort Wayne is in　　　　④ Fort Wayne, in

20. Gorillas are quiet animals, _____ they are able to make about twenty different sounds.

　① how　　　　　　　② in spite of
　③ because of　　　　④ even though

21. Farmers rotate their crops _____ the soil will remain fertile.

　① because of　　　　② in order to
　③ so that　　　　　④ rather than

22. It matters little who finds the truth _____ the truth is found.

　① because　　　　② so long as
　③ so that　　　　④ even if

23. No serious claim has yet been made _____ by cloud-seeding unless favourable natural clouds were already present.

① producing rain   ② rain has been produced

③ that rain produces   ④ that rain has been produced

24. Advertising is distinguished from other forms of communication _____ the advertiser pays for the message to be delivered.

① where as   ② which

③ because of   ④ in that

19. 병치 · 도치 · 생략

※ 다음 빈칸에 알맞은 것은?

1. Authorities hung dozens of conspicuous posters to warn the people about China's new crime wave, _____ women and selling them for wives.

   ① to kidnap   ② kidnapping

   ③ that is to kidnap   ④ which kidnaps

2. Physical training is good _____.

   ① for both body and mind   ② both for body and for mind

   ③ for both body and for mind   ④ both for body and mind

3. It is better to lose one's life than _____.

   ① if you lose your spirit   ② to lose one's spirit

   ③ losing his spirit   ④ your spirit getting lost

4. She didn't know whether to sell her books or _____.

   ① to keep them for reference

   ② if she should keep them for reference

   ③ keeping them for reference

   ④ kept for reference

5. Answering accurately is more important than _____.

   ① a quick finish   ② you finish quickly

   ③ finishing quickly   ④ to finish quickly

6. The cement and sand are first mixed thoroughly ; _____.

    ① then added the water is   ② then add the water

    ③ then the water is added   ④ the adding of water is followed

7. Only under special circumstances _____ to test out of freshman composition and literature.

    ① freshmen permitted   ② permitted are freshmen

    ③ are freshmen permitted   ④ are permitted freshmen

8. "Does Fred want to go fishing tomorrow?"

   "No, he doesn't, and _____."

    ① either I   ② either do I   ③ neither do I   ④ neither I

9. Closely related to the sociology of science _____ a field that, though it scarcely yet exists, is widely described as the science of science.

    ① does   ② for   ③ of   ④ is

10. The clay burial vessels from the early Hopewell culture of North America are decorated with zigzag, grooved, and _____.

    ① designs are geometric   ② geometrically designed

    ③ geometric designs   ④ geometry designed

11. While still in kindergarten _____.

    ① I learned to read   ② reading was learned by me

    ③ they taught me to read   ④ I was learned to read

12. _____ have a chance to meet the great musician.

    ① Until then did I   ② Until then did I not

    ③ Not until then did I   ④ Not until then I did

13. "Have you ever seen a house burnt down so fast?"

"No, Never _____ anything like it."

① have I seen   ② I have seen

③ seen I have   ④ have seen I

14. The rhinoceros has a rather poor sense of smell, nor _____.

① can it see well   ② it well can see

③ it can see well   ④ well can it see

15. No sooner _____ gone home than it began to rain heavily.

① had I   ② have I   ③ I had   ④ I have

16. _____ exerted by tornadoes that they have been known to lift railroad locomotives off their tracks.

① So great is the force   ② The great force is

③ How great the force is   ④ The force is great

특례영어
실전문제 총정리

PART Ⅱ

Written Expression

1. 동사의 종류

※ 다음 밑줄 친 부분 중 문법적으로 잘못된 부분을 찾아 고치시오.

1. Pollution <u>effects</u> more people <u>living</u> in <u>today's society</u> than it did <u>those</u> in previous
            ①   ②   ③   ④

   years.

2. The student <u>made</u> his homework <u>quickly</u> so that he <u>could</u> play football before
             ①   ②   ③

   <u>bedtime</u>.
   ④

3. A good <u>tutor</u> can <u>learn</u> students vital information which will enable <u>them</u> to pass
        ①   ②   ③

   <u>the</u> entrance examination.
 ④

4. <u>Teaching and learning</u> are part of the <u>same</u> educational experience, but unfortunately
          ①   ②

   <u>they</u> are often thought of <u>to be</u> separate.
  ③   ④

5. <u>After</u> working <u>for</u> the company <u>for</u> one year, he married <u>with</u> the boss's daughter.
  ①   ②   ③   ④

6. <u>Early</u> this morning I <u>asked to</u> Mr. Smith what time <u>to begin</u> the meeting and he said
  ①   ②   ③

   he <u>was not sure</u>.
     ④

2. 동사의 시제

※ 다음 밑줄 친 부분 중 문법적으로 잘못된 부분을 찾아 고치시오.

1. The National Education Association conduct extensive research on a great many
　 ①　　　　　　　　　　　　　　　②　　　　③

   aspects of education.
　　　　　　　④

2. He tried to remember exactly what he had done from the time he left the store until
　　 ①　　　　　　　　　　　　②　　　③

   the time he gets home.
　　　　　　 ④

3. I have to deposit this money in my check account or else the check I just wrote will
　　　　 ①　　　　　　　　②　　　　　③　　　　　　　④

   bounce.

4. Systematic investigations have prove that many American Indian languages are highly
　 ①　　　　　　　　　②　　　　　　　　　　　　　③

   developed in the phonology and grammar.
　　④

5. When I met him yesterday, he told me that his father died three weeks before.
　　　 ①　　　　　　　　②　　　　　　　③　　　　　④

6. The first zoological garden in the United States had established in Philadelphia in 1874.
　　 ①　　　　　　　　　　　　　　　②　　　③　　　　　④

7. In 1884 and 1888, the National Equal Rights Party nominally Belva Lockwood for
　　　 ①　　　　　　　　　　　　　　　②　　　　　　　③
   President of the United States.
　　 ④

8. In 1872, when Congress passes the Yellow Stone Act, the world's first national park
　　　　　　　　①　　　　　　　　　　　　②　　　　　③

   was created.
　 ④

69

3. 조동사

※ 다음 밑줄 친 부분 중 문법적으로 잘못된 부분을 찾아 고치시오.

1. "Must you go?"   "I must. But you mustn't fear I'll be away for long. I have a
   ①   ②   ③

   conference here next week that I mustn't miss."
                                            ④

2. It would be a good thing if the two opposition parties could field a single candidate.
      ①   ②

   However, should that prove impossible, they may at least refrain from smearing each
                ③   ④

   other.

3. I would rather staying at home than go for a walk.
      ①   ②   ③   ④

4. He demanded that he was given the right to express his opinion.
                    ①   ②   ③   ④

5. Not until the 19th and 20th centuries did modern nationalism in Europe produced its
   ①   ②   ③

   ripest fruit and its lethal poisons.
                        ④

6. The law I am referring to requires that everyone who owns a car has accident
               ①   ②   ③   ④

   insurance.

4. 태

※ 다음 밑줄 친 부분 중 문법적으로 잘못된 부분을 찾아 고치시오.

1. A table <u>put</u> in a garden and on the table a piece of blue cardboard <u>is placed</u>,
   ①   ②

   <u>on which</u> there is a watch-glass <u>containing</u> a drop of syrup.
   ③   ④

2. <u>You can't</u> <u>take possession of</u> the house <u>until</u> <u>all the papers</u> <u>have signed</u>.
   ①   ②   ③   ④   ⑤

3. Thomas Nast <u>was known</u> <u>primarily</u> <u>for</u> a <u>political</u> cartoonist.
                ①   ②   ③   ④

4. As soon as the child <u>goes to</u> school, he is <u>quickly</u> aware of how important <u>it is</u> to be
                         ①   ②   ③

   <u>think</u> well of.
   ④

5. The first <u>fossilized</u> dinosaur <u>bones</u> were <u>discovery</u> in the <u>1700's</u>.
               ①   ②   ③   ④

6. Her husband was <u>so completely</u> <u>addict</u> to alcohol that he lost his job and <u>had</u> trouble
                   ①   ②   ③

   finding <u>another</u> one.
           ④

71

5. 가정법

※ 다음 밑줄 친 부분 중 문법적으로 잘못된 부분을 찾아 고치시오.

1. I <u>intend to move</u> that our committee <u>appoints</u> Tom <u>as chairman</u>, and I hope that you
           ①   ②   ③

   <u>will second</u> my motion.
       ④

2. I would go to visit <u>that</u> beautiful lake <u>but</u> I <u>couldn't</u> get in <u>touch</u> with you while I am
                      ①   ②   ③   ④

   now in Boston.

3. If you <u>would have</u> listened, you too would have concluded that Tom was <u>more</u>
        ①   ②

   <u>capable</u> than any other <u>boy</u> in <u>his</u> class.
     ③   ④

4. If it <u>had not rained</u> so hard, we <u>would have liked</u> to <u>have gone</u> on a picnic at
        ①   ②   ③

   Lake Tahoe.
    ④

5. The law <u>requires</u> that everyone <u>has</u> his car <u>checked</u> at least once <u>a</u> year.
        ①   ②   ③   ④

6. <u>Had I have been</u> in my <u>brother's</u> position, I would have <u>hung up</u> the phone <u>in the</u>
       ①   ②   ③   ④

   <u>middle of</u> the conversation.

7. If you <u>knew</u> how many pieces John <u>ate</u> for breakfast this morning, you would never
        ①   ②

   <u>have doubted</u> why he is <u>overweight</u>.
     ③   ④

72

8. I wish that he <u>wasn't</u> so lazy ; he <u>would</u> find <u>learning</u> a language <u>easier</u>.
               ①   ②   ③   ④

9. If Greg <u>would have tried</u> <u>harder</u> to reach the opposited shore, we would not have <u>had</u>
                 ①   ②   ③   ④

    to pick him up in the boat.

10. If you <u>saw</u> the amount of food he ate <u>for breakfast</u> this morning, you <u>would understand</u>
             ①   ②   ③

    why he <u>has grown</u> so fat.
            ④

11. <u>Was</u> I a millionaire, I <u>should</u> be able <u>to have</u> a large house <u>of my own</u>.
     ①   ②   ③   ④

※ 다음 밑줄 친 부분 중 문법적으로 잘못된 부분을 찾아 고치시오.

1. My supervisor, <u>just recently</u> employed, made us <u>working</u> <u>overtime</u> two <u>times</u> in the
　　　　　　　　　①　　　　　　　　　　　　　　　　　②　　　　③　　　　　　④
   previous month.

2. His failure <u>is</u> not to <u>being</u> ascribed <u>to</u> lack of <u>diligence</u>.
　　　　　　①　　　　②　　　　　　③　　　　④

3. <u>When Miss Kim</u> was sick with the flue, her mother made <u>her</u> <u>to eat</u> chicken soup and
　　①　　　　　　　　　　　　　　　　　　　　　　　　　　　②　　③
   <u>rest</u> in bed.
　　④

4. There <u>is</u>, it seems, <u>no</u> limit to the satisfaction to be <u>finding</u> in the pursuit of <u>knowledge</u>.
　　　　①　　　　　②　　　　　　　　　　　　　　③　　　　　　　　　　　④

5. The policeman <u>allows</u> people <u>to stay</u>, but he does not <u>leave</u> them <u>enter</u> easily.
　　　　　　　①　　　　　　②　　　　　　　　　③　　　　④

6. The students <u>in the dormitories</u> were forbidden, <u>unless</u> they had <u>special passes</u>,
　　　　　　　①　　　　　　　　　　　　　　②　　　　　　　③
   <u>from staying</u> out after 11:30 p.m.
　　④

7. 동명사

※ 다음 밑줄 친 부분 중 문법적으로 잘못된 부분을 찾아 고치시오.

1. Neither rain <u>nor</u> snow nor sleet <u>keeps</u> the postman <u>from</u> delivering our letters which
     ①   ②   ③

 we so much look forward to <u>receive</u>.
         ④

2. <u>In</u> many <u>Christian</u> countries, Christmas <u>is</u> a day <u>for given</u> gifts.
  ①   ②   ③   ④

3. Mr. Brown often <u>wore</u> a <u>heavy coat</u> because he was not used <u>to live</u> in <u>such</u> a cold
       ①   ②   ③ ④

 climate.

4. <u>Most</u> measurements <u>involved</u> <u>to read</u> some <u>type of</u> scale.
  ①   ② ③   ④

5. Cowboys in <u>movies</u> never seem to have <u>any</u> trouble <u>to drawing</u> guns <u>out of</u> their
     ①   ②   ③   ④

 holsters.

6. Children may not enjoy <u>to eat</u> sweets after a meal <u>so much as</u> <u>at</u> other times, but it is
        ①   ②   ③

 healthier for them <u>to do</u> so.
       ④

7. Do you <u>mind</u> <u>that</u> I <u>open</u> the window <u>now</u>?
     ① ② ③   ④

8. The purpose of the organization <u>is</u> <u>greeting</u> all newcomers to the city and to provide
                                                ①   ②

   <u>them</u> with <u>any</u> necessary information.
     ③   ④

9. <u>The purpose</u> of the instructions is <u>making</u> it <u>easy</u> for newcomers to find <u>their</u> way
        ①   ②   ③   ④

   around the city.

8. 분사

※ 다음 밑줄 친 부분 중 문법적으로 잘못된 부분을 찾아 고치시오.

1. The average age of the Mediterranean olive trees grow today is two hundred years.
   ①   ②   ③   ④

2. After waiting in line for three hours, much to our disgust, the tickets had been sold
   ①   ②   ③   ④

   out when we reached the window.

3. His cap was blown off by the wind while walking down a wide street.
           ①   ②   ③   ④

4. We can supplement our own ideas with information and data gathering from our
                                    ①   ②   ③

   reading, our observation, and so forth.
                             ④

5. Consider all the possibilities, I really believe that I would prefer not to make any changes.
   ①   ②   ③   ④

6. The boiled point of any liquid is determined by the pressure of the surrounding gases.
       ①   ②   ③   ④

7. The first short story publish by Washington Irving was "Rip Van Winkle," which
       ①   ②

   appeared in 1819.
   ③   ④

8. Considered all possible cases, I came to believe that I would rather not to make any
   ①   ②   ③   ④

   changes in my method of research.

77

9. Looking back, the house seemed to have been engulfed by the snow, which fell
     ①   ②   ③   ④

   faster and faster.

10. Coffee is my favorite hot drink, even though it kept me awake at night.
          ①   ②   ③   ④

11. Being that the United States has a food surplus, it is hard to see why anyone in our
      ①   ②   ③

   country should go hungry.
          ④

9. 명사

※ 다음 밑줄 친 부분 중 문법적으로 잘못된 부분을 찾아 고치시오.

1. The new policy <u>is</u> that all <u>visitor</u> must show identification <u>at</u> the <u>receptionist's</u> desk.
                  ①   ②   ③   ④

2. The <u>affect</u> of the bomb was <u>so</u> devastating that it took <u>nearly</u> a month to clear <u>out</u> the
        ①   ②   ③   ④

   debris.

3. In Korea, the <u>individual</u> income tax is the <u>governmental</u> largest <u>source</u> of <u>revenue</u>.
               ①   ②   ③   ④

4. Blood transfusions from one individual to <u>another</u> <u>serve</u> to supply various <u>material</u>
                                 ①   ②   ③

   that the recipient <u>lacks</u>.
               ④

5. <u>In the spirit</u> of the <u>naturalist</u> writers, that <u>author's</u> work portrays man's struggle for
     ①   ②   ③

   <u>surviving</u>.
    ④

6. <u>Classification</u> is a useful approach to the <u>organization</u> of <u>knowledges</u> in <u>any</u> field.
   ①   ②   ③   ④

7. Advertising <u>falls into</u> two <u>main</u> <u>category</u> ; consumer advertising and trade <u>advertising</u>.
           ①   ②   ③   ④

8. Encyclopedias may be used to <u>answer question</u>, <u>to solve</u> problems, or to <u>obtain</u>
                         ①   ②   ③

   <u>information</u> on a particular topic.
    ④

9. In the United States, <u>inches</u> and <u>feets</u> <u>are</u> still <u>used as</u> units of measurement.
                      ①   ② ③   ④

10. <u>At</u> birth, an infant <u>exhibits</u> a <u>remarkable</u> number of motor <u>response</u>.
      ①   ②   ③   ④

11. <u>During</u> the 1936 Olympics, Jesse Owens set <u>a world new</u> <u>record</u> in track and won
       ①   ②   ③

    four gold <u>medals</u>.
           ④

12. There <u>will</u> be a <u>fifteen-minutes</u> intermission <u>after</u> the first <u>act</u>.
         ①   ②   ③   ④

13. <u>Nobody</u> who will not try to help the other <u>people</u> develop <u>his</u> abilities <u>deserves</u> to
       ①   ②   ③   ④

    have friends.

10. 관사

※ 다음 밑줄 친 부분 중 문법적으로 잘못된 부분을 찾아 고치시오.

1. Jimmy has <u>an</u> unique <u>ability</u> to make people <u>feel</u> <u>at</u> ease.
             ①   ②   ③ ④

2. <u>Little</u> is known about <u>her</u> background and <u>early</u> life <u>of</u> prison reformer Jessie D. Hodder.
     ①   ②   ③   ④

3. <u>She felt that</u> she was as <u>good swimmer</u> <u>as he was,</u> <u>if not better.</u>
       ①   ②   ③   ④

4. <u>In a hour's time</u> I had done the work <u>to</u> my satisfaction, I got my hat <u>in</u> the hall and
         ①   ②   ③

   <u>slipped</u> out unnoticed.
     ④

11. 대명사 I

※ 다음 밑줄 친 부분 중 문법적으로 잘못된 부분을 찾아 고치시오.

1. <u>Each</u> man and woman <u>must sign</u> <u>their</u> full name <u>before entering</u> the examination
   ①   ②   ③   ④
   room.

2. Many doctors stopped <u>smoking</u> because <u>there is</u> a lot of evidence that <u>this</u> is a prime
                       ①   ②   ③
   cause of <u>lung cancer</u>.
          ④

3. A scientist bases <u>its</u> work on <u>hypotheses</u> that <u>have been checked</u> through <u>careful</u>
              ①   ②   ③   ④
   experimentation.

4. <u>During</u> the course of a day, <u>the average man</u> takes 17,300 breaths, <u>whereas</u> the
   ①   ②   ③
   average woman, with <u>their</u> smaller lungs, takes 28,800.
            ④

5. <u>It</u> was <u>her</u> <u>who</u> represented her country in the United Nations and <u>later</u> became
   ①   ② ③   ④
   ambassador to the United States.

6. People are usually <u>interested</u> <u>in seeing</u> a movie star <u>just as</u> <u>they are</u> in real life.
                 ①   ②   ③   ④

7. When Rhodesia declared <u>their</u> independence from England, <u>few</u> though that the
                    ①   ②
   new government <u>would last</u> <u>even a month</u>.
          ③   ④

82

8. Although Alice <u>has been</u> to the mountains <u>many times</u> before, <u>she still</u> likes to climb <u>it</u>.
                                  ①   ②   ③   ④

9. It is a <u>real</u> pleasure <u>to have met</u> you and <u>he</u> during your visit <u>to</u> this city.
          ①   ②   ③   ④

10. Everyone <u>is expected</u> <u>to attend</u> the afternoon session <u>but</u> the field supervisor, the
               ①   ②   ③

sales manager, and <u>I</u>.
          ④

11. Each nation has <u>its</u> own peculiar character <u>which</u> <u>distinguishes</u> <u>them</u> from others.
               ①   ②   ③   ④

12. Ground squirrels <u>live</u> in colonies <u>in which</u> each animal <u>have</u> <u>its own</u> under ground
                ①   ②   ③   ④

burrow.

13. It was during the 1920's <u>that</u> the friendship <u>between</u> Hemingway and Fitzerald
                          ①   ②

reached <u>their</u> <u>highest</u> point.
      ③   ④

14. The Democratic Party <u>has controlled</u> <u>the most</u> of elected positions <u>at</u> state and local
                    ①   ②   ③

levels in South Carolina <u>since</u> the Reconstruction.
                    ④

※ 다음 밑줄 친 부분 중 문법적으로 잘못된 부분을 찾아 고치시오.

1. When choosing a major, college students <u>should consider</u> how good <u>are they</u> at
                                           ①   ②

   different subjects as well as what the <u>job market</u> <u>will be</u> when they graduate.
                                       ③   ④

2. <u>Of all the nurses</u> who applied for the Frontier Nursing Program, <u>only those which</u>
        ①   ②

   <u>had had experience</u> in working in intensive care units were <u>called in for interviews</u>.
         ③   ④

3. <u>On</u> finishing your thesis, <u>be sure to</u> take it to <u>whomever</u> asks for <u>it</u>.
    ①   ②   ③   ④

4. He <u>whom</u> this emotion is <u>a stranger</u>, who can no longer pause <u>to wonder</u> and stand
       ①   ②   ③

   rapt <u>in awe</u>, is as good as dead : his eyes are closed.
        ④

5. There <u>are</u> not many people in this city <u>who</u> <u>own</u> the houses they <u>live</u>.
       ①   ② ③   ④

6. The United States is <u>composed of</u> fifty states, two <u>of those</u> are <u>separated</u> from
                         ①   ②   ③

   <u>the others</u> by land or water.
      ④

7. <u>Some</u> experts have <u>already</u> predicted <u>that</u> the next president <u>will</u> be.
     ①   ②   ③   ④

8. Today <u>the number of</u> workers <u>which</u> go on strike for higher wages <u>is</u> <u>almost twice</u>
          ①   ②   ③   ④

that of twenty tears ago.

9. A boy <u>who</u> you must <u>meet right</u> away is Freddy Thompson, <u>the best</u> math student
         ①   ②   ③

<u>in our</u> dormitory.
  ④

10. So Louisa's brother, to <u>who</u> the dog <u>had belonged</u>, <u>had</u> built a little house for him
                ①   ②   ③

and <u>tied</u> a chain to him.
    ④

11. The Tartar chief <u>controls</u> a thousand men, all of <u>which</u> must obey <u>his</u> orders <u>in both</u>
             ①   ②   ③   ④

war and peace.

12. A metropolitan region <u>is</u> defined <u>as</u> a central city and the territory <u>where</u> <u>surrounds it</u>.
           ①   ②   ③   ④

13. The period during <u>when</u> people <u>learned to</u> melt iron <u>is called</u> the <u>Iron Age</u>.
           ①   ②   ③   ④

※ 다음 밑줄 친 부분 중 문법적으로 잘못된 부분을 찾아 고치시오.

1. There <u>have</u> been many an <u>argument</u> <u>about</u> <u>its</u> proper usage.
          ①   ②   ③ ④

2. There is no <u>logical</u> reason why this house <u>costs</u> twice <u>more than</u> it <u>did</u> last years.
          ①   ②   ③   ④

3. The sun seems to <u>have been formed</u> <u>when</u> the universe was <u>already</u> ten billion <u>years</u>.
               ①   ②   ③   ④

4. Shells have served <u>as</u> currency <u>in</u> many lands and <u>among</u> many <u>differently</u> peoples.
                ①   ②   ③   ④

5. <u>I'm</u> <u>certainly</u> that you are <u>a</u> good student <u>in</u> my class.
   ①   ②   ③   ④

6. Flight <u>is</u> a very difficult <u>activity</u> <u>for</u> most <u>alive</u> things.
        ①   ② ③   ④

7. <u>Much</u> <u>alike</u> the elephant, the mastodon <u>was</u> a forest-dwelling <u>animal</u>.
   ①   ②   ③   ④

8. <u>The same</u> other beans, limas <u>are</u> seeds <u>that</u> <u>grow in</u> pods.
   ①   ②   ③   ④

9. <u>Many</u> of Gauguin's work <u>was lost</u> <u>on</u> the South Sea island where he lived <u>until</u> his
   ①   ②   ③   ④

death.

14. 형용사 Ⅱ / 비교구문

※ 다음 밑줄 친 부분 중 문법적으로 잘못된 부분을 찾아 고치시오.

1. Some people <u>are able to</u> make more <u>money</u> <u>in</u> five years <u>as</u> most people can in a
                ①   ② ③   ④

    lifetime.

2. <u>The more difficulty</u> the questions are, <u>the less likely</u> I am to <u>be able to</u> answer <u>them</u>.
            ①   ②   ③   ④

3. A rabbit <u>moves about</u> <u>by running</u> on its hind legs, <u>which are</u> much longer and
            ①   ②   ③

    <u>more strong</u> than its front legs.
      ④

4. Last year the country <u>had</u> fewer imports <u>as</u> it did <u>the year before last</u> <u>due to</u> the
                  ①   ②   ③   ④

    energy crisis.

5. The songs of Bob Dylan are very popular <u>among young people</u>, <u>who regard him</u>
                                     ①   ②

    <u>as more superior</u> <u>to other musicians</u>.
        ③   ④

6. <u>The price</u> of gold on the <u>world market</u> <u>has been rising</u> <u>highest</u> each year.
     ①   ②   ③   ④

7. Of the two cars that the Smiths <u>have</u>, the Plymouth is, <u>without any question</u>,
                          ①   ②

    <u>the cheapest</u> <u>to run</u>.
       ③   ④

8. <u>All</u> English words of two or more <u>syllables</u> <u>have</u> <u>at less</u> one accented syllable.
   ①   ②   ③ ④

15. 부사

※ 다음 밑줄 친 부분 중 문법적으로 잘못된 부분을 찾아 고치시오.

1. He insists that his secretary <u>is probable</u> responsible for <u>writing</u> all <u>reports</u> as well as
                                       ①   ②   ③

  <u>for</u> balancing the books.
  ④

2. Medicine <u>tends</u> <u>not to</u> work very <u>good</u> when it is not used exactly <u>as</u> prescribed.
             ①   ②   ③   ④

3. The popularity of "E.T." grew so <u>fast</u> and <u>unexpected</u> that stores <u>swiftly</u> <u>ran out of</u>
                             ①   ②   ③   ④

  E.T. dolls.

4. <u>During</u> dreams the body is asleep <u>but</u> the <u>thinking part</u> of the brain is <u>awake wide</u>.
   ①   ②   ③   ④

5. He is always <u>worried</u> about <u>being</u> late, so he leaves <u>early</u> <u>than anyone</u> else.
             ①   ②   ③   ④

6. Because George <u>ate</u> <u>faster</u> than <u>me</u>, he <u>was able to</u> leave the cafeteria sooner.
          ① ②   ③   ④

7. I don't mind if we <u>go</u> to <u>the</u> Philippines, but it would be <u>more</u> better if we <u>went</u>
              ①   ②   ③   ④

  to Hong Kong.

8. The plane is <u>scheduled</u> to arrive <u>lately</u> <u>because of</u> bad weather.
         ①   ②   ③   ④

9. Habits <u>formed</u> while we are <u>young</u> become <u>firm</u> fixed <u>as</u> we grow older.
              ①   ②   ③   ④

10. Certain types of computers <u>work</u> <u>properly</u> only <u>in environment</u> with <u>controlled precisely</u>
                                    ①   ②   ③   ④

   temperatures.

11. His face marked and his head <u>bald</u>, he <u>looked</u> <u>some</u> older than I <u>had expected</u>.
                                  ①   ②   ③   ④

12. First aid experts stress that <u>knowing</u> what <u>to do</u> in an emergency can <u>often save</u>
                              ①   ②   ③

   a life, <u>very especially</u> in accident cases.
          ④

13. Profound changes such as these go forward <u>rapid</u> in the social and <u>economic</u>
                                    ①   ②

   spheres, <u>whereas</u> the arts remain cautious, conservative and <u>European</u>.
         ③   ④

※ 다음 밑줄 친 부분 중 문법적으로 잘못된 부분을 찾아 고치시오.

1. The writer always starts <u>from</u> observations of everyday incidents and objects <u>around</u>
   ①   ②

   her and concludes <u>with</u> some fresh or profound insight <u>upon</u> basic human nature.
   ③   ④

2. Our supervisor told <u>us</u> that we <u>had to</u> finish the report <u>completely</u> <u>at</u> tomorrow.
   ①   ②   ③   ④

3. <u>Fast-food restaurants</u> originated <u>in the 1920s</u> to serve <u>hurrying tourists</u> who didn't
   ①   ②   ③

   want <u>to waste</u> time <u>off the road</u>.
   ④   ⑤

4. <u>Since</u> four years, Mr. Michael <u>has</u> been <u>handling</u> all foreign <u>accounts</u>.
   ①   ②   ③   ④

5. The Rose Bowl parade <u>takes place</u> every year <u>in Pasadena</u> <u>in</u> <u>New Year's Day</u>.
   ①   ②   ③   ④

6. No one who <u>has seen</u> him work in the laboratory <u>can deny</u> that Williams has an
   ①   ②

   <u>interest</u> and an <u>aptitude</u> for chemical experimentation.
   ③   ④

7. During hard <u>times</u>, one can count <u>in</u> his friends to give <u>him</u> the aid <u>which</u> he needs.
   ①   ②   ③   ④

8. <u>In generally</u>, the climate of <u>the</u> Rocky Mountain area <u>becomes</u> <u>windier</u> at high altitudes.
   ①   ②   ③   ④

17. 일치와 화법

※ 다음 밑줄 친 부분 중 문법적으로 잘못된 부분을 찾아 고치시오.

1. Martha on <u>violin</u>, accompanied by Saul on piano, <u>were</u> a great hit at the <u>annual recital</u>
           ①   ②   ③

   <u>last week</u>.
     ④

2. A good teacher thinks that all of <u>his</u> students <u>has</u> good minds, at least <u>as good as</u> his,
                               ①   ②   ③

   <u>if not better</u>.
      ④

3. There <u>is</u> a number of things <u>that</u> will be discussed <u>at</u> <u>the</u> policy council meeting
         ①   ②   ③ ④

   tomorrow.

4. The shift <u>in</u> population from rural <u>to</u> urban areas <u>have become</u> <u>more or less</u> worldwide.
             ①   ②   ③   ④

5. <u>Whether or not</u> Marx's understanding of social conflicts <u>are</u> in any way "scientific"
        ①   ②

   <u>remains</u> a <u>vexing</u> question.
     ③   ④

6. Mr. Park said that <u>if he had to</u> do <u>another</u> homework tonight, he <u>would not be able</u>
                        ①   ②   ③

   <u>to attend</u> the concert.
     ④

7. It <u>has been estimated</u> that the efforts of only one percent of the <u>world's population</u>
         ①   ②

   <u>moves</u> civilization <u>forward</u>.
     ③   ④

8. Sociological studies <u>has found</u> that deeply <u>hold</u> values and principles <u>are</u> <u>highly</u>
                                ①   ②   ③ ④

resistant to change.

9. The president, <u>with</u> his wife and daughters, <u>are</u> returning from a brief vacation at
              ①   ②

Sokcho so as <u>to attend</u> a press conference <u>this morning</u>.
              ③   ④

10. <u>Neither</u> of the two candidates <u>who</u> <u>had applied</u> for admission to the Department
    ①   ②   ③

of English Language and Literature <u>were</u> eligible for scholarship.
                       ④

11. Neither your unkind remarks <u>nor</u> your <u>unfriendly</u> attitude <u>have</u> caused me any <u>great</u>
                   ①   ②   ③   ④

distress.

12. One of the requirements for foreign students whose native language <u>is</u> not English
                                             ①

and who <u>wish</u> to enter American universities <u>are</u> <u>to take</u> the TOEFL.
    ②   ③   ④

13. John Dewey is generally <u>considered</u> one of the <u>greatest</u> modern <u>educational</u>
                         ①   ②   ③

<u>philosopher</u>.
  ④

14. One of Mark Twin's <u>most</u> <u>startling</u> and sarcastic <u>work</u> <u>is</u> "Letters from the Earth"
                ①   ②   ③ ④

15. The Woman <u>in</u> the kitchen motioned <u>to</u> the doctor <u>that</u> the water <u>is</u> hot.
             ①   ②   ③   ④

16. Peter, <u>as well as</u> his <u>two</u> sisters Sandra and Emily, <u>are</u> <u>left-handed</u>.
       ①   ②   ③   ④

18. 접속사

※ 다음 밑줄 친 부분 중 문법적으로 잘못된 부분을 찾아 고치시오.

1. Despite <u>of</u> what you may <u>have heard</u>, they won't go <u>on</u> strike <u>even if</u> their demands
        ①   ②   ③   ④

   aren't met.

2. <u>It made</u> <u>fearful noises</u>, they said, <u>like neither man</u> <u>or</u> woman.
      ①   ②   ③   ④

3. <u>Despite of</u> the pills <u>which</u> the doctor prescribed, Ellen <u>still</u> has trouble <u>sleeping</u>.
      ①   ②   ③   ④

4. Lincoln continued to take care <u>of</u> the mill and store, <u>by</u> his <u>employer</u> had a series of
                             ①   ②   ③

   misfortunes and <u>had to</u> give up his business.
                ④

5. <u>The</u> onion <u>has</u> both <u>a</u> distinctive flavor <u>or</u> odor.
     ①   ②   ③   ④

6. No visitor <u>or</u> relative can <u>enter</u> <u>the patient's room</u> unless he is <u>not invited</u> by the
           ①   ②   ③   ④

   doctor.

7. <u>The reason</u> he has been <u>such a success</u> is <u>because</u> he never <u>gives up</u>.
      ①   ②   ③   ④

8. I <u>object to</u> war not <u>because</u> it drains the economy, <u>but that</u> it seems <u>inhuman</u>.
    ①   ②   ③   ④

※ 다음 밑줄 친 부분 중 문법적으로 잘못된 부분을 찾아 고치시오.

1. The purpose of <u>the United Nations</u>, <u>broadly speaking</u>, is <u>to maintain</u> peace and
   ①   ②   ③

   <u>encouraging</u> respect <u>for basic human rights</u>.
   ④   ⑤

2. My father <u>enjoys</u> fresh air, <u>sunshine</u>, and <u>to take</u> long <u>walks</u>.
   ①   ②   ③   ④

3. People planning <u>to travel</u> <u>by car</u> to north Dakota <u>in the winter</u> are advised to equip
   ①   ②   ③

   their cars with snow tires and <u>bringing</u> warm clothing.
   ④

4. Family problems, <u>business</u> worries, and, <u>more than</u> anything else, <u>desiring</u> to paint,
   ①   ②   ③

   <u>motivated</u> Gauguin's flight to Tahiti.
   ④

5. The Korea Department of Agriculture <u>supervises</u> the quality, <u>clean</u>, and <u>purity of</u> <u>meat</u>.
   ①   ②   ③   ④

6. Try to copy the gentleness, the <u>patience</u>, and the long-suffering of the Buddha and
   ①

   Jesus and <u>of other</u> great souls, <u>such as</u> Ghandi, who <u>appeared</u> among us in our own
   ②   ③   ④

   time.

7. In the <u>early</u> morning the first thing that <u>both</u> my brother and <u>me</u> did was to go out
      ①   ②   ③

<u>to see</u> the pony.
  ④

8. The juvenile offender <u>was released</u> <u>from custody</u> on condition that he find a job
                          ①   ②

<u>immediately</u> and <u>stayed</u> out of trouble for six months.
  ③   ④

9. The bottling company sponsors an essay competition <u>in which</u> students submit papers,
                                                        ①

a parcel of historians <u>will judge from</u> them <u>on the basis of</u> style and content, and
                         ②   ③

the winners receive <u>gift certificates</u>.
                      ④

10. Then and there the <u>wise old</u> doctor made the man <u>write to</u> his brother, <u>asked</u>
                        ①   ②   ③

forgiveness, and <u>closing</u> a check as the first step in reparation.
                   ④

11. <u>Lots of</u> people <u>find</u> that renting a car is <u>actually</u> cheaper than <u>to buy</u> one.
      ①   ②   ③   ④

12. <u>Because of</u> <u>its</u> extra long nose, the anteater <u>has and possesses</u> a good sense of <u>smell</u>.
      ①   ②   ③   ④

13. Mark Twain is <u>a good</u> representative <u>of</u> post-civil War authors because of his
                   ①   ②

place <u>of birth</u>, education, and <u>how he wrote</u>.
        ③   ④

특례영어
실전문제 총정리

PART III

종합 문법

METRO

※ 다음 문장 중 문법적으로 틀린 문장을 고르시오? (1~37)

1. ① By next Christmas I'll have been here for seven years.
   ② The hotel has been closed many years ago.
   ③ Everything I like is either illegal, immoral, or fattening.
   ④ She did nothing except complain the whole time she was here.

2. ① Good medicine always tastes <u>bitterly</u>.
   ② <u>None</u> but the best need apply.
   ③ I always take two <u>spoonfuls</u> of sugar in my office.
   ④ Give my best <u>regards</u> to your parents when you return.

3. ① I must insist that she <u>go</u> first.
   ② Never put off till tomorrow what you can <u>do</u> today.
   ③ During my absence, try to <u>be</u> on your best behavior.
   ④ Mr. Kim went <u>to</u> abroad to study.

4. ① I always make the children pick up their toys.
   ② He was not used to living alone.
   ③ I am about to seeing you soon.
   ④ One should avoid eating a heavy meal late in the evening.

5. ① My sister <u>married with</u> a wealth man.
   ② I have nothing <u>in common with</u> my parents.
   ③ David was <u>born of</u> a royal family.
   ④ Sue <u>majors in</u> physical education.

6. ① Can you tell me if it would be cheaper to travel by train or by bus?
   ② I hope to send a year in America after I leave school.
   ③ Mont Blanc is the tallest mountain in Europe.
   ④ If you've got exams tomorrow, why aren't you studying?

7. ① I cannot but <u>frowning</u> at his mistake.

   ② I enjoy <u>listening</u> to classical music.

   ③ Never stop <u>heeding</u> your first instincts.

   ④ Buying a new car can be a <u>trying</u> experience.

8. ① When I returned home, I found the window open and something stolen.

   ② The soils in many our dry lands are rich, but they cannot grow crops.

   ③ When you popcorn, the small hard kernels suddenly burst into large, soft, snowwhite bodies.

   ④ I've had ten years off experience in repairing small appliances.

9. ① Having earned the teacher's praise, the student went home content.

   ② My having refused the boss's unreasonable request cost me my job.

   ③ Being misinformed, he blamed the wrong person for his loss.

   ④ He being knave or fool, I will stand by him all the same.

10. ① Try not to take his words so <u>literally</u>.

   ② <u>Raise</u> your hands if you have a question.

   ③ The <u>affect</u> of the bomb was devastating.

   ④ The theatre was <u>filled</u> with people.

11. ① Mathematics is more difficult than physics.

   ② Part of the spectators was excited.

   ③ Bread and butter is his main diet.

   ④ Half of the vacation was spent in the country.

   ⑤ A lot of people have come to see you.

12. ① Norwegian women are <u>breaking into</u> one of the last male bastions - the military.

   ② Women have <u>taken jobs as</u> fighter pilots and submarine officers.

   ③ If a war erupts, Norwegian women are not <u>barred from</u> combat as they are in several other European states.

   ④ So, few of them <u>feel discriminated apart</u>.

13. ① I gave some books to the boys whom I thought were students.

② If the boy had lain quite, he would not have been hurt.

③ His brother doesn't act the way he should.

④ Please lie down.

14. ① I gave him that I have in my pocket.

② He is a walking dictionary.

③ I said nothing that made him angry.

④ Do not praise such men as praise you to your face.

15. ① Young people go to picnics in the summer.

② Boys and girls go dancing.

③ Students and professors go to football games.

④ Go past the drugstore on the corner.

16. ① I cannot buy it for such a price.

② Half the year is nearly finished.

③ I bought a book for seven dollars.

④ There was a fight between two boys.

17. ① The job wasn't very interesting, but on the contrary it was well-paid.

② You've got the most money, so you can pay for the rest of us.

③ Most pop music drives me out of my mind.

④ I don't think any more of them want to come.

18. ① Illness prevented him from graduating in March.

② They will bear this pain as they have borne so many greater ones.

③ Let it lay there.

④ Whomever they send will be welcome.

19. ① He is supposed to come at 8:00 this morning.

② The mere mention of his name is surprised.

③ Things are not going well.

④ He cut his foot on the broken glass.

20. ① He attended the meeting yesterday.

    ② We entered into conversation with them.

    ③ A boy of eighteen is approaching manhood.

    ④ He will be married with her tomorrow.

21. ① I was told that many persons had been wounded by the accident the day before.

    ② It's a long time since I saw you last. Where have you been, and when have you come back?

    ③ Will you wait till I have finished this work?

    ④ If you had not helped them, they would still be poor.

22. ① I don't like Paul because he always tries to take advantage of me

    ② Either you go to the party with John, or you go there with James.

    ③ She did not like the idea but she went along with her colleagues.

    ④ Since this is my birthday party, I'll invite whom I like.

23. ① I don't like much sugar in my coffee.

    ② Nowadays much women are becoming lawyers.

    ③ I usually have little money at the end of the month.

    ④ She has little water in the bucket.

24. ① She has grown into a beautiful woman.

    ② The boy grew out of his earlier interests.

    ③ Dinner was followed dancing.

    ④ The book bored me to distraction.

25. ① It is you who are responsible for the accident.

    ② Is the climate of Korea similar to that of Italy?

    ③ How old do you think she is?

    ④ She told that she would be late.

26. ① Is the climate of Korea similar to Italy?

② You'll find it difficult to finish your job.

③ I took it for granted that he would come home.

④ How was it that the automobile accident happened?

27. ① Left to herself, she began to weep.

② I never see this watch without thinking of you.

③ He narrowly escaped from running over by a taxi.

④ Bill, as well as his friends, was injured.

28. ① I expect to hear from Mary soon.

② This is superior than that.

③ Prices continue to rise.

④ Would you mind repeating that?

29. ① Do you know which way to take?

② How foolish you are to quarrel with him?

③ I intended visiting there on Sunday.

④ You are to be back by 10 O'clock.

30. ① He said, "My blood ran cold."

② She enjoys teaching and to write.

③ You are old enough to know better.

④ We wish you a safe journey.

31. ① I must have my hair cut.

② I make it a rule to take a walk every morning.

③ I expected Susan to marry John.

④ No one can make him to do the work.

32. ① I regret she failed in the test again.

② I believe she failed in the test again.

③ I regret her having failed in the test again.

④ I believe her having failed in the test again.

33. ① It is possible to persuade him.

　② It is impossible to persuade him.

　③ He is possible to persuade.

　④ He is impossible to persuade.

34. ① This is too good a story to be true.

　② I have never before met so gentle a person.

　③ I've never met such delightful a person before.

　④ There's quite a good film on down the road.

35. ① This cattle were grazing.

　② It is careless of John to do so.

　③ John was given anything by no one.

　④ He had his pocket picked.

36. ① I like red wine better than white one.

　② There are five books. One is mine, and the others are his.

　③ He said that he takes a walk every morning.

　④ There is no rule but has some exceptions.

37. ① Nothing is so precious than time.

　② It is the more useful of the two.

　③ The lake is deepest here.

　④ This is superior in quality to that.

※ 다음 문장 중 문법적으로 맞는 문장을 고르시오? (38~54)

38. ① He repented of having been idle in youth.

　② Are you sure of that he will come?

　③ I regret having not been able to help him.

　④ I never see you without think of my brother.

39. ① The poison, using in a small quantity, will prove to be a medicine.

② You must make yourself respected.

③ Have you ever seen towns destroying by bombing?

④ Being a fine day, I went out for a walk.

40. ① The reason why he was absent was because he was ill.

② He had scarcely seen me than he left the room.

③ Important as sugar is, we can't live on it

④ His only fault is what he has no fault.

41. ① All day long the book laid on the desk, yet no one saw it.

② He asked us not to mention about his failure in the examination.

③ His sister has married an American.

④ Please sit the flower-pot on the wind-sill.

42. ① So far as I concern, the steps you suggest leave nothing to be desired.

② She looks beautifully in her pink dress.

③ He said me that he was busy.

④ He looked me in the face.

43. ① It is not you that I am angry with.

② Be careful of that you don't fall asleep.

③ I wish I were there yesterday.

④ Many a year have passed since then.

44. ① We are glad of your company.

② My father is good of English.

③ The big jar was full with oil.

④ The beautiful lady was dressed with white.

45. ① What do you do since last Saturday?

② My sister plays the piano very good.

③ We can feel the wind push against us.

④ That's the book my brother bought it to me.

46. ① I always avoid to make any promise.

    ② I used to practice to pronounce English words.

    ③ He admitted to have stolen the money.

    ④ My uncle has promised to help us.

47. ① Tom and his friends enjoyed to play football.

    ② In many ways, riding a bicycle is similar to drive a car.

    ③ The speaker is well acquainted with subject.

    ④ They plan going to the grocery store this afternoon.

48. ① It goes without saying that a friend in need is a friend indeed.

    ② My grandmother seems to glad to talk in English to anyone.

    ③ She usually studies English with tape recorder besides her.

    ④ My father was gardened with a pipe in his mouth.

49. ① The greater the demand, higher is the price.

    ② Calcium is necessary for the development of strong bones.

    ③ Almost everyone fail to pass his driver's test on the first try.

    ④ Violence on American campuses had abated in 1970.

50. ① Here you are allowed talking in a loud voice.

    ② Tell him the best way which to express my thanks.

    ③ She has no fountain pen to write with.

    ④ This book is so difficult that he can't read.

51. ① Each of us must do our duty.

    ② His both friends succeeded in the examination.

    ③ Never could any of my friends solve this problem.

    ④ Nobody volunteered except Tom and I.

52. ① He is well spoken by all his classmates.

    ② I explained to him that we could not stay any longer.

    ③ You ought not be careless when you are driving a car.

    ④ If she had time enough, she would have come to help us.

53. ① We can't see anything in the sky.　　= Anything can't be seen in the sky.

　　② Nobody can do the work.　　= The work can be done by nobody.

　　③ They robbed him of his watch.　　= He was robbed of his watch.

　　④ The hot debate resulted in quarrel.　= A quarrel was resulted from the hot debate.

54. ① We need not hurry yesterday.

　　② You should have worked harder when young.

　　③ The story is well known by all Korean people.

　　④ She is married with a rich businessman.

※ 다음 문장 중 문법에 맞으면 O, 틀리면 X를 하시오? (55~65)

55. All of us were exciting with the result of the experiment.

56. The police is searching for a tall dark man with a beard.

57. Whoever visits Seoul goes back satisfied.

58. The accident cost him his life.

59. The class could not help to laugh when the teacher dropped all his papers.

60. The teacher advised us to read books as many as possible.

61. I must write down his address before I don't forget it.

62. They employed a man whose past they knew nothing.

63. Don't forget to bring your dictionary next time you're here.

64. We cannot be too careful in choosing friends.

65. It is three years since my dog died.

※ 다음 두 문장 중 같은 뜻이 되게 하려면 빈칸에 알맞은 것은? (66~91)

66. Whenever I see this picture, it makes me think of my native town.

    = This picture always _____ me of my native town.

67. To my _____, he failed in the attempt.

    = I was disappointed that he had tried in _____.

68. It seems that he did not think of it seriously.

    = He seems not to _____ of it seriously.

69. I supported him as much as I could.

    = I supported him to the best of my _____.

70. If I had not worked hard, I would have dropped out.

    = I worked hard, _____ I would have dropped out.

71. A : He was too modest to make his feelings known to her.
    B : His modesty _____ him from making his feelings known to her.

    ① made   ② brought
    ③ prevented   ④ put

72. The stone was so heavy that I could not lift it

    = The stone was _____ heavy for me to lift.

73. Because of rain, I couldn't go out.

= The rain prevented me _____ going out.

74. That is why they study English.

= That is _____ they study English _____.

75. Brave as he was, he turned pale at the sight.

= _____ he was brave, he turned pale at the sight.

76. He _____ what he is today to his wife's great assistance.

= As his wife assisted him a great deal, he is what he is today.

77. It interests me that they eat food from cans.

= It is _____ to me that they eat food from cans.

78. He isn't here yet.

= He _____ isn' t here.

79. He had the courage to go there alone.

= He was so _____ that he went there _____ himself.

80. She looks just like her aunt, doesn't she?

= She closely _____ her aunt, doesn't she?

81. It is of no use to cry over split milk.

= It is _____ to cry over split milk.

82. Yesterday he went to Seoul on urgent business.

= Urgent business _____ him go to Seoul yesterday.

83. These two packages weigh exactly the same.

    = There is _____ _____ in weight between these two packages.

84. Every day he reads the Bible.

    = Not a day passed _____ his reading the Bible.

85. My watch is out of order.

    = There is something _____ with my watch.

86. This book is worth reading again.

    = It is worth _____ to read this book again.

87. He is not too poor to buy it.

    = He is not so poor as to be _____ to buy it.

88. However humble it may be, there is no place like home.

    = _____ it _____ _____ humble, there is no place like home.

89. He said, "I wish I were rich enough to buy the picture."

    = He said that he wished he _____ rich enough to buy the picture.

90. I supported him as much as I could.

    = I supported him to the best of my _____.

91. He knows _____ _____ to do such a foolish thing.

    = He is too wise to do such a foolish thing.

92. I am sorry for having been idle in my youth.

    ① I am sorry that I was idle in my youth.

    ② I am sorry that I have been idle in my youth.

    ③ I am sorry for that I was idle in my youth.

    ④ I am sorry for that I had been idle in my youth.

    ⑤ I am sorry that I am idle in my youth.

93. She might have been drowned.

    ① She was drowned.

    ② She was not drowned.

    ③ She will probably be drowned.

    ④ She is sure to have been drowned.

※ 다음 밑줄 친 부분과 같은 뜻을 지닌 것은?

94. When <u>it comes to</u> spending money, he refuses.

    ① he concentrates on   ② he has a doubt

    ③ there is a reason for   ④ there is question of

※ 다음 문장과 같은 뜻을 지닌 것은?

95. You ought to come early.

    ① You came early.   ② You come early.

    ③ You did not come early.   ④ You are likely to come early.

※ 다음 A, B 두 문장을 합쳐서 뜻이 같은 한 문장이 되게 하시오? (96~98)

96. A: In fact, Henry didn't see the accident.
    B: But he insists that.

    → He insists _____.

97. A: I walked to school.
    B: It took half an hour.

    → It _____.

98. A: It started snowing yesterday.
    B: It's still snowing.

    → It _____.

99. 다음 주어진 문장을 복문으로 바꾸시오.

    The task was too hard for 12-year old boy to carry out.

    → _____.

100. 다음 주어진 문장을 단문으로 바꾸시오.

    I stayed home because it was raining.

    → _____.

101. 다음 주어진 문장을 단문으로 바꾸시오.

    We went on a picnic although the weather was cool.

    → _____.

102. 다음 주어진 문장을 분사구문으로 바꾸시오.

    As I did not know what to say, I remained silent.

    → _____.

103. 다음 주어진 문장을 동명사를 사용하여 단문으로 바꾸시오.

He not only holds an important office, but often writes good novels.

→ _____.

104. 다음 주어진 문장을 I wish를 사용하여 바꾸시오.

I am sorry my father was not alive then.

→ _____.

※ 다음 빈칸에 알맞은 단어는? (105~135)

105. What if life were perfect? What if you lived in a perfect world of perfect people and perfect possessions, with everyone and everything doing the perfect thing at the perfect time? What _____ you had everything you wanted, and only what you wanted, exactly as you wanted, precisely when you wanted it?

106. He is well spoken _____ by everybody.

107. Mary likes a man _____ eyes are blue.

108. He does not really like her much and _____ the time the play is over he almost hates her.

109. Pop music is extremely popular among young people and may be listened to for hours every day. It is quite common, for example, to find boys and girls studying, or doing homework, _____ a radio beside them.

110. A: She will soon return home.
    B: It will not be _____ before she returns home.

111. I am not living in a bigger apartment because I _____ afford it.

112. I would do anything to make you happy.

= _____ would I not do to make you happy?

113. It is very good _____ you to say so.

114. She is lazy so she is not getting _____ very well in her job.

115. Book, like friends, must be carefully chosen, for bad books do more harm than bad companions. A man who picks up and reads any book that he happens to come across, is in danger of being poisoned by it. We cannot read a good book _____ being the better.

116. Indeed the quarrels are a necessary part of the process, for the pace would never be kept up if everyone did not accuse everyone _____ of idling.

117. I wasn't watching television _____ usual when you phoned at half-past eight.

118. As she though of things her eyes grew dinner _____ ever and she could hardly see at all.

119. George Bernard Shaw was interested in English words and sounds. He was not pleased with the way in _____ English was written.

120. She said to herself. "We must fight for _____ we believe."

121. In a few days I had grapsed the main principles on _____ the hotel was run.

122. The best teacher in the college in the world cannot give a student a real education. He can lead the way to the mine from _____ it can be dug, provide him with the proper tools, and help him make more vigorous effort, but the student will own only as much of the precious metal as he digs for himself.

123. He is no more ashamed of recording his actions, good and bad, _____ of seeing himself in his bath.

124. The knife is the most useful _____ all the simple tools.

125. A: Mr. Brown is not a scholar.
    B: He is rather a poet.

    "Mr. Brown _____."

126. Business improves at the Bober store and Morris attributes the increase to Frank's popularity _____ the customers.

127. We secure the dead whale alongside and fight _____ the hungry sharks till morning.

128. Hogarth is impressed with Langdon's work and _____ Hogarth'd influence and Franklin's Langdon gets a commission to paint a panel.

129. Potter is quite content to let Langdon care _____ her.

130. Langdon picks _____ Billy at Fort Number 4 and they go to Portsmouth.

131. He wanted fer found only so that he could extort money _____ his former wife.

132. Newland chats with Ellen at the dinner and she asks him to call _____ on her the next day.

133. The fact that his wife is Southern member of the Mingott clan has made him acceptable _____ New York society.

134. She receives a letter telling her that Chuck died _____ influenza.

135. The English Bible has had much more influence than Shakespeare _____ the written and spoken language of the English race.

136. 빈칸에 compare의 올바른 형태를 쓰시오.

He thinks that philosophy is useless as _____ with science.

137. 빈칸에 trace의 올바른 형태를 쓰시오.

I have been able to gather something of this by _____ with my fingers the lines in the sculptured marble.

138. 빈칸에 적당한 전치사는?

The team didn't take part _____ the game.

139. 빈칸에 lead의 올바른 형태를 쓰시오.

On that Sunday afternoon in Korea I walked toward the bridge _____ to the outskirts of the city, Bellock carts moved far to one side to make way for the lorries.

140. 빈칸에 power의 올바른 형태를 쓰시오.

No one, no matter how much _____ physically he was than I, would sway me.

141. 빈칸에 read의 올바른 형태를 쓰시오.

I would like to see the books which have been _____ to me, and which have revealed to me the deepest channels of life.

※ 다음 빈칸에 알맞은 전치사는? (142~146)

142. They look _____ the cause of a traffic accident.

143. You have to make up _____ the loss.

144. They are indifferent _____ pro-baseball.

145. One should abide _____ one's promise.

146. Don't look down _____ the weak.

147. 빈칸에 call의 올바른 형태를 쓰시오.

I heard my name _____.

148. 빈칸에 sit의 올바른 형태를 쓰시오.

I saw him _____ motionless in his chaur.

149. 다음 글을 읽고 물음에 답하시오.

What hunger __①__ relation __②__ food, zest is __①__ relation __②__ life. The man who enjoys __③__ football is to that extent superior to the man who does not.

(1) 빈칸 ①에 공통으로 들어갈 전치사는?

(2) 빈칸 ②에 공통으로 들어갈 전치사는?

116

(3) 윗글의 첫 문장을 우리말로 옮기시오?

(4) ③에 알맞은 말은?
① watch   ② to watch   ③ to have watch   ④ watching

150. 빈칸에 use의 올바른 형태를 쓰시오.

He found the book especially _____ and relaxing.

151. 다음 빈칸에 적당한 것은?

I suffer daily as a result of never ___(1)___ formed habits even in such simple things as putting money, tickets, and such things in one particular pocket.

It is perfectly ___(2)___ to know that one has plenty of money on one's person and yet not to be able to find it without ___(3)___ as fuss as if one were chasing biting insects all over one's body.

(1) ① having   ② being   ③ have   ④ having been

(2) ① attractive   ② absurd   ③ peaceful   ④ wise

(3) ① reading   ② asking   ③ learning   ④ making

152. 다음 글을 읽고 물음에 답하시오.

Read for main ideas. Stop to waste time on details. When you read a short story, follow the thread of the plot. When you read a novel, get a quick, overall view. When you read nonfiction, be intent on getting the ___①___ .

(1) 밑줄 친 main ideas와 같은 의미를 가진 단어로 빈칸 ①에 들어갈 가장 알맞은 것은?
① love   ② imagination   ③ plot   ④ theme

(2) 밑줄 친 to waste를 문맥에 맞게 바르게 고친 것은?
① wasting   ② on wasting   ③ wasted   ④ by wasting

(3) 밑줄 친 <u>be intent on</u>과 가장 가까운 뜻을 가진 것은?

① keep on   ② understand   ③ read   ④ concentrate on

153. 다음 문장의 밑줄 친 곳에 주어진 단어의 적당한 꼴을 쓰시오.

Instead of <u>(1) roll</u> up her sleeve she began to <u>(2) fasten</u> a pin that held her dress together over her chest.

154. 다음 글에서 괄호 안에 있는 단어를 문맥에 맞는 형태로 고치시오.

I was 18 years old, (travel) with friends around Europe to fill in time before university. We'd (run) out of money and (take) a boat-painting job in Cannes, though I spent much of my time (draw).

특례영어

실전문제 총정리

PART IV

재 진술

1. That the educated person is happier than the uneducated is by no means self-evident.

   ① The educated person is definitely happier than the uneducated.
   ② The uneducated person is definitely happier than the educated.
   ③ It is clear that The educated person is happier than the uneducated.
   ④ It is not clear whether educated person is happier than the uneducated.

2. Philadelphia is the third largest city in the United States.

   ① No city is larger than Philadelphia in America.
   ② The United States has only two large cities.
   ③ Two cities are larger than Philadelphia in America.
   ④ Philadelphia is not so large as most American cities.

3. One day Leonore fell ill of surfeit of raspberry tarts.

   ① Leonore made herself ill by drinking raspberry tarts.
   ② Leonore became ill because she missed raspberry tarts.
   ③ Leonore made herself ill by overeating raspberry tarts.
   ④ Leonore died of raspberry tarts.

4. Beautiful clothes do not make a fine gentleman any more than beautiful feathers make a fine bird.

   ① Although beautiful clothes make a fine gentleman, beautiful feathers do not make a fine bird.
   ② Either beautiful clothes make a fine gentleman, or beautiful feathers make a fine bird.
   ③ Beautiful clothes do not make a fine gentleman, but beautiful feathers can make a fine bird.
   ④ Just as beautiful clothes do not make a fine gentleman, so beautiful feathers do not make a fine bird.

5. The essential virtue, if you are to make anything of your life, is diligence : it does not matter what word you choose if you understand what mean by it. Concentration, industry, hard work, are all synonyms : or if you like to draw on the vocabulary of the street, "plugging" or "sticking it" will give you the essential meaning with less elegance but more vigor.

   ① The writer thinks one has to be diligent if he wants to achieve something in his life.
   ② "Diligent", "plugging", "sticking it", "industry" are not taken as synonyms.
   ③ "Sticking it" is not a necessary virtue for someone who wants to succeed in his life.
   ④ If you choose the word "plugging" instead of "concentration", it will distort the main point of the passage.

6. There is no doubt that primitive man used his fingers for counting.

   ① It is of no suspicion that ancient man used his fingers for counting.
   ② That uneducated man used his fingers for counting is doubtful.
   ③ It is true that most people count numbers by fingers.
   ④ We have no doubt that finger-counting methods are frequently used.

7. Few scientists have played as important a part in the history of science as did Newton.

   ① The few scientists greatly influenced the history of science.
   ② Few scientists have had much influence on the development of science.
   ③ Newton had a major role in the history of only a few scientists.
   ④ Newton had more of a historical impact than did most other scientists.

8. After the war there has been a tendency to adopt indiscriminately foreign customs and fashions, but it is to be regretted that they often destroy the old beautiful customs of our country.

   ① Preservation of old customs is useless.
   ② Foreign customs are not to be adopted blindly.
   ③ War plays an important role in bringing in foreign customs.
   ④ We should stick to our old customs regardless of the change of times.

9. Turn-ups and downs of economic conditions have a great effect on our daily life.

   ① Economic fluctuation is common.

   ② Economic situation changes have a very important impact on our life.

   ③ We dislike economic turn-ups and downs.

   ④ We recently suffered from economic changes.

10. I heard my father say to mummy once that only eternity could cure him of his deep sorrow.

   ① Anything on earth could give him some relief.

   ② Even God could not give him any comfort.

   ③ Nothing but death could lessen his grief.

   ④ Even death could not release him from suffering.

11. The British were braced for particularly heavy attacks against the fleet on May 25, to coincide with Argentina's National Day celebrations.

   ① The readiness of the British to attack Argentina.

   ② The British abstention from attacks on Argentina's National Day celebrations.

   ③ The British intention to exploit a good opportunity.

   ④ The readiness of the British for the Argentine attacks.

※ 다음 밑줄 친 부분과 뜻이 같은 것은? (12~17)

12. <u>A proper sense of proportion leaves no room for superstition.</u>

   ① If one has a suitable sense of balance, superstition cannot influence him at all.

   ② If one believes in superstition, no one allows an appropriate sense of proportion.

   ③ If one has a proper sense of balance, on superstition can live in any room.

   ④ If one is superstitious, he really needs a suitable sense of proportion.

13. Mary tried to convince her father that she was telling the truth, but <u>it was all to no end</u>.

    ① her talking continued   ② her father believed her

    ③ it was all in vain   ④ it was a lie

14. There are many people who hate violence, and are convinced that it is one of their most hopeful tasks to work for its reduction, if possible, for its elimination from human life. <u>I am among these hopeful enemies of violence</u>.

    ① I believe that the fight against violence is not at all hopeless.

    ② I think that it is impossible to eliminate violence from human life.

    ③ I realize that I must fight against the enemies of violence.

    ④ I think that there are too many enemies in the fight against violence.

15. Looking at the baby, the driver said, "My goodness! What an ugly baby! <u>I don't think I have ever seen an uglier baby</u>."

    ① I don't think it's an ugly baby I have ever seen.

    ② I remember it's the ugly baby I have seen.

    ③ I'm afraid it's the ugliest baby I've ever seen.

    ④ I think it's an ugly baby I have ever seen.

16. Someone has said that a poor decision is better than no decision at all. If you find your decision is wrong you can usually change it to the right decision and go forward, while <u>the person who straddles fence</u> never finds out which is the right decision and thus seldom gets very far.

    ① the person who commits himself decisively

    ② the person who does not make a decision at all

    ③ the person who put off his determination

    ④ the person who hold fast to his decision

17. His hand fell away from his weapon, his head slowly dropped until his face rested on the leaves in which he lay. This courageous gentleman and hardy soldier was near swooning from intensity of emotion.

① became almost paint as to feel the intensity of emotion

② lost consciousness because of intensive attention

③ became dizzy for him to put up with intensity of emotion

④ lost his heart from the intensity of emotion

특례영어
실전문제 총정리

PART V
영작문

※ 다음 우리말을 옳게 영작한 것을 고르시오. (1~16)

1. "오랫동안 기다리게 해서 미안합니다."

   ① I am sorry for you waited me so long.
   ② I am sorry to have kept you waiting so long.
   ③ It is great pity that you should wait for long.
   ④ Excuse me. You waited for me so long.

2. "당신은 거기에 언제 가시는 게 편리하시겠습니까?"

   ① When shall you be convenient to there?
   ② When will you go there conveniently?
   ③ When to go there will be convenient to you?
   ④ When will it be convenient for you to go there?

3. "아무도 미래에 무슨 일이 일어날지 알 수 없다."

   ① Not anyone know what will happen in the future.
   ② Anyone hardly knows what will happen in the future.
   ③ No one knows what will happen in the future.
   ④ Any one doesn't know what will happen in the future.

4. "당신은 이 소설을 누가 썼다고 생각하십니까?"

   ① Do you think who wrote this novel?
   ② Do you think whom wrote this novel?
   ③ Who do you think wrote this novel?
   ④ Whom do you think wrote this novel?

5. "네가 그의 비열한 짓을 보고 꾸중을 한 것은 당연하다."

   ① It is natural that you were angry with his mean acts.
   ② You might as well scold his childish acts.
   ③ You may well scold him in regard to his mean acts.
   ④ He should be scolded by his mean acts.

6. "건강의 중요성은 아무리 강조해도 지나칠 것이 없다."의 영작이 어색한 것은?

① Too much can be estimated about the importance of health.

② It is impossible to overstate the importance of health.

③ We cannot state the importance of health too much.

④ The importance of health cannot be exaggerated.

7. "얼마 동안 출장 다녀오셨습니까?"

① How long did you have taken a business trip?

② How long do you have taken a business trip?

③ How long were you being on a business trip?

④ How long have you been on a business trip?

8. "그의 견해는 나의 견해와 완전히 달랐다."

① His viewpoint was one thing and mine was the other.

② His viewpoint was quite different from me.

③ His viewpoint was quite different from mine

④ His viewpoint was quite different from that of mine.

9. "그는 나보다 다섯 배나 많은 책을 가지고 있다."의 영작이 어색한 것은?

① He has five times as many books as I have.

② He has five times so many books that I have.

③ He has five times the number of books that I have.

④ He has five times more books than I have.

10. "그녀는 어제 도착한 것 같다."

① She seemed to have got there yesterday.

② She seemed to get there yesterday.

③ She seems to have got there yesterday.

④ It seemed that she arrived there yesterday.

11. "우리 집 이웃 사람은 친절합니다."

    ① My next-door neighbor is kind.

    ② My neighboring in the next door is kind.

    ③ My neighborhood on the next door is kind.

    ④ A neighboring man of my house is kind.

12. "점수가 어떻게 되지요?"

    ① What's the score?   ② How's the score?

    ③ How did the score turn out? ④ What did the score do?

13. "거북하게 생각 마시고 편할 대로 하세요."

    ① Please enjoy peace without bothering.

    ② Don't think bothered and enjoy.

    ③ Please make yourself at home.

    ④ Be not difficult and enjoy.

14. "네가 할 일이나 해라."의 영작이 어색한 것은?

    ① You have something to do with this.

    ② This is none of your business.

    ③ This is no business of yours.

    ④ Mind your own business.

15. "나의 옛 모교를 지나가기만 하면 담임선생님이 생각난다."의 영작이 어색한 것은?

    ① I never go past my old school but I think of my homeroom teacher.

    ② I never go past my old school that I think of my homeroom teacher.

    ③ I never go past my old school without I thinking of my homeroom teacher.

    ④ Whenever I go past my old school, I think of my homeroom teacher.

16. "나는 고전음악을 듣는 습관이 있다."의 영작이 어색한 것은?

    ① I was in the habit of listening to classical music.

    ② I made a habit of listening to classical music.

    ③ I made it a habit to listen to classical music.

    ④ I made it a habit of listening to classical music.

※ 다음 우리말을 영작할 때 빈칸에 알맞은 것은? (17~27)

17. "여기 무슨 일로 오셨습니까?"

    = _____ _____ you here?

18. "내 애들은 항상 실수를 저지른다."

    = My kids always _____ a mistake.

19. "중요한 것은 최선을 다하는 것이다."

    = _____ is important is to do your _____.

20. "이 책은 읽을 가치가 있다."

    = This book is _____ reading well.

21. "그 사람은 유머 감각이 뛰어나다."

    = He has a _____ _____ _____ _____ .

22. "밖에 비가 오고 있습니다."

    = _____ is _____ outside.

23. "그는 결코 거짓말 할 사람이 아니다."

    = He is the _____ man to tell a lie.

    = He is above telling a lie.

24. "이렇게 오래 기다리게 해서 미안합니다."

= I am sorry to have _____ you _____ so long.

25. "당신 사진 찍을 줄 아십니까?"

= Can you _____ a picture?

26. "텔레비전을 보십니까?"

= Do you _____ TV?

27. "한국의 대기오염은 어느 지역 못지않게 심각하다."

= The air pollution in Korea is no _____ serious than any other area.

※ Translate into English : Put the following Korean sentences into English. (28~40)

28. 우리들 중에 우리가 무엇을 해야 할 것인가에 대하여 견해가 다른 사람들은 거의 없는 것 같다.

29. 많은 사람들이 거대한 현대 사회에서 개인이 할 수 있는 중요한 일은 없다고 느끼는 것은 어쩌면 당연한 일이다.

30. 대부분의 사람들은 살기 위하여 일해야 한다.

31. 우리 모두 신한국 창조에 참여합시다.

32. 인간은 하나님의 형상으로 창조되었다.

33. 모든 사람이 죄를 범하였으매 하나님의 영광에 이르지 못하더니….

34. 인간은 반드시 환경의 영향을 받는다고는 말할 수 없다.

35. 모든 사람은 날 때부터 자유롭고 동등한 존엄성과 권리를 가지고 있다.

36. 요즈음은 겨울이 전만큼 춥지가 않다. 여러 가지 원인이 있겠지만 분명히 공해도 그 원인 중의 하나일 것이다.

37. 나는 주말에는 반드시 등산을 간다. 산에서 맑은 공기를 마실 수 있는 것도 좋지만 무엇보다도 자연과 친할 수 있는 기회를 갖게 되는 것이 즐겁다.

38. 긴 안목으로 볼 때 국가의 모든 시책 중에서 교육이 제일 중요하다. 왜냐하면 교육이야말로 국민의 의식 수준을 높이며 모든 어려운 문제를 해결할 수 있는 능력을 키워 주기 때문이다.

39. 나는 매일 아침 일찍 일어나서 뒷산에 올라간다. 아침 공기는 매우 맑아서 여간 개운하지가 않다. 나는 앞으로도 이 습관을 계속해 나갈 작정이다.

40. 내 방 친구 중 한 명은 공학을, 또 한 명은 경제학을, 또 한 명은 전자 계산학을 공부하고 있다.

※ **다음 주어진 단어를 사용하여 영작하시오. (41~46)**

41. 가능한 한 빨리 알려 주시면 감사하겠습니다.(your ~ing)

42. 해가 서쪽에서 뜬다 해도, 저는 약속을 지킵니다.(break)

43. 우리의 제안에 대해서 어떻게 생각하시는지 말해 주십시오.(suggestion)

44. "조심하세요! 무모한 운전자들을 조심하세요!"(watch)

45. 그는 시계 내부를 아무렇게나 다루어서 망가뜨려 버렸다.(tamper)

46. 그 세 사람은 돌아가면서 운전을 하여 한 사람이 너무 피곤하지 않도록 했다.(turns)

※ 다음을 영작하시오. (47~51)

47. 일찍 자고 일찍 일어나는 것은 사람을 건강하게 해 준다.

48. 둘 중에서 그는 더 비싼 것을 택했다.

49. 역에 도착하기 전에 얼마나 더 많은 버스 정류장이 있느냐?

50. 관광은 한국의 중요한 수입 원천이다.

51. 어떤 책이든 흥미만 있으면 괜찮습니다.

52. 문장의 뜻이 통하도록 괄호 안의 단어들을 올바른 순서로 배열할 때 세 번째 오는 단어는?

    The boy was young (several, Tom, years, than, by)

53. 괄호 속의 단어들을 뜻이 통하도록 올바른 순서대로 쓰시오.

    Nadia has just informed her boss that, because she is pregnant, she will be taking four (absence, mother's, of, leave) in about two months.

54. 문장의 뜻이 통하도록 괄호 안의 단어들을 올바른 순서로 배열할 때 그 순서가 맞는 것은?

    (further/information/to be seen/remains) but very soon they will know the truth.
      ①   ②   ③   ④

    ① ① - ④ - ② - ③   ② ① - ② - ④ - ③
    ③ ① - ③ - ④ - ②   ④ ① - ④ - ③ - ②

55. 문장의 뜻이 통하도록 괄호 안의 단어들을 올바른 순서로 배열할 때 세 번째 오는 단어는?

She had (them, difficulty, persuading, great, in) to stop it.

56. 밑줄 친 네 개의 단어를 옳게 배열하여 "그것들이 서로 다르기는 하지만"의 뜻이 되도록 하시오.

Brotherly love is love among equals ; motherly love is love for the helpless. are / as / different / they from each other, they have in common that they are by their very nature not restricted to one person.

57. 주어진 단어로 밑줄 친 부분에 알맞은 영문을 작성하되 번호로 답을 쓰시오.

(1) The Republic _____.
　　① be　　　　② democratic　　　③ of　　　④ shall
　　⑤ Korea　　 ⑥ a　　　　　　　⑦ republic

(2) But _____ succeeded.
　　① have　　　② for　　　　　　③ help　　　④ I
　　⑤ might　　 ⑥ your　　　　　⑦ not

(3) It _____ work.
　　① an　　　　② finish　　　　　③ hour　　　④ takes
　　⑤ to　　　　⑥ this　　　　　 ⑦ you

(4) He _____ Siberia.
　　① by　　　　② Germany　　　　③ of　　　　④ to
　　⑤ way　　　 ⑥ went

58. 주어진 단어를 올바로 배열하여 아래 속담을 영작하시오.

(1) 유유상종
　　(of, feather, flock, birds, together, a)

134

(2) 하늘은 스스로 돕는 자를 돕는다.

   (those, helps, themselves, heaven, help, who)

(3) 학문에는 왕도가 없다.

   (no, to, road, is, learning, royal, there)

(4) 사공이 많으면 배가 산으로 간다.

   (cooks, the, spoil, too, broth, many)

(5) 백문이 불여일견

   (the, is, in, proof, of, eating, pudding)

특례영어
실전문제 총정리

PART VI

생활영어

※ 다음 빈 곳에 알맞은 것은? (1~7)

1. A : Hello? May I talk to Susan?
   B : _____.
   A : Oh, I've finally got you.

   ① You're welcome   ② This is I
   ③ Speaking   ④ Sorry, wrong number

2. "Do you want Mrs. Kim to pay for the call?
   "No, I want her to call me _____."

   ① collectly   ② collective   ③ collectively   ④ collect

3. A: "May I speak to Mr. Brown?"
   B: "He's not in now. Would you like to ____ a message?"

   ① tell   ② leave   ③ take   ④put

4. A: Hello, is this the Brown residence?
   B: Yes, it is.
   A: May I speak to Mr. Brown please?
   B: Sorry, he's not in right now. _____.
   A: No, just tell him that Mr. Smith called.

   ① Why are you calling please?
   ② May I take a message?
   ③ Are you calling long distance?
   ④ Do you wish to know when he'll be back?

5. A: Mr. White isn't in this department.
   Do you know his extension?
   B: _____.

   ① What about Miss Lee?
   ② I don't know whether his department is extended
   ③ Of course, I know his friends
   ④ I'm afraid not

6. A: May I speak to Anne, please?

   B: Sure. _____ I'll call her.

   ① Hang up.

   ② Hold on, please.

   ③ Nice to meet you here.

   ④ What's your phone number?

7. A: How can I contact you?

   B: _____.

   ① Call me at 010-7372-2221. I'm at this number from noon to p.m. 6 daily

   ② Call me at 010-7372-2221. I'm at this number from noon to 6 p.m. daily

   ③ You can contact

   ④ I'd like to talk you about the job

※ 다음 우리말에 적당한 영어 표현은? (8~9)

8. "그분이 지금 안 계시는데, 전하실 말씀이 있습니까?"

   ① "He's not being here now. Can I tell him anything?"

   ② "He's not in right now. May I take your message?"

   ③ "He's absent right now. What business have you with him?"

   ④ "He's gone right now. What business have you with him?"

9. A: May I talk to Barbara?

   B: She's upstairs. 끊지 말고 기다려 주십시오.

   ① Wait, please   ② Don't cut and wait

   ③ Hold on, please   ④ Hang up, please

10. 전화가 울려서 수화기를 들고 상대방이 누구인지를 묻는 말은?

    ① Who is calling, please?   ② Who are you, please?

    ③ What do you want, please?   ④ Can I help you, please?

11. He went to the nearest phone and called home. He said, "Jimmy, ___(1)___.
Please open the door for me. I've left my keys inside." Without a word, the boy
___(2)___.

    (1)에 들어갈 가장 알맞은 말은?
      ① This is your Dad   ② It is your Dad
      ③ I'm your true Dad   ④ I'm no one at your Dad

    (2)에 들어갈 가장 알맞은 말은?
      ① cut the phone   ② put down
      ③ hung dawn   ④ hung up

12. A: Please connect me with Mr. Kim at Extension 153.
    B: Your _____ is on the phone.

    ① caller   ② receive   ③ speaker   ④ party

13. A: May I use your telephone?
    B: Sure, go right _____.

14. "212-8303번을 대 주세요."의 적합한 표현은?

    ① Ring me up 212-8303   ② Give me 212-8303
    ③ Call me 212-8303   ④ Engage me 212-8303

15. 다음 문장에서 일반적으로 쓰이지 않는 표현은?

    ① 통화중입니다 : This line is busy.
    ② 통화 다 끝났습니까? : Are you through?
    ③ 잠깐 기다리세요. : Please wait a moment.
    ④ 나중에 다시 전화하겠습니다 : I'll dial again later.

16. A: Hello.

    B: Hello. Can I speak to John, please?

    A: Yes, _____. Who's calling, please?

    ① that is he   ② he is him   ③ this is he   ④ you got him

17. Person　: San Francisco. 031-212-8303

    Operator：_____.

    Person　: No, station-to-station, please.

    ① Is this a person-to-person?
    ② Is this a collect call?
    ③ Is this a paid call?
    ④ Who's calling please?

18. A: "Do you mind closing the window?"

    B: "_____, for we have enough fresh air."

    ① Yes, I do   ② Yes, I don't
    ③ No, I don't   ④ No, I do

19. A: Aren't you fond of dogs?

    B: _____.

    ① Yes, I'm not   ② No, I am
    ③ Yes, I am   ④ No, I don't

20. A: "Would you mind opening the window?"

    B: "_____. I wish you wouldn't have a cold."

    ① Certainly not   ② Yes
    ③ No, not at all   ④ Not in the least

21. _____ if we talk on the grass?

    ① Do you want   ② Do they mind
    ③ Are we minded   ④ Can you allow

22. A: Did you decide to apply for the position?

    B: _____.

    ① Thanks for offering

    ② Yes, my boss talked me into it

    ③ You won't regret telling me about it

    ④ Yes, my boss talked me out of it

23. A: Aren't you ready yet, dear?

    B: No not yet. I can't remember where I left my handbag.

    A: You take too much time to get ready.

    B: _____.

    A: No, we have plenty of time to get to the theater the play begins.

    ① Are you in a hurry?

    ② But I don't like waiting

    ③ What time is it now?

    ④ The play begins at nine o'clock

24. A: Bill isn't married, is he?

    B: _____(1)_____.

    A: What's his wife's name?

    B: Mary. No, Glo....ria. Gee, it's on the tip of my __(2)__, But I can' t quite remember.

    A: That's OK. It'll come to you

    B: Ginger! Her name is Ginger!

    (1) ① Yes, he does   ② No, he isn't
        ③ I don't know   ④ Sure, he is

    (2) ① mouth   ② lips
        ③ tongue   ④ throat

25. A: You look tired. Did you have a hard day?

    B: (1) Sort of. I've been painting all day.

    A: Why don't you take a short break?

        Would you like a cup of coffee?

    B: ___(2)___. It's just what I need.

    A: How would you like it?

    B: I'll take it black.

    (1) 밑줄 친 Sort of와 뜻이 같은 것은?

       ① Never   ② Scarcely   ③ Very much   ④ A little

    (2) ① Yes, please   ② No, thank you

        ③ Never mind   ④ Certainly not

26. 다음 중에서 답이 될 수 없는 것은?

    A: Doesn't he like to take a rest right away?

    B: _____.

    ① No, he likes to   ② Yes, he does
    ③ Yes, he likes to   ④ No, he doesn't

27. A: Would you mind moving your elbow, please?

    B: Oh, _____. I am sorry.

    ① of course not   ② of course
    ③ certainly   ④ never mind

28. A: "Don't you know where the Baltic Sea is?"

    B: "_____"

    ① Yes, I don't know. Could you tell me where it is?

    ② No, I know very well where it is.

    ③ Yes, but not exactly. Isn't it somewhere in the south?

    ④ No, I sailed on it five years ago.

29. A: Don't forget to lock the door.

 B: _____.

 ① Yes, I won't   ② Not at all

 ③ No, I don't   ④ That's all

30. 다음 중에서 답이 될 수 없는 것은?

 A: Would you like to stop now?

 B: _____.

 ① Yes, I would.

 ② No, I'd like to keep on.

 ③ Yes, I wouldn't like to.

 ④ No, I wouldn't like to stop now.

31. 다음 중에서 답이 될 수 없는 것은?

 A: Do you ever come on time?

 B: _____.

 ① No, I never come on time.

 ② No, I don't ever come on time.

 ③ Yes, I scarcely ever come on time.

 ④ Yes, I always come on time.

32. A: "Let's meet somewhere later."

 B: "How about in front of the City Hall?"

 A: "OK. What time shall we _____?"

 ① meet   ② make it   ③ decide   ④ make

33. 상대방에게 고마운 마음을 표현한 말로 적당하지 않은 것을 고르시오.

 ① I'm extremely obliged to you.

 ② Thanks a million.

 ③ That was really nice of you.

 ④ I don't think we've met.

34. 상대방의 기분에 대해 물어보고 싶을 때 적당하지 않은 말은?

    ① You, idiot!   ② What's up

    ③ How do you feel?   ④ Are you okay?

35. 작별 인사로 적당하지 않는 말은?

    ① So long.   ② Good to see you.

    ③ Good-bye.   ④ Take care.

36. A: "What's the weather forecast for today?"
    B: "_____."

    ① They say it's going to rain all day

    ② Sun

    ③ Overcast with some showers

    ④ Humid and dry

37. A: You look beautiful today.
    B: _____.

    ① Thanks. You've made my day

    ② Thanks. I've managed to do it

    ③ Thanks. I live up to my expectation

    ④ I do that in return for your compliment

38. A: I am afraid I'm disturbing you.
    B: _____.

    ① It's my pleasure   ② Not in the least

    ③ Don't be sorry   ④ That'll be good

39. A: "I think John was fired yesterday."
    B: "_____"

    ① What makes you say that?   ② Sure!

    ③ Is he still working?   ④ I don't know.

40. A: The new secretary doesn't keep up to our standard.

    B: _____.

    ① She doesn't work the office

    ② She is wrong with work

    ③ Give her a break. She has a lot of work to do

    ④ I couldn't say! She was a secretary

41. "이제 그만 가겠습니다"의 작별 인사로 쓰이지 않는 것은?

    ① I must be going.

    ② I must take leave of you.

    ③ I really must go.

    ④ I'd like to go now.

42. A: "It's beautiful day, isn't it?"

    B: "_____."

    ① No, it's not   ② Yes, it's a little cloudy
    ③ Yes, it couldn't be better   ④ No, I don't know about it

43. A: What can I do for you?

    B: I've got a problem.

       I bought a ticket to London, but I lost it.

    A: No problem. Just buy another ticket.

    B: _____

    A: Just buy another ticket.

    ① Go ahead, please.   ② I beg your pardon?
    ③ What's the matter?   ④ Don't mention it.

44. I'm terrible sorry에 대한 응답으로 알맞은 것은?

    ① That's quite all right.   ② You're welcome.
    ③ No, thanks.   ④ Fine, Thanks.

45. A: Excuse me, but do you have the time?

    B: _____.

    A: That's all right.

    ① No, I don't have plenty of time

    ② Well, I am awfully busy right now

    ③ Sorry, but my watch has stopped

    ④ Sure, but it's high time to leave

46. 다음 밑줄 친 뜻과 반대되는 것은?

    My watch <u>gains</u> five minutes a day.

    ① loses   ② slows   ③ lacks   ④ shortens

47. There is _____ with him. ; he looks sick.

    ① nothing the matter   ② all the matter

    ③ something the matter   ④ None of these

    ⑤ something to do

48. 다음 대화 중 밑줄 친 부분을 영어로 바꾸시오.

    Salesperson : Can I help you?

       J ane : No, thanks. (1) <u>단순히 구경만 하려구요.</u>

    Salesperson : Okay. If you find anything you like, (2) <u>곧 말씀해 주세요.</u>

       Jane : Well. I'll do so. Thanks.

  (1) ① I'm only seeing good now

     ② I'm only looking at the shop now

     ③ I'm just looking around

     ④ I'm just looking into good now

  (2) ① just let me know

     ② just let's know

     ③ Will you make me know soon?

     ④ Please tell me anything

49. 밑줄 친 우리말을 영어로 바꾸시오. (At a department store)

A: Can I try this coat on ?

B: <u>예, 입어 보세요</u>.

① Sure, go ahead ② Yes, please wear that
③ Yes, you are welcome ④ No, I don't mind

※ 다음 빈 곳에 알맞은 것은? (50~54)

50. A: "_____"

B: "No, this is on me."

① Let's go Dutch. ② Will that be all?
③ Will you have this bill? ④ Shall I take this bill?

51. "Is the restaurant still open?"

"_____."

① It's time to leave ② I'm afraid it closed ten minutes ago
③ Ten minutes later ④ I know

52. "Why don't you let me treat you to lunch today, Jane?"

"_____."

① No, I'm not. That would be a good time for me

② I wish I could, but I have another commitment today

③ Good. I'll put it on my calendar so I don't forget

④ OK. I'll check with you on Tuesday

53. "Are you ready to order?"

"_____."

① Of course. The steak comes with soup and salad

② Yes, what are your dinner specials tonight?

③ I'll pay the check

④ I'll pay cash

54. A: Are you going to the discotheque tonight?

    B: Yes, why don't you come too?

    A: Isn't it pretty expensive?

    B: _____.

    A: Okay. I'll see you later.

    ① No, it's cheap   ② Yes, it's cheap
    ③ No, it's pretty   ④ Yes, it's pretty

55. What does the woman mean in the following dialogue?

    Man : "What would you say to a cup of coffee?"

    Woman : "Great idea!"

    ① She'll sell him a cup of coffee
    ② The coffee cup's too full
    ③ She'd like some coffee
    ④ Coffee's hard on her nerves

56. 상대방에게 병원에 가도록 충고할 때 다음 중 가장 적당한 말은?

    ① If I were you, I wouldn't see a doctor.
    ② I think you should see a doctor.
    ③ Do you prefer to see a doctor?
    ④ I'm very grateful to you for seeing a doctor.

57. 다음 빈 곳에 알맞은 것은?

    A: I'm having a toothache again. I can't stand it.

    B: _____.

    A: I'd love to , if it's your tooth.

    ① I'll take you to the dentist this afternoon
    ② You should have brushed your teeth every day
    ③ I've been advising you to have the painful tooth pulled out
    ④ You might ruin the bone surrounding the painful tooth if you leave it untreated

58. 다음 글을 읽고 물음에 답하시오.

A: I'd like to make an appointment with Dr. Moon.

B: All right . What is your name, please?

A: Bonny Lee.

B: And have you been a patient here before, Miss Lee?

A: _____(1)_____ .

B: Then may I have your address and phon number, please?

A: I live at 9-16 Shinsa-dong, Eunpyung-ku. My phon number is 212-8303.

B: All right. I can fit you at two-thirty this afternoon.

A: _____(2)_____ I'll be in class then.

B: Well, the next free spot wouldn't be until next Thursday.

A: Then I suppose we'd better (3) <u>make it</u> this afternoon.

(1), (1)에 알맞은 대화는?

① Yes, I have been once

② I don't know exactly, but I wish to know

③ No, I haven't

④ No, I have never seen one

(2), (2)에 알맞은 대화는?

① Thank you very much.

② Is there any other time?

③ I don't like you to examine me.

④ I hope you to consult me.

(3), (3)의 뜻을 가장 잘 표현한 것은?

① 결정하다   ② 재촉하다

③ 성공하다   ④ 변경하다

(4) 대화의 내용으로 보아 B는 다음 중 누구인가?

① Dr. Moon   ② nurse

③ operator   ④ receptionist

59. "정찰제입니다."라고 할 때 올바르지 않은 표현은?

① We never ask two prices.

② We are a one-price store.

③ We ask only one price.

④ We receive only one order.

60. "거스름돈을 주세요."라고 할 때 올바른 표현은?

① Give me the rest, please.

② Give me the remainder.

③ Give me the change, please.

④ Give me the exchange, please.

61. "지금 품절입니다."라고 할 때 올바른 표현은?

① That article is stopped now.

② We are out of that article now.

③ We have no article now.

④ That article is cut out now.

62. 회화의 관용 상 적합하지 않은 표현은?

① 「물건을 건네줄 때」 : "Here you are."

② 「값을 물을 때」 : "How much does it cost."

③ 「거스름돈을 내 줄 때」 : "Here is the rest money."

④ 「손님이 들어 왔을 때」 : "Welcome, sir. Can I help you."

63. "Pass me the sugar, please." 에 대한 옳은 대답은?

① Here it is.

② Help yourself to it.

③ No, thanks.

④ It's over there.

64. When you offer your guest something to eat or drink, what do you say?

① I say, "Make yourself at home."

② I say, "Please help yourself."

③ I say, "Don't you have appetite?"

④ I say, "I want you eat much."

65. 회화의 관용상 적합하지 않은 표현은?

① 「스테이크를 어떻게 해 그릴까요?」 : "How do you like your steak?"

② 「커피를 어떻게 해드릴까요?」 : "What can I do for your coffee?"

③ 「주문하십시오.」 : "May I take your order."

④ 「많이 먹었습니다.」 : "I've had enough."

66. When you are at table and you want to get some salt far from you, what do you do?

① I reach my hand across the table to take it myself.

② I say, "Will you pass me the salt, please?"

③ I stand up and go to take it.

④ I ask the servant to bring me another salt bottle.

67. 「식욕이 어떻습니까?」의 영어로 가장 적합한 것은?

① How much do you eat?

② What is your appetite?

③ How's your appetite?

④ What is your passion for eating?

68. 환자에게 "오늘은 기분이 좀 어떻습니까?"라고 할 때에 가장 적합한 표현은?

① What about your health today?

② How do you feel today?

③ How do you do today?

④ How are you today?

69. 다음 대화 중 빈칸에 알맞은 것은?

    A: May I help you?

    B: Do you have something for a cold?

    A: Do you have a fever?

    B: No, I just have a ____(1)____ nose.

    A: Why don't you ____(2)____ an antihistamine?

    B: That ____(3)____ like a good idea.

    (1) ① keen   ② runny   ③ sharp   ④ saucy

    (2) ① experiment   ② eat   ③ drink   ④ try

    (3) ① sounds   ② is   ③ looks   ④ seen

※ 다음 빈 곳에 알맞은 것은? (70~73)

70. A: Excuse me. Can you tell me the wat to the City Hall?
    B: I'm sorry. I am a _____ here myself.

    ① walker   ② guide   ③ resident   ④ stranger

71. "Could you tell me how to get to East Gate Market?"
    "_____"

    ① Sure. I'm from East Coast myself.
    ② I'm sorry. I'm from West Coast.
    ③ I'm sorry. I am a stranger here myself.
    ④ Why don't you do to West Gate Market?

72. "How long does it take to walk to the post office from here?"
    "_____"

    ① About two blocks.   ② Why don't you catch a taxi?
    ③ You can't miss it   ④ About thirty minutes.

73. A: Something wrong, officer?

    B: You just broke the speed limit.

    A: But I was only driving 40 miles an hour.

    B: The speed limit's _____ on this road.

    ① 30   ② 40
    ③ 50   ④ 60

74. What is the woman's advice in the following dialogue?

    Man : "I've got to find myself an apartment today."

    Woman : "But you can't take just any apartment.
             You need one near the university."

    ① Apply to just one university.

    ② Stay in the university dormitory.

    ③ Take any apartment that is available.

    ④ Rent an apartment near the university.

75. Read the dialogue and choose the one that is suitable to the underlined parts (1), (2) and (3)

    A: What's the matter, sir?

    B: My waller' s gone!

    A: Let's ___(1)___. Where did you last have it?

    B: On the bus. Uh oh! Someone ___(2)___ it.

    A: Let's ___(3)___ it to the police.

    B: Okay. I've got to call the bank and tell them, too.

    (1) ① hurry up   ② retrace your steps
        ③ go back   ④ return

    (2), (3)
        ① lost, report   ② lost, declare
        ③ lifted, report   ④ lifted, declare

76. 다음 대화가 일어날 수 있는 가장 적절한 장소는?

A: Come on. We're late. What were you doing?

B: I was just buying a couple of books.

A: The flight goes in two minutes. Come on.

① a bus terminal   ② a station

③ a bookstore   ④ an airport

※ 다음 대화 중 빈 곳에 알맞은 것은? (77~78)

77. "The plane is scheduled to leave at 9 a.m. Are you ready to go?"
"_____"

① Really.

② Can you hold on a minute?

③ Yes, I am packing.

④ Don't leave me!

78. A: How do you get to work?

B: _____.

A: When do you have to be at work?

B: At nine.

① To make money   ② I like it very much

③ By bus   ④ I enjoy working

79. 해당 단어를 영어로 쓰시오.

(1) _____ : 호텔의 숙박 '요금'

(2) _____ : 짐표에 붙이는 '꼬리표'

(3) _____ : 호텔에 들어가는 '숙박 절차'

(4) _____ : 호텔을 나오는 '퇴숙 절차'

80. 다음 대화문을 읽고 물음에 답하시오.

A: Welcome home!

B: Thank you.

A: Did you have any problems on the journey?

B: Well, <u>we didn't have any serious problems but it certainly wasn't a holiday</u>.

A: Of course, not.

B: We don't have a wash or a shave for two weeks!

A: Really?

B: Yes, It wasn't very comfortable!

A: What about food? Was that a problem?

B: Well, we didn't have any normal food.

A: What did you have?

B: Well, we had some food tablets.

A: Are you going to the moon again?

B: I hope _____. It was wonderful!

(1) 대화자 A와 B의 직업으로 가장 그럴듯한 것은?
　　① 기자와 우주비행사　　　　　② 아들과 아버지
　　③ 학생과 교사　　　　　　　　④ 여행객과 여행사 직원

(2) B가 여행한 곳은 어디인가?
　　① 이국땅　　　　② 농장　　　　③ 달나라　　　　④ 남극

(3) B가 여행 중 먹은 음식은 무엇인가?
　　① fresh vegetable　　　　　　② soup and rice
　　③ normal food　　　　　　　　④ artificial food

(4) 밑줄 친 문장의 뜻으로 가장 적당한 것은?
　　① 큰 문제가 많이 있었지만, 불편하지도 않았다.
　　② 휴일이 아니었기 때문에 큰 문제가 없었다.
　　③ 큰 문제도 없었고, 휴일도 전혀 없었다.
　　④ 큰 문제는 없었지만, 그렇게 편한 것은 아니었다.

(5) 빈 칸에 들어 갈 가장 적절한 것은?
　　① as　　　　　② such　　　　　③ it　　　　　④ so

81. "삼일빌딩이 어디입니까?"라고 길을 물을 때 부적절한 표현은?

① Could you tell me the way to the Samil Building?

② Which way is the Samil Building?

③ Where is the Samil Building, please?

④ Could you tell me where can I go to the Samil Building?

82. "아빠, 여기가 어디인지 몰라도 저는 무사해요."의 적절한 표현은?

"Hello, Dad. I don't know _____, but I'm OK."

① where this is   ② where is here

③ where I am   ④ where are we

83. "부산행 급행은 언제 들어옵니까?"의 올바른 문장은?

① What time is the express for Busan supposed to arrive here?

② When is he express for Busan due here?

③ What time will the express for Busan come here?

④ What is the time that the express for Busan will arrive here?

84. A, B의 대화에서 밑줄 친 곳에 적합한 말은?

A: "Do you have any vacancies?"

B: "I am sorry, _____. You will find it hard to fine a room on holidays."

① this way, please

② you will have no vacancy

③ all the rooms are booked up

④ you can register at the front desk

85. "독방은 얼마입니까?"의 영어로 적합하지 않은 것은?

① How much do you charge for a single room?

② What's the rate for a single room?

③ What is the charge for a single room?

④ What does a single room charge?

157

86. "몇 시에 돈을 치르고 나가야 합니까?"의 영어로 적합하지 않은 것은?

① What time do we have to check out?

② What time so you take the bill?

③ What is your check-out time?

④ What time do we have to pay the bill and leave?

87. "차로 모시러 가겠습니다."의 올바른 문장은?

① We'll call you up.　　② We'll pick you up.

③ We'll bring you by car.　　④ We'll take you by car.

88. 상대방의 동의를 구할 때 적절하지 않은 표현은?

① No way!

② Do you feel the same way?

③ Am I talking nonsense?

④ I wonder if you agree entirely.

89. "무엇을 도와 드릴까요?"의 영어 표현으로 가장 자연스러운 것은?

① What do you want?　　② What help do you need?

③ What can I do for you?　　④ do you need my help?

※ 다음 대화 중 빈 곳에 알맞은 것은? (90~97)

90. A: Hurry up or we'll miss the show.

　　B: I can't find my glasses. Do you know where they are?

　　A: _____. But you won't need them, anyway.

　　　You'll fall asleep as soon as the show starts.

① I have no idea　　② You deserve it

③ Go for it　　④ Good for you

91. A: Rennie doesn't sing as beautiful as Jim.

   B: Sure he does.

   A: _____.

   ① I agree with you

   ② I disagree. Rennie's voice is better

   ③ No, Rennie's voice definitely isn't as beautiful as Jim's

   ④ Rennie doesn't sing about beautiful things.

92. "How did you like new art exhibition?"

   "_____."

   ① At the Seoul Gallery   ② By looking around the streets

   ③ It was very good   ④ By subway

93. A: I have a confession to make.

   B:_____.

   ① Not at all   ② Go ahead

   ③ By now   ④ It's my pleasure

94. A: Excuse me, do you have change for a dollar?

   B: _____

   A: Thank you. Anything will do fine.

   ① I don't have any change right now.

   ② There is a coin machine just around the corner.

   ③ I'm not sure just what it is your're asking for?

   ④ I only have quarters and dimes. Will that do?

95. "Where is the report?"

   "_____."

   ① There it is   ② There the report is

   ③ There is it   ④ Is the report there

96. A: Let's go to the University Bookstore.

    B: I'm sorry, I can't.

    A: _____?

    B: I have to meet someone here.

    ① How about you   ② What for

    ③ Who do you meet   ④ Why not

97. "What is your nationality?"

    "I am _____."

    ① the Korean   ② Korean

    ③ Koreans   ④ Korea

98. "How"가 들어갈 수 없는 문장은?

    ① _____ would you like to have your haircut?

    ② _____ do you think about it?

    ③ _____ do you like your steak?

    ④ _____ about taking a walk?

99. "당신의 가족에게 안부 전해 주세요." 에 부적절한 표현은?

    ① Please remember me to all your family.

    ② Give my kindest regards to all your family.

    ③ Say hello to all your family.

    ④ Please remind me of all your family.

100. 상대방에게 「먼저 쓰십시오./하십시오./타십시오.」라고 할 때의 표현은?

    ① After you, sir.   ② Go ahead, sir.

    ③ I'm second, sir.   ④ You are first, sir.

101. "지금 TV에 무엇이 나옵니까?" 의 올바른 표현은?

    ① What's on TV now?   ② What's doing in TV now?

    ③ What's appearing in TV now?   ④ What's coming out of TV now?

102. "얼마입니까?"라고 물건 값을 물을 때 부적절한 표현은?

① What's the price?   ② How much does it cost?

③ How much is it?   ④ What is the rate?

103. 상점에서 "모자 좀 봅시다."라고 할 때 부적절한 표현은?

① Let me see hats.   ② Make me look at your hats.

③ I'd like to see hats.   ④ Show me hats, please.

※ 다음 대화중 빈 곳에 알맞은 것은? (104~106)

104. A: Do you have the time?

B: _____.

① It's 4:50   ② No, I don't have enough

③ Tonight will be OK   ④ Yes, I have a good watch

105. A: I wish you a Merry Christmas.

B: _____.

① The same to you   ② Congratulations

③ Thanks to you   ④ Many happy returns

106. A: Could you please help me correct my speech?

B: _____.

① I was happy to do it   ② I'd be happy to

③ You don't have to thank me   ④ Yes, that's correct

특례 영어
실전문제 총정리

PART Ⅶ

단문 독해

※ 다음 글을 읽고 물음에 답하시오.

1.

> We cannot travel every path. <u>Success must be won along one line.</u> To live with ideal is a successful life. Success grows less and less dependent on luck and chance. Self-distrust is the cause of most of our failures. The great and indispensable help to success is character.

(1) 밑줄 친 문장과 가장 비슷한 뜻을 지닌 격언은?

① 백지장도 맞들면 낫다.

② 실패는 성공의 어머니다.

③ 한 우물을 파라.

④ 성공은 1%의 영감과 99%의 땀이다.

(2) 필자가 성공의 가장 큰 요인이라고 여기는 것은?

① luck   ② self-distrust

③ character   ④ chance

2.

> Especially well-suited for those who should not take aspirin or aspirin-containing products. DOSAGE : Adults, 1 to 2 tablets 4 times daily. Consult a physician for use by children under 6 or for use longer than 10 days.

(1) The phrase that in closest in meaning to the word <u>DOSAGE</u> is

① be careful   ② notice this

③ two ages of life   ④ recommended amount

(2) What should you do if you want to give this medication to a four-year-old child?

① Ask a doctor

② Give him half of the adult dosage

③ Wait for ten days before giving it to him

④ Be sure that it does not contain aspirin.

3. 다음 영문에 등장하는 주인공의 직업은?

> At 22 she published her first book, on the mythical King Arthur. Her typewriter never cooled down, even after she married Hugh Fraser, a Conservative Member of Parliament, and produced three sons and two daughters. The result : 23 volumes.

   ① a typewriter   ② a member of parliament
   ③ a publisher   ④ an author

4.

> Only a fool like John would believe Robert's statement.

  (1) John thought Robert's statement was _____.
     ① foolish   ② exaggerated
     ③ true   ④ clever

  (2) Robert's statement was _____.
     ① indisputable   ② implausible
     ③ misinterpreted   ④ unfair

5. Who should be prosecuted for soul murder?

> The literary side of a technical education should consist in an effort to make the pupils enjoy literature. It does not matter what they know, but the enjoyment is vital. The great English universities, under whose direct authority school children are examined in plays of Shakespeare, to the certain destruction of their enjoyment, should be prosecuted for soul murder.

   ① school children who do not enjoy literature
   ② some great English universities
   ③ Shakespeare
   ④ plays of Shakespeare

6.

Just as myths glorify the accomplishments of people, epics assert that the accomplishments of human beings are admirable and worthy of retelling.

(1) Myths tell about the _____.

    ① similarities between gods and people

    ② difference between gods and people

    ③ glorious actions of people

    ④ praiseworthy deeds of gods

(2) Myths differ from epics in _____.

    ① value of greatness   ② judgements

    ③ main characters   ④ praising deeds

(3) Epics and myths are similar in _____ .

    ① recording pre-history of people

    ② making people seem admirable

    ③ glorifying gods

    ④ praising deeds

7. 다음 글에서 영국인에 대한 일반론으로 옳지 <u>않은</u> 것은?

Here are a couple of generalizations about England that would be accepted by almost all observers. One is that the English are not gifted artistically. They are not as musical as the Germans or Italians. Painting and sculpture have never flourished in England as they have in France. Another is that as Europeans go, the English are not intellectual. They have a horror of abstract thought. They feel no need for any philosophy or systematic "world-view". Nor is this because they are "practical", as they are so fond of claiming for themselves.

① 영국인은 예술적인 재능이 없다.

② 영국인은 철학의 필요성을 느끼지 못한다.

③ 영국인은 추상적인 사고방식을 싫어한다.

④ 영국인은 실용적인 국민성이 결여되어 있다.

8. 다음 글에서 사업가가 가장 중요시 하는 것은?

The milkman has a rival in the early calling, and that rival is the newspaperboy. Both milk and news are required for breakfast and the London businessman would as soon do without the one as the other, the first being for his bodily refreshment and the second for his mental.

① 신문 배달부　　② 신문　　③ 우유 배달부　　④ 우유

9. 다음 글을 읽고 물음에 답하시오.

In the 1940's, three Frenchmen sailed down the Niger River in a native canoe. During the 2,600mile voyage, they stopped often to visit with <u>cooperative African natives</u>. The explorers recorded interviews and took thousands of   photographs that tell about native life along the Niger.

(1) 세 명의 불란서인들이 여행한 곳은?
　　① Europe　　② America　　③ Asia　　④ Africa

(2) 밑줄 친 부분의 원주민을 묘사하는 가장 적절한 말은?
　　① warlike　　② helpful　　③ jealous　　④ sailors

10. 다음을 일고 표현하고자 하는 답을 고르시오.

Love is not a relationship with a specific person. Love of the helpless one is the beginning of brotherly love. To love one's own flesh and blood is no achievement. Only in the love of those who do not serve a purpose does love begin to unfold. By having compassion for the helpless one, man begins to develop love for his brother.

① 자기 자신을 사랑해야 남도 사랑할 줄 안다.
② 자기 형제를 사랑할 줄 모르는 사람이 어찌 남을 사랑할 것인가.
③ 맹목적인 사랑이 진정한 사랑이다.
④ 자기에게 도움이 되지 않는 사람들 까지도 사랑하게 되어야 진정한 사랑이 되기 시작한다.

11. 다음 글을 가장 잘 요약한 것은?

We are so accustomed to newspapers and books and magazines that we take it for granted that the world has always been able to read and write. Actually, writing, the most important of all inventions, is relatively new in the long history of mankind.

① Writing is a difficult art.
② Writing is a recent invention.
③ Everybody can both read and write.
④ Books have been a part of human life.

12. 다음 글에서 필자가 언급하지 <u>않은</u> 것은?

The word liberty is often interpreted incorrectly. The dictionary gives many exact definitions of the world : briefly, it means "freedom from restraint or control." Such a brief definition leads to misinterpretation. Many people think liberty means that may do whatever they like regardless of the effects. Liberty is not uncontrolled freedom.

① 자유   ② 방종
③ 제약   ④ 의무

13. 다음 글을 읽고 물음에 답하시오.

The second leading cause of death in this country, cancer claims the lives of over 385,000 Americans every year.

(1) 윗글에 의하면, 암보다 더 높은 사망원인을 가진 것은 몇 가지가 있는가?
    ① one   ② two
    ③ three   ④ none

(2) 향후 5년간 암으로 사망하게 될 미국인의 수는 얼마로 추정되는가?
    ① 385,000   ② 1 million
    ③ 2 millions   ④ 1.5 millions

14.

> Two miners trapped 200 feet underground for 28 days in a collapsed gold mine were rescued today. Both were muddy but smiling when, wrapped in white bed sheets, they were carried out of the mine on stretchers.

(1) 왜 광부는 지하에 갇혀 있게 되었나?

   ① 그들이 원했기 때문이다.   ② 금을 채굴하기 위해서이다.

   ③ 금광이 붕괴되었기 때문이다.   ④ 그들이 잠이 들었기 때문이다.

(2) 광부들은 결국 어떻게 되었나?

   ① 구조원들에 의해 들것에 실려 구조되었다.

   ② 구조반들의 도움으로 갱내의 열린 구멍으로 올라와 빠져나왔다.

   ③ 갱내의 통로를 통해 기어 나왔다.

   ④ 진흙으로 뒤덮인 굴을 지나 걸어 나왔다.

15.

> Muscles produce heat when the body is in motion, but when the body is at rest, very little heat is generated except by the metabolic activity of he internal organs.

(1) 윗글에 의하면 몸이 쉬고 있을 때 일어나는 현상은?

   ① Muscles require heat.

   ② The metabolic activity of the internal organ is at rest.

   ③ Internal organs generate heat.

   ④ The metabolic rate increases.

(2) 몸이 움직이고 있을 때 일어나는 현상은?

   ① Internal organs are at rest.

   ② Muscles generate very little heat.

   ③ The liver suffers quite a lot.

   ④ Muscles produce heat.

PART VIII

문장 완성형 독해

※ 문맥상 빈 곳에 가장 잘 어울리는 것을 고르시오.

1. Since the beginning of time, men have tried to convince others to adopt their point of view. They have become masters in the art of _____.

   ① discussion   ② education
   ③ persuasion   ④ compulsion

2. Iron, coal and oil are examples of our abundant _____.

   ① resources   ② minerals
   ③ heritage   ④ mines

3. For many years man has been able to make astronomical observation from the earth. It is now possible to send to great heights unmanned telescopes in balloons and to make observations not possible from observatories _____.

   ① in the sky   ② on earth
   ③ in space   ④ by automation

4. The sea sparkled with brightly colored lights. _____ the sky was cloudless.

   ① But   ② Therefore
   ③ Above   ④ Next

5. There is a(n) _____ pattern of growth in reading ability, although it does not necessarily progress exactly according to age.

   ① immoderate   ② consistent
   ③ accidental   ④ reluctant

6. Surely human affairs would be far happier if the power in men to be silent were the same as that to speak. But experience more than sufficiency teaches that men govern nothing with more difficulty than their _____.

   ① affairs   ② minds
   ③ tongues   ④ offspring

7. Changes in a developing science are not to be compared to the tearing down of old buildings to make way for new ones, but rather to the gradual evolution of a zoological type. We must not believe that discarded theories have been _____.

① used in molding new ideas
② of any importance in present research
③ seriously considered
④ either sterile or in vain

8. Athletic games are often so close that they are decided in the last few seconds of play. In such games the players who maintain their self-control under pressure are most likely to _____.

① lose   ② win
③ play   ④ tie

9. Although there is not much oxygen in the ocean, all that there is comes from the air. Thus, there is more free oxygen in the water near the surface and less free oxygen _____.

① above the surface   ② on top of mountains
③ in the air   ④ down below

10. Not to know what has been transacted in former times is to be always a child. If no use is made of the labors of past ages, the world must remain always in the infancy of _____.

① ignorance   ② progress
③ knowledge   ④ despair

11. An author would rather be attacked than be unnoticed. The worst thing the world can do to him is to be silent about his _____.

① faults   ② successes
③ books   ④ complaints

12. Education was one of the functions of the church at that time; therefore, the majority of teachers were _____.

   ① ministers   ② classicists

   ③ scientists   ④ educators

13. Before the dam _____, the river overflowed its banks every summer.

   ① be built   ② builds

   ③ was built   ④ has built

14. Some illnesses may be caused by physical or mental stress, whereas others may occur without a readily recognizable _____.

   ① point of origin   ② result

   ③ behavior pattern   ④ symptom

15. They would say that his visit to the upper world had ruined his sight, and the _____was not worth even attempting.

   ① progress   ② ascent

   ③ process   ④ conception

16. Those who _____ in the affairs of others are one of the most insensitive people in the world.

   ① mingle   ② mutter

   ③ meager   ④ meddle

17. If we hurry, we can _____ him in no time.

   ① outdo   ② outwit

   ③ overcome   ④ overtake

18. Closely tied to the population problem is the problem of food. The world's total supply of food, and particularly _____, has at last come to be seen as a massive problem.

① oil   ② protein

③ clothes   ④ shelter

19. To place Herbert Spencer's philosophy it is necessary not only to _____ his relation to Darwin but also to contrast him with his philosophical predecessors, in particular Hegel and Comte.

① proceed   ② owe

③ contribute   ④ trace

20. If man does something that conduces to his welfare he does something that _____.

① buy some security   ② is harmful to his well-being

③ adds to his well-being   ④ makes him prosperous

21. When we say that an argument is invalidated by scientific evidence, we mean that _____.

① the argument is destroyed

② the argument is supported

③ the argument is neither destroyed nor supported

④ the argument should be validated

22. I felt that diagnosis was correct, but I doubted that the remedy offered would_____.

① cure the disease   ② heal the opposition

③ solve the problem   ④ soothe the flame

23. In social systems, there is likely to be fundamental _____ between the short-term and long-term consequences of a policy.

① agreement   ② conflict
③ harmony   ④ problem

24. People have one thing in common; they are _____.

① different   ② generous
③ concerned   ④ thoughtful

25. I am always ready to learn, although I do not always like being _____.

① right   ② taught
③ lenient   ④ seen

26. A house without books is a mindless and characterless house, no matter how rich the Persian carpets and how elegant the furniture may be. The Persian carpets only tell you that the owner has got money, but the books will tell you whether he has got _____.

① a large capital   ② a mind as well
③ lots of courage   ④ fine furniture

27. Above all, make your study a habit, like getting dressed or undressed, combing your hair or brushing your teeth, and it will become so much a part of your life that you will feel guilty if you _____.

① look dirty   ② want to succeed
③ continue for good   ④ skip a single time

28. Although the local gambling club contributed large sums of money to civic projects, the new mayor firmly refused to _____ its activities.

① confirm   ② condemn
③ condone   ④ control

29. Some take no thought of the value of money until they have come to an end of it, and many do the same with their time. Lost wealth may be replaced by industry and economy, lost knowledge by study, lost health by temperance or medicine, but lost _____ is forever lost.

30. We are making bombs and bombs are making hate and suspicion. We are keeping secrets and secrets breed _____.

    ① happiness   ② distrust   ③ bombs
    ④ trust   ⑤ blessings

31. A good reader is active in his effort to understand. Any book is a problem, a puzzle. The reader's attitude is that of _____ looking for clues to its basic ideas.

    ① a publisher   ② a writer   ③ a listener
    ④ a detective   ⑤ a citizen

32. Our life is not short, but we make it so. Just as great wealth is scattered in a moment when it comes into the hands of a bad owner, while wealth, however small, if it is entrusted to a good keeper, increases by use, so our life is long enough for him who _____.

    ① lives at random   ② uses it properly
    ③ aimlessly   ④ feels life uninteresting

33. The best teacher in the best college in the world cannot give a student a real education. He can lead the way to the mine from which it can be dug, provide him with the power tools, and help him make more vigorous effort, but the student will own only as much of the precious metal as _____.

    ① the teacher gives him   ② he wants to have
    ③ the college curriculum supplies ④ he digs for himself

34. According to the laws of heredity, characteristics possessed by parents will appear in the progeny. Since the parent leopard is spotted, we expect that its offspring will be _____.

① plain   ② speckled
③ vicious   ④ docile

35. Even when we make an inference from known facts, the truth of the inference is never certain. If the body of evidence from which we draw a conclusion is sufficiently large and reliable, we may accept the conclusion as _____.

① immediately obvious   ② enhancing the criteria
③ unquestionably proved   ④ reasonably probable

36. If the blind lead the blind, both shall fall into the ditch. Of the following, this proverb means most nearly; _____.

① Two blacks do not make white.
② None are so blind as those who will not see.
③ One cannot get sympathy from a hard- or cold-hearted person.
④ If the ignorant are led by the ignorant, both will come to disaster.

37. Beggars cannot be choosers. Of the following, this proverb means most nearly;

_____.

① If one is in a weak and dependent situation, one can't lay down conditions or be exacting in demands or terms.
② There must always be stages in which a person gradually goes from bad to worse.
③ A wise person when alone has all the occupation and interest he needs.
④ A man's life lasts only a short time, but art with its manifestations goes on forever.

38. Time is to Season as Space is to _____.

① Travel   ② Area   ③ Hour   ④ Universe

39. Paradoxically, all the local residents demonstrating for world peace _____ gun control.

① represent　　② condone　　③ oppose　　④ need

40. "The only unchanging truth is that everything changes" is a _____.

① paradigm　　② pretext　　③ paradox　　④ predilection

41. When you look back over a long period, you seem to see human beings always fixed in some special place and some characteristic attitude. It seems to you that they were always doing _____.

① exactly the same thing　　② good for human beings
③ things that are dull　　④ a thing different

42. The aim of science is to foresee, and not, as often been said, to understand. Science describes facts, objects and phenomena minutely, and tries to join them by what we call laws, so as to be able to predict events in the _____.

① past　　② present　　③ space　　④ future

43. Since their first appearance on earth, men have gathered information and have attempted to pass useful ideas to other men. The carving of word pictures on the walls of ancient caves represents some of men's efforts _____.

① to show their first arrival on earth
② to convey information
③ to put down the stories of heroes
④ to gather information

44. Religion is based, I think, primarily and mainly upon _____. It is partly the terror of the unknown and partly the wish to feel that you have a kind of elder brother who will stand by you in all your troubles and disputes.

① belief　　② science　　③ peace　　④ fear

45. In adolescence, I hated life and was continually on the verge of suicide. Now, ____ I enjoy life and with every year that passes I enjoy it more.

① on second thoughts   ② in addition

③ on the contrary   ④ in advance

46. With the exception of the inhabitants of the southeastern districts, the people are almost purely Celtic, descendants of the early Britons, who were escaped _____ with the _____.

① slavery — others   ② infiltration — northerners

③ civilization — Normans   ④ intermixture — invaders

47. They that can give up essential liberty to obtain a little temporary safety deserve neither _____ nor _____.

① pity — justice   ② wealth — health

③ kindness — consideration   ④ liberty — safety

48. College graduates have a debt to pay for, they must know that the education they have received is not _____.

① biased   ② complete

③ free   ④ creditable

49. The old lady who owned the pet shop did not like children to come in with their noise and dirt. This was too bad, for children are a pet shop's best _____.

① customers   ② pets

③ watchers   ④ owners

50. Pussy crept toward the mouse hole on soft padded feet. She was hungry. She watched the mouse hole for a long time. What was she waiting for?

① dog   ② bone

③ mouse   ④ hole

51. It has been said that "Knowledge is power", but greater power lies in the ability to utilize this knowledge. A trained and powerful mind surely contains something, but its chief value consists in what it _____.

① can do   ② contains   ③ forgets   ④ retains

52. I once met woman who, having been left with a fortune, said that she would never feel free till she had got rid of her property. She maintained that one became possessions' servant and not their _____.

① friend   ② master   ③ colleague   ④ accountant

53. The prevention of tooth decay is at present an unsolved problem. Though cavities are easily identified, attempts to isolate the agent responsible for their occurrence have not yet been _____.

① successful   ② refuted   ③ undertaken   ④ discussed

54. The trapdoor spider builds her home in the ground. It is lined with silk cobwebs and has a little door that opens. The trapdoor spider is a good _____.

① buyer   ② builder   ③ singer   ④ trapper

55. It has been said that tyranny has no enemy as formidable as the pen. One of freedom's most important safeguards is _____.

① a free press   ② universal suffrage
③ adult education   ④ the secret ballot

56. Although it is always a mistake to consider misfortune good for an artist, Van Gogh's legend is so dramatic that we are tempted to do so. If it were madness that enabled him to paint with the perfection shown in some of his very late landscapes, we are apt to say welcome to madness, for it _____.

① turned him from portraiture   ② made a greater painter of him
③ led to the one love of his life   ④ increased the drama of his story

57. People with fixed incomes are fortunate in times of falling prices. Their real incomes increase because their dollars will buy more goods and services than they did _____.

① when goods were plentiful   ② after a war
③ when the prices were high   ④ during deflation

58. You can't _____ in the dark, because in order to see, the eye must receive light. Since darkness is the absence of light, there is no light in the darkness to be reflected from chairs, tables or people to your eyes, and therefore you can't see these objects.

59. Nothing grows or lives on the moon, for there is no water and no air. There are no clouds on the moon, for clouds are made from water. There is complete silence on the moon, for there can be no sound without _____.

60. Tom is still a _____ in golf because he has only started playing about a month or so ago.

① novice   ② veteran   ③ host   ④ intrepid

61. People have always found it difficult to govern themselves, which explains why there are so few truly _____ societies around today.

① democratic   ② technocratic
③ plebeian   ④ autocratic

62. Propaganda, however effective, is in effect a _____ of the truth and cannot be long sustained.

① perversion   ② inversion
③ subversion   ④ diversion

63. He _____ his property as a direct result of taxes unpaid.

   ① foreshadowed   ② forfeited

   ③ foresaw   ④ fornicated

64. Sound is a form of energy that travels in waves away from a vibrating source through the surrounding _____.

   ① waves   ② vibrations

   ③ medium   ④ compression

65. Play in old age marks an atrophy of human nature, that is, _____.

   ① a failure of man to grow

   ② a tendency of man to be frivolous

   ③ an inclination of man to waste time

   ④ a refusal of man to accept the responsibility

66. Because she had never worked before, she had to find a job requiring a minimum of _____.

   ① ambition   ② money

   ③ education   ④ experience

67. The well-fed child says to the hungry child, "Keep good cheer." Of the following, this proverb means most nearly: _____.

   ① We can all endure the misfortune of others.

   ② It is very good to have companions in misery.

   ③ Every man thinks his cross the heaviest.

   ④ Every man must bear his own burden.

68. Julius Caesar cannot be called a "champion of liberty." He was a soldier and a great leader. He did away with some of the obstacles to the progress of the state, but he did not promote the cause of _____.

   ① war   ② power   ③ government   ④ freedom

69. Travelling is easy and pleasant today. We enjoy traveling on land by train, bus, or automobile. On the ocean, great ships offer very comfortable accommodations to _____.

① friends   ② sleepers   ③ teachers   ④ dignitaries

70. Some illnesses may be caused by physical or mental stress, whereas others may occur without a readily recognizable _____.

① result   ② symptom
③ points of origin   ④ behavior pattern

71. It is unfortunate that we frequently differentiate between "pure science" and "applied science" as if they were two types of science, and one were more valuable than the other. It is my hope that we may _____.

① abolish this distinction   ② evaluate them separately
③ emphasize theoretical studies   ④ clearly distinguish between them

72. _____. Some are caused by lightning, but most are caused by careless people. They often throw away burning cigarettes and do not put out campfires when they leave their campsites. The forests must not be damaged or destroyed, for they are our public property.

① Fires destroy many forests every year.
② Young trees should be planted when old ones are cut out.
③ The forests provide us with many things.
④ The forests should be taken good care of.

73. Among life's most difficult and important kinds of analysis are those which we perform when we read an essay carefully. It is true that we cannot avoid performing analysis, no matter how unconsciously we may go about it, for all reading goes from part to part, and parts fit together in some way to make up _____.

① an analysis   ② a life   ③ a part   ④ a whole

74. If you want to have a personal wage/salary increase you put in for a raise. A group of workers makes a wage-claim. If the employer does not want to increase wages, there may be a pay dispute, eventually lead into a walk-out. Usually, however, the union officials and the management will enter into _____ to discuss ways of resolving the conflict.

① a fight
② negotiation
③ unemployment
④ a strike

75. A very trivial circumstance will serve to exemplify this. Suppose you go into a fruiter's shop, wanting an apple. You take up one, and on biting it, you find it sour; you look at it, and see that it is hard and green. You take up another one, and that too is hard, green and sour. The shopman offers you a third; but before biting it, you examine it, and find that it is hard and green, and you immediately say that you will not have it as it must be _____, like those that you have already tried.

① bitter
② sweet
③ red
④ sour

76. One of the most important weapons used during the Second World War was not a weapon used against people, but rather a drug used against _____.

① disease
② gas
③ accidents
④ pollution

77. Animals have different ways to keep themselves warm. Some mammals have fur to help keep their bodies warm. Feathers help keep birds' bodies warm. People use clothes to protect themselves from the _____.

① heat
② cold
③ coolness
④ warmth

78. Almost all of the world's civilized populations believe that the earth is a sphere. Only among isolated primitive tribes is the theory that the earth is flat _____.

① rejected
② changed
③ criticized
④ accepted

79. During the American Revolution, the people of Canada remained loyal to England, although the rebelling colonies tried to persuade them to _____.

① sell their territory to the colonies

② state exactly how they stood on the issue

③ help England fight the uprising against the crown

④ join the war of independence

80. In the early days of this country, large areas were cleared of trees in order to make more land available for cultivation. Eastern forests were the first to suffer, and then as the frontier was extended, western forests also echoed with the _____.

① sleigh bells   ② dinner gong

③ woodman's ax   ④ children's voices

81. Every human society has rules covering marriage. In Britain it is illegal to marry under the age of 18 without your parents' _____.

① understanding   ② submission

③ permission   ④ praise

82. The magnificent qualities of the Vikings were as striking as their _____.

① laws   ② defects

③ cowardice   ④ history

83. The urban population of the United States slowly _____, the urban decline in births being more than balanced by migration from the rural areas.

① decreased   ② consolidated

③ disintegrated   ④ increased

84. The winter afternoon was no longer bright and sunny. The sun was _____.

① bright and warm   ② melting the snow

③ rising in the east   ④ hidden by clouds

85. Although he knew himself to be _____, Arnold feared he would be accused of the crime.

    ① guilty   ② suspicious   ③ blameless   ④ stolid

86. He suffered all his life from bad health but learned to endure it with _____.

    ① great fortitude   ② proper therapy
    ③ ill grace   ④ regular exercise

87. In attempting to establish relationships between known and unknown factors, most workers in the various fields of scientific research believe that the most reliable findings are based on _____.

    ① perceptive flashes of insight   ② direct observation
    ③ prior knowledge   ④ authoritative information

88. History reveals that freedom has often resulted from the successful use of force; yet we hate war as strongly as we love liberty. Is there a resolution to this _____?

    ① paradox   ② history
    ③ ambiguity   ④ necessity

89. During a thunder and lightning storm, one is fairly safe indoors. But since a chimney rises unprotected above the roof, it is more likely to be struck by the lighting than are other parts of the house. It is therefore wise to _____?

    ① avoid open places   ② stay outside all the time
    ③ close all doors and window ④ keep away from open fire-places

90. Belief in God is not essential to belief in immortality, but it is difficult to dissociate one from the other. These two notions have been so _____ connected that a life after death has always been looked upon as the most powerful instrument to God's hand in his dealings with the human race.

    ① ingenuously   ② unfriendly
    ③ miserly   ④ inseparably

특례영어
실전문제 총정리

PART IX

중 · 장문 독해

■ 독해 1.

Bill Clinton had won the election but lost his voice, so it was a good thing Boris Yeltsin did most of the talking, "I think that my warm and good relationship with George Bush will not prevent our relationship from being even better," said the President of Russia in a phone call on Nov. 5. "The political boldness and firm rejection of old dogmas and stereotypes that you stand _____(4)_____ match the principles of Russian-American relations." These gracious sentiments were in marked contrast to what Yelstin had been saying only a few weeks earlier. In conversations with his own aids and at least one Western diplomat, he had dismissed the Arkansas Governor as too young, too inexperienced and -get this-too much of a "socialist." That's a peculiar epithet from someone who, until two years ago, was a card-carrying communist ; but now that Russia has repudiated Karl Marx and embraced Adam Smith, its leader is apparently susceptible to Republican propaganda about democrats.

1. Why was it a "good thing" that Clinton had lost his voice, and for whom was it good?

① For Clinton because he speaks poor Russian while Yelstin speaks fluent English.

② For Clinton because Clinton would have lost a debate with Yelstin, the old fox.

③ For Yelstin because he always likes to do most of the talking.

④ For Yelstin because it prevented Clinton's pointing out Yelstin's former hostile remarks about Clinton.

2. What was Yelstin's attitude to Clinton in that telephone conversation?

① conciliatory   ② distant and formal

③ challenging   ④ condescending

3. Why did the writer call the readers' attention to Yelstin's having labeled Clinton a "socialist"?

① Because not many Americans are aware that Clinton is a socialist.

② Because it is deliciously ironical that a lifelong communist should have objected to a politician for being a socialist.

③ Because Yelstin is duped by Republican propaganda about Clinton.

④ Because Clinton refuses to carry a card that identifies his political sympathies.

4. Which of the following prepositions best fits blank(4)?

① on   ② for
③ by   ④ against

5. Which of the following most probably was the Republican propaganda about democrats?

① That the democrats are bold and firm.

② That they are warm and human.

③ That they are hasty reformers without a sense of reality.

④ That they are disciples of Adam Smith.

■ 독해 2.

Even the fairest and most impartial newspaper is a medium of propaganda. Every daily newspaper has an editorial page. Here opinion is expressed on events and personalities in the news. But editorial judgement is so persuasively presented that many people accept these opinions as facts.

Good journalists uphold a code of ethics which distinguishes between news and editorial opinion. This code holds that in an editorial column the publisher is entitled to advocate any cause he chooses. It is understood that there he is speaking as a partisan and may express any view he desires.

Because a modern newspaper is so expensive to produce and so costly to establish, newspapers have increasingly become big business organizations.

Although there are exceptions, these large newspapers tend to reflect the views of their owners in their editorials on economic and political matters. In the news columns, however, the complete and unbiased facts should be reported. The better metropolitan newspapers and the great press associations usually can be relied on to keep their news impartial. But the less ethical publications often deliberately "color" the news to favor or oppose certain groups or movements.

1. The author states that no modern newspaper _____.

   ① is free of propaganda

   ② is controlled by big business interests

   ③ separates fact and opinion

   ④ operates according to a code of ethics

2. According to the passage, all daily newspapers _____.

   ① have an editorial page

   ② follow a code of ethics

   ③ are operated by an unbiased publisher

   ④ are supported by a big business organization

3. According to the journalistic code of ethics, a newspaper must _____.

   ① accept only responsible advertisers

   ② separate editorials from news

   ③ interpret news according to its editorial viewpoint

   ④ determine what reader should know about the news

4. According to the passage, a newspaper publisher may use the editorial page to support _____.

   ① only the cause which is most popular

   ② any cause supported by the advertisers

   ③ any cause he believes in

   ④ only the cause of the owners

5. Newspapers have entered the category of large business organizations because of

   _____.

   ① their influence on the reading public
   ② their reports of stock market activity
   ③ the millions of papers sold daily
   ④ the tremendous costs of production

6. When only one side of the news is regularly presented in a newspaper, the reader may assume that the _____.

   ① paper is a member of a large press association
   ② paper's ethical standards are suspect
   ③ paper is in financial trouble
   ④ paper upholds a journalistic code of ethics

7. In context, the underlined word "<u>color</u>" most nearly means _____.

   ① dye   ② tint   ③ describe   ④ distort

■ 독해 3.

   Part of what is at risk is the promise first made on this continent : All, regardless of race or class or economic status, are entitled to a fair chance and to the tools for developing their individual powers of mind and spirit to the utmost. This promise means that all children by virtue of their own efforts, competently guided, can hope to attain the mature and informed judgement needed to secure gainful employment and to manage their own lives, thereby serving not only their own interests but also the progress of society itself.

1. Which of the following best restates the author's thesis in this essay?

① Some people need to be educated in order to make informed decisions.

② It is the promise of the Declaration of Independence that everybody will have equal opportunity.

③ Our children need to be well educated in order to be gainfully employed and manage their own lives, thereby serving their own interests and the progress of society as well.

④ Race, class, and economic status shall determine who will be able to develop their powers of mind and spirit.

2. If we do not provide a high level education for all, we risk losing ;

① a free, democratic society

② a high standard of living

③ the ability to manage our own lives

④ all of the above

3. The author's primary purpose in this selection is to ;

① inform   ② persuade   ③ entertain   ④ dream

4. In his effort to convince us the author uses ;

① logic (facts)   ② emotion (opinions)
③ both logic and emotion   ④ neither logic nor emotion

■ 독해 4.

Help Wanted: A part-time secretary at a law firm. No prior experience required. Must have a B. A. degree, preferably in accounting.

Special consideration given to applicants with working knowledge of computers and a second language. Starting Salary : $20/hour (approximately 15 hours/week). (a) Working hours are non-negotiable.

1. Based on the ad above, what kind of worker is the firm seeking?

　　① a law clerk to handle legal research.
　　② an accountant who can deal with tax matters.
　　③ an office assistant to handle secretarial work.
　　④ a college student to deal with investigations.

2. Who among the four applicants listed below would have the most advantage?

　　① a college student seeking a part-time job for the summer vacation.
　　② a computer expert looking for a position in computer programming.
　　③ an expert in linguistics seeking a teaching position.
　　④ a former accounting firm secretary seeking to reenter the job market on a part-time base.

3. Approximately how much money could one make in the position?

　　① $50 a week　　② $200 a week　　③ $20 a day　　④ $1,200 a month

4. Which among the following is not required by the hiring firm?

　　① a college degree　　　　　② knowledge of computers
　　③ skill in English　　　　　④ book keeping skills

5. What is indicated by the underlined (a)?

　　① that the hours are flexible
　　② that the hours are set by the employee
　　③ that the hours are determined by the employer
　　④ that the hours may change without notification

■ 독해 5.

　　It has been documented that, almost twelve million years ago at the beginning of the Pliocene Age, a horse, about midway through its evolutionary development, crossed a land bridge where the Bering Straits are now located, from Alaska into the grasslands of Europe. The horse was the hipparion about the size of a modern-day pony with three toes and specialized cheek teeth for grazing. In Europe the hipparion encountered another less advanced horse called the anchitheres which had previously invaded Europe by the same route, probably during the Miocene Period. Less developed and smaller than the hipparion, the anchitheres was completely replaced by it. By the end of the Pleistocene Age both the anchitheres and the hipparion had become extinct in North America where they had originated. In Europe they had evolved into an animal very similar to the horse as we know it today. It was the descendant of this horse that was brought by the European colonists to the Americas.

1. Both the hipparion and the anchitheres _____.

   ① were the size of a modern pony
   ② were native to North America
   ③ migrated to Europe in the Pliocene Period
   ④ had unspecialized teeth

2. According to this passage, the hipparions were _____.

   ① five-toed animals
   ② not as highly developed as the anchitheres
   ③ larger than the anchitheres
   ④ about the size of a small dog

3. The author suggests that the hipparion and the anchitheres migrated to Europe _____.

   ① by means of a land route which is now non-existent
   ② on the ships of European colonists
   ③ because of a very cold climate in North America
   ④ during the Miocene Period

4. The word <u>extinct</u> in line 10 most nearly means?

   ① having died out   ② large and strong
   ③ different   ④ tame

5. It can be concluded from this passage that the _____.

   ① Miocene Period was prior to the Pliocene

   ② Pleistocene Period was prior to the Miocene

   ③ Pleistocene Period was prior to the Pliocene

   ④ Pliocene Period was prior to the Miocene

■ 독해 6.

> For many engineers, sitting at desks and making precise designs on paper is no longer necessary. Instead, they can use computer terminals to create infinitely more complicated designs. These engineers are taking advantage of a rapid emerging electronic data processing technology called computer graphics.
>
> Computer graphics have been used to test various design of cars, planes, even buildings. Corporate executives have turned to computer graphics to convert financial data into charts and graphs. Even film animators have begun to use computer graphics to create special effects of test colors by pushing a button.

1. Automobile engineers have used computer graphics to _____.

   ① examine complex designs   ② decide market availability

   ③ produce car finishes   ④ compile economic information

2. The main idea of the passage is a _____.

   ① sort of engineering jobs   ② new method of drawing

   ③ different way to business   ④ change in industry

3. We can infer from the passage that computer graphics will be a _____.

   ① generally expensive business

   ② carefully controlled industry

   ③ continually expanding technology

   ④ highly complex structure

Norway has one of the toughest drunk-driving laws in western world. Any driver who is found to have more than 0.05 percent alcohol in his blood automatically spends a minimum of three weeks confined in a special facility. There offenders make furniture, stud snow tires, do electrical work, or perform household chores. In addition to serving time, they lose their license for one year on the first offense, and permanently if convicted again within five years.

Hardly anyone, no matter how influential he might be, beats the rap. Of some 20,000 Norwegians sentenced to such facilities in the past four years, several have been celebrities, including members of the parliament.

1. The Norwegian drivers lose their license permanently when _____.

   ① he is convicted against drunk-driving laws on the first offense

   ② his car crashes that of others

   ③ he is accused of drunk-driving again within five years after the first offense

   ④ he run away after committing traffic accidents

2. During his confinement, the Norwegian drivers _____.

   ① enjoy social meeting with other prisoners

   ② suffer from physical affliction

   ③ read and meditate freely

   ④ are forced to do serving activities

3. Which statement is wrong in accordance with the upper paragraph?

   ① even members of the parliament cannot evade the punishment if he or she is convicted of drunk-driving laws.

   ② The drunk-driving drivers having 0.07 alcohol in their blood should be confined in a special facility for at least three weeks.

   ③ The Norwegian drunk-driving laws seem to be tougher than those of others in the western world.

   ④ The celebrities in Norway are free form drunk-driving laws.

The substitution of machines ___(1)___ human labour raises problems which are likely to become acute ___(2)___ the not very distant future. (a) <u>These problems</u> are not new. They began with the Industrial Revolution, which ruined large numbers of skilled and industrious handicraftsmen, inflicting upon them hardships that they had in no way deserved and that (b) <u>they</u> bitterly resented. The sufferers had no political power and were not able ___(3)___ offer any effective resistance to progress. Nowadays, in democratic countries, the political situation is different and wage-earners cannot be expected to submit tamely ___(4)___ starvation. But if we are to believe Norbert Wiener's book on cybernetics-and I see no reason why we should not-(c) <u>it</u> should soon be possible to keep up the existing level of production with a very much smaller number of workers. The more economic methods, one may suppose, would be introduced during a war while the workers were at front, if such a war were not quickly ended by H-bomb extermination, and when the survivors returned their former jobs would no longer be available. The social discontent resulting ___(5)___ such a situation would be very grave. It could be dealt with in a totalitarian country, but a democracy could only deal with (d) <u>it</u> by radical changes in its social philosophy and even in its ethics.

1. Fill in the blanks with the appropriate word.

   (1)   (2)   (3)   (4)   (5)

2. What do the underlined parts (a) (b) (c) and (d) refer to? (Answer in English)

   (a)

   (b)

   (c)

   (d)

3. What was the influence of the Industrial Revolution upon handicraftsmen? (Answer in Korean)

4. Write the difference between the sufferers in the past and wage earners in modern democratic countries. (in Korean)

5. From the context of above paragraph, what do you suppose Norbert Wiener's book on cybernetics deals with? (in Korean)

■ 독해 9.

The fixed stars were distinguished from the planets even in ancient times because the planets move seasonally through the constellations, which are relatively nonchanging arrangements of stars in the sky. Planets are cold, solid bodies that shine by reflecting sunlight. Stars, on the other hand, contain much more matter, but they are so hot that they are entirely gaseous, and they emit light by incandescence.

1. Relatively nonchanging arrangements of stars in the sky are called _____.

   ① fixed stars   ② planets
   ③ constellation   ④ incandescence

2. Planets are _____.

   ① stationary   ② self-luminous
   ③ entirely gaseous   ④ nonluminous

3. What is stated in the above sentence is _____

   ① stars are heavier than planets
   ② planets are solid heavenly bodies
   ③ stars emit light by reflection
   ④ planets were fixed in ancient times

■ 독해 10.

As the nation's economy recovers from the current slowdown, conservation will become our major concern. The demand for our natural resources will increase. In order to help conserve our dwindling natural resources, we will need everyone's help and cooperation in such ventures as recycling newspapers and glass so that they can be used again. If we want to continue to enjoy our open spaces and woodlands, then we must support conservation legislation and join local organizations which promote these laws. Every little bit that individuals do now will help all of us in the future.

1. What is the speaker's main concern?

　① some future economic problems.
　② the membership of local organization.
　③ conservation legislation
　④ the necessity for conservation

2. According to the speaker, why is conservation particularly important at this time?

　① We need to develop woodland.
　② Resources are limited.
　③ Support is needed for new laws.
　④ The economic lookout is poor.

3. What is one way we can save some of our natural resources?

　① By slowing down the economy.
　② By encouraging more industry.
　③ By recycling newspapers and glass.
　④ By using open spaces.

4. How can we preserve open spaces and woodlands?

　① By supporting conservation laws
　② By using them frequently
　③ By using their natural resources
　④ By increasing their animal populations

5. What does the speaker suggest regarding conservation?

    ① Individuals can help very little.

    ② Recycling newspapers and glass is the answer.

    ③ Economists must participate.

    ④ Everyone should help.

■ 독해 11.

    He was a boy of eighteen when he dropped down into London, with no money and no connections except the address of a cousin who was supposed to be working at a baker's. When he went to the bakery shop, however, he found that the cousin had gone to America. Anton tramped the streets for several days, sleeping in doorways and on park benches, until he was in utter despair. He knew no English, and the sound of the strange language all about him confused him. By chance he met a poor German tailor who had learned his trade in Vienna, and could speak a little Czech. This tailor kept a repair shop in London basement. He didn't much need an apprentice, but he was sorry for the boy and took him in for no wages.

1. Anton was _____.

    ① a poor German tailor   ② a shoemaker

    ③ an English gentleman   ④ a boy of eighteen

2. Anton was able to understand _____.

    ① some English   ② easy English conversation

    ③ No English   ④ English with a Czech accent

3. The German tailor hired Anton _____.

    ① because he needed a helper badly

    ② because he had a lot of money

    ③ because Anton was a skilled tailor

    ④ because he felt pity toward him

4. Anton's cousin _____.

   ① had already moved to America

   ② owned a bakery in London

   ③ took him in for no wages

   ④ got him a job at a repair shop

■ 독해 12.

> Unquestionably, it is possible to do without happiness ; it is done involuntarily by nineteen-twentieths of mankind, and voluntarily by the hero or martyr for the sake of something which he prizes more than his individual happiness. But what is this something but the happiness of others, or some the requisites of happiness?

1. In this paragraph, it is argued that _____.

   ① no one is really self-sacrificing

   ② men always act for the sake of happiness

   ③ it is better to seek another's happiness than your own

   ④ some men choose to be unhappy

2. Which of the following does not contradict the paragraph?

   ① Martyrdom never makes anyone happy.

   ② Most people are happy.

   ③ Everyone prizes his individual happiness.

   ④ Only the hero makes men happy.

3. Which of the following statements is true about a martyr?

   ① a person who chooses to die against the government.

   ② a person who loves his country.

   ③ a person who chooses to die or suffer rather than renounce his faith.

   ④ a person who dies.

4. Requisites refer to _____.

① something needed   ② something worthless

③ something valuable   ④ something not required

■ 독해 13.

A revolution is under way. We are in the era of the computers-an information age that will change forever the way people work, play, travel and even think. Just as the industrial revolution dramatically expanded the strength of man's muscles and the reach of his hand, so the computers revolution will magnify the power of his brain. But unlike the industrial revolution, which depended on finite resources such as iron and oil, the new information age will be fired by a seemingly limitless resource : the inexhaustible supply of knowledge itself.

1. The revolution which this passage says is now under way is occurring in the field of _____.

① travel   ② information

③ industry   ④ management

2. The development of the computers is termed a revolution because it is expected to _____.

① greatly change the way people live.

② encourage people to play more.

③ finally end the need to work.

④ result in the growth of tourism.

3. Above passage indicates that the computers revolution will enable the human brain to

.

① become larger   ② calculate more quickly

③ understand itself better   ④ solve problems more effectively

4. Which of the following was especially important in the development of the industrial revolution?

① mineral resources   ② computers

③ human muscle-power   ④ electrical energy

■ 독해 14.

Some of you still enjoy reading fairy tales, but you are not so deeply absorbed in them as you were a few years ago. It is an interesting part of growing up to keep adding to our enthusiasm never wholly discarding what we outgrow, but tying on new pieces of muslin to the tail of our kite. The age of fairy tales belongs to a period when we are interested chiefly in a world of unreality. Goblins, wizards, dwarfs- all those creatures of the imagination- seem to children so much more engaging than water lilies or tadpoles or bread and butter.

Grown people find pleasure in remembering their childish imaginings. But other interests have displaced those early flights of fancy. In fairy tales, you know, all one needs for success or happiness is a fairy godmother. Then everything always turns out all right for the hero or heroine. But as we grow older, these imaginary victories which once satisfied us lose their power of enchantment. We want real success and real happiness. It is this growing interest in a real world in contrast to the fanciful world of fairy lore that marks the first great advance made in reading taste. The world of real people, real problems, real victories, real facts-these are the reading interest of a man growing up.

1. The title that best expresses the main idea of this selection is _____.

① Fairy tales   ② Growing up in reading taste

③ Real happiness   ④ Winning imaginary victories

2. "Tying new pieces of muslin to the tail of our kite" means _____.

① adding new interest to our lives   ② finding new excuses

③ forgetting the past   ④ Flying a kite rather than reading

3. According to the selection, grown people remember their childish imaginings with _____.

① difficulty   ② enchantment

③ enthusiasm   ④ pleasure

4. In a fairy tale all one needs for success or happiness is a _____.

① wizard   ② hero

③ fairy godmother   ④ heroine

5. According to the author, realistic stories appeal chiefly to a person who is _____.

① childish   ② successful and happy

③ becoming mature   ④ reading fairy tales

■ 독해 15.

A few years ago a shortage of natural gas drove prices sky high. Likewise, gasoline prices rose when demands exceeded supplies. A glut in the oil market drove prices back down. The law of supply and demand functioned according to textbook description in the case of oil, but the situation is otherwise in the current natural gas market. Natural gas consumers are finding their heating bills more of a burden than last year, in spite of a dramatic increase in supplies. There is so much natural gas available that many suppliers are closing down their plants for lack of a market, and it is rumored that some suppliers are even burning off their surplus gas.

1. The author's purpose is to _____.

① discuss oil prices   ② discuss gas shortage.

③ question high gas prices.   ④ compare gas and oil prices.

2. You can infer that gas suppliers are burning their surplus gas in order to _____.

① lower the prices on their product.

② create a shortage to sustain high prices.

③ get rid of an inferior product.

④ create a glut in the market.

3. Many suppliers of natural gas are _____.

    ① reducing their prices   ② going out of business

    ③ running out of gas   ④ converting to the oil business

4. The cost of heating with natural gas this year _____.

    ① has risen   ② depends on supply and demand

    ③ is easier to bear   ④ has remained the same as last year

5. The amount of natural gas currently available is _____.

    ① more than last year's supply

    ② equal to last year's supply

    ③ less than last year's supply

    ④ none of the above

■ 독해 16.

When used for studies of learning and memory, the octopus is a more interesting subject than the squid. Unlike the free-swimming squid, which relies exclusively on its eyes to guide it to a tasty fish or crab, the octopus often feeds off the bottom of the sea. It uses not only its eyes but its tentacles to identify a likely meal. The brain of the octopus has two separate memory-storage areas-one for visual memories and the other for tactile memories.

1. How does the squid find its food?

    ① By memory only   ② By touch only

    ③ Both by sight and touch   ④ By sight only

2. The passage is mainly about _____.

    ① a new way of feeding deep-sea fish

    ② biological differences between two animals

    ③ how to use visual and tactile memories

    ④ a warning to deep-sea divers

3. According to the passage, which if the following can describe the octopus?

　　① Its brain is simpler than that of squid.

　　② It cannot look and touch at the same time.

　　③ Its brain does now function very well.

　　④ The memory of what it has seen and touched is contained in separate areas.

■ 독해 17.

A large part of the food we eat keeps us going and provides the body with its heat and energy. It has precisely the same function as fuel performs with our modern machinery. For this fuel purpose of food we are concerned particularly with carbohydrates-our daily bread. In the second place, we consume food for building up the machine itself; that is to say, for the development of the body. It is for this purpose that we require particularly the complex substances known as proteins, builders of muscles and other tissues. We have come to realize in recent years the important part played also by those essential substances to which the term vitamin is applied. They are diverse in chemical composition and in function, and they are only required in small quantities.

1. What is the use of carbohydrates?

　　① They are used for builders of muscles

　　② They are used in small quantities.

　　③ They keep us going and provide the body with heat and energy.

　　④ They are used for building up the machine.

2. What is the use of proteins?

　　① They are used for builders of muscles and other tissues.

　　② They are complex substances in body.

　　③ They are used for the fuel purpose of food.

　　④ They are diverse in chemical composition and in function.

3. What is vitamin?

　① It is a term which can be applied to food.

　② It is the important part which makes up our body.

　③ It is a kind of fuel to make food.

　④ It is a substance diverse in composition and function.

■ 독해 18.

　　In dim far-off times when our forefathers were wild, naked savages, they had no books. Like ourselves, when we were tiny, they could neither read nor write. But at night, when the day's work was done, when the fight or the chase was over, they gathered around the wood fire and listened to the tales of the story-teller. These stories were all of war. They told of combat with fierce men or with strange beasts. They were filled with passion and revenge. There was no tenderness and no love. For the life of man in those far-off days was wild and rough. It was one long struggle against nature and man.

1. The word which means ancestors is _____.

　① far-off　　　　　　　② savages

　③ forefathers　　　　　④ ourselves

2. Why were the stories about war?

　① Their life was a continuous battle.

　② They were at war with the animals.

　③ Their life was pleasant.

　④ They were chased all day.

3. A title for this passage might be _____.

　① Savage Tales of Tenderness

　② Tales Our Ancestors Told

　③ Fireside Stories

　④ The Long Struggle

4. What sentiment was missing from their stories?

   ① Passion   ② Revenge

   ③ Hatred   ④ Tenderness

5. How did our ancestors learn about other places and people?

   ① They told stories.   ② They listened to stories.

   ③ They read books.   ④ They wrote to each other.

■ 독해 19.

Another important function of the terrestrial atmosphere is that it turns the earth into a giant greenhouse, keeping it at a mean temperature of about 60°F, higher than it would be otherwise. The functioning of greenhouse is based on the fact that glass, being almost completely transparent to visible light, which brings most of the sun's energy, is opaque to the heat rays which are emitted by the object warmed up by the sun's radiation. Thus, solar energy entering through the glass roof of a greenhouse is trapped inside and maintains a temperature well above that of the outside air.

In the case of our atmosphere, the role of glass is played by carbon dioxide and water vapour which, even though present in minor amounts, absorb very strongly heat rays emitted from the earth's warm surface and radiate them back to the earth. Thus the excess heat which is removed from the earth's surface during the daytime by the convective air currents is resupplied during the cold nights.

The moderating effect of the atmosphere can be demonstrated by comparing the earth with the moon, which gets exactly the same amount of heat but has no atmosphere. Measurements of the moon's surface temperature show that on the illuminated side of the moon the temperature of the rocks rises to 214°F, while it drops to -243°F on the moon's dark side. If our earth had no atmosphere, water would boil during the daytime and alcohol would freeze during the night.

1. What is meant by "it turns the earth into a giant greenhouse"?

  ① It enables the earth to grow tropical plants at all times of the year.
  ② It turns the earth green by stimulating the growth of trees and plants.
  ③ It protects the earth from both excessive heat and cold.
  ④ It provides a green roof over the earth.

2. What is the effect of glass being "opaque" to heat rays?

  ① Heat rays can pass in and out freely through glass.
  ② Only about half of all heat rays can pass through glass.
  ③ Heat rays brought in by light cannot pass out through glass.
  ④ One cannot see through a pane of glass while it lets heat rays pass in and out.

3. What is the source of the heat that we have during the night?

  ① the sun   ② the moon
  ③ the core of the earth   ④ the atmosphere

4. What would be the appropriate title of the article containing this passage?

  ① Greenhouse Farming   ② Heat Therapy
  ③ The Earth's Atmosphere   ④ The Moon, the Cold Goddess

5. Which of the following statement cannot be inferred from the passage above?

  ① The sun's energy is brought to the earth by light rays.
  ② Alcohol freezes at a very low temperature.
  ③ Air circulates up and down, carrying heat with it.
  ④ It is best to release as much carbon dioxide into the air as we can.

■ 독해 20.

A university training is the key to many doors, both of knowledge and of wisdom. A man's education should be the guiding line for the reading of his whole life, and I am certain that those who have made good use of their university studies will be convinced of the importance of reading the world's great books and the literature of their own land.

They will know what to read and how to understand it. He who has received a university training possesses a rich choice. He needs never be inactive or bored; there is no reason for him to seek refuge in the clack and chatter of our modern life. He needs not be dependent on headlines which give him something new every day. He has the wisdom of all time to drink from to enjoy as long as he lives.

1. Headlines which gives us something new every day are _____.

   ① , for the most part, of little value to us

   ② always against our interests

   ③ at any time instructive to us

   ④ of utmost importance to our daily life

2. The importance of reading the world's great books and the literature of our own land _____.

   ① is being lost day by day

   ② can be forgotten nowadays

   ③ is not so great as present as it was in the past

   ④ cannot be emphasized too strongly

3. A university training _____.

   ① greatly helps a man to acquire knowledge and wisdom

   ② prevents a man from acquiring knowledge and wisdom

   ③ has nothing to do with a man acquiring knowledge and wisdom

   ④ enormously helps a man to depend on headlines

The environment is everything about you. An environment may have such living things as birds, fish and planets. It has such non-living things as air, soil and water. Many animals and planets are found in only one kind of environment. Man, however, can be found in almost all environments. He can even visit places where he needs special things to live, such as the moon. It is clear that people have the power to change an environment. What they do has an effect on all the living and non-living things there. This is why it is important to think about the changes before we make them. When people make wise choices, the environment stays healthy.

1. Choose the best title for this article.

① The Environment and You   ② Pollution is Everywhere

③ Water and Air to Clean   ④ Non-living Environments

2. This article hints that man _____.

① does not enjoy living on the planet earth

② ignores the non-living environments around us

③ can travel from one environment to another

④ prefers one environment to another

3. Man cannot live on the moon unless he has special _____.

① friends   ② equipment

③ problems   ④ weapons

4. We can see that an environment can easily be destroyed by _____.

① disease   ② nature

③ God   ④ man

5. In order to save the environment for our future need, we must _____.

① destroy all non-living things

② keep our environment healthy

③ change our environment

④ kill all animals of prey

■ 독해 22.

After inventing dynamite, Swedish-born Alfred Nobel became a very rich man. However, he foresaw its universally destructive powers too late. Nobel preferred not to be remembered as the inventor of dynamite. So in 1895, just two weeks before his death, he created a fund to be used for awarding prizes to people who had made worthwhile contributions to mankind. Originally there were five awards; literature, physics, chemistry, medicine, and peace. Economics was added in 1968, just sixty-seven years after the first awards ceremony. Nobel's original legacy of nine million dollars was invested, and the interest on this sum is used for the award which vary from $30,000 to $125,000. Every year on December 10, the anniversary of Nobel's death, the awards(gold medal, illuminated diploma, and money) are presented to the winners. Sometimes politics plays an important role in the judges' decision. Americans have won numerous science awards, but relatively few literature prizes. No awards were presented from 1940 to 1942 at the beginning of the World War II. Some people have won two prizes, but this is rare; others have shared their prizes.

1. When did the first award ceremony take place?

① 1895   ② 1901

③ 1962   ④ 1968

2. Why was the Nobel prize established?

① to recognize worthwhile contributions to humanity

② to resolve political differences

③ to spend money

④ to honor the inventor of dynamite

3. In which area have Americans received the most awards?

   ① literature   ② peace

   ③ economics   ④ science

4. Which of the following statements is not true?

   ① Awards vary in monetary value.

   ② Ceremonies are held on December 10 to commemorate Nobel's inventions

   ③ Politics can play an important role in selecting the winners.

   ④ A few individuals have won two awards.

5. In how many fields are prizes bestowed?

   ① 2   ② 5

   ③ 6   ④ 10

■ 독해 23.

> The early history of human race is most clearly and readily studied by observing the stages of human technological progress. That is why it was a long-standing convention to divide early history into broad periods according to the hard materials-stone, copper, bronze, and iron, in that order-from which cutting tools and weapons were made. Then, as knowledge of the past increased, the broad periods were further subdivided. The Stone Age was divided into the Old(Paleolithic) period and the New(Neolithic) period when it was noticed that the technique of sharpening flint and other stones changed from flaking to grinding.

1. Historians have divided early human history into broad periods according to terms that refer to _____.

   ① how long the materials used lasted

   ② how living quarters were built

   ③ the kind of shaping method used

   ④ materials used for making utensils and weapons

2. Which of the following is said of the system used for dividing early history into periods?

① It has been recently devised.

② It is not based on cultural developments.

③ It is intended to indicate technological progress.

④ It refers to materials that have lasted to the present.

■ 독해 24.

Jefferson's belief in science and reason was a firm conviction. He wrote, "I join you therefore in regarding as cowardly the idea that the human mind is incapable of further advances··· that it is not probable that anything better will be discovered than what was known to our fathers··· Thank heaven the American mind is already too much opened th listen to these impostures, and while the art of printing is left to us, science can never be retrograde; what is once acquired of real knowledge can never be lost. To preserve the freedom of the human mind then, and freedom of the press, every spirit should be ready to devote itself to martyrdom···"

1. Jefferson believed that _____.

① there is nothing new under the sun

② there were advances to be made by mankind in the future

③ the American mind was inventive

④ science was becoming retrograde

2. The idea that everything worthwhile has already been thought of _____.

① was propounded by Jefferson

② was attributed to the free press by Jefferson

③ was characterized by Jefferson as cowardly

④ was worthy of martyrdom, according to Jefferson

3. Jefferson implied that the freedom of thought and of the press _____.

  ① would cultivate and promote mankind's progress

  ② were impostures

  ③ were the basis of the art of printing

  ④ paved the road to martyrdom

4. What quality of the American mind did Jefferson express gratitude for?

  ① its knowledge

  ② its readiness to protect its freedom

  ③ its ability to listen to impostures

  ④ its openness

■ 독해 25.

　　All summer the children play on the beaches. They are happy and friendly; as each wave sweeps in across the sand, the smaller ones turn their backs to the seas, and run sensibly away. When the water, edged with foam, draws back again, they go running after it, with an air of driving the ocean before them. But at the next wave, they flee as before, with shrill alarm, and fresh surprise. The sun warms their small brown legs, and they collect colored stones _____ by the tide with enthusiasm. The larger children plunge into the waves like little dolphins. The water is clear and cold.

1. As each wave floods in across the sand, the smaller children _____ the seas.

  ① confront   ② turn away from
  ③ plunge into   ④ turn around

2. "with an air of driving the ocean" means _____.

① driving the ocean as lightly as air

② ready to dive into the ocean

③ as if they were driving the ocean

④ getting on the ocean like a car

3. The proper word for the blank is _____.

① putting   ② put

③ wearing   ④ worn

4. The manner in which above passage describes the children on the beach is _____.

① picturesque   ② fantastic

③ surrealistic   ④ expressionistic

■ 독해 26

Unlike most butterflies, the remarkable black and orange Monarchs migrate southward each fall. Like birds, they follow regular migration routes down major river valleys, along coast lines, and across plains. In the East, the Monarchs travel the length of Cape Cod, cross to Long Island, follow its length, then cross to lower New Jersey, and go on down the coast. No one is sure why these butterflies migrate or how they navigate. All we know is that Monarchs migrate by the millions and that they come back every spring. There are too many things we don't know why, aren't there?

1. The Monarch migration route in the East extended from _____.

① Cape Cod to states south of New Jersey

② New Jersey to states farther south

③ Long Island to New Jersey

④ Cape Cod to Long Island

2. The migration of the Monarchs and the route they follow are _____.

   ① predictable and periodic   ② uncharted but frequent

   ③ haphazard and sporadic   ④ significant but infrequent

3. The reasons for the migration of the Monarch butterfly are _____.

   ① the same as for most other butterflies

   ② related to the existence of predators on Cape Cod

   ③ related to feeding areas along coastlines

   ④ still a mystery

■ 독해 27.

The United States developed from a predominantly rural nation at the end of the Civil War in 1865 to the world's largest and wealthiest industrial power by the time it entered World War Ⅰ in 1917. Among the key factors for this major transformation were a huge population increase, discovery and exploitation of enormous mineral resources, consolidation of the vast Great Plains and Western settlements, and the construction of the extensive railroad networks.

1. This passage is mainly about _____.

   ① why the United States entered World War Ⅰ

   ② how the United States became an industrial power

   ③ how the Great Plains and the West were settled

   ④ why the railroads were built

2. You can infer that between 1865 and 1917, many people _____.

   ① left the cities   ② died in the war

   ③ went to work by train   ④ moved to the cities

Many people know that Ben Franklin's kite experiment helped to prove that lightning is electricity. Kites have been used for scientific purposes since the middle 1700's-for testing weather conditions, taking aerial photographs, etc. They have also been employed in many interesting ways during wartime. Centuries ago, a Korean general sent a kite, with line attached, to the opposite bank of a river. A cable followed the line, forming the nucleus from which a bridge was built. The Japanese developed a man-carrying kite, invaluable in scouting the enemy's position. Many armies used to employ kites for signaling purposes. Now some airline lifeboats are equipped with kites carrying radio antennas which automatically signal S.O.S.

1. The title below that best expresses the main theme or subject of this passage is :

① Kite making as a hobby   ② Methods of signaling
③ Uses of kites through the years   ④ Our debt to Ben Franklin

2. The most recent use of kites mentioned is carrying _____.

① bridge cables   ② Soldiers
③ Photographers   ④ radio antennas

Pearls are found in many seas, but the best and the greatest number come from the Persian Gulf. There are many fine points about a pearl that contribute to determining its value. First, though not most important, is color. Then there is shape, which may be round, pear-shaped, pendant, oval or flat. Further, there is size, which does not determine value except as found in combination with color and shape. But the determining factor is _____, and the luster of a really valuable pearl is unmistakable.

Just what makes a pearl? Arab poets say that as the oyster comes to the surface of the sea on a summer evening, a dewdrop falls into its heart and eventually becomes a gem. As a matter of fact, to an oyster a pearl is foreign article made tolerable, but one it would gladly be rid of. A grain of sand or a parasite gets into the shell, and to rid itself of the irritation the oyster moves and squirms, and in doing so covers the irritating object with a secretion. As the secretion hardens, it becomes round and forms a pearl. The more effort the oyster makes to expel the nuisance, the more abundant is the secretion and the larger the pearl becomes.

1. The title that expresses the main theme of this selection is :

　① Persian jewels

　② Where pearls are found

　③ Why pearls are valuable

　④ The qualities and formation of pearls

2. Which would best complete the blank?

　① shape　　　　　　　　　② size

　③ color and shape　　　　④ luster

3. The value of a pearl depends chiefly on its _____.

　① size　　　　　　　　　② age

　③ color　　　　　　　　　④ luster

4. The making of a pearl is started by _____.

　① a hard place in the shell　　② a drop of dew

　③ an irritating object　　　　④ an oyster wound

5. The size of a pearl is chiefly affected by the _____.

　① length of time in forming　　② amount of secretion produced

　③ rapidly of motion　　　　　④ size of the oyster

Having spent seven years in analyzing a survey of the views of some 4,500 America women, Shere Hite has concluded that they are fed up with the male. "What is going on right now in the minds of women is a large scale cultural revolution," writes Hite, "Over and over, women of all ages express their increasing emotional frustration and gradual disillusionment with their personal relationships with men."

Hite insists that despite women's liberation and the sexual revolution, women remain oppressed and even abused by men. Nearly four out of five women in her study said they still had to fight for their rights within relationships, though an even greater proportion (87%) maintained that men actually tended to become more emotionally dependent than women. They complained that they were expected to play the traditional nurturing, love-giving roles while helping out as breadwinners.

In Hite's view, one of her most disturbing and important discoveries was the pervasiveness of "private emotional violence" inflicted by men upon women. Such violence, she says, is conveyed through insults, hostility, teasing and aggressive behavior. Virtually all her respondents (92%) complained that men communicate with women in language that indicated "condescending, judgemental attitudes."

1. Hite asserts that American women are _____.

① tired of the male-chauvinist attitude

② more liberated than those in other countries

③ assertive and aggressive like men nowadays

④ organizing a revolution to make men more dependent than ever

2. American women, are complaining that _____.

① they have to take care of the family and earn money at the same time

② men do not help them at home

③ they are not allowed to have their own career because of nurturing and love-giving role

④ they can't get a professional job because of men's prejudice

3. According to the passage, which of the following is NOT TRUE?

   ① Emotionally, men are more dependent than women.

   ② Many women are beaten by their husbands.

   ③ Women of all ages are frustrated by man's attitude.

   ④ Women are suffered from men's prejudice and their sense of superiority.

4. The underlined words, <u>breadwinners</u> means _____.

   ① those who deliver bread   ② those who earn money

   ③ housewives   ④ those who cook at home

5. Translate the underlined part.

■ 독해 31.

   A young woman who was about to wed decided at the last moment to test her sweetheart. So selecting the prettiest girl she knew, she said to her, though she knew it was a great _____;

   "I'll arrange for Jack to take you out tonight… a walk on the beach in the moonlight, a lobster supper and all that sort of thing… and I want you, in order to put his faithfulness to the proof, to ask him for a kiss."

   The other girl laughed, blushed, and assented. The dangerous plot was carried out. Then the next day the girl in love visited the pretty one and said anxiously : "Well, did you ask him?" "No, I didn't get a chance. He asked me first."

1. The most suitable word in _____ is _____.

   ① risk   ② safety

   ③ test   ④ moment

2. As a result Jack turned to be _____.

  ① faithful   ② unfaithful

  ③ humorous   ④ courageous

3. Probably the girl in love should be _____.

  ① disappointed   ② encouraged

  ③ concentrated   ④ interested

4. The best title for this passage is _____.

  ① A Romantic Moonlight   ② A Dangerous Wedding

  ③ A Test of Sweetheart   ④ A Walk on the Beach

■독해 32.

    Issac Newton's supreme scientific work was his system of universal gravitation. He went to his farm in 1665 to avoid the plague, and during this time he worked out the law gravity and its consequences for the solar system. He later remarked to a friend that he got the idea while watching an apple fall from a tree in his orchard. Every particle of matter in the universe, he wrote, attracts every other particle with a force varying in inverse proportion to the square of the distance between them, and directly proportional to the product of their masses.

1. Where did Newton find his law of gravity?

  ① On his farm   ② In his laboratory

  ③ In his study   ④ In his friend's orchard

2. The phrase "every particle of matter attracts every other particle" means that every particle _____.

  ① repels other particles   ② seeks other particles

  ③ draws other particles to itself   ④ evades other particles

3. According to the passage, the system of universal gravitation is Newton's _____.

① least important scientific work

② most disputed scientific work

③ most misunderstood scientific work

④ most important scientific work

4. Issac Newton can best be described as a _____.

① biologist   ② geologist

③ physician   ④ physicist

5. Newton discovered the system of universal gravitation in which century?

① Sixteenth   ② Seventeenth

③ Eighteenth   ④ Nineteenth

■ 독해 33.

It is no secret that I am not one of those naturalists who suffer from cities, or affect to do so, nor do I find a city unnatural or uninteresting, or a rubbish heap of follies. It has always seemed to me that there is something more than mechanically admirable about a train that arrives on time, a fire department that comes when you call it, a light that leaps into the room at a touch, and a clinic that will fight for the health of a penniless man and mass for him the agencies of mercy, the X ray, the precious radium, the anesthetics and the surgical skill. Far beyond any pay these services receive stands out the pride in perfect performances. And above all, I admire the noble impersonality of civilization that does not inquire where the recipient stands on religion or politics or race. I call this beauty, and I call it spirit··· not some mystical soulfulness that nobody can define but the spirit of man that has been a million years growing.

1. The aspect of city life most commendable to this author is its _____.

   ① impartial   ② agencies of mercy

   ③ free benefits   ④ mechanical improvement

2. The author makes a defense of _____.

   ① cities   ② prompt trains

   ③ free clinics   ④ religion or politics

3. The author implies that efficient operation of public utilities is _____.

   ① expensive   ② mechanically commendable

   ③ spiritual in quality   ④ unnatural or uninteresting

4. The title best expressing the idea of this paragraph is _____.

   ① Admirable Characteristic of Cities

   ② Disadvantages of a Rural Home

   ③ Tolerance in the City

   ④ Encouragement for Living in the City

■ 독해 34.

The general principles of dynamics are rules which demonstrate a relationship between the motions of bodies and the forces which produce those motions. Based in large part on the work of his predecessors, Sir Issac Newton deduced three laws of dynamics which he published in 1687 in his famous "Principia".

Prior to Newton, Aristotle had established that the natural state of a body was a state of rest, and that unless a force acted upon it to maintain motion, a moving body would come to rest. Galileo had succeeded in correctly describing the behavior of falling objects and in recording that no force was required maintain a body in motion. He noted that the effect of force was to change motion. Huygens recognized that a change in the direction of motion involved acceleration, just as did a change in speed, and further, that the action of a force was required. Kepler deduced the laws describing the motion of planets around the sun. It was primarily from Galileo and Kepler that Newton borrowed.

1. Huygens stated that acceleration was required _____.

  ① for either a change in direction or a change in speed

  ② only for a change in speed

  ③ only for a change in direction

  ④ neither for a change in direction nor for a change in speed

2. According to this passage, Newton based his laws primarily upon the work of _____.

  ① Galileo and Copernicus   ② Ptolemy and Copernicus

  ③ Huygens and Kepler   ④ Galileo and Kepler

3. What was the main purpose of the passage?

  ① To demonstrate the development of Newton's laws

  ② To establish Newton as the authority in the field of physics

  ③ To discredit Newton's laws of motion

  ④ To describe the motion of planets around the sun

■ 독해 35.

No matter how decisively the Gulf war ends, turmoil and bloodshed are likely to persist in the Middle East unless the anit-Iraq alliance accepts the need for profound political change.

Experts of widely varying viewpoints agree on some basic challenges that will face the United States and its friends, both Western and Arab, whenever they complete their onslaught on Saddam Hussein.

These include democratic reform in such countries as Saudi Arabia and Kuwait, redistribution of oil wealth to the Arab world's resentful have-nots, and some sort of accommodation for the Palestinians.

"Nothing in the Middle East will return to the status quo." said Egypt's Tahseen Beshir, a former presidential spokesman. "The key will be whether the Americans and their allies put the same effort into building the peace as they did in launching the war."

To many Arabs and Muslims, the war has elevated Saddam to the status of holy warrior, the only man willing to take on the might of the Western world.

"A defeated Saddam, particularly a dead one, will take on a much more favorable image," wrote Robert O' Neill, an Oxford University history professor, in Britain's Financial Times.

"We should be prepared after a Gulf war to face a long and uncertain period as a new system of regional security is built."

1. The passage is mainly concerned with the _____.

① political change in the United States　② Gulf war

③ Arab world's have-nots　　　　　　　④ Britain's finance

2. Which of the following is not mentioned as a basic challenge that will face the United States when it defeats Iraq?

① democratic reform in Saudi Arabia　② redistribution of oil wealth

③ accommodation for the Palestinians　④ preparation for the Gulf war

3. Professor O'Neill believes that if Saddam were defeated he would _____.

① die immediately　　　　　　　　　② return the status quo the Middle East

③ launch another war　　　　　　　　④ take on a much more favorable image

4. Tahseen Beshir was a _____.

① politician of Egypt　　　　　　　② history professor

③ reporter of the Financial Times　④ holy warrior

■ 독해 36.

One of the most disappointing aspects of computers today is that so few people have access to them. Even those who do are usually responsible for getting a particular job done and have no access to computers for personal use.

One of the electronics distributor hopes to change this situation with a home computer system that will sell for approximately six hundred dollars. The HC 30 will be a basic system with many of the characteristics of the large computers. Once the customer is familiar with the standard program, he can purchase options that expand the machine's capabilities.

1. According to the passage, the HC 30 has _____.

① optional equipment   ② disappointing aspects
③ limited access to information   ④ familiar programs

2. The machine that is being described is one that _____.

① has little similarity to other computers
② will be available soon
③ is available soon
④ has been used as toy

3. How does the HC probably compare with other computers?

① It is more versatile.   ② It is more complex.
③ It is larger.   ④ It is cheaper.

■ 독해 37.

Younger people cannot look upon their traditions with nostalgia as they did not experience them firsthand. Neither do they have ⓐ the complex of defeat that plagues the wartime generation. Their Japan has always been a rich nation, and war and hunger seem as __(1)__ as the tradition they never saw, largely because their fathers worked so hard to leave it behind. They look dispassionately at their cultural traditions and simply ⓑ pull out the elements that they like, changing their context. The older generation sees this as a loss of identity, but it could as easily be interpreted as a search for a new identity __(2)__ one does not fit himself to the past but makes the past fit him. This is not a rejection of that past, but neither is it ⓒ an uncritical embrace.

※ (1~2) Fill in the blank with a suitable word.

1. (1) ① appealing   ② significant
       ③ remote   ④ expensive

2. (2) ① not only   ② in which
       ③ save that   ④ for whom

※ (3~5) Choose the one that is nearest to the meaning of the underlined parts.
   ⓐ, ⓑ and ⓒ.

3. ⓐ ① the pain of defeat the wartime generation suffers from
      ② the sense of defeat almost ignored by the wartime generation
      ③ the sense of failure the wartime generation regards as trifling
      ④ the agony of defeat with which the wartime generation is hardly tormented

4. ⓑ ① exclude the parts which seem impressive for them
      ② select the factor attractive for them
      ③ pass on the elements that they are fond of
      ④ miss the areas they regard as desirable

5. ⓒ ① an unquestioning acceptance
      ② a rash judgement
      ③ an unfavorable interpretation
      ④ a negative opinion

■독해 38.

Among the hazards which confront workers are the so-called occupational diseases. One of these, for example, is lead poisoning, which sometimes affects people who work for long periods with lead dust or with preparations like glaze or paint containing lead. Since the lead is eliminated slowly, the poison accumulates and finally causes great weakness, loss of power in the hands, kidney disease, or other serious disorders. Workers should make special precautions to avoid such dangers.

1. To what general danger does the paragraph call our attention?

    ① accidents at work   ② occupational diseases

    ③ traffic hazards   ④ financial losses

2. What is mentioned as accumulative effect of the specific difficulty described?

    ① kidney disease   ② poverty

    ③ defective vision   ④ anxiety

3. What danger mentioned in the paragraph should a man who paints a large building be careful to avoid?

    ① weak ladders   ② laed poisoning

    ③ exposure to winds   ④ car accidents

4. Which element of paint is mentioned?

    ① glaze   ② dust

    ③ lead   ④ artistic value

We Japanese are very egoistic. It must be said. Especially we Japanese men. We are self-centered and introspective and concerned with our own inner feelings. We are extremely sensitive to anything that reflects on us personally, good or bad. We are a subtle people, and all Japanese are keenly aware of the nuances of anything that is said about us or happens around us.

1. Generally, the Japanese are interested in _____.

    ① the events of the world

    ② physical appearance of himself

    ③ natural landscape

    ④ his own emotion

2. The reason why the Japanese can recognize the delicate difference of the meaning of talks and events around them is _____.

    ① their rough national character

    ② their feeble physical power

    ③ their keen neurotic troubles

    ④ the subtlety of their national character

There can be little doubt that malaria was prevalent in all American colonies during the seventeenth century. Toward the end of the century and continuing into the eighteenth, a rising incidence marked parts of Pennsylvania, New Jersey, Maryland, Delaware, and other colonies situated in the coastal plains region, while a corresponding decline characterized New England. The significance of malaria in colonial history can scarcely be overrated, for it was a major hurdle in the development of the American colonies. To the newly arrived settlers of "fresh European", it frequently proved fatal, and epidemics of pernicious malaria took a heavy toll of old and new colonists alike. In endemic regions the regular succession of spring and fall outbreaks, with the concomitant sickness and disability, deprived the colonies of much sorely needed labor.

(Note) endemic=found regularly in a particular place
concomitant=existing or happening together

1. Malaria occurred _____.

① only in the spring   ② in almost any season

③ in periodic outbreaks   ④ only in the fall

2. During the late seventeenth and early eighteenth centuries _____.

① the number of malaria cases in Maryland declined

② the number of malaria cases in New England increased

③ the number of malaria cases in the coastal plains region declined

④ the number of malaria cases in New Jersey increased

3. The words "endemic regions" (line 9) means most nearly _____.

① extensive regions

② regions with poor climate

③ regions where malaria was common

④ regions where malaria was rare

4. The importance of malaria in colonial history _____.

① is difficult to exaggerate

② was minimal

③ has never been assessed

④ is difficult to determine

5. Malaria affected _____.

① only "fresh Europeans"
② only old colonists
③ only newly arrived settlers
④ both old and new colonists

■ 독해 41.

Human environmental interference has halted the approach of a new ice age and will mean a warmer global climate, a local researcher has said. Among the possible consequences, Professor David G. Bridges believes, will be a shrinking of the Great Lakes and inland water, a northward shift of the agricultural belt into Canada, and a melting of glacial ice that could raise ocean levels. A future increase of atmospheric carbon dioxide, caused by the burning of coal, oil, and gas, will be an overwhelming weather influence. The effect of this use of fossil fuels will be a drier Midwest climate with drastic effects on agriculture, commerce, and recreation. "After overpopulation and the shortage of food, this is probably the most serious problem mankind faces", Professor Bridges said.

1. The main idea of the passage is the _____.

① world's changing climate
② approaching ice age
③ shrinking of the Great Lakes
④ Canadian agricultural belt

2. A possible result of the interference may be the _____.

① raising of the levels of the Great Lakes and inland waters
② shrinking oceans
③ increase of glacial ice
④ movement of farming areas to the north

3. Professor Bridges believes that the interference is due to _____.

① new agricultural methods

② the recent increase in temperatures

③ less carbon dioxide in the air

④ the burning of coal, oil and gas

4. According to the passage, the entire earth's climate should _____.

① become much cooler   ② grow somewhat warmer

③ remain the same   ④ change only slightly

5. Who or what is primarily responsible for the interference?

① Researchers   ② The new ice age

③ Mankind   ④ A drier climate

■ 독해 42.

Another evolutionary puzzle was a good deal more difficult to solve until recently. This is the problem of how the flightless ratites became so widerspread geographically. The ratites were once regarded as primitive birds separated by oceans that they could not cross. It seemed necessary in those days to construct hypotheses explained the independent evolution of each member of the group. The biologist T.H. Huxley was almost alone in opposing such hypotheses. He based his opposition on his studies of the birds' bone structures.

1. It can be inferred from the passage that quite recently scientists' views of the ratites have _____.

① influenced world opinion

② changed substantially

③ led to disagreement

④ been widely published

2. According to the passage, T.H. Huxley disagreed with other scientists because of his observations of the ratites _____.

① anatomy   ② feeding habits

③ enemies   ④ nesting places

3. According to the passage, T.H. Huxley believed that _____.

① ratites were related to other birds

② ratites were unable to fly across oceans

③ it was impossible for the ratites to survive

④ ratites had a common ancestor

4. The paragraph preceding this one most probably discussed _____.

① other theories of T.H. Huxley

② how ratites became unable to fly

③ the evolution of another animal

④ the scientific method

5. It can be inferred that the problem discussed in the paragraph just prior to this passage was _____.

① more difficult   ② less difficult

③ more important   ④ less important

■ 독해 43.

There is a public library in every town in Britain. There are branch libraries in many villages. Anyone may borrow books, and no charge is made for borrowing. In some places you may borrow as many books as you are likely to want, but in others you are limited to a certain number, of which some may be kept for as long as is reasonable, so there is no difficulty in having all the reading that is needed.

If the book you want is out, you may ask for it to be kept for you, and if you pay the cost of sending a postcard, the librarian will let you know when the book has been returned and is ready for you.

1. How much does it cost to borrow books from a public library in Britain?

① 5 pence   ② 10 pence

③ Nothing   ④ Variable

2. What must a borrower do if he wants the librarian to let him know when a book has been returned?

① He must pay the cost of sending the book.

② He must pay postage fee for a postcard.

③ He must be ready to buy the book.

④ He must go to the library every day.

■ 독해 44.

When was the last time you saw a lawman on a horse? From San Francisco to New York, mounted Police Forces are reappearing in the cities. Many cities are rediscovering the benefits of using horses as opposed to patrol cars. In New York the number of horses has grown from 80 in 1976 to 150 today.

One reason for the switch over is the financial difficulties many cities face. A horse costs about $1,500 and $11 a day to take care of. The average daily cost to maintain a patrol car is $45 a day.

Visibility is another advantage. An officer on top of horse can see ever fences and the heads of a crowd. Being able to look into someone's backyard for suspicious activity has led to a reduction in residential burglaries.

The biggest benefit has been the positive P.R. created with the public. Almost everyone likes horses and will come up and talk to the officer about the horse. In a sense, the horse serves as a go-between and helps to break down the animosity between the public and the police.

1. How much is the average daily cost to maintain a patrol car?

① $1,500   ② $1,100

③ $45   ④ $11

2. How has the horse contributed to a drop in home breaking?

   ① The police officer is high enough to see over a wall or fence.

   ② Many robbers are afraid of horses.

   ③ Officers can ride into people's backyards.

   ④ All of the above.

3. What is the best service the horse provides to the community?

   ① It helps to balance the city budget.

   ② It improves community relations.

   ③ It catches criminals.

   ④ It doesn't cause any pollution.

4. Which of the following is not true?

   ① In New York the number of horses has grown from 80 in 1976 to 150 today.

   ② A horse costs about $1,500 and $11 a day to take care of.

   ③ Many cities are recommending the use of patrol cars.

   ④ An officer on top of horse can see over fences and the heads of a crowd.

5. If you have "animosity" in your heart, you have a feeling of _____.

   ① compassion   ② hatred

   ③ patience   ④ irritation

■ 독해 45.

Democracy is not a beloved Republic really, and never will be. But it is less hateful than other contemporary forms of government, and to that extent it __(1)__ our support. It does start from the assumption that the individual is important, and that all types are needed to make a civilization. It does not divide its citizens into the bossers and the bossed-as an efficiency-regime tends to go. The people I admire most are those who are sensitive and want to create something or discover something, and do not see life __(2)__ power, and such people get more of a chance under a democracy then elsewhere.

1. People love democracy not because it is perfect but because it is less _____ than other regimes.

   ① immaculate   ② craven

   ③ fictitious   ④ abominable

2. The suitable word for the blank (1) is _____.

   ① deserves   ② stands

   ③ asks   ④ reserves

3. The suitable word for the blank (2) is _____.

   ① in   ② in terms of

   ③ by dint of   ④ as

■ 독해 46.

Doubling reading speed can increase comprehension by about eight percent. Increased reading speed sharpens the mind generally and helps a person become mentally more efficient.

Almost anyone can be trained to read better, doubling and sometimes even tripling his or her reading speed. Poor reading may be the result of a person's not having read enough. Such a reader usually lacks vocabulary and has bad reading habits. Some unconsciously resist change because they think slow readers get more out of what they read.

The best readers tend to have a broad vocabulary, to be familiar with sentence patterns, and to have had a variety of life experiences. These persons can quickly learn to read 1,800 to 2,400 words per minute with excellent comprehension. The 10,000-words-a-minute speed reader is very rare; most people read about 250 words per minute. In order to get their assignments done, college students should be able to read about 600 words per minute.

1. Most people read about how many words per minutes?

   ① 10,000   ② 2,400
   ③ 600   ④ 250

2. According to the passage, one reason for poor reading is that poor readers _____.

   ① are familiar with sentence patterns
   ② lack an adequate vocabulary
   ③ do not have sharp minds
   ④ are familiar with what they read

3. According to the passage, one reason for good reading is that good readers tend to _____.

   ① read up to 10,000 words a minute
   ② read about 8 percent faster than poor readers
   ③ have had many different kinds of experiences
   ④ have gone to college to learn speed reading

4. The passage contends that increasing reading speed will also probably lead to _____.

   ① an increase in comprehension
   ② the ability to do college work
   ③ a familiarity with life
   ④ the desire to read more

5. It can be inferred form the passage that a program to increase a poor reader's reading speed would probably include _____.

   ① some vocabulary words
   ② practice in the speaking of complete sentences
   ③ exercises that require a good mental outlook
   ④ college-level materials for lessons in reading

Prior to Newton, Aristotle had established that the natural state of a body was a state of rest, and that unless a force acted upon it to maintain motion, a moving body would come to rest. Galileo had succeeded in correctly describing the behavior of falling objects and in recording that no force was required to maintain a body in motion. He noted that the effect of force was to change motion. Huygens recognized that a change in the direction of motion involved acceleration, just as did a change in speed, and further, that the action of a force was required. Kepler deduced the laws describing the motion of planets around the sun. It was primarily from Galileo and Kepler that Newtom borrowed.

1. Which of the following scientists established that the natural state of a body was a state of rest?

① Galileo   ② Aristotle

③ Kepler   ④ Newton

2. Huygen stated that acceleration was required _____.

① for either a change in direction or a change in speed

② only for a change in speed

③ only for a change in direction

④ neither for a change in direction nor for a change in speed

3. The first scientist to correctly describe the behavior of falling objects was _____.

① Aristotle   ② Kepler

③ Newton   ④ Galileo

4. According to this passage, Newton based his laws primarily upon the work of _____.

① Galileo and Copernicus   ② Huygens and Kepler

③ Ptolemy and Copernicus   ④ Galileo and Kepler

5. What was the main purpose of this passage?

　① To discredit Newton's laws of motion
　② To establish Newton as the authority in the field of physics
　③ To demonstrate the development of Newton's laws
　④ To describe the motion of planets around the sun

■ 독해 48.

　It has been said that an invention goes through three stages : doubt of its existence, denial of its importance, and finally, credit of its discovery going to someone else.

　An example of the truth of the third part ot this assertion is the invention of the "Pullman", the railroad sleeping car. The first sleeper was actually built by Richard Imlay of Philadelphian in 1838. There were at least eight different railroads that advertised some kind of sleeping car before 1850 and George Pullman's first car was not built until 1858. Also, Pullman patented the folding upper berth as late as 1863. Pullman, nevertheless, seems to have been a better businessman and a better promoter than Imlay.

1. This main idea expressed in this passage is that the Pullman car _____.

　① was used by eight railroads
　② contained three compartments
　③ competed with other types of sleeping cars
　④ had an origin typical of most inventions

2. Pullman's actual contribution to the sleeping car was a special _____.

　① window　　　　　　　　　　　② engine
　③ bed　　　　　　　　　　　　　④ wheel

3. In what year was Pullman's first sleeping car produced?

　① 1838　　　　　　　　　　　　② 1850
　③ 1858　　　　　　　　　　　　④ 1863

■ 독해 49.

People often dream of living in a perfect place where no one would be poor, no one would be rich, and everyone would be considerate of everyone else. Such a place, however, is too good to be true : such a place is no where, and that's what the word 'utopia' means. It is made up of two Greek words meaning 'not a place'.

The word was first used by Sir Thomas More, a sixteenth century English writer whose book UTOPIA, published in 1516, described a perfect island country. More's idea for his tale came from the ancient Greek philosopher Plato. Plato's THE REPUBLIC described what would be a perfect state.

Early legends among the Norse, Celtic and Arab people told of a perfect place existing somewhere in the Atlantic. These legends were no longer believed when explorations of the Americans began, but after More's time it became common for writers to imagine and describe perfect places.

Today when people want certain changes in government or society, their ideas are sometimes labeled 'utopian'. Usually the critics mean that the change, if effected, would not suddenly make everything perfect because people are by nature imperfect.

1. Conditions in a utopian country would be such that _____.

① everyone would be happy all the time

② people would be self-governing

③ no one would be either rich or poor

④ All of the above

2. According to the author, Utopia is _____.

① somewhere in the Atlantic   ② in people's imaginations

③ no longer dreams of   ④ no longer in existence

3. More's UTOPIA was based on _____.

① a philosopher's earlier work   ② an original idea

③ an Arab legend   ④ a theory explained to him

4. THE REPUBLIC described _____.

① the perfection of the state in which Plato lived
② Plato's theory of a perfect place
③ a perfect island country
④ a perfect government in office

5. In modern usage, any idea labeled 'utopian' is considered _____.

① unnecessary   ② inconsiderate
③ impractical   ④ imperfect

■ 독해 50.

Stress is with us all the time. It comes from mental or emotional activity as well as physical activity. It is unique and personal to each of us. So personal, in fact, that what may be relaxing to one person may be stressful to another. For example, if you're a busy executive who likes to keep occupied all of the time, "taking it easy" at the beach on a beautiful day may feel extremely frustrating, nonproductive, and upsetting. You may be emotionally distressed from "doing nothing". Too much emotional stress can cause physical illnesses such as high blood pressure, ulcers, or even heart disease. Physical stress from work or exercise is not likely to cause such ailments. The truth is that physical exercise can help you to relax and to better handle you mental or emotional stress.

1. Stress is _____.

① optional   ② relaxing
③ manageable   ④ the same for all people

2. A source of stress not specifically mentioned in this passage is _____.

① physical activity   ② educational activity
③ mental activity   ④ emotional activity

3. Physical problems caused by emotional stress can appear as all of the following except _____.

    ① ulcers   ② pregnancy

    ③ heart disease   ④ high blood pressure

4. One method mentioned to help handle stress is _____.

    ① physical exercise   ② sleeping

    ③ drugs   ④ taking it easy

5. Which statement is NOT correct according to the above passage?

    ① Too much physical stress may cause ulcers or heart disease.

    ② Too much emotional stress may be the cause of physical illnesses.

    ③ The source of stress to one person may not be the source of stress to another person.

    ④ The emotional stress is more harmful than the physical stress.

■ 독해 51.

    The bus passenger, trying to save a few cents, hurried her young daughter aboard without (pay) the child's fare.

    "How old are you, little girl?" The bus driver asked.

    "Four and a half." She answered.

    "And when will you be five?" He asked again.

    "Just as soon as I get off the bus."

1. The suitable form of (pay) is _____.

    ① payment   ② to pay

    ③ being paid   ④ paying

2. The actual age of the girl may be _____.

   ① less than four and a half   ② between four and five

   ③ four and a half   ④ at least five

■ 독해 52.

Today's telephone is very different from the one Bell made almost one hundred years ago. A picture phone lets you see the person you are speaking to. If you have one of the newest phones, you don't have to dial again when you get a busy signal. Your call goes through itself when the line is free. On some phones you can talk to three of four people at once.

1. The underlined part means _____.

   ① immediately   ② once or twice

   ③ at the same time   ④ one after the other

2. The best title of this passage is _____.

   ① Passing Time Over the Phone   ② Who Invented the Phone?

   ③ Today's Newer Phones   ④ Telephone Operators

■ 독해 53.

According to the best historical and archaeological evidence, it is estimated that it took about 800 thousand to 1 million years for the earth's population to reach the 250 million total which existed at the end of the first century after Christ. For some time after that, disease, famine, and war kept the population increase down to a fraction of 1 percent a year. So that more than 15 centuries passed before the population reached 500 million. But the next 250 years, up to 1850, the population of the world shot up to the billion mark, and today it has reached 3 billion. It is predicted by U.N. investigators that in the next 35 years the population of the world will double, reaching almost 7 billion by the year 2000.

When experts are asked what the most effective measure which overpopulation poses, they reply that at least three measures can be considered ; (1) increasing sources and supply of food for underdeveloped countries ; (2) increasing the industrialization of underdeveloped countries ; (3) regulating conception and births. The experts add, however, that none of the proposed measures can be effective by itself, that all must be combined into an integrated program. They also agree that without some regulation of conceptions and births, any other measures are doomed to failure.

1. Our information about the population of the earth before the first century after Christ comes mainly from _____.

   ① estimates based on current population growth
   ② references in literature and mythology
   ③ estimates based on previous population growth
   ④ written records and cultural remains

2. It is estimated that in the year A.D. 100 the population of the earth was about _____.

   ① 800 thousand   ② 1 million
   ③ 250 million   ④ 500 million

3. The population of the world doubled between the year _____.

   ① 1850 and today   ② 100 and the year 1600
   ③ 100 and the year 1400   ④ 1 and the year 100

4. By the year 2000, the earth's population will probably exceed its present population by _____.

   ① 1 billion   ② 3 billion
   ③ 4 billion   ④ 7 billion

5. Population growth was most restricted in the period from _____.

    ① 100 B.C. to A.D. 100   ② A.D. 100 to A.D. 1600

    ③ A.D. 1600 to A.D. 1850   ④ A.D. 1850 to the present

6. Which of the following would be most likely to discover "archaeological evidence"?

    ① an architect   ② an explorer

    ③ a physician   ④ a physicist

7. The word "famine" means _____.

    ① infection   ② destruction

    ③ slaughter   ④ starvation

8. The word "integrated" means _____.

    ① coordinated   ② biased

    ③ effective   ④ impartial

9. The expression "doomed to failure" means _____.

    ① will not succeed   ② have failed in the past

    ③ will probably succeed   ④ have succeeded in the past

10. In the expression "which overpopulation poses···", poses is used as _____.

    ① a noun   ② ad adjective

    ③ a verb   ④ an adverb

■독해 54.

> Premack cities an experiment in which Sarah was given a real apple and asked to select those symbols-red or green, round or square-that characterized the apple. She did this readily. Then the apple was replaced with its symbol, the blue triangle, and Sarah was again invited to select its qualities. With unfailing confidence, she attributed to this totally unapple-like symbol the same qualities of roundness and

redness-evidence that the chimp thinks of the word not as its literal form (blue plastic) but as the thing it represents (red apple).

1. When Sarah saw the blue triangle, she _____.

   ① could only pick up another blue triangle exactly the same
   ② picked up the symbol that meant "round", and "red" in order to describe what an apple looked like
   ③ picked up a real apple
   ④ could not understand what it meant

2. Sarah thinks of words as _____.

   ① pieces of plastic   ② games
   ③ representations of ideas   ④ literature

■ 독해 55.

   Solar energy is rapidly becoming a logical alternative source of heat as the unavailability of conventional fuels becomes a major problem in industrial countries. Getting energy from the sun is not a new idea. Most people have had the experience of getting a sunburn on a cloudy day, much to their surprise ; the energy is always there. Technology has now brought the cost of harnessing the sun closer to being economically competitive. Finally, the fact that solar heating and solar cooling are very attractive environmentally provides another reason to switch from conventional fuels.

1. What is the source of solar energy?

   ① the earth   ② the sun
   ③ the oil   ④ the nucleus

2. In this passage, "harnessing the sun" is another way of saying _____.

   ① "controlling the sun"   ② "riding the sun"

   ③ "using the sun's energy"   ④ "trying down the sun"

3. According to the passage, energy from the sun is evidenced physically by _____.

   ① getting sunburned   ② seeing the shadow

   ③ sunshine passing through clouds   ④ seeing the sun behind clouds

4. Solar heat is becoming a logical source of energy because _____.

   ① conventional fuels are not expensive enough

   ② conventional fuels are becoming unavailable

   ③ conventional fuels are too expensive

   ④ conventional fuels are attractive environmentally

5. What is one advantage of using solar energy?

   ① It is not dangerous.

   ② It does not pollute the environment.

   ③ It can generate electricity.

   ④ It is economically competitive.

■ 독해 56.

    To accept passively an unjust system is to cooperate with that system ; thereby the oppressed become (1) the oppressor.

    Non-cooperation with evil is much a moral obligation as is cooperation with good. The oppressed must never allow the conscience of the oppressor to <u>slumber</u>. Religion reminds every man that he is his brother's keeper. To accept injustice or <u>segregation</u> passively is to say to the oppressor that his actions are morally right. It is a way of allowing his conscience to fall asleep. At this moment the oppressed fails to be his brother's keeper. So <u>acquiescence</u>-while often the easier way-is not the moral way. It is the way of the coward.

1. 빈칸 (1)에 가장 알맞은 것은?

　① as evil as　　② as good as　　③ as strong as　　④ as weak as

2. 밑줄 친 slumber의 뜻은?

　① are quickly　　② move slowly　　③ prick painfully　④ sleep quietly

3. 밑줄 친 segregation의 뜻을 우리말로 쓰시오.

4. 밑줄 친 acquiescence의 뜻은?

　① accepting without protest　　② enduring for ever and ever
　③ looking for an opportunity　　④ running away from danger

5. 윗글의 내용을 우리말로 2~3줄 분량으로 요약하시오.

■ 독해 57.

※ 다음 빈칸에 적당한 것은?

　　Many people talk, not because they have anything to say but (1) the mere love of talking. Talking should be an exercise of the brain rather (2) of the tongue. Talkativeness, the love of talking's sake, is almost fatal to success. Men are plainly hurried on, in the heat of their talk, to say quite different things from (3) they first intended.

1. ① before　　　　　　　　② because
　③ for　　　　　　　　　④ as

2. ① than   ② that
   ③ like   ④ just as

3. ① that   ② whenever
   ③ whether   ④ what

■ 독해 58.

   History proves that dictatorships do not grow out of strong and successful governments, but out of weak and helpless ones. If by democratic methods people get a government strong enough to protect them from fear and starvation, their democracy succeeds : but if they do not, they grow impatient. Therefore, the only sure <u>bulwark</u> of continuing liberty is a government strong enough to protect the interests of the people and a people, strong enough and well enough informed to maintain <u>its sovereign control</u> over its government.

1. 밑줄 친 <u>bulwark</u>의 뜻은?

   ① bulldog   ② intermediary
   ③ something that defends or protects   ④ value or price

2. 밑줄 친 <u>its sovereign control</u>이 가리키는 것은?

   ① 국민의 주권행사   ② 대통령의 수완
   ③ 왕권의 통치   ④ 독재자의 통제

3. 전체의 뜻을 우리말로 2~3줄 분량으로 요약하시오.

Much as I liked Antonia, I hated a superior tone that she sometimes took (a) me. She was four years older than I and (b) <u>had seen more of the world</u> ; but I was a boy and she was a girl, and I resented her protecting manner.

Before the autumn was over, she began to treat me more like an equal and to (c) <u>defer</u> to me in other things than reading lessons.

One day when I rode over to the Shimerdas' I found Antonia starting off (d) for Russians Peter's house, to borrow a spade. I offered to take her on the pony, and she got up behind me.

1. 괄호 (a) 안에 가장 적합한 말을 고르시오.

① of   ② with

③ about   ④ in

2. 밑줄 친 (b)의 의미와 가장 가까운 것을 고르시오.

① had made a trip around the world

② had witnessed great events

③ had lived for a long time

④ had more knowledge about the ways of the world

3. 화자가 자신이 Antonia보다 오히려 낫다고 생각하는 것은 무엇인가?

① that he is from a wealthy family

② that he knows how to get to Peter's house

③ that he is older than she is

④ that he is a boy

4. 윗글의 내용과 관계가 가장 먼 것을 고르시오.

① Peter, who owns a spade, is from another country.

② Antonia's attitude towards the narrator did not change with time.

③ The narrator owns a pony and offered to give Antonia a ride.

④ The narrator has warm regards for Antonia despite her often condescending attitude.

5. 밑줄 친 (c)의 명사형을 고르시오.

① deferment   ② deference

③ deferant   ④ defersion

6. 괄호 (d) 안에 가장 알맞은 말을 고르시오.

① on foot   ② on walking

③ by feet   ④ by walk

■ 독해 60.

I read everything on the topic of the college education with (a) <u>mounting</u> impatience. I am exasperated by the critics, but I am even more exasperated by the professed friends of (b) <u>liberal education</u>. I can understand the type of a man who asserts that a B.A. degree (c) <u>isn't worth a nickel in the pay envelope</u>, but I am downright annoyed with the professed friends of the colleges who accepts the challenge and tries to prove that a diploma does have cash value, after all. Even if he succeeds in proving (d) <u>the point</u> I am very disappointed in him.

I never went to college. I shall always regret the fact. I don't think I should have a cent more (e) my name today if I had graduated from Harvard. I'm no economic royalist, but I'm doing all right.

1. 윗글의 내용과 가장 거리가 먼 것을 고르시오.

① The author is not a graduate of a prestigious university but does not think he would have become richer had he done so.

② The author is more angry with the proponents of college education than he is with the opponents.

③ The author seems to disagree with much of what he reads about college education.

④ The author is of the view that a college diploma is the key to financial success.

2. 밑줄 친 (a)의 뜻이 가장 가까운 것을 고르시오.

① worsening   ② increasing

③ formulating   ④ materializing

3. 밑줄 친 (b)의 가장 정확한 정의를 고르시오.

① academic training pertaining to general cultural concerns such as philosophy.

② education geared toward the promotion of the political goals of the liberal party.

③ open-minded and forward looking education.

④ education dedicated to the well-being of the masses.

4. 밑줄 친 (c)와 뜻이 가장 가까운 것을 고르시오.

① has less value than five cents.

② has nothing to do with living.

③ has little monetary value.

④ has profit generating propensities.

5. 밑줄 친 (d)가 구체적으로 가리키는 것을 고르시오.

① that the critics of college education can be proven wrong.

② that there are other things more important than money.

③ that college education is necessary for all.

④ that college education has a monetary significance.

6. 괄호 (e) 속에 가장 알맞은 말을 고르시오.

① to   ② of
③ from   ④ at

■ 독해 61.

A community depends on communication. The citizens must be able to understand one another. ① This means more than ② that they must be able ③ to effect a ready translation of the dialects of the country. They must have a common culture. ④ They must have the intellectual training needed to comprehend it and to communicate with those who ⑤ share it.

1. ①의 This가 가리키는 것은?

① community
② communication
③ A community에서 communication까지
④ The citizens에서 another까지

2. ②의 that은?

① This를 선행사로 하여 종속절을 인도하는 관계대명사이다.
② 명사절을 인도하는 접속사이다.
③ communication을 가리키는 대명사이다.
④ 전문의 내용을 가리키는 대명사이다.

3. ③의 to affect의 뜻은?

① to influence   ② to pretend
③ to produce   ④ to endeavor

4. ④와 동일한 의미의 내용을 가진 영문은?

① The citizens must make their intellectual training necessary to understand the common culture.

② The citizens must have the intellectual training and need to understand it.

③ The citizens must be so educated as to understand the common culture.

④ It was necessary for the citizens to understand the intellectual training they must have.

5. ⑤의 share와 가장 뜻이 가까운 우리말은?

① 분배한다.　　　　　　　　② 준다.

③ 같이 한다.　　　　　　　　④ 할당한다.

■ 독해 62.

The (1) minute investigation of the historians, the political scientist, even the sociologists have not (a) succeeded in (b) destroying or even seriously (c) modifying the mind-pictures (d) created by the romantic Southerner.

1. 의미상 (1) minute와 가장 거리가 먼 것은?

① careful　　　　　　　　② thorough

③ idle　　　　　　　　　　④ detailed

2. Who created the mind-pictures?

① the political scientists　　② the romantic Southerner

③ the historians　　　　　　④ the sociologists

3. 본문 속의 밑줄 친 단어 (a),(b),(c),(d)의 명사형이 잘못된 것은?

① succeeded-succession　　② destroying-destruction

③ modifying-modification　　④ created-creation

■독해 63.

We know now that the Milky Way is a vast belt of distant stars, each star a sun more or less like our own. Most of stars are too far away to be counted, even in a large telescope, but-strange (a) it may be seen-it is possible to weigh the lot.

1. 윗글의 내용과 뜻이 어긋나는 문장을 고르시오.

   ① There are lots of stars in the Milky Way.
   ② The stars in the Milky Way can't be counted.
   ③ It is not possible to know the weight of the stars in the Milky Way.
   ④ Each star in the Milky Way is not like our own sun.

2. (a)에 들어갈 가장 적당한 말은?

   ① enough   ② however
   ③ therefore   ④ though

■독해 64.

That morning, I was sure the end of the world had come. My boss had (a) fired me; and, with pessimism of youth, I was convinced that I would never find another job. I was marked for failure (I was 19 years old). That evening I had a date to meet a friend at Lewis Stadium to hear the New York Philharmonic. (b)_____, I decided to go.

1. (a) fired와 비슷한 말은?

   ① fined   ② dismissed
   ③ scolded   ④ beat

2. (b)의 빈칸에 들어갈 가장 알맞은 말은?

   ① Happily   ② Sadly
   ③ Job or no job   ④ However

258

■ 독해 65.

Mastery of English is not something solely achieved in college. But (1) <u>this essential skill surely should mature at a very rapid rate while at college</u> and should be nearing optimum efficiency by time of graduation.

Foreign tongues are also extremely important. (2) <u>Knowledge of French, Russian, Chinese or any other language provides a far deeper knowledge of our own language.</u> Moreover, a real insight into foreign culture is only possible when one knows the language of that culture.

Then there are (A) <u>nonlinguistic languages</u> that the student must master. (3) <u>Statistics and mathematics are clearly indispensable to roles in technology or science.</u> But these languages are also __(B)__ for social sciences and arts. The humanist who assumes that he can safely ignore math is sadly mistaken and will be shut off from much of the modern world.

A campus is not the only possible setting for higher education. Actually, (4) <u>if college has any value at all, the student's higher education will continue throughout life.</u>

College's great significance is that it can __(C)__ a systematic way and in a conductive environment introduce the student to the educational process. Above all else, this means establishing a taste for human excellence. (5) <u>This is the foundation of a real and continuing education.</u>

1. 윗글의 내용과 일치하지 않는 것은?

① 영어를 숙달하는 것은 대학에서만 가능하다.
② 외국문화를 이해하려면 그 문화의 언어를 알아야 한다.
③ 수학을 무시해도 괜찮다고 생각하는 사람은 잘못이다.
④ 대학에서는 교육을 체계적으로 실시할 수 있다.

2. 밑줄 친 (A) <u>nonlinguistic languages</u>에 해당되지 않는 것은?

① winks　　　　　　　② gestures
③ nodding　　　　　　④ esperanto

3. 괄호 (B)에 들어갈 가장 적당한 것은?

① essence   ② essential

③ essencable   ④ essentiality

4. 괄호 (C)에 들어갈 가장 적당한 것은?

① at   ② for

③ in   ④ on

5. 학생이 반드시 마스터해야 할 사항이 아닌 것은?

① sciences   ② English

③ math   ④ nonlinguistic languages

※ 윗글에서 밑줄 친 부분 (1)~(5)을 우리말로 옮기시오.

6. (1)

7. (2)

8. (3)

9. (4)

10. (5)

<u>Middle of the roaders</u> look for the middle ground in any conflict. They try to find a compromise for any position and feel that no matter what the situation, each side should be gaining something. Often as a result of there compromises, neither group wins anything and both may _____.

1. 밑줄 친 부분 <u>Middle of the roaders</u>의 어구를 우리말로 옮길 때 적절한 것은?

① 강경론자   ② 편견주의자

③ 온건주의자   ④ 무관심주의자

2. 밑줄 친 부분에 들어갈 단어는?

① gain   ② lose

③ win   ④ benefit

■ 독해 67.

When I was seven years old, my father died and my mother sent us children to stay with my grandmother is Scotland. Her house was an old converted farm, one storied, with a thatched roof and fairy tale windows like Hans Anderson house. I still have many photographs that bring back, vivid memories of that stay in Scotland. On all of them, the figure of my grandmother stands out in sharp contrast to the surrounding relatives and children. She was a tall and stern-looking Scotswoman. Her expression in the photographs was always the same-a sort of disapproving watchfulness which seemed to say that although she might relax at times, she would never allow the slighest degree of what she called nonsense.

1. Grandmother lived in _____.

   ① a fashionable house

   ② a big apartment

   ③ a small cottage that was once a farm house

   ④ an old house which once belonged to Hans Andreson

2. 할머니의 성격을 가장 잘 대변해 주는 단어는?

   ① vividness   ② contrast

   ③ relaxation   ④ watchfulness

3. 다음 글 중 본문의 내용과 일치하는 것은?

   ① I was brought up at my grandmother's.

   ② My mother died before my father.

   ③ My grandmother was very kind to me.

   ④ My grandmother shared the house with relatives,

■ 독해 68.

A college is a community, and a community consists of people who are bound together by personal ties. The relation between teacher and student is a personal relation. There must be a mutual interests, a mutual helpfulness. (a) No mechanical device can ever take the place of this personal connection. No TV screen can (b)_____ to your responses, or share your joys and sorrows, or chat with you over a coke or coffee in the Commodore Room.

To mechanize education, to depersonalize it, is to deprive (c) it of its most precious ingredient. (d)_____. (e) Vanderbilt, fortunately, is not too big for us to know one another, and take an interest in one another, Vanderbilt is not too big for us to be friends.

1. 밑줄 친 (a)를 우리말로 번역하여 답란에 쓰시오.

2. (b)_____에 (response)라는 단어를 어휘 변형시켜 답란에 써넣으시오.

3. (c)it는 무엇을 가리키나? 본문에서 찾아서 답란에 쓰시오. (영어로)

4. (d)_____에 다음에 주어진 단어들의 순서를 바로잡아 "우리는 어떤 대가를 치르더라도 이러한 개인적인 요소를 소중히 간직합시다."라고 영작하여 답란에 써넣으시오.

(Let, element, costs, cherish, at, us, personal, this, all)

5. 밑줄 친 (e)를 우리말로 번역하여 답란에 써넣으시오.

■ 독해 69.

※ 다음 영문을 읽고 주어진 질문의 내용이 본문의 내용과 일치하면 ○를, 일치하지 않으면 ×를 답란에 쓰시오.

When Golda graduated as the best student of the class, her mother was pleased. Now the girl could work full time in the grocery store. Even in America girls were not expected to go to high school!

Golda, however, expected to go. And after some tearful arguments, her parents agreed. Papa had, for once, sided with her-albeit rather faintly. Perhaps he felt guilty that he, the breadwinner, actually earned so little. He was a wise, gentle, and scholarly man, but not cut out for business……

She had decided to become a teacher because such a profession was "intellectually and socially useful". Mama, however, had found out that married women were not permitted to teach in the local schools. "You want to be an old maid?" she had screamed at Golda. "That's what you're studying for?"

Papa now sided strongly with Mama. Either Golda must quit school and go to work like other sensible girls her age, or she must transfer to a business school to be trained in subjects which would help her get a job and, who knows, a husband too······.

After running away from home and living with married sister in Denver for two years, Golda won this battle too. She returned to Milwaukee to finish high school.

1. As a young girl, Golda had a willingness to do anything to please her parents.

2. Golda went to Denver because she had a strong desire to get married.

3. Golda was an excellent student and wanted to go to high school to become a teacher.

4. Golda's father always supported her-even against her mother's wishes.

5. Golda's mother wanted Golda to work full time after her graduation.

No one knows exactly (a) <u>what new changes machines will bring in the life</u> of future generations, but we can be sure that life will not be the same as it is now. The lives of our grandchildren will be as different from our lives as ours are from (b) <u>those</u> of our grandparents.

1. (a) <u>what new changes machines will bring in the life</u>에 대한 우리말의 적절한 번역은?

　① 새롭게 변화한 기계들이 생활에 어떤 부담을 줄 것인가
　② 기계들의 생활에 어떤 새로운 변화를 가져올 것인가
　③ 기계들이 새로운 변화에 어떻게 대처해야 하는가
　④ 생활에서 얻은 변화는 기계와 어떤 관계를 갖게 되는가

2. 윗글의 내용과 일치하지 <u>않는</u> 것은?

　① The life of future generations will be different from our modern living.
　② We are sure that the life of future generations will be the same as the life of our generation.
　③ Machines will make possible some change of the lives of our grandchildren.
　④ The use of machines in future living will play an important part to change the ways of living.

3. (b) <u>those</u>가 이 글에서 나타내는 뜻은?

　① the lives　　　　　　② new changes
　③ ours　　　　　　　　④ future generations

(a) <u>It</u> is no good talking about the greatness of our fatherland, pretending to be proud of it, unless we who live in the country do something to make (b) <u>it</u> great.

1. (a) <u>It</u> 가 가리키는 것은?

   ① talking   ② pretending

   ③ fatherland   ④ talking 과 pretending

2. (b) <u>it</u> 가 가리키는 것은?

   ① talking   ② fatherland

   ③ pretending   ④ something

■ 독해 72.

> One day, a beggar followed a lady and asked her some money. She refused; so he turned away with a sigh saying he must do what he made up his mind to do.
>
> At this word, the lady was greatly frightened (a) <u>lest he should take his own life</u>. So she called him back, gave him a shilling, and asked (b) <u>what he meant.</u> The beggar took the money, put it into his pocket and said; "Madam, I have been begging all day in vain, and __(c)__ you not given me this shilling I should have been obliged to go to work."

1. 밑줄 친 (a)의 뜻에 가장 가까운 것은?

   ① so that he might not take his own life

   ② not to kill himself

   ③ for fear of his committing suicide

   ④ for fear of his killing her

2. 밑줄 친 (b)에 이을 수 있는 말은?

   ① to do in the future   ② to do with her

   ③ to do with money   ④ by the word

3. 빈칸 (c)에 알맞은 것은?

   ① unless   ② if

   ③ but for   ④ had

4. 윗글의 내용에 부합되는 것은?

   ① The beggar was dying of starvation.

   ② The beggar was denied a job though he was willing to work.

   ③ considering the result, the lady should not have given the money.

   ④ It was wise of the lady to give the money.

■ 독해 73.

> A train stopped at a small station, and a lady opened the window. There was a boy outside, and the lady said to him, "I can't walk very fast, so I don't want to get out of this train. Please run to the station restaurant and get me an icecream, and get one for yourself, too. (   ) twenty cents."
>
> The boy went. He came back a few seconds before the train started again. He was eating an icecream. He ran to the lady's window, gave her ten cents and said to her, "There was only one icecream in the restaurant."

1. 윗글의 (   )에 알맞은 것은?

   ① Here is   ② Here are

   ③ The amount of   ④ Money is

※윗글의 내용에 따라 다음 문장을 완성시키기에 가장 알맞은 것은?

2. The lady in the train _____.

   ① asked if he sold an icecream

   ② asked whether he could run to the station

   ③ asked for an icecream from the boy

   ④ asked the boy to get her an icecream

3. The money the lady gave to the boy was for _____.

　① an errand the boy was going to run

　② two icecreams, one for each

　③ the anxiety the boy would cause

　④ one icecream for the lady herself

4. If the lady had gotten out of the train. She might have lost it because _____.

　① there were so many trains at the station then.

　② she could not walk very fast.

　③ the train stopped on time.

　④ she liked icecream very much.

■ 독해 74.

　Parents have come to do much less for their children today, and (a) home has become much less of a workshop. Clothes can be brought ready-made, washing can go to the (b) , cooked or canned food can be bought, bread is baked and delivered by the baker, milk arrives on the door step, and (c) can be had at the restaurant and the school diningroom.

1. 밑줄 친 (a)의 뜻과 같은 것은?

　① 가정이 소규모의 공장으로 변했다.

　② 가정에서 공장 일을 하는 사람의 수가 훨씬 줄었다.

　③ 가정에서 만들어지는 것들의 수가 훨씬 줄었다.

　④ 가정에서 공장까지의 거리가 훨씬 가까워졌다.

2. 빈칸 (b)와 (c)에 알맞은 것은?

	(b)	(c)
①	factory	tickets
②	dormitory	experiments
③	observatory	home
④	laundry	meals

3. 본문의 내용과 일치하는 것은?

① Parents must have done much less in the past than now for their children.

② In the past, parents themselves had to make clothes for their children.

③ More things should be made at home now than in the past.

④ Canned food is more delicious than home-made food.

■ 독해 75.

There are countries in which unnecessary poverty prevails because the people as a whole are unaware of methods whereby <u>it</u> can be relieved. There are vast tracts of land, abandoned or never cultivated, which could support a thriving community <u>if full use was made of the knowledge and skill of scientists</u>.

There are innumerable people suffering from disease which can be cured, and from <u>which</u>, by following simple scientific rules of hygiene, they never again suffer. There are vast storehouses of natural power, such as the wind, waterfalls and the heat of the sun, which science can show how to harness for the relief of human drudgery and for raising the standard of living. The possibilities are enormous.

1. <u>it</u>이 지시하는 내용을 우리말로 쓰시오.

2. <u>if</u> 이하 밑줄 친 부분을 if they로 시작되는 글로 바꾸시오.

3. which의 선행사를 찾아 우리말로 쓰시오.

■ 독해 76.

I read everything on the topic that comes to my notice, but of late I read with growing impatience. I am exasperated by <u>the critics</u> but I am even more exasperated by the professed friends of liberal education. I can understand the type of a man who asserts that B.A. degree isn't worth a nickel in the pay envelope, and I think he is quite right in asserting that a college education is no good to his sort. But I am downright annoyed with the professed friend of the colleges who accepts the challenge and tries to prove that a diploma does have cash value, after all. Even if he succeeds in proving <u>the point</u>, I am very disappointed in him.

1. <u>the critics</u>의 비판 내용을 우리말로 간략히 설명하시오.

2. <u>the point</u>의 내용을 우리말로 간략히 설명하시오.

■ 독해 77.

※ 다음 영문의 빈칸(1~6)에 넣기에 알맞은 전치사를 (a~f)에서 하나씩 골라 별지 해답란에 그 기호를 쓰고, 밑줄 친 부분을 국문으로 번역하여 해답란에 쓰시오.

As a child I could never understand why grownups took dreaming so calmly when they could make such a fuss (1) any holiday. This still puzzles me. I am mystified (2) people who say they never dream and appear (3) have no interest in the subject. It

270

is much more astonishing me if they said they never went out (4) a walk.

 The dream life, though queer and bewildering and unsatisfactory (5) many respects, has its own advantages. The dead are there, smiling and talking. The past is there, sometimes all broken and confused occasionally as fresh as a daisy. And perhaps the future it there too, winking (6) us.

a. about   b. at   c. by   d. for
e. in   f. to

번역 :

■ 독해 78.

 Wellington is said to have chosen his officers by their noses and chins. The standard for them in noses must have been rather high to judge by the portraits of the Duke, but no doubt he made allowances. Anyhow, by this method he got the men he wanted. Some people, however, may think that he would have done better to have let the mouth be the deciding test. The lines of one's nose are more or less arranged for one at birth. A baby, born with a snub nose, would feel it hard that the decision that he would be no use to Wellington should be come to so early. And even if he arrived in the world with a Roman nose he might smash it up in childhood, and with it his chances of military fame. This, I think you will agree with me, would be unfair.

1. The feminine form of the word "Duke" is _____.

2. Turn the phrase, "to have let the mouth be the deciding test", into a clause.

3. Translate the underlined sentence, beginning with "a baby", into Korean:

4. The original name of "Roman nose" is _____. (Write in English.)

5. What does the underlined "it" stand for in the sentence? (Write in English.)

■ 독해 79.

> Your opinions are important to many of other people, too. This is because you are part of that group of people called the public, and your ideas help to make up public opinion. Public opinion on any subject is a mass judgement or conclusion on that subject-the opinion reached when most of the people make up their minds. Public opinion is one of the most powerful forces in _____ what happens in a democracy such as ours.

1. 밑줄 친 make up과 가장 뜻이 가까운 것은?

① dispose   ② compose   ③ compensate

④ decide   ⑤ influence

2. 밑줄 친 mass judgement와 가장 뜻이 가까운 것은?

① judgement on the quality of some material

② judgement that can be relied upon

③ judgement made by many people

④ judgement made by the politicians

⑤ judgement made carelessly

3. 빈칸에 알맞은 것은?

　　① ignoring　　　　　② demonstrating　　　　　③ deciding
　　④ promising　　　　　⑤ probing

■ 독해 80.

(A) <u>Smokers stand a good chance of dying from lung-cancer</u>. Now a report from the University of Hawaii, in Honolulu, says male smokers (B) <u>drive up</u> their lung-cancer risk even ___(c)___ by eating a lot of high-cholesterol foods. The researchers compared 326 (D) <u>people who had been diagnosed with lung cancer to</u> 865 healthy people. By examining the food each person ate in a normal mouth, the scientists discovered that the risk for lung-cancer increased dramatically in male smokers who ate the most cholesterol compared to male smokers who ate the least cholesterol.

1. 밑줄 친 부분 (A)를 우리말로 옮기시오.

2. 밑줄 친 부분 (B)와 뜻이 가장 가까운 단어를 본문에서 찾아 쓰시오.

3. 빈칸 (C)에 high를 적절히 변형시켜 써넣으시오.

4. 밑줄 친 부분 (D)를 우리말로 옮기시오.

It is simply that the values in the East and in the West are different. The man in the East wants more out of life itself than the man in the West (a) <u>does</u>. If anything, the East is more materialistic than the West. The East, (b) <u>being so old</u>, knows how short life is. Man's years pass so soon. Therefore, enjoyment of life cannot be (c) <u>put off</u>, for in old age the senses are (d) <u>dulled</u>.

1. Select the sentence that is least consistent with the passage above.

① The man in the East thinks more about material things than does the man in the West.
② The East is not as old as the West.
③ The man in the East is willing to put off enjoyment of life.
④ Values in the East is not the same as those in the West.

2. Which of the following does the underlined (a) indicate?

① are different
② wants more out of life
③ has values
④ is simple

3. Select the clause that is closest to the underlined (b).

① because it is so old
② when it is so old
③ despite the fact that it is old
④ no matter how old it is

4. Select the term that has the same meaning as (c).

① neglect
② abolish
③ postpone
④ cancel

5. Which of the following has the opposite of (d)?

① sharp
② slim
③ big
④ tiny

There are many ways in which we can be peacemakers. One way is to tolerate the opinions and desires of the others, Many quarrels result form arguments in which men become angry with the opinion others express. Every man has a right to express his opinion. However foolish an opinion may seem, we should allow it to be expressed, and should not (1) take offence because others do not think as we (2) do.

1. 밑줄 친 (1) take offence의 뜻은?

　　① attack　　　　　　② agree　　　　　　③ be angry
　　④ express　　　　　　⑤understand

2. 다음 중 윗글과 같은 내용인 것은?

　　① Peacemakers are the best things we can be.
　　② We must allow different opinions to be expressed.
　　③ Foolish opinions make quarrels.
　　④ You must tolerate others to get what you desire.
　　⑤ You should not take offence when someone is foolish.

3. 밑줄 친 (2) do 가 대신하고 있는 것은?

　　① take　　　　　　② think　　　　　　③ offence
　　④ should　　　　　　⑤ seem

※다음 ＿＿＿에 들어갈 어구를 (a)~(g)에서 고르시오.

　　The age ＿1＿ has been called the machine age, the age of the science, and even the atomic age. It could as reasonably be called the verbal age. For today words are the mightiest and yet the commonest tools in the world. ＿2＿, electric and atomic power are relatively unimportant in our daily lives. This, of course, has been true of other ages. But __3__, the more its existence depends on the power of words. And today their power is immense. We often fail to understand this __4__. Familiarity breeds, if not contempt, at least indifference. Yet, stop a moment and consider how much we live in a verbal world. The university education, __5__, is almost entirely a verbal experience. You read books, you listen to lectures, you formulate your outlook on life with word.

    a. contrasted with the power of words

    b. the greater progress men make

    c. the more complex a civilization becomes

    d. because we take words for granted

    e. we live in

    f. because we set great value on the power of words

    g. which, you feel, has so much importance to your future

■ 독해 84.

It has long been a fashion to say that the East is "spiritual" and the West is "material". But like many things that are carelessly said, (1) it is not true. The East is neither more nor less spiritual than the West, and the West is neither more nor less materialistic than the East. This may be said of all men alike : they prefer to have food rather than to starve, to have shelter than to be homeless, to be healthy rather than diseased, to live long rather than short lives, to be happy rather than sorrowful.

Then where did this myth about the spiritual East and the material West come from? (2) It has its roots in a sort of truth, and this truth can be simply stated: people in the East like to enjoy life. They will not work so hard __(3)__ they have no time for simple pleasure in living, in eating, in sleeping, in playing with their children, and in talking with their wives and families. They will not __(4)__ two jobs if (5) they can pay their bills with one, for two jobs consume their time and distract their minds.

1. 본문 중에서 밑줄 친 (1) <u>it</u>이 가리키는 것은?

   ① that the East is "spiritual"

   ② that the West if "material"

   ③ a fashion to say that the East is "spiritual" and the West is "material"

   ④ that the East is "spiritual" and the West is "material"

2. 본문 중에서 밑줄 친 (2) <u>It</u>가 가리키는 것은?

   ① this myth about the spiritual East and the material West

   ② the material West

   ③ this myth about the material East and the spiritual West

   ④ the spiritual East

3. 본문 중에서 밑줄 친 (3)에 가장 알맞은 접속사를 쓰시오,

4. 본문 중에서 밑줄 친 (4)에 들어갈 가장 적당한 어구는?

   ① take over   ② take out

   ③ take on   ④ take off

5. 본문 중에서 밑줄 친 (5)가 가리키는 것을 본문에서 찾아 쓰시오.(영어로)

■ 독해 85.

The United States probably suffers more injury __(1)__ insects than any other country in the world, because as people migrated here a large number of insects came with them, but these pests' natural enemies, by which they would be destroyed, were left behind. In this country alone insects destroy yearly materials and goods estimated to be worth many millions of dollars. the damage done to our crops by their activities amounts to even more. Insects are especially active as disease carriers. The household fly carries numerous diseases and parasites. Mosquitoes are responsible __(2)__ malaria, and the tick for Rocky Mountain fever. Insects also carry diseases to many important crops. It is hard to fight insects (3) <u>because they adapt themselves to all sorts of conditions</u>, and because their size has so often obscured their destructive powers.

This country has gone a long way in its scientific study of insects. France and Italy have shown themselves keenly alive to the importance of the work, and Great Britain is developing many workers in (4) <u>her commonwealth</u>. Some insecticide has been developed for almost every injurious insect __(5)__ the United States but the fight call __(6)__ more trained workers and a large expenditure of money.

1. According to this article insects cause great damage to _____.

① stored foods   ② clothing

③ forests   ④ cultivated plants

2. Insects are hard to fight because they _____.

① are so small   ② live outdoors

③ run so fast   ④ hide in the park

3. Foreign insects cause the greatest losses in this country because they came _____.

① in large numbers   ② without their native foes

③ to a temperate climate   ④ to a good eating ground

4. 밑줄 친 (1)에 들어갈 적당한 전치사는?

5. 밑줄 친 (2)에 들어갈 적당한 전치사는?

6. 밑줄 친 (3)을 번역하여라.

7. 밑줄 친 (4)의 뜻은?

8. 밑줄 친 (5)에 들어갈 적당한 전치사는?

9. 밑줄 친 (6)에 들어갈 적당한 전치사는?

■ 독해 86.

In the cities the African loses his tribal sense more quickly and easily than in the country, and he has a greater opportunity for feeling himself a part of the new and wider political unit, the nation. It helps to be able to look on a leader, such as Nkrumah, as if he were a tribal chief; but again it is just a matter of practical expediency. There was an inner strength in the old system that is still lacking in the new.

There are, then, inherent conflicts in the new way that prevent complete acceptance, and this is not surprising considering how <u>it</u> has been imposed <u>from without</u>, with not the slightest consideration for the old way. At the same time it is obvious that the old has gone for good, and in the cities the Africans have come to look upon it with shame, so that it is no longer even a source of pride, let alone of moral or spiritual strength.

1. Africa인들이 새로운 제도에서 상실한 것은?

   ① a leader   ② inner strength

   ③ political unit   ④ tribal chief

2. 밑줄 친 <u>it</u>이 가리키는 것은?

   ① inherent conflict   ② the old way

   ③ the new way   ④ complete acceptance

3. 밑줄 친 <u>from without</u>의 뜻과 가장 가까운 것은?

   ① 아무 생각 없이   ② 무(無)로부터

   ③ 빈곤으로부터   ④ 밖으로부터

4. 도시에 사는 Africa인들이 수치로 생각하는 것은?

   ① the old   ② living in the city

   ③ new system   ④ moral or spiritual strength

■ 독해 87.

Last week I had for about the hundredth time an experience that always disturbs me. Riding on the train, I found myself talking with my seat-mate, who asked me what I did _(1)_ a living. "I teach English." Do you have any trouble predicting his response? His face fell, and groaned, "Oh, dear, I'll have to __(2)__." In my experience there are only two other possible reactions. The first is even less __(3)__. : "I hated English in school. It was my worst subject." The second, so rare as to make an honest English teacher almost burst __(4)__ tears of gratitude when it occurs, is an animated conversation about literature, or ideas, or the American language-the kind of conversation that shows a continuing respect for "English" as something more than being sure about 'who' and 'whom', 'lie' and 'lay'.

1. (1)에 들어갈 알맞은 단어는?

   ① on   ② with
   ③ for   ④ by

2. (2)에 들어갈 가장 적당한 표현은?

   ① keep my mouth shut   ② watch my language
   ③ be prepared for your questions   ④ change my seat-mate

3. (3)에 들어갈 수 <u>없는</u> 단어는?

   ① inspiring   ② encouraging
   ③ stimulating   ④ aspiring

4. (4)에 들어갈 수 <u>있는</u> 단어는?

   ① into   ② out
   ③ on   ④ with

5. 윗글의 취지와 일치하는 항목은?

   ① As a teacher of English, the writer wants to share conversations about literature or ideas rather than about the rules of words.
   ② As a teacher of English, the writer is more interested in the correct knowledge of English grammar.
   ③ The writer feels gratitude when his partner is sure about the correct usage of 'who' and 'whom', 'lie' and 'lay' etc.
   ④ The writer is unsatisfied with all of the three reactions that his partners show when they have discovered that he is a teacher of English.

※ 다음 ____에 들어갈 알맞을 단어를 고르시오.

The scene in the kitchen was a shocking sight. In one corner stood a frightened little kitchen maid, in another the housekeeper. At the table sat my cook, waving a ladle and singing, __1__ his foot. His eyes were glazed and he was far away in some other sphere. The table __2__ pieces of chicken.

I was furious. It was __3__ to say. "Get out. You're dismissed!" when I thought of the counsel that had calmed me so many times. If I lost control, I would only hurt myself. I __4__. "Let's get something on the table." I said. Everyone __5__. Soon the dinner table was ready.

1. ① stepping   ② beating time with
   ③ dancing   ④ jumping

2. ① was littered with   ② was full
   ③ was clean with   ④ decorated with

3. ① right there   ② on my head
   ③ in my thought   ④ on the tip of my tongue

4. ① shouted   ② screamed
   ③ pulled myself together   ④ lost myself

5. ① jumped and ran   ② patched in
   ③ sat quietly   ④ cooked the chicken

■독해 89.

She stuck up her wet face to be kissed, and I gazed down at her with the warm intention of kissing her. But when I looked into her face, I saw two little rivulets, running from Mamie's nose to her pouted upper lip. I had never noticed (1) <u>them</u> before, although I had often observed her sticking her tongue out and upward, whenever she sniffed. For (2) <u>ours</u> was a catarrhal climate. Now I looked and saw. But I have always been proud in later days that, even at this early age, I mastered (3) <u>repulsion</u> and kissed Mamie on her salty lips.

1. 밑줄 친 부분 (1)이 가리키는 것을 영어로 답하라.

2. 밑줄 친 부분 (2)를 두 단어로 표시하라.

3. 밑줄 친 부분 (3)을 구체적으로 설명하라.

■ 독해 90.

Every day, in all kinds of weather, many thousand of men and women jog. Why has jogging become so popular? Most joggers begin because they hear it is very good exercise. Jogging makes the heart stronger and helps people lose weight. <u>It</u> can also help them feel better about themselves.

Donald Robbins, who is forty-two years old and works in an office, began jogging a few years ago, because he felt he was too fat. At first he could only run about 100 yards. It took him three months to be able to run a mile. But two years later, he ran tin an marathon race-over twenty-six miles. Many joggers, like Donald Robbins, feel that if they can succeed at jogging, they can succeed at other things, and often <u>this feeling</u> helps them at their jobs.

1. 밑줄 친 <u>It</u>이 가리키는 것은?

2. 조깅이 가져다 주는 효과로 본문에서 언급된 것은?

① 인내심을 키워 준다.

② 심장을 튼튼하게 하여 준다.

③ 다리의 근육을 발달시켜 준다.

④ 소화를 촉진시켜 준다.

3. Why did Donald Robbins begin jogging?

① Because he had a heart disease.

② Because he wanted to lose weight.

③ Because he liked running.

④ Because he lost his job.

4. Donald Robbins finally _____.

① stopped jogging　　　　② lost his job

③ succeeded at jogging　　④ recovered from his disease

5. 밑줄 친 this feeling이 나타내는 것을 우리말 세 음절 단어로 써넣으시오.(○○감)

■ 독해 91.

　　Fir4st of all, it is often confused with the explosive experience of "falling" in love, the sudden collapse of the barriers which existed until that moment between two strangers. But, as it was pointed out before, this ___(1)___ of sudden intimacy is by its very nature short-lived. After the stranger has become an intimately known person, there are no more ___(2)___ to be overcome, there is no more sudden closeness to be achieved.

※ 빈칸에 알맞은 단어를 본문 안에서 찾아 쓰시오.

(1) :　　　　　　　　　　(2) :

■ 독해 92.

Not only can the computer gather facts, it can also store them as fast as they are gathered and can pour them out whenever they are needed. The ___(1)___ is a really high-powered "memory" machine that "has all the answers" -or almost all. What is the most efficient speed for driving a car through the New York-New Jersey tunnels? What brand of canned goods is the ___(2)___ popular in a particular supermarket? What kind of weather will we have tomorrow? The computer will flash out the ___(3)___ in a fraction of a second.

※ 빈칸에 알맞은 단어를 본문 안에서 찾아 쓰시오.

(1) :   (2) :   (3) :

■ 독해 93.

I was enjoying a ride on my new bicycle when the sky suddenly blackened and a few drops of rain fell. Realizing that I would never reach home before the storm broke, I decided to take the bus. "How much is the ___(a)__?" I asked the driver. "Twenty five cents", he said. (b) To my relief I found a solitary quarter in my pocket. "Can I take my bike on the bus?" I asked. "Well," he said, "I suppose If you paid separately for it, it would be all right." "All I have is a quarter." I confessed. He made a face as a loud ___(c)___ of thunder sounded, and I resigned myself to a long, wet ride home. "That bicycle looks brand-new." he commented as I turned to go. "It is." I replied. "In that case," he said jovially, "bring it aboard. Children under six years old ride free."

1. 빈칸 (a)에 적당한 단어는?

① wage   ② fare
③ cost   ④ fee

2. 밑줄 친 (b)를 바꿔 쓴 것으로 옳은 것은?

① my relief in finding   ② I found relief in

③ I found myself relieved   ④ I was relieved to find

3. 빈칸 (c)에 적당한 단어는?

① clap   ② beat

③ clang   ④ tick

4. Why do you think the driver made a face?

I think it was because _____.

① he made it a rule never to allow a bicycle in his bus

② he felt happy doing a child an unusual service

③ he felt it difficult to deal with my situation

④ he was afraid lest a heavy storm might overtake him

5. 윗글의 내용에 부합되는 문장을 고르시오.

① The trouble with me was that I had barely enough money for my bicycle.

② Without my bike, I couldn't have found a way out of difficulty.

③ The driver must have a sense of humor to allow me to take the bike into the bus.

④ No additional charge was made for my bike because I was under six.

■ 독해 94.

A poor farmer who had always lived in the country and had never visited a big town won a lot of money, so he decided that he could now (a) <u>afford</u> a holiday in an excellent hotel by the sea. When lunchtime came on his first day there, he decided to go and eat in the restaurant of the hotel.

The headwaiter showed him to his table, __(b)__ his order and went away when he looked at the farmer again, he had a surprise. The farmer __(c)__.

The headwaiter was very annoyed at this and immediately told one of the other waiters in the restaurant to go to the man and inform him, without being in any way

(d) <u>insulting</u>, that people did not do such a thing in restaurants of that quality. The waiter went to the farmer and said in a friendly voice, "Good morning, Sir. Would you like a shave, or a haircut?"

1. 밑줄 친 (a)와 가까운 뜻으로 쓰인 afford가 들어 있는 문장은?

   ① Olives afford oil. ② We can afford a car.
   ③ I can afford to speak frankly.   ④ Music affords her pleasure.

2. 빈칸 (b)에 들어가기에 적당한 낱말은?

   ① took   ② passed
   ③ supplied   ④ sent

3. 문맥상 빈자리 (c)에 들어가기에 적당한 낱말은?

   ① had cleared his table
   ② had some honey on his biscuits
   ③ wiped his mouth with a handkerchief
   ④ had tied his napkin around his neck

4. 밑줄 친 (d)의 낱말 대신 쓸 수 있는 것은?

   ① polite   ② respectful
   ③ rude   ④ scolding

5. The tone of the above passage is _____.

   ① embarrassing   ② humorous
   ③ grim   ④ melancholy

Two shops in the same neighborhood have undergone a similar experience. The fathers who owned the shops died toward the end of last year (a) <u>and their only sons have taken over</u>. One is a barber shop and the other is a pizza shop.

In doing so, the two suns have given up whatever dreams they may have had about doing to a university. But they do not seem to mind (b) <u>it</u>. They have both married, and filled with a new sense of responsibility. They are earnestly carrying on their fathers' work and taking care of their mothers.

It has meant an entirely new life for these two young man. In the case of the barber shop, the new owner has become accustomed by now to the many problems of management, including his relations with the other barbers working there. For the son at the pizza shop, it means, besides making and delivering pizza and maintaining good customer relations, getting up before sawn everyday to buy fresh meat and vegetable at the central wholesale market.

(c) <u>Both have a new recognition of all that their fathers went through over the years</u>. The two fathers were well known in the neighborhood. Both sons grew up in the neighborhood. People remember them in their school days. They were active in neighborhood young men's associations, taking an active part in local festivals and volunteering their service in an emergency such as a fire broke out.

The two fathers (d) <u>passed on</u> but they were fortunate to have fine sons. Life goes on, but we would prefer to have the future of our country placed in the hands of such young men-not those roaring around on motorcycles or in sports cars, not those causing trouble on and off the campus.

1. 밑줄 친 (a)를 우리말로 번역하여 답란에 쓰시오.

2. 밑줄 친 (b) it는 무엇을 말하는 것인지 우리말로 설명하시오.

3. 밑줄 친 (c)를 우리말로 번역하여 답란에 쓰시오.

4. 밑줄 친 (d) passed on 와 같은 뜻을 가진 단어를 본문에서 찾아 쓰시오.

5. 다음에서 본문의 내용과 일치하지 않는 것은?

① Of the two shops, one is an eating place.

② The sons, when they were young, used to roar around on motorcycles.

③ The people in the neighborhood seem to like the two sons.

④ The writer of this article is praising the devotion of the sons to their parents.

■ 독해 96.

Automobiles and trains, airplanes and ocean liners are on the move, day and night, (a) around the clock. But this has not always been so. There was a time in which man had no vehicles and no roads. The Stone Age people used streams and lakes as roadways. And they traveled on logs, one alone, or (b) several tied together. Logs were the first vehicles of transportation.

1. 밑줄 친 (a) around the clock 의 뜻과 같은 것은?

① here and there   ② for twelve hours

③ without a stop   ④ behind schedule

2. 밑줄 친 (b) several 이 구체적으로 가리키는 것은?

① people   ② logs

③ streams   ④ vehicles

3. In a time when there was no vehicles and no roads, man may have _____.

① worked together in order to make some airplanes

② stayed at home without any movement

③ traveled in a boat using streams and lakes

④ used logs by way of transportation

■ 독해 97.

Birds are able sometimes to discriminate between protectors and persecutors, but (A) seldom very well I should imagine ; they do not view the face only, but the whole form, and our frequent change of dress must make it difficult for (B) them to distinguish the individuals they know and trust from strangers. Even a dog is occasionally at fault when his master, last (C) see in a black suit, reappears in white with a straw hat on.

1. 밑줄 친 부분 (A)을 우리말로 옮기시오.

2. 밑줄 친 단어 (B)의 them이 가리키는 것을 영어로 쓰시오.

3. 밑줄 친 단어 (C)의 see를 문맥에 맞는 형태로 고치시오.

■ 독해 98.

Alice Hinderman, a woman of twenty-seven (1) when George Willard was a mere boy, had lived in Winesburg all her life. She clerked in Winney's Dry Goods Store and lived with her mother who married a second husband. Alice's stepfather was a carriage painter, and ___(2)___ drink. His story is an (3) <u>odd</u> one. It will be worth telling one day. At twenty-seven Alice was tall and somewhat slight. Her head was large and overshadowed her body. Her shoulders were a little stooped and her hair and eyes brown. She was quiet but beneath a placid exterior a continual ferment went ___(4)___.

1. Which of the following is closest to the meaning of the underlined (1)?

   ① When George Willard was only a boy

   ② When George Willard was truly a boy

   ③ When George Willard was a small boy

   ④ When George Willard was on only child

2. Select a statement that is least consistent with the passage above.

   ① Alice Hinderman grew up in Winesburg.

   ② Alice's mother married a man who made a living painting carriages.

   ③ Alice owned and operated a dry goods store in Winesburg.

   ④ Alice's hair and eyes are of the same color.

3. Which of the following is the most appropriate in (2)?

   ① gave to   ② given to

   ③ giving to   ④ give to

4. Which of the following is closest to the meaning of (3)?

   ① uneven   ② forgotten

   ③ more   ④ strange

5. Select the most appropriate word for (4)?

   ① off   ② over

   ③ on   ④ away

Every year in many developing countries large areas of land that once produced food become completely ___(A)___ . The hungry residents of these areas have to move or die. The problem is not caused by pollution; it is not the result of poisonous chemicals which (B) <u>contaminate</u> the land. Pollution is not the only way to destroy the environment. It can be destroyed by humans who disturb the ecological balance of an area in other ways. In any area there is a balance in nature. Each part of the natural system depends on other parts.

1. 빈칸 (A)에 produce를 적절히 변형시켜 써넣으시오.

2. 밑줄 친 부분 (B)를 우리말로 옮기시오.

3. 환경을 파괴시키는 두 가지 요인을 본문에 나오는 단어로 각각 쓰시오.

The scientifically valid procedure in language learning involves listening first, to be followed __(1)__ speaking. Then comes reading, and finally the writing of the language. This is just the order in which a child learns his mother tongue-first hearing, then speaking; (2) <u>and only after he has acquired considerable facility in understanding and speaking, dose he learn to read and write</u>. However, most traditional methods of teaching languages to adults have almost completely reversed (3) <u>this process</u>-first comes reading, closely linked with writing. Then, after (4) <u>one is supposed to have acquired a knowledge of reading and writing</u>, classes are offered in conversation. This major deficiency in language teaching is in large measure the result of our classical tradition of Greek and Latin studies, languages which are only known to us in the dead forms of written documents. It was falsely assumed that ___(5)___ the classical tongues were taught exclusively through the printed page, modern, living languages should be introduced in the same way.

1. 본문 중에서 밑줄 친 (1)에 가장 알맞은 전치사는?

　① in　　　　　　　　　② with
　③ of　　　　　　　　　④ by

2. 본문 중에서 밑줄 친 (2)을 우리말로 옮기시오.

3. 본문 중에서 밑줄 친 (3)가 구체적으로 무엇을 뜻하는지 우리말로 쓰시오.

4. 본문 중에서 밑줄 친 (4) 'one is supposed to have acquired a knowledge of reading and writing' 을 'it' 으로 시작되는 문장으로 바꿔 쓰시오.

5. 본문 중에서 밑줄 친 (5)에 가장 알맞은 접속사는?

　① when　　　　　　　② while
　③ since　　　　　　　④ so

■ 독해 101.

　The south Italian town dweller is, of course, a somewhat different character. He has the alleged advantages and conveniences of town life, but <u>one can hardly drive through the crowded slums of Naples without thinking that the peasant, despite the primitive living conditions, is better off</u>. The struggle to survive is terrific in these populations southern cities, and though the city dweller may not have to labor quite so hard physically as the farmer, he must be considerably shrewder and much more alive, even to the smallest opportunity, if he is to succeed in wangling a living.

1. 밑줄 친 문장과 뜻이 같도록 바꾸어 쓸 때 빈칸에 적합한 것은?

Whenever one drives through the crowded slums of Naples, one thinks _____.

① the peasant is very poor because of his primitive living conditions

② the peasant's primitive living conditions are getting better

③ the peasant is richer in spite of his primitive living conditions

④ the peasant is in good health due to his primitive living conditions

2. 빈칸에 이어질 말로 적당치 않는 것은?

The South Italian town dweller _____.

① is poorer when he lives in the slum than the peasant

② labors harder physically than the peasant

③ is much more clever and active in living

④ enjoy so-called conveniences of town life

3. 밑줄 친 부분을 우리말로 번역하라.

■ 독해 102.

As a people there is nothing in which we take a juster pride than our educational system. It is our boast that every boy or girl has the chance to get a school training, and we feel it is a prime national duty to furnish this training free, because only thereby can we secure the proper type of citizenship in the average American. Our public schools and our colleges have done their work well, and there is no class of our citizens deserving of heartier praise than the men and women who teach in them.

1. thereby가 의미하는 것은?

① by furnishing a school training free

② by taking pride in our educational system

③ by praising teachers and professors

④ by securing the proper type of citizenship

2. 밑줄 친 문장과 뜻이 가장 가까운 것은?

① It is strange that teachers and professors should be praised.

② No citizens praise teachers and professors with all their hearts.

③ It is right and proper that teachers and professors should receive the heartiest praise.

④ Our citizens should be praised for providing classes to teachers and professors.

■ 독해 103.

A college is a community, and a community consists of people who are bound together by personal ties. The relation between teacher and student is personal relation. There must be a mutual interest, a mutual helpfulness. No mechanical device can ever take the place of this personal connection. No TV screen can respond to your responses, or share your joys and sorrows, or chat with you over a coke or coffee in the Commodore Room. To mechanize education, to depersonalize it, is to deprive (1) it of its most precious (2) ingredient. Let us cherish this personal element at all costs. Vanderbilt, fortunately, is not too big for us to know one another, and take an interest in one another, Vanderbilt is not too big for us to be friends.

1. (1)의 "it" 이 무엇을 가리키는지 본문에서 찾아 한단어로 답하라.(영어로)

2. (2)의 "ingredient" 와 같은 뜻을 가진 단어 하나를 본문에서 찾아 써라.(영어로)

3. 필자는 사제 관계를 어떻게 보고 있는지 본문에서 찾아 두 단어로 답하라.(영어로)

4. 필자는 교육의 가장 귀중한 요소를 무엇으로 보는지 본문에서 찾아 두 단어로 답하라.
   (영어로)

At certain times of year, foods in China are eaten <u>not so much for nourishment</u> <u>as   (1)   their meaning</u>. This is especially so on New Year's Day, the first day of the Chinese lunar calendar.

1. (1)에 들어갈 단어 하나를 본문에서 찾아 써넣어라.

2. 밑줄 친 부분만 우리말로 옮겨라.

I missed the opportunity of association and friendship with men of wide culture and high ideals in an atmosphere of quiet and detachment. I went to work when I was 16 years old because at that age it seems important to eat ravenously and regularly-seems more important than (1) <u>it really is</u>. My associations thenceforth were with folk who were neither scholars nor gentlemen. It was many years before I ever had opportunity of close and friendly contact with men whose intellect and whose culture were superior to my <u>own   (2)   </u>.

1. 밑줄 친 부분 (1) 다음에 생략된 단어는?

2. 밑줄 친 부분 (2) 다음에 생략된 두 개의 단어는?

■ 독해 106.

The road itself is a brilliant achievement of modern technology. It runs for several hundred miles into the mountains, winding like a snake round steep sides up to the top and then down again to be valleys beyond. I remember one spot in it where there is a sheer cliff of more than a thousand feet. As the road is only wide enough for one vehicle, open spaces have been cut into the sides of the mountains at intervals. Should two vehicles meet, as often happens, it is necessary ___(1)___ one to reverse to the nearest open space in order to let the other pass. In bad weather, it is quite terrifying to feel the vehicle travel across the road towards a horrifying cliff. The drivers are quite unconcerned, however. ___(2)___, I have never heard of a serious accident.

* vehicle=car

1. (1) 안에 알맞은 전치사를 써넣으시오.

2. (2) 안에 "사실대로 말하면" 이란 뜻의 관용어 (4단어)를 써넣으시오.

3. Bad weather makes the road frightening, because _____.

   ① the road becomes very dangerous

   ② one vehicle has to reverse

   ③ the drivers travel carelessly

   ④ open spaces have been cut into the sides of the mountains

4. The drivers are _____.

   ① nervous in bad weather

   ② terrified of the sheer cliffs

   ③ not worried

   ④ always talking about the achievement of modern technology

5. The road _____.

   ① winds up hill all the way

   ② climbs straight to the top of the mountain

   ③ has numerous open spaces

   ④ winds gradually up to the top and then down again

PART X

영문 번역

※다음 영문 중 밑줄 친 부분만 우리말로 번역하시오.

1. Deep in the forest a hunter picked up big pieces of raw meat and put them in ah basket. (A) <u>For many days at a time he had eaten nothing but meat.</u> Now he was hungry for vegetables and grain. He picked up the basket and walked through the deep shade toward the edge of the forest (B) <u>where trees stood close together to form a triangle.</u> There the hunter took the meat from the basket and fastened a piece to each of the three trees. Then he turned and walked back into the forest.

   (A):

   (B):

2. Change in the whole social system is inevitable not merely because conditions change-though partly for that reason-but because people themselves change. We change, you and I, we change and change vitally, as the years go on. New feelings arise in us, old values depreciate, new values arise. <u>Things we thought we wanted most intensely we realize we don't care about. The things we built our lives on crumble and disappear, and the process is painful.</u>

   번역

3. As a scientist it is his business to discover facts, to invent techniques, to devise means. In contrast, <u>it is business of philosophy to help mankind to decide upon those ends toward the realization of which all scientific facts and knowledge of techniques ought to be used as means</u>, for philosophy does concern itself with values and with what ought to be as well as with what is.

   번역

4. At the beginning of the last strike the papers announced that Public Opinion opposed to dictation by a minority. <u>Towards the end of the strike the papers said that Public Opinion was strongly in favor of a settlement which would leave neither side with a sense of defeat. I do not complain of either of these statements, but I have been wondering, as I have always wondered before, how a leader-writer discovers what the Public Opinion is.</u>

5. <u>It is the small matters of conduct, in the observance of the rule of the road, that we pass judgement upon ourselves, and declare that we are civilized or uncivilized. The great moments of heroism and sacrifice are rare.</u> It is the little habits of commonplace intercourse that make up the great sum of life and sweeten or make bitter the journey.

6. We understand that <u>the U.S. forces cut is designed to reduce enormous deficits in federal budgets and to stimulate economic recovery,</u> seeing that it is unnecessary to maintain the present U.S. military strength in the post-Cold War era brought on by the collapse of communism in Europe.

7. The most important task all mankind must tackle in the process of industrialization is preserving the environment from worsening pollution. <u>Essential to this end is international cooperation since environmental problems are not limited to individual</u>

countries but are global and regional in nature as pollution spreads beyond national boundaries.

번역

8. As far as our environment is concerned, pollution is a real threat to human health and well-being. Indeed, many scientists believe that, if we do not soon change our ways, the earth will one day so polluted that human beings will no longer able to survive on it. Not until we learn about conservation can mankind be safe.

번역

9. Television now plays such an important part in so many people's lives that it is essential for us to try to decide whether it is a blessing or a curse. Obviously television has both advantages and disadvantages. But do the former outweigh the latter? And does it corrupt or instruct our children? I think we must realize that television itself is neither good nor bad. It is the uses to which it is put that determine its value to society.

번역

10. Many young people, it is true, do not seem to value freedom. But some of us still believe that, without freedom, human beings cannot become fully human and that freedom is therefore supremely valuable. Perhaps the forces that now menace* freedom are too strong to be resisted for very long. It is still out duty to do whatever we can to resist them. (* menace=threaten)

번역

302

11. Computers can be used for work with languages. The sentences of the English language are being studied on a machine. <u>The results of this study will be of interest to teachers in other countries.</u>

   번역

12. <u>Similarly</u> it is not always easy today to see that <u>the satisfaction of a scholar's curiosity is worth the disruption of society that may result from it.</u> And scholars have learned that they cannot engage in it without an occasional fight.

   번역

13. (A) They grew up <u>in revolt against</u> the Mass Communication antics of their age.

   번역

   (B) To change a tire you must <u>jack up</u> the car.

   번역

14. Whoever has to deal with young children learns that too much sympathy is a mistake. Children readily understand that an adult who is sometimes a little stern is best for them; their instinct tells them whether they are loved or not, and <u>from those whom they feel to be affectionate they will put up with whatever strictness results from genuine desire for their proper development.</u>

   번역

15. (A) <u>We aspire for a world of peace free of nuclear weapons.</u>

    번역

    (B) We will participate in international efforts toward <u>the total elimination of chemical-biological weapons.</u>

    번역

16. In the three short decades between now and the 21st century, millions of ordinary, psychologically normal people will face an abrupt collision with the future. <u>Many of them will find it increasingly painful to keep up with the incessant demand for change that now characterizes our time.</u> This acceleration of change is a concrete force that reaches deep into our personal lives, compels us to act out new roles, and confronts us with the danger of a new and powerfully upsetting disease. This new disease can be called "future shock".

    번역

17. A friend of mine dropped around the other day, highly indignant because "the newspapers" had said six months ago that <u>a certain road was going to be paved and it hasn't been.</u>

    번역

18. I do not believe we can have any freedom at all in the philosophical sense, <u>for we act not only under external compulsion but also by inner necessity.</u>

    번역

19. According to the Freudian theory and that of many others whose writings have preceded his by hundreds or even thousands of years, <u>dreams do not reveal anything about the future.</u>

　[번역]

20. The great agent of change and, from our point or view, destruction, has actually been the machine. No doubt the machine has brought us many advantages, but <u>it has destroyed the old ways of living, and by reason of the continual rapid change it involves, prevented the growth of new.</u>

　[번역]

21. (A) His more active rate of energy does not wreck him; <u>for the organism adapts itself, and as the rate of waste augments, augments correspondingly the rate of repair.</u>

　[번역]

　(B) <u>If he should discard as irrelevant the ideals which by tradition we profess,</u> what virtues would be name?

　[번역]

　(C) <u>Liberty is to faction what air is to fire, an aliment without which it instantly expires.</u>

　[번역]

※ 다음 지문을 우리말로 번역하시오.

22. The basic function of advertising is its use as a selling tool. Purposes of advertising may vary from company to company, depending upon specific needs. Many businesses use advertising to sell a product or to promote the company name or image.

   Corporate advertising refers to a company promoting its name and image. The goal is to sell the corporation as a whole. Specific factors are not considered. On the other hand, a company may advertise in order to promote a specific product. Price, uses, description, availability, and uniqueness of the product are emphasized.

23. History is the historian's experience. It is 'made' by nobody save the historian: to write history is the only way of making it.

24. We are accustomed to take progress for granted: to assume without hesitation that the changes which have happened during the last hundred years were for the better.

25. During the past quarter century this power has not only increased to one of disturbing magnitude but it has changed in character. The most alarming of all man's assaults upon the environment is the contamination of air, earth, rivers and sea with dangerous and even lethal materials. This pollution is for the most part irrevocable; the chain of evil it initiates not only in the world that must support life but in living tissues is for the most part irreversible. In this now universal contamination of the environment, chemicals are the sinister and little-recognized partner of radiation in changing the very nature of the world-the very nature of its life.

26. The seventh month of the year, July is named after Julius Caesar. Julius Caesar was a famous general. He became emperor of Rome. Before the time of Caesar another calendar was used. The year began I March instead of in January. The present month of July was then the fifth month instead of the seventh month. Caesar changed this. He made a new calendar. This is the calendar we use at present. Caesar himself was born in July. He gave the name of July to this month, the seventh month of the new calendar.

27. Human beings communicate in many ways. One of these ways is the gesture. Men communicate approval by winking an eye, by clapping their hands, by whistling, by smiling or laughing. They communicate disapproval by pointing a thumb toward the ground, by putting the tongue out of the mouth and blowing, by holding the nose with the fingers, or by grimacing. They indicate direction by pointing and they often communicate size by holding their hands a certain distance apart. There are many other gestures. Some communicate ideas, some communicate attitudes or feelings.

28. (A) But many movies are still made to give sheer pleasure and excitement. As we watch them, we forget about our own troubles. We laugh: we cry: we live other people's lives awhile.

(B) It is important to learn early to rely upon yourself; for little has been done in the world by those who are always looking out for someone to help them.

29. (A) People are like stained-glass window; they sparkle and shine when the sun is out, but when the darkness sets in, their true beauty is revealed only if there is a light from within.

　　번역

(B) And the word became flesh and dwelt among us, full of grace and truth; we have beheld his glory, glory as of the only son from the Father. And from his fullness have we all received, grace upon grace. For the law was given through Moses; grace and truth came through Jesus Christ.

No one has ever seen God; the only Son, who is in the bosom of the Father, he has made him know.

　　번역

30. What does "living" mean? A teacher asked his class that question. The discussion of the question made the students thoughtful. Living things move by themselves. Plants and animals are living things. The students had a lively discussion.

　　번역

31. (A) To know is one thing, to act is another. Many people know that it is good for the health to keep early hours, but very few put it into practice.

　　번역

(B) A book may be compared to the life of your neighbor. If it be good, it cannot last too long; if bad, you cannot get rid of it too early.

번역

32. (A) No doubt some cannibals had been there, killing and feasting upon the poor prisoners who had fallen into their hands, for I had heard before that among some savages it was often an established custom to kill and eat the roasted bodies of their enemies they caught in a war. When I looked around, I saw many bones lying about here and there.

번역

(B) For all the cautions, however, most of the conference participants agreed on two reasons that an India-Pakistan war is unlikely in the near future. One is that both countries face economic problems because large fiscal deficits have forced them to accept bitter IMF prescriptions. In real terms, India has cut its defense budget 9%. Pakistan keeps its defense costs secret, but is also under pressure to shrink military expenditures.

번역

33. The influenza virus is a single molecule composed of millions of individual atoms. While bacteria can be considered as a type of plant secreting poisonous substances into the body of the organism they attack, virus, like the influenza virus, are living organisms themselves. We may consider them as regular chemical molecules since they have strictly defined atomic structure; but on the other hand, we must also consider them as being alove since they are able to multiply in unlimited quantities.

34. (A) Many eminent historians have done harm than good because they viewed facts through the distorting medium of their passions.

(B) In short, reading as a writer involves reading thoroughly, imaginatively, and creatively. It implies a consideration of subject matter, style, and technique.

35. Probably the first intellectual revolution in the history of mankind was the transition from the prelogical basis of primitive religion to the type of religious thinking which rests upon a belief in benevolent gods and a philosophical explanation of the universe. How the transition was accomplished, no one knows. Apparently some tribes developed the idea that supernatural beings in manlike form would be more capable of hearing and answering entreaties than disembodied spirits or ghosts.

Since prehistoric man almost universally assumed that the spirit of a human being survived the death of his body, and since medicine men were widely revered, it seems possible that the spirits of some of these may have been transferred to mountain tops or to homes in the sky and worshiped as gods.

36. The world now knows that danger is shinning through the sky. The evidence is overwhelming that the earth's stratospheric ozone layer-our shield against the sun's hazardous ultraviolet rays-is being eaten away by man-made chemicals far faster than any scientist had predicted.

37. (A) His codes for boys were detailed and demanding. They had to be honest, trust-worth and self-reliant, of course. But I suspect it was courage that Father admired above all other qualities.

(B) The primary channel of transmission of culture is the family; no man wholly escapes from the kind, or wholly surpass the degree, of culture which he acquired from his early environment.

38. People propose to themselves some one paramount objective, and restrain all impulses that do not minister to it. A businessman may be so anxious to grow rich that to this end he sacrifices health and private affections. When at last he has become rich, no pleasure remains to him except harrying other people by exhortations to imitate his noble example.

39. This sovereign, anticipating activity of God is seen in many ways. He has taken the initiative in creation, bringing the universe and its contents into exercise; "In the beginning God created the heavens and the earth."

40. Looking back on one's own life, it is difficult to fit all the events and chronologies accurately into their places. If one tries to realize too much at once, the impression is apt to grow chaotic and unmeaning in its complexity; you can't get the proportions of events; and perhaps, indeed, one of the compensating constituents of all our various existences consists in that very disproportion which passing impressions most happily take for us, and which they often retain notwithstanding the experiences of years.

41. (A) It was not until the following morning when the sun rose that I came to my senses.

(B) When it comes to English, he is second to none in his class.

(C) The vastness of modern knowledge keeps us from being experts in more than one or two subjects.

314

(D) I was caught in a shower on my way home from school, and drenched to the skin.

42. But the socialists face a dilemma: in a generally healthy economy of low inflation and a positive trade balance, their own social policies have encouraged joblessness. For example, companies must make benefit payments totaling more than 40 percent of salaries, which hardly promotes new hiring. French workers who have lost their jobs enjoy unemployment benefits equal to 60 percent of their former salaries for 30 months-a longer period than anywhere else in Europe. That lulls thousands into life on the dole: more than half of the claimants find work suspiciously near the end of their 30 month limit. Even France's day-care programs may aggravate the problem. In Germany, new mothers typically stay at home for years after a birth, creating job openings for others. But in France where cheap day care is more available, many mothers return to the office immediately after their six-week pregnancy leave.

43. Then I had to turn my mind to my clothes, which by this time had quite worn out. So I had to think of making a new suit for myself. I have told you I kept and dried the skins of the beasts I shot, and these served my purpose. The first thing I made was a great fur cap. I did it so well that I set to work and made a whole suit.

44. Accordingly, it is necessary to distinguish between the manifest dream, i.e. the dream as experienced and perhaps written down, and the latent dream, i.e. the thoughts, wishes and desires expressed in the dream with their disguises remove. The task of the analyst and interpreter on this view is to explain the manifest dream in terms of the latent dream.

45. So far in world history a life of empty pleasure was possible for only a small elite, and they remained essentially sane because they knew they had power and that they had to think and to act in order not to lose their power. Today, the empty life of consumption is that of the whole middle class, which economically and politically

316

has no power and little personal responsibility. The major part of the western world knows the benefits of the consumer type of happiness, and growing numbers of those who benefit from it are finding it wanting.

46. To understand the nature of these diseconomics, we must examine the three broad areas of pollution-air, water, and soil-that make up the main constituent elements of our planetary life. The atmosphere of air and climates; the hydrosphere of rivers, lakes, and oceans; the lithosphere from which rock has crumbled away over the millennia to give us our thin and fragile envelope of soil-all three are inextricably interwoven in the systems which support organic life.

47. Dating has an important role in educational and social maturation. Boys and girls benefit from this experience, provided that it is not carried on to the exclusion of all others. The individual who has a reasonably comprehensive dating experience

during his formative years tends to broaden his experience, enrich his personality, gain poise and balance, increase his ability to adjust to others under varied circumstances, reduce his emotional excitement on meeting or associating with those of the opposite sex, enhance his ability to judge others objectively and sensibly, add to his prestige among those of his own age, and obtain a wider acquaintance from which a mate may be selected.

실전문제 총정리

PART XI

단어

1. 단어 (동의어 · 반의어)

※ 다음 밑줄 친 부분과 뜻이 가장 가까운 것은?

1. He ended his speech <u>abruptly</u>.

   ① gradually   ② quietly   ③ suddenly   ④ boldly

2. It's not easy to read prof. Kim's writing, because he often <u>abbreviates</u> words where other professors normally wouldn't.

   ① omits   ② shortens   ③ misses   ④ invents

3. Jefferson's embargo of 1807 <u>abruptly</u> halted the New England maritime trade.

   ① barely   ② temporarily   ③ briefly   ④ suddenly

4. My dentist said I would have fewer decayed teeth if I <u>abstained</u> from eating candy.

   ① discouraged   ② prohibited   ③ refrained   ④ didn't vote

5. It was foolish of you to suggest such an <u>absurd</u> thing.

   ① abhorrent   ② prejudiced   ③ ridiculous   ④ absolute

6. Angry citizens protested the <u>abuse</u> of helpless animals.

   ① bad treatment   ② strict training   ③ proper care   ④ good care

7. When he was an executive of the company, his first <u>accomplishment</u> was to bring about better working conditions.

   ① duty   ② achievement   ③ accumulation   ④ imposition

8. They showed themselves <u>adept</u> at many stratagems for obtaining them.

   ① suitable   ② skillful   ③ appropriate   ④ timely

9. <u>Adult</u> students require less supervision.

   ① Adolescent　　② Juvenile　　③ Infantile　　④ Mature

10. Having come from on <u>affluent</u> society, Dick found it difficult to adjust to a small country town.

   ① big　　② overpopulated　③ wealthy　　④ formal

11. It is a simple matter to <u>alter</u> the pattern to fit you.

   ① enlarge　　② change　　③ shorten　　④ design

12. My <u>ambition</u> inspired me to go to night college.

   ① fortune　　② pride　　③ ignorance　　④ desire to succeed

13. AMELIORATE ;

   ① hasten　　② macerate　　③ improve　　④ ruin

14. Most plants depend upon their roots to <u>anchor</u> themselves in the soil and to absorb water and inorganic chemicals.

   ① secure　　② reproduce　　③ moisten　　④ distribute

15. An <u>anonymous</u> donor.

   ① generous　　　　　　② well-known
   ③ one whose name is not known　　④ reluctant

16. I was bitter toward those members of my family who supported this <u>antiquated</u> law.

   ① outworn　　② new　　③ outward　　④ fresh

17. APPAREL ;

   ① clothing　　② knowledge　　③ fear　　④ shelter

18. The solution to the problem was <u>apparent</u> to all.

    ① obvious   ② complicated   ③ easy   ④ difficult

19. The teacher made an <u>apt</u> remark about that issue.

    ① antagonistic   ② adept   ③ bad   ④ appropriate

20. It is hard to play fair in a game, but it is still harder to play fair in an <u>argument</u>.

    ① war   ② lecture   ③ conversation   ④ controversy

21. Most members of the camel family are found in <u>arid</u> habitats.

    ① dirty   ② dry   ③ sandy   ④ harsh

22. John is <u>a skilled worker</u>.

    ① a novice   ② an artisan   ③ a vessel   ④ a partisan

23. From primitive times man has been making an <u>assault</u> on his environment with fire.

    ① benefit   ② wealth   ③ supply   ④ aggression

24. ASSETS ;

    ① results   ② debts   ③ total resources   ④ monies owed

25. The scientific study of the stars.

    ① astrology   ② astronomy   ③ anthropology   ④ archaeology

26. ATHEISM ;

    ① disorder   ② envy   ③ unbelief   ④ weak purpose

27. The city council recently <u>banned</u> the sale of all tobacco products to minors.

    ① recommended   ② promoted   ③ prohibited   ④ legalized

28. Farm machinery has eliminated much <u>backbreaking</u> work.

① strenuous   ② hazardous   ③ time-consuming   ④ pacesetting

29. The American Medical Association has called for the sport of boxing to be <u>banned</u>.

① forbidden   ② regulated   ③ studied   ④ reorganized

30. At the beginning the land was extremely <u>barren</u>, but after many years' hard work, it has finally become fertile.

① empty   ② vacant   ③ vain   ④ sterile

31. BEATIFIC ;

① giving bliss   ② beautiful   ③ eager   ④ hesitant

32. BENIGN ;

① visual   ② popular   ③ kind   ④ surpassing

33. artistic <u>bent</u> ;

① design   ② course   ③ taste   ④ aptitude

34. BOMBASTIC ; (반의어)

① solicitous   ② unimpassioned   ③ rhapsodic   ④ weightless

35. Prices of the necessities of life were <u>boosted</u> again last month.

① attacked   ② fixed   ③ raised   ④ stabilized

36. Can a small lifeboat <u>brave</u> the towering waves and save the stranded sailors?(우리말로)

37. The foot ball match was <u>cancelled</u> owing to the storm.

① called in   ② called off   ③ closed up   ④ cast off

38. CAPRICIOUS ;

① active   ② fickle   ③ sheeplike   ④ slippery

39. After he had been fined $100 for <u>careless</u> driving, he began to observe the traffic signs with more caution.

① jealous   ② vicarious   ③ amicable   ④ reckless

40. Plants without leaves, such as algae and fungi, are the first forms of life to grow back after a natural <u>catastrophe</u>.

① disaster   ② event   ③ phenomenon   ④ explosion

41. The 1989 <u>census</u> showed that about ten million people lived in seoul.

① opinion poll   ② birth record   ③ payroll register   ④ population count

42. Seeds are contained in the <u>center</u> of fleshy fruit such as apples and pears.

① core   ② focus   ③ nucleus   ④ median

43. CHARITABLE ;

① violent   ② generous   ③ vicious   ④constructive

44. His report was organized <u>chronologically</u>.

① by contrasts   ② in terms of comparisons
③ according to significance   ④ according to a time sequence

45. The first term on the campus <u>commences</u> in April.

① begins   ② ends   ③ observes   ④ expels

46. In spite of the <u>complexity</u> of the problem, the mathematician solved it quickly.

① completeness   ② community   ③ complication   ④ compression

324

47. He was punished because he refused to comply.

① deploy   ② reply   ③ deplore   ④ obey

48. I conceded that it had failed.

① admitted   ② feared   ③ announced   ④ doubted

49. The school conferred an award on him.

① compromised   ② corrupted   ③ collaborated   ④ gave

50. CONFRONT ;

① face   ② argue   ③ accuse   ④ rebuke

51. Growth of Korea has slowed considerably in the early 1990's.

① greatly   ② for a while   ③ a little   ④ with no doubts

52. What he did was contrary to what he said.

① pertinent   ② similar   ③ opposite   ④ relevant

53. What he said was contrary to what we expected.

① ironic   ② innate   ③ opposite   ④ real

54. By what criterion will you judge the theory?

① consideration   ② standard   ③ result   ④ decision

55. Professor Baker is a critical judge of fine arts.

① connoisseur   ② artist   ③ philatelist   ④ prodigious

56. The wheels of the first road vehicles were fashioned from crude stone disks.

① hand-carved   ② roughly made   ③ flat   ④ heavy

57. The doctor was unable to <u>cure</u> the patient.

    ① restore health to   ② wait for   ③ talk with   ④ collect his fee from

58. DEGRADE ;

    ① evaluate   ② downhill   ③ lower in esteem   ④ rough terrain

59. During the <u>decade</u> of the 1960's the economy expanded by about 2.4times.

    ① ten months   ② ten days   ③ ten years   ④ one year

60. Every <u>decent</u> man has a number of secrets which he is afraid to tell even to his friends.

    ① impatient   ② proud   ③ respectable   ④ timid

61. Committing a <u>deception</u> in obtaining car insurance is against the law.

    ① perjury   ② treason   ③ infidelity   ④ fraud

62. Novelist Ernest Hemingway <u>deftly</u> depicted the human misery that the superficial gaiety of the 1920's.

    ① skillfully   ② prudently   ③ occasionally   ④ humorously

63. DENUNCIATION

    ① condemn openly   ② speak loudly
    ③ reason pooly   ④ perform poorly

64. Almost half of Nevada has a <u>desert</u> climate.

    ① an arid   ② a humid   ③ a cold   ④ an unpredictable

65. They <u>destroyed</u> the old building to construct a new one in its place.

    ① tore down   ② tore up   ③ tore off   ④ tore round

66. DETER ;

    ① retain   ② decide   ③ possess   ④ give up

67. wide <u>discrepancy</u>.

    ① reduction   ② increase   ③ agreement   ④ variation

68. <u>Dissenting</u> opinion.

    ① harsh   ② foolish   ③ disagreeing   ④ hasty

69. DIURNAL ;

    ① daily   ② empty   ③ flushing   ④ two-fold

70. Be sure to take correct <u>dose</u>.

    ① kind   ② amount   ③ size   ④ shape

71. For centuries, its soft feathers and <u>down</u> provided lightest, most efficient insulation available.(우리말로)

72. The government took <u>drastic</u> measures to stop crime.

    ① strong   ② thoughtful   ③ clever   ④ consistent

73. We <u>eased</u> through the patch of thorny bushes.

    ① ran quickly   ② hurried   ③ moved carefully   ④ passed

74. The number of United States citizens who are <u>eligible</u> to vote continues to increase.

    ① manifest   ② convertible   ③ effusive   ④ entitled

75. ELIMINATE ;

    ① make better   ② make a difference   ③ refuse to do   ④ rule out

76. The wisdom of life consists in the <u>elimination</u> of nonessentials.

    ① contempt   ② refusing   ③ discrimination   ④ removing

77. John gave a(n) _____ speech that was profoundly moving.

    ① loquacious   ② colloquial   ③ eloquent   ④ fluent

78. A mature tulip bulb contains the <u>embryo</u> of a plant.

    ① a flower bud   ② waste product
    ③ complete undeveloped form   ④ color producing pigment

79. We often <u>encounter</u> someone's views on our colleges.

    ① adopt   ② advocate   ③ meet   ④ abandon

80. Albert Schweitzer remains something of an <u>enigma</u>.

    ① genius   ② saint   ③ puzzle   ④ center of an criticism

81. The mysteries of the Universe are an <u>enigma</u> to man

    ① puzzle   ② trouble   ③ genius   ④ present

82. Plays that <u>entail</u> direct interaction between actor and audience present no unusual difficulties for actors.

    ① advocate   ② involve   ③ exaggerate   ④ announce

83. EQUIVOCAL ;

    ① doubtful   ② monotonous   ③ equal   ④ talkative

84. The Salk vaccine is a major factor in the fight to <u>eradicate</u> polio.

    ① completely destroy   ② carefully disguise
    ③ sustain   ④ contain

85. Anyone who helps others with no thought to personal gain is <u>essentially</u> an altruist.

① possibly   ② eagerly   ③ basically   ④ ordinarily

86. The examination will begin <u>exactly</u> at eight thirty.

① consequently   ② equitably   ③ precisely   ④ exceedingly

87. In literature, caricatures usually contain verbal <u>exaggeration</u> through which the writer achieves comic and often satiric effects.

① banter   ② interaction   ③ humor   ④ overstatement

88. It is <u>exhilarating</u> to be alive in a time of awakening consciousness, but it can also be painful, confusing, and disorienting.

① exhausting   ② cheerful   ③ burdensome   ④ melancholy

89. EXORBITANT ;

① vicious   ② forceful   ③ excessive   ④ absorbing

90. EXTIRPATE ;

① clean   ② eradicate   ③ favor   ④ subdivide

91. When he learned that a tornado was approaching his town, he ran to his house and <u>evacuated</u> his elderly mother immediately.

① anticipated   ② removed   ③ comforted   ④ escaped

92. His pulse was very <u>feeble</u>.

① slow   ② weak   ③ fast   ④ strong

93. Hard work is an important <u>factor</u> of success.

① kind   ② result   ③ part   ④ sign

94. The little red colt belongs to that brown <u>female horse</u>.

    ① hog   ② gander   ③ rooster   ④ mare

95. A good statesman always learns more from his opponents than from his <u>fervent</u> supporters.

    ① elite   ② ardent   ③ strategic   ④ manipulating

96. The sculptor carved the <u>figurine</u> of child from a piece of driftwood.

    ① tall monument   ② lucky charm
    ③ form   ④ small statue

97. In the book the author describes his <u>firsthand</u> impression of Korea.

    ① distinct   ② direct   ③ intensive   ④ extensive

98. I also have to get my watch <u>fixed</u>.

    ① settled   ② secured   ③ mended   ④ made firm

99. FLANK ;

    ① company   ② fence   ③ fresh   ④ side

100. He <u>flatters</u> anyone whose position is high.

    ① blames too much   ② talks too much
    ③ praises too much   ④ annoys too much

101. FLATTERY ;

    ① praise   ② light   ③ bird   ④ attack

102. Diamonds that are <u>flawed</u> or are too small for jewelry are used to cut very hard metals.

    ① tiny   ② imperfect   ③ lustrous   ④ crude

103. Small <u>flaws</u> in an object show that it is handmade.

    ① acquirements ② details   ③ defects   ④ trademarks

104. Monetary policy was controlled primarily through the <u>flexible</u> use of both open market operations and adjustment in the discount rate.

    ① equitable   ② stiff   ③ rigid   ④ elastic

105. There are in excess of fifty species of <u>fluorescent</u> fungi.

    ① microscopic ② poisonous   ③ luminous   ④ aquatic

106. Many tourists are attracted to the New England states by the autumn <u>foliage</u>.

    ① weather   ② leaves   ③ festivals   ④ harvest

107. In case of emergency, please <u>follow</u> the orders of the train crew.

    ① post   ② transfer   ③ confirm   ④ obey

108. In 1965 California replaced New York as the <u>foremost</u> state in the export of manufactured goods.

    ① most accessible   ② aforementioned
    ③ fourth   ④ leading

109. FRATERNAL ;

    ① friendly   ② brotherly   ③ relative   ④ grouped

110. FRUGALITY ;

    ① exception   ② high cost   ③ relative   ④ spending little

111. Grounded whales often struggle <u>fruitlessly</u> to reenter deep water.

    ① violently   ② desperately   ③ in vain   ④ at length

112. <u>Furthermore</u>, I feel that his behavior is upsetting the entire classroom.

　① Nevertheless　② However　　③ In spite of this　④ In addition

113. If one aids and abets a criminal, he is also considered <u>guilty of</u> the crime.

　① malignant　　② decrepit　　③ versatile　　④ culpable

114. GALLANT ;

　① swift　　　② brave　　　③ ugly　　　④ watery

115. The passionate few have a <u>genuine</u> interest in literature.

　① real　　　② sustained　　③ lively　　④ growing

116. GERMANE ;(반의어)

　① biological　② penitent　　③ irrelevant　④ gruesome

117. That is a problem really beyond my <u>grasp</u>.

　① comprehension　　　　② concentration
　③ compliment　　　　　 ④ compromise

118. Science without philosophy, facts without perspective and valuation, cannot save
　　us from <u>havoc</u> and despair.

　① ordeal　　　② travail　　　③ disorder　　④ fear

119. HALLOW ;

　① pick out　　② seek　　　③ shatter　　④ make holy

120. Grouping stars by constellations is a <u>handy</u> way of mapping the sky.

　① nice　　　② convenient　③ manual　　④ mutual

121. Hang-over ;

    ① string of rope   ② suspending object
    ③ surviving trace   ④ alliance

122. Leaves are not distributed <u>haphazardly</u> on a plant stem, but are arranged in a very precise way that assures them the maximum light.

    ① dangerously   ② densely   ③ randomly   ④ linearly

123. HARRY ;

    ① plunder   ② deny   ③ hurry   ④ prey

124. They moved to Florida because they <u>hated</u> the cold winters in the Midwest.

    ① tugged   ② heeded   ③ loathed   ④ shrugged

125. How long an animal or plant can live is governed by <u>heredity</u>, environment, and chance.

    ① history   ② altitude   ③ climate   ④ genetics

126. They were <u>hesitant</u> to move because they could not get a good price for their old house.

    ① incessant   ② negligent   ③ reluctant   ④ exorbitant

127. HETEROGENEOUS ; (반의어)

    ① able   ② putrid   ③ simulate   ④ uniform

128. HIATUS ;

    ① branch   ② disease   ③ gaiety   ④ opening

129. HIDEOUS ;

    ① ugly   ② noisy   ③ selfish   ④ stormy

130. She wants to <u>hitch</u> her trailer to your car.

    ① wreck   ② hatch   ③ connect   ④ thatch

131. HOMOGENEOUS ;

    ① doubtful   ② same kind   ③ different   ④ gigantic

132. HOSTILE ;

    ① friendly   ② unfriendly   ③ harsh   ④ tough

133. I found it at the <u>identical</u> place where I left it.

    ① hidden   ② dark   ③ same   ④ unknown

134. Twins Pete and Rick appear to be <u>identical</u> and often fool even their friends.

    ① exactly alike   ② together often   ③ well-dressed   ④ ironical

135. A state of laziness.

    ① idyll   ② idol   ③ idle   ④ ideal

136. Few composers have been so <u>idolized</u> during their life time as was Edward MacDowell.

    ① dissatisfied   ② reviewed   ③ misguided   ④ worshipped

137. <u>Ignoring</u> something will not make it go away.

    ① Taking an interest in   ② Looking closely at
    ③ Paying no attention to   ④ Studying the causes of

138. ILLEGIBLE ;

    ① not able to be read   ② allowed by law
    ③ against the law   ④ not allowed by the rules

139. When I answered the telephone this morning, I knew <u>immediately</u> the lady had the wrong number.

① right away　　② right now　　③ right along　　④ right down

140. I don't think it is <u>impartial</u> for the professor to flunk my chemistry test.

① excessive　　② effusive　　③ unbiased　　④ compatible

141. A lot depends on what happens during the <u>impending</u> days.

① coming　　② exploding　　③ applauding　　④ repeating

142. The difference in the greenness of leaves in the morning and in the evening is almost <u>imperceptible</u>.

① strange　　② unattractive　　③ unnoticeable　　④ imperfect

143. By today's standards, early farmers were <u>imprudent</u> because they planted the same crop repeatedly, exhausting the soil after a few harvests.

① stubborn　　② rotated　　③ imprecise　　④ unwise

144. <u>incessant</u> chatter.

① worthless　　② illogical　　③ unceasing　　④ noisy

145. Many weak and <u>incompetent</u> rulers were overthrown by more powerful forces.

① incapable　　② dictatorial　　③ unfortunate　　④ greedy

146. I look upon <u>indolence</u> as a sort of suicide.

① idleness　　② arrogance　　③ quality　　④ gambling

147. She is a very <u>industrious</u> student.

① intelligent　　② careful　　③ hardworking　　④ interesting

148. It was <u>inevitable</u> that women would be sent into space along with men.

    ① unavoidable   ② unlikely   ③ influential   ④ fantastic

149. She follows orders well, but she seldom <u>initiates</u> action.

    ① relates   ② introduces   ③ starts   ④ infuriates

150. The <u>inscribed</u> the words on the wall.

    ① wrote   ② read   ③ translated   ④ fragmentary

151. INTEGRAL ; (반의어)

    ① shy   ② profane   ③ lofty   ④ fragmentary

152. In the northeastern United States, it rains <u>intermittently</u> throughout the spring.

    ① abundantly   ② steadily   ③ periodically   ④ steadily

153. Workers are given frequent <u>intervals</u> of rest.

    ① interviews   ② periods   ③ promises   ④ pleasure

154. Members of the <u>intrigue</u> met in secret so that their conspiracy would not be discovered.

    ① team   ② band   ③ cabal   ④ mob

155. What will you <u>introduce</u> in tomorrow's meeting?

    ① bring to   ② bring up   ③ bring off   ④ bring back

156. Her services are <u>invaluable</u> to the poor in distress for money.

    ① helpful   ② priceless   ③ valueless   ④ useful

157. I learned <u>invaluable</u> lesson one night in Seoul.

    ① very expensive   ② very intensive   ③ valueless   ④ very valuable

158. He <u>did something repeatedly</u> in the past.

   ① iterated   ② shrieked   ③ divested   ④ chided

159. There is a pleasure in philosophy, and a <u>lure</u> in the mirages of metaphysics.

   ① satisfactory   ② attraction   ③ significance   ④ wisdom

160. JEOPARDY ;

   ① freedom   ② danger   ③ flower   ④ wonder

161. The new mayor is known to have a <u>keen</u> sense of humor.

   ① useful   ② simple   ③ sour   ④ sharp

162. LACONIC ; (반의어)

   ① radial   ② tangible   ③ minute   ④ pompous

163. The extreme heat made everyone quite <u>languid</u>.

   ① gruff   ② bothersome   ③ selfish   ④ listless

164. The rich and powerful minority would <u>league</u> together to hold down the poor and back - ward majority.(우리말로)

165. The Brazilian government <u>levies</u> a uniform 70% tax on all imported pianos.

   ① imposes   ② takes off   ③ requests   ④ correlates

166. LIABILITIES ;

   ① debts   ② credits   ③ cadavers   ④ abilities

167. It is expected that so much import of rice last year will <u>lower</u> food costs.

   ① raise   ② reduce   ③ increase   ④ refine

168. When the Korea stock market fell in 1989, many stockholders were forced to sell their shares at <u>ludicrously</u> low prices.

① predictably   ② relatively   ③ suspiciously   ④ ridiculously

169. The teacher was <u>mortified</u> by his own inability to answer such a simple question.

① distressed   ② humiliated   ③ surprised   ④ satisfied

170. The meal he served was rather <u>meager</u>.

① scanty   ② dull   ③ dingy   ④ lifeless

171. Time to <u>meditate</u>

① withdraw   ② reflect   ③ rest   ④ change

172. MEDIUM ;

① faction   ② a panacea   ③ a charlatan   ④ a means of doing

173. I had planned everything <u>meticulously</u>.

① carefully   ② quickly   ③ busily   ④ awkwardly

174. The Egyptian government wants to clear the Suez Canal of <u>mines</u> and sunken vessels. (우리말로)

175. MINUET ;

① comb   ② clock   ③ weapon   ④ dance

176. Many airlines have made <u>modifications</u> in the interior of the 747 to provide greater luxury and comfort for their passengers.

① artworks   ② alterations   ③ improvements   ④ many windows

177. MOISTURE ; (반의어)

① dryness   ② fairness   ③ darkness   ④ humidity

178. That college will <u>mold</u> his opinions

① respect   ② form   ③ measure   ④ break

179. The committee has made a most <u>momentous</u> decision.

① momentary   ② important   ③ light   ④ quick

180. She looked <u>mournful</u>.

① tired   ② dead   ③ brave   ④ sad

181. MUTINY ;

① level off   ② rebel   ③ squawk   ④ replace

182. The old man said he was going to <u>sleep briefly</u>.

① nap   ② hurry   ③ dissent   ④ depart

183. The old man said he was going to <u>sleep for a short time</u>.

① nap   ② neglect   ③ nod   ④ notify

184. He is <u>noted</u> for his honesty in business matters.

① famous   ② wise   ③ bad   ④ dreadful

185. The <u>onset</u> of sleep is determined by many factors.

① confusion   ② fragment   ③ delicacy   ④ beginning

186. In Korea there are more people who are <u>obese</u> today than twenty years ago.

① gainfully employed   ② upwardly mobile
③ excessively overweight   ④ privately educated

187. OBSOLETE ; (반의어)

    ① outworn   ② novel   ③ urban   ④ wrong

188. He was too <u>obstinate</u> to admit to admit he had been wrong.

    ① stubborn   ② frightened   ③ selfish   ④ cautious

189. When equipment becomes <u>obsolete</u>, it is time to replace it.

    ① run down   ② badly rusted
    ③ out of date   ④ expensive to repair

190. He <u>offended</u> me by the way he spoke and behaved.

    ① displeased   ② impressed   ③ assisted   ④ defended

191. Those dark clouds look <u>ominous</u>; it will probably rain before evening.

    ① promising   ② mysterious   ③ gathering   ④ threatening

192. Less food is necessary to maintain <u>optimum</u> body temperature during warm weather than during cold weather.

    ① necessary   ② healthy   ③ the best favorable   ④ the highest

193. ORIENTAL ; (반의어)

    ① southern   ② occidental   ③ religious   ④ eastern

194. When did that new style of dancing <u>originate</u>?

    ① start   ② open   ③ happen   ④ disappear

195. He must have an operation, <u>otherwise</u> his condition will become worse and worse.

    ① different   ② but   ③ if not   ④ when

196. I was surprised and <u>outraged</u> to see that she had gone ahead with her plans without consulting us first.

    ① excited   ② unhappy   ③ angered   ④ relieved

197. Lukewarm acceptance is much more bewildering than <u>outright</u> rejection.

    ① resentful   ② prudent   ③ judicious   ④ direct

198. Mary sometimes hurts others when she criticizes their work because she is too <u>outspoken</u>.

    ① sever   ② strict   ③ frank   ④ reserved

199. The supreme Court has the power to <u>overrule</u> the decisions of lower court.

    ① criticize   ② reverse   ③ delay   ④ inspect

200. The candidate's victory at the polls was <u>overwhelming</u>.

    ① treacherous   ② defeating   ③ triumphal   ④ popular

201. If someone suffered from a <u>protracted</u> illness.

    ① the person was ill for a long time.
    ② the person was ill from time to time.
    ③ the person's vitality was low, though the illness was invisible.
    ④ the person's body surface got swollen all over.

202. Rustic or rural life.

    ① pasture   ② pastille   ③ pastoral   ④ patrol

203. When it comes to cultural heritage, jazz seems to be the only <u>peculiarly</u> American phenomenon.

    ① oddly   ② uniquely   ③ suspiciously   ④ patriotically

204. A laser beam is used to <u>penetrate</u> even the hardest substances.

① light up   ② identify   ③ repair   ④ pass through

205. Every effort is being made to insure <u>permanent</u> world peace.

① assistant   ② fortunate   ③ wanton   ④ lasting

206. That was a <u>perpetual</u> problem.

① additional   ② occasional   ③ constant   ④ common

207. The <u>perpetual</u> motion of the earth as it turns on its axis creates the change of seasons.

① ancient   ② leisurely   ③ constant   ④ rhythmic

208. The lawyer wanted to know all the <u>pertinent</u> details.

① suitable   ② essential   ③ innumerable   ④ exact

209. Donald's father refused to let his son <u>pierce</u> his ear.

① listen   ② clean   ③ cut   ④ puncture

210. We know what makes some answers <u>plausible</u> and others not.

① reasonable   ② pleasant   ③ false   ④ confident

211. PLENARY ;

① easy   ② empty   ③ full   ④ untrustworthy

212. Despite advanced techniques, manual packing is still <u>predominant</u>.

① long-sighted   ② available   ③ prevalent   ④ specific

213. The choir sang as a <u>preliminary</u> event to the ceremony.

① prelude   ② precaution   ③ precept   ④ precise

214. Weight lifting is the gymnastic sport of lifting weights in a prescribed manner.

   ① vigorous   ② popular   ③ certain   ④ careful

215. presumed guilt

   ① supposed   ② obvious   ③ proved   ④ limited

216. This day devoted to the memory of Robert Frost, offers an opportunity for reflection which is prized by politicians as well as by others, and even by poets.

   ① encouraged   ② won   ③ sought after   ④ valued highly

217. An opportunity for reflection is prized by politicians as well as by poets.

   ① welcomed   ② highly valued   ③ provided   ④ eagerly seized

218. procrastinating manner

   ① insolent   ② perverse   ③ compliant   ④ postponing

219. PRODIGAL ; (반의어)

   ① abstinent   ② gallant   ③ free   ④ neurotic

220. He ate a prodigious amount of the homemade bread.

   ① slight   ② huge   ③ tiny   ④ moderate

221. We all share the leader's profound concern with regard to the danger of nuclear catastrophe.

   ① imminent   ② serious   ③ strong   ④ emergent

222. Richard Rogers, one of the most prolific writers on Broadway, played a major role in the evolution of the American musical theater.

   ① young   ② productive   ③ able   ④ promising

223. PROPONENTS ;

　　① voters　　　② supporters　　　③ critics　　　④ constituents

224. <u>Punctuality</u> is imperative in your new job.

　　① being efficient　　　　② being on time
　　③ being courteous　　　　④ being cheerful

225. PUNDIT ;

　　① businessman　　② savant　　　③ politician　　　④ magician

226. "Why dose the apple fall down rather than go up?" many children find this question
　　<u>puzzling</u>.

　　① penetrating　　② perplexing　　③ strange　　　④ attractive

227. Swarms of locusts <u>ravaged</u> the crops.

　　① raided　　　② landed on　　③ flew over　　④ destroyed

228. During the recent petroleum embargo, motor fuels had to be <u>rationed</u>.(우리말로)

229. Can animals think, <u>reason</u> and remember as humans do? (우리말로)

230. He tried, but he couldn't <u>recollect</u> the story.

　　① repeat　　　② understand　　③ remember　　④ change

231. After the quarrel, they finally <u>reconciled</u> and became friends again.

　　① made off　　② made up　　③ made through　　④ made good

232. The patient has <u>recovered</u> very quickly.

① got on   ② got off   ③ got over   ④ got out

233. She politely <u>refused</u> my proposal to dine out together,

① turned in   ② turned against   ③ turned off   ④ turned down

234. When required by their parents to eat spinach and other green vegetables, many children only do so <u>reluctantly</u>.

① imitatively   ② impatiently   ③ unwillingly   ④ unknowingly

235. REMORSE ;

① recover   ② regret   ③ redesign   ④ defy

236. Geronimo was a <u>renowned</u> chief of the Apache tribe.

① a youthful   ② an inventive   ③ a knowledgeable   ④ an acclaimed

237. He <u>resolved</u> to act at once

① hesitated   ② offered   ③ refused   ④ determined

238. A witness provided the clue that <u>resolved</u> the mystery.

① promised   ② solved   ③ consented   ④ complicated

239. Her will and <u>resolve</u> are an inspiration to all burn victims. (우리말로)

240. Excessive humidity <u>retards</u> evaporation of perspiration from the body.

① slows   ② prevents   ③ disturbs   ④ restrains

241. Developed in 1895, the X-ray tube <u>revealed</u> the structure of matter on the atomic scale.

① changed   ② arranged   ③ disclosed   ④ photographed

242. During the Civil War steamboating on the lower Mississippi River was <u>ruined</u>.

    ① taxed   ② enjoyed   ③ delayed   ④ destroyed

243. They were <u>summoned</u> on 5 February this year.

    ① cared for   ② called for   ③ called after   ④ called up

244. SANGUINE ;

    ① muddy   ② red   ③ stealthy   ④ light

245. She must have early learned to <u>school</u> and repress her emotion. (우리말로)

246. They learned how to buy meat, and <u>season</u> it. and cook it, and serve it. (우리말로)

247. SENTIENT ;

    ① very emotional   ② capable of feeling

    ③ hostile   ④ sympathetic

248. The house by the sea had a mysterious air of <u>serenity</u> about it.

    ① obesity   ② fitness   ③ climate   ④ calmness

249. Although her mother gave the coat to her, it looked rather <u>shabby</u>.

    ① large   ② worn-out   ③ dirty   ④ old -fashioned

250. It means a heightened awareness of people and their moods, a sensitivity to all sorts of subtle <u>shadings</u>.

    ① profession   ② small variations   ③ fate   ④ recorded music

251. She felt very <u>silly</u> when everyone laughed at her question.

① clever   ② foolish   ③ twofold   ④ prudent

252. The two men turned around <u>simultaneously</u> at the sound of the whistle.

① one after another   ② in a hurry

③ in a similar manner   ④ at the same time

253. Some species of diving beetle, when attacked, secrete an irritating substance from special glands <u>situated</u> on the front of their bodies.

① rotating   ② isolated   ③ emptying   ④ positioned

254. Since he didn't have enough time to read the newspaper before going to woke, he just <u>looked at it quickly</u> on the bus.

① shifted it   ② skimmed it   ③ slapped it   ④ threw it

255. He doesn't like <u>skinny</u> women.

① quite   ② thin   ③ fat   ④ talkative

256. SLACKEN ;

① wash   ② whip   ③ cool off   ④ slow up

257. By eating large quantities of sardine, you can improve you memory and <u>slow</u> the aging process.(우리말로)

258. Diesel engines provide excellent mileage, but they are relatively noisy and their acceleration is <u>sluggish</u>.

① uneven   ② loud   ③ slow   ④ unreliable

259. SOMNOLENT ;

    ① angry   ② sleepy   ③ foolish   ④ honest

260. The unhappy child was <u>soothed</u> by the promise of a treat

    ① annoyed   ② calmed   ③ surprised   ④ cried

261. Unless you are more <u>specific</u>, we do not know which one to send you.

    ① definite   ② clear   ③ articulate   ④ responsive

262. SPECIOUS;

    ① particular   ② plausible   ③ suspicious   ④ vigorous

263. SPECTRUM;

    ① an electronic device   ② broad range
    ③ eyeglasses   ④ onlooker

264. The introduction of <u>standardized</u> parts was a great contribution to the automobile industry.

    ① neutralized   ② production   ③ uniform   ④ spare

265. This old guy is very <u>hard to deal with</u>.

    ① sensitive   ② sterile   ③ stubborn   ④ corruptible

266. SUBLIME ;

    ① highly praised   ② extreme   ③ noble   ④ quiet

267. Since none of the poll had predicted the winner, everyone was <u>surprised</u> by the results of the election.

    ① astounded   ② asserted   ③ aroused   ④ assuaged

268. Let us <u>suspend</u> judgment until we know all the facts.

    ① be through   ② put off   ③ announce   ④ conclude

269. Don't bother me with <u>trivial</u> matter.

    ① troublesome   ② not important   ③ mutual   ④ complicated

270. TANTALIZE ;

    ① tease   ② oppress   ③ confine   ④ transform

271. I think this music is very <u>tedious</u>.

    ① dull   ② familiar   ③ unusual   ④ pleasant

272. <u>temporary</u> filling

    ① not intended to last   ② enduring
    ③ fragile   ④ not painful

273. His <u>tenacious</u> personality made him top salesperson in the company.

    ① tenable   ② persistent   ③ explosive   ④ charming

274. The job was <u>terminated</u>.

    ① filled   ② ended   ③ begun   ④ listed

275. I remember that <u>thrift</u> and saving were ideals which our parents considered important enough to urge upon us.

    ① wasting money   ② spending money carefully
    ③ earning much money   ④ enjoying expensive things

276. He is <u>thrifty</u>.

    ① economical   ② careless   ③ wasteful   ④ drift

277. Her teacher scolded her because she could not <u>tolerate</u> her rudeness.

① put up at   ② put up with   ③ put on   ④ put off

278. Benjamin Franklin has <u>traits</u> that have come to be admired by many people over the years.

① stories   ② inventions   ③ adventurers   ④ characters

279. A series of rifle shots disturbed the <u>tranquility</u> of the camp grounds.

① solidarity   ② equanimity   ③ excitement   ④ peacefulness

280. The elegant inner decorations <u>transformed</u> the airliner's cabin into a luxurious hotel room.

① diverted   ② changed   ③ transported   ④ returned

281. Don't argue with me? I'm <u>treating</u> this time.

① playing   ② complaining   ③ going to phone   ④ planning to leave

282. I thought Lucy would be nervous when she made her speech, but she delivered it without <u>trepidation</u>.

① dexterity   ② fortitude   ③ fright   ④ avarice

283. TRIUMPH ;

① victory   ② loss   ③ fault   ④ noise

284. Doctors encourage their patients not to get upset about <u>trivial</u> matters.

① unusual   ② unimportant   ③ uncertain   ④ unexpected

285. Truth as <u>ultimate</u> reality, if such there is, must be eternal, imperishable, unchanging.

① fundamental   ② stern   ③ sober   ④ absolute

286. The court hands down a <u>unanimous</u> opinion.

    ① sharp   ② sudden   ③ effective   ④ of one mind

287. UNCOUTH ; (반의어)

    ① refined   ② boor   ③ buffoon   ④ clown

288. According to a man's experience of life, the book will <u>unfold</u> new meanings to him.

    ① reveal   ② instruct   ③ conceal   ④ teach

289. She always gets upset about <u>unimportant</u> matters.

    ① trivial   ② stunted   ③ prevalent   ④ trenchant

290. There mush be some <u>universal</u> appeal in the name of democracy.

    ① general   ② pathetic   ③ irresistible   ④ direct

291. If economic conditions do not improve, there will be widespread <u>unrest</u>.

    ① tranquility   ② disorder   ③ satisfaction   ④ hindrance

292. William Faulkner's stories reflect his Mississippi <u>upbringing</u>.

    ① visits   ② cousins   ③ education   ④ accent

293. All the young men in the district have been arrested after the <u>upheaval</u>.

    ① bump   ② vendor   ③ violent disturbance   ④ accent

294. Many doctors and nurses were <u>utterly</u> convinced of the medicine's effect.

    ① hardly   ② finally   ③ rapidly   ④ completely

295. <u>Everyone engaged in selling</u> must have a proper license.

    ① Operators   ② Debtors   ③ Auditors   ④ Vendors

296. The man <u>vanished</u> when the policeman appeared.

① disappeared   ② finished   ③ reduced   ④ visited

297. The <u>vacuous</u> remarks of the politician annoyed the audience, which had hoped to hear more than empty platitudes.

① empty   ② candid   ③ acute   ④ superficial

298. <u>Vanity</u> keeps us from seeing our own faults

① great success   ② friendship   ③ excessive pride   ④ superficial

299. <u>Vast</u> amounts of money are being invested in the local market.

① enormous   ② constant   ③ unknown   ④ sufficient

300. Mercury's <u>velocity</u> is so much greater than the Earth's that it completes more than four revolutions around the Sun in the time it takes Earth to complete on.

① speed   ② orbit   ③ weight   ④ diameter

301. <u>versatile</u> leader

① unskilled   ② timid   ③ many-sided   ④ audacious

302. The current <u>vogue</u> of country music originated primarily in Thenesse.

① voice   ② popularity   ③ sound   ④ tempo

303. North American fur trade <u>wanted</u> in the early 1800's mainly due to the diminishing number of fur-bearing animals.

① staggered   ② ceased   ③ declined   ④ collapsed

304. Stop justifying selfishness because "the world is a jungle." It can also be a garden, depending on whether one wants to plant and <u>water</u> or to plunder and uproot. (우리말로)

305. WEARY ;

   ① early   ② beautiful   ③ tired   ④ unhappy

306. Not everyone can be <u>well-to-do</u>.

   ① rich   ② beautiful   ③ healthy   ④ neutral

307. WHIT ;

   ① method   ② sense   ③ note   ④ very small amount

308. George went to the bank to <u>withdraw</u> some money.

   ① take out   ② take in   ③ rotted   ④ glistened

309. The grapes <u>withered</u> on the vine.

   ① matured   ② shriveled   ③ rotted   ④ glistened

※ 다음 빈칸에 알맞은 것은?

1. The father's refusal to respect his son's privacy resulted in the boy's _____ from his parents.

　① rebellion　　② alienation　　③ delinquency　　④ conflict

2. I'd like to go with you but I can't _____ (to buy) the plane fare.

　① lend　　② allow　　③ afford　　④ append

3. A quarrel over an inheritance _____ the brothers for many years.

　① compromised　② angered　　③ befriended　　④ alienated

4. His _____ directions misled us : we did not know which of the two roads to take.

　① ambiguous　　② extenuating　　③ detailed　　④ expedient

5. The lover of democracy has an _____ toward totalitarianism.

　① antipathy　　② empathy　　③ sympathy　　④ predilection

6. When the concert was over, the audience _____ enthusiastically.

　① advertised　　② appreciated　　③ applauded　　④ assembled

7. "I can't meet you today. I have a previous _____."

　① appointment　② promise　　③ time　　④ promises

8. A few of the critics _____ the play, but in general they either disregarded or ridiculed it.

　① appreciated　　② criticized　　③ denounced　　④ discredited

9. The police _____ a middle-aged man armed with a shot gun.

① apprehended   ② interfered   ③ comprehended ④ preoccupied

10. A student who is talented in one subject may have little or no _____ in another.

① valor   ② aptitude   ③ honor   ④ pride

11. The old view that every point of light in the sky represented a possible home for life
    is quite foreign to modern _____.

① archeology   ② astrology   ③ astronomy   ④ ethics

12. Her secretary said that she would not be _____ until the next week.

① available   ② unavoidable   ③ unquestionable   ④ answerable

13. As the _____ of the ax bit into the trunk, the tree quivered.

① point   ② shaft   ③ handle   ④ blade

14. His boots gave him _____ on his heels.

① blisters   ② pimples   ③ clusters   ④ ripples

15. I thought we still had some milk, but the bottle is _____.

① level   ② bare   ③ empty   ④ cold

16. I should finish the book tonight, for I've read all but last _____.

① copy   ② title   ③ measure   ④ chapter

17. The workers were _____ in their demand for better conditions.

① united   ② combined   ③ joined   ④ stuck

18. Memorial Day is observed in ____ of the soldiers and sailors who died for their country.

① commemoration   ② regard
③ distribution   ④ defiance

19. _____ for the orphans caused him to give money for their support.

① Compassion   ② Cruelty   ③ Indifference   ④ Honesty

20. They sent me a couple of _____ tickets for the concert.

① communicative   ② commentary
③ complimentary   ④ compulsory

21. An electric motor _____ electric energy into mechanical energy,

① diverts   ② produces   ③ lubricates   ④ converts

22. A group of people organized to consider affairs.

① council   ② company   ③ cabinet   ④ counsel

23. The two drivers were injured in the _____.

① speed   ② carelessness   ③ cross   ④ crash

24. The recent wet weather made the ground very _____.

① damp   ② harsh   ③ rusty   ④ decayed

25. Laziness, luxury, and a lack of initiative are characteristics of a _____ society.

① fashionable   ② vehement   ③ cultivated   ④ decadent

26. The dictionary lists more than one _____ for that word.

① define   ② definite   ③ definition   ④ defining

27. Gloria is too _____ : she always insists she is right.

① incompetent   ② honest   ③ dogmatic   ④ punctual

28. To be _____, a theatrical setting must resemble reality.

① believable   ② effective   ③ reasonable   ④ respectable

29. One who leaves one country to enter another.

① emigrant   ② native   ③ patriot   ④ immigrant

30. John asked for some soda, but the bottle was _____.

① clean   ② cold   ③ empty   ④ full

31. Over 600 students _____ for evening classes this term.

① enlisted   ② recorded   ③ graded   ④ enrolled

32. The art students were ____ by the sheer beauty of the portrait which hung before them.

① enthralled   ②disappointed   ③ depersonalized   ④ guaranteed

33. Years ago many people held the _____ belief that the earth is flat.

① truthful   ② everlasting   ③ erroneous   ④ strengthening

34. Heat _____ the metal, while cold contracts it.

① soils   ② expands   ③ rots   ④ rusts

35. That animal now has become _____.

① extinct   ② interior   ③ stark   ④ animated

36. A millennium is _____.

① a period of one thousand years   ② a period of thousands years
③ a period of ten thousand years   ④ a million year

37. Tom used to be so cheerful, but now he has become so _____.

① energetic   ② gloomy   ③ placid   ④ lofty

38. The luggage was much too heavy for the old man to _____.

① handle   ② send   ③ open   ④ fix

39. If there is much traffic in the street, we say in English that the traffic is _____.

① big   ② large   ③ strong   ④ heavy

40. The ____ to the Brown fortune will be a millionaire, when Mr. Brown dies.

① winner   ② heir   ③ descendant   ④ peer

41. Many airplanes are _____ by manufacturing company and model number.

① secured   ② influenced   ③ utilized   ④ identified

42. The opening ceremony was canceled because of the ____ rain.

① protective   ② promising   ③ impending   ④ upending

43. English continues to be a fundamental tool for obtaining entrance and business communities all over the world. As a result, thousand of students are studying English in both formal and ____ setting in every country around the globe.

44. If you continue to accept help without expressing any thanks or appreciation, you may be accused of _____.

① dependent   ② rational   ③ ingratitude   ④ impunity

45. "A professional writer for or editor of a newspaper" is a ____.

① novelist   ② journalist   ③ typewriter   ④ essayist

46. The literal meaning of a word is its _____.

① original meaning   ② colloquial meaning

③ distorted meaning   ④ meaning in literature

47. Malice cannot exist between _____.

    ① old rivals   ② obvious enemies
    ③ true friends   ④ apparent competitors

48. We are interested only in the efficiency of the shoes salesman in _____ our needs.

    ① making   ② contacting   ③ pointing   ④ meeting

49. The night was so _____ that the thief was easily able to escape his pursuers.

    ① misty   ② moist   ③ mild   ④ messy

50. These are not _____ melons : they are shipped from abroad.

    ① native   ② foreign   ③ stale   ④ strange

51. You may go : I have no _____ to your going.

52. We all go through life wearing spectacles colored by our own tastes, our own
    calling, and our own prejudices. We see subjectively, not _____.

53. A(n) _____ tries to see a little good in everything.

    ① pessimist   ② chauvinist   ③ optimist   ④ feminist

54. Seeing the murderer kill his victim was a terrible _____ for the child.

    ① guest   ② ordeal   ③ plague   ④ litter

55. Mahatma Gandhi urged his followers to pursue a program of _____ resistance as he
    felt that it was more effective than violence and acts of terrorism.

    ① pastoral   ② patent   ③ penitent   ④ passive

56. Whatever profession one may engage in, one can not succeed without _____.

① prejudice   ② pride   ③ patience   ④ examination

57. Video signals have to do with _____.

① sounds   ② pictures   ③ railroads   ④ money

58. In human relations, nothing is of greater _____ value than a smile.

① negative   ② native   ③ conservative   ④ positive

59. His immense _____ of knowledge fascinated me.

① range   ② quality   ③ density   ④ degree

60. She decided to help him, _____ in him a great talent for painting.

① realizing   ② looking   ③ recognizing   ④ searching

61. He had a strong _____ regard the gardener as a thief.

① reluctance to   ② feeling to   ③ attitude not   ④ negation

62. I expected the customer to ___ on the lateness of the delivery but he said nothing.

① remark   ② notice   ③ talk   ④ tell

63. I wan you to instruct me how to _____ a bicycle.

① repair   ② prepare   ③ decline   ④ incline

64. Apparently the long drought has _____ this tree's growth.

① retarded   ② rebuked   ③ retreated   ④ retained

65. "Fish" and "dish" are examples of words which _____.

① parallel   ② imitate   ③ rhyme   ④ define

66. The trip to school is generally shorter for _____ children than those living in the country.

① rural   ② urban   ③ city   ④ cosmopolitan

67. Paul likes ships and the sea do much that he has decided to become a _____.

① servant   ② soldier   ③ secretary   ④ sailor

68. A boycott of other countries' sporting events appears a politically more expedient from of protest than trade _____.

① blocks   ② treaties   ③ sanctions   ④ actions

69. An undisciplined child lacks _____.

① action   ② opinion   ③ courage   ④ self-control

70. The _____ of the sleepy town was shattered by a tremendous explosion.

① seraph   ② severance   ③ serenity   ④ similitude

71. It is impossible for a parent to _____ his children from every danger.

① conserve   ② spoil   ③ shield   ④ absolve

72. He was such a_____ businessman that he never lost money in any transaction.

① conscientious   ② shrewd   ③ reckless   ④ moderate

73. You _____ a generous person when you call him a sting person.

① dissent   ② apprise   ③ slander   ④ slake

74. Is there any sight more ludicrous than the _____ of a woman stumbling _____ on a pair of high heels?

① show, around   ② pride, about

③ spectacle, along   ④ foolishness, aside

75. The policeman was very _____ when he saw a light in the shop.

① suggestive   ② suspicious   ③ deductive   ④ disturbing

76. It is usually Tom who does most of _____ in our conversation.

① talking   ② the talking   ③ talk   ④ the talk

77. My knees were _____ as I entered the cave.

① inquiring   ② enchanting   ③ glimmering   ④ trembling

78. Moving about in a boat may _____ it.

① uphold   ② upset   ③ upstart   ④ upgrade

79. Very hot water makes a kind of gas which is called _____.

80. A person who is rich is a _____ man.

81. Before the bank lent the customer money, it _____ that he was the true owner of the house.

① affirmed   ② assumed   ③ verified   ④ proposed

PART XII

숙어

※ 다음 밑줄 친 부분과 뜻이 같은 것은?

1. Mr. Rogers is <u>associated</u> with a well-known law firm.

   ① supported   ② connected   ③ disappointed   ④ appreciated

2. He will <u>abide by</u> his promise if he gives it.

   ① renege on   ② allow for   ③ renew   ④ stick to

3. How do you <u>account for</u> the result of experiment?

   ① examine   ② explain   ③ execute   ④ exhibit

4. I don't think I am <u>acquainted with</u> the situation.

   ① of compassion   ② worried about
   ③ concerned over   ④ informed about

5. The tribute is nominal, but it is an acknowledgment <u>all the same</u>.

   ① simultaneously   ② nonetheless
   ③ after all   ④ similarly

6. There are dark bodies <u>as well as</u> shining bodies in the sky.

   ① may as well   ② speak well of   ③ stand well with   ④ in addition to

7. The street lights come on automatically <u>in the evening just before dark</u>.

   ① at nadir   ② at outbreak   ③ at dusk   ④ at relapse

8. I got the news <u>at first hand</u>.

    ① on its emergence   ② from a person who knows it

    ③ from a reliable source   ④ urgently

9. That can be said of mankind <u>at large</u>.

    ① in general   ② in a mass   ③ in public   ④ in profusion

10. What she is going through is called <u>being in labour</u>.

    ① acting with ease   ② working in too great detail

    ③ the act of feeding babies   ④ the act of giving birth

11. To <u>beat about the bush</u> is to

    ① go hunting   ② work about the bush

    ③ be direct in approaching something   ④ be indirect in approaching something

12. The student <u>broke in on</u> the conversation without waiting for the speaker to stop talking.

    ① seized   ② regarded   ③ interrupted   ④ withdrew from

13. When are you going to <u>break the news</u> to your family?

    ① leave   ② have news about

    ③ tell   ④ see

14. By the time the war <u>began</u>, most of the people already left.

    ① broke out   ② broke off   ③ broke up   ④ broke short

15. His father died young, and he was <u>brought up</u> by his mother. (=r   )

16. It is not clear that he <u>is up to</u> the trip.

    ① going to enjoy ② on   ③ planning   ④ able to make

17. This tool is <u>by no means</u> satisfactory.

　　① far from being　② incredibly　　③ at all costs　　④ certainly

18. <u>By sheer practice</u>, he became expert at squad manoeuvres.

　　① By determined effort　　　　② By moderate practice
　　③ By practice alone　　　　　　④ By hard practice

19. You'll have to hurry up to <u>compensate for</u> the time you lost.

　　① make the best of　　　　　　② make up for
　　③ make it up with　　　　　　④ be punished for

20. The meeting was <u>called off</u> because of the rain.

　　① demanded　　② cancelled　　③ postponed　　④ held

21. You must <u>carry out</u> his order.

　　① leave　　　② allow　　　③ accept　　　④ perform

22. The hair-style has <u>caught on</u> with the girl students.

　　① been charmed　　　　　　② become popular
　　③ become familiar　　　　　　④ been satisfied

23. Starfish <u>cling to</u> stones by the suction of their innumerable tube feet.

　　① attract　　② destroy　　③ hold fast to　　④ swim over to

24. He <u>came across</u> a very curious book in a second-hand bookshop.

　　① bought　　　　　　　　　② sold at a low price
　　③ found by chance　　　　　④ paid lots of money for

25. George <u>come down with</u> malaria when he was travelling in Vietnam.

　　① confided　　② contracted　　③ recited　　④ flattered

26. The gentleman is said to have <u>come of</u> a noble family.

    ① become of   ② break off   ③ break out   ④ descended from

27. His lectures are interesting, but he never seems to <u>come to the point</u>.

    ① be definite in telling something   ② remain constant in arguing

    ③ bring to a close   ④ discuss seriously

28. She usually <u>comes up with</u> some practical suggestions.

    ① adopts   ② acts upon   ③ presents   ④ turns away from

29. The mining company <u>complied with</u> the regulation.

    ① voted for   ② conformed to   ③ defied   ④ appealed

30. All of them agreed to <u>comply with</u> the regulation.(해석)

    ① 개정하기   ② 논의하기   ③ 따르기   ④ 불만을 표시하기

31. The man didn't have enough experience to <u>cope</u> with the problems of his job.

    ① be concerned   ② deal successfully

    ③ be finished   ④ be caught

32. Tom is reliable, you can <u>count on</u> him.

    ① trust   ② vilify   ③ skulk   ④ recant

33. In <u>covering a lot of ground</u>, a lecturer

    ① takes a long walk   ② discusses many issues

    ③ hides his real feelings   ④ walks up and down the platform

34. Haskins <u>wasn't cut out for</u> journalism.

    ① wasn't suited for   ② wasn't trained for

    ③ wasn't intelligent enough for   ④ was born for

35. Drop me a line the next time you're in town.

    ① serve as a conduit   ② come over for a visit
    ③ contact me on the phone   ④ provide assistance to me

36. You must study English regularly day in and day out to improve your English.

    ① very often   ② every other day
    ③ once in a while   ④ every day

37. The United States is trying to deal sith the serious problems brought on by the energy crisis.

    ① dispense   ② cope   ③ cooperate   ④ interact

38. Seoul maintains a basic agreement on aviation cooperation with Rome, but it is devoid of specifics such as designation of carriers.

    ① lacking in   ② wading into   ③ turning in   ④ standing for

39. Unfair laws must eventually be done away with.

    ① examined   ② abolished   ③ reversed   ④ belittled

40. My wife wants me to do away with this nice old hat.

    ① discard   ② keep   ③ preserve   ④ retain

41. To draw up a contract is to

    ① sign a contract   ② look over a contract
    ③ prepare a contract   ④ talk over a contract

42. I must drop a line to John, asking him to come.

    ① give a call   ② pay a visit
    ③ write a short letter   ④ send a telegram

43. He sometimes <u>drops in</u> to see me in the evening.

   ① falls in drops   ② falls down in
   ③ comes down in   ④ pays an unexpected visit

44. "As soon as I arrive, I'll <u>drop you a line</u>", said her brother at the airport.

   ① take a picture of you   ② write you a letter
   ③ telephone you   ④ send you a gift

45. I was tired of the grandeur of the Forbidden City, and <u>fed up with</u> the crush and noise of the Chinese City outside the Tartar wall.

   ① afraid of   ② impatient for
   ③ puzzled with   ④ bored with

46. You ought to keep that old icebox. You can <u>fall back on</u> it if anything happens to your new refrigerator.

   ① keep it as second-hand   ② paint it fresh
   ③ sell it out   ④ use it in an emergency

47. I <u>fell in with</u> an old friend of mine at a hotel in London.

   ① called on   ② met by chance   ③ was fond of
   ④ fought with   ⑤ competed with

48. <u>Far be it from me</u> to correct you, but I think you've made a serious mistake.

   ① 거리가 멀다   ② 외람되다   ③ 불가능하다   ④ 정반대가 되다

49. Mary said that she was <u>fed up</u>.

   ① disgusted   ② satisfied   ③ ravenous   ④ full

50. Before beginning classes, each student must <u>fill out</u> many forms.

   ① complete   ② eliminate   ③ produce   ④ distribute

51. I bought that house <u>for a song</u>.

    ① at a very high price   ② at a very low price

    ③ for composing the music   ④ for some musical production

52. She says she is leaving Korea <u>for good</u>.

    ① quickly   ② forever   ③ purposely   ④ really

53. <u>For the life of me</u>, I cannot solve the problem on my own.

    ① All throughout my life   ② Try as I may

    ③ According to my life style   ④ From as ling as I can remember

54. We have <u>gone into</u> the matter very thoroughly but still can't find an answer.

    ① solved   ② investigated

    ③ replied   ④ proceeded

55. Sooner or later everything <u>ganged up</u> on me.

    ① came together in   ② went away from

    ③ got together against   ④ got together for

56. They can't <u>get along</u> without money.

    ① agree   ② contend   ③ manage   ④ consent

57. The old man will not <u>get over</u> his cancer.

    ① recover from   ② be immune from

    ③ clear up   ④ die of

58. If, in buying something, I <u>get stuck</u>, I

    ① get a good bargain   ② can't resist it

    ③ pay too much for it   ④ am cheated

59. We have to get through with it today.

    ① endure   ② finish   ③ continue   ④ pass through

60. The bell rang when the student got to the last question on the exam.

    ① arrived at   ② solved   ③ encountered   ④ understood

61. Could you give me a hand with the door?

    ① Could you fix   ② Could you direct me to
    ③ Could you go out   ④ Could you help me open

62. I hope you will give me a ring as soon as you get there.

    ① let me say   ② call me down
    ③ call me up   ④ ask after me

63. Mr. Jackson wants to give out this news as soon as possible.

    ① furnish   ② announce   ③ emit   ④ abandon

64. Such conduct may give rise to misunderstandings.

    ① erase   ② strengthen   ③ cause   ④ control

65. When the King gave up his throne, his brother succeeded him.

    ① pardoned   ② neglected   ③ released   ④ abdicated

66. Helen stopped working for the company because she felt that the employees were not treated fairly.

    ① went through   ② went on
    ③ went out for   ④ gave up

67. You must not give way to your feelings.

    ① yield to   ② hold up   ③ overcome   ④ live up to

68. I would say it is necessary for the young painter to go through a period of imitation.

① put an end to ② experience   ③ be let into   ④ accomplish

69. My brother's tie does not go with his suit.

① match   ② affect   ③ distinguish   ④ concern

70. The accused man held back important information.

① checked   ② contracted   ③ concealed   ④ revealed

71. This ring has been handed down from generation to generation.

① rebuked   ② bequeathed   ③ preserved   ④ collected

72. You will have to speak up. he manager is rather hard of hearing.

① not listening to others   ② partly deaf
③ a fast speaker   ④ not speaking clearly

73. Einstein's theory of relativity seemed hard to believe at the time that he first introduced it.

① incredible   ② brutal   ③ congenial   ④ invariable

74. When you drive, you have to follow several rules. If another vehicle cuts in front of you, you have to jam on the brakes to stop suddenly. If another vehicle has the right of way, you must yield or give up.

① turns right   ② has to move before you
③ is running in the right lane   ④ has some trouble on the way

75. Poor nutrition in the early states of can hold back adult growth.

① reject   ② retard   ③ resist   ④ restore

76. If an offer still <u>holds good</u>, it

    ① remains in effect   ② is cancelled

    ③ has been accepted   ④ has been put off

77. <u>Hold on</u> for a few more minutes until Mary comes in.

    ① walk   ② stand   ③ sit   ④ wait

78. How long can the enemy <u>hold out</u>?

    ① resist   ② persist   ③ consist   ④ desist

79. <u>In retrospect</u>, I think she made the right decision.

    ① All things considered   ② In general

    ③ In spite of everything   ④ Looking back

80. Our economy is proving surprisingly <u>immune to</u> political pressures from America and other big countries.

    ① dependent on   ② affected by

    ③ free from   ④ responsible for

81. My grandmother has been <u>in a coma</u> for several days.

    ① very angry   ② unconscious   ③ distracted   ④ very busy

82. The old man often <u>indulges in</u> the luxury of a good cigar.

    ① allows himself to enjoy   ② imagines

    ③ longs for   ④ planes to give up

83. Everyone was <u>in high spirits</u> when we went on a picnic.

    ① depressed   ② drunk   ③ angry   ④ cheerful

84. He realized, in retrospect, that the battle could have been won.

    ① looking back   ② in general

    ③ in spite of everything   ④ all things considered

85. You must have insight into the international market.

    ① experience with   ② identification with

    ③ understanding of   ④ hostility toward

86. I thought of him in terms of the children of his age I knew in the States.

    ① on behalf of   ② by means of

    ③ from the standpoint of   ④ by way of

87. The most important thing is to think and plan in terms of a permanent peace.

    ① for the sake of   ② with the scope of

    ③ from the standpoint of   ④ as soon as possible

88. In the end the misunderstanding was gone.

    ① Finally   ② Secretly   ③ At first   ④ Generally

89. Moreover, they were attacked by various diseases in the wake of the war.

    ① following   ② aggravated by   ③ preceding   ④ alleviated by

90. Disco is now in vogue among the young people.

    ① vague   ② enthusiastic   ③ popular   ④ passionate

91. We will have the work done, irrespective of cost.

    ① instead of   ② regardless of   ③ in spite of   ④ with regard to

92. She has been complaining about her neighbours talking about her behind her back, but if you ask me, <u>it's six of one and half a dozen of the other</u>.

① 계산상으로는 착오가 없다.　　② 당연한 이치로서 이상할 것이 없다.

③ 양편의 흑백을 가려보면 된다.　　④ 서로 대동소이. 피장파장이다.

93. If Barry has any time <u>left over</u>, he will help me with my French lesson.

① to spare　　② at the end　　③ by the clock　　④ at all

94. Robert asked Nancy <u>to keep him company</u>.

① to sympathize with him　　② to visit his company

③ to watch him　　④ to accompany him

95. The international situation changes so quickly nowadays that you cannot <u>keep up with</u> it without reading news materials.

①give an account of　　② remain informed about

③ take care of　　④ inquire of

96. Please <u>keep an eye on</u> my purse while I telephone.

① hold　　② watch　　③ look through　　④ clean out

97. You have <u>left off</u> vital information in the application form.

① curtailed　　② enlarged　　③ scribbled　　④ omitted

98. Most of the professors <u>were lenient with him</u>.

① were very unfair　　② were very impatient

③ were not severe　　④ were very hard

99. In order to cope with ever increasing competition, the business firms have been endeavoring to <u>level up</u> their computerized system.

① endure　　② make　　③ enhance　　④ renounce

100. To know a piece of music well, it is necessary to <u>listen to</u> it several times.

    ① perform   ② hear   ③ practice   ④ comprehend

101. Children should not be <u>looked down on</u> by their parents.

    ① taken care of   ② come over   ③ despised   ④ respected

102. If I <u>look forward to</u> something, I

    ① look it over   ② look it up   ③ look for it   ④ anticipate it

103. He was often told he <u>looked like</u> his father.

    ① reproached   ② restrained   ③ resembled   ④ reconciled

104. John <u>lost his temper</u> and kicked the vending machine.

    ① became angry   ② lost his dime
    ③ misplaced his wallet   ④ was late

105. If a man <u>loses his touch</u>, he

    ① loses his attractiveness or influence with others.
    ② loses all his money.
    ③ loses his sense of touch
    ④ loses his friendship with others.

106. She <u>was lost in</u> deep thoughts of her mother's death for a few minutes.

    ① went away with   ② was absorbed in
    ③ despaired of   ④ gave up

107. You had better <u>make a clean breast of</u> what you have done.

    ① forget   ② remember   ③ understand   ④ confess

108. It does not <u>make any difference</u> which college you choose.

    ① prove   ② matter   ③ wonder   ④ explain

109. She <u>made believe</u> not to hear me.

    ① seemed   ② refused   ③ pretended   ④ insisted

110. <u>Make great efforts</u> for excellence.

    ① Strive   ② Coerce   ③ Falter   ④ Swerve

111. I can not <u>make out</u> what he wanted.

    ① help   ② inherit   ③ deny   ④ understand

112. I cannot <u>understand</u> what the writing means.
① make with   ② make over   ③ make out   ④ make believe

113. I couldn't <u>make out</u> what he said.

    ① explain   ② remember   ③ believe   ④ understand

114. We understand why people <u>make so much of</u> the place.

    ① admire   ② respect   ③ frequent   ④ neglect

115. Maybe that's enough to <u>make the point</u> that mine isn't a case of sour grapes.

    ① suggest   ② prove   ③ point out   ④ show plainly

116. You'll have to work very hard to <u>make up for</u> the lost time.

    ① summon   ② compensate for ③ call together ④ arrange for

117. The visiting group <u>was made up of</u> five members.

    ① consisted in   ② consisted with ③ conferred with ④ consisted of

118. I hope David will finally <u>make up his mind</u>.

① arrive   ② decide   ③ get well   ④ wake up

119. The waitress had the orders <u>mixed up</u>.

① cooked   ② taken away   ③ confused   ④ filled

120. The pitiful sigh <u>moved us to</u> tears.

① made - cry   ② made - laugh
③ made - move   ④ made - sweat

121. It's <u>next to</u> impossible to do such a thing.

① probably   ② almost   ③ quite   ④ not

122. In English he is <u>next to none</u> in his class.

① the better   ② the worse   ③ the best   ④ the worst

123. John said he was <u>obliged</u> to his neighbors for all their help.

① polite   ② opposed   ③ accepted   ④ thankful

124. I've been working at the store <u>off and on</u> for the past three years.

① irregularly   ② industriously   ③ imperceptibly   ④ unceasingly

125. I am surprised that he offered to assist her <u>of his own accord</u>.

① by himself   ② voluntarily   ③ without my consent   ④ automatically

126. How many bottles of champagne do you have <u>on hand</u>?

① in your hand   ② available   ③ chilled   ④ for the party

127. She will be <u>on pins and needles</u> until the baby is born.

① waiting   ② sewing   ③ very anxious   ④ working

128. I planned to go to Busan be car. But, <u>on second thought</u>, I went there by bus.

    ① changing my mind   ② at second hand

    ③ by the way   ④ by no means

129. I decided to go the party <u>on the spur of the moment</u>.

    ① without previous thought   ② for only a short time

    ③ at the earliest possible moment   ④ after careful thought

130. Susan and Robert Jones have one young son and another child <u>on the way</u>.

    ① about to be born   ② playing in the street

    ③ to be dead   ④ not commonly known

131. I <u>am open to any suggestions</u> that you might want to share with me.

    ① am willing to accept any suggestions

    ② tend to ignore suggestions

    ③ never fail to heed any suggestions

    ④ always pass on any suggestions

132. The machine has been <u>out of order</u>.

    ① operating   ② broken   ③ outside   ④ repaired

133. May felt <u>out of place</u> among the young students.

    ① crowded   ② superior   ③ ancient   ④ uncomfortable

134. Such a thing is <u>out of the question</u>.

    ① very easy   ② impossible   ③ without question   ④ sure

135. He is worse off than ever before, because he <u>is out of work</u>.

    ① is off duty   ② has finished the work

    ③ is unemployed   ④ has retired from work

136. What are your expenditures <u>over and above</u> those for room and board?

    ① along with   ② beside   ③ besides   ④ instead of

137. My mother gave me the same advice <u>over and over again</u>.

    ① once more   ② over and above
    ③ still more   ④ repeatedly

138. I can no longer <u>put up with</u> such a behaviour.

    ① avoid   ② like   ③ throw   ④ tolerate

139. Did he <u>participate in</u> the plot?

    ① take part in   ② reveal   ③ find out   ④ tell about

140. When did your father <u>pass away</u>?

    ① marry   ② call   ③ die   ④ divorce

141. A laser beam is used to <u>pass through</u> even the hardest substances.

    ① illuminate   ② reiterate   ③ deprecate   ④ penetrate

142. John <u>paid court to</u> her for at least two years before she agreed to marry him.

    ① were in contact with   ② wooed
    ③ loved   ④ were in company with

143. The child <u>picked out</u> the red pencil.

    ① brake   ② chose   ③ held   ④ pushed

144. We can hardly <u>picture to ourselves</u> a time in which printing was unknown.

    ① imagine   ② recognize   ③ guess   ④ draw

145. I never know he is <u>pulling my leg</u>.

    ① teasing me   ② attacking me

    ③ looking down on me   ④ insulting me

146. My friend told me to <u>pull myself together</u>.

    ① to get hold of myself   ② to stop feeling sorry for myself

    ③ to avoid worrying about myself   ④ to be held of myself

147. After being startled, Kate paused and <u>pulled herself together</u>.

    ① pulled in her arms and legs   ② got control of her emotions

    ③ pulled on her clothes   ④ continued doing her work

148. The plane was fatally crippled when the rear cargo door was <u>pulled off</u> in flight.

    ① jammed   ② opened   ③ torn away   ④ crumpled up

149. The parents were given little hope that their son would <u>pull through</u> his illness.

    ① get up from   ② get away with   ③ get over   ④ get out of

150. Here's my statement-please <u>put it down</u>.

    ① make note of it   ② deny it

    ③ contradict it   ④ suppress it

151. Shall we <u>put off</u> the program?

    ① withhold   ② dispose of   ③ advance   ④ postpone

152. There are things that teachers will not <u>put up with</u>.

    ① tolerate   ② contribute to

    ③ become members of   ④ agree with

153. We move to the country, because we couldn't <u>put up with</u> the city smoke any longer.

    ① breathe   ② like   ③ hate   ④ endure

154. <u>Regardless of</u> his diligence, he failed in his enterprise.

    ① In comparison with   ② Despite of
    ③ Except for   ④ In regard with

155. All organisms <u>react to</u> changes in their environment.

    ① cause   ② respond to   ③ require   ④ submit to

156. You had better <u>read up on</u> Freud before you take your psychology examination.

    ① become informed about by reading   ② study about
    ③ translate   ④ write about

157. You are expected to <u>refrain from talking</u> during briefings.

    ① repeat   ② speak aloud
    ③ keep yourself from talking   ④ explain your opinion clearly

158. The Mikasuki Indians will have to <u>reside on</u> the reservation for the time being.

    ① work on   ② visit   ③ live on   ④ protect

159. Judy <u>ran across</u> an old friend today.

    ① ran over   ② talked to   ③ happened to meet   ④ trampled

160. She <u>ran out of</u> food supplies before winter came.

    ① used up   ② sent for   ③ gave up   ④ asked for

161. Look out, or you will be <u>run over</u>.

    ① driving over   ② run fast
    ③ passing by   ④ knocked down and passed over

162. The chairman did not <u>rule out</u> the possibility of an agreement.

① promise   ② accept   ③ forestall   ④ reject

163. Her bright red hair made her <u>stand out</u> from the others.

① separated   ② insulted   ③ isolated   ④ distinguished

164. Mary is <u>second to none</u> in dancing.

① fair   ② excellent   ③ the best   ④ fine

165. The Iranians did not <u>see eye to eye</u> with the Americans about releasing the hostages.

① view   ② scare   ③ agree   ④ quarrel

166. I will <u>see into</u> the matter tomorrow.

① conjecture   ② consider   ③ investigate   ④ solve

167. We must <u>send for</u> a doctor right now.

① come and see   ② visit to see
③ send a man to fetch   ④ send a man to talk

168. Shall we <u>set up</u> next week's meeting?

① arrange   ② cancel   ③ race   ④ discard

169. Who can <u>shed light on</u> the reasons?

① turn on   ② explain   ③ dissipate   ④ appall

170. At one time a composer of abstract music, Aaron Copland later <u>shifted to</u> a style that more people could understand.

① exaggerated   ② converted to   ③ imitated   ④ refused to work with

171. You may find him charming at the moment, but he will <u>show his true colors</u> soon enough.

    ① have a change of heart   ② reveal his real nature

    ③ get very angry and agitated   ④ become remorseful and confess everything

172. I was supposed to phone Mary this morning but <u>it slipped my mind</u>.

    ① I changed my mind

    ② she phone me

    ③ I couldn't remember her phone number

    ④ I forget it

173. The stars in the American flag <u>stand for</u> the States.

    ① represent   ② support   ③ replace   ④ endeavor

174. Tom is so intelligent that he <u>stands out</u> in his class.

    ① is diligent   ② is prominent   ③ is intelligent   ④ is proud

175. Several point <u>stand out</u> in his arguments.

    ① are noteworthy   ② are omitted

    ③ don' t make sense   ④ seem to be false

176. He <u>stood up for</u> his friend means that arguments.

    ① gave his friend his seat.   ② defended him

    ③ went out with him.   ④ took care of him

177. Those who <u>straddle the fence</u> are not to be trusted.

    ① break the barrier between men

    ② destroy private property

    ③ build a wall around themselves

    ④ take both sides of an issue

178. In Nathaniel Hawthorne's "The Scarlet Letter", Reverend Dimmesdale <u>succumbed to</u> Hester's charms.

    ① appealed to   ② conversed about

    ③ yielded to   ④ cared nothing for

179. The poor girl <u>took to her heels</u>.

    ① fled   ② arrived   ③ spoken   ④ commanded

180. She has <u>taken a fancy</u> to my house.

    ① called at   ② spoken highly of

    ③ had a liking for   ④ caught sight of

181. Tom <u>takes after</u> his father in many ways.

    ① follows   ② observes   ③ resembles   ④ neglects

182. Jean <u>takes after</u> her mother in character.

    ① humiliates   ② initiates   ③ resembles   ④ receive

183. She <u>takes after</u> her mother.

    ① resembles   ② hates   ③ loves   ④ respects

184. He spoke so quickly that it was difficult to <u>take down</u> what he was saying.

    ① translate   ② record   ③ follow   ④ interpret

185. In the dark, I <u>took him for</u> George.

    ① cheated him for   ② went to see

    ③ confused him with   ④ introduced him to

186. I <u>took it</u> that the ship was wrecked in the storm.

    ① believed   ② assumed   ③ suggested   ④ introduced him to

187. In making the final decision, each applicant's age, health condition, and job experience are <u>taken into account</u>.

    ① numbered   ② stabilized   ③ contrasted   ④ considered

188. She <u>took off</u> her coat the entrance.

    ① removed   ② reached   ③ regain   ④ retain

189. The plane for Rio De Janeiro will <u>take off</u> at 6 : 00 p.m.

    ① depart   ② land   ③ approach   ④ refuse

190. She <u>took off</u> her coat at the entrance.

    ① got on   ② reached   ③ removed   ④ supposed

191. We <u>took our time</u> coming up with the solution.

    ① were engaged in   ② spent a short time
    ③ did not hurry   ④ did out best

192. He <u>took over</u> his father's trade.

    ① released   ② finished   ③ managed   ④ succeeded to

193. I couldn't <u>think of</u> her name at the moment.

    ① invent   ② suggest   ③ remember   ④ consider

194. Why do you want to <u>throw away</u> those books?

    ① imitate   ② discuss   ③ extract   ④ discard

195. Why did you <u>turn down</u> my request?

    ① not more   ② no more   ③ any more   ④ not less

196. The Minister <u>turned down</u> the committee's suggestions.

    ① agreed to accept   ② decided to consider

    ③ refused to agree to   ④ determined to send back

197. He didn't <u>turn up</u> until for five o'clock.

    ① give up   ② show up   ③ call up   ④ bring up

198. He <u>turns up</u> late for everything.

    ① arrives   ② contemplates   ③ departs   ④ acts

199. The plane for New York will <u>take off</u> at 6 : 00 p.m.

    ① As   ② Though   ③ When   ④ Since

200. The employee was told to finished the job <u>without fail</u>.

    ① for certain   ② without complaining

    ③ immediately   ④ without asking

201. She has been feeling <u>under the weather</u>.

    ① cold   ② confused   ③ ill   ④ regretful

202. If something is <u>up for grabs</u>, it is

    ① available to any bidder.   ② higher in price.

    ③ available to thieves only.   ④ available to workers only.

203. John : I thought your plans for winter vacation were all set.

    Mary : They were all set, but now <u>they're up in the air</u>.

    ① 겨울 휴가 계획은 취소되었다.

    ② 겨울 휴가 계획은 아직 미정이다.

    ③ 겨울 휴가 계획은 거의 마무리 단계이다.

    ④ 겨울 휴가 계획은 예정대로 진행되고 있다.

204. If someone <u>is up to something</u>, he is

    ① upstairs doing something.   ② in prison.

    ③ plotting something.   ④ approaching to something.

205. Capitalism has its <u>virtues and vices</u>.

    ① tricks and policies   ② closeness and openness

    ③ theories and practices   ④ merits and shortcomings

※ 다음 빈칸에 적당한 것은?

1. They _____ a brilliant idea for preventing heat loss.

   ① invented   ② came up with   ③ arrived at   ④ made up

2. No, you're not early. As a _____ of fact, you're thirty minutes late

3. I entirely _____ you ; driving in Seoul is really dangerous.

   ① agree with   ② disagree   ③ agree for   ④ agree about

4. This supermarket sells goods _____.
   (이 슈퍼마켓에서는 물건을 할인해서 팔고 있습니다.)

   ① at most   ② at a discount   ③ at all events
   ④ at random   ⑤ at least

5. I must confess I was _____ myself with rage.

   ① outside   ② beside   ③ above   ④ beyond

6. To require or demand something is to call _____ something.

   ① for   ② up   ③ on   ④ in

7. We have to _____ the garden party on account of rain.

   ① call up   ② call for   ③ call off   ④ call upon

8. To obtain something is to come _____ it.

   ① by   ② on   ③ of   ④ over

9. Mary _____ a bad cold while on a visit to Vancouver.

   ① came by   ② came into   ③ came off with   ④ came down with

10. The traffic came to a _____ while the train passed by.

   ① spin   ② glimmer   ③ gallop   ④ halt

11. _____ my good advice, Jim walked home in the rain.

   ① Away from   ② Contrary to
   ③ The reverse of   ④ Rejecting himself of

12. If one is not able to cope with his environment he is _____.

   ① not able to stand it   ② not able to change it
   ③ not a match for it   ④ not satisfied with it

13. To depend on someone is to count _____ him.

   ① with   ② of   ③ on   ④ in

14. That book dealt with the natives' lives (=t_____)

   ① until   ② as far as   ③ for   ④ by

15. The answer was so different _____ what he expected, that the king was much surprised.

   ① is   ② that   ③ from   ④ to

16. Yesterday our daughter-in-law _____ birth to a six-pound baby boy.

   ① got   ② had   ③ gave   ④ produced

17. To surrender is to give _____.

    ① down   ② up   ③ over   ④ after

18. Tom never _____ his discontent.(톰은 결코 불만을 드러내지 않습니다.)

    ① gives in   ② gives up   ③ gives vent to   ④ gives himself

19. In China, a daughter _____ in her marriage.

    ① cannot say so   ② has nothing to say

    ③ has no say   ④ does no say no

20. The Negro lives on an island of poverty _____ the midst of a vast ocean of material prosperity.

21. The old man _____.(그 노인은 홀로 살고 있었습니다.)

    ① kept the house   ② kept his peace   ③ kept in order

    ④ kept to himself   ⑤ kept in mind

22. To be disappointed is to experience a let _____.

    ① down   ② off   ③ alone   ④ over

23. The boss suggested that the company _____ off ten workers.

    ① get   ② take   ③ lay   ④ put

24. He looked everywhere _____ his lost book.

    ① at   ② to   ③ towards   ④ for

25. I'm really looking forward _____ my vacation this year.

26. To make peace with someone is to make _____.

 ① over ② with ③ though ④ up

27. Her success in the entrance examination seems to be out _____ question.

28. Along with other native woman I had participated _____ years with men _____ the national struggle for freedom, working and suffering side _____ side with them until it had finally been achieved.

 ① in, with, by ② for, in, by ③ for, at, with ④ during, with, by

29. To recover from a serious illness is to pull _____.

 ① over ② in ③ off ④ through

30. The prisoners were all put to death. (=k_____).

31. _____ how great they may be, the earth's supplies of coal, oil and natutal gas are finite.

 ① In spite of ② As a result of ③ On account of ④ Regardless of

32. Each star in the American flag _____ for one of the fifty states.

 ① means ② point ③ appeals ④ stands

33. We set out for next destination. (=s_____)

 ① with ② on ③ at ④ to

특례영어 실전문제 총정리

정답 및 해설

PART I : English Structure

1. 동사의 종류

1. **정답** ③
   word affect (= influence = have an influence on = have an effect on = have an impact on) : ~에 영향을 미치다
   해석 그 환자는 약이 자기 신체에 어떠한 영향을 미치는가에 대해 알고 싶어 했다.

2. **정답** ④
   tips He died a beggar. (= He was a beggar when he died.) : 유사보어 (준보어) 에 관한 문제
   해석 그는 너무 가난하게 죽어서 친구들이 장례비를 치러야 했다.

3. **정답** ②
   word raise : (문제를) 제기하다
   해석 비록 법률 위반 행위는 발견되지 않았지만, 그것은 정치 도의상 복잡한 문제를 제기하고 있다.

4. **정답** ②
   word matter (= count = be important) : ~이 중요하다
        It doesn't matter to me : 나는 상관없어
   해석 이것과 저것 중에서 어느 것을 원하세요?

5. **정답** ①
   word turf : 잔디밭 / shiver : (추위, 공포로) 떨다
        glee : 기쁨 (= delight) / elastic : 유연한, 탄력 있는
        do (= be good enough) : ~하기에 좋다
   해석 정신이 건강한 아이는 여름날 잔디에서 손바닥을 펴 그것을 만져 보며 지구의 탄력성 있는 단단함에 은밀한 희열을 느끼며 가볍게 떨 것이다. 그는 그 잔디밭이 어떤 놀이에 적합할까라든지 양이 풀을 뜯어먹기에 적합할까에 대하여 생각하는 것이 아니다.

6. **정답** ①
   word until (you are) spoken to : 누가 당신에게 말을 걸 때까지 speak to (= talk to) : ~에게 말을 걸다

7. **정답** ③
   word play a trick on : ~에게 장난치다, ~를 속이다
        innocent : 무죄인, 결백한, 순수한

8. **정답** ④
   word set oneself up as~ : ~라고 자처하다
        expert : 전문가 ↔ layman : 비전문가, 문외한
        share A with B : A를 B와 나누어 가지다
   해석 전문가들은 기술적, 사회적, 혹은 정치적 문제와 같은 어떤 문제에 대하여 권위자로 자처한다. 그들은 모든 해결책을 가지고 있는 것 같아 보이고, 조언하고 제안하는 것을 즐기는 것처럼 보인다. 그들은 아주 기쁜 마음으로 어떤 문제에 대해서든 조언을 하고 동료들과 광범위한 지식을 함께 나누는 것을 꺼리지 않는다. 그들의 좌우명은 "내게 무엇이든 물어보라,

내가 답을 주겠노라." 이다.

9. **정답** ②
   word declare : 과세품을 신고하다
        custom officer : 세관
   해석 "신고할 것 있습니까?"라고 세관 직원은 대게 묻는다.

10. **정답** ②
    word lie on one's back : 벌떡 드러눕다
    해석 타일 바닥에 벌떡 드러누워 있을 때, 나의 머리는 온통 걱정스러운 일들로 가득 차 있었다.

11. **정답** ②
    tips consider, take, acknowledge, … + 목적어
         + to be (혹은 as) + 목적보어
    해석 MIT 교수인 Noam Chomsky는 미국의 가장 위대한 언어학자 중의 한 사람으로 여겨지고 있다.

12. **정답** ④
    word lend : 빌려 주다 / borrow : 빌리다
         loan : 대부하다
    해석 우리가 샌프란시스코에 살았을 때 아파트를 빌려서 썼는데 매우 비쌌다.

13. **정답** ①
    word welcome : (사람을) 환영한다
         grudge : ~을 싫어하다, 시기하다
    tips thank는 사람을 목적어로 받고, appreciate는 행위나 사물을 목적어로 받는다.

14. **정답** ②
    word hand in (= turn in = submit) : 제출하다
         give in (= surrender) : 굴복하다
         not A but B : A가 아니라 B이다
         counter (= matter = be important) : ~이 중요하다
    해석 중요한 것은 당신이 소유하고 있는 재산이 아니라 당신의 인격이다.

15. **정답** ④
    tips there는 부사이므로 목적어를 취해야 하는 전치사 to와 함께 쓰이지 않는다.

16. **정답** ①
    word fall asleep : 잠들다
         as soon as : ~하자 마자
    해석 난 늘 침대에 눕자마자 잠들어 버린다.

17. **정답** ①
    tips equal이 형용사보어로 쓰이고 있다.
    해석 일반적으로 인간은 동등하게 태어난다고 믿어진다.

18. **정답** ③
    word resemble (= take after) : 닮다

19. **정답** ③
    word make haste : 서두르다
         make haste slowly : 급하면 돌아가라

20. **정답** ③
    word do good : 이로움을 준다

21. **정답** ②
    word pay respect to : ~를 존경하다
    tips thank는 사람을 목적어로 받고, appreciate는 행위
    나 사물을 목적어로 받는다.
    해석 그것은 또한 40년 동안 충실히 봉사해 오신 선생님
    에 대한 감사와 사라져 가는 조국에 대한 우리의 존
    경심을 보여 주는 한 방법이었다.

22. **정답** ②
    word convert A into B : A를 B로 전환시키다

23. **정답** ④
    tips My mother made me a cake. (4형식)
        → My mother made a cake for me. (3형식)

24. **정답** ③
    tips details~observe는 make의 목적어인데 뒤로 도치
    되었으며, 빈 곳에는 목적보어가 와야 한다.
    해석 X레이는 물체를 통과할 수 있으며 X레이가 아니면
    관찰하기 힘든 세부적인 것을 볼 수 있게 해 준다.

25. **정답** ②
    해석 A : 사업에 실패해서 그는 무일푼이 되었다.
        B : 사업의 실패가 그를 무일푼이 되게 했다.

2. 동사의 시제

1. **정답** ③
    tips 시간이나 조건을 나타내는 부사절에서는 현재시제
    를 사용하여 미래시제를 대신한다.

2. **정답** ②
    tips 동작의 완료를 의미하는 과거완료시제이어야 한다.

3. **정답** ②
    tips 불변의 진리를 나타낼 때 현재시제를 사용한다.

4. **정답** ②

5. **정답** ③
    tips 접속사 before나 after가 이끄는 부사절에서는 과거
    완료 대신 과거시제가 쓰인다.

6. **정답** ③
    해석 1928년에 대통령이 되기 전에 허버트 후버는 상무
    장관으로 일했다.

7. **정답** ①

8. **정답** ③
    tips 경험을 나타내는 현재완료시제의 용법이다.

9. **정답** ④
    tips 계속을 나타내는 완료시제와 함께 쓰이는 전치사는
    since

10. **정답** ④
    tips earlier가 있으니 과거보다 하나 앞선 과거완료시제
    가 와야 한다.

11. **정답** ②
    tips 시간이나 조건을 나타내는 부사절에서는 현재완료
    시제를 사용하여 미래완료시제를 대신한다.
    해석 땅이 마르면 우리가 갈 수 있다.

12. **정답** ③
    tips for over three years라는 기간 표시의 부사구가 있으
    므로 완료형이 와야 하는데 기준 시점이 되는 when
    이하가 과거이므로 과거완료가 되어야 한다.
    해석 그녀가 의사 자격을 얻겠다는 결심을 했을 때는 3년
    이상 동안 간호사 생활을 해 왔던 시기였다.

13. **정답** ③
    tips 현재시제로 물으니 현재시제로 답한다.

14. **정답** ①
    tips 현재시제의 형식을 묻는 문제다. 주어가 복수이니
    복수동사가 온다.

15. **정답** ①
    tips 시간이나 조건을 나타내는 부사절에서는 현재시제
    를 사용하여 미래시제를 대신한다.

16. **정답** ④
    word make a noise : 소란을 피우다

17. **정답** ②

18. **정답** ③
    tips 특정 순간에 측정 동작이 일시적으로 계속됨을 나
    타낼 때 진행형이 쓰인다.
    just now : 과거시제 / now : 현재시제
    right now : 시점에서 일어나는 시제

19. **정답** ④
    해석 "조지가 오늘 오후 어디로 갈까?"
        "자유의 여신상을 보러 가는데 데려가 질꺼야."

20. **정답** ④
    word be supposed to (= be going to = be about to) :
    ~하기로 되어 있다

21. **정답** ③
    tips 의미상 경험을 나타내는 현재완료시제이어야 하며,
    서수사 앞에는 정관사 the가 와야 한다.

22. **정답** ①

    tips ②번 before는 과거완료와 함께 쓰이고, ③번 〈~이래로〉의 뜻인 since 다음에는 기간을 나타내는 말을 쓸 수 없으며, ④번 ago는 항상 과거시제와 함께 쓰인다.

          그는 죽은 지 3년이 지났다

          = He has been dead for three years.

          = It is three years since he died.

          = Ten years have passed since he died.

          = He died ten years ago.

23. **정답** ③

    tips ①번 have gone to의 주어가 되는 것은 3인칭뿐이다.

          have been to : 경험, 완료 모두 쓰인다.

          have been in : 경험

    해석 비행기 안에서 서있어 본 적이 있느냐?

24. **정답** ③

    tips and가 있는 문장은 과거보다 앞선 시제라도 같은 시제를 사용하여 나열한다.

25. **정답** ④

    word search for (= look for = in search of) : ~를 찾다

    tips 계속을 의미하는 과거완료진행이어야 한다.

    해석 그녀가 집에 도착했을 때 그들이 그녀를 3일 동안 계속 찾고 있었다는 것을 그녀는 알았다.

26. **정답** ③

    tips (up) until은 ~까지 계속을 의미함으로 진행형과 함께 쓰인다.

27. **정답** ②

    tips ②번 be동사가 come의 뜻으로 쓰인다.

    해석 A : 벌써 새 도서관에 다녀왔니?

          B : 바로 어제 다녀왔어.

3. 조동사

1. **정답** ④

    tips 과거의 강한 추측을 나타낼 때 must have + pp 〈~임에 틀림없다〉가 쓰인다.

    해석 그곳에서 당신을 만날 것이라고 내가 말한 적이 없기 때문에 당신이 나를 오해했음에 틀림없다.

2. **정답** ②

    tips would rather have pp : (과거의 하지 않은 일에 대해서) ~했으면 좋을 텐데.

          would rather + 동사원형 (= had better + 동사원형) : ~하는 편이 낫겠다.

    해석 "당신 부인은 어떤 양탄자를 샀습니까?"

          "푸른색을 샀습니다. 그러나 나는 갈색을 샀으면 했습니다."

3. **정답** ③

    word oversleep oneself : 늦잠자다

4. **정답** ④

    word ought to have pp = should have pp

          : ~했어야만 했는데 (안했다)

5. **정답** ④

    word be used to (= be accustomed to) : ~하는데 익숙하다

          used to : ~하곤 했다 (과거의 규칙적인 습관)

6. **정답** ①

    tips would you like~ ? : 권유를 나타내는 표현이다.

7. **정답** ②

    tips but Charles can't (go to the lecture)

    해석 Susan과 나는 강의를 들으러 갈 수 있으나 Charles는 갈 수 없다.

8. **정답** ④

    해석 오늘날 지구로부터 달까지의 거리는 레이더나 레이더 광선을 통하여 쉽게 측정될수 있다.

9. **정답** ①

    word A is no more B than C is (B) : A가 B가 아닌 것은 C가 B가 아닌 것과 같다

    해석 우리가 눈먼 사람에게 빛을 설명할 수 없듯이 열정을 경험해 본 적이 없는 사람에게 열정을 설명할 수는 없다.

10. **정답** ③

    해석 오늘 아침 땅이 젖은 걸 보니 간밤에 비가 왔음에 틀림없다.

11. **정답** ②

    tips 주절의 주어와 동사가 It is이므로 부가의문문은 isn't it이 되어야 한다.

    해석 그녀가 미국에 다녀온 것은 이번이 처음이지요, 그렇죠?

12. **정답** ④

    tips 부기의문문 문제이다.

13. **정답** ②

    tips had better의 부가의문문은 hadn't이다.

    해석 당신이 머무르는 것이 낫겠어요, 그렇지요?

14. **정답** ④

    tips 청유형에서 like, love, prefer 등의 동사는 will이나 won't와 함께 사용하지 않고, would나 wouldn't와 함께 쓴다.

    해석 당신의 방 친구가 이번 주말 가족을 방문할 예정이라니, 오늘 밤 우리와 함께 식사나 하지 않으시렵니까?

15. **정답** ④

tips ought to have pp = should have pp
: ~했어야만 했는데 (안했다)

해석 우리는 어제 그 편지를 받았어야 했는데 편지가 도착
하지 않았다.

4. 태

1. 정답 ③

tips music이 could의 주어이므로 hear의 수동형이 와야
한다.

해석 그 파티에서 음악이 너무 커 멀리서도 들을 수 있었다.

2. 정답 ④

word be married to : ~와 결혼하다

3. 정답 ③

word be drowned : (물에 빠져 익사하다) 는 항상 수동
형을 취한다.

4. 정답 ②

tips 사람의 감정을 나타낼 때 관용적으로 수동태가 쓰
인다. (사람의 감정은 외부의 요인에 의해 지배받으
므로)

5. 정답 ③

word be seated = seat oneself = sit : ~에 착석하다

5. 가정법

1. 정답 ③

tips 주장, 요구, 명령 등을 나타내는 insist, suggest,
propose, demand, order, desire, request 등의 동
사는 that이하 절에서 〈(should) 동사원형〉을 쓴다.
가정법 현재를 나타낸다.

해석 그의 의사는 그가 짧은 휴식시간을 가지도록 제안
하였다.

2. 정답 ②

word refund : 반환금 (= repayment)

해석 사라는 반환금을 돌려 달라고 요구했다.

3. 정답 ①

4. 정답 ②

tips 주절의 내용과 would를 봐서 가정법 과거임을 알
수 있다.
if 생략 : If he were to leave (= Were he to leave)
he would get ~

해석 그가 오늘 떠난다면, 금요일까지는 그곳에 도착할
텐데.

5. 정답 ②

word I don' t have any idea
(= I have no idea = I don' t know)
nervous breakdown : 신경쇠약

해석 A : 미스 박은 300명의 고용인을 거느리고 있어.
B : ② 만약 내가 그렇게 된다면, 신경쇠약에 걸리고
말거야.

6. 정답 ④

tips 가정법 과거이므로 be동사는 were이 되어야 하고,
〈조금 더 검다면〉은 긍정의 표현이 와야 하므로 a
little이다.

해석 너의 머리가 조금 더 검다면, 너는 내 여동생과 거
의 똑같아 보일 것이다.

7. 정답 ②

word for the time being
(= for the present = temporarily) : 당분간

tips would rather 다음에 절이 오면 가정법 과거시제가
온다.

해석 나는 당신이 당분간은 그것에 대해서는 전혀 손대지
않는 게 좋을 것 같아요.

8. 정답 ②

tips 가정법 과거완료 문장이므로 주절에는 might have
pp

해석 "불쌍한 브리안, 그가 시합에 졌어."
"운이 조금만 더 있었더라도 이길 수 있었을 텐데."

9. 정답 ④

tips 과거 사실의 반대를 의미할 때 가정법 과거완료시제
를 사용한다.

해석 나에게 시간이 조금 더 있었더라면 더 잘할 수 있었
을 텐데.

10. 정답 ④

tips 가정법 과거완료와 가정법 과거가 합쳐진 혼합가정
이다.
= As you did not go to bed earlier, you are more
tired.

해석 "난 매우 피곤해."
"네가 더 일찍 잠자리에 들었더라면, 좀 덜 피곤할
텐데."

11. 정답 ①

tips 〈그렇지 않았더라면〉의 내용이 와야 would have
pp의 가정법 과거완료와 어울려 쓸 수 있다.

해석 그들 차에 고장이 생긴 것이 틀림없다. 그렇지 않았
더라면 손님들이 오래전에 도착했었을 텐데.

12. 정답 ①

tips 가정법 미래를 나타내는 표현은 if절에 should가 오
는 것이 원칙이다.

해석 "무엇을 도와드릴까요?"
"혹시 알렌씨를 보거든 안부 전해 주십시오."

13. **정답** ④

tips 가정법 과거를 묻는 문제이다.
해석 나에게 시간이 있다면, 대학극장에서 그 새로 나온 영화를 볼 텐데.

14. **정답** ③

tips It is time (that) ~ 이하는 가정법 과거가 온다.
It is time that we went home.
= It is time that we should go home. (should는 생략할 수 없다)
= It is time for us to go home.

15. **정답** ①

word What if~ ? : 만약 ~하면 어찌될까? (염려를 나타내는 표현)
해석 "그가 널 만나러 올 거야." "만약 그가 오지 않으면 어떡하지?"

16. **정답** ①

tips as if 가정법 과거는 주절과 같은 시제를 의미한다.

17. **정답** ③

tips 주절의 시제가 would have pp인 것으로 봐서 가정법 과거완료 문장이다.
해석 "어젯밤 연구회에 갔었니?" "아니, 그러나 만약 갔더라면, 음악을 즐겼을 텐데."

18. **정답** ③

tips 과거사실에 대한 가정이므로 가정법 과거완료 이어야 한다.
해석 "당신이 그 상을 못 탔다니, 정말 안됐군요."
"정말 그래요. 그 상을 받았더라면 새 차를 샀을 텐데."

19. **정답** ③

해석 만약 당신이 내게 전화하라고 말하지 않았다면 그녀에게 전화하지 않았을 것이다.

20. **정답** ①

tips 조건 절은 가정법 과거완료 (과거사실의 반대), 주절은 가정법 과거 (현재사실의 반대) 이다.
해석 만약 미국에서 1955년에 가난한 사람을 위해 더 많은 집을 지었더라면, 지금쯤이 나라의 일부지역의 경우 주택문제가 그렇게 심각하지 않을 텐데.

21. **정답** ③

tips provided, providing은 if를 대용하는 표현으로 if only (~하기만 한다면) 의 뜻이다.
해석 "대부를 받을 수 있습니까?" "좋은 담보를 제공한 다면요."

6. 부정사

1. **정답** ②

tips 부정사를 부정하는 never나 not의 위치는 (원형) 부정사 앞에 온다.
②는 let's not go인데 원형부정사 go가 생략된 형태이다.

2. **정답** ③

tips have no choice 〈 = alternative〉 but to 동사원형~
: ~하지 않을 수 없다.
해석 우리는 그의 엄격한 조건을 수락하는 수밖에 없다.

3. **정답** ②

tips remember나 forget은 부정사를 목적어로 취할 때는 미래, 동명사를 목적어로 취할 때는 과거를 의미한다.
해석 나는 존에게 정원에 물주는 것을 상기시키는 것을 잊지 말아야 한다.

4. **정답** ④

tips 부정사의 형용사적 용법을 묻는 문제.
해석 존. F. 케네디는 미국대통령으로 선출된 최초의 가톨릭교도이다.

5. **정답** ①

tips be to 부정사 용법으로 의미상은 운명을 나타내는 표현이다.

6. **정답** ④

word talk to (= speak to = address) : ~에게 말을 걸다, ~와 이야기를 나누다
tips 부정사의 형용사적 용법으로 의미상은 an easy man이 전치사 to의 목적어이다.
해석 나는 아저씨와 그 문제를 논의하고 싶었지만, 아저씨는 같이 대화를 나누기에 쉬운분이 아니었다.

7. **정답** ③

tips It is believed that she is very kind-hearted.

8. **정답** ②

tips see는 지각동사이므로 원형부정사, 혹은 분사가 목적보어로 온다.
재귀대명사 myself는 강조용법으로 쓰인 것이다.
해석 "이 신발이 수제품이라는 것을 어떻게 압니까?"
"내 자신이 직접 그것이 만들어지는 것을 보았습니다."

9. **정답** ④

tips 목적보어가 원형부정사 go이니까 사역동사 let이 와야 한다.
해석 나는 어머니에게 송년 파티에 가는 것을 허락해 달라고 요청했다.

10. **정답** ①
   tips 〈let (사역동사) + 목적어 + 원형부정사〉구문
   해석 그 의사는 환자가 그를 부르기 전에 상태를 그렇게 악화되게 방치한 것에 놀랐다.

11. **정답** ④
   tips 〈make (사역동사) + 목적어 + 원형부정사〉구문
   그가 understand의 주체이므로 동사원형이 온다.
   해석 나는 그에게 그 단어의 의미를 이해하도록 만들 수가 없었다.

12. **정답** ③
   tips 〈had better + 원형부정사〉구문
   해석 비자기간이 만료되기 전에 기간을 연장 받는 것이 좋겠다.

13. **정답** ③
   tips 〈warn (경고하다) + 목적어 + to 동사원형〉구문
   부정사를 부정하는 not의 위치는 부정사 앞에 와야 한다.

14. **정답** ①
   tips 〈would rather + 원형부정사〉구문
   원형부정사를 부정하는 not의 위치는 원형부정사 앞에 와야 한다.
   해석 빌은 내년에는 다시 그의 룸메이트와 함께 지내고 싶지 않다고 말했다.

15. **정답** ③
   tips 〈too~to~〉용법인데 to buy가 생략되어 있다.
   해석 "축구 경기에 갈 예정입니까?"
   "아뇨, 입장표가 나한테는 너무나 비싸 구할 수 없어요."

16. **정답** ①
   word don't forget to 동사원형 : 반드시 ~한다

17. **정답** ④
   word make A of B : B를 A로 만들다
   해석 "톰의 아버지는 그를 의과대학에 보내기를 원해."
   "그래, 그의 아버지는 그를 의사로 만들고 싶어 해."

18. **정답** ①
   word make use of : ~를 이용하다
   tips ③은 in a way which is wise가 필요 없다.
   ④는 wise ways in his time's use를 wise ways in using his time으로 바꾸어야 한다.
   해석 학생은 시간을 현명하게 활용하는 법을 배워야 한다.

19. **정답** ①
   tips 형용사 interesting을 수식하는 부정사의 부사적용법이다.
   해석 질은 같이 이야기를 나누기에 매우 재미있다.

20. **정답** ④

21. **정답** ③
   tips 〈want + 목적어 + to 동사원형〉구문
   He wants the doctor to come. (O)
   He wants that the doctor comes. (X)

22. **정답** ③
   word come along with : ~와 함께 가다
   tips 〈get + 목적어 + to 동사원형〉 : ~에게 ~하게 시키다 (준사역동사)
   해석 "메기도 당신과 함께 올 것입니까?"
   "나는 다음번 여행에 그녀를 데리고 갈 예정입니다."

23. **정답** ④
   tips permit (허락하다) 는 부정사를 목적어로 취하는 대표적인 동사 중의 하나다.

24. **정답** ③
   tips 〈like + 목적어 + to 동사원형〉구문
   exercise가 finish의 객체이므로 수동형인 to be finished가 되어야 한다.
   해석 나는 모든 사람들이 그 연습문제를 내일 이전에 끝내 놓기를 바란다.

25. **정답** ④
   tips 〈want + 목적어 + to 동사원형〉구문
   해석 교장 선생님은 당신이 즉시 자기 사무실로 오기를 원한다.

26. **정답** ①
   tips For~는 의미상의 주어이고, to dry가 진 주어인 구문이다.
   해석 옷이 잘 마르기 위해서는 햇빛 아래 널어야 한다.

27. **정답** ④
   tips let은 사역동사니까 원형부정사가 와야 하고, 형용사 friendly와 연결되어야 하니 be동사가 와야 한다.
   해석 당신의 관심을 끄는 사람이나 사물에 대한 반응은 가능하면 적대적인 것보다는 친근한 것이 되도록 하라.

28. **정답** ③
   tips 대부정사를 묻는 문제다.
   해석 그가 시험에 합격하지 못했지만 지금도 여전히 합격하기를 원하고 있다.

29. **정답** ②
   tips 부정사 앞에 not이 와야 한다.
   해석 그녀는 나에게 다른 사람에게는 어떤 일이 있었는지에 대하여 이야기하지 말라고 요구했다.

1. 정답 ④

tips look forward to (= anticipate = expect) 의 to는 전치 사이므로 동명사가 목적어로 와야 한다. 또한 watch 는 지각동사라 원형부정사가 목적보어로 온다.

해석 나는 정말이지 챔피언이 경기하는 것을 보기를 기대하고 있다.

2. 정답 ①

word be similar to : ~와 비슷하다 (전치사 뒤에는 동명사 온다)

tips drive는 타동사라서 전치사 of없이 목적어를 취한다. 비교되는 것은 같은 품사, 같은 형태를 지녀야 한다. 주어가 동명사 구문 이므로 to 이하도 동명사구가 와야 한다.

3. 정답 ②

tips look forward to (= anticipate = expect) 는 동명사를 목적어로 취하는 숙어이다.

4. 정답 ②

5. 정답 ④

tips approve of (승인하다) 의 of는 전치사이므로 동명사가 목적어로 와야 하며, 동명사의 의미상의 주어는 소유격이 원칙이다.

6. 정답 ④

tips 동명사 spending이 이 문장의 주어이며, our는 그 의미상 주어이다.

해석 우리가 허가 없이 돈을 쓰는 것은 비판을 받을 것이다.

7. 정답 ④

해석 그녀는 대학 공부를 마친 후 유럽으로 가기를 기대하고 있다.

8. 정답 ③

tips They never meet but they quarrel.
= Whenever they meet, they quarrel.
= When they meet, they always quarrel.
= Everytime (= Each time) they meet, they quarrel.

9. 정답 ③

tips resist (~에 저항하다) 는 동명사를 목적어로 취하는 동사다.

10. 정답 ④

tips risk (~의 위험을 무릅쓰다) 는 동명사를 목적어로 취하는 동사다.

해석 "저런 일을 해 보는 게 어때 ?"
"저는 지금당장 위험을 무릅쓰고 어떤 새로운 일을 감행할 수가 없습니다."

11. 정답 ④

tips consider (~를 고려하다) 는 동명사를 목적어로 취하는 동사다.

해석 나는 너의 제안을 받아들일 것을 고려 중이다.

12. 정답 ②

tips go climbing : 등산하다
go swimming : 수영가다
go fishing : 낚시가다

13. 정답 ②

tips 동명사의 의미상의 주어는 소유격이 원칙이며, Jack's returning the book이 이 문장의 주어이다.

해석 "브라운 여사는 지금 행복합니까?"
"잭이 책을 돌려준 것이 그녀를 매우 기쁘게 해 주었답니다."

14. 정답 ③

tips appreciate는 동명사를 목적어로 취하는 동사다. you는 동명사의 의미상 주어이다.

해석 저는 당신이 저를 도와주겠다고 제안한 것을 진심으로 감사드립니다. 그러나 저 혼자서 그럭저럭 꾸려나갈 수 있을 것이라고 저는 확신합니다.

15. 정답 ③

word be busy (in) + 동명사 : ~하느라고 바쁘다
(= be busy with + 명사)

16. 정답 ②

word have difficulty (= trouble) (in) +동명사
: ~하느라고 애를 먹다

8. 분사

1. 정답 ①

tips 〈found + 목적어 + 목적보어〉의 5형식 구문인데 목적어인 something은 steal의 주체가 아니고 대상임으로 과거분사가 목적보어로 와야 한다.

2. 정답 ①

tips 분사가 주격보어로 쓰이고 있는 서술용법인데 수동의 뜻이니 과거분사이어야 한다.

해석 그는 어쩌다 그 스캔들에 말려들게 되었다.

3. 정답 ③

tips 사람의 감정을 일으키는 동사 interest, surprise, bewilder, confuse 등은 사물을 수식할 때는 현재분사를 쓴다.

4. 정답 ③

word hibernation : 겨울잠, 동면
warm-blooded : 온혈의 ↔ cold-blooded : 냉혈의

tips 과거분사 blooded가 warm과 합쳐진 의사분사이다.
해석 겨울잠은 심지어 온혈동물들 중에서도 발생한다.

5. 정답 ③
word keep + 목적어 + ~ing : 계속 ~하게 하다
tips 분사가 목적보어로 쓰이고 있는 서술용법인데 능동의 뜻이니 현재분사이어야 한다.

6. 정답 ①
word How do you like~? (= What do you think of~?)
: ~을 어떻게 생각합니까?
해석 "새로운 일이 어때요?" "매우 재미있습니다."

7. 정답 ④
tips 목적어 the work의 입장에서 보면 수동의 뜻이니 과거분사가 목적보어로 오는 서술용법이다.
해석 나는 그 일이 내일까지 완성되기를 원한다.

8. 정답 ④
tips 〈have (사역동사) + 목적어 + pp〉구문이며 「당하다」의 뜻으로 쓰였다.
해석 조지는 싸움에서 코가 부러졌다.

9. 정답 ③
tips baggage는 carry의 객체이므로 과거분사 carried가 와야 한다.
해석 나는 짐꾼이 짐을 옮기도록 했다.

10. 정답 ③
tips excite, disappoint, satisfy, bore등과 같은 사람의 감정을 나타내는 동사는 사람이 주어이면 과거분사 (원인격 분사), 사물이 주어이면 현재분사 (경험격 분사) 가 주격보어로 쓰인다.
The game was exciting. (경험격 분사)
I was excited over the game. (원인격 분사)

11. 정답 ④
해석 두 시간 뒤 나는 교수님의 강의에 싫증이 나기 시작했다.

12. 정답 ③
tips As he had been an ardent admirer of Tolstoy, ~
= Having been an ardent admirer of Tolstoy, ~
해석 톨스토이의 열렬한 숭배자였기 때문에, 챔프만은 그가 역에서 그 위대한 사람과 마주서 있다는 것을 알게 되었을 때 기뻐서 어쩔 줄 몰랐다.

13. 정답 ②
tips If one is given these characteristics, ~
= (Being) given these characteristics, ~

14. 정답 ②
word cylinder : 원통 / wick : (양초의) 심지
tips 〈with +목적어 + 수식어구〉로 묘사적 독립분사구문이다.

해석 가장 흔한 양초의 형태는 중심에 심지가 박혀 있는 단단한 원통형의 파라핀이다.

15. 정답 ④
tips As all the plans were laid out, ~
해석 모든 계획이 입안되었으니, 우리는 일을 시작할 준비가 다 되었다.

16. 정답 ②
word fall-fell-fallen : (자동사) 떨어지다
fell-felled-felled : (타동사) 넘어뜨리다
tips 분사의 한정용법으로 수동의 뜻이므로 과거분사 fallen이 tree를 수식하여 쓰러진 나무의 뜻이 된다.
해석 어느 날 그녀가 쓰러진 나무위에 앉아있을 때, 숲 뒤쪽에서 목소리를 들었다.

17. 정답 ①
tips 분사가 보어, 목적어 혹은 부사적 수식 어구를 동반할 때는 보통 뒤에서 수식 (후치 수식) 을 하는데 능동의 뜻이면 현재분사, 수동의 뜻이면 과거분사가 쓰인다.

18. 정답 ①
해석 탁자 위에 놓여 있는 그 펜은 내 것이다.

19. 정답 ③
해석 "나는 어제 가게에서 몇 권의 책을 사고 있는 존을 만났어."
"왜 너는 그와 인사를 하지 않았니?"

20. 정답 ②
tips 분사가 주격보어로 쓰이고 있는 서술용법인데 수동의 뜻이니 과거분사이어야 한다.
해석 그 대문은 수년 동안 닫혀 있었다.

21. 정답 ②
해석 마음속으로 나는 학우들이 해변에 서 있는 것을 그려 볼 수 있었다.

22. 정답 ①
해석 그 이빨을 빼어 버리는 것이 낫겠다.

23. 정답 ③
tips 〈get (준 사역동사) +목적어 (사물) + pp〉 구문
〈get (준 사역동사) +목적어 (사람) + to 동사원형〉
해석 이 접시들을 세척하고 난 뒤 갈 거야.

24. 정답 ③
해석 메어리는 재빨리 일을 해냈다.

25. 정답 ②
tips I cannot make myself understood.
(= They do not understand what I meant.)
I cannot make myself understood in English.
(나는 영어로 의사소통이 된다.)

해석 너무나 소음이 많아서 연사의 목소리가 들리지 않았다. (연사는 자신의 목소리가 들리게 할 수 없었다.)

26. 정답 ②
해석 내가 백만장자가 될 때까지는 결코 만족하지 않을 것이다.

27. 정답 ①
word upon (= on) + ~ing : ~하자마자
tips 분사구문의 의미상의 주어는 주절의 주어와 동일해야 생략이 가능하므로 returning의 주어는 사람이므로 사람이 주어로 오는 문장이어야 한다.

28. 정답 ②
tips 분사구문의 주어는 주절의 주어와 일치할 때 생략한다. 이 문제의 경우 standing의 주어는 사람이므로 사람이 주어로 오는 문장이어야 한다.
해석 그 초행자는 바쁘게 움직이는 거리의 모퉁이에 서서 어둠 속을 응시하고 있을 때 갈 곳이 없다는 것을 깨달았다.

29. 정답 ①
tips (Being) born and educated의 주어는 사람이므로 사람이 주어인 문장이 와야 한다.

30. 정답 ③
word anthropological : 인류학 상의
be involved with : ~에 관련되다
tips 종속절의 빈 곳에 주어, 동사가 오면 접속사가 필요하게 된다.
해석 비록 마가렛 미드는 주로 인류학 연구로 알려져 있지만, 정신건강세계연맹에도 가입하고 있었다.

31. 정답 ②
tips As the job had been done, they~
= The job (having been) done, they~
해석 "그들이 왜 모든 장비를 가져갑니까?"
"그 일이 다 끝났기 때문에 떠나려고 짐을 꾸리는 겁니다."

32. 정답 ④
tips = If weather permits, ~ (독립분사구문)

33. 정답 ②
tips As the day's work had been done, Mary~
= The day's work (having been) done, Mary~

34. 정답 ④
tips = As his health failed, Henry Lee~
해석 건강이 악화되었기 때문에, 헨리는 군에서 휴가를 떠났다.

9. 명사

1. 정답 ①
tips 「수학 선생」은 mathematics teacher이며, 주어가 복수이므로 teachers가 된다.

2. 정답 ②
tips equipment는 집합적 물질명사이므로 two pieces of equipment가 되어야 한다.
해석 Jones 박사는 연구실에 비치할 두 개의 장비를 주문했다.

3. 정답 ②
tips 〈수사 + 명사〉가 명사 앞에서 형용사 역할을 할 때 하이픈을 사용하며 단수명사가 온다.
해석 드물게 발견되는 네잎 클로버는 행운의 표시로 여겨진다.

4. 정답 ④
tips Physics is my favorite subject.
= Physics is my favorite.
= Physics is my preference.
= Physics is a favorite of mine.
(물리학은 내가 좋아하는 과목이다.)

5. 정답 relieved
tips 〈to one's + 추상명사〉 : ~가 ~하게도
to one's relief : 다행스럽게도
to one's wonder (= surprise) : 놀랍게도
to one's sadness : 슬프게도
to one's disappointment : 실망스럽게도
to one's regret : 후회스럽게도
해석 매우 다행스럽게도 그 어린이는 안전했다.
= 그 어린이가 안전하다는 것을 알고 안심했다.

6. 정답 ②
tips 〈상호복수〉를 묻는 문제다.
shake hands with : 악수하다
change cars : 차를 갈아타다
be on good terms with : ~와 사이가 좋다
해석 그들은 서로 악수하고 화해하였다.

7. 정답 ②
word restlessness : 불안감
insomnia : 불면증
delirium : 일시적인 정신착란
tips An excessive consumption of caffeine에서 of는 목적격의 of로써 「카페인을 지나치게 복용하는 것」으로 해석한다.
해석 카페인을 지나치게 복용하면 불안감, 불면증, 그리고 일시적인 정신착란까지 초래할 수 있다.

8. **정답** ②

    tips   Two-thirds of, The rest of, Most of, The portion of… 와 같은 부분을 나타내는 표현은 of 다음에 단수명사가 오면 단수동사, 복수명사가 오면 복수동사가 온다.

    해석   "그 일은 어떻게 되었습니까?"
              "그 일의 2 / 3가 완료되었습니다."

9. **정답** ②

    tips   〈수사 + 명사〉가 명사 앞에서 형용사 역할을 할 때 하이픈을 사용하며 단수명사가 온다.

10. **정답** ③

11. **정답** ①

    tips   when은 접속사이므로 절이 이어져야 하니 ③④는 정답이 될 수 없고, California의 소유격은 its가 되어야 한다.

    해석   스페인이 캘리포니아를 자신의 영토라고 주장하게 된 것은 카르릴로가 캘리포니아를 발견했던 1542년부터이다.

12. **정답** ②

    tips   명사가 of~로 수식받을 때 유일한 것이면 정관사, 여럿이 있을 수 있을 때는 부정관사를 쓴다.

    해석   당신은 이 색상의 옷을 입으면 제일 멋있어 보인다.

10. 관사

1. **정답** ③

    tips   half〔all, both, double〕+ the + 명사의 순이다.

2. **정답** ①

    tips   관계대명사 that 이하 절의 한정을 받고 있으므로 정관사 the가 와야 한다.

3. **정답** ③

    tips   so〔as, how, however〕+ (형용사) + a〔an〕+ 명사의 순이다.
              이때 명사가 불가산명사이면 부정관사는 생략된다.

    해석   Lindon부인은 소양이 부족하여 일자리를 구할 수가 없다.

4. **정답** ③

    word get in touch with : 접촉하다

    tips   〈관사의 생략〉을 묻는 문제이다.
              by phone, by letter, by bus, by train, by telegram…

5. **정답** ②

    해석   제임스 조이스는 많은 책을 쓴 작가였다.

6. **정답** ③

    word make a mistake : 실수하다

    tips   such〔what〕+ (형용사) +a〔an〕+ 명사의 순이다.

11. 대명사 I

1. **정답** ②

    tips   앞 문장을 받을 수 있는 대명사는 so이며, 첫 동사가 is이니 and 이하의 동사도 is로 이어져야 한다.

    해석   오로지 자신에게만 관심이 잇는 사람은 칭찬받을만하지 못하며, 그렇게 여겨지지도 않는다.

2. **정답** ②

    tips   his family를 받는 소유대명사 his가 주어가 되어야 한다.

3. **정답** ②

    tips   조건문에는 any를 쓴다.

4. **정답** ②

    tips   권유나 부탁을 할 때는 의문문이라도 some을 쓴다.

5. **정답** ③

    word every five minutes (= every fifth minute) : 매 5분마다

    해석   그 짐승은 매 5분마다 오직 한번만 호흡할지도 모른다.

6. **정답** ②

    word (The) same to you : 당신도요

7. **정답** ②

    word the same as : ~과 꼭 같은

8. **정답** ②

    word the same ~ as : ~과 똑같은 종류의

9. **정답** ①

    word cultivation : 경작 / survival : 생존
              dispersal : 퍼뜨림

    tips   관사 없이 뒤의 명사와 연결될 수 있는 것은 no뿐이다.

    해석   옥수수는 씨를 퍼뜨릴 믿음직스러운 방법이 없으므로 생존을 위해 인간의 경작에 의존하고 있다.

10. **정답** ①

    tips   not ~ either = neither

    해석   캐나다는 미국시민들이 이 나라에 들어올 여권을 얻도록 요구하지 않으며, 멕시코 역시 그러하다.

11. **정답** ③

    tips   〈find + it (가목적어) + 목적보어 + to 부정사 (진목적어) 〉구문이다.

12. **정답** ②
    word make oneself at home
           (= make oneself comfortable) : 편히 하다
    해석 앉아서 편히 쉬십시오.

13. **정답** ③
    word entangle oneself with : ~와 관계를 가지다
         plug : 밀어 넣다
         module : 치수 기본단위
    해석 우리는 한 사람의 전체에 관심을 갖기보다 그 사람
        의 성격이라는 기본단위를 취급한다.

14. **정답** ③
    tips none = not~any이고, nothing = not~anything인데
        milk라는 물질명사를 받아 줄 대명사이어야 하니
        none이다.

15. **정답** ③
    tips 대명사 they의 소유격은 their이다.

16. **정답** ②
    tips 〈It was ~ that~〉 강조구문이다.
    해석 현대적인 신문이 탄생한 것은 1830년과 1835년 사
        이였다.

17. **정답** ③
    tips 〈It was ~ who~〉 강조구문이다.
    해석 "차에 타고 있던 세 사람 모두 사고로 다쳤습니까?"
        "아뇨, 다친 것은 오직 두 명의 승객뿐입니다."

18. **정답** ①
    tips 긍정문에는 some, 부정문ㆍ의문문ㆍ조건문에는
        any를 쓰나, 부탁이나 권유일 때는 의문문이라도
        some을 쓴다.

19. **정답** ③
    tips so will I. (= I will go, too.) : 나도 역시 갈 것이다.

20. **정답** ④
    tips So did I. (= I went, too)

21. **정답** ①
    tips every나 each가 주어일 때 단수취급한다.

22. **정답** ②
    tips ① both는 「둘 다」이므로 of the three와 연결될 수
        없고, ④ every는 형용사로 쓰일 뿐 주어가 될 수
        없고, a few 역시 of the three와 연결해 쓰기 곤란
        하다.

23. **정답** ③
    word regardless of : ~에 상관없이
    tips 문장의 주어가 되는 것이어야 하고, 동사가 is이니
        ③ each state라야 한다.
    해석 미국 상원에서는 각 주가 인구에 개의치 않고 동등
        하게 취급받는다.

24. **정답** ①
    word by surprise : 불시에 (= unexpectedly)
    tips almost, nearly는 everyone과 함께 쓰일 수 있다.
    해석 현재의 경제 위기는 불시에 거의 모든 사람에게 닥
        쳤다.

25. **정답** ③
    tips 〈such~as〉구문이며, rely on의 목적이니 him이어
        야 한다.

26. **정답** ④
    tips I have no children. (보통의 의미)
        I have not a children. (강조의 의미)

27. **정답** ①
    tips Mr. Lee isn't, either. (= Neither is he.) : 부정
        I am, too. (= So am I) : 긍정

28. **정답** ③
    tips this kind of flower이거나 these kinds for flowers이
        어야 한다.

29. **정답** ③
    tips 비교되는 것이 Hawaii Mauna Loa의 크기와
        Everest산의 크기이므로 volume을 대신하는
        지시대명사 that이 쓰여야 한다.

30. **정답** ②
    tips 복수명사 libraries를 받는 지시대명사가 필요하다.
    해석 오늘날 도서관들은 과거의 것들과는 상당히 다르다.

31. **정답** ③
    tips 〈there is〉구문의 주어이며 내용상 적합한 것은
        none뿐이다.
    해석 남아 있는 것이 전혀 없어서 아무것도 줄 수가 없다.

12. 대명사 II

1. **정답** ①
    word beneficial : 유용한, 도움이 되는
    tips 선행사가 the areas이니 관계대명사는 which인데,
        이때 which는 전치사 in의 목적이다.
    해석 댐은 그것들이 세워지는 지역에 많은 도움을 줄 수
        있다.

2. **정답** ④
    해석 이것은 한국말로 무엇이라고 하지요 ?

3. **정답** ②
    word on business : 사업 때문에
         on foot : 걸어서
    tips How는 방법을 묻는 의문사이다.

4. **정답** ①

    tips 의문문이 문장의 한 요소가 된 것을 간접의문이라 하는데 이때 어순은 「의문사 + 주어 + 동사」가 된다. 한편, finish는 동명사를 목적어로 취하는 동사이므로 ④도 정답이 될 수 없다.

    해석 "우리가 외출하기 전에 옷을 바꿔 입을 시간이 나에게 있을까요?"
        "그것은 우리가 얼마나 빨리 식사를 마치느냐에 달려있지요."

5. **정답** ②

    tips I believe는 삽입이고, 동사 is의 주어이므로 주격관계대명사 who가 온다.

6. **정답** ③

    tips 앞 문장 전체가 선행사이며, 이때 관계대명사는 which이다.

    해석 그가 30분 늦게 도착했는데, 이것이 우리를 매우 화나게 했다.

7. **정답** ③

    word dispense with (= do without = manage without) : ~없이 지내다

    tips 선행사 〈no + 명사〉이고 전치사 with의 목적이니 목적격관계대명사 that이어야 한다.

    해석 금과 은은 만약 이것들이 없다면 우리가 불편해지는 그런 기능을 갖고 있지는 않다.

8. **정답** ③

    word stitch : 한 바늘 / even : 고른, 평탄한

    tips as는 such, the same, as, so 등과 함께 쓰여 관계대명사의 구실을 한다. (유사관계대명사)

    해석 작은 바늘하나로 그는 어떤 기계로 할 수 있는 것 못지않게 작고 고른 바느질을 하고 있었다.

9. **정답** ④

    해석 병사들은 어떤 사람이 상관이 되던 그에게 복종해야 한다.

10. **정답** ④

    tips 선행사가 사람이고, 동사 lives의 주어이므로 who가 와야 한다.

    해석 옆집에 사는 그 남자는 매우 친절하다.

11. **정답** ②

    tips ~, what clothes to take
        = ~, what clothes I will take

12. **정답** ④

    tips 간접의문문의 어순은 〈의문사 + 주어 + 동사〉순이 되어야 한다.

    해석 이 구두들의 값이 얼마나 되는지 나는 의문스럽다.

13. **정답** ②

    tips 간접의문문의 어순은 〈의문사 + 주어 + 동사〉순이 되어야 한다.

해석 그들이 거기서 기다리고 있을 때 그들이 어떻게 보였는지 나는 상상할 수 있다.

14. **정답** ④

    tips think, suppose, imagine, believe, guess 등의 동사가 있는 의문문에 의문사가 포함된 의문문이 목적어로 삽입될 때 의문사는 문두로 나온다.

    해석 네가 생각건대 누가 제일 나은 학급 반장이 될 것 같으냐?

15. **정답** ④

    tips 선행사가 a house이니 which가 되어야 하고, 내용상 전치사 in의 목적어이다.

    해석 그 농부는 곡물을 넣어 둘 집을 짓고 있다.

16. **정답** ②

    tips 선행사가 all일 때 관계대명사는 that이 온다.

    해석 필요한 모든 것은 계속적인 연료용 기름의 공급이다.

17. **정답** ②

    tips 선행사가 the only일 때 관계대명사는 that이 온다.

18. **정답** ③

    tips 주어와 선행사의 역할을 겸하고 있는 관계대명사는 what이다.

    해석 아마도 그 인류학자의 업무 중 가장 중요한 것은 늘 혼자라는 사실이다.

19. **정답** ③

    word out of joint : 연관이 안 되는

    tips and 전 · 후에는 유사한 표현이 온다. (병치)

    해석 우리가 말하는 것과 행동하는 것이 다소 연관이 안 되는 것 같다.

20. **정답** ③

    word A is to B as〔what〕C is to D : A와 B의 관계는 C와 D의 관계와 같다.

    해석 빵과 빵 만드는 사람과의 관계는 옷과 옷 만드는 사람의 관계와 같다.

21. **정답** ④

    word superficial : 피상적인 / artificial : 인위적인

    tips no matter what = whatever

    해석 태도가 피상적이며 인위적이고 억지로 하는 것일 때는 어떤 형태라 할지라도 그것은 좋지 못한 태도다.

13. 형용사 Ⅰ

1. **정답** ④

word authentic (= genuine) : 진짜의

tips 형용사의 어순을 묻는 문제

〈수량형용사 + 성질형용사〉「대소 + 형상 + 색체 + 재료」의 순서이다
해석 "미국 식당에서 제공하는 중국 음식은 어떻습니까?"
"나쁘지 않지만 나는 진짜 중국 음식을 더 좋아합니다."

2. **정답** ①
tips alive는 한정용법에 쓸 수 없다.
명사 앞에서 수식할 수 있는 한정용법에 쓰이는 형용사는 living이다.
①의 tree alive는 tree (which is) alive에서 which is가 생략된 표현인데 living tree와 같은 표현이다.

3. **정답** ③
tips 〈수량 + 대소 + 형상 + 색체 + 재료형용사〉의 어순이다.

4. **정답** ①
tips 〈배수사〉를 묻는 문제이다.
This is three times as large(long, wide,…) as that.
= This is three times the size(length, width,…) of that.
해석 호텔에 묵는 것이 기숙사 방을 빌리는 것보다 두 배나 비싸다.

5. **정답** ③
word traveler check : 여행자 수표
tips few는 「거의 없는」, a few는 「some, any」, not a few는 「많은」, quite a few는 「약간, 조금」의 뜻이다.
해석 호텔에 묵는 것이 기숙사 방을 빌리는 것보다 두 배나 비싸다.

6. **정답** ②
tips a-로 시작되는 형용사는 서술용법 즉, 주격보어나 목적격보어로 사용된다.
해석 게릴라의 의도는 그녀를 산채로 잡는 것이다.

7. **정답** ③
해석 이번 여름에는 해변에 사람들이 아주 많다.

8. **정답** ①
word be indifferent to (= be uninterested in) : ~에 무관심하다

9. **정답** ④
word be concerned with : ~에 관심을 가지다
be pleased with : ~에 기뻐하다
be critical of : ~을 비판하다
해석 "빌의 생각은 우스꽝스러워."
"베이커 교수가 그 생각을 비판하니?"

10. **정답** ③
tips Gate Three (= The Third Gate) World War Two
(= The Second World War)
a third world war (아직 일어나지 않아서 소문자로 쓴다)

11. **정답** ②
word come easy : 쉬워지다
해석 그가 더 많은 연습을 하고 나면 이 일은 그에게 쉬워질 것이다.

12. **정답** ④
word chapter fifteen (= the fifteen chapter) : 제15과
해석 "시험은 그 책의 전반부에 대해 볼 거야."
"그 말은 15과를 끝내야 한다는 거지."

13. **정답** ①
해석 짠 바닷물에서 자라는 열대나무 맹글로브는 해안 땅에서 건축할 때 사용된다.

14. **정답** ④
word be known for (= pass for) : ~로 알려지다
해석 율리시스 심프슨은 전통적으로 훈련받은 고전음악 작곡가이며 심금을 울리는 교향음악의 창시자로 알려져 있다.

15. **정답** ①
tips 〈관사 · 소유격 · 지시형용사 + 수량형용사 + 성질형용사 + 명사〉의 순이다.
성질형용사는 〈대 · 소 + 형상 + 신 · 구 + 색체 + 재료〉의 순이다.
해석 저 검붉은 사과들은 맛이 있고 즙이 많다.

16. **정답** ②
tips worth는 목적어를 취하는 형용사이다.
해석 그녀는 당신의 코트가 그 가격만큼의 가치가 있다고 생각하지 않는다.

17. **정답** ④
word sensible : 지각 있는
sensual : 관능적인
sensitive : 민감한
plight : 곤경
be sensitive to : ~에 대해 신경 쓰다
해석 우리는 가끔 주변에 있는 다른 사람들의 곤경에 대해 신경 쓰는 것을 잊을 때가 있다.

18. **정답** ④
word 3월 5일 : the fifth of March 또는 March the fifth

19. **정답** ①
word not A so much as B (= not so much A as B = B rather than A) : A라기보다는 오히려 B다.
해석 "그 트럼펫 연주자의 연주 소리가 매우 시끄럽죠."
"시끄러운 소리가 아니라 재능 부족 때문에 신경이 거슬렸습니다."

14. 형용사 II / 비교구문

1. 정답 ③
- word wealthy (= well-to-do = well off)
  : 부유한 ↔ badly off : 가난한
- tips 주어가 few people이니 동사는 are가 되어야 하고, than으로 이어지니 비교급 better off가 와야 한다.
- 해석 협동조합에 근무하는 사람들이 노동자로 살았을 때 보다 경제적으로 더 유복한 사람은 거의 없다.

2. 정답 ②
- tips 동등비교에 as~as를 사용하며, and (it is) as ancient (as language) 에서 괄호안의 표현이 생략된 것이다.

3. 정답 ④
- word well-behaved : 예의가 바른, 행실이 바른
- 해석 네, 두 살배기 치고는 (예의가 바릅니다.)

4. 정답 ①
- tips He is as good as his word.
  = He is a man of his word.
  : 그는 약속을 잘 지킨다.
- 해석 스티브는 약속을 꼭 지키는 사람이다.
  그가 당신을 돕겠다고 애기했다면, 그렇게 할 것이다.

5. 정답 ③
- tips As~, so~ : ~한 것처럼 ~하다.
- 해석 A : 너는 나를 왜 그렇게 대하는 거냐?
  B : 네가 나에게 대한 그대로 나도 너를 대할 것이다.

6. 정답 ④
- tips ①원급비교일 때는 as~as가 되어야 하고, ②than 앞에는 비교급이 와야 하며, ③비교급 다음에는 than이 와야 한다.
- 해석 "시험이 매우 어려웠습니다."
  "변명하지 마. 너보다 더 똑똑하지 않은 다른 애들도 다 합격했더라."

7. 정답 ①
- tips 「하물며, 더욱이」의 뜻으로 긍정문에는 much more 가, 부정문에는 much less가 쓰인다.
- 해석 저 학생들은 교과서는 고사하고 소설책 읽기도 좋아하지 않는다.

8. 정답 ④
- tips 「the + 형용사의 최상급 + of + all + (the) + 복수명사」: 최상급 표현
- 해석 영어권 작가들 중에는 셰익스피어가 가장 널리 알려져 있다.

9. 정답 ②
- tips 「the + 형용사의 최상급 + of + all + (the) + 복수명사」: 최상급 표현

- 해석 이 소녀는 내가 여태 만나 본 적이 있는 모든 소녀들 중에서 가장 매력적이다.

10. 정답 ④
- tips 동등비교가 사용된 as large as~가 his eyes를 수식하고 있다.
- 해석 그는 그의 할머니의 눈만큼이나 큰 눈으로 슬픈 듯이 우리를 쳐다보았다.

11. 정답 ②
- word A as well as B : B뿐만 아니라 A도
  chemist : 화학자
- 해석 로버트 씨는 유능한 교사일 뿐만 아니라 훌륭한 화학자이기도 하다.

12. 정답 ③
- word not ~ any more (= no more) : 더 이상 ~이 아니다
- 해석 나는 네가 그 문제에 대해서 아는 것 이상으로 다 잘 알지는 못한다.

13. 정답 ④
- tips 〈the + 비교급, the + 비교급〉
  : ~하면 할수록, 더욱 ~하다.
- 해석 "그 약이 당신을 좀 더 낫게 해 주었습니까?"
  "아니요, 그 약을 먹으면 먹을수록 더욱더 좋지 않았습니다."

14. 정답 ①
- word let alone (= not to mention
  = not to speak of = to say nothing of)
  : ~는 말할 것도 없이
  worth + ~ing : ~할 가치가 있는
- 해석 그러한 질문은 세상 사람들에게 대답하는 것도 말할 것도 없고 거의 물어볼 가치도 없는 것 같아 보인다.

15. 정답 ③
- tips that was ever recorded인데 관계대명사와 be동사가 생략된 형태이다.
- 해석 그것은 지금까지 역사에 기록된 것 중에서 최악의 태풍이었다.

15. 부사

1. 정답 ③
- tips 주어로서 명사절을 이끌 수 있는 것은 의문부사 when뿐이다.
- 해석 무명의 용사들을 추모하기 위해 바쳐진 그 기념비가 언제 산기슭에 건립되었는지는 마을 사람들에게까지도 아직 수수께끼로 남아 있다.

2. **정답** ②

word forbid + 목적어 + to 동사원형
= prohibit + 목적어 + from + ~ing
: ~가 ~하는 것을 금지하다

tips 동사 forbid를 수식하니 부사이어야 하며 부사의 위치는 일반 동사 앞에 온다.

해석 그들은 절대 남편이 아내를 구타하는 것을 금지하고 있다.

3. **정답** ①

tips 부사 enough는 수식하는 형용사, 동사, 부사 뒤에 위치한다.

4. **정답** ③

word active volcano : 활화산

tips only는 강조어구 바로 앞에 위치한다.

해석 현재 북미에는 단 33개의 활화산만 존재한다.

5. **정답** ①

tips call it off (O) / call off it (X)

해석 "내일 비가 오면 어떻게 합니까?" "그것을 취소시켜야 될 것 같아요."

6. **정답** ①

tips ③④는 much는 형용사의 비교급·과거분사를 수식하니 expensive와 함께 쓸 수 없고, ②의 a lot of 도 형용사를 수식할 수 없다.

7. **정답** ③

tips 부정부사의 부사가 문두에 오니 도치되어야 하고, 과거보다 앞선 시제이므로 과거 완료를 쓴다.

해석 나는 아내를 만나기 전에는 사랑에 빠져 본 적이 없다.

8. **정답** ②

해석 조지는 시험성적을 올릴 방법을 알았지만, 공부할 시간이 충분하지 않았다.

9. **정답** ②

tips 주어로서 명사절을 이끌 수 있는 것은 의문부사 When뿐이다.

해석 그 기념물이 언제 세워졌는가 하는 점이 여전히 모든 사람들에게 수수께끼이다.

10. **정답** ②

tips 문맥상 양보구문이 와야 한다.

해석 식사하는 사람이 단지 짜증스러운 것인 사람들이 있습니다.
아무리 훌륭한 식사라도 그들은 그것이 지루한 것이라고 생각할 것입니다.

11. **정답** ②

tips 부사의 최상급은 the를 붙이지 않아도 된다.

해석 나는 9월에 태어났고, 그래서 모든 달 중에서 9월을 가장 좋아한다.

12. **정답** ②

tips 형용사 right와 어울려 쓸 수 있는 부사는 quite인데 「전혀·극히」의 뜻이다.

해석 "헬렌, 당신 옷 참 멋지네요."
"네, 그런데 목 주변이 전혀 맞지 않아요."

13. **정답** ③

tips 동사 think를 수식하므로 부사가 와야 하고, 「~와 다르다」는 from이다.

14. **정답** ④

tips so나 not은 문장을 대신하여 쓰이는 표현인데, ④의 not은 your arm is not broken 대신 쓰이고 있다.

15. **정답** ②

해석 교육영화의 국제적 교환이 증가하고 있다.

16. **정답** ④

tips 장소를 나타내는 부사 또는 부사구가 문두에 오면 도치된다.
그러나, 주어가 대명사이면 도치되지 않는다.
(Here he comes.)

17. **정답** ①

tips ago는 항상 과거형 동사와 함께 쓰인다.

18. **정답** ②

word so far (= up to now) : 지금까지

tips Not yet (= I have not finished my homework yet)
: 아직 못했어

19. **정답** ①

tips be leaving은 가까운 미래를 나타내는 표현으로 쓰이고 있다.

해석 당신은 곧 런던으로 떠날 겁니까?

16. 전치사

1. **정답** ④

word congratulate A on B : A에게 B를 축하해 주다.

2. **정답** ④

tips by는 동작·상태의 완료, till (until) 은 계속을 의미하는 전치사로 쓰인다.

해석 "당신은 그곳에 필과 같이 걸어갈 겁니까?"
"네, 그가 6시까지 이곳에 도착하면요."

3. **정답** ③

word arrive at (= get to = reach) : ~에 도착하다

4. **정답** ②

word the things which are behind : 지난 일들
(= what are behind)
what lies ahead : 앞으로 닥칠 일 / reach for
: ~을 향해 나아가다
해석 지난 일들은 잊고, 앞으로 다가올 일을 위해 노력하라.

5. **정답** ③
word retreat (= withdraw) : 퇴각 (철수) 하다
tips 행위자 앞의 전치사는 by
해석 퇴각하는 군대에 의한 다리파괴는 그들이 안전하게 도망칠 시간을 두었다.

6. **정답** ②
word as to : ~에 관해서 / labor union : 노동조합
해석 그는 노동자들이 노동조합을 결성했는지 아닌지에 대해 전혀 몰랐다.

7. **정답** ②
해석 많은 어리둥절한 상황들은 오해로 인하여 발생된 것이다.

8. **정답** ①
word consent to (= assent = agree) : ~에 동의하다
supervisor : 감독
leave : 휴가
해석 감독은 2주일 동안의 무급휴가를 나에게 주는 것에 동의했다.

9. **정답** ①
word in public : 공개적으로
beneath my dignity : 품위에 어울리지 않는, 체면이 손상되는
해석 "당신은 공개적으로 저렇게 춤을 춘 적이 있습니까?"
"물론 없지요! 그것은 내 품위에 맞지 않는 일입니다."

10. **정답** ③
word in time : 시간 이내에, 제때에 / on time
: (= punctually) : 정각에

11. **정답** ②
word by then : 그때까지 / share : 몫
해석 그 사무실의 어느 누구도 그때까지 그 계획 중 자기 몫을 다 해내지 못했다.

12. **정답** ③
word before a crowd : 군중 앞에서

13. **정답** ②
word controversy : 논쟁
tips between은 둘 사이, among은 셋 이상 사이를 나타낼 때 쓰이는 전치사다.
해석 이러한 결론이 교수들 사이에 큰 논쟁을 불러 일으켰다.

14. **정답** ②

tips 시간이나 수량의 단위를 나타낼 때 by를 쓴다.
by the week, by the pound...
해석 그는 주급으로 100달러를 번다.

15. **정답** ③
tips 친척관계를 의미하는 전치사는 to이다.

16. **정답** ①
word be proud of (= take pride in = pride oneself on) :
~를 자랑하다

17. **정답** ④
word because of (= on account of = owing to)
: ~ 때문에
as a result of : ~의 결과로
from A to B : A에서 B까지
해석 뉴욕에서 로스앤젤레스로 가는 비행기가 짙은 안개로 인하여 지연되었다.

18. **정답** ①
word without (a) doubt (= certainly) : 의심할 여지없이

19. **정답** ③
word beneath contempt : 경멸할 가치도 없는
해석 어제 파티에서의 그의 행동은 경멸할 가치도 없는 것이었다.

20. **정답** ②
tips congratulate A on B : A에게 B를 축하해 주다.
해석 당신의 성공을 축하드리고 싶습니다.

21. **정답** ②
tips spend〔waste〕+목적어+ on + 명사
spend〔waste〕+목적어+ (in) + ~ing

22. **정답** ④
word in contrast to : ~와 대조적으로, ~와는 달리
해석 그의 초기 연구와는 대조적으로 멜론 박사의 새로운 연구는 지구 온도가 전반적으로 더워지고 있는 경향을 나타내 보여 주고 있다.

23. **정답** ②
tips 감사를 나타내는 전치사는 for이다.

17. 일치와 화법

1. **정답** ①
tips The number of~ (~의 숫자) 는 단수 취급
A number of~ (많은~) 는 복수 취급
해석 자동차 수가 현저하게 증가하고 있다.

2. **정답** ②

tips 〈one of 복수형〉이 주어일 때 단수동사가 오며, 시제는 현재이다.
해석 오늘날의 학자들이 지적하는 과거 생활 수준을 가장 잘 보여 주는 지표 중 하나가 바로 신장이다.

3. **정답** ④
tips Wool processing이 주어이니 동사가 이어져야 하고 〈one of 복수형〉이어야 한다.
해석 모직물을 처리하는 과정은 인간에 의해 개발된 최초의 기술 중 하나이다.

4. **정답** ②
tips 〈one of 복수형〉이어야 하며, sellers 앞에 those나 their 둘 다 문법적으로 가능하나 내용상 their는 부적당하다.

18. 접속사

1. **정답** ①
word Unless (= if ~ not) : 만약 ~이 아니라면
해석 만약 그녀가 즉시 떠나지 않는다면 결코 시간 내에 그곳에 도착하지 못할 것이다.

2. **정답** ①
tips A, B, and C로 되어 있는 병치구문으로 빈칸에는 and가 적합하다.

3. **정답** ③
해석 그린피스는 우리 모두가 다른 인간들과가 아니라 모든 지구상의 아름다운 동물들과 평화롭게 사는 법을 터득해야 된다고 믿고 있다. 우리는 오늘날 지구의 미래를 보호하기 위하여 일해야 한다. 그렇지 않으면 너무 때가 늦고 말 것이다.

4. **정답** ④
word at once A and B
(= both A and B = alike A and B) : A, B 둘 다

5. **정답** ③
tips 〈both A and B〉의 구문에서 A와 B는 같은 품사, 같은 형태이어야 한다.

6. **정답** ③
tips 〈so ~ that〉구문이다.

7. **정답** ①
word 〈whether ~ or~〉 : ~인지 어떤지
해석 어떤 책이 좋은 책인가 아닌가 하는 것은 우리가 그 책을 단 한 번만 읽기를 원하는지 한 번 이상 읽기를 원하는지에 달려 있다.

8. **정답** ①
tips 접속사 although가 이끄는 부사절 다음에 주절이 와야 한다.
해석 "당신이 메리에게 왜 화를 내죠?"
"내가 그녀에게 편지를 세 번이나 썼지만, 그녀가 답장을 전혀 하지 않았기 때문입니다."

9. **정답** ①
tips 문맥상 양보의 접속사가 와야 한다.
해석 로드아일랜드는 비록 텍사스 주보다 훨씬 작지만 상원의원의 수는 같다.

10. **정답** ①
word 〔so, in order〕that ~ may : ~하기 위하여
해석 그는 성공하기 위하여 열심히 공부한다.

11. **정답** ②
word 〈so that ~ can〉 : ~하기 위하여
해석 인생에서 성공하기 위해서는 열심히 공부해야 한다.

12. **정답** ③
word specimen : 견본 / embryonic fluid : 양수
fetus : 태아
해석 견본으로 약간의 양수가 태아로부터 채취된다면, 아이가 결점을 가지고 태어날지 아닐지를 결정할 수 있게 될 것이다.

13. **정답** ④
word blade : (칼날 같은) 잎
tips neither, not, never, no와 같은 부정어 뒤에 사용하여 부정의 연속을 나타내는 것은 nor 이다
해석 꽃도 잔디도 이 사막에서는 자라지 않을 것이다.

14. **정답** ②
tips 〈so ~ that〉구문이다.

15. **정답** ③
word whether ~ or (not) : ~인지 아닌지
can afford : (~할) 능력이 있다
해석 그는 선물을 살 능력이 있든 없든 친척을 위한 산물을 산다.

16. **정답** ①
word split : 분열시키다 / protoplasm : 원형질
해석 박테리아가 너무 커지게 되면, 반으로 쪼개져 두 개의 새로운 박테리아를 형성하며, 또 각각의 박테리아는 그 자체의 세포, 벽, 원형질을 가진다.

17. **정답** ②
tips Since (= Now that) : ~이기 때문에

18. **정답** ③
tips 내용상 이유를 나타내는 종속접속사가 필요하다.
해석 그는 매우 빨리 말하기 때문에 (그의 말을) 이해하기가 어렵다.

19. **정답** ②

tips it is primarily~ 이하의 문장이 주절이므로, 그 앞은 종속절이어야 하므로 종속접 속사가 있는 것을 선택한다.

해석 인디애나 주 포트웨인은 비옥한 농업과 낙농지역이었지만, 근본적으로 그곳은 다양한 산업의 중심지이다.

20. **정답** ④

word make a sound : 소리를 내다
make a noise : 소란을 피우다

해석 고릴라는 약 20가지의 다른 소리를 낼 수 있지만, 매우 조용한 동물이다.

21. **정답** ③

word 〈so that~ will〉: ~하기 위해서
fertile : 비옥한 ↔ barren, sterile : 황폐한

해석 토양을 비옥하게 유지하기 위해서 농부들은 윤작을 한다.

22. **정답** ②

word 〈so long as〉: ~이기만 한다면, ~인한
matter (= count = be important) : 중요하다

해석 진리는 발견되기만 한다면 누가 발견하든 그건 별로 중요한 것이 아니다.

23. **정답** ④

word cloud-seeding : 인공강우를 조성하기 위해 구름에 드라이아이스 등을 뿌리는 것

tips 문맥상 No serious claim과 동격관계를 유지하는 것이어야 하니 접속사 that이 이끄는 절이어야 한다.

해석 적당한 천연의 구름이 사전에 조성되지 않으면 인공강우법에 의해 비가 생성되었다는 믿을만한 주장은 이제껏 없었다.

24. **정답** ④

word be distinguished from : 구별하다
in that~ : ~라는 점에서
pay for : ~의 대금을 치르다

해석 광고는 광고주가 전달되는 메시지의 대금을 치른다는 점에서 다른 형태의 통신과 구별이 된다.

19. 병치 · 도치 · 생략

1. **정답** ②

word kidnap : 유괴하다

tips 접속사 and 전 · 후에는 비슷한 형태의 표현이 쓰여야 한다. (병치)
and 이후가 동명사 구문이므로 and 앞에도 동명사 구문이 와야 한다.

해석 당국은 부녀자를 납치하여 마누라로 팔아 넘겨 버리는 중국의 새로운 범죄흐름을 사람들에게 경고하기 위해 눈에 잘 띄는 벽보를 수십 장 붙였다.

2. **정답** ①

word be good for : ~에 좋다

tips both A and B에서 A와 B는 유사한 표현을 써야 한다. (병치)

3. **정답** ②

tips It는 가주어이고, 진주어가 to lose one's life이므로 비교의 대상도 부정사가 와야 한다. (병치)

해석 영혼을 잃기보다 목숨을 잃는 것이 더 낫다.

4. **정답** ①

tips whether A or B에서 A와 B는 유사한 표현이 와야 하는데 A가 부정사이니 B도 부정사가 와야 한다. (병치)

5. **정답** ③

tips 주어가 Answering accurately로써 동명사이니 비교의 대상이 되는 than 이하도 동명사가 와야 한다. (병치)

해석 정확하게 답변하는 것이 답변을 빨리 끝내는 것보다 더 중요하다.

6. **정답** ③

tips 세미콜론 (:) 은 접속사와 동일한 역할을 하니 앞문장과 뒷문장이 동일한 형태〔태 · 시제 · 구조 등등〕이어야 한다.

7. **정답** ③

tips Only under special circumstances라는 부사구 (전치사구) 가 문두에 오면 도치된다.

8. **정답** ③

해석 나도 역시 가지 않을 것이다.
(Neither do I. = I don't go, either.)

9. **정답** ④

tips 도치된 문장인데 주어는 a field이다.

해석 아직 존재하지는 않지만, 과학의 과학으로 널리 묘사되고 있는 한 분야가 사회학과 밀접하게 관련되어 있다.

10. **정답** ③

word clay : 점토 / vessel : 용기 / groove : 흠, 자국
geometric : 기하학의

tips are decorated with의 목적어로서 명사 design을 수식하는 형용사가 필요한데 zigzag, grooved and~로 연결되는 ③의 geometric이 적합하다.

해석 북미의 초기 Hopewell 문화에서 나온 점토매장용기는 지그재그모양으로 홈이파여 있는 기하학적인 디자인으로 장식되어져 있다.

11. **정답** ①

tips 분사구문에서 주어를 생략하는 것은 주절의 주어와 일치되는 경우이므로 주절의 주어가 I이어야 한다.

While in kindergarten = While I was in kindergarten

12. **정답** ③
   tips 부정의 부사구 Not until then이 문두에 오니 도치된다.

13. **정답** ①
   tips 부정의 부사 never가 문두에 왔으므로 도치가 이루어진다.
   해석 "당신은 집이 그렇게 빨리 타버리는 것을 본 적이 있습니까?"
        "아뇨, 결코 그와 같은 것은 본 적이 없습니다."

14. **정답** ①
   tips 부정의 부사 nor가 문두에 왔으므로 도치가 이루어

진다.
〈부정의 부사 + 조동사 + 주어 + 본동사〉의 어순이 된다.
해석 코뿔소는 냄새도 잘 맡지 못하고, 잘 보지도 못한다.

15. **정답** ①
   tips 부정의 부사구 No sooner가 문두에 왔으므로 도치가 이루어진다.

16. **정답** ①
   tips The force exerted by tornadoes is so great that~
        locomotive : 기관차
   해석 폭풍으로 발휘되는 힘은 너무도 커서 철도기관차를 철로에서 이탈시킬 수도 있다고 알려져 있다. (The force exerted by tornadoes is so great that~)

PART Ⅱ : Written Expression

1. 동사의 종류

1. **정답** ① effects → affects
   word affect (= influence = have an influence on = have an effect on = have an impact on) : ~에 영향을 미치다
   해석 공해는 이전에 살았던 사람들 보다 현대에 살고 있는 사람들에게 더 많은 영향을 끼치고 있다.

2. **정답** ① made → did
   word do homework : 숙제하다

3. **정답** ② learn → teach
   tips learn은 4형식 문장에 쓰지 못한다.
   해석 훌륭한 가정교사는 학생들에게 입학시험에 합격하는데 매우 중요한 정보를 가르쳐 줄 수 있다.

4. **정답** ④ to be → as
   word think of(look upon, regard, consider) A as B : A를 B로 간주하다
   해석 가르치는 것과 배우는 것은 같은 교육경험의 일부인데, 불행하게도 그것들이 분리되어 있는 것처럼 여겨지고 있다.

5. **정답** ④ with를 없앤다.
   tips 수동태일 때는 be married to가 된다.
   해석 그 회사에서 1년 동안 근무한 후 그는 사장 딸과 결혼했다.

6. **정답** ② asked to → asked
   tips ask는 4형식 문장에서 수여동사로 쓰인다.
   해석 오늘 아침 일찍 나는 스미스 씨에게 언제 모임이

시작되느냐고 물었는데 그는 확실히 모르겠다고 말했다.

2. 동사의 시제

1. **정답** ② conduct → conducts
   tips 주어인 The National Education Association이 단수이므로 conduct는 단수형을 취해야 한다.
   해석 국립교육협회는 교육 제반의 양상에 대해서 광범위하게 조사하고 있다.

2. **정답** ④ gets → get
   word from A until B : A로부터 B일 때까지
   해석 그는 그 상점을 떠나서 집에 도착할 때까지 했던 일을 정확히 기억해 내려고 노력했다.

3. **정답** ④ just wrote → have just written
   word deposit : 예금하다
        or else (= otherwise) : 그렇지 않으면
        check account : 당좌예금
        saving account : 저축예금
        write : 수표를 발행하다
        bounce : (공이) 튀다, 부도나다
   tips 내가 방금 발행한 것이므로 just wrote는 have just written (완료형) 이어야 한다.
   해석 나는 이 돈이 내 당좌에 입금시켜야 한다. 그렇지 않으면 내가 지금 발행한 수표가 부도가 날 것이다.

4. **정답** ② have prove → have proved
   tips 현재완료시제는 have 동사 뒤에 오는 동사는 과거 분사 형이어야 한다.
   해석 조직적인 연구를 통하여 많은 미국 인디언의 언어가 음성학적인 면에 있어서나 문법적인 면에 있어서나 매우 발달된 것이라는 것이 증명되었다.

5. **정답** ③ died → had died
   tips that 이하의 절의 사건이 주절의 시제 told보다 먼저 발생한 것이니 과거완료시제를 써야 한다.
   해석 어제 그를 만났더니 자기아버지가 3년 전에 돌아가셨다고 말했다.

6. **정답** ② had established → was established
   tips 과거의 특정 시점 in 1874가 있으니 과거시제가 와야 한다. 한편, 주어가 garden이니 수동태이기도 하다.
   해석 미국의 첫 번째 동물원이 1874년 필라델피아에 건립되었다.

7. **정답** ② nominally → nominated
   tips 명사인 Party와 목적어인 Belva Lockwood를 연결시켜줄 동사가 필요하며, 시제는 In 1884 and 1888가 있으니 과거이다.
   해석 1884년과 1888년에 National Equal Rights Party는 벨바 록우드를 미국 대통령으로 지명했다.

8. **정답** ① passes → passed
   tips when은 관계부사, 그 선행사는 1872년 이라는 과거의 특정 시점, 따라서 when이 이끄는 절의 시제는 과거가 되어야 한다.
   해석 의회가 Yellow Stone Act를 통과시켰던 1872년에 세계 최초의 국립공원이 건립되었다.

3. 조동사

1. **정답** ③ mustn't → need not
   tips must의 부정은 need not (~할 필요가 없다) 이다.
   해석 "가야만 하니?" "가야 해. 그러나 내가 오랫동안 떠나있을 거라고 두려워할 필요는 없어. 다음 주 이곳에서 놓쳐서는 안 되는 모임이 있어."

2. **정답** ④ may → might
   word field : (전투에) 배치하다
        refrain from : ~을 삼가다 / smear : 중상하다
   tips should that prove impossible은 if that should prove impossible에서 if가 생략되어 도치된 형태이다.
   해석 만약 두 반대 당이 단일 후보를 내세울 수 있다면 좋을 것이다. 그러나 만일 그것이 불가능한 것으로 판명되면 적어도 서로 중상 비방하는 것이라도 삼가야 할 것이다.

3. **정답** ② staying → stay
   word would rather A than B : B하는 것보다는 차라리 A 하는 게 낫다.
   해석 나는 산책하기보다 차라리 집에 있는 게 낫다.

4. **정답** ② was → (should) be
   tips demand, require, urge, suggest, recommend 등의 동사 다음의 that절에서는 (should) + 동사원형이 온다.
   해석 그는 자신의 견해를 밝힐 수 있는 권리를 부여받아야 한다고 요구했다.

5. **정답** ③ produced → produce
   word ripe : 익은, 성숙한 / lethal (= fatal) : 치명적인
   tips 부정의 부사 not till이 문두에 와서 도치된 문장인데, 일반 동사가 주절의 동사라서 조동사 did를 주어 앞에 사용했으므로 produced는 원형동사가 되어야 한다.
   해석 19C, 20C에 이르러서야 비로소 유럽의 근대 민족주의는 최고로 좋은 결과를 낳았으며, 동시에 (인류에) 치명적인 해악도 끼쳤다.

6. **정답** ④ has → have
   tips 4번 참조
   해석 내가 언급하고 있는 법에 의하면 차를 소유하고 있는 모든 사람은 자동차보험에 들어야 한다.

4. 태

1. **정답** ① put → in put
   tips put은 '놓다' 뜻의 타동사. table에 놓여 있으니 수동으로 바뀌어야 한다.
   해석 탁자가 정원에 놓여 있고, 탁자 위에 푸른 판지가 있다. 그 판지 위에는 한 방울의 시럽을 담고 있는 시계의 유리 뚜껑이 놓여 있다.

2. **정답** ⑤ have signed → have been signed
   tips 서류에 서명되어지는 것이므로 ⑤ have signed → have been signed
   해석 모든 서류에 서명이 될 때까지는 당신이 이 집을 소유할 수 없습니다.

3. **정답** ③ for → as
   tips be known as : ~로 알려지다 (= pass for)
        be known for : ~로 유명하다
        be known to : ~에게 알려지다
        be known as : ~를 보면 안다
   해석 토머스 네스트는 주로 정치 풍자 만화가로 알려져 있다.

4. **정답** ④ think → thought

해석 아이들이 학교에 입학하자마자, 남들이 자기를 잘 봐주는 것이 얼마나 중요한 것인지를 곧 알게 된다.

5. **정답** ③ discovery → discovered

word fossilize : 화석이 되게 하다

dinosaur : 공룡

해석 최초의 화석이 된 공룡 뼈가 1700년대에 발견되었다.

6. **정답** ② addict → addicted

word be addicted to : ~에 중독되다, ~에 빠지다

해석 그녀의 남편은 완전히 술에 중독되어 실직하였으며 새 직장을 찾기도 힘이 들었다.

5. 가정법

1. **정답** ② appoints → appoint

word appoint A as B : A를 B로 지명하다

motion : 동의안

tips insist, ask, suggest, demand, recommend, move (동의하다), second (제청하다) 등은 동사의 목적어로 that절이 올 때 동사원형을 써서 가정법 현재를 나타낸다.

해석 우리 위원회가 톰을 의장으로 지명하는데 동의할까 하니 여러분도 저의 동의에 찬성해 주면 좋겠습니다.

2. **정답** ③ couldn't → can't

tips 가정법과거와 직설법이 결합된 문장이다. but 이하는 직설법이 와야 한다.

해석 나는 그 아름다운 호수를 방문하고 싶지만 보스턴에 있는 지금은 당신과 연락을 취할 수가 없습니다.

3. **정답** ① would have → had

tips 주절의 동사 would have concluded에서 가정법과거완료임을 알 수 있다.

해석 네가 들어보았더라면, 너도 톰이 자기반에서 다른 어떤 아이보다 더 능력이 있는 아이라는 결론을 곧 내릴 수가 있었을 텐데.

4. **정답** ③ have gone → go

tips 가정법과거완료의 문장이다.

해석 비가 그렇게 심하게 오지 않았더라면, Tahoe 호수에 소풍 가고 싶었을 텐데.

5. **정답** ② has → have

tips insist, ask, suggest, demand, recommend, move, advice 등은 동사의 목적어로 that절이 올 때 동사원형을 써서 가정법 현재를 나타낸다.

해석 법은 사람들이 적어도 1년에 한 번은 차를 점검할 것을 요구하고 있다.

6. **정답** ① Had I have been → Had I been

tips Had I been~ = If I had been → if 생략

해석 내가 내 동생이었다면, 대화 중에 전화를 끊었을 것이다.

7. **정답** ③ have doubted → doubt

tips If절 속에 this morning이 있으니 현재 사실임을 알 수 있고, 현재 사실의 반대를 나타낼 때 가정법 과거가 쓰인다.

해석 존이 오늘 아침식사로 얼마나 많은 음식을 먹었는지 안다면, 그가 왜 체중이 불었는지 의심하지 않을 것이다.

8. **정답** ① wasn't → were not

tips I wish 가정법 과거완료 문장이다. 현재 사실의 반대를 의미하니 I am sorry that he is not so lazy의 뜻이다.

해석 그가 그렇게 게으르지 않으면 좋을 텐데, 그러면 언어 배우기가 더 쉽다는 것을 알 텐데.

9. **정답** ① would have tried → had tried

tips 가정법 과거완료문장이므로 If + 주어 + had + pp가 되어야 한다.

해석 그레그가 반대편 해안에 도달할 수 있도록 좀 더 노력했더라면, 우리가 그를 배에 끌어올리지 않아도 되었을 텐데.

10. **정답** ① saw → had seen

해석 만약 당신이 그가 오늘아침 먹었던 식사량을 보았더라면 그가 왜 그렇게 뚱뚱해지게 되었는지 알 수가 있을 텐데.

11. **정답** ① was → were

tips Were I a millionaire

= If I were a millionaire → if 생략

6. 부정사

1. **정답** ② working → work

word work overtime : 초과근무하다

tips 〈make (사역동사) + 목적어 + 원형부정사〉구문이다. just recently employed는 분사구문으로 삽입된 문장이다.

해석 나의 감독은 겨우 최근에 고용된 사람인데, 지난달에 두 번 우리를 초과 근무시켰다.

2. **정답** ② being → be

word be ascribed to : ~의 탓으로 여기다

tips be to 부정사 용법으로 의무 · 당연을 의미하는 구문이다.

해석 그의 실패가 근면함의 부족 탓으로 여겨져서는 안 된다.

3. **정답** ③ to eat → eat

   tips 〈make (사역동사) + 목적어 + 원형부정사〉 구문이다.

   해석 김양이 유행성감기로 아팠을 때, 그녀의 어머니는 그녀에게 닭 수프를 먹고 침대에서 쉬게 했다.

4. **정답** ③ finding → found

   tips 부정사의 수동형을 묻는 문제이다.

   해석 지식을 추구하는 과정에서 나타나는 만족에는 어떤 한계도 없는 것 같아 보인다.

5. **정답** ④ enter → to enter

   tips 〈leave (~하도록 내버려 두다) + 목적어 + to부정사〉 구문이다.

   해석 그 경찰관은 사람들을 머무르도록 허락하나 손쉽게 출입하도록 내버려 두지는 않는다.

6. **정답** ④ from staying → to stay

   word forbid + 목적어 + to부정사 : ~가 ~하는 것을 금지하다

   해석 기숙사에 있는 학생들은 특별한 통행증이 없으면 밤 11시 30분 이후에는 출입이 금지되어 있다.

7. 동명사

1. **정답** ④ receive → receiving

   word sleet : 진눈깨비
   〈keep (= prevent) + 목적어 + from ~ing〉
   : ~가 ~하는 것을 막다

   tips look forward to (= anticipate, expect) 에서 to는 전치사이므로 동명사를 목적어로 취한다.

   해석 비이건 눈이건 진눈깨비건 그것이 우리가 그리도 받아보기를 기대하고 있는 편지를 집배원이 배달하는 것을 막지는 못한다.

2. **정답** ④ for given → for giving

   tips 전치사 for의 목적어이니 동명사가 와야 한다.

3. **정답** ③ to live → to living

   tips 〈be used to (~에 익숙하다)〉는 동명사를 목적어로 취하는 숙어이다.

   해석 브라운 씨는 그런 추운 날씨에 익숙하지 못했기 때문에 종종 두툼한 코트를 입었다.

4. **정답** ③ to read → reading

   tips involve는 동명사를 목적어로 취하는 동사이다.

   해석 대부분의 계측법은 특정한 형태의 눈금 읽기가 포함된다.

5. **정답** ③ to drawing → (in) drawing

   word have trouble〔difficulty〕(in) ~ing : ~하는데 있어 곤란함을 겪다

holster : 권총집

   해석 영화에서는 카우보이들이 권총집에서 별 어려움 없이 빼내는 것처럼 보인다.

6. **정답** ① to eat → eating

   word not A so much as B : A라기보다는 오히려 B이다

   tips enjoy는 동명사를 목적어로 취하는 동사이다.

   해석 어린이들은 식사 후에 사탕을 먹으려하기보다는 오히려 다른 때에 먹고 싶어 하는데 어린이들이 그렇게 하는 것이 건강에 더 도움이 된다.

7. **정답** ② that → if

   tips Do you mind ~ing = Do you mind if~
   : ~해도 괜찮겠습니까?

8. **정답** ② greeting → to greet

   tips 부정사나 동명사는 모두 문장의 주어나 보어로 쓰일 수 있으나 동명사는 일반적인 의미, 부정사는 일시적·구체적인 의미로 사용된다. 이 문장은 '그 조직의 목적'이라는 구체적인 의미를 지니므로 부정사가 보어로 쓰여야 한다.

   해석 그 조직의 목적은 그 도시를 처음 방문하는 사람들을 맞이하고 또 그들에게 필요한 어떤 정보라도 모두 제공해 주는 것이다.

9. **정답** ② making → to make

   tips 문제 8번 참조

   해석 그 지시문의 목적은 그 도시를 처음 방문하는 사람들이 그 도시 주변의 길을 찾는 것을 쉽게 해 주는 것이다.

8. 분사

1. **정답** ③ grow → growing

   tips 분사가 보어, 목적어 혹은 부사적 수식 어구를 동반할 때는 보통 뒤에서 수식한다.
   한편, 이 문장에서 grow는 능동의 뜻이니 현재분사를 써야 한다.

   해석 오늘날 자라고 있는 지중해 올리브나무의 평균연령은 200세이다.

2. **정답** ① After waiting → After we waited

   tips 주절의 주어 tickets은 분사구문의 주어와 다르므로 After waiting은 After we waited로 고쳐야 한다.

   해석 3시간이나 줄을 서서 기다린 뒤 창구에 도착했을 때 매우 유감스럽게도 표는 다 팔리고 없었다.

3. **정답** ③ walking → he was walking

   tips 주절의 주어는 his cap이고, 분사구문 while 이하의 주어는 he라서 주어가 다르므로 생략할 수 없다.

   해석 폭이 넓은 도로를 거닐다가 그의 모자가 바람에 날려갔다.

4. **정답** ③ gathering → gathered

   word   supplement : 보충하다

            and so forth (= etc, and the like) : 기타 등등

   tips   from our~so forth까지 부사적 수식 어구를 동반하니 후치하며, 수동의 뜻이니 과거분사 gathered가 되어야 한다.

   해석   우리는 독서, 관찰 그리고 기타 등등을 통하여 모은 정보나 데이터로 우리의 생각을 보충할 수 있다.

5. **정답** ① Consider → Considering

   tips   시간을 나타내는 분사구문 Considering all the possibilities,~이어야 한다.

   해석   모든 가능성을 고려해 볼 때, 나는 정말 어떠한 변화도 만들지 않는 편이 오히려 나을 것이라고 믿는다.

6. **정답** ① boiled → boiling

   word   boiling point : 끓는 점

   tips   분사의 한정용법을 묻는 문제인데 능동의 뜻이니 현재분사 boiling이어야 한다.

   해석   어떤 액체이건 액체의 비등점은 둘러싸고 있는 기체의 압력에 의해 결정된다.

7. **정답** ② publish by → published by

   tips   by Washington Irvin이라는 부사적 수식 어구를 동반하니 후치하며, 수동의 뜻이니 과거분사 published이어야 한다.

   해석   워싱턴 어빙에 의하여 출간된 첫 번째 단편소설은 1819년에 나온 "립 반 윙클" 이었다.

8. **정답** ① considered → Considering 과 ④ to make → make

   tips   ①의 considered~뒤에 목적어가 있으므로 능동의 분사구문을 이끄는 Considering으로 바꿔야 한다. would rather 다음에는 원형부정사가 와야 하니 ④에서 to를 없애야 한다.

   해석   가능한 모든 경우들을 고려해 본 뒤 나는 나의 연구 방법을 바꾸지 않는 것이 좋겠다고 믿게 되었다.

9. **정답** ① Looking back → when I looked back

   tips   분사구문의 주어가 주절의 주어인 the house와 같을 수 없으니 Looking back은 when I looked back으로 고쳐야 한다.

   해석   뒤 돌아보았을 때 그 집은 눈에 삼켜진 듯 보였고, 눈은 더욱더 빠르게 내리고 있었다.

10. **정답** ④ awake → awaking

   word   〈keep +목적어 + ~ing〉

            : ~로 하여금 계속 ~하게 하다

   해석   커피는 나를 밤에 잠들지 못하게 하지만 내가 좋아하는 음료다.

11. **정답** ① Being that → Seeing that 또는 As

   word   surplus : 과잉

9. 명사

1. **정답** ② visitor → visitors

   tips   all은 복수의 의미이니 그 다음에 보통명사가 오면 복수가 되어야 한다.

   해석   새로운 정책은 모든 방문객들이 이제는 접수처에서 신분증을 제시해야 한다.

2. **정답** ① affect → effect

   word   affect : ~에 영향을 미치다

            (명사로 쓰일 경우는 '애정' 의 뜻이다)

            effect : 결과 (동사로 쓰일 경우는 '~의 결과를 낳다' 의 뜻이다)

            devastating : 파괴적인 / debris : 잔해

   해석   폭탄의 결과는 너무 참혹해서 잔해를 치우는데 거의 한 달이 걸렸다.

3. **정답** ② governmental → governmental's

   word   individual income tax : 개인 소득세

   해석   한국에서는 개인 소득세가 정부의 가장 큰 세입이다.

4. **정답** ③ material → materials

   word   blood transfusion : 수혈 / recipient : 수혜자

   tips   material은 가산명사이고, various의 수식을 받으니 복수가 되어야 한다.

   해석   한 사람으로부터 다른 사람에게 수혈하는 것은 그 수혜자에게 부족한 여러 물질들을 공급해 주는데 도움이 된다.

5. **정답** ③ that author's work → that work of author's

   tips   이중소유격을 묻는 문제이다. ex) a friend of mine

   해석   자연주의 작가들의 정신을 보면, 그러한 작가들의 작품은 생존에 대한 인간의 투쟁을 묘사하고 있다.

6. **정답** ③ knowledges → knowledge

   word   classification : 분류 (법)

   tips   knowledge는 불가산명사라서 복수를 쓸 수 없다.

   해석   분류법은 특정분야의 정보를 조직화하는데 있어서 유용한 접근법이다.

7. **정답** ③ category → categories

   word   advertising : 광고 / fall into : ~로 나뉘다

   tips   category는 가산명사이고, two의 수식을 받으니 복수가 되어야 한다.

   해석   광고는 두 개의 주 영역으로 나뉜다. 즉 소비자광고와 상업광고이다.

8. **정답** ① answer question → answer questions

   tips   A, B, and C의 병치구문인데, question은 가산명사이므로 복수가 되어야 한다.

   해석   사전은 질문에 답하고 문제를 풀며, 특정한 주제에 대한 정보를 얻는데 사용될 수 있다.

9. 정답 ② feets → feet
   tips 도량형 feet는 foot에서 온 말이다. feets는 그 자체가 복수형이다.
   해석 미국에서는 인치와 피트가 여전히 측정 단위로 사용되고 있다.

10. 정답 ④ response → responses
   word motor response : 운동 반응
   tips a number of (= many) 의 수식을 받으니 복수형의 명사가 와야 한다.
   해석 출생 시 신생아는 상당히 많은 운동 반응을 보여 준다.

11. 정답 ② a world new → a new world
   tips world record (세계적인 기록) 는 〈명사 + 명사〉의 형태로 복합명사이다. 따라서 형용사 new는 두 명사사이에 들어갈 수 없다.
   해석 1936년 올림픽 경기에서 제시 오웬스는 트랙경기에서 세계신기록을 수립하고 4개의 금메달을 획득했다.

12. 정답 ② fifteen-minutes → fifteen-minute
   word intermission : 휴식시간
   tips 수사 다음의 명사는 단수형을 쓰지만 복수의 뜻을 지니며 hyphen으로 연결하는 것이 일반적이다.
      ex) a five-dollar bill / a ten-mile race
         a five act drama
   해석 제1막이 끝난 뒤 15분간의 휴식시간이 있을 것이다.

13. 정답 ③ his → their
   tips other people의 소유격은 their이어야 한다.
   해석 다른 사람들이 자신의 능력을 개발하려는 것을 도와주려고 하지 않는 사람은 친구를 가질 자격이 없다.

10. 관사

1. 정답 ① an → a
   tips unique의 첫 음이 자음이므로 부정관사 a가 와야 한다.
      an MP / an LP / an honest man
      an hour / an 18 / an X-ray...
      a Union / a European / a useful
      a united / a one...
   해석 지미는 사람들에게 편안한 기분이 들게 해 주는 독특한 능력을 가지고 있다.

2. 정답 ② her → the
   tips 한정된 명사 앞에는 정관사 the가 온다. 형용사구 of prison reformer Jessie D. Hodder가 background and early life를 한정하므로 ②의 her은 부적절 하다.
   해석 교도소 개혁론자인 Jessie D. Hodder의 배경과 어린 시절에 관해서는 알려져 있는 바가 거의 없다.

3. 정답 ② good swimmer → good a swimmer
   tips 〈as, so, too, how, however + 형용사 + a (an) + 명사〉의 어순이다.
   해석 그녀는 자신이 그 사람보다 더 낫지는 못해도 그 사람만큼은 훌륭한 선수라고 생각했다.

4. 정답 ① a → an
   해석 한 시간 뒤 나는 그 일을 만족스럽게 끝마치고 나서 현관에 있는 모자를 쓰고 눈치 채지 않게 살짝 빠져 나왔다.

11. 대명사 I

1. 정답 ③ their → his
   tips each, every로 수식되는 명사는 항상 단수 취급한다. 따라서 their는 his로 바꾸어야 한다.
   해석 모든 남녀는 시험장에 들어가기 전에 성과 이름 모두 다 써야 한다.

2. 정답 ④ this → it
   word prime : 주요한 / cancer : 암
   tips 앞에 나온 명사 smoking을 받는 대명사는 it이므로 ④ this → it이어야 한다.
   해석 흡연이 폐암의 주요 원인이라는 많은 증거가 있기 때문에 많은 의사들이 흡연을 그만두었다.

3. 정답 ① its → his
   tips a scientist가 주어이니 그의 소유격은 his가 와야 한다.
   해석 과학자는 주의 깊은 실험을 통해 검증된 가설에 연구의 근거를 두고 있다.

4. 정답 ④ their → her
   tips their가 가리키는 명사는 the average man, 즉 단수이므로 소유격도 단수가 와야 한다.
   해석 하루 중 보통남자는 17,300번 호흡을 하고, 반면 폐가 더 작은 보통여자는 28,000번 호흡을 한다.

5. 정답 ② her → she
   tips 〈It was ~ who (that)〉강조구문인데 강조되는 것이 주격이니 she를 써야 한다.
   해석 UN에서 자기 나라를 대표하고 이후에 주미대사가 된 사람이 바로 그 여자다.

6. 정답 ④ they are → he is
   tips a movie star를 받는 대명사는 he이어야 한다.
   해석 사람들은 보통 영화배우를 실제 생활에서 있는 그대로 보는데 관심을 가진다.

7. 정답 ① their → her

tips 국가가 정치적 · 경제적 의미로 쓰이면 her, 자연환경 · 국토 · 지리의 의미로 쓰이면 its가 쓰이는 것이 원칙이다.

해석 로디지아가 영국으로부터 독립을 선언했을 때 새 정부가 한 달 이상 계속될 것이라고 생각했던 사람은 거의 없었다.

8. **정답** ④ it → them
   tips 대명사 ④번 it가 가리키는 것은 the mountains이니 복수형 them으로 바뀌어야 한다.

9. **정답** ③ he → him
   tips you and he는 동사 has met의 목적어이니 you and him이어야 한다.
   해석 이 도시를 방문하는 동안 당신과 그를 만난 것은 정말 즐거운 일이다.

10. **정답** ④ I → me
    word session : 회기, 학기 / field supervisor : 현장 감독
    tips 전치사 but (= except, save) 의 목적이나 목적격이 와야 한다.
    해석 현장 감독, 판매담당 지배인, 그리고 나 외에는 모두 다 오후 모임에 참석해 줄 것이 요망된다.

11. **정답** ④ them → it
    tips Each나 every~가 주어일 때는 의미는 복수이나 형태는 단수 취급을 한다.
    해석 모든 민족은 자신과 다른 민족들을 구분지어 주는 독특한 특징을 지니고 있다.

12. **정답** ③ have → has
    tips each나 every는 단수 취급하므로 each animal을 받는 동사인 have가 has로 되어야 한다.
    해석 줄무늬 다람쥐는 식민지 지역에 사는데 그곳에서는 모든 동물들이 각자 자신의 지하 굴을 가지고 있다.

13. **정답** ③ their → its
    tips 〈It was ~ who (that)〉강조구문인데 대명사 their는 friendship을 가리키므로 its가 되어야 한다.
    해석 헤밍웨이와 피츠제럴드의 우정이 최고에 달한 것은 1920년대였다.

14. **정답** ② the most → most
    word the Reconstruction : 1866~1877년간의 미국 남부 주들의 재 편입 Democratic Party : 민주당
    tips most가 대명사로 쓰일 때는 부정대명사이므로 정관사 the를 사용할 수 없다.
    해석 남부 주들의 재 편입기이래 남부 캘리포니아 주와 그 하급조직의 선거직 대부분을 민주당이 장악해 왔다.

12. 대명사 Ⅱ

1. **정답** ② are they → they are
   word major : 전공 / be good at : ~에 능숙하다
   tips 간접의문문의 어순은 〈의문사 + 주어 + 동사〉이다.
   해석 대학생들은 전공을 선택할 때 그들이 졸업할 즈음 취업 시장이 어떠할 것인지 뿐만 아니라 (전공을 제외한) 다른 과목도 잘할 수 있는지도 고려해 봐야 한다.

2. **정답** ② only those which → only those who
   word those who~ : ~하는 사람들 / apply for : ~에 지원하다
   intensive care unit : 중환자실 / call in (= summon) : 소환하다
   해석 Frontier Nursing Program에 지원한 간호사들 중에 중환자실에서 근무한 경험이 있는 사람들만 면접을 받았다.

3. **정답** ③ whomever → whoever
   word be sure to : 반드시 ~하다
   tips 전치사 to의 목적은 whomever가 아니라 whomever asks for it이며, 따라서 asks의 주어이어야 하니 whomever는 whoever이어야 한다.
   해석 논문을 끝마치거든 반드시 그것을 요구하는 사람이면 누구든지 다 주어라.

4. **정답** ① whom → to whom
   word be a stranger to : ~에 낯설다 / rapt : 황홀한
   as good as (= nearly, almost) : 거의 ~와 같은
   tips whom 이하의 문장 this emotion is a stranger는 완전한 문장이므로 소유격관계 대명사도 가능하다고 생각할 수 있으나 한정사는 겹쳐 쓰지 못하므로 전치사 to whom이어야 한다.
   ex) a my friend (X) / whose this (X)
   해석 이런 감정에 낯설고, 더 이상 감탄하여 경외심에 넋을 잃을 줄 모르는 사람은 죽은 것과 같다. 그러한 사람의 두 눈은 감겨져 있는 것이다.

5. **정답** ④ live → live in
   tips ~the houses they live에서 houses와 they사이에는 목적격 관계대명사 which가 생략되어 있는데 이때 which는 전치사 in의 목적이므로 in을 생략할 수 없다.
   해석 이 도시에는 자기들이 살고 있는 집을 소유하고 있는 사람이 많지 않다.

6. **정답** ② of those → of which
   word be composed of (= be made up of = consist of = comprise) : ~로 구성되다
   be separate from : ~와 분리되다
   tips fifty states가 선행사이니 ②번 of those → of which 이어야 하며 이때 which는 부분을 나타내는 전치사 of의 목적이다.

해석 미국은 50개의 주로 구성되어 있는데 이들 중 2개
의 주가 땅이나 물에 의해서 나머지 다른 주들과 분
리되어 있다.

7. **정답** ③ that → who
   word expert : 전문가 ↔ layman : 문외한
   tips that이 의문사 who (의문대명사) 가 되어 간접의문
   문의 형태로 문장이 성립된다.
   해석 몇몇 전문가들은 이미 누가 차기 대통령이 될지를
   예측해 왔다.

8. **정답** ② which → who
   word go on strike : 파업하다
   tips 관계대명사 which의 선행사는 workers이므로 who
   가 와야 한다.
   해석 임금인상을 위해 파업한 노동자들의 수는 20년 전
   의 수보다 거의 2배 가까이 된다.

9. **정답** ① who → whom
   word dormitory : 기숙사
   tips meet의 목적어이므로 ①은 목적격 whom이어야 한
   다.
   해석 당신이 곧 만나야 하는 소년은 우리 기숙사에서 수
   학을 가장 잘하는 학생인 프레디 톰슨이다.

10. **정답** ① who → whom
    word belong to : ~에 속하다
    tips 관계대명사 who는 전치사 to의 목적어이므로 목적
    격인 whom이 되어야 한다.
    해석 그래서 그 개의 주인인 루이자의 오빠는 작은 개집
    을 만들고, 그 개를 줄에 묶어 놓았다.

11. **정답** ② which → whom
    tips 선행사가 a thousand men이고 전치사 of의 목적이
    므로 목적격 whom이 와야 한다. 이때 of는 부분을
    나타내는 전치사이며 부분을 나타내는 of의 목적이
    면 목적격관계대명사는 생략할 수 없다.
    해석 타타르 추장은 천 명의 남자를 통솔하는데 그들 모
    두 전시든 평시든 그의 명령에 따라야 한다.

12. **정답** ③ where → which
    word metropolitan : 대도시권 / territory : 지역, 영역
    tips ③번 where는 surround의 주어가 되어야 하므로 관
    계부사가 아니라 주격 관계대명사가 와야 한다. 관
    계부사는〈전치사 + 관계대명사〉로 바꿀 수 있는 것
    이어야 하므로 목적격인 경우이어야 한다.
    해석 대도시권역은 중심이 되는 도시와 또 그곳을 둘러싸
    고 있는 지역이라고 규정지을 수 있다.

13. **정답** ① when → which
    tips during은 전치사이므로 관계부사인 when은 목적어
    로 올 수 없고 관계대명사 which이어야 한다.
    해석 사람들이 철을 녹이는 것을 배웠던 시기를 철기시
    대라고 부른다.

13. 형용사 Ⅰ

1. **정답** ① have → has
   tips Many a boat has been wrecked here.
   = Many boats have been wrecked here.
   해석 그것의 적절한 사용법에 대한 많은 논쟁이 있다.

2. **정답** ③ more than → as much as
   tips 배수사 twice의 경우에는 as~as가 온다.
   2배 이상일 경우는〈배수사 + as~as〉
   3배 이상일 경우는〈배수사 + as~as〉
   또는〈배수사 +비교급~than〉를 쓴다.
   This is three times as large as that.
   = This is three times the size of that.
   해석 왜 이 집의 가격이 작년의 2배가 되는지에 대하여
   논리적인 근거가 없다.

3. **정답** ④ years → years old
   해석 태양은 우주의 역사가 이미 100억 년이 되었을 때
   형성된 것으로 보인다.

4. **정답** ④ differently → different
   word currency : 통화, 화폐
   tips 명사 peoples를 수식하는 것은 형용사이어야 한다.
   해석 조개 껍질은 여러 지역, 그리고 여러 민족들 사이에
   서 화폐로 쓰였다.

5. **정답** ② certainly → certain
   word be certain of : ~를 확신하다
   tips certain은 서술 용법에 쓰이는 형용사이다.

6. **정답** ④ alive → living
   tips a-로 시작하는 형용사는 제한적 용법으로 사용하지
   않고 서술적 용법으로 사용한다.
   해석 비행은 대부분의 살아 있는 생물체에게는 매우 어
   려운 행동이다.

7. **정답** ② alike → like
   tips like (~처럼) 는 목적어를 취하는 형용사이며, alike
   는 보어로 쓰인다.
   해석 코끼리와 거의 같은 마스터돈은 숲에서 서식하는
   동물이다.

8. **정답** ① the same → like
   word bean : 콩 / pod : 콩깍지
   tips 내용상 '다른 콩깍지' 의 의미이며, 형태상 목적어
   를 취하는 형용사 like이어야 한다.
   해석 다른 콩처럼 리마도 콩깍지에서 자라는 씨앗이다.

9. **정답** ① many → much
   tips '고갱이 남긴 많은 작품' 은 추상적인 의미라서
   much가 수식한다.
   해석 고갱이 남긴 많은 작품이 그가 죽을 때까지 살았던
   South Sea섬에서 분실되었다.

1. **정답** ④ as → than
   tips 비교 문장으로 앞에 more라는 비교급을 썼으므로
   ④의 as는 than이 와야 한다.
   해석 어떤 사람들은 대부분의 사람들이 일생 동안 번 돈
   보다 더 많은 돈을 5년 이내에 벌 수 있다.

2. **정답** ① The more difficulty → The more difficult
   tips 〈The + 비교급~, the + 비교급~〉
   : ~하면 할수록 더욱 ~하다
   해석 문제가 어려우면 어려울수록 나는 그것들에 대한
   답을 더욱더 할 수 없을 것이다.

3. **정답** ④ more strong → stronger
   word hind leg : 뒷다리 / front leg : 앞다리
   tips 형용사 strong은 단음절이므로 비교급, 최상급이
   stronger, strongest가 된다.
   해석 토끼는 뒷다리로 달려서 여기저기 움직이는데 뒷다
   리는 앞다리보다 훨씬 더 길고 힘도 세다.

4. **정답** ② as → than
   word the year before last : 재작년
   tips fewer라는 비교급이 있으므로 as → than이어야 한
   다.
   해석 그 나라는 에너지 위기 때문에 재작년보다 수입이
   더 작았다.

5. **정답** ③ as more superior → as superior
   word regard A as B : A를 B로 간주하다
   superior to : ~보다 뛰어난
   tips superior는 라틴계 비교급으로 그 앞에 more는 필
   요 없다.
   해석 밥 딜런의 노래가 젊은이들 사이에 유행하고 있는
   데, 젊은이들은 그를 다른 가수보다 뛰어나다고 여
   기고 있다.

6. **정답** ④ highest → higher
   tips '매년 (전해보다) 조금 더' 의 의미이므로 비교급이
   와야 한다. 둘 사이 (of the two) 를 비교할 때에는
   비교급이 최상급의 의미를 가진다.
   해석 세계시장에서의 금 가격이 매년 조금씩 상승해 왔다.

7. **정답** ③ the cheapest → the cheaper
   word without question : 의심할 여지없이
   tips 〈of the two〉가 있을 경우 최상급을 쓰지 않고
   〈the + 비교급〉을 쓴다.

8. **정답** ④ at less → at least
   해석 둘 혹은 그 이상의 음절을 지니고 있는 모든 영어
   단어들은 적어도 강세가 있는 음절을 하나 가지고
   있다.

1. **정답** ① is probable → is probably
   tips probable은 형용사 responsible을 수식하므로 부사
   가 되어야 한다.
   해석 그는 그의 비서가 장부정리뿐만 아니라 보고서작성
   을 책임지고 있을 것이라고 주장한다.

2. **정답** ② good → well
   word tend to 동사원형 : ~하는 경향이 있다
   tips 동사 work를 수식해야 하므로 부사가 와야 한다.
   해석 약은 처방대로 정확히 사용되지 않으면 잘 듣지 않
   는 경향이 있다.

3. **정답** ② unexpected → unexpectedly
   word run out of (= use up) : 다 써 버리다
   tips unexpected는 동사 grew를 수식하므로 부사가 되
   어야 한다.
   해석 영화 'E.T.'의 인기가 예상치도 못하게 빠른 속도로
   높아져서 가게의 E.T.인형이 재빨리 다 팔려졌다.

4. **정답** ④ awake wide → wide awake
   tips 형용사를 수식하는 부사는 형용사 앞에 오는 것이
   원칙이다.
   해석 꿈을 꾸는 동안 신체는 잠들어 있지만 두뇌의 생각
   하는 부분은 완전히 깨어 있다.

5. **정답** ③ early → earlier
   tips than으로 이어지니 early는 비교급으로 바뀌어야 한
   다.
   해석 그는 늘 지각하는 것을 걱정한다. 그래서 다른 어느
   누구보다 일찍 일어난다.

6. **정답** ③ me → I
   tips 비교의 대상은 주어이므로 me가 아니라 주격이 와
   야 한다.

7. **정답** ③ more → much
   tips very는 원급이나 현재분사를 수식하고, much는 비
   교급이나 과거분사를 수식한다.
   해석 우리가 필리핀에 가더라도 나는 상관없지만 홍콩에
   간다면 훨씬 더 좋겠다.

8. **정답** ③ lately → late
   word late : 늦은 / lately : 최근에
   해석 날씨가 나빠 비행기가 늦게 도착하도록 예정되어
   있다.

9. **정답** ③ firm → firmly
   tips 형용사 fixed를 수식하므로 부사가 되어야 한다.
   해석 어려서 형성된 습관은 나이가 들어감에 따라 확고
   하게 굳어진다.

10. **정답** ④ controlled precisely → precisely controlled
   tips 부사 precisely는 형용사 화된 과거분사 controlled 를 수식하므로 전치수식이 되어져야 한다.
   해석 어떤 종류의 컴퓨터는 온도가 정확하게 유지되는 환경에서만 제대로 작동한다.

11. **정답** ③ some → somewhat
   tips 형용사 older를 수식하므로 부사가 와야 한다.
   해석 그의 얼굴은 두드러지고 머리는 벗겨졌기 때문에 그는 내가 기대했던 것보다 다소 나이가 더 들어 보였다.

12. **정답** ④ very especially → especially
   word first aid : 응급처치 / emergency : 비상사태
   tips especially는 '특히'의 뜻으로 부사 very를 수식하는 것이 논리상 불가능하다.
   해석 응급처치 전문가들은 비상사태 때 해야 할 일을 알아두는 것이 특히 사고 시 인명을 구할 수 있는 경우가 많다는 것을 역설하고 있다.

13. **정답** ① rapid → rapidly
   word sphere : 분야 / whereas : 반면
       conservative : 보수적인

해석 마이클 씨는 4년 동안 모든 해외 계정을 취급해 왔다.

5. **정답** ③ in → on
   tips 특정한 날을 의미할 때 on을 쓴다.
       on New Year's Day : 1월 1일에

6. **정답** ③ interest → interest in
   word have an interest in : ~에 관심을 가지다
   해석 윌리엄이 연구실에서 작업하는 것을 본 사람이라면 어느 누구도 그가 화학 실험에 관심과 재능을 가지고 있다는 것을 부인할 수 없다.

7. **정답** ② in → on
   word count on : ~에 의존하다
       hard times : 어려운 시기
   해석 어려운 시기에는 자기가 필요로 하는 도움을 줄 수 있는 친구에게 의존할 수 있다.

8. **정답** ① In generally → In general
   word in general : 일반적으로 / windy : 바람이 부는
       altitude : 고도
   해석 일반적으로 로키산 지역의 기후는 고도가 높은 지역일수록 바람이 더 많이 분다.

16. 전치사

1. **정답** ④ upon → into
   word insight into~ : ~에 대한 통찰력
   해석 작가가 늘 일상적인 일들이나 주변의 사물들에 대한 관찰들로부터 시작하여, 기본적인 인간성에 대한 어떤 신선하고 심오한 통찰을 가지고 결론을 내린다.

2. **정답** ④ at → by
   tips 완료의의미가 있을 때는 by, 계속의 의미가 있을 때는 until이 쓰인다.
   해석 우이 감독은 우리들에게 보고서를 내일까지 완전히 끝내라고 말했다.

3. **정답** ⑤ off the road → on the road
   tips 길에서는 on the road를 쓴다.
   해석 패스트푸드 음식점은 길에서 시간을 소비하기를 원치 않는 시간이 바쁜 방문객들을 만족시키기 위해 1920년대에 처음 시작되었다.

4. **정답** ① Since → For
   tips since는 '과거 특정 시점 이래 지금까지'의 의미이므로 그 다음에 과거의 특정시점이 와야 하며, 일정 기간을 표시하는 표현이 올 때는 for를 쓴다.
       ex) since last year / since 1972 / since last summer

17. 일치와 화법

1. **정답** ② were → was
   tips were의 주어가 Martha이므로 단수동사가 와야 한다.
   해석 사울의 피아노 반주에 맞춘 마르타의 바이올린연주로 지난 주 연례 공연이 있었는데 대성공이었다.

2. **정답** ② has → have
   tips 주어가 all of his students로 복수이므로 복수동사가 와야 한다.
   해석 훌륭한 선생님은 그의 학생들 모두가 자기보다 낫지는 않더라도 적어도 자기만큼은 훌륭한 마음을 갖고 있다고 생각한다.

3. **정답** ① is → are
   tips a number of~ (많은~) 가 주어이면 복수 취급, the number of~ (~의 숫자) 가 주어이면 단수 취급한다.
   해석 내일 정책위원회에서 논의될 안건이 많이 있다.

4. **정답** ③ have become → has become
   word shift : 이동
       mote or less : 다소
   tips 주어는 단수인 The shift이므로 단수동사가 와야 한다.
   해석 시골에서 도시로의 인구 이동이 다소 세계적인 현상이 되었다.

5. **정답** ② are → is
   tips ‘Where or not~scientific’ 까지가 주어로서 동사는 remains이다.
   한편, 내 ②번 are의 주어는 understanding이므로 단수동사 is가 되어야 한다.
   해석 사회적 갈등에 대한 마르크스의 이해가 어떤 면에서 ‘과학적’인 것인가 아닌가 하는 문제는 하나의 난처한 문제이다.

6. **정답** ① if he had to → if he should 또는 if he were to
   tips 간접화법이라도 가정법은 시제 일치의 원칙에 해당되지 않는다. (시제 일치의 예외)
   해석 Mr. Park은 ‘만약 오늘밤 다른 숙제를 해야 한다면, 그 연주회에 갈 수 없었을 텐데’ 라고 말했다.

7. **정답** ③ moves → move
   tips 주어가 복수인 efforts이므로 복수동사가 와야 한다.
   해석 세계인구 중 오직 1%만의 노력으로 문명이 진전된다고 평가되어 왔다.

8. **정답** ① has found → have found
   tips 주어가 복수인 Sociological studies이므로 복수동사가 와야 한다.
   해석 사회학적 연구를 통하여 깊게 뿌리박힌 가치나 원리원칙들은 변화에 매우 저항적이라는 것이 밝혀져 왔다.

9. **정답** ② are → is
   tips 주어가 단수인 The president이므로 단수동사가 와야 한다.
   해석 대통령이 부인과 딸을 동반하고 오늘 오후에 있을 기자회견에 참석하기 위해 속초에서의 짧은 휴가를 마치고 돌아올 예정이다.

10. **정답** ④ were → was
   word candidate : 후보자 / eligible : 적임의
   tips neither는 단수의 개념을 지니므로 단수동사를 받는다.
   해석 영어영문학과에 신청한 두 지원자 중 어느 한 명도 장학금을 받을 자격이 없다.

11. **정답** ③ have → has
   tips 〈neither~nor〉는 단수취급 한다.
   해석 당신의 불친절한 말이나 불친절한 태도 그 어느 것도 나에게 큰 고통을 안겨 주지 못했다.

12. **정답** ③ are → is
   tips 〈One of + 복수명사〉가 주어일 때는 단수동사가 온다.
   해석 모국어가 영어가 아니면서 미국 대학에 입학하고자 하는 외국 학생에게 요구되는 것이 TOEFL시험을 보는 것이다.

13. **정답** ④ philosopher → philosophers
   tips One of 다음에는 항상 복수명사가 온다.

14. **정답** ③ philosopher → philosophers
   word sarcastic : 풍자적인
   startling : 놀랄만한, 뛰어난
   tips One of 다음에는 항상 복수명사가 온다.
   해석 마크 트웨인의 몹시 뛰어나고 풍자적인 작품들 중의 하나가 ‘지구로 부터의 편지들’ 이라는 작품이다.

15. **정답** ④ is → was
   tips 주절의 시제가 과거이므로 that이하 절의 시제도 과거이어야 한다.
   해석 부엌에 있는 부인이 그 의사에게 물이 뜨겁다는 것을 몸짓으로 알렸다.

16. **정답** ③ are → is
   tips B as well as A (= not only A but also B) 가 주어일 때 동사는 B에 수를 일치시킨다.

18. 접속사

1. **정답** ① of → of의 삭제
   word despite (= in spite of = with all = for all)
   : ~에도 불구하고
   meet (= satisfy) : 충족시키다
   해석 당신이 들었을지도 모르는 것과는 상관없이 그들은 그들의 요구가 충족되지 않더라도 파업을 하지는 않을 것이다.

2. **정답** ④ or woman → nor woman
   해석 그것은 남자이건 여자이건 사람이 내는 소리와는 전혀 다른 무서운 소음을 내었다고들 했다.

3. **정답** ① In spite → In spite of
   word prescribe : 처방하다
   have trouble (in) ~ing : ~하는데 애를 먹다
   해석 의사가 처방해 준 약을 먹었는데 엘렌은 여전히 잠이 들지 않아 애를 먹고 있다.

4. **정답** ② by → because 또는 for
   tips 내용상 by는 이유를 나타내는 등위접속사 for로 바뀌어야 한다.
   해석 링컨은 제분소와 가게를 계속 돌보아야 했다. 왜냐하면 연속되는 불행으로 주인이 사업을 포기할 수밖에 없었기 때문이다.

5. **정답** ④ or → and
   word both A and B
   (= alike A and B = at once A as B) : A, B둘 다
   onion : 양파 / flavor : 맛 (= taste)

odor : 향기 (= fragrance)

해석 양파는 독특한 맛과 향기를 지니고 있다.

6. **정답** ④ not invited → invited

    tips unless 는 if not의 의미이므로 not이 없어져야 한다.

    해석 어떤 방문객이나 친척도 의사의 허락이 없다면 환자 방에 들어갈 수 없다.

7. **정답** ③ because → that

    tips The reason의 주어이고 절이 보어로 올 때는 that이 이끄는 명사절이 와야 한다.

    해석 그가 그러한 성공을 한 사람이 된 것은 그가 결코 포기를 하지 않았기 때문이다.

8. **정답** ③ but that → but because

    word not because A but because B

      : A이기 때문이 아니고 B이기 때문이다

      drain : 파탄시키다

      inhuman : 비인간적인

19. 병치·생략·도치·삽입·강조

1. **정답** ④ encouraging → to encourage

    tips and로 연결된 병치구조이다. and앞에 to maintain으로 부정사이면 and뒤도 부정사가 와야 한다.

    해석 대략적으로 말해서 UN의 목적은 평화를 유지하고 기본적인 인권에 대한 존중을 촉진시키는 것이다.

2. **정답** ③ to take → to take 삭제

    tips 〈명사, 명사 and 명사〉가 와야 하는 병치구문이다.

3. **정답** ④ bringing → to bring

    tips 〈부정사 and 부정사〉로 된 병치구문이다.

    해석 겨울에 차로 다코타 북부 지역을 여행하고자 하는 사람은 차에 스노타이어를 달고, 두툼한 옷을 가져가도록 요구된다.

4. **정답** ③ desiring → to desire

    tips 〈명사, 명사 and 명사〉로 된 병치구문이다.

    해석 가족 문제, 사업에 대한 걱정, 그리고 무엇보다도 그림을 그리고 싶은 욕망 때문에 고갱은 타이티로 날아갔다.

5. **정답** ② clean → cleanness

    tips 〈명사, 명사 and 명사〉로 된 병치구문이다. quality, purity와 함께 supervise의 목적어가 되어야 하므로 clean은 명사 cleanness가 되어야 한다.

    해석 한국의 농수산부는 곡물의 질과 청결함과 순도를 감독한다.

6. **정답** ② of other → other

    tips the Buddha, Jesus, other great souls모두 of의 목적어로서 같은 형태 이어야 하므로 (병치) other 앞의 of가 없어져야 한다.

    해석 부처나 예수, 그리고 우리 시대에 나타났던 간디와 같은 또 다른 성인들이 지녔던 관대함과 인내 그리고 오랜 끈기를 닮으려고 노력하라.

7. **정답** ③ me → I

    tips 〈A and B〉로 된 병치구문이다. my brother and me가 주어이므로 me가 주격이 되어야 한다.

    해석 이른 아침 동생과 내가 했던 첫 번째 일은 망아지를 보러 나가는 것이었다.

8. **정답** ④ stayed → stay

    word juvenile offender : 청소년 범죄자 / custody : 감금

      on condition that~ : ~라는 조건으로

    tips that~이하의 절은 〈동사 and 동사〉로 된 병치구문이다.

      stayed는 fine과 함께 fine를 주어로 하는 동사이니 원형을 써야 한다.

    해석 그 청소년 범죄자는 즉시 직장을 구하고 6개월 동안 말썽을 피우지 않겠다는 조건으로 감금에서 풀려났다.

9. **정답** ② will judge from → judge from

    word essay competition : 백일장

      a parcel of : 한 덩어리의

      gift certificate : 상품권

    tips and전·후의 동사는 같은 시제를 쓴다. (병치)

    해석 병 만드는 회사가 백일장을 지원하는데, 이 백일장에서 학생들이 글을 제출하면 일련의 역사학자들이 이 글의 문체와 내용을 근거로 글을 심사하고, 입상자는 상품권을 받게 된다.

10. **정답** ④ closing → closed

    word then and there (= there and then) : 즉석에서

      reparation : 배상

    tips and전·후의 동사는 시제와 형이 같아야 한다. (병치)

    해석 즉석에서 나이 든 그 현명한 의사는 그 남자로 하여금 형에게 편지를 쓰게 했고, 용서를 빌었으며, 배상의 첫 단계로 수표를 끊어 주었다.

11. **정답** ③ has and possess → has

    word extra : 여분의

      anteater : 개미핥기

      sense of smell : 후각

    해석 개미핥기는 특이하게 긴 코 때문에 뛰어난 후각을 가지고 있다.

12. **정답** ④ how he wrote → way of writing

    word post-civil War : (미국의) 남북전쟁 이후

PART Ⅲ : 종합 문법

1. **정답** ② many tears ago → for many years
   word ④ did nothing except + 동사원형 (= did nothing but +동사원형)
   : ~하지 않을 수 없었다, ~할 수 밖에 없다
   tips ② many tears ago는 명백한 과거를 의미하는 부사구이므로 현재완료시제와 함께 사용할 수 없다.

2. **정답** ① bitterly → bitter
   tips ① 불완전 자동사 taste 다음에는 보어로서 형용사가 와야 한다.

3. **정답** ④ to abroad → abroad
   word ③ be on one's best behavior : 얌전하게 굴다
   go abroad : 해외에 나가다
   tips ④ 부사 abroad 앞에는 전치사가 필요 없다.

4. **정답** ③ seeing → see
   word ③ be about to + 동사원형 : ~할 예정이다

5. **정답** ① marry with → marry
   word ② in common with : ~와 공통으로
   ④ major in : ~를 전공하다
   tips ① marry는 자동사로 착각하기 쉬운 타동사로서 전치사 with가 필요 없다.

6. **정답** ① would → will
   tips ①에서 주절의 시제가 현재이므로 목적어인 if~절의 조동사는 would일 수가 없다.
   ④ If you've got~
   = If you have (have got = have)

7. **정답** ① frowning → frown
   tips ① cannot but + 동사원형 : ~하지 않을 수 없다.
   frown : 인상 쓰다, 찡그리다
   ④ a trying experiment : 성가신 일

8. **정답** ① open → opened

9. **정답** ④ knave or fool → a knave or a fool
   tips ④에서 knave와 fool은 보통명사이므로 앞에 부정관사가 와야 한다.

10. **정답** ③ affect → effect (효과, 결과, 영향)
    word ③ affect : ~에 영향을 끼치다
    devastating : 황폐화시키는

11. **정답** ② was → were
    tips ②에서 Part of는 부분을 나타내는 표현으로서 그 다음에 복수명사 the spectators 와 수를 일치시킨다.

12. **정답** ② taken jobs as → taken jobs such as
    word break into : 침입하다 / bastion : 요새
    submarine : 해군 장교
    bar A from B : A가 B하는 것을 금지하다

13. **정답** ① whom → who
    word ① give~to : ~를 ~에게 주다
    tips ①에서 I thought는 삽입 절이며, 관계대명사는 주격 (who) 이 되어야 한다.

14. **정답** ① that → what
    word ② a walking dictionary : 박식한 사람
    ④ to one's face : 면전에서

15. **정답** ① go to picnics → go on a picnic
    word ① go (out) on a picnic : 소풍 가다

16. **정답** ① for such a price → at such a price

17. **정답** ④ any more of them ~.
    → (that) they any more want to come.
    word ① on the contrary (문두)
    = to the contrary (문미) : 그와는 반대로
    ③ drive me out of my mind
    = make me crazy : 나를 미치게 만든다.

18. **정답** ④ whomever → whoever
    tips ④에서복합관계대명사가 주격으로 쓰였으므로 whoever로 고쳐야 한다.

19. **정답** ②
    → He is surprised at the mere mention of his name.
    word ② be surprised (at) : '~에 놀라다' 는 항상 사람을 주어로 한다.

20. **정답** ④
    → He will be married to her. 또는 He will marry her.

21. **정답** ②
    when have you come back → when did you come back
    tips 의문사 when은 현재완료시제와 함께 쓰이지 못한다.

22. **정답** ④ whom → whomever 또는 anyone who
    tips ④에서 동사 invite의 목적이 되려면 선행사가 포함된 관계대명사가 와야 한다.

23. **정답** ② much → many
    tips ②에서 가산명사 women앞에는 수를 나타내는 many가 와야 한다.

24. **정답** ③ followed → followed by
    word ① grow into : 자라서 ~이 되다
    ② grow out of~ (= become too old for)
    : ~하기에는 너무 나이가 들다
    ④의 해석은 그 책은 미칠 정도로 따분했다.

25. **정답** ④ told → said
    tips say는 3형식 동사이고, tell은 4형식 동사이다.
    She said that~ (O) / She told that~ (X)
    She told me that~ (O) / She said me that~ (X)
    She said to me that~ (O)

26. 정답 ① to Italy → to that of Italy
    word ① be similar to : ~와 유사하다
    　　③ take it for granted that~ : ~을 당연히 여기다
    tips ①에서 비교되는 것은 한국의 기후와 이태리의 기
    　　후이므로 Italy는 that of Italy가 되어야 한다.

27. 정답 ③ running over → being run over
    word ③ narrowly escape ~ing : 하마터면 ~할 뻔하다

28. 정답 ② than → to
    tips ②에서 라틴계 비교급 표현은 be superior to가 되
    　　어야 한다.

29. 정답 ③ intended visiting → intended to visit
    word ③ intend to + 동사원형 : ~하려고 의도하다

30. 정답 ② to write → writing
    tips ②에서 enjoy는 동명사를 목적어로 취하는 동사다.

31. 정답 ④ make him to do → make him do
    word ② make it a rule to + 동사원형
    　　　　: 반드시 ~하기로 하고 있다
    tips ④에서 make는 사역동사이므로 목적보어로 원형
    　　부정사가 와야 한다.

32. 정답 ④ having failed → to have failed

33. 정답 ③
    tips ③에서 possible이라는 형용사는 to 부정사의 목적
    　　어를 주어로 하는 문장에 쓸 수 없다.

34. 정답 ③ such delight a person → such a delight person
    tips 〈such + a (an) + 형용사 + 명사〉의 어순이다.

35. 정답 ③ anything by no one → nothing by anyone
    해석 John은 어느 누구에게도 전혀 받은 것이 없다.

36. 정답 ① white one → white
    tips ①에서 one은 물질명사 wine을 대신할 수 없다.

37. 정답 ① than → as
    tips ①은 최상급을 나타내는 표현이다.

38. 정답 ①
    tips ② sure of → sure
    　　 (be sure of + 명사 = be sure that + ⓢ + ⓥ~)
    　　③ having not → not having
    　　 (준동사의 부정은 준 동사 바로 앞에 한다)
    　　④ think → thinking
    　　 (without은 전치사이므로 동명사가 와야 한다)

39. 정답 ②
    tips ① using → used
    　　③ destroying → destroyed /
    　　④ Being a fine day → It being a fine day
    　　 (= As It was a fine day)

40. 정답 ③
    tips ① why → that
    　　② than → when 또는
    　　before 〈scarcely ~ when (before) 〉: ~하자 마자
    　　④ what → that

41. 정답 ③
    tips ① laid → lay / ② mention about → mention
    　　(mention은 타동사다)
    　　④ sit → sat

42. 정답 ④
    word ① so far as I am concerned = as for me
    　　 = for my part : 나로서는
    tips ① I → I am
    　　② beautifully → beautiful (look은 불완전 자동사)
    　　③ said → told 또는 said to

43. 정답 ①
    tips ② careful of → careful
    　　(be careful of + 명사 = be careful that + ⓢ + ⓥ~)
    　　③ were → had been
    　　(yesterday가 있으니 가정법 과거완료의 형태이다)
    　　④ have → has (many a + 명사는 단수 취급한다)

44. 정답 ①
    tips ② of → at (be good at : ~를 잘한다)
    　　③ with → of
    　　 (be full of = be filled with : ~로 가득 차 있다)
    　　④ with → in (be dressed in : ~의 옷을 입고 있다)

45. 정답 ③
    tips ① What do you do~? → What have you been~?
    　　② very good → very well
    　　④ bought it to me → bought it for me

46. 정답 ④
    tips ① to make → making
    　　② to pronounce → pronouncing
    　　③ to have → having

47. 정답 ③
    word ③ be acquaint with : ~와 친숙하다
    tips ① to play → playing
    　　② drive → driving
    　　④ going → to go

48. 정답 ①
    word ① It goes without saying that~
    　　　　: ~는 말할 필요조차 없다
    　　④ with a pipe in his mouth : 입에 파이프를 물고서
    tips ② seems to glad → seems to be glad
    　　③ besides → beside
    　　④ was gardened → gardened

49. 정답 ②
    tips ① higher → the higher
        ③ fail → fails 또는 failed
        ④ had abated → abated

50. 정답 ③
    tips ① talking → to talk / ② which를 없앤다.
        ④ read → read it (that절 안에 this book을 받는 대
        명사가 있어야 한다.)

51. 정답 ③
    tips ① our → his
        ② His both friends → both of his friends
        ④ I → me

52. 정답 ②
    tips ① spoken by → spoken of by
        ③ ought not be → ought not to be
        ④ had → had had (가정법 과거완료)

53. 정답 ③
    tips ① → Nothing can be seen in the sky.
        ② → The work cannot be done by anybody.
        ④ → A quarrel resulted from the debate.

54. 정답 ②
    tips ① → We need not have hurried yesterday.
        ③ → The story is well known to all Korean
            people.
        ④ → She is married to a rich businessman.

55. 정답 X (exciting → excited)
    tips 사람이 주어이니 과거분사 excited가 되어야 한다.
        (원인 격 분사)
        The game is exciting. (경험 격 분사)
    해석 우리 모두는 그 실험결과를 듣고 흥분했다.

56. 정답 X (is → are)
    tips police형 집합명사는 항상 정관사 the와 함께 쓰이
        며, 복수 취급한다.

57. 정답 O
    tips 감정동사 (excite, satisfy, …) 는 사람이 주어일 때는
        과거분사가 보어로 쓰인다.
    해석 서울을 방문하는 사람이면 누구나 만족스럽게 돌아
        간다.

58. 정답 O
    해석 그 사고로 그는 목숨을 잃었다.

59. 정답 X (to laugh → laughing)
    word cannot help ~ing : ~하지 않을 수 없다

60. 정답 X (books as many as possible
            → as many books as possible)

해석 선생님이 우리에게 가능한 한 많은 책을 읽으라고
    충고해 주셨다.

61. 정답 X (의미상 don't 삭제)
    해석 그의 주소를 잊어버리기 전에 적어 두어야 겠다.

62. 정답 X
    tips nothing 다음에 전치사 about이나 of가 와야 한다.
    해석 그들은 그들의 과거에 대하여 전혀 아는 바가 없는
        어떤 사람을 고용했다.

63. 정답 O
    word Don't forget to + 동사원형 : 반드시 ~한다.
    해석 다음에 여기에 올 때는 잊지 말고 사전을 가져오
        너라.

64. 정답 O
    word cannot ~ too~
        : 아무리 ~하여도 결코 지나침이 없다
    해석 친구를 선택하는데 있어서 아무리 신중하여도 결코
        지나침이 없다.

65. 정답 O
    tips = Three years have passed since my dog die.
        = My dog has been dead for three years.
        = My dog died three years ago.

66. 정답 reminds
    word remind A of B : A에게 B를 상기시켜 주다

67. 정답 disappointment, vain
    word to one's disappointment : ~가 실망하게도
        in vain : 헛되이

68. 정답 have thought

69. 정답 ability
    word as much as one can
        = to the best one's ability : ~능력껏 최선을 다하여
    해석 나는 최선을 다하여 그를 도왔다.

70. 정답 otherwise
    tips 가정법 과거완료는 과거 사실의 반대를 의미한다.

71. 정답 ③
    word prevent A from ~ing : A가 ~하는 것을 방해하다.
    해석 A : 그는 너무 수줍어서 자신의 감정을 그녀에게 알
            릴 수가 없었다.
        B : 그의 수줍음이 자신의 감정을 그녀에게 알리는
            것을 방해했다.

72. 정답 too
    word so~ that~can't
        = too~to : 너무 ~해서 ~할 수 없다

73. **정답** from

74. **정답** what, for
    tips   Why ~? = What ~ for?

75. **정답** Though
    tips   Brave as he was, ~ = Though he was brave ~
    해석 그는 아무리 용감하다 해도, 그 광경을 보았을 때 그의 얼굴은 창백해졌다.

76. **정답** owed
    해석 그는 오늘날의 자신이 된 것은 아내의 많은 도움 때문으로 여기고 있다.

77. **정답** interesting

78. **정답** still
    tips   still은 '여전히' 라는 부사로 부정문에서는 be동사나 조동사 앞에 온다.

79. **정답** brave, by
    word by oneself (= alone) : 홀로, 혼자서

80. **정답** resembles
    word look like (= take after = resemble) : 닮다

81. **정답** useless
    word It is of no use to + 동사원형
            = It is useless to + 동사원형
            = It is no use ~ing : ~해도 소용없다

82. **정답** made
    word on urgent business : 급한 볼일 때문에
    tips   목적어 him 다음에 go라는 동사원형이 왔으므로 사역동사가 와야 한다.

83. **정답** no difference
    해석 두 짐은 무게가 꼭 같다.
          = 두 짐에는 무게의 차이가 없다.

84. **정답** without
    해석 그는 매일 성경을 읽는다.
          = 그가 성경을 읽지 않고 지나는 날은 거의 없다.

85. **정답** wrong
    word out of order : 고장 난
            something wrong with : 뭔가 잘못된

86. **정답** while
    tips   be worth ~ing = be worthy of ~ing
            = be worthy to be pp
            = It is worth while to + 동사원형 : ~할 가치가 있다
    해석 이 책은 읽을 만한 가치가 있다.

87. **정답** unable

88. **정답** Be, ever, so
    해석 아무리 초라하다 할지라도 집만 한 곳은 없다.

89. **정답** were
    tips   가정법은 시제 일치의 예외이다.

90. **정답** ability
    word to the best of my ability : 나의 능력껏

91. **정답** better, than
    word know better than to + 동사원형
            : ~할 만큼 어리석지 않다

92. **정답** ①
    tips   동명사의 완료형 (having pp) 은 주절보다 앞선 시제를 의미하는데 문장에 in my youth라는 명백한 과거를 의미하는 부사구가 있으므로 ①이 답이다.

93. **정답** 없음
    tips   might have pp는 과거사실에 대한 추측을 나타내는 표현으로서 '~이었을 지도 모른다.' 는 뜻인데 같은 뜻을 지닌 표현이 보기에는 없다.

94. **정답** ④
    word when it comes to ~ing : ~라는 문제에 있어서, ~관해서
    해석 그는 돈을 쓰는 문제라면 거절한다.

95. **정답** ③
    word ought to have pp = should have pp
            : ~했어야 했는데 (못했다)
            : 이루지 못한 과거사실에 대한 유감이나 후회를 나타낼 때 쓰인다.
    해석 너는 일찍 왔어야 했다.

96. **정답** that he saw the accident

97. **정답** took me half an hour to walk to school

98. **정답** has been snowing since yesterday

99. **정답** The task was so hard that 12-year old boy could not carry it out.

100. **정답** I stayed home because of rain

101. **정답** We went on a picnic in spite of the cool weather
    word in spite of = Despite = with all = for all
            : ~에도 불구하고

102. **정답** Not knowing what to say, I remained silent
   tips 분사구문을 부정하는 not의 위치는 분사구문 앞에
       위치한다.

103. **정답** Besides holding an important office, he often
       writes good novels

104. **정답** I wish my father had been alive then

105. **정답** if
   tips whit if~ ? : 만약 ~라면 어떻게 될까?
       (염려를 나타내는 표현)
   해석 만약 인생이 완벽하다면 어떻게 될까? 만약 완벽한
       사람들과 완벽한 소유가 있는 완벽한 세상에 살게
       되어, 모든 사람과 모든 사물이 완벽한 시기에 완벽
       한 일을 한다면 어떻게 될까? 만약 원하는 모든 것
       을, 그리고 오직 원하고 있는 것을 정확히 원하는
       시기에 갖게 된다면 어떻게 될까?

106. **정답** of
   tips speak well of (= praise) 가 수동태로 바뀐 문장이다.

107. **정답** whose
   tips 관계대명사 소유격이 온다.

108. **정답** by
   word by the time : 일 때 까지
   해석 그는 사실 그녀를 몹시 싫어했고, 연극이 끝날 때
       쯤 되어서는 그녀를 거의 증오하다시피 했다.

109. **정답** by
   word with a radio beside them : 라디오를 곁에 켜놓고
   tips 부대상황을 의미하는 전치사로 with가 쓰인다.
   해석 팝송은 젊은이들 사이에 대단한 인기가 있는데, 매일
       여러 시간을 들을 수도 있다. 이를테면 곁에 라디오
       를 켜놓고 공부를 하거나 숙제를 하는 청소년들을
       보는 것은 흔한 일이다.

110. **정답** long
   word It will not be ling before~ (= soon) : 머지않아, 곧
   해석 그녀는 머지않아 곧 집으로 돌아올 것이다.

111. **정답** cannot
   해석 나는 여유가 없기 때문에 큰 아파트에서 살고 있지
       못하다.

112. **정답** what 또는 whatever
   tips 주절의 동사가 would be인 것에서 가정법이라는
       힌트를 얻을 수 있고, 부정사구 to make you happy
       속에 가정의 의미가 포함된 문장이다.
   해석 당신을 행복하게 해 주기 위해서라면 어떤 짓이라도
       나는 할 것이다.
       = 당신을 행복하게 해 주기 위해서라면 내가 무슨
       짓을 못하겠는가?

113. **정답** of
   tips 사람을 성질을 나타내는 형용사가 오면 부정사의
       의미상의 주어 앞에 of가 온다.

114. **정답** on
   해석 그녀는 게으르다. 그래서 맡은 일을 잘 해내지 못하
       고 있다.

115. **정답** without
   해석 책도 친구와 마찬가지로 조심스레 골라야 한다.
       왜냐하면 나쁜 책은 나쁜 친구들보다 더 많은 해를
       입히기 때문이다. 우연히 마주치는 책을 아무것이나
       집어서 읽는 사람은 그 책에 중독될 위험송이 있다.
       우리가 좋은 책을 읽으면 반드시 그로 인하여 우리는
       더 나아진다.

116. **정답** else
   word accuse A of B : A를 B라 하여 고소하다
       keep up : 지속하다, 유지하다
   해석 사실 논쟁은 발전에 없어서는 안 될 부분이다. 왜냐
       하면 모든 사람들이 자신을 제외한 나머지 사람들이
       게으르다고 비난하지 않으면 (발전) 속도는 계속 유
       지될 수 없을 것이다.

117. **정답** as
   word as usual : 늘 그러하듯이

118. **정답** as

119. **정답** which
   tips the way in which~ = the way (that) ~
       = the way how = the way~ = how~
   해석 조지 버나드 쇼는 영어의 단어와 발음에 관심이 있
       었다. 그는 영어를 쓰는 방법에 대해서는 만족하지
       못했었다.

120. **정답** what
   tips 관계대명사 what이 이끄는 명사절이 전치사 for의
       목적이 되고 있다.

121. **정답** which
   word grasp (= comprehend, understand, make out,
       figure out) : 이해하다
       run : 경영하다
   해석 나는 수일 내에 그 호텔을 운영하는 주된 원리가
       되는 것을 이해하게 되었다.

122. **정답** which
   word mine : 광산 / dig : 파다 / vigorous : 활기에 찬
   tips 전치사 from의 목적이며 두 문장을 연결하는 역할도
       해야 하므로 관계대명사가 와야 한다.
   해석 세계에서 가장 훌륭한 대학의 가장 훌륭한 선생이라
       면 학생들에게 실제적인 가르침을 주지는 않을 것이
       다. 그는 학생에게 파 들어가야 할 광산에 이르는 길
       을 인도하고, 파 들어가는데 필요한 도구를 제공해

주고, 학생들이 보다 열성적으로 노력할 수 있도록 도울 것이다. 그러나 학생들은 자신의 힘으로 캐낸 만큼만 소중한 것들을 가지게 될 것이다.

123. **정답** than
　word no more ~ than~
　　　: ~가 아닌 것은 ~가 아닌 것과 마찬가지다
　　　be ashamed of : ~을 부끄러워하다
　해석 자신의 행위가 옳든 그르든, 자신의 행위를 기록하는 것을 부끄러워하지 않는 것은 목욕탕에서 자신의 모습을 부끄러워하지 않는 것과 같다.

124. **정답** of
　word 〈the + 형용사의 최상급 + of + (all the) 복수명사〉
　　　: 최상급 표현

125. **정답** is a poet rather than a scholar

126. **정답** among
　tips among : ~사이에 (셋 이상)
　　　between : ~사이에 (둘 이상)
　해석 봅 가게의 사업은 향상되었는데 모리스는 사업이 향상된 것을 고객들 사이에서의 인기의 탓으로 돌렸다.

127. **정답** with
　word fight with : ~와 싸우다 / shark : 상어
　해석 우리는 죽은 고래를 옆에서 지키며 아침이 될 때까지 굶주린 상어와 싸웠다.

128. **정답** through
　word through one's influence : ~의 덕분으로
　해석 호가드는 랑돈의 작품에 감명을 받았고 호가드와 프랭클린 덕택에 랑돈은 판넬 화를 그려 수수료를 받았다.

129. **정답** for
　word care for : 돌보다
　　　be content to : ~에 만족하다
　해석 포터는 랑돈이 그녀를 돌보게 한 것에 대해 매우 흡족해한다.

130. **정답** up
　word pick up : ~를 차로 데리러 갔다
　해석 랑돈은 빌리를 Fort 4번에서 차에 태워 포츠머스로 갔다.

131. **정답** from
　word extort A from B : B로부터 A를 강탈해 가다
　해석 그는 전 아내로부터 돈을 강탈하기 위하여 아내를 찾기 원했다.

132. **정답** on
　word call on : 방문하다
　　　chat : 대화를 나누다

133. **정답** in
　tips 좁은 장소는 at, 넓은 장소는 in을 쓴다.
　해석 그의 아내가 Mingott가문의 남부사람이라는 사실 때문에 뉴욕사회에서 그는 인정 받았다.

134. **정답** of
　word die of : (병) 으로 죽다
　해석 그녀는 척크가 인플루엔자로 죽었다는 내용의 편지를 받았다.

135. **정답** on 또는 upon
　word have an influence = have an effect on = have an impact on = influence = affect : ~에 영향을 끼치다
　해석 영어로 된 성경이 셰익스피어가 영국민족의 구어와 문어에 영향을 끼친 것보다 더 많은 영향을 끼쳤다.

136. **정답** compared
　tips ~as compared with science
　　　= ~as it is compared with science

137. **정답** tracing
　word trace the lines : 선을 따라 더듬다
　tips 전치사 뒤에 동명사가 와야 한다.
　해석 나는 손가락으로 그 대리석 조각품의 윤곽을 더듬어 봄으로써 이와 같은 것을 알아낼 수 있었다.

138. **정답** in
　word take part in : ~에 참가하다

139. **정답** leading
　tips 현재분사가 부사구를 동반할 때는 후치하며, 의미상 능동이니 현재분사가 온다.
　해석 한국에서의 그 일요일 오후 내가 그 도시의 교외로 이르는 다리 쪽으로 걷고 있었는데 Bellock마차가 화물차에게 길을 내주기 위해 한쪽으로 급히 움직였다.

140. **정답** more powerful
　tips than이 있으므로 형용사의 비교급이 필요하다.
　해석 그가 비록 육체적으로는 나보다 훨씬 힘이 세다 할지라도 그 어느 누구도 결코 나를 움직일 수 없을 것이다.

141. **정답** read
　해석 나는 남들이 나에게 읽어 주었던, 그리고 인생의 가장 깊은 곳을 보여 주었던 그런 책들을 읽고 싶다.

142. **정답** into
　word look into (= investigate) : 조사하다

143. **정답** for
　word make up for (= compensate for = atone for)
　　　: 보상 (보충) 하다

144. **정답** to

word be indifferent to (= be uninterested in)
: ~에 무관심하다

145. **정답** to

word abide by : 준수하다, (약속을) 지키다

146. **정답** on

word look down on (= despise) : 멸시하다

147. **정답** called

tips   my name은 call의 대상이므로 과거분사가 와야
한다.

148. **정답** sit 또는 sitting

tips   see는 지각동사로서 목적보어로 원형부정사, 분사
모두 올 수 있다.

149. **정답** (1) in, (2) to, (3) 해석 참조, (4) ④

word A is to B what(as)C is to D : A와 B의 관계는 C와
D의 관계와 같다
be in relation to : ~와 관계가 있는
be superior to : ~보다 우수한

해석 굶주림이 음식과 관계가 있듯이 열정은 인생과 관계
가 있다. 축구 보기를 좋아하는 사람은 그렇지 못한
사람보다 그만큼 더 나은 것이다.

150. **정답** useful

tips   목적보어이므로 형용사가 와야 한다.

151. **정답** (1) ①, (2) ②, (3) ④

word as a result of : ~의 결과로서

make fuss : 소동을 피우다
chase (= run after) : 추격하다

해석 나는 돈이나 표와 같은 간단한 것을 특정 주머니 속
에 넣어두는 단순한 습관마저도 들여놓지 못해서 매
일 고통을 받는다. 어떤 사람은 자신의 몸에 많은 돈
을 휴대하고 있음을 알면서도 몸을 무는 벌레를 좇
아 온몸을 뒤지는 사람처럼 야단법석을 떨지 않고서
는 돈을 찾아낼 수 없다는 것이 매우 어처구니없는
일이다.

152. **정답** (1) ④, (2) ①, (3) ④

해석 큰 줄기를 좇아 글을 읽고 세세한 것에 시간을 낭비
하지 마라. 단편을 읽을 때는 구성의 줄거리를 따르
라. 장편을 읽을 때는 전체에 대한 개략적인 관점을
재빨리 이해하도록 하라. 논픽션을 읽을 대는 주제
를 파악하는데 전념해야 한다.

153. **정답** (1) rolling, (2) fasten

tips   (1) 은 전치사 of의 목적이니 동명사 rolling이 와야
하고, (2) 는 to부정사의 형태이니 동사원형인 fasten
이 와야 한다.

해석 소매를 말아 올리는 대신 그녀는 옷을 가슴께에 묶
어둘 수 있도록 핀을 꽂았다.

154. **정답** travel → travelling / run → run
take → took / draw → drawing

해석 내가 친구와 함께 대학 입학하기 전의 시간을 보내
기 위해 유럽 여행을 했을 때의 나이가 18세였다. 대
부분 시간을 그림 그리는데 보냈지만 돈을 다 써버
렸기 때문에 칸에서는 그림 그리는 일을 했다.

PART Ⅳ : 재 진술

1. **정답** ④

word by no means (= anything but = on no account
= not at all = far from ~ing
= not ~ by any means = never) : 결코 ~이 아닌
self- evident : 명백한

해석 교육을 받은 사람이 그렇지 못한 사람보다 행복하
다는 것은 결코 확실한 게 아니다.

2. **정답** ③

tips   ① = Philadelphia is the largest city in America.

3. **정답** ③

word surfeit : 과음, 과식 / raspberry : 나무딸기
tart : (과일이 든) 파이
fall ill : 병이 나다

해석 어느 날 Leonore는 나무딸기가 든 파이를 과식해서
병이 났다.

4. **정답** ④

word A is not B any more than C is D
= A is not any more B than C is D
= A is no more B than C is D
= A is not B just as C is D
: A가 B가 아닌 것은 C가 D가 아닌 것과 같다

해석 아름다운 깃털이 있다고 하여 아름다운 새가 아닌
것처럼 멋진 옷을 입었다고 하여 훌륭한 신사인 것
은 아니다.

5. **정답** ①

word make A of B : B를 A가 되게 하다
plug : 꾸준히 일하다
vigor : 활력
the vocabulary of street : 거리에서 보통 사람들이
쓰는 말
stick to : (구어) 참다, 견디다

해석 만약 당신의 인생을 무엇인가 중요한 인생이 되게 하고 싶으면, 꼭 필요한 덕목이 근면이다. 근면이란 말이 어떤 뜻인지 알기만 하면, 어떤 단어를 택하는 가는 중요한 게 아니다. concentration, industry, hard work는 모두 diligent의 동의어들이 혹은 일상의 속된 표현을 쓰고 싶다면 plugging, sticking it와 같은 말들은 세련미는 덜하지만 보다 힘 있게 그 핵심적인 의미를 전달해 줄 것이다.

6. **정답** ①

word there is no doubt that~ : ~을 의심할 여지가 없다
    primitive man : 원시인
    of no suspicious (= not suspicious) : 의심할 바 없는
해석 원시인들이 수를 셀 때 손가락을 이용했다는 것은 분명하다.

7. **정답** ④

word play a part (= play a role) : ~한 역할을 하다
tips 〈부정의 주어 (Few~) + as ~ as〉는 최상급의 의미이다.
해석 과학역사에 있어서 뉴턴만큼 중요한 역할을 한 과학자는 거의 없다.

8. **정답** ②

word indiscriminately : 무분별하게
tips '외국의 문물을 맹목적으로 수용해서는 안 된다' 는 내용의 글이다.
해석 전후 무분별하게 외국의 관습과 유행을 받아들이는 경향이 있는데, 이로 인하여 우리나라의 미풍이 종종 파괴되어 참 섭섭하다.

9. **정답** ②

word turn-ups and downs fo economic conditions
    : 경제상황의 변동

10. **정답** ③

word eternity : 영원한 세계, 내세
    cure A of B : ㅁ에게서 B를 고치다

11. **정답** ③

word The British : 영국인들 / brace for~ : ~을 감행하다
    coincide with~ : ~와 때를 맞추다

12. **정답** ①

word leave no room for~ : ~할 여지가 없다
    superstition : 미신
해석 균형 있는 적절한 감각을 가지면 미신에 대한 여지를 가질 틈이 없다.

13. **정답** ③

word to no end (= in vain) : 헛된, 허사의
해석 메리는 그녀의 아버지에게 그녀가 사실을 말하고 있다는 것을 확신시키려 했다. 그러나 그것은 모두 허사였다.

14. **정답** ①

word elimination : 제거 / not at all : 결코 ~이 아닌
해석 폭력을 싫어하여 이를 감소시키고 가능하다면 완전히 없애버리기 위해 노력하는 것을 가장 바람직한 일의 하나로 여기는 사람들이 많다. 나는 이러한 폭력을 없애고 싶어 하는 바람을 가진 사람들 중의 하나이다.

15. **정답** ③

tips 〈부정어 (don't) + 비교급 (uglier) + (than the boy)〉로 되어 있는 의미상 최상급의 표현이다.
해석 아기를 보며 그 운전사는 말했다. "오 맙소사! 정말 못생긴 아이로군! 이보다 더못생긴 아기는 본 적이 없는 것 같다."

16. **정답** ②

word a poor decision : 잘못된 판단
    straddle the fence : 우물쭈물하다
    find out : 알아내다
    hold fast to (= adhere to = stick to = cling to)
    : 고수하다

17. **정답** ②

word weapon : 무기 / hardy : 강건한
    swoon : 의식을 잃어버리다

PART Ⅴ : 영작문

1. **정답** ②

tips 〈keep +목적어 + ~ing〉구문이며, 시제는 기다리게 한 것이 미안한 것보다 앞선 시제이니 부정사의 완료시제가 와야 한다.

2. **정답** ④

tips convenient는 사람을 주어로 하지 못하는 형용사이다.

3. **정답** ③

tips no = not~any이지만 any가 포함된 표현을 주어로 하여 부정문을 만들지 못한다.
    No one knows = God knows = Who know~?

4. **정답** ③

tips think, believe, imagine, guess, say가 주절의 동사일 때 간접의문문의 의문사는 문두로 나간다.

5. **정답** ③

   tips ① It's natural 뒤의 that절에는 should가 쓰인다.
   (이성적 판단의 의미)
   ② might as well은 had better와 같은 의미로「~하
   는 편이 낫겠다.」의 뜻이다.
   ③ may well + 동사원형은「~하는 것은 당연하다」
   의 뜻이다.
   ④ 전치사 by는 for로 바뀌어야 한다.

6. **정답** ①

   tips = We cannot overstate the importance of health.
   = It is impossible for us to state the importance of
   health too much.
   = Too much cannot be estimated about the
   importance of health.

7. **정답** ④

   tips How long~은 계속을 나타내는 완료시제에 쓰이는
   표현이다.

8. **정답** ③

   tips A is different from B (A와 B는 다르다) 에서 A와 B
   는 같은 표현이어야 한다.
   (병치) mine = my viewpoint

9. **정답** ②

   tips = A is five times as many as B
   = A is five times more than B
   = A is five times the number of B

10. **정답** ③

   tips ③ = It seems that she got there yesterday.

11. **정답** ①

   word a next-door neighbor : 이웃사람
   neighborhood : 근처
   neighboring : 이웃의

12. **정답** ①

13. **정답** ③

   tips make yourself at home
   = make yourself comfortable

14. **정답** ①

   tips ② = ③ = ④ = You have nothing to do with this.
   = This is no concern of yours.

15. **정답** ②

16. **정답** ④

17. **정답** What, brought

18. **정답** make

   word make a mistake (= make a blunder = commit an
   error = commit a blunder) : 실수하다

19. **정답** What, best

   word do one's best (= try one's best = do all that one
   can do) : 최선을 다하다

20. **정답** worth

   word be worth ~ing
   (= be worthy to be pp = be worthy of ~ing = It is
   worth while to 동사원형 = deserve to be pp)
   : ~할 가치가 있다

21. **정답** sharp, sense, of, humor

22. **정답** It, raining

23. **정답** last

24. **정답** kept, waiting

25. **정답** take

   tips have one's picture taken
   : '남에게 자신의 사진이 찍히다' 의 뜻

26. **정답** watch

27. **정답** ④

   tips A is no more B than C
   : C가 B가 아니듯이 A도 B가 아니다
   A is no less B than C
   : C가 B이듯이 A도 B하다

28. **정답** It seems that few of us have different view about
   what we should do.

29. **정답** It may be natural that many people (should) feel that
   there is nothing important one can do in the great
   modern society.

30. **정답** Most people have to work to live.

31. **정답** Let's take part in creating new korea.

32. **정답** Man was created in the images of God.

33. **정답** Since all (men) have sinned and fall short of the glory
   God…

34. **정답** People cannot say that man is necessarily
   influenced by environment.

35. **정답** All people naturally have freedom, equal dignity and
   right.

36. **정답** Nowadays, weather is not so cold as it was.
   Among the various reasons, air pollution evidently
   seems to be one of them.

37. **정답** I make it a rule to go climbing every weekend. It is
   very delightful to be familiar with nature, much more
   to have fresh air.

38. **정답** From the long term point of view, education is the most important of all the policies. Because it is education that improves people's level of consciousness and the ability to solve all the difficult problems.

39. **정답** I get up early every morning and go up the mountain. The morning air is so clear as to feel refreshed. I will keep this habit as usual.

40. **정답** One of my roommates is studying engineering, another economics, and a third, electronic engineering (or electronics).

41. **정답** I will thank you for your informing me of something as soon as possible.

42. **정답** If the sun were to rise in the west, I would not break my promise.

43. **정답** Would you please tell us what you think of our suggestion? 또는 Would you please tell us what your opinion about our suggestion is?

44. **정답** "Watch out! Watch for careless drivers!"

45. **정답** He tampered with the inside of a watch so carelessly that he broke it.

46. **정답** Three of the men took turns at driving to prevent one person from feeling so tired.

47. **정답** To keep early hours makes a man healthy.

48. **정답** Of the two, he chose the more expensive.

49. **정답** How may more bus stops do we have before we get to the station?

50. **정답** Tourism is an important source of revenue for Korea.

51. **정답** Any book will do so long as it is interesting.

52. **정답** by
  tips The boy was younger than Tom by several years.

53. **정답** months' leave of absence
  word pregnant : 임신한
        leave : 휴가
        leave of absence : 휴가 기간
  해석 나디아는 사장에게 자기가 임신해서 2개월쯤 후 4개월간의 휴가를 얻겠다고 방금 알렸다.

54. **정답** ②
  tips Further information remains to be seen

55. **정답** in
  tips She had great difficulty in persuading them to stop it.

56. **정답** different as they are (= though they are different)

57. **정답** (1) ③-⑤-④-①-⑥-②-⑦
        (2) ②-⑥-③-④-⑤-⑦-①
        (3) ④-⑦-①-③-⑤-②-⑥
        (4) ⑥-④-②-①-⑤-③

58. **정답** (1) Birds of a feather flock together.
        (2) Heaven helps those who help themselves.
        (3) There is no royal road to learning.
        (4) Too many cooks spoil the broth.
        (5) The proof of the pudding is in the eating.

PART Ⅵ : 생활영어

전화의 상대편에게 좀 기다려 달라고 할 때
→ Please hold the line a moment.

전화로 전갈을 부탁할 때
→ Would you mind taking a message for me?

전화 걸려온 사람이 다른 전화를 받고 있을 때
→ I'm sorry, but Mr. Ha is speaking on another line.

전화가 잘못 걸려 왔을 때
→ I'm afraid you have the wrong number.

(당신이) 전화를 잘못 거셨습니다.
→ You (must) have the wrong number.
→ You dialed / called / phoned the wrong number.

(제가) 전화를 잘못 걸었습니다.
→ You are / must be a wring number.
→ I have the wrong number.

전화를 뒤에 걸어 달라고 할 때
→ Please call me up later.

내선에 연결해 달라고 부탁할 때
→ Please give me Extension Two-Seven-Five.

사람을 전화로 불러 달라고 부탁할 때
→ May I speak / talk to a person.
→ Will you call a person to the phone.

1. **정답** ③
   tips This is Susan speaking : 제가 수잔입니다.
         This is she / he : 접니다.

2. **정답** ④
   tips call a person collect : 요금 수신인 지불로 전화를
         걸다.
         collect : (전화 / 전보 / 소포) 요금 수령인 지불로

3. **정답** ②
   tips leave a message : 전언을 남기다
         take a message : 전언을 받다

4. **정답** ②
   tips May I take a message : 전하실 말씀이 있습니까?
         Are you calling long distance : 장거리 전화입니까?

5. **정답** ④
   tips Extension : 구내전화
         Do you know his extension?
         : 그의 교환번호를 아십니까?

6. **정답** ②
   tips Hold on : 기다리세요.
         Hang up : 전화를 끊으세요.

7. **정답** ②
   tips How can I (contact / reach / catch / find / see) you?
         : 어떻게 연락을 드릴까요?

8. **정답** ②
   tips right now : 지금 당장 (동사는 현재형 / 완료형)
         just now : 지금 막, 방금 (동사는 과거형)

9. **정답** ③
10. **정답** ①
11. **정답** (1) ①, (2) ④

12. **정답** ④
    tips Your party is on the phone / line. party : 관계자
          Call me at the office, extension four two.
          : 회사의 내선 42번으로 전화해 주세요.
          Go ahead, please : (교환이) 나왔습니다, 말씀하십
          시오.

13. **정답** ahead
    tips Go right ahead or Go ahead : 네, 그렇게 하세요.

14. **정답** ②

15. **정답** ④
    tips ④ → I'll phone again. 또는 I'll call you back.

16. **정답** ③

17. **정답** ①
    tips station-to-station : 번호통화
          person-to-person : 지명통화

18. **정답** ①
    tips Would / Do you mind ~ing?에 대한 전형적인 대답
          → 거절할 때 : Yes, I am sorry
          → 승낙할 때 : (No), certainly not,
                        (No), of course not
                        (No), not at all
                        (No), not in the least

19. **정답** ③
    tips 의문문에 대한 응답 시 긍정으로 묻건, 부정으로 묻
          건 그 대답은 [Yes , 긍정문] 또는 [No , 부정문]의 형
          태가 된다.

20. **정답** ②

21. **정답** ②
    tips Do you mind my opening the door?
          = Do you mind if I open the door?

22. **정답** ②
    tips apply for : ~에 지원하다
          apply to : ~에 적용하다
          talk~into… : ~에게 …하도록 설득하다
          talk~out of… : ~에 …하지 않도록 설득하다

23. **정답** ①
    tips A의 마지막 대답이 No이니 빈 곳은 Yes나 No를 요
          하는 질문이 와야 한다.

24. **정답** (1) ④, (2) ③
    tips on the tip of one's tongue
          : 금방 입에서 나올 것 같은
          It'll come to you : 생각나겠죠.
          Gee : (구어) 체, 허, 이런, 아이 깜짝이야

25. **정답** (1) ④, (2) ①
    tips sort of : (부사) 얼마간, 다소, 약간 (= a little) ex)
          I sort of like music.
          How would you like it? : 어떻게 해드릴까요?
          I will take it black. : 블랙으로 하겠습니다.
          a break : 휴식

26. **정답** ①
27. **정답** ①
28. **정답** ③
29. **정답** ①
30. **정답** ③
31. **정답** ③

32. **정답** ②
    tips What time shall we make it?
          : (약속할 때) 몇 시로 할까요?
          Let's make it at six : 6시로 합시다.
          the City Hall : 시청

33. **정답** ④
    tips be obliged to a person : ~에게 감사하다.
          be obliged to 동사원형 : ~하지 않으면 아니 되다.
          oblige : ~에게 강요하다, ~을 고맙게 여기게 하다
          (수동형)

34. **정답** ①
    tips You, idiot! : 이 바보야!

35. **정답** ②
    tips (I am) good / glad to see you. : 만나서 반갑습니
          다.

36. **정답** ①

37. **정답** ①
    word make one's day : ~을 매우 행복하게 하다
         live up to : ~에 따라 살아가다
         in return for : ~의 답례로

38. **정답** ②
    word Make oneself at home
          (= Make oneself comfortable)
          : 편히 하다, 어려워하지 않다.

39. **정답** ①
    tips fire (= dismiss) : 해고하다
          What makes you say that.
          : 무슨 근거로 그렇게 이야기하니?

40. **정답** ②
    tips keep up to one's standard : ~의 수준에 미치다.
          work the office : 사무실을 운영하다.
          She is wrong with work : 그녀는 일을 잘 못한다.
          give one's a break : ~에게 휴식시간을 주다.

41. **정답** ④
    tips take leave of : ~와 작별 인사하다

42. **정답** ③

43. **정답** ②

44. **정답** ①
    tips Iam sorry에 대한 응답
          → That's (quite) all right. / That's OK.
          Don't worry (about it).
          I beg you pardon?
          (= Pardon me? = Excuse me?) 는 끝이 올라간다.

: 다시 한 번 말씀해 주세요?

45. **정답** ③
    tips Do you have the time? : 몇 시입니까?
          → Yes, I have it at six : 여섯 시입니다
          What time do you have? : 몇 시입니까?
          → I have it at six : 여섯 시입니다.

46. **정답** ①
    tips 시계가 빠를 때 : My watch gains five minutes a day.
          = My watch goes(is) five minutes fast a day.
          시계가 느릴 때 : My watch loses five minutes a day.
          = My watch goes(is) five minutes slow a day.

47. **정답** ③
    tips There is something the matter with him.
          : ~이 고장 나다, 아프다
          = There is something wrong with him.

48. **정답** (1) ③, (2) ①

49. **정답** ①
    word go ahead : 해 보세요
          I don't mind : 나는 상관하지 않습니다.

50. **정답** ①
    해석 "각자 내기로 합시다."
          "아닙니다. 이것은 내가 내겠습니다."

51. **정답** ②

52. **정답** ②
    word let me treat you to lunch : 제가 점심대접을 하겠습
          니다.
    해석 "내가 오늘 점심을 대접하려고 하는데 어때요?"
          "나도 그러고 싶지만, 오늘은 다른 일이 있어요."

53. **정답** ②
54. **정답** ②

55. **정답** ③
    word What would(do) you say to~?
          = What do you think about~?
          : ~하는 것이 어떻겠습니까? (권유를 나타내는 표현)

56. **정답** ②
57. **정답** ③

58. **정답** (1) ③, (2) ②, (3) ①, (4) ②
    tips Have you been a patient here?
          : 이 병원에서 진찰받은 적이 있나요?
          What time shall we make it?
          : (약속을) 몇 시로 할까요?
          Let's make it this afternoon
          : 오늘 오후로 합시다.

59. **정답** ④
60. **정답** ③
61. **정답** ②
62. **정답** ③
63. **정답** ①
64. **정답** ②

65. **정답** ②
   tips ② → How do you like your coffee?
      (어떻게 해드릴까요?)

66. **정답** ②
67. **정답** ③
68. **정답** ②

69. **정답** (1) ②, (2) ④, (3) ①
   tips have a runny nose : 콧물이 흐르다
      try an antihistamine : 항히스타민제를 복용하다

70. **정답** ④
   word the City Hall : 시청 / I'm a stranger here myself
       : 나도 여기는 처음입니다
      resident : 주민

71. **정답** ③
72. **정답** ④
73. **정답** ①
74. **정답** ④

75. **정답** (1) ②, (2) ④
   word trace one's step : 왔던 길을 더듬어 살피다
      wallet : 지갑
      lift : 소매치기하다 / declare : 신고하다

76. **정답** ④
77. **정답** ③
78. **정답** ③

79. **정답** (1) hotel charge, or hotel bill (2) label
      (3) check-in (4) check-out

80. **정답** (1) ① (2) ③ (3) ④ (4) ④ (5) ④

81. **정답** ④ → Could you tell me where I can go to the Samil
      Building ?

82. **정답** ③
83. **정답** ②
84. **정답** ③
85. **정답** ④
86. **정답** ②
87. **정답** ②

88. **정답** ①
   word No way ! : 절대 안 돼 !

89. **정답** ③
   tips ③ = May I help you?

90. **정답** ①
   word I have no idea = I don't know
      I have an idea = I know

91. **정답** ①

92. **정답** ③
   word How did you like~? : ~이 어떠했니?

93. **정답** ②
   word make a confession : 고백하다

94. **정답** ④
   해석 A : 실례합니다. 1달러짜리 바꿀 잔돈이 있으세요?
      B : _____.
      A : 고맙습니다. 어떤 것이든 좋습니다.
      ① 지금 잔돈이 없습니다.
      ② 저 구석에 동전교환기가 있습니다.
      ③ 무엇을 필요로 하는지 모르겠습니다.
      ④ 25센트짜리와 10센트짜리뿐인데 괜찮으시겠습
        니까?

95. **정답** ①

96. **정답** ②
   tips What for~ = Why~

97. **정답** ②
   tips nationality (국적) 을 묻는 질문에는 무관사로 표현한
      다.

98. **정답** ②
99. **정답** ④
100. **정답** ①
101. **정답** ①
102. **정답** ④
103. **정답** ②

104. **정답** ①
   word Do you have the time? = What time is it?

105. **정답** ①
   word (The) sane to you : 당신도요

106. **정답** ②
   word I'd be happy to : 도움요청을 받았을 때 쾌히 승낙
      할 때 쓰이는 정중한 표현

PART Ⅶ : 단문 독해

1. **정답** (1) ③, (2) ③
   - **word** not~every : 모두 ~인 것은 아니다 (부분 부정)
     self-distrust : 자기 불신
     indispensable : 필수불가결한
   - **해석** 우리가 모든 길을 다 가 볼 수는 없다. 성공은 한 우물을 팔 때 가능해진다. 이상을 갖고 살면 성공적인 삶을 살 수 있다. 성공이 행운이나 우연에 매달리는 경우가 줄어 들고 있다. 자기 불신이 대부분 실패의 원인이다. 성공의 중요한 그리고 없어서는 안 될 요소는 인격인 것이다.

2. **정답** (1) ④, (2) ①
   - **word** well-suited : 적절한 / adult : 성인
     dosage : (1회) 복용량
     consult : ~에게 조언을 구하다
   - **tips** (1) dosage와 비슷한 것은? → ④ : 추천되는 양
     (2) 이 약을 4세 어린이에게 복용코자 할 때 어떻게 해야 하는가?
     →① : 의사와 상담하다
   - **해석** 아스피린이나 아스피린이 들어있는 약을 복용할 수 없는 사람에게 특히 적합함.
     복용량 : 성인-매일 4번씩 한번에 1~2정, 6세 이하 어린이가 사용하거나 10일 이상 사용할 시에는 의사와 상담할 것.

3. **정답** ④
   - **word** mythical : 신화적인 / cool down : 식다
     Conservative Member of Parliament : 보수당 의원
   - **해석** 22세 때 그녀는 신화적인 아더 왕을 주제로 한 첫 번째 책을 출간했다. 그녀는 보수당 의원인 휴 프레이저와 결혼한 후 세 명의 아들과 두 명의 딸을 낳은 후에도 계속 글을 썼다. 그 결과 저작이 23권이다.

4. **정답** (1) ③, (2) ②
   - **word** indisputable : 의문의 여지가 없는
     implausible : 받아들이기 어려운
     misinterpreted : 오역된
   - **해석** 존과 로레타의 이야기를 믿을 것이다.

5. **정답** ②
   - **word** consist in (= lie in) : ~에 있다
     vital : 필수적인, 중요한
     matter (= count = be important) : 중요하다
     soul murder : 정신적인 살인행위
   - **해석** 기술교육의 문화적 측면은 학생들로 하여금 문학을 즐기게 하려는 노력 속에 존재해야 한다. 그들이 무엇을 알고 있나 하는 것은 중요하지 않지만, 흥미는 필수적인 것이다. 영국의 유명 대학들은 그들의 직접적인 권위 하에 학생들에게 셰익스피어 희곡에 관한 시험을 치르게 하여 흥미를 얼마 만큼은 상실케 하고 있으니, 정신적인 살인 행위로 기소되어 마땅하다.

6. **정답** (1) ④, (2) ③, (3) ④

7. **정답** ④
   - **word** generalization : 일반론 / observer : 관찰자
     abstract thought : 추상적 사고
     world view : 세계관
     be fond of (= have a liking to = like) : 좋아하다
   - **해석** 거의 모든 관찰자들이 받아들이게 될 영국에 대한 두 가지 일반론이 있다. 첫째는 영국인이 재능을 지니지 못했다는 점이다. 그들은 이태리인이나 독일인처럼 음악적이지 못하고 그림이나 조각도 프랑스에서처럼 번성했던 적이 없었다. 둘째는 영국인은 유럽인들처럼 지적이지 못하다는 점이다. 영국인들은 추상적인 사고에 대해 공포심을 가지고 있으며 철학이나 체계적인 '세계관'을 가져야겠다는 필요성도 느끼지 못하고 있다. 영국인들이 자신들을 위한 주장을 펴기 좋아하는, 실용적 사람들이라는 점에서 그들이 지성적이지 않다는 것을 또한 알 수 있다.

myth / glorify
   - **word** myth : 신화 / glorify : 찬양하다
     epic : 서사시 / accomplishment : 업적
     deed : 행위 / character : 등장인물, 성격
   - **해석** 신화가 신의 업적을 찬양하는 것인 것과 마찬가지로, 서사시는 인간의 업적이야 말로 훌륭하고 다시 이야기할 만한 가치가 있는 것임을 노래하고 있는 것이다.

8. **정답** ②
   - **word** calling (= vocation) : 직업
     would as soon A as B (= would rather A than B)
     : B하느니 차라리 A하는 게 더 낫다.
     do without (= manage without = dispense with)
     : ~없이 지내다
     the first being~ = for the first is~
     bodily refreshment : 신체적인 청량제
   - **해석** 우유 배달부는 아침 일찍 배달해야 하는 직업인데 경쟁자가 하나도 없다. 그 경쟁자는 바로 신문 배달 소년이다. 우유와 신문 둘 다 아침식사 시간에 필요한 것인데 런던의 사업가는 후자 (신문) 보다 전자 (우유) 없이 지내는 것이 더 낫다고 여길 것이다. 우유가 신체적인 청량제라면 신문은 정신적인 청량제이기 때문이다.

9. **정답** (1) ④, (2) ②
   - **word** 1940's : 1940년대 / native : 원시적인
     explorer : 탐험가 / jealous : 시기심이 많은
     warlike : 호전적인
   - **해석** 1940년대 세 명의 불란서인 들이 원시적인 카누를 타고 니제르 강을 항해했다. 2,600마일을 항해하는 동안 그들은 그들에게 협조적인 아프리카 원주민들을 방문하곤 했다. 탐험가들은 그들과의 대화 내용을 기록하고 니제르 강 주변의 원시생활을 보여 주는 수천 장의 사진을 찍었다.

10. **정답** ④
   - **word** specific : 특정한

helpless : 어쩔 수 없는, 속수무책의
brotherly love : 형제애 / unfold (= open) : 펼치다
by ~ing : ~ 함으로써
compassion for : ~에 대한 연민
해석 사랑은 특정 개인과의 관계가 아니다. 아무런 힘이 없는 사람에 대한 사랑이 형제애의 시작이다. 자신의 살과 피를 사랑하는 것은 어떤 성취를 얻지 못한다. 어떤 목적에 도움이 되지 않는 사람에 대한 사람에 대한 사랑 안에서만 사랑은 구현 되기 시작한다. 의지할 곳 없는 사람에 대한 연민을 가짐으로써, 인간은 형제를 위한 사랑을 시작하는 것이다.

11. 정답 ②
word be accustomed to : ~에 익숙해지다
actually : 사실상 / invention : 발명
take it for granted that~ : ~을 당연한 것으로 여기다
해석 우리는 신문, 책, 잡지 등에 너무 익숙해 있기 때문에 늘 읽고, 쓸 수 있음을 당연히 여기고 있다. 사실상 모든 발명품 중 가장 중요한 것인 문자는 인류의 긴 역사에서 보면 비교적 최근의 것이다.

12. 정답 ④
word interpret : 해석하다 / definition : 정의
briefly : 간략히 말해서
restraint : 제지, 구속
control : 지배, 통제
misinterpretation : 잘못된 해석
regardless of : ~에 상관없이

해석 자유라는 단어는 종종 잘못 해석되고 있다. 사전에는 이에 대한 많은 해석이 있는데 요약하면 자유는 구속이나 통제로부터의 자유를 의미한다. 이러한 간략한 정의 때문에 잘못된 해석이 생기고 있다. 많은 사람들은 자유란 결과에 상관없이 좋아하는 것은 무엇이든 할 수 있다는 것을 의미한다고 생각한다. 자유는 결코 통제없이 마음대로 하는 것은 아니다.

13. 정답 (1) ①, (2) ③
word cancer : 암
해석 미국의 사망 원인 중 두 번째인 암으로 인하여 매년 385,000명의 미국인이 죽고 있다.

14. 정답 (1) ③, (2) ①
word miner : 광부 / trap : 갇히다 / collapse : 붕괴하다
rescue : 구출하다 / stretcher : 들것
해석 붕괴된 금광 속 지하 200피트에서 28일 동안 갇혀 있던 두 명의 광부가 오늘 구출됐다. 그들은 진흙투성이였지만, 하얀 시트에 싸여 들것에 실려 금광 밖으로 운송될 때 웃고 있었다.

15. 정답 (1) ③, (2) ④
word muscle : 근육 / at rest : 쉴 때
generate : 발산하다
internal organ : 신체 내부기관
metabolic activity : 신진대사
해석 몸이 움직일 때는 근육에서 열이 나지만 쉬고 있을 때는 신체 내부기관들이 신진대사를 할 때를 제외하면 거의 열이 나지 않는다.

PART Ⅷ : 문장 완성형 독해

1. 정답 ③
word point of view : 견해 / compulsion : 강세, 강요
해석 태초부터 사람들은 다른 사람들에게 자신의 견해를 받아들이도록 설득시키려고 노력해 왔다. 그들은 이제 설득 기술의 숙달 자가 되었다.

2. 정답 ①
word abundant : 풍부한 / resource : 자원 / mineral : 광물 mine : 광산 / heritage : 유물, 유산
해석 철, 석탄, 석유는 우리의 풍부한 자원들의 보기이다.

3. 정답 ②
word astronomical observation : 천체 관측 / unmanned telescopes : 무인 망원경 / make observations (which are) not possible / observatory : 관측소
해석 오랫동안 인간은 지상에서 천체를 관측할 수 있었다. 현재는 기구 속에 무인 망원경을 하늘 높이 보내 지상의 관측소에서는 불가능한 관찰을 할 수 있다.

4. 정답 ③

word sparkle : 반짝이다
해석 바다는 매우 밝은 색의 빛들로 반짝였다. 그 위로 하늘에는 구름 한 점 없었다.

5. 정답 ②
word immoderate : 과도한
consistent : 일관된, 모순되지 않는
reluctant : 꺼리는 (= unwilling)
according to : ~에 따라서
해석 독서력 신장이 반드시 나이에 따라 향상되는 것은 아니지만 어떤 일정한 패턴이 있다.

6. 정답 ③
word (by) far : 훨씬 더 / more than sufficiency : 충분하고도 남는 / offspring : 자녀
해석 만일 인간의 침묵할 줄 아는 능력이 말하는 능력과 동일하다면 인간사는 틀림없이 더욱 명랑해질 것이다. 그러나 사람들이 혀를 다스리는 일이야 말로 가장 어렵다는 것을 우리는 경험을 통하여 익히 알고도 남음이 있다.

7. **정답** ④

word be compared to : ~에 비유되다
tear down : 철거하다
make way for : ~에게 길을 내주다
evolution : 진화 / zoological : 동물학적인
discarded : 버려진
not A but B : A가 아니고 B

해석 발전해 가는 과학에서의 변화는 새 건물에 밀려나 헐리는 건물과 비유하지 말고, 오히려 동물적 형태의 점진적 진화에 비유하여야 한다. 우리는 버려진 이론들이 쓸모없다거나 헛된 것이라고 생각해서는 안 된다.

8. **정답** ②

word athletic game : 육상경기 / self-control : 자제심
be likely to : ~하기 쉬운

해석 육상경기는 종종 너무나 치열하여 경기의 마지막 몇 초에 승부가 결정된다. 그런 경기에서는 압박 소에서도 자제력을 잃지 않는 선수들이 가장 경기에 이기기 쉽다.

9. **정답** ④

word free oxygen : (공기 속에) 유리된 산소
surface : 표면

해석 바다 속에서는 산소가 많지 않지만, 바다 속의 모든 산소는 공기 중에서 오는 것이다. 따라서 수면 가까이에 유리된 산소가 더 많으며, 그 아래 깊은 곳에 유리된 산소가 더 적다.

10. **정답** ②

word transact : 행하다
make use of : ~을 이용하다 (= take advantage of)
infancy : 유아기 / infant : 유아 / despair : 절망

해석 과거에 어떤 일들이 행하여졌는지 모르는 것은 언제나 어린이로 남아 있는 것과 다름이 없다. 만약 과거의 수고를 이용하지 않는다면, 이 세상은 늘 초보적 발전 단계에 머물러 있어야 한다.

11. **정답** ③

word would rather A than B : B 하느니 차라리 A 하는 것이 낫다 / fault : 결점

해석 작가는 무관심한 것보다 차라리 비판받는 것이 더 낫다고 여긴다. 세상 사람들이 자기 글에 대해 보일 수 있는 가장 나쁜 것은 그가 쓴 책에 대해 침묵을 지키는 것이다.

12. **정답** ①

word minister : 목사 사제 / majority (다수) ↔ minority (소수)

해석 그 시대에는 교육이 교회가 하던 역할들 중 하나였다. 따라서 대다수 선생님들이 사제였다.

13. **정답** ③

word overflow : 넘쳐흐르다 / bank : 둑, 제방

해석 그 댐이 건설되기 전에는 매년 여름 그 강이 둑을 넘쳐흘렀다.

14. **정답** ①

word physical : 육체적인 / mental : 정신적인
whereas : 반면 / symptom : 증세, 징후

해석 육체적 혹은 정신적 스트레스 때문에 생기는 병이 더러 있다. 반면 즉시 알아볼 수 있는 원인 없이 생기는 병도 더러 있다.

15. **정답** ②

word the upper world : 지상의 세계 / ascent : 상승

해석 그들은 그가 지상 세계로 올라갔기 때문에 시력을 버렸다며 (지상 세계로) 올라가는 것은 시도해 볼 가치조차 없는 것이라고 말했다.

16. **정답** ④

word insensitive : 무감한 / mingle : 혼입하다
mutter : 중얼거리다 / meager : 빈약한, 희박한
meddle : 간섭하다

해석 다른 사람들의 일에 참견하는 사람들은 세상에서 가장 무감한 사람들 중 하나일 것이다.

17. **정답** ④

word outdo : 능가하다 (= excel)
outwit : ~의 의표를 찌르다 / overtake : 따라잡다
in no time (= out of hand = out of control = at once = immediately) : 즉시

해석 우리가 서두르면 곧 그를 따라 잡을 수 있을 것이다.

18. **정답** ①

word be tied to : ~에 연관되다
a massive problem : 중대한 문제 / shelter : 은신처

해석 식량 문제는 인구 문제와 밀접하게 연관되어 있다. 식량과 특히 원유를 전 세계적 차원에서 공급하는 것이 마침내 중대한 문제로 인식되게 되었다.

19. **정답** ④

word not only A but (also) B : A 뿐만 아니라 B 또한
contrast A with B : A와 B를 대조하다
predecessor : 선조, 조상
proceed : 앞으로 나아가다
trace : 흔적, ~을 추적하다

해석 허버트 스펜서의 철학이 점하는 위치를 알기 위해서는 그와 다윈과의 관계를 조사하는 것뿐만 아니라 그와 철학적 선배들 특히 헤겔과 콩트를 대조해 봐야 할 필요가 있다.

20. **정답** ③

word conduce to : ~에 공헌하다 (= contribute to)
welfare : 복지 / add to : 첨가하다

해석 인간의 복지에 이바지하는 어떤 일을 한다는 것은 인간의 복지를 증대시키는 일을 하는 것이다.

21. **정답** ①

word invalidate : 무효화하다

해석 어떤 주장이 과학적 증거를 통하여 무효화된 것이라고 말할 때, 그 주장은 폐기된 것임을 의미하는 것이다.

22. 정답 ①
word diagnosis : 진단 / remedy : 치료, 요법
soothe : 달래다, 누그러뜨리다
해석 나는 그 진단이 옳다고 생각했으나 제공된 요법으로 그 병을 치료할 수 있을 것인지 의심스러웠다.

23. 정답 ②
word short-term (단기적인) ↔ long-term (장기적인)
해석 사회 제도에 있어서, 어떤 정책의 단기적 결과와 장기적 결과 사이에는 근본적인 갈등이 있기 쉽다.

24. 정답 ①
word in common : 공통된
해석 사람들은 공통적인 면을 하나 갖고 있는데, 그것은 그들이 다 서로 다르다는 점이다.

25. 정답 ②
word be taught : 배우다 cf. be told : 듣다, be beaten : 맞다, 지다
해석 나는 비록 항상 배우는 것을 좋아하지는 않지만, 언제나 배울 준비가 되어 있다.

26. 정답 ②
word elegant : 우아한 / capital : 자본
해석 책이 없는 집은 아무리 비싼 페르시아산 카펫이 있고, 아무리 우아한 가구가 있다 하더라도 지성이 없고, 개성이 없는 집이다. 페르시아산 카펫은 그 집 주인이 돈이 많다는 것을 알려 주지만, 책은 주인이 훌륭한 지성을 가지고 있음을 알려 준다.

27. 정답 ④
word above all : 우선, 먼저 / like 명사 ? 동명사 : ~처럼
cf. as+절 : ~처럼 / skip : 건너뛰다
해석 우선 공부가 옷을 입거나 벗고, 머리 빗질을 하고 이를 닦는 것과 같은 습관이 되도록 만들어라. 그래서 공부하는 습관이 생활의 한 부분이 되게 하면, 만약 한 번이라도 빼먹으면 죄의식을 느끼게 될 것이다.

28. 정답 ①
word gambling club : 도박장
contribute A to B : A를 B에 기여하다
civic project : 도시 계획
confirm : (법적으로) 승인하다, 확고히 하다
condemn : 비난하다 / condone : 용서하다
해석 지방 도박장이 많은 돈을 도시 계획을 하는 데에 희사했지만, 신임 시장은 그들의 활동을 승인하기를 확고하게 거부했다.

29. 정답 time
word take no thought of (= ignore) : 무시하다
come to an end : 다 써버리다 / temperance : 절제
해석 돈을 다 써 버리고 나서야 비로소 돈의 가치를 생각하는 사람들이 더러 있다. 시간의 경우도 마찬가지인 사람들이 많다. 잃어버린 재산은 근면과 절약을 통하여 되찾을 수 있고, 잃어버린 지식은 공부로, 잃어버린 건강은 절제와 약으로 되찾을 수 있지만 잃어버린 시간은 영원히 다시 찾을 수 없다.

30. 정답 ②
word suspicion : 의심 / keep secret : 비밀을 간직하다
distrust : 불신
해석 우리는 폭탄을 만들고 폭탄은 증오와 의심을 낳는다. 우리는 비밀을 지니고 있는데 비밀은 불신을 낳는다.

31. 정답 ④
word look for (= search for = in search of) : ~를 찾다
clue : 단서 / detective : 형사
해석 훌륭한 독서가는 (책을) 이해하기 위해 적극적으로 노력한다. 어떤 책이든 문제를 지니고 있으며, 수수께끼 같은 내용을 지니고 있다. 독자의 태도는 그 책의 근본이 되는 사상에 대한 단서를 찾는 탐정의 태도와 같은 것이 되어야 한다.

32. 정답 ②
word (Just) as A, so B : 마치 A이듯이 B이다
scatter : 흩어 버리다
come into the hands of : ~의 손에 들어가다
be entrusted to : ~에 맡겨지다
at random : 함부로
해석 우리의 인생은 짧지 않지만 우리가 인생을 그렇게 만든다. 아무리 많은 재산이라도 관리를 잘 못하는 사람의 손에 들어갔을 때 금방 없어지고, 반면 아무리 작은 재산이라도 관리를 잘 하는 사람 손에 맡겨지면 늘어나는 것처럼 우리 인생도 그것을 잘 이용하는 사람에게는 충분히 길다.

33. 정답 ④
word mine : 광산 / dig (-dug-dug) : (땅을) 파다
provide A with B : A에게 B를 제공하다
precious metal : 귀금속 / curriculum : 교과과정
해석 세계에서 가장 좋은 대학의 가장 훌륭한 선생님이라면 학생들에게 직접적인 가르침을 주지 않을 것이다. 그는 학생들에게 (귀중한 것을) 파낼 수 있는 광산으로 가는 길을 인도하고, 팔 수 있는 도구를 제공하고, 열심히 살 수 있도록 도와 줄 것이다. 학생은 혼자의 힘으로 파낸 만큼의 귀금속만을 가지게 될 것이다.

34. 정답 ②
word according to : ~에 의하면 / heredity : 유전
progeny : 자식, 계승자 / spotted : 얼룩이 있는
offspring : 후손 / speckle : 반점, 얼룩덜룩하게 하다
vicious : 악의가 있는 / docile : 유순한 (= obedient)
해석 유전 법칙에 의하면 부모가 지는 특질은 후손에게 나타난다고 한다. 부모인 표범에게 얼룩이 있으면 그 새끼에게도 얼룩이 있을 것으로 기대된다.

35. 정답 ④

word inference : 추론
draw a conclusion : 결론을 도출하다
obvious : 명백한 / enhance : 강화하다
accept A as B : A를 B라고 받아들이다
criteria : (criterion의 복수형) 표준
해석 알려진 사실을 가지고 추론할 때 그 추론이 진실인
지 아닌지의 여부는 결코 확실히 알 수 없다. 우리가
결론을 도출하는 증거들이 충분히 많고 믿을 만하
면, 그 결론은 상당히 믿을 만한 것이라고 받아들일
것이다.

36. **정답** ④
word the blind : 눈 먼 사람 / disaster : 재난
해석 눈 먼 사람이 눈 먼 사람을 인도하면 둘 다 도랑에 빠
질 것이다. 다음 중 이 속담이 의미하는 바와 가장 가
까운 것은?→ ④ 무지한 사람이 무지한 사람을 인도
하면 둘 다 재난에 빠지게 될 것이다.

37. **정답** ①
word term : 조건 / from bad to worse : 점점 악화되는
manifestation : 구현
해석 거지는 선택할 수 있는 사람이 될 수 없다. 다음 중
이 속담이 의미하는 바와 가장 가까운 것은?→ ① 만
약 허약하여 의존할 수밖에 없는 입장에 처하게 되
면 조건을 거절할 수도 없고 자신의 요구나 조건을
정확하게 챙길 수가 없다.

38. **정답** ②
word A is to B as[what] C is to D : A와 B의 관계는 C와
D의 관계와 같다.
해석 시간과 계절의 관계는 공간과 지역의 관계와 같다.

39. **정답** ①
word paradoxically : 역설적으로
represent : ~을 나타내다 / condone : ~을 용서하
다
해석 역설적으로 세계 평화를 위한다고 주장하는 모든
지여 주민들이 무력 통제를 표방하고 있다.

40. **정답** ③
word paradigm : 전형적인 예 / pretext : 구실
paradox : 역설 / predilection : 편애
해석 "변하지 않는 유일한 진리는 모든 것은 변한다는 것
이다" 라고 하는 것은 역설이다.

41. **정답** ①
word look back over : 뒤돌아보다
해석 오랜 세월을 돌이켜보면 사람은 어떤 특정 장소에
특정적인 태도에 늘 고정되어 있는 것처럼 보인다.
그래서 그들은 늘 똑같은 일만 하고 있는 것처럼 보
인다.

42. **정답** ④
word foresee : 예견하다
as often been said : 종종 얘기되듯이

minutely : 세세하게
what we[you, they] call (= what is called = so called)
: 소위
해석 과학의 목적은 조종 얘기되듯이 이해하는 것이 아니
고 예견하는 것이다. 과학은 사실과 사물과 현상을
세세하게 묘사하고 미래에 일어날 일들을 예측할 수
있기 위하여 그것들을 소위 법칙으로 연결시키려고
시도하는 것이다.

43. **정답** ②
word appearance : 출현 / gather (모으다) ↔ scatter,
disperse (흩어 버리다)
해석 지구상에 처음 출현한 이래 인간은 계속 정보를 모
아 왔고, 유용한 생각들을 다른 사람에게 전하려고
노력해 왔다. 고대 동굴 벽에 새겨진 그림문자는 정
보를 전달하려는 인간의 노력 중 일부를 보여 주는
것이다.

44. **정답** ④
word be based upon[on] : ~에 근거하다
stand by : 지지하다 (= support)
해석 종교는 주로 두려움에 근거하고 있다고 나는 생각한
다. 이는 부분적으로는 미지의 세계에 대한 두려움
이고 또 부분적으로는 곤란에 빠지거나 분쟁에 휘말
리게 되었을 때 당신을 지원해 줄 수 있는 형님 한 분
을 갖고 싶다는 바람이다.

45. **정답** ③
word in adolescence : 청년기에
on the verge of : 막 ~하려고 하다
suicide : 자살
on second thoughts : 다시 생각하여
in addition to : ~에 덧붙여 (= besides)
on the contrary : 그와는 반대로
in advance : 미리, 먼저 (= beforehand)
해석 젊은 시절에 나는 인생을 혐오하여 항상 자살 직전에
이르곤 했다. 지금은 정반대로 인생을 즐기고 있으
며 해가 더해 갈수록 인생을 더욱 더 즐기고 있다.

46. **정답** ④
word with the exception of : ~을 제외하고는
district : 지역
해석 남동부 지역의 거주자를 제외하면 그 주민들은 거의
가 순수 켈트족으로 초기 브리튼의 후손인데 그들은
침략자들과의 혼합을 면했다.

47. **정답** ④
word give up : 포기하다 / obtain : 얻다 (= come by)
temporary : 일시적인 / deserve : ~할 가치가 있다
neither A nor B : A도 B도 아니다
해석 하찮고 순간적인 안전을 위해 필수적인 자유를 포
기할 수 있는 사람들은 자유도 안전도 가질 자격이
없다.

48. **정답** ③

441

word college graduate : 대학 졸업생
pay for : ~의 대가를 지불하다
biased : 치우친, 편견을 가진 / free : 무료의
creditable : 칭찬할 만한
해석 대학 졸업생들은 갚을 빚이 있는데, 그들은 그들이 받은 교육이 공짜가 아님을 알아야 한다.

49. 정답 ①
word pet shop : 애완동물 가게
customer : 고객, 단골손님
해석 애완동물 상점 주인인 나이든 그 여자는 아이들이 시끄럽게 굴며 더러운 채 들어오는 것을 싫어했다. 이는 매우 딱한 일인데, 왜냐하면 아이들이 애완동물 상점의 최고 고객이기 때문이다.

50. 정답 ③
word pussy : 고양이 / mouse hole : 쥐구멍
padded : 푹신한
해석 고양이는 쥐구멍을 향해 살금살금 기어갔다. 그녀는 배가 고팠다. 그녀는 오랫동안 쥐구멍을 노려보았다. 그녀가 무엇을 기다리고 있을까?

51. 정답 ①
word utilize : 이용하다
something : 꽤 중요한 것 (사람)
consist in (= lie in) : ~에 놓여 있다.
해석 "아는 것이 힘이다"라고들 한다. 그러나 더 큰 힘은 이러한 지식을 활용할 수 있는 능력에 있다. 지식 있고 힘 있는 사람은 틀림없이 뭔가 중요한 능력을 지니고 있을 것이다. 그러나 그 능력의 진정한 가치는 그것이 무엇을 할 수 있는가에 달려 있다.

52. 정답 ②
word fortune : 재산
having been left with a fortune
= though she had been left with a fortune
get rid of (= do away with = remove = abolish = eliminate = exclude) : 제거하다
maintain : 주장하다 / colleague : 동료
accountant : 회계원
해석 나는 언젠가 한 부인을 만났는데, 그녀는 많은 재산을 물려받았지만 그 재산을 다 처분해 버릴 때까지는 결코 마음이 자유롭지 못할 것이라고 말했다. 그녀는 사람은 소유하고 있는 재산의 하인이지 주인이 되지 못하고 있다고 주장했다.

53. 정답 ①
word cavity : 충치의 구멍
identify : 찾아내다, 신원을 확인하다
be responsible for : ~에 책임이 있는
해석 이빨이 썩는 것을 방지하는 것은 현재에도 미결의 과제이다. 충치의 구멍은 쉽게 찾아낼 수 있지만, 충치를 발생시키는 원인이 되는 것을 없애려는 시도는 아직 성공하지 못했다.

54. 정답 ②

word trapdoor : 작은 문 / be lined with : ~로 줄쳐 있다
cobweb : 거미줄
해석 trapdoor 거미는 땅에 집을 짓는다. 그 집은 실크 거미줄로 쳐져 있는데 열리는 작은 문도 있다. 이 거미는 훌륭한 건축가이다.

55. 정답 ①
word tyranny : 폭군 / formidable : 무서운
safeguard : 보호자
universal suffrage : 보통 선거권 / ballot : 투표
해석 폭정에 대해서는 언론만큼 강력한 적은 없다고들 한다. 자유를 지키는 가장 중요한 보호 장치 중의 하나가 언론의 자유이다.

56. 정답 ②
word misfortune : 불행 cf. unfortunately : 불행하게도
legend : 전설, 전해오는 이야기 / tempt : 유혹하다
landscape : 풍경화 / be apt to : ~하기 쉽다
portraiture : 초상화법
해석 불행이 화가에게는 좋은 것이라고 말하는 것은 분명 잘못된 생각이겠지만, 반 고흐의 이야기는 너무 극적이어서 그런 단정을 내리게끔 충동받는다. 만약 그가 후기의 일부 풍경화에서 보여 준 완벽함을 가지고 그림을 그릴 수 있게 해 준 것이 광기라면 우리도 기꺼이 미치고 싶다고 쉽게 말할 것 같다. 왜냐하면 광기가 그를 훌륭한 화가로 만들었기 때문이다.

57. 정답 ③
word fixed income : 고정된 수입
해석 고정된 수입을 가진 사람들은 가격이 떨어지는 시기에는 운이 좋다. 그들은 같은 수입으로 가격이 높을 때보다 더 많은 상품과 서비스를 살 수 있기 때문에 그들의 실질 수업이 올라간 것이 되기 때문이다.

58. 정답 see
word Since (= Now that) : ~이기 때문에
be reflected from : ~로부터 반사되다
해석 볼 수 있기 위해서는 눈이 빛을 받아야 함으로 어둠 속에서는 볼 수가 없다. 어둠이란 빛이 없는 것인데 어둠 속에서는 의자나 탁자, 사람들로부터 눈으로 반사될 빛이 전혀 없다. 그래서 이런 사물들을 볼 수가 없는 것이다.

59. 정답 air
word be made from : ~로 만들어지다 (화학적 변화)
해석 달에서는 어떤 것도 자라거나 살 수가 없다. 물과 공기가 없기 때문이다. 달에는 구름도 없다. 구름도 물로 만들어지기 때문이다. 달에는 완벽한 침묵만 있을 뿐인데 공기가 없으면 소리도 존재할 수 없기 때문이다.

60. 정답 ①
word a month or so = about a month
novice (= beginners) : 초보자
intrepid : 용기 있는
해석 Tom은 약 한 달 전 골프를 치기 시작했으니 아직 초보자이다.

61. **정답** ①
    word technocratic : 기술자 지배의 / plebeian : 평민의
        autocratic : 독재의
    해석 사람들은 늘 스스로를 다스리는 것이 어렵다는 것을
        깨달아 왔다. 이것이 오늘날 주변에 진정으로 민주
        적인 사회가 왜 거의 없는가를 설명해 준다.

62. **정답** ①
    word propaganda : 광고 / in effect : 사실상
        perversion : 왜곡 / inversion : 전도, 도치
        subversion : 전복 / diversion : 전환
    해석 선전은 아무리 효과적이라 하더라도 진실을 왜곡시
        킨 것이어서는 오래 지속될 수 없다.

63. **정답** ②
    word foreshadow : 미리 암시하다 / forfeit : 몰수하다
        foresee : 예견하다 / fornicate : 간통하다
    해석 그는 세금을 납부하지 않았기 때문에 재산을 몰수
        당했다.

64. **정답** ③
    word vibrating source : 진동원 / medium : 매체
        compression : 압축
    해석 소리는 진동원으로부터 그를 둘러싸고 있는 매체를
        통해 파동의 형태로 멀리까지 이동하는 형태의 에너
        지이다.

65. **정답** ①
    word atrophy : 쇠퇴
        that is (= that is to say, so to speak, in other words)
        : 즉, 다시 말하면
        frivolous : 하찮은 / inclination : 성향
    해석 노년에 놀고 지낸다는 것은 인간 정신의 쇠퇴, 즉
        인간이 성장하지 못한다는 것을 말해 주는 것이다.

66. **정답** ④
    word minimum (최소) ↔ maximum (최대)
    해석 그녀는 이전에 일해 본 적이 없기 때문에 가장 적은
        경험을 요구하는 직업을 찾아야 했다.

67. **정답** ①
    word well-fed : 뚱뚱한
        Keep good cheer. : 기운을 잃지 마.
    해석 살찐 아이가 굶주린 아이에게 "기운을 잃지 마" 라
        고 말하는 것은 다음 어느 속담과 비슷한가? → ①
        우리가 다른 사람의 불행은 견딜 수 있다.

68. **정답** ④
    word do away with (= get rid of = abolish = remove =
        eliminate = exclude) : 제거하다
        promote : 조장하다, 촉진하다
    해석 줄리어스 시저를 "자유의 투사"라고 부를 수는 없
        다. 그는 군인이자 위대한 지도자였다. 그는 국가 발
        전에 방해가 되는 것들 중 일부를 없앴지만 자유의
        토대가 될 만한 것을 촉진하지는 않았다.

69. **정답** ②
    word accommodation : 숙박시설, 편의
        dignitaries : 고위층
    해석 오늘날은 여행이 쉽고 즐겁다. 육지에서는 기차나
        버스, 또 다른 자동차를 타고 여행을 즐긴다. 바다에
        서는 큰 배가 잠을 자려는 사람에게 매우 안락한 숙
        박시설을 제공해 준다.

70. **정답** ③
    word physical : 육체적인 / mental : 정신적인
        whereas : 반면에 / symptom : 증세
        point of origin : 발생원인
    해석 어떤 병은 육체적인 혹은 정신적인 스트레스에 의해
        일어나지만 반면에 어떤 병들은 즉시 알 수 있는 원
        인 없이 발생할 수 있다.

71. **정답** ①
    word differentiate : 구별 짓다 / pure science : 순수과학
        applied science : 응용과학 / evaluate : 평가하다
    해석 불행하게도 우리는 자주 순수과학과 응용과학이 과
        학에 다른 두 형태이며 한 쪽이 다른 한 쪽보다 더
        소중한 것인 것처럼 이 둘을 구분 짓고자 한다. 그래
        서 이러한 구분을 없애고자 하는 것이 나의 희망이
        다.

72. **정답** ①
    word put out (= extinguish) : 불을 끄다
        public property : 공공재산
    해석 매년 많은 숲이 산불로 파손된다. 일부는 번개에 의
        해 일어나기도 하지만 대부분은 사람들의 부주의함
        때문에 발생한다. 사람들은 종종 불이 꺼지지 않은
        담배꽁초를 버리고, 모닥불을 끄지 않고서 야영지를
        떠나기도 한다. 산림은 공공재산이므로 손상되거나,
        파손 되서는 안 된다.

73. **정답** ④
    word analysis : 분석
    해석 우리가 살아가는 동안 하게 되는 분석 중 가장 어렵
        고 중요한 것들 중에서는 에세이를 주의 깊게 읽을
        때 하는 분석이 있다. 아무리 무의식적으로 에세이
        를 접하더라도 분석하기를 피할 수 없다는 것이 사
        실이다. 왜냐하면 도서를 할 때 부분 부분을 읽지만,
        각 부분은 전체의 통일성을 보여 줄 수 있도록 서로
        조화를 이루고 있기 때문이다.

74. **정답** ②
    word put in for : ~를 신청하다 / walk-out : 파업
        enter into : 시작하다 / negotiation : 협상
    해석 만약 당신이 개인적으로 임금 인상을 원하면 인상을
        신청한다. 노동단체는 인상 요구를 한다. 사용자측
        이 임금 인상을 원치 않게 되면 임금 분쟁이 발생하
        고 결국 파업에 이르게 된다. 그러나 대개의 경우 노
        동조합 간부와 경영자는 분쟁을 타결할 방법을 의논
        하기 위해 협상을 시작할 것이다.

75. 정답 ④

word trivial : 사소한 / exemplify : 입증하다

해석 아주 사소한 상황이 이것을 입증하는 데 도움이 된다. 당신이 사과가 필요하며 과일 가게에 갔다고 가정해 보자. 사과 하나를 집어 깨물어 보니 맛이 시다. 그것을 자세히 살펴보면 그것이 단단하고 푸른색이라는 것을 알게 된다. 또 다른 사과를 하나 집어 들어 본다. 그것 역시 단단하고 푸른색이어서 시다. 가게 주인이 세 번째로 사과를 권한다. 사과를 깨물어 보기 전에 살펴보니 단단하고 푸른색이다. 그래서 이것도 이미 깨물어 봤던 사과들처럼 분명히 맛이 시다는 생각이 들어 가져가지 않겠다고 말하게 된다.

76. 정답 ①

word pollution : 공해

해석 제2차 세계대전 중 사용된 가장 중요한 무기 중의 하나는 사람을 상대로 사용한 무기가 아니라 질병을 퇴치하기 위해 사용된 약이었다.

77. 정답 ②

word mammal : 포유동물 / fur : 모피, 털

feather : (새의) 깃

해석 동물들은 자신을 따뜻하게 유지하는 여러 방식을 갖고 있다. 어떤 포유동물들은 체온을 유지하기 위해 털을 갖고 있으며 깃털은 새의 몸을 따뜻하게 유지하는 데 도움이 된다. 사람들은 자신을 추위로부터 보호하기 위해서 옷을 사용한다.

78. 정답 ④

word sphere : 구 / primitive : 원시적인 / tribe : 종족

해석 전 세계 문명인들은 거의 대부분이 지구가 둥글다고 믿고 있다. 지구가 평편하다는 이론은 단지 고립된 미개 부족들 사이에서만 받아들여지고 있다.

79. 정답 ④

word loyal : 충성스러운 / rebel : 반란 / territory : 영토

해석 미국 독립전쟁 중 캐나다 민족은 반란을 일으킨 식민지 사람들이 그들이 독립운동에 가담할 것을 설득하려 했음에도 불구하고 영국에 대해 계속 충성을 다했다.

80. 정답 ③

word clear A of B : A에서 B를 제거 (박멸) 하다

cultivation : 경작

frontier : (19세기 미국 서부 개척지의) 변경

echo : 메아리치다 / ax : 도끼 (소리)

해석 이 나라의 초기 시대에 경작이 가능한 땅을 더 많이 만들기 위해서 넓은 지역에서 나무를 베어 없앴다. 동부의 숲이 첫 대상이었고, 변경이 확대되어 감에 따라 서부의 숲도 역시 나무꾼의 도끼 소리가 울려 퍼졌다.

81. 정답 ③

word illegal : 불법적인 / submission : 굴복

permission : 허락

해석 모든 인간 사회는 결혼에 관한 규칙을 가지고 있다. 영국에서는 18세가 되기 전에 부모의 허락 없이 결혼하는 것은 불법이다.

82. 정답 ④

word magnificent : 장엄한, 훌륭한 / striking : 현저한

defect : 결점 / cowardice : 겁, 소심함

해석 바이킹족의 두드러진 특징은 그들의 역사만큼이나 두드러진 것이었다.

83. 정답 ①

word urban (도시의) ↔ rural (시골의)

migration : 이주, 이동

해석 미국의 도시 인구는 서서히 감소하였고, 도시의 출생 감소는 시골 지역으로부터의 이주로 인하여 더욱 균형이 잡혔다.

84. 정답 ④

word no longer (= no more) : 더 이상 ~이 아니다

melt : 녹이다

해석 겨울의 오후는 더 이상 밝고 화창하지 않았다. 태양이 구름에 가려졌던 것이다.

85. 정답 ③

word be accused of : ~로 고발당하다

suspicious : 의심스러운 / stolid : 신경이 무딘

해석 비록 아놀드는 자신이 결백함을 알았지만, 죄로 인하여 고발당할 것을 두려워했다.

86. 정답 ①

word suffer from : ~를 겪다 / fortitude : 용기

therapy : 치료

해석 그는 일평생 좋지 못한 건강으로 고통 받았지만 대단한 용기로 그것을 견뎌내는 것을 배웠다.

87. 정답 ②

word scientific research : 과학 연구

be based on : ~에 근거를 두고 있다

insight : 통찰력

해석 알려진 사실과 알려지지 않은 사실 사이의 관계를 수립하려고 시도할 때, 여러 과학 분야에 종사하고 있는 대다수의 사람들은 가장 확실한 발견은 직접적인 관찰에 근거를 둔다고 믿고 있다.

88. 정답 ①

word result from : ~에서 비롯되다 / resolution : 해결책

해석 자유는 종종 무력의 성공적인 사용에서 비롯된 것임을 역사는 보여 주고 있다. 그러나 우리는 자유를 사랑하는 만큼 강렬하게 전쟁을 미워한다. 이러한 역설을 해결해 줄 해결책이 과연 있을까?

89. 정답 ④

word chimney : 굴뚝

keep away from : ~에서 멀리 떨어져 있다.

해석 천둥과 번개를 동반한 폭우가 있는 동안에는 사람은 옥내에 있는 것이 안전하다. 그러나 지붕 위에 굴뚝이 보호 장치 없이 솟아 있다면 그 집은 다른 부분보다 지붕에 벼락 맞기 쉽다. 따라서 노출되어 있는 인화 물질을 피하는 것이 현명하다.

90. **정답** ④
   word immortality : 불멸
   dissociate A from B : A와 B를 분리키시다

ingenuously : 교묘하게 / miserly : 인색한
inseparably : 밀접하게

해석 신에 대한 믿음이 반드시 불멸에 대한 믿음인 것은 아니다. 그러나 전자(신에 대한 믿음)와 후자(불멸에 대한 믿음)는 따로 떼어 내어서 생각하기 어렵다. 이 두 가지 관념은 너무 밀접하게 관련되어 있어서 죽음 뒤에 삶은 항상 신과 인류와의 관계에서 신의 수중에 들어 있는 가장 강력한 도구로 간주되어 왔다.

PART Ⅸ : 중 · 장문 독해

1. **정답** 1. ④ 2. ① 3. ② 4. ③ 5. ③
   word lose one's voice : 목이 쉬어 말을 못하다
   boldness : 대담함, 무모함 (↔ cowardness, timidity)
   dogma : 교리, 교조
   stereotype : 상투적인 것 (생각) (정형화된) 인습
   match : ~와 어울리다 (= go with)
   gracious : 우아한, 정중한 (= benign, courteous, polite)
   sentiments : 소감
   in marked contrast : 두드러지게 대조되는
   dismiss A as B : A를 B로 성급히 단정하다
   much of socialist : 대단한 사회주의자
   epithet : 명칭, 별칭 / card-carrying : 전형적인
   embrace : 껴안다, 채택하다
   repudiate : ~을 부인 (부정) 하다
   be susceptible to : ~에 쉽게 영향을 받다

해석 빌 클린턴은 선거에서 이겼지만 목소리가 쉬어서 말을 할 수 없었다. 그래서 보리스 옐친 대통령이 대부분 말을 하게 되었는데 이는 옐친 대통령에게는 잘된 일이었다. "내가 부시 대통령과 좋은 관계를 유지했다고 해서 당신과의 관계를 개선할 수 없을 것이라고 생각하지 않습니다." "당신은 정치적인 면에서 과감하다 정도로 낡은 도그마와 정형화된 인습을 확고히 거부해 왔는데 이는 러시아와 미국 간의 관계의 원칙과 잘 부합합니다."라고 러시아 대통령은 11월 5일의 전화 통화에서 말했다. 이런 호의적인 소감은 옐친이 불과 수주 전에 얘기했던 것과 뚜렷이 대조되는 것이었다. 옐친은 그의 측근과 적어도 한 명의 서방 외교관이 포함된 사람들과 대화를 나눌 때 알칸사스 주지사 (클린턴) 을 너무 어리고 경험이 없는 풋내기로 치부하면서-이 점을 잘 이해해야 하는데-대단한 '사회주의자' 라고 대수롭지 않게 치부했다. 이는 2년 전만 해도 전형적인 공산주의자였던 사람이 한 말로는 놀라운 언사이다. 그러나 러시아가 칼 마르크스의 공산주의 이론을 버리고 아담 스미스의 자본주의 이론을 도입하고 있기 때문에 그 지도자가 민주당을 (사회주의적이라고) 공격하는 공화당의 선전을 민감하게 받아들이게 된 것으로 보인다.

해답 1. 클린턴이 말을 할 수 없게 된 것이 왜 좋은 일이며, 누구에게 다행스런 일이었나? → ④ 옐친에게 : 클린턴이 옐친이 전에 자기에게 했던 혹평을 지적할

수 없게 되어서
2. 전화 통화에서 옐친이 클린턴에게 보인 태도는? → ①유화적이었다.
3. 저자는 왜 옐친이 클린턴을 사회주의자로 규정했다는 점에 독자를 주목하도록 했는가? → ②평생 공산주의자였던 사람이 사회주의자라는 이유 때문에 한 정치인을 반대한다는 것이 무척 역설적이기 때문에
5. 다음 중 민주당(원) 에 대한 공화당의 선전으로 볼 수 있는 것은? → ③그들은 현실적인 감각이 없는 성급한 개혁론자들이다.

2. **정답** 1. ① 2. ③ 3. ② 4. ③ 5. ④ 6. ② 7. ④
   word impartial : 공정한 (= fair, unprejudiced, unbiased)
   medium : 매개체 / propaganda : 선전
   editorial column : (신문의) 사설
   persuasively : 설득력 있게
   uphold : 지지하다
   a code of ethics : 윤리 강령
   distinguish A and B (= distinguish A from B) : A와 B를 구별하다 / entitle : 권한을 부여하다
   tend to (= have a tendency to = be inclined to) : ~하는 경향이 있다 / partisan : 열성당원
   metropolitan : 대도시의, 수도의
   deliberately : 고의로 (= on purpose, intentionally, purposely, consciously)
   color : 채색하다, 왜곡하다

해석 아무리 공정하고 사심 없는 신문이라도, 신문은 하나의 선전 매개체이다. 모든 일간신문에는 사설란이 있다. 이곳에서 뉴스에 나오는 사건과 인물에 대한 의견이 표현된다. 그러나 사설의 판단은 너무도 설득력 있게 제시되기 때문에 많은 사람들이 이 견해들을 사실로 받아들인다. 훌륭한 언론인들은 뉴스와 사실의 의견을 구분하게 하는 윤리 강령을 준수한다. 이 강령에 의하면 사설란에서 발행인은 그가 원하는 어떤 명분도 옹호할 권한이 있다고 주장한다. 이 말은 사설에서 그는 한 분파의 일원으로 말하고 있으며 그리하여 그가 원하는 어떤 견해도 피력할 수 있다는 말로 이해된다. 현대의 신문은 제작하는 데 매우 많은 비용이 들고, 신문사를 설립하는 데도

돈이 많이 들기 때문에, 신문사는 더욱 대기업화되어 왔다. 예외가 있긴 하나, 이 거대한 신문사들은 경제적, 정치적 문제에 있어 그들의 사설에 사주 (社主)의 견해를 반영하는 경향이 있다. 그러나 뉴스란은 완전한 편견 없는 사실들이 보도되어야 한다. 우수한 대도시의 신문들과 거대한 언론협회들은 뉴스를 공정하게 유지한다고 믿을 수 있다. 하지만 덜 윤리적인 출판물 (신문) 들이 종종 어떤 특정 집단이나 운동에 유리하거나 불리하게 뉴스를 고의로 왜곡시키는 경우가 있다.

해답 1. 필자는 현대의 어떤 신문도 ①선전성을 벗어나지 못하고 있다고 말한다.
2. 모든 일간신문에는 ①사설란이 있다.
3. 언론 윤리 강령에 따르면 신문은 ②뉴스와 사설을 구분해야 한다.
4. 윗글에 따르면 신문 발행인은 신문 사설란을 이용하여 ③그가 믿는 어떤 명분도 옹호할 수 있다.
5. 신문사가 대기업 범주에 속하게 된 것은 ④엄청난 제작비 때문이다.
6. 뉴스의 어느 한 측면만 신문에 정기적으로 게재되면, 독자는 그 신문의 ②윤리적 수준이 의심스럽다고 생각할 수 있다.
7. 문장 속에서 밑줄 친 "color" 라는 단어는 ④왜곡시키다를 의미한다.

3. **정답** 1. ③ 2. ④ 3. ② 4. ②
word at risk (= at a stake = in a danger) : 위험에 처해 있는 / make a promise : 약속하다
regardless of (= irrespective of) : ~에 관계없이
status : 지위 / be entitled to : ~을 부여받다
to the utmost : 최고도로
by virtue of (= by means of = by dint of = with the help of) : ~에 의해서
mature : 성숙된 / informed : 유식한
secure : ~을 안전하게 하다, ~을 확보하다
gainful employment : (돈벌이가 잘 되는) 좋은 직장
해석 위협받고 있는 것 중의 하나는 이 대륙에서 가장 먼저 보장되었던 다음과 같은 약속이다. 모든 사람들은 인종과 계급, 경제적 지위에 관계없이 공정한 기회와 개개인의 실력을 최고로 발전시키는 데 필요한 수단을 부여받을 수 있다. 이 약속은 훌륭한 지도를 받는다면 모든 어린이들은 스스로의 노력을 통하여 좋은 직장을 얻고 자신의 삶을 영위하는 데 필요한 성숙함과 풍부한 판단력을 얻게 되기를 희망할 수 있고 그리하여 자기 자신의 이익뿐 아니라 사회 전체의 발전에도 기여하게 되기를 희망할 수 있다는 것을 의미하는 것이다.
해답 1. 다음 중 윗글의 주제를 잘 나타내는 것은?
→ ③우리 어린이들은 좋은 직장을 얻고 자신의 삶을 잘 영위해서 자신의 이익과 사회의 발전에 기여하기 위해 교육을 잘 받아야 할 필요가 있다.
2. 모든 사람들을 위한 높은 수준의 교육을 제공하지 않으면 _____ 을 잃을 위험에 처하게 된다.
→ ④ 보기 전부
3. 저자가 윗글을 쓴 주목적은? → ② 설득시키기 위한 것

4. 우리를 확신시키기 위해 저자는 _____ 을 사용하고 있다. → ② 정서 (견해)

4. **정답** 1. ③ 2. ④ 3. ④ 4. ④ 5. ③
word wanted : 사람 구함 / B.A. degree : 학사학위
non-negotiable : 협상할 수 없는
book keeping : 부기
해석 사람 구함 : 법률회사의 시간제 비서직임. 경력은 필요하지 않음. 학사학위 있어야 함. 회계학 전공이면 더 좋음. 컴퓨터를 다룰 줄 알고 제2외국어를 할 수 있는 지원자에게 가산점 부여. 초임 : 시간당 $20 (주당 약 15시간 근무함) . 근무시간은 회사에서 정함.
해답 1. 위 광고에 의하면 회사에서 어떤 사람을 구하고 있나? → ③비서 업무를 취급할 사람
2. 다음 중 네 명의 지원자 중 위 회사가 가장 선호할 지원자는? → ④시간제 일을 찾고 있는 전직 회계사 비서
4. 다음 중 회사가 요구하지 않고 있는 것은?
→ ④부기 능력

5. **정답** 1. ② 2. ③ 3. ① 4. ① 5. ①
word document : 서류로 입증하다
evolutionary : 진화의 / the Berling Straits : 베링해협
cheek tooth : 어금니 / graze : 풀을 뜯다
invade : 침공하다
extinct : 소멸한 (= died out) cf. extinction : 멸종
midway through its evolutionary development : 진화의 단계에서 중간에 있는
the Oligocene Period : 점신세
the Miocene Period : 중신세
the Pliocene Period : 선신세
the Pleistocene Period : 홍적세
해석 선신세 (Pliocene Age) 초기인 약 1200만 년 전 진화의 중간 단계쯤에 이른 말이 지금 베링해협이 위치한 육로를 통해 알래스카에서 유럽의 초원으로 건넜다는 기록이 있다. 그 말은 발가락이 셋이고 풀을 뜯는 데 쓰이는 특별한 어금니가 있는 오늘날 망아지 크기의 히파리온 (hipparion) 이었다. 유럽에서 히파리온은 아마도 중신세 (Miocene Period) 동안에 같은 통로로 먼저 유럽에 온 안키테레스라 불리는 덜 진화된 말을 만나게 되었다. 홍적세 (Pleistocene Period) 말기에 히파리온과 안키테레스 모두 그것이 기원한 북미에서 멸종하였다. 유럽에서는 그들이 오늘날 우리가 알고 있는 말과 매우 유사한 동물로 진화하게 되었다. 유럽 식민주의자들에 의해 미국으로 도입된 것이 바로 이 말의 후예였다.
해답 1. 히파리온과 알키테레스 둘 다 ②북미가 원산이다.
2. 이 글에 따르면 히파리온은 ③안키테레스보다 더 컸다.
3. 저자는 히패리온과 안키테레스가 유럽으로 ①지금은 존재하지 않는 육로를 통해 이주했음을 암시하고 있다.
5. 윗글에서 ①중신세 (Miocene Period) 가 선신세 (Pliocene Period) 보다 앞선다는 것을 추론할 수 있다.

6. **정답** 1. ① 2. ② 3. ③
   word precise : 정확한
   no longer : 더 이상 ~이 아니다 (= not ~any longer)
   infinitely : 무한히
   complicated : 복잡한 (= complex, intricate)
   take advantage of : ~을 이용하다
   corporate : 기업체 / executive : 이사, 임원
   turn to : ~에 의존하다
   convert A into B : A를 B로 전환하다
   film animator : 만화영화 제작자
   해석 많은 기술자들이 책상에 앉아 종이 위에 정확한 디자인 작업을 할 필요가 없어졌다, 대신 컴퓨터를 이용하여 복잡한 디자인을 무한정 만들어 낼 수 있게 되었다. 이런 기술자들은 컴퓨터 그래픽이라 불리는 화면에 신속히 나타나는 전자식 자료 전송 기술을 이용하고 있다. 컴퓨터 그래픽은 자동차, 비행기, 심지어는 건물의 다양한 디자인을 시험해 보는 데에 사용되어 왔다. 회사 임원들은 회사의 재정적인 자료를 도표나 그래프로 바꾸는 데 컴퓨터 그래픽에 의존한다. 심지어 만화영화 제작자들도 컴퓨터 그래픽을 사용하기 시작하였는데, 버튼만 누르면 색상의 시험 효과를 얻을 수 있게 되었다.
   해답 1. 자동차 기술자들은 ①복잡한 디자인을 검사하기 위해 컴퓨터 그래픽을 사용해 왔다.
   2. 윗글의 주제는? →②새로운 디자인 방법
   3. 우리는 컴퓨터 그래픽이 ③끊임없이 확장되는 기술이 될 것이라고 이 문장을 통하여 추론할 수 있다.

7. **정답** 1. ③ 2. ④ 3. ④
   word drunk-driving law : 음주운전에 관한 법률
   confine : 감금하다 (= imprison)
   special facility : 특수 수용시설
   offender : 범죄자, 위반자
   stud : 장식용 못, 장식용 못을 박다
   chore : 자질구레한 일
   in addition to : ~뿐만 아니라 (= besides)
   convict : 유죄 판결을 내리다 / influential : 유력한
   beat the rap : (미국 속어) 형벌을 면하다
   sentence : (형을) 선고하다 (= condemn)
   celebrity : 유명인사, 명성 (= fame) / parliament : 국회
   해석 노르웨이는 서방 세계에서 가장 엄한 음주운전에 관한 법률을 가진 나라 중 하나이다. 혈중 알코올 농도가 0.05퍼센트 이상으로 밝혀진 운전자는 누구이든 자동적으로 특수 수용시설에 감금되어 최소한 3주일을 보내게 된다. 그곳에서 위반자들은 기구를 만들거나, 스노우 타이어에 못을 박거나, 전기 공사를 하거나 아니면 허드렛일을 해야 한다. 이와 같은 봉사 근무 외에도, 초범일 경우 일 년간 면허가 정지되며, 5년 이내 다시 유죄 판결을 받으면 영구적으로 면허가 정지된다.

8. **정답** 1. (1) for (2) in (3) to (4) to (5) from
   2. (a) Problems that result from the substitution of machines for human labour
   (b) handicraftsmen
   (c) to keep up the existing level of ~ number of workers.
   (d) the social discontent
   3. 일거리를 빼앗아 매우 어려운 지경에 처하도록 했다.
   4. 과거 피해자들은 정치적 힘이 없어 효과적으로 저항할 수 없었지만 오늘날 임금 노동자들은 상황에 쉽게 굴복하지 않는다.
   5. 더 적은 노동력으로 같은 생산력을 유지하는 경제적인 생산 방법을 취급하고 있다.
   word substitute A for B (= replace B with A) : B를 A로 대체하다 / be likely to : ~할 것 같은
   acute : 날카로운, 심각한
   in the not very distant future : 그다지 멀지 않은 장래에 / handicraftsman : 수공업자
   inflict [impose] A on [upon] B : B에게 A를 가하다
   offer a resistance to : ~에 저항하다
   submit to (= yield to) : ~에 굴복하다
   starvation : 기아 / keep up : ~을 계속 유지하다
   H-bomb : 수소폭탄 / extermination : 근절, 박멸
   cybernetics : 인공두뇌학 / survivor : 생존자
   해석 인간의 노동력을 기계로 대체하는 것이 그리 멀지 않은 장래에 심각한 문제를 불러일으킬지도 모른다. 이러한 문제들이 지금 새로 생긴 것은 아니다. 이는 산업혁명 때부터 시작되었는데 산업혁명은 숙련되고 부지런한 많은 수공업자들의 일거리를 빼앗아 그들이 겪지 않아도 될 그리고 그들이 몹시 원망한 역경을 그들에게 안겨 주었다. 고통을 받게 된 자들은 정치적인 힘이 없어 진보에 효과적으로 저항할 수 없었다. 오늘날 민주국가에서는 정치적 상황이 그때와 임금 노동자들이 직장을 잃고 굶어 죽게 되는데도 얌전히 굴복만 하고 있기를 기대할 수 없을 것이다. 그러나 우리가 인공두뇌학에 대해 쓴 Norber Wiener의 책을 믿는다면-믿지 못할 이유가 전혀 없기도 하지만-지금보다 훨씬 더 적은 수의 근로자로 같은 생산량의 수준을 유지하는 것이 곧 가능해질 것이다. 그런데 만약 전쟁이 발생하여 근로자들이 전선으로 나가고, 전쟁이 수소폭탄 같은 결정타로 쉽게 끝나지 않게 된다면 경제적인 방법이 보다 많이 개발될 것이다. 그렇게 되면 생존자들이 귀환했을 때 그들이 이전에 했던 일을 더 이상 할 수 없게 될 것이다. 그런 상황에서 야기되는 사회적 불만이 매우 심각한 수준에 이를 것이다. 독재 국가에서는 쉽게 다룰 수 있겠지만 민주국가에서는 사회 철학과 윤리가 급격한 변화의 소용돌이를 겪고 나서야 이 문제가 해결될 수 있는 것이다.

9. **정답** 1. ③ 2. ④ 3. ②
   word be distinguished from : 구별하다
   constellation : 별자리, 성좌
   emit : (빛, 향기를) 발산하다
   on the other hand : 한편
   gaseous : 가스의, 기체의
   incandescence : 백열 상태

해석 고정되어 있는 항성은 고대에도 행성과 구별이 되었는데, 이는 행성은 계절마다 별자리 사이를 움직이는데 비해, 별자리는 하늘의 항성으로 이루어지는 비교적 불변하는 배열이었기 때문이다. 행성은 태양의 빛을 반사시킴으로 인해 반짝이는 차고 단단한 천체이다. 반면, 항성은 훨씬 많은 물질을 함유하고 있지만, 너무도 뜨거워 전체가 기체 상태이며, 백열함으로써 빛을 발한다.

해답 1. 하늘의 비교적 불변하는 항성의 배열이 ③별자리라고 불리고 있다.
2. 행성은 ④빛을 발하지 못한다.
3. 윗글에 기술된 내용을 통하여 볼 때 ②행성은 단단한 고체로 되어있는 천체이다.

10. **정답** 1. ④ 2. ② 3. ③ 4. ① 5. ④
word slowdown : 침체 / conservation : 자연 보존
dwindling : 줄어드는
venture : 모험적인 사업, 감히 ~하다
recycle : 재생하다 / legislation : 법률 제정

해석 국가 경제가 최근 침체에서 벗어나게 됨에 따라 자연 보존이 주요 관심사가 될 것이다. 천연자원에 대한 수요는 계속 증가할 것이다. 점점 줄어들고 있는 천연 자원의 보존을 돕기 위해서는 신문이나 유리재생 같은 모험적인 사업에 모든 사람이 협력하고 이를 도와야 한다. 그리하여 그것들이 다시 사용될 수가 있다. 우리가 탁 트인 공간과 숲을 계속 누리려면 자연 보존을 위한 입법을 돕고 이런 법률 제정을 추진하는 단체에 가입해야 한다. 지금 개개인이 하는 조그만 노력이 미래에 우리 모두에게 도움이 될 것이다.

해답 1. 저자의 주요 관심사는? → ④자연 보존의 필요성
2. 오늘날 자연 보존이 특히 중요한 이유는?
→ ②자원이 한정되어 있으므로
3. 우리가 자원을 보존할 수 있는 방법 중 하나는?
→ ③신문과 유리의 재생
4. 깨끗한 공간과 숲을 어떻게 보존할 수 있는가?
→ ①자연 보호 법률을 지원함으로써
5. 저자는 자연 보존에 관해 무엇을 할 것을 제안하고 있는가? → ④모든 사람이 도와야 한다.

11. **정답** 1. ④ 2. ③ 3. ④ 4. ①
word drop into : ~에 잠깐 들르다 / connection : 친척
be supposed to : ~로 여겨지다
tramp : 터벅터벅 걷다 / utter : 완전한
despair : 절망 / by chance (= by accident) : 우연히
Czech : 체코인, 체코어 / apprentice : 견습생, 도제

해석 그가 18세 때 돈 한 푼 없이, 그리고 한 빵집에서 일하고 있을 것이라고 여겨지는 사촌의 주소 이외에는 전혀 친척이 없는 런던에 들렀다. 하지만 그가 그 빵집을 찾아갔을 때 그 사촌은 이미 미국으로 가 버린 것을 알았다. 안톤은 여러 날을 터벅터벅 길을 걸어 다니며, 현관 입구와 공원 벤치에서 잠을 잤다. 마침내 그는 완전히 절망에 빠지고 말았다. 그는 영어를 몰랐으며, 주위에서 들려오는 그 낯선 언어는 그를 혼동시켰다. 그는 비엔나에서 장사를 배우고 체코어를 조금 할 줄 아는 가난한 한 독일인 재단사

를 만났다. 그 양복 재단사는 런던의 한 지하실에 수선점을 경영하고 있었다. 그는 견습공이 별로 필요치 않았지만, 그 아이가 불쌍해서 급료 없이 그를 받아들였다.

12. **정답** 1. ③ 2. ③ 3. ③ 4. ①
word do without (= manage without = dispense with)
: ~없이 지내다 / involuntarily : 어쩔 수 없이
voluntarily : 자발적으로 / martyr : 순교자
for the sake of : ~을 위해서
requisite : 필수 불가결한
something : 대단한 것
but (= except, save) : ~이외에 / martyrdom : 순교
renounce : 포기하다

해석 의심할 여지없이 행복 없이 지낼 수도 있다. 세상 사람들 중 20분의 19는 어쩔 수 없이 행복 없이 지내고, 자신의 행복보다 더 소중히 여기는 것을 위해서 사는 영웅이나 순교자는 스스로 원해서 그렇게 산다. 다른 사람들의 행복이나 행복이라는 필수불가결한 것보다 더 소중한 것이 도대체 어떤 게 있을까?

해답 1. 윗글에서 주장하는 내용은? → ③자신의 행복보다 타인의 행복을 추구하는 것이 더 좋다.
2. 다음 중 윗글에 반대되는 내용은? → ③모든 사람들이 자신의 개인적 행복을 더 소중히 여긴다.
3. 다음 중 순교자에 대해 옳은 설명인 것은?
→ ③신념을 포기하기 보다는 차라리 고통을 받거나 죽음을 선택하는 사람들

13. **정답** 1. ② 2. ① 3. ① 4. ①
word under way : 진행 중인 / era : 시대 / muscle : 근육
magnify : 확대시키다 / unlike : ~와는 달리
inexhaustible : 무한정한

해석 혁명이 진행 중에 있다. 우리는 컴퓨터의 시대 즉 정보시대에 살고 있는데 이는 사람들이 일하고 놀고 여행하고 생각하는 방식을 완전히 변화시킬 것이다. 산업혁명이 인간의 물리적인 힘을 극적으로 확대시켜 주었듯이 컴퓨터 혁명은 인간 두뇌의 힘을 확대시켜 줄 것이다. 그러나 철과 기름과 같은 한정된 자원에 의존했던 산업혁명과는 달리 새로운 정보 시대는 외관상 무한정해 보이는 자원인 지식의 무한정한 공급에 의해 불붙을 것이다.

해답 1. 지금 진행되고 있는 혁명은 ②정보 분야에서 일어나고 있다.
2. 컴퓨터의 발달은 하나의 혁명으로 규정되는데 그것은 ①인간의 생활 방식을 크게 변화시킬 것으로 예상되기 때문이다.
3. 윗글은 컴퓨터 혁명이 인간 두뇌가 ①더욱 확대되는 것을 가능케 해 줄 것이라고 지적하고 있다.
4. 산업혁명의 발달에서 특히 중요한 것은?
→ ① 광물자원

14. **정답** 1. ② 2. ① 3. ④ 4. ③ 5. ③
word fairy tale : 동화 / be absorbed in : ~에 열중한
growing up : 성장 / keep[go] -ing : 계속 ~하다
add to : ~을 더하다

outgrow : 나이를 먹어 ~을 알다

muslin : 모슬린 (속이 거의 다 비치는 고운 면직물)

kite : 솔개, 연 / goblin : 도깨비

wizard : 마법사 / dwarf : 난쟁이

engaging : 매력적인 / water lily : 수련

tadpole : 올챙이

childish : 유치한 cf. childlike : 순수한

displace : 대신하다 / fancy : 공상

flight : (상상) 비약

fairy godmother : 요정 대모 (이름을 숨기고 대모처럼 친절을 베푸는 사람)

in contrast to : ~와 대조하여

enchantment : 매력 / fairy lore : 동화

해석 여러분 중의 일부는 아직도 동화를 즐겨 읽을 것이다. 그러나 옛날처럼 깊게 몰두하지는 못한다. 나이가 들어 잃어버렸던 것을 완전히 버리는 않고 우리의 연 꼬리에 새로운 모슬린 조각을 계속 붙여 가면서, 흥미를 더욱 더해 가는 것은 성장의 흥미로운 한 부분이다. 동화를 읽는 나이는 우리가 주로 비현실적인 세계에 관심이 있을 때이다. 도깨비, 마술사, 난쟁이 등, 이 모든 상상의 창조물들은 어린이들에게 수련이나 올챙이 혹은 버터 바른 빵보다 훨씬 더 매력적인 것 같다. 성장한 어른들은 그들의 유치한 상상들을 기억해 내면서 즐거움을 느낀다. 그러나 다른 즐거움들이 이러한 어린 시절의 상상의 날개를 대신하게 되었다. 아는 바처럼 동화 속에서는 성공이나 행복을 위해서는 단지 요정 대모만 있으면 된다. 그러면 모든 것이 주인공에게 좋게 된다. 그러나 나이가 듦에 따라 한때 우리를 만족시켰던 이러한 가공의 승리는 매력의 힘을 잃게 된다. 우리는 실제의 승리와 행복을 원한다. 이와 같이 동화 속에서의 상상의 세계와 대조적으로 현실 세계에 대한 관심이 성장해 간다는 사실이 바로 독서 취향에 있어서의 최초의 커다란 진전임을 나타내 주는 것이다. 실제 인물, 실제의 문제, 실제의 승리, 실제의 사실들의 세계-이런 것들이 성장해 가는 사람의 독서 취향이 되는 것이다.

해답 1. 윗글에 가장 적합한 제목은? → ② 독서 취향의 성장

2. "우리의 연 꼬리에 새로운 모슬린 조각을 붙인다."가 의미하는 바는? → ① 인생에 새로운 흥미를 더해 나간다는 뜻

3. 성장한 어른들은 어린 시절의 유치한 상상에 ④ 즐거움을 느끼며 기억한다.

5. 글쓴이에 의하면 현실적인 이야기들은 주로 ③ 성숙해 가는 사람들에게 호소력을 느낀다.

15. **정답** 1. ③ 2. ③ 3. ② 4. ① 5. ①

word shortage : 부족 / natural gas : 천연가스

likewise : 마찬가지로 (= similarly) / glut : 공급 과잉

the law of supply and demand : 수요·공급의 법칙

dramatic : 극적인, 엄청난

heating bill : 난방비 / close down : 폐쇄하다

rumor : 풍문 / burn off : ~을 불태워 버리다

해석 몇 년 전 천연가스의 공급이 달려서 그 가격이 하늘 높이 치솟았다. 마찬가지로 가솔린도 수요가 공급을 초과할 때 가격이 상승했다. 원유 시장에서 공급이 과잉하게 되면 가격은 내렸다. 원유의 경우 수요·공급의 법칙이 교과서에 나오는 것과 똑같이 작용한다. 그러나 최근 천연가스 시장은 다르다. 천연가스 사용자들은 공급이 엄청 증가했음에도 불구하고 난방비 부담이 작년보다 늘었다는 것을 알게 될 것이다. 이용할 수 있는 천연가스가 너무 늘어나 천연가스 공급자들은 시장 부족 때문에 공장 문을 닫고 있다. 그래서 남은 가스를 태워 없애는 공급자도 있다는 소문이 나돌고 있다.

해답 1. 글쓴이의 목적은? → ③가스 가격이 높은데 대하여 의문을 제기하고 있다.

2. 우리는 가스 공급자들이 ②높은 가격을 유지할 수 있도록 공급 부족을 형성하기 위해 남은 가스를 태우고 있다고 추측할 수 있다.

3. 많은 가스 공급자들은? → ②사업을 그만두려 하고 있다.

4. 올해 천연가스 난방비는? → ①작년보다 올랐다.

5. 최근 이용할 수 있는 천연가스의 양은? → ①작년 공급분보다 더 많아졌다.

16. **정답** 1. ④ 2. ② 3. ④

word when (it is) used for studies of~ : ~에 관한 연구용으로 사용되는 경우 / octopus : 낙지

squid : 오징어 / unlike : ~와 달리 / crab : 게

exclusively : 전적으로 (= entirely)

rely on : ~에 의존하다 / tentacle : (동물) 촉수

identify : (신원을) 확인하다

visual : 시각의 / tactile : 촉각의

해석 학습과 기억에 관한 연구용으로 사용되는 경우, 낙지가 오징어보다 흥미로운 대상이다. 맛있는 물고기나 게를 찾기 위해 전적으로 눈에 의존하며 자유로이 수영하는 오징어와 달리, 낙지는 종종 바다 밑바닥 근처에서 먹이를 찾는다. 낙지는 먹이를 찾는 데 눈뿐만 아니라 촉수도 이용한다. 낙지의 두뇌는 따로 떨어진 두 기억저장 부분이 있는데, 한 곳을 시각적 기억을 저장하고, 또 한 곳은 촉각에 의한 기억을 저장하는 곳이다.

17. **정답** 1. ③ 2. ① 3. ④

word provide A with B : A에게 B를 공급하다

precisely : 정확하게 / fuel : 연료

perform : 이행하다

be concerned with : ~와 관련이 있다

in the second place : 둘째로

that is to say : 즉, 다시 말해서 (= in other words, that is) / carbohydrate : 탄수화물

protein : 단백질 / muscle : 근육 / tissue : 조직

해석 우리가 먹는 상당량의 음식이 우리를 지탱시켜 주며 우리 신체에 열과 에너지를 공급해 준다. 이는 연료가 현대적인 기계를 움직이게 하는 역할과 아주 똑같은 것이다. 음식의 이런 연료 역할은 특히 탄수화물 다시 말하면 우리가 일용하는 빵과 관련이 깊다.

449

둘째, 우리는 그 기계 자체를 지탱하기 위하여, 즉 신체를 발달시키기 위하여 음식을 소화한다. 바로 이런 목적 때문에 우리는 특히 근육 및 다른 신체 조직의 구성인자인 단백질이라 알려진 복잡한 물질을 필요로 한다. 최근 우리는 비타민이라는 용어로 불리는 물질들이 행하는 중요한 역할을 인식하게 되었다. 비타민은 화학적 구성과 그 기능이 다양하며, 단지 소량만 필요할 뿐이다.

18. **정답** 1. ③ 2. ① 3. ④ 4. ④ 5. ②

word in dim far off times : 아주 먼 옛날
　　forefather : 선조 (= ancestor)
　　savage : 미개인 / tiny : 작은
　　chase : 사냥, 추격 / combat : 전투
　　be filled with : ~로 가득 차 있다 / revenge : 복수

해석 아주 먼 옛날 우리의 선조가 야생적이고 벌거벗은 야만인이었을 때 그들에게는 책이 없었다. 어렸을 때의 우리가 그러했던 것처럼 그들은 읽을 줄도 쓸 줄도 몰랐다. 그러나 하루의 일과가 끝나거나 싸움과 수렵이 끝난 밤 모닥불 주변에 모여서 이야기꾼들이 해 주는 이야기에 귀를 기울였다. 이야기들은 모두 전쟁에 관한 것이었다. 그들은 사나운 사람이나 이상한 짐승들과 싸웠던 일에 대해 이야기했다. 그 얘기는 열정과 복수로 가득 차 있었고 부드러움이라든가 사랑에 대한 것은 없었다. 왜냐하면 이 시대의 사람들의 삶은 사납고 거친 것이었기 때문이다. 그것은 자연과 인간과의 오랜 투쟁이었던 것이다.

해답 1. 선조 (ancestor) 를 의미하는 단어는?
　　2. 왜 이야기가 전부 전쟁에 관한 것이었나?
　　→ ①그들의 생활은 끊임없는 투쟁의 연속이었기 때문이다.
　　3. 윗글의 제목은? → ③노변 이야기들
　　4. 노변 이야기에 들어있지 않던 내용은? → ④부드러움
　　5. 선조들은 다른 지역이나 사람들에 대해 어떤 방식으로 배웠는가? → ②이야기꾼들이 하는 이야기에 귀를 기울임으로써

19. **정답** 1. ③ 2. ③ 3. ④ 4. ③ 5. ④

word terrestrial : 지구상의 / atmosphere : 대기
　　turn A into B : A를 B로 바꾸다
　　green house : 온실
　　be based on : ~에 근거를 두고 있는
　　transparent : 투명한 / opaque : 부전도성의
　　trap inside : 안에 갇히다
　　carbon dioxide : 이산화탄소
　　radiate : (열을) 발하다, 복사하다
　　convective : 환류의 / moderate : 알맞은
　　illuminate : ~을 밝게 해 주다

해석 지구를 둘러싸고 있는 대기가 하는 또 다른 중요한 기능은 지구를 거대한 온실로 변화시켜 온도를 그렇지 않았을 경우보다 조금 더 높은 대략 60℉로 유지시켜 주고 있다. 대기가 온실 기능을 한다는 것은 다음과 같은 사실에 근거한다. 즉, 유리는 태양에너지의 대부분을 옮기는 가시적인 빛에는 거의 완전히 투

명하기 때문에 태양의 복사열에 의해 데워진 물체가 방출하는 열선에 전도되지 않는다는 것이다. 그래서 온실의 유리 천장을 통해 온실로 들어 간 태양에너지는 온실 내부에 갇혀서 내분의 온도를 외부 공기의 온도보다 높게 유지되게 해 준다. 대기의 경우 이산화탄소와 수증기가 유리의 역할을 하는데 대기 속의 이들의 양이 비록 미미하지만, 지구의 따뜻한 표면에서 방출되는 열을 많이 흡수해서 이를 다시 지구로 복사시킨다. 이처럼 낮 동안 환류하는 공기 흐름에 의해 지구 표면을 떠난 초과열이 차가운 밤 동안 재공급되는 것이다. 대기의 온도 조절 효과는 지구와 거의 같은 양의 열을 받지만 대기가 없는 달을 비교함으로써 잘 드러난다. 달 표면의 온도의 측정치를 보면 밝은 쪽 표면의 바위 온도가 214℉까지 올라가는 반면 어두운 쪽의 바위 온도는 -243℉까지 떨어진다. 만약 지구에 대기가 없으면 낮에는 물이 끓을 것이고 밤에는 알코올이 얼 것이다.

해답 1. "지구를 거대한 온실로 변화시킨다." 의 의미는? → ③지구를 지나친 더위와 추위로부터 보호해 준다.
　　2. 유리가 열선에 "반투명체의 역할"을 한다는 의미는? → ③빛이 수반하고 있는 열은 유리를 통과할 수 없다.
　　3. 우리가 밤 동안 누리는 열의 원천은? → ④대기
　　4. 윗글을 포함한 본문의 적절한 제목은? → ③지구의 대기
　　5. 다음 중 윗글에서 추론할 수 없는 것은? → ④가능한 한 많은 이산화탄소를 대기 속에 방출하는 것은 아주 좋은 일이다.

20. **정답** 1. ① 2. ④ 3. ①

word a key to door : 문을 여는 열쇠
　　guiding line : 지침
　　those who~ : ~인 사람들
　　cf. he[one] who~ : ~인 사람
　　make good use of : ~을 잘 활용하다
　　be convinced of : ~을 확신하다
　　be dependent on : ~에 의존하다
　　clack : 재잘거림
　　as long as : ~인 동안, ~인 한

해석 대학 교육은 지식과 지혜의 여러 문을 여는 열쇠이다. 교육은 한 사람이 일생 동안 하게 될 독서의 지침을 제공해 주는 것이 되어야 한다. 그래서 나는 대학교육을 잘 받은 사람들은 전 세계의 훌륭한 책들과 자기 나라의 문학 책을 읽은 것이 얼마나 중요한지 확실히 알고 있을 것이라고 생각한다. 그들은 무엇을 읽을 것인지 그것을 어떻게 이해해야 하는지 알 것이다. 대학 교육을 받은 사람은 폭넓은 선택을 한다. 그는 무기력하게 가만히 있거나 지루해 할 필요가 없다. 그가 현대사회의 쓸데없는 잡담 속에 시간을 보낼 리는 결코 없다. 매일매일 새로운 것을 전달해 주는 신문의 머리기사에 의존할 필요도 없다. 그는 그가 살아 있는 한 누릴 수 있는 모든 시대의 지혜를 갖고 있다.

해답 1. 매일 새로운 것을 전달해 주는 신문은? → ①대부분 우리에게 가치가 없다.

2. 세계의 훌륭한 책들과 자기 나라의 문학작품을 읽는 것은? → ④아무리 강조해도 지나침이 없다.
3. 대학 교육은? → ①사람이 지식과 지혜를 얻는 데 큰 도움이 된다.

21. **정답** 1. ① 2. ③ 3. ② 4. ④ 5. ②
word environment : 환경 / living things : 생물체
non-living things : 무생물체
have an effect on (= have an influence on = have an impact on = affect = influence) : ~에 영향을 미치다
해석 환경이란 주변에 있는 모든 것이다. 환경에는 새, 물고기, 나무와 같은 생물체도 있고 공기, 흙, 물과 같은 무생물체도 있다. 많은 동·식물들은 오직 한 가지 형태의 환경에서만 발견된다. 그러나 인간은 거의 모든 환경 속에서 발견될 수 있다. 인간의 심지어 생존하기 위해서 특별한 장비가 필요한 이를테면 달도 방문할 수 있다. 사람이 환경을 변화시킬 수 있는 힘을 지니고 있다는 것은 분명하다. 인간이 하는 것은 그곳에 있는 생물체와 무생물체에 영향을 미칠 수 있다. 이것이 인간이 변화를 추구하기 전에 먼저 변화에 대해 생각해 보는 것이 왜 중요한가 하는 이유다. 인간이 현명한 선택을 했을 때 비로소 환경은 건전한 상태로 남아 있을 수 있는 것이다.
해답 1. 이글의 가장 좋은 주제는? → ①환경과 인간
2. 윗글이 암시하고 있는 것은? → ③인간은 한 가지 형태의 환경에서 다른 형태의 환경으로 여행할 수 있다.
3. 인간은 특별한 ②장비가 없으면 달에서 살 수가 없다.
4. 우리는 환경이 ④인간에 의하여 쉽게 파괴될 수 있다는 것을 알 수 있다.
5. 미래를 위해 환경이 구하기 위해서 우리는 ②환경을 건전하게 유지해야 한다.

22. **정답** 1. ② 2. ① 3. ④ 4. ② 5. ③
word foresee : 예견하다
prefer to : ~하기를 더 좋아하다 / fund : 기금
make contribution to : 기여하다 (= contribute to)
worthwhile : 훌륭한, 가치가 있는
award ceremony : 시상식 / legacy : 유산
illuminated : 빛나는 / diploma : 상패
play a role : ~한 역할을 하다
해석 스웨덴 태생의 알프레드 노벨은 다이너마이트를 발명하고 난 후 부자가 되었다. 그러나 다이너마이트가 엄청난 파괴력을 지녔다는 것을 뒤늦게 알았다. 노벨은 다이너마이트를 발명한 사람으로 후세에 기억되기 싫었다. 그래서 죽기 2주 전인 1895년 인류에게 중대한 기여를 한 사람에게 상을 주는 데 쓰일 기금을 만들었다. 처음에는 문학, 물리학, 화학, 의학 그리고 평화 등 5개 분야의 상이었다. 경제학상은 처음 시상식이 있었던 해로부터 꼭 67년이 지난해인 1968년에 추가되었다. 기금에 투자된 노벨의 최초 유산은 900만 불이었고, 그에 대한 이자가 3만 불에서 15만 천 불까지 다양한 상금을 지불하는 데 사용

된다. 노벨이 죽은 날을 기념하는 날인 매년 10월 10일에 상 (금메달, 빛나는 상패, 그리고 상금) 이 수상자에게 수여된다. 때로는 수상자를 결정하는 데 정치 상황이 개입되기도 한다. 미국인은 과학상을 많이 받았지만 문학상은 비교적 적게 받았다. 제2차대전이 시작되었던 1940년부터 1942년까지는 상을 수여하지 않았다. 상을 두 번씩이나 수상한 사람도 있지만, 이런 경우는 드물고, 여러 사람이 골고루 수상했다.
해답 1. 첫 번째 시상식은 언제 있었나? → ②첫 번째 시상식은 경제학 분야가 추가된 1968년보다 67년 전이니 1901년이 답이다.
2. 노벨상이 만들어진 이유는? → ①인류에 대한 훌륭한 업적을 기리기 위해
3. 미국인이 많은 상을 받은 분야는? → ④과학 분야
4. 다음 중 사실이 아닌 것은? → ②기념식은 노벨의 발명을 기념하기 위해 10월 10일에 열린다.
5. 상을 몇 개 분야에서 주어지는가? → ③6개 분야

23. **정답** 1. ④ 2. ③
word stages of human technological progress : 인류의 기술 발전 단계
long-standing : 오랫동안 지속된
convention : 관습
divide A into B : A를 B로 나누다
n that order : 이 순서대로
subdivide : 세분하다 / Stone Age : 석기시대
flint : 부싯돌 / flake : 얇게 조각내다 / grind : 갈다
from A to B : A에서 B로 / utensil : 도구
해석 인류의 기술 발전 단계를 관찰함으로써 인류의 초기 역사를 매우 쉽게 그리고 분명하게 연구할 수 있다. 이는 절단 도구나 무기를 만드는 데 사용된 단단한 재료-돌, 구리, 청동, 철의 순서로-에 따라 초기 역사를 광범위한 기간으로 나누는 것이 오랫동안 지속되어 온 관습이기 때문이다. 과거에 대한 지식이 증가함에 따라, 광범위한 기간은 좀 더 세분화되었다. 부싯돌과 다른 용도의 돌을 만드는 기술이 돌을 그저 깨부수는 것 (flaking) 에서 연마하는 것 (grinding) 으로 변했다는 것을 알게 되었을 때 석기시대는 구석기 시대와 신석기 시대로 나누어졌다.
해답 1. 역사가는 ④도구나 무기를 만드는 데 사용된 재료에 따라 인류의 초기 역사를 광범위한 기간으로 나누었다.
2. 다음 중 초기 역사를 시대로 구분하는 데 사용된 체계에 대하여 논한 것은? → ③그것은 기술적 발전을 보여 주려는 것이다.

24. **정답** 1. ② 2. ③ 3. ① 4. ④
word belief in : ~에 대한 믿음 / conviction : 확신
join : 결합하다
regard A as B : A를 B로 간주하다
cowardly : 겁 많은 / be incapable of : ~할 수 없는
imposture : 사기, 협잡 / retrograde : 후퇴하다
be ready to : 기꺼이 ~하다 (= be willing to)
devote oneself to : ~에 전념하다
martyrdom : 순교

해석 제퍼슨의 과학과 이성에 대한 믿음은 확고한 신념이었다. 제퍼슨은 다음과 같은 글을 썼다. "나는 '인간은 더 이상 발전할 수 없으며, 과거 우리 조상들이 알았던 것보다 더 나은 것을 발견할 수는 없을 것이다' 는 생각은 겁쟁이들이나 하는 것으로 여긴다는 점에서 당신과 견해를 같이한다. 우리 미국인들의 정신은 매우 개방적이어서 이런 사기 같은 말에 귀를 기울이지 않는다는 점에서 하늘에 감사드리고 싶다. 그리고 우리가 인쇄술을 지니고 있기에 과학은 결코 퇴화할 수 없을 것이다. 왜냐하면 우리가 한 번 획득한 지식이 (인쇄술을 통해 보존되기 때문에) 다시 상실되는 경우란 결코 있을 수 없을 것이기 때문이다. 그러므로 사상의 자유와 언론의 자유를 지키기 위해 우리 모두 기꺼이 자신을 바쳐야 할 것이다."

해답 1. 제퍼슨은 ②인류는 미래에도 진보할 수 있을 것이다라고 믿었다.
2. 가치 있는 것은 모두 이전에 다 밝혀졌다는 생각은? → ③제퍼슨은 겁쟁이나 하는 생각이라고 여겼다.
3. 제퍼슨은 사상과 언론의 자유가 ①인류의 진보를 촉진시킬 것이다라는 것을 암시했다.
4. 제퍼슨은 미국인의 어떤 정신에 대해 감사를 보냈는가? → ④개방적인 면

25. **정답** 1. ② 2. ③ 3. ④ 4. ①
word all summer : 여름 내내 / sweep : 쓸다
sensibly : 상당히 / edged with : ~로 테를 두른
foam : 거품 / with an air of : ~한 기분으로
as before : 이전처럼 / shrill : 시끄러운
tide : 조수 / with enthusiasm : 열정적으로
plunge into : ~로 뛰어들다 / dolphin : 돌고래

해석 여름 내내 어린이들은 해변에서 논다. 그들은 행복하고 우호적이다. 파도가 모래 위를 휩쓸고 올 때면 작은 아이들은 바다로 등을 돌리고 상당히 멀리까지 달아난다. 거품으로 테를 두른 물이 바다로 되돌아갈 때 그들은 앞에 있는 바다를 몰고 간다는 기분으로 물을 뒤따라 뛰어 들어간다. 그러나 또다시 파도가 쳐오면 시끄러운 비명 소리를 내며 또다시 놀라며 이전처럼 달아난다. 태양이 그들의 작고 갈색 빛다리를 뜨겁게 내리 쬐이는데도 그들은 조수에 마모된 색깔이 있는 돌을 아주 열심히 모은다. 좀 더 큰 아이들은 작은 돌고래처럼 파도 속으로 뛰어든다. 물은 맑고 차갑다.

해답 1. 파도가 모래 위로 밀려 올 때면 작은 아이들은 바다로부터 ②멀리 도망간다.
2. "바다를 몰고 간다는 기분으로"라는 말의 의미는? → ③마리 그들이 바다를 몰고 있는 것처럼
4. 윗글에서 해변의 어린이들을 묘사한 방식은?
→ ①그림 같은

26. **정답** 1. ① 2. ① 3. ④
word unlike : ~와 달리 / butterfly : 나비
migrate : 이동하다 / fall : 가을
navigate : 항해하다

해석 대부분의 나비와는 달리 오렌지색과 검은색이 섞여 유난히 눈에 띄는 Monarch는 매년 가을 남쪽으로 이동한다. 그들은 새처럼 큰 강의 계곡 아래로, 해안선을 따라서 평원을 가로지르는 규칙적인 이동 경로를 따른다. 동부에서는 코드 곶을 길이대로 여행하고 롱 아일랜드로 건너가서는 길이대로 여행하고 더 낮은 지역인 뉴저지로 건너갔다가 해안으로 내려온다. 어느 누구도 이 나비들이 왜 이동하고 어떻게 항해하는지 확실히 모른다. 우리가 알고 있는 것이라고는 Monarch가 수백만 마리씩 이동하고 있으며 매년 봄에 다시 돌아온다는 것이다. 우리가 이유를 모르는 것이 너무도 많다.

해답 1. 동부에서의 Monarch 이동 경로는 ①코드 곶에서 뉴저지 남부 지역까지 뻗쳐있다.
2. Monarch의 이동과 그들이 따르는 경로는 ①예측할 수 있으며, 주기적이다.
3. Monarch라는 나비가 이동하는 이유는 ④여전히 수수께끼이다.

27. **정답** 1. ② 2. ④
word predominantly : 주로 / from A to B : A에서 B까지
rural (시골의) ↔ urban (도시의)
transformation : 변화
exploitation : 개발, 이용 / enormous : 거대한
consolidation : 통합 / extensive : 광범위한

해석 미국은 1865년 남북전쟁이 끝날 무렵에는 농업 국가였으나, 세계 1차 대전에 참가했던 1917년에 이르러서는 세계에서 제일 거대하고 부유한 공업국가로 발전했다. 이러한 큰 변화의 주요인들은 엄청난 인구 증가, 무한정한 광물 자원의 발전과 개발, 거대한 대평원과 서부 정착지의 통합, 광범위한 철도망의 건설 등이다.

해답 1. 윗글은 주로 ②미국이 어떻게 공업국이 되었는가에 대해 쓰고 있다.
2. 우리는 1865년과 1917년 사이에 많은 사람들이 ④도시로 이주했다고 추론해 볼 수 있다.

28. **정답** 1. ③ 2. ④
word kite : 연 / lightning : 번개 / aerial : 공중의
general : 육군 (공군) 대장 / bank : 둑
nucleus : 핵심, 중심
invaluable (= priceless, valuable) : 귀중한
scout : 정찰하다 / life-boat : 구명정
be equipped with : ~을 구비하다

해석 많은 사람들은 프랭클린의 연 실험 덕분에 번개가 전기라는 것이 입증되었다는 것을 알고 있다. 1700년대 중반 이래 연은 기후 조건 측정이나 공중사진 촬영 같은 과학적인 목적을 위해 사용되어 왔다. 연은 또 전시에도 여러 재미있는 방식으로 사용되었다. 수세기 전 한 한국군 장군이 줄이 부착된 연을 반대편 강둑으로 보냈다. 줄에 이어 굵은 밧줄을 보냈는데 이것이 다리를 만드는 중심부를 형성했다. 일본인은 사람이 타고 나르는 연을 만들었는데 이는 적의 위치를 정찰하는 데 매우 귀중한 것이었다. 많은 군대들이 신호 수단으로 연을 사용하곤 했다. 지

금은 비행기 구명정에 자동적으로 SOS를 보내는 안테나가 장착된 연을 달아 놓고 있다.

29. **정답** 1. ④ 2. ④ 3. ④ 4. ③ 5. ②
　　word pearl : 진주 / pear-shaped : 배 모양의
　　　　pendant : 매달려있는 / oval : 타원형의
　　　　in combination with : ~와 조화를 이루다
　　　　luster : 광택 / unmistakable : 틀릴 여지가 없는
　　　　oyster : 굴 / dewdrop : 이슬방울
　　　　gem : 보석 (= jewel) / as a matter of fact : 사실상
　　　　foreign article : 이물질 / parasite : 기생충
　　　　irritation : 짜증 / squirm : 꿈틀거리다
　　　　secretion : 분비 (물) / nuisance : 귀찮은 것
　　　　expel : 내몰아 버리다
　　　　the+비교급~, the+비교급~ : ~하면 할수록 더욱더 ~하다.
　　해석 진주는 많은 바다에서 발견되지만 질도 제일이고 수량도 최고인 것은 페르시아만산이다. 진주의 가치를 판단하는 기준은 여러 가지이다. 첫째, 가장 중요한 것은 아니지만 우선 색상을 들 수 있다. 그 다음은 모양인데 둥근 것, 배처럼 생긴 것, 타원형인 것 혹은 납작한 것 등이 있다. 다음으로 크기를 들 수 있는데 색상, 모양과 조화를 이루었을 때에만 가치를 지니게 된다. 그러나 가장 결정적인 기준은 광택이다. 진정 가치 있는 진주의 광택은 매우 뚜렷해서 잘못 판단할 수가 없다. 진주는 어떻게 만들어지는가? 아랍의 시인들은 굴이 여러 날 밤 바다 표면으로 올라와 있을 때 이슬이 그 속으로 들어가 보석이 된다고 말한다. 사실 굴에게는 진주가 참으면서 만든 이물질이지만 제거하려고 하면 기꺼이 제거할 수 있는 것이다. 모래알이나 기생충이 굴 속에 들어가면 굴은 이 짜증나는 것들을 없애기 위해 움직이고 몸부림친다. 그 과정에서 분비물이 나와 이 물질을 둘러싸게 된다. 분비물이 단단해져서 둥글게 되면 진주가 된다. 굴이 이 귀찮은 것을 몰아내려고 애를 쓰면 쓸수록 분비물의 양이 더 많아지고, 진주는 더 커지는 것이다.
　　해답 1. 윗글의 제목은? → ④진주의 질과 그 형성
　　　　3. 진주의 가치는 주로 ④광택에 있다.
　　　　4. 진주는 ③짜증나게 만드는 이물질이 조개 속으로 들어가는 것에 의해 만들어지기 시작한다.
　　　　5. 진주의 크기는 주로 ②분비물의 양의 영향을 받는다.

30. **정답** 1. ① 2. ① 3. ② 4. ② 5. 지금 부인들의 마음속에 진행되고 있는 것은 대규모의 문화혁명이다.
　　word be fed up with : ~에 혐오감을 느끼다
　　　　male (남성) ↔ female (여성)
　　　　what is going on : 진행되고 있는 것
　　　　frustration : 좌절감 / disillusionment : 환멸감
　　　　despite (= in spite of = with all = for all) : ~에도 불구하고
　　　　oppress : 억압하다 / abuse : 남용하다, 학대하다
　　　　fight for : ~을 위하여 투쟁하다
　　　　maintain : 주장하다 / nurture : (영양을 주어) 키우다

breadwinner : 가족 부양자
pervasiveness : 만연, 널리 퍼짐
disturbing : 걱정스러운
inflict : (타격, 고통을) 가하다 / insult : 모욕감, 욕
hostility : 적개심 / tease : 조롱
aggressive : 공격적인 / respondent : 응답자
condescending : (사람·행위가) 잘난 체하는
　　해석 약 4500명의 미국 부인들의 견해를 조사한 것을 7년 동안 분석하고 난 후 S. 하이트는 그들이 남성에 대하여 혐오감을 지니고 있다고 결론 내렸다. 지금 부인들의 마음속에 진행되고 있는 것은 대규모의 문화혁명이다. 더욱 모든 연령층의 부인들이 남자들과 개인적인 관계에 있어 좌절감이 늘고, 환멸이 증대하고 있다는 견해를 밝혔다고 하이트는 적고 있다. 하이트는 여성의 해방과 성적 혁명에도 불구하고 여성은 여전히 남성에게 억눌리고 학대받고 있다고 주장한다. 그녀의 연구에 의하면 더 많은 비율인 87%의 여성들이 감정적인 면에 있어서 실제로 남성이 여성보다 훨씬 의존적이라고 주장하지만 5명 중 4명의 여성이 남성과의 관계에 있어 여성의 권리를 쟁취하기 위하여 투쟁해야 한다고 주장했다. 그들은 가족 부양자로서 가족의 생계를 돕고 있으면서도 전통적으로 여성의 일로 여겨져 온 요리하기, 자녀양육, 자녀가 남편에게 사랑스런 손길을 제공해야 하는 것 등의 일도 함께해야 한다고 불평한다. 하이트의 견해에 따르면, 몹시 속상하지만 중대한 발견의 하나가 남성이 여성에게 가하는 개인적이고, "감정적인 폭력"이 만연해 있다는 사실이다. 그러한 폭력은 욕이라든가 적개심, 조롱, 공격적인 태도를 통해 가해진다고 그녀는 밝히고 있다. 응답자 중 거의 전부라고 할 수 있는 92%의 여성들이 남성은 잘난 체하는 태도나 모든 판단을 자신이 내리는 듯한 태도로 여성들과 대화한다고 불만을 터뜨리고 있다.
　　해답 1. 하이트는 미국의 여성은 ①남성 우월적인 태도에 싫증나있다고 주장한다.
　　　　2. 미국 여성들은 ①그들이 돈도 벌고 동시에 가족을 돌보아야 한다는 것을 불평하고 있다.
　　　　3. 본문의 내용을 통해 볼 때 다음 중 옳지 않은 것은? → ②많은 부인들이 남편에게 매를 맞는다.

31. **정답** 1. ① 2. ② 3. ① 4. ③
　　word be about to : 막 ~하려는 중이다
　　　　sweet heart : 연인 / arrange : 계획 (준비) 하다
　　　　lobster : 왕새우 / faithfulness : 충실함
　　　　put~ to the proof : ~을 시험하다
　　　　ask A for B : A에게 B해 달라고 요구하다
　　　　blush : 얼굴을 붉히다 / in love : 사랑에 빠진
　　　　plot : 은밀한 계획
　　해석 곧 결혼하기로 되어 있는 젊은 여인이 마지막 순간 애인을 시험해 보기로 결심했다. 그래서 그녀가 아는 소녀 중 제일 예쁜 소녀를 골라 그것이 매우 큰 모험이라는 것을 알면서도 다음과 같이 말했다. "잭이 오늘 저녁 너를 데리고 나가 달빛 아래서 해변을 산책하고, 왕새우를 곁들인 정찬을 먹는 그런 일들을 모두 하기로 약속되어 있어. 그의 마음이 변함없는

지 시험해 보고 싶으니 네가 그에게 키스해 달라고 요청해 주길 바래." 얘기를 듣던 소녀는 웃다가 얼굴을 붉히며 그렇게 하겠노라고 동의했다. 그래서 그 위험천만한 음모는 진행되었다. 그 다음 날 책의 애인인 소녀가 예쁜 소녀를 찾아가 걱정스럽게 물었다. "네가 그에게 키스를 청했니?" "아니, 기회가 없었어. 그가 먼저 요청했거든."

해답 2. 결과적으로 책은 ②충실하지 않은 것으로 판명났다.
3. 책과 연애하던 소녀는 아마 ①실망했을 것이다.
4. 윗글의 제목으로 적절한 것은? → ③애인의 시험

32. **정답** 1. ① 2. ③ 3. ④ 4. ④ 5. ②
word supreme : 최고의
universal gravitation : 만유인력
plague : 전염병 / law of gravity : 중력의 법칙
consequence : 결과 / solar system : 태양계
orchard : 과수원 / particle : 입자
in inverse proportion to : ~에 반비례하여
directly proportional to : ~에 정비례하는
product of masses : 질량의 곱

해석 아이작 뉴턴의 최고의 과학적 업적은 그의 만유인력의 법칙이다. 그는 1665년 전염병을 피하여 농장으로 갔는데 이 기간 동안 중력의 법칙과 태양계에서의 그것의 결과를 도출해 냈다. 그는 나중에 친구에게 과수원에서 사과가 사과나무에서 떨어지는 것을 보다가 그 생각을 하게 됐다고 이야기하였다. 우주에 있는 물체의 모든 입자는 다른 입자를 끌어당기는데 이때 작용하는 힘은 입자 사이의 거리의 곱에 반비례하고, 질량의 곱에 정비례한다고 그는 밝혔다.

해답 1. 뉴턴은 중력의 법칙을 어디서 발견했는가?
→ ①농장에서
2. "모든 입자는 다른 입자를 끌어당긴다."는 구절이 의미하는 것은? → ③모든 입자는 다른 모든 입자들을 끌어당긴다.
3. 윗글에 따르면, 만유인력의 체계는 뉴턴의 ④가장 중요한 과학 업적이다.
4. 뉴턴은 ④물리학자로 가장 잘 묘사될 수 있다.
5. 뉴턴이 만유인력 체계를 몇 세기에 발견했는가?
→ ②17세기

33. **정답** 1. ② 2. ③ 3. ④ 4. ①
word suffer from : ~로 고통 받다
affect to do so : 그러는 체하다
a rubbish heap : 쓰레기 더미
on time (= punctual) : 정각에 cf. in time (= sooner or later) : 조만간에
anesthetics : 마취제 / stand out : 두드러지다
above all : 무엇보다도 / stand on : ~에 의거하다
recipient : 수령인 / impersonality : 비인간성
soulfulness : 정신세계
commendable : 칭찬할 만한
impartial : 공평한 / agencies of mercy : 자선기관
free benefits : 무료 혜택
make a defense : 방어하다 / imply : 암시하다

efficient operation : 효율적 운영
public utility : 공익사업

해석 내가 도시 생활로 고통 받거나 그런 체하는 자연주의자들 중 하나가 아닌 것은 결코 비밀이 아니며, 또한 도시 생활이 부자연스럽고 흥미 없으며 우둔한 자들로 이루어진 쓰레기 더미라고 생각하지도 않는다. 정각이면 도착하는 기차, 부르기만 하면 오는 소방서, 손을 대면 방을 밝혀 주는 불빛, 돈 없는 사람의 건강을 위해 일하는 진료소와 자선단체, X-ray, 비싼 라듐, 마취제, 외과 기술 등과 같은 저절로 경탄할만한 이상의 것들이 있다고 늘 여겨진다. 어떠한 지불 이상으로 이러한 봉사는 완벽한 수행에의 자부심을 두드러지게 한다. 그리고 무엇보다 나는 그 수령인이 종교, 정치, 인종에 있어 어디에 의거하는지를 묻지 않는 문명의 숭고한 비인격성을 경탄한다. 나는 이것이 아름다움이며, 아무도 정의할 수 없는 어떤 신비로운 정신세계일 뿐만 아니라 백만 년간 성장해 온 인간의 정신인 영혼이라 부른다.

해답 1. 이 글을 쓴 이에게 있어서 가장 칭찬할 만한 도시생활의 양상은 ①공평한 봉사이다.
2. 글쓴이는 ①도시 생활을 옹호하고 있다.
3. 글쓴이는 공익사업의 효율적인 운영이 ③질적으로 정신적인 것임을 암시하고 있다.
4. 이 글의 견해를 가장 잘 나타내는 제목은 ①도시의 경탄할 만한 특질이다.

34. **정답** 1. ① 2. ④ 3. ②
word dynamics : 역학 / predecessor : 선조, 선
deduce : 연역하다 / prior to : ~에 앞서서

해석 역학의 일반 원리들은 물체의 운동 및 운동을 촉발하는 힘과의 관계를 설명하는 규칙이다. 선학들의 업적에 많은 것을 토대로 하여 아이작 뉴턴경은 1678년 출판된 그의 유명한 저서 'Principia'에서 역학의 3가지 법칙을 연역해 놓았다. 뉴턴에 앞서서 아리스토텔레스는 물체의 자연 상태는 정지 상태이며 만약 물체의 운동을 유지하기 위해 힘이 작용하지 않으면 움직이는 물체는 정지하게 된다고 설정했었다. 갈릴레오는 낙하물의 운동을 바르게 묘사하고 물체의 운동을 계속하게 만드는 데는 어떠한 힘도 요구되지 않는다는 것을 기록하는데 성공했다. 그는 힘의 효과가 운동을 변화시키는 것이라고 기록했다. Huygens는 운동 방향의 변화는 속도의 변화와 마찬가지로 가속을 포함하며 더 나아가 힘의 작용을 필요로 한다는 것을 알았다. 케플러는 태양 주위의 혹성 운동을 묘사하는 법칙을 도출해 냈다. 뉴턴이 빌려 쓴 것은 주로 갈릴레오와 케플러였다.

해답 1. Huygen은 가속이 ①운동 방향의 변화 혹은 속도의 변화에 필요하다고 말했다.
2. 이글에 의하면, 뉴턴은 주로 ④갈릴레오와 케플러의 작업에 토대를 둔 법칙에 기초를 두고 있다.
3. 이글의 주된 목적은? → ②뉴턴을 물리학 분야의 권위자로 위치를 굳히기 위해서

35. **정답** 1. ② 2. ④ 3. ④ 4. ①
word turmoil : 혼란 / bloodshed : 학살

454

persist : 지속되다 / alliance : 동맹
profound : 심원한
expert (전문가) ↔ layman (문외한)
onslaught : 맹공격 / reform : 개혁
accommodation : 적응, 조정
have-nots : 가진 것 없는 나라
status quo : 원상태
launch the war : 전쟁을 개시하다
take on : ~한 모습을 띠다

해석 아무리 걸프전이 확실하게 끝난다고 해도 반이라크 동맹국이 심오한 정치적 변화의 필요성을 받아들이지 않는다면 중동에서의 혼란과 학살은 지속될 것 같다. 폭넓고 다양한 견해를 가진 전문가들은 사담 후세인에 대한 맹공격을 완료할 때마다 미국과 그 우방 및 서부와 아랍 세계가 직면할 몇 가지 기본적 도전에 동의한다. 여기에는 사우디아라비아와 쿠웨이트 같은 나라의 민주적 개혁, 아랍 세계의 분개한 비산유국에 대한 오일 달러의 재분배, 팔레스타인에 대한 일종의 조정 문제 등이 포함된다. 이집트의 전 대통령 대변인 Tahseen Beshir는 이렇게 말한다. "중동에서는 아무것도 원상태로 돌아오지 않을 것이다. 문제의 핵심은 미국과 그 동맹국들이 전쟁 개시에 했던 것처럼 평화 건설에도 같은 노력을 기울일 것인지에 있는 것이다." 많은 아랍인과 회교도인에게 있어, 전쟁은 사담을 성스러운 전사의 위치로 올려놓았으며, 그는 서방 세계의 무력에 기꺼이 맞서고자 하는 유일한 사람이었다. 옥스퍼드대학의 사학과 교수인 로버트 오닐 씨는 영국의 Financial Times에서 다음과 같이 썼다. "패배한, 특히 죽은 사담은 훨씬 더 영예로운 이미지로 남을 것이다. 우리는 지역 안정의 새 체계가 이뤄짐에 따라 걸프전 후의 길고 불확실한 기간에 직면할 준비를 해야 한다."

해답 1. 이 글은 주로 ②걸프전과 관련된 것이다.
2. 미국이 이라크를 물리치고 난 후 직면하게 될 기본적인 도전으로 언급되지 않은 것은? → ④걸프전 준비
3. 오닐 교수는 사담이 패배당하면 ④훨씬 더 명예로운 이미지로 여겨질 것으로 믿고 있다.
4. Tahseen Beshir는 ①이집트의 정치인이다.

36. 정답 1. ① 2. ② 3. ④
word access to : ~에 접근하다
those who~ : ~인 사람들
be responsible for : ~에 책임이 있는
approximately : 대략
option : 선택 품목

해석 오늘날 컴퓨터의 가장 실망스러운 면 중 하나는 컴퓨터에 접근할 수 있는 사람이 거의 없다는 것이다. 그렇게 하는 사람들조차도 보통 어떤 특수 업무를 완수하도록 해야 하는 책임을 맡고 있고, 개인적 용도로는 컴퓨터에 가까이 할 수 없다는 것이다. 전자제품 도매업자 중 한 사람이 약 $600에 팔릴 수 있는 가정용 컴퓨터 시스템을 가지고 이 상황을 변화시키길 바라고 있다. HC 30 기종은 대형컴퓨터의

많은 특성을 지닌 기본 시스템이 될 것이다. 고객이 일단 표준 프로그램에 익숙해지면, 그 기계의 기능을 확장시킬 수 있는 선택 품목을 구입할 수 있다.

37. 정답 1.
word nostalgia : 향수
first-hand : 직접적으로 (= directly)
↔ second-hand : 간접적으로 (= indirectly)
complex : 열등감 / plague : 질병, 괴롭히다
leave ~ behind : 뒤에 남기다
dispassionately : 냉정하게 / pull out : 뽑아내다
identity : 주체성 / see A as B : A를 B로 보다
interpret : 해석하다 / fit oneself to : ~에 맞추다
uncritical : 무비판적인 / embrace : 수용 (하다)

해석 젊은이들은 그들이 직접 겪지 못했기 때문에 전통을 향수를 가지고 바라보지 않는다. 그들은 또한 전쟁 세대를 괴롭혔던 패배의 열등감도 가지고 있지 않다. 그들의 일본은 언제나 부유한 나라였고, 전쟁과 기아는 그들의 아버지가 그것을 극복하려고 열심히 일했기 때문에, 전통만큼이나 멀게 보였다. 그들은 문화적 전통을 냉정하게 보고 그들이 원하는 요소만을 뽑아내어 맥락을 바꾸어 놓는다. 구세대는 이것을 주체성의 상실로 여긴다. 그러나 이것은 그 가운데에서 자신을 과거에 맞추는 게 아니라 과거를 자신에게 맞추려는 새로운 주체성의 모색으로 해석될 수 있다. 이것은 결코 과거를 거부하는 것이 아니고 무비판적인 수용도 아니다.

38. 정답 1. ② 2. ① 3. ② 4. ③
word hazard : 위험 / confront : ~에 직면하다
so-called : 소위 / occupational disease : 직업병
lead poisoning : 납중독
preparation : (화장품, 식품, 약품 따위의) 조제품
glaze : 유약 / since (= now that) : ~이기 때문에
eliminate : 제거하다 / accumulate : 누적되다
kidney : 신장, 콩팥 / disorder : 무질서, 질병
precaution : 조심, 예방

해석 근로자들이 직면하고 있는 위험 중 소위 직업병이라는 것이 있다. 가령 이들 중 하나가 납중독인데, 이것은 때때로 납 먼저 혹은 유약이나 납을 함유한 페인트 같은 제품 등과 더불어 오랫동안 작업하는 사람들에게 영향을 미친다. 납은 서서히 없어지기 때문에, 독소가 쌓여서 결국 엄청난 무력감이나 손힘의 상실, 신장병 혹은 다른 심각한 질병을 유발한다. 근로자들은 그러한 위험들을 막기 위해 각별한 주의를 해야 한다.

해답 1. 이 글은 일반적으로 어떤 위험에 대하여 우리의 주위를 환기시키고 있는가? → ②직업병
2. 특정 장애가 쌓인 결과로써 윗글에서 언급되고 있는 것은? → ①신장병
3. 큰 선물에서 페인트칠을 하는 사람은 윗글에서 언급된 어떤 위험을 피하기 위해 주의해야 하는가? → ②납중독
4. 페인트의 성분으로 언급된 것은? → ③납

39. **정답** 1. ④ 2. ④

    word egoistic : 이기적인

       self-centered : 자기중심적인

       introspective : 내성적인

       be concerned with : ~에 관심이 있다

       reflect on : ~에 영향을 미치다

       good or bad : 좋건 나쁘건 / subtle : 민감한

       be aware of : ~를 의식하다, ~를 알다

       nuance : 뉘앙스

    해석 우리 일본인들은 상당히 이기적이라고 말할 수밖에 없다. 특히 우리 일본인들이 그렇다. 우리는 자기중심적이고, 내성적이며, 자신의 내적인 감정에 관심이 있다. 우리는 좋건 나쁘건 개인적으로 우리에게 영향을 미치는 어떤 일에 지나치게 예민하다. 우리는 민감한 사람들로서, 모든 일본인들은 우리들에 대해 말하는 어떤 이야기나 우리 주변에서 일어나는 어떤 일의 미묘한 뉘앙스를 날카롭게 인식하고 있다.

    해답 2. 일본인들이 자기 주변에서 일어나는 대화나 사건들의 미묘한 의미 차이를 인식할 수 있는 것은 ④그들의 민감한 국민성 때문이다.

40. **정답** 1. ③ 2. ④ 3. ③ 4. ① 5. ④

    word prevalent : 만연하다 / toward : ~경

       a rising incidence : 발병하는 경우의 증대

       mark : ~을 특징짓다

       coastal plains region : 해안 평원 지역

       overrate : 과대평가하다 (= overestimate)

       hurdle : 장애물 / epidemic : 유행병

       pernicious : 해로운

       take a heavy toll of~ : 많은 희생이 나게 하다

       endemic : 풍토의, 고유의, 풍토병의

       outbreak : (병의) 발병

       concomitant : 수반하는 (= accompanying)

       deprive A of B : A로부터 B를 박탈하다

    해석 17세기 동안 미국 식민지에서 말라리아가 만연했다는 것은 의심의 여지가 없다. 17세기 말경부터 18세기로 이어지면서 펜실베이니아, 뉴저지, 메릴랜드, 델라웨어 등과 해안 평안 지역에 위치한 식민지들에서 말라리아 발병 건수가 증가했고, 뉴잉글랜드 지역에서는 감소했다. 말라리아가 식민지대에 중요한 의미를 지닌다는 것은 아무리 과장해서 이야기해도 모자랄 지경이다. 왜냐하면 이는 미국 식민지의 발달에 큰 장애요인이 되었기 때문이다. 말라리아라는 해로운 유행병은 '유럽에서 막 건너온' 새로운 정착민에게 치명적인 것이 되곤 해서, 이미 정착해있던 사람들과 새로 건너 온 사람 할 것 없이 많은 사람의 목숨을 빼앗아갔다. 말라리아가 풍토병인 지역에서는 말라리아가 봄, 가을 연속해서 발생하여, 사람들을 병들게 하고 죽게 함으로써 식민지에서 아주 필요로 하였던 노동력을 박탈해 버렸다.

    해답 1. 말라리아는 ③주기적으로 발생했다.

       2. 17세기 후반과 18세기 초반에 ④뉴저지의 말라리아 발병 건수가 증가했다.

       3. "endemic region" 이란 ③말라리아 풍토병이 있는 지역을 의미한다.

       4. 식민지 시대 역사에서 말라리아의 중요성은?

       → ①과장할 필요가 없을 정도이다.

       5. 말라리아는 ④식민지의 신·구 정착민 모두에게 영향을 미쳤다.

41. **정답** 1. ① 2. ④ 3. ④ 4. ② 5. ③

    word environmental interference : 환경 파괴

       halt : 중지시키다 / shrinking : 축소

       agricultural belt : 농업지역 / glacial ice : 빙하

       carbon dioxide : 이산화탄소

       overwhelming : 압도적인

       fossil fuel : 화석연료

       drastic : 강렬한 / commerce : 상업

    해석 인간의 환경 파괴가 새로운 빙하기의 도래를 막았지만 이로 인하여 지구의 기후는 더 따뜻해질 것이라고 한 지역 연구가 밝혔다. David G. Bridges 교수는 지구가 더 따뜻해짐으로써 야기될 결과로 Great Lakes와 내륙 호수의 축소, 농업 지역의 북쪽으로의 이동, 즉 Canada로의 이동, 바다의 수면을 상승시킬 수 있는 빙하의 해빙 등이 있을 것으로 믿고 있다. 석탄, 석유, 가스 등을 연소시킬 때 발생하는 이산화탄소 양의 미래의 증대가 날씨의 영향을 미치는 가장 중요한 요인이 될 것이다. 이런 화석연료의 사용은 중서부의 기후를 더욱 건조하게 만들어 농업, 상업, 그리고 오락에 많은 영향을 미칠 것이다. 인구 과잉과 식량 부족 이후 환경 파괴나 이로 인한 문제가 인류가 직면한 가장 심각한 문제가 될 것이라고 Bridges 교수는 말했다.

    해답 1. 윗글의 주제는? → ①변화하는 세계의 기후

       2. 환경 파괴의 결과로 가능한 것은? → ④농업 지역의 북쪽으로의 이동

       3. Bridges 교수는 환경 파괴가 ④석탄, 석유, 가스의 연소 때문이라고 믿고 있다.

       4. 윗글에 따르면 지구 전체의 기후는 ②다소 더 따뜻해진다.

       5. 환경 파괴에 주로 책임이 있는 것 혹은 사람은? → ③인류

42. **정답** 1. ② 2. ① 3. ④ 4. ③ 5. ②

    word evolutionary : 진화의 / puzzle : 수수께끼

       flightless : 날 수 없는 / ratite : 주조류의 새

       widespread : 널리 퍼진

       be regarded as : ~로 여겨지다 / hypothesis : 가설

       biologist : 생물학자 / bone structure : 뼈구조

    해석 진화에 관한 또 하나의 수수께끼는 최근까지도 매우 해결하기 어려웠다. 이것은 날 수 없는 주조류의 새들이 어떻게 해서 지리적으로 그렇게 광범위하게 퍼져 있는가 하는 것이다. 주조류들은 한때 그들이 건널 수 없는 대양에 의하여 분리된 원시 조류로 간주되었다. 이 점은 그 당시 주조류 각각의 집단의 독자적인 진화를 설명하는 가설을 설정하는 데 필수적인 것처럼 보였다. 생물학자 T.H. 헉슬리는 그러한 가설에 반대한 거의 유일한 사람이었다. 그는 새의 뼈대 구조에 관한 그의 연구를 토대로 하여 반대론을 폈다.

해답 1. 윗글로 미루어 보아 주조류에 대한 아주 최근 과학자들의 견해는 ②근본적으로 바뀌었다.
2. 윗글에 의하면 헉슬리는 주조류의 ①조직 구조 관찰을 통하여 다른 과학자들과 견해를 달리하고 있다.
3. 윗글에 의하면 헉슬리는 주조류는 ④공통의 조상을 가지고 있다고 믿었다. (힌트) 헉슬리는 다른 과학자들이 주조류의 새들을 별도의 독자적인 진화 과정을 가졌다고 본 견해에 반대했음을 상기.
4. 이 글의 앞에는 아마도 ③다른 동물의 진화를 논했을 것이다.
5. 윗글로 미루어 이 글 앞에 논의된 문제는 ②이보다 덜 어려웠을 것이다.

43. **정답** 1. ③ 2. ②
word public library : 공동 도서관 / branch : 지점
charge : 부담, 요금 / librarian : 사서 직원
let you know : 알려주다
해석 영국의 모든 도시에는 공동 도서관이 있다. 많은 마을에 도서관 지점이 있다. 누구나 책을 빌릴 수 있고 대출 요금은 없다. 어떤 곳에서는 원하는 만큼 책을 빌릴 수 있지만, 어떤 곳에서는 일정한 권수까지 제한되어 있는데 그중 몇 권은 합당한 기한만큼 대출 받을 수 있다. 따라서 필요한 모든 독서를 하는 데 어려움이 없다. 만일 대출받고자 하는 책이 대출 중이면, 그 책을 당신을 위해 보관해 달라고 요청할 수 있고, 우편 요금을 지불하면, 도서관 직원은 그 책이 반납되어 당신을 기다리게 될 때에 당신에게 그 사실을 알려 줄 것이다.

44. **정답** 1. ③ 2. ① 3. ② 4. ③ 5. ②
word lawman : 법의 집행관 / mounted : 말을 타고 있는
opposed to : ~와 반대되는 / switch : 교체
visibility : 가시도 (可視渡) / suspicious : 수상쩍은
residential burglary : 주거지역의 도둑
positive P.R. : 긍정적인 선전 효과
talk to (= speak to, address) : ~에 말을 걸다
go between : 중매자 / animosity : 적대감
compassion : 동정심 / irritation : 짜증
해석 여러분이 말을 탄 경관을 마지막으로 본 것이 언제입니까? 샌프란시스코에서 뉴욕까지 말을 탄 경찰의 모습이 여러 도시에서 다시 등장하고 있다. 많은 도시들은 순찰차 대신 말을 사용할 경우 이점이 있다는 것을 다시 인식하고 있다. 뉴욕에서는 말의 숫자가 1976년 80마리였던 것이 지금은 150마리로 늘었다. 순찰차를 말로 교체하는 이유 중 하나는 많은 도시가 직면하고 있는 재정적인 어려움이다. 말은 구입비용이 1500달러이고 유지비는 매일 11달러가 든다. 반면 순찰차를 유지하는 데 드는 비용은 일일 평균 45달러이다. 볼 수 있는 범위가 넓다는 것이 또 다른 이유 중 하나이다. 말을 타고 있는 경관은 울타리와 군중의 머리 너머로 볼 수 있다. 뭔가 수상쩍은 일이 있나 없나 알기 위해 뒤뜰을 조사할 수 있게 됨으로써 주거 지역에서의 좀도둑 숫자는 감소하게 되었다. 무엇보다 가장 큰 이점은 대중과의 관

계에서 생기는 긍정적인 선전 효과이다. 거의 모든 사람들이 말을 좋아하기 때문에 다가와서 말에 대하여 경관과 대화를 나눌 것이다. 이런 의미에서 많은 경찰과 대중을 연결하는 중개자 역할을 하고 나아가서 경찰과 대중 사이에 존재하는 적대감을 없애는 데 도움을 줄 것이다.
해답 1. 순찰차를 유지하는 데 매일 평균적으로 드는 비용은? → ③45달러
2. 말이 주거지역 범죄 감소에 어떤 방식으로 공헌했는가? → ①경관이 울타리 너머로 볼 수 있을 만큼 높은 위치에 있게함으로써
3. 말이 지역 사회에 제공해 주는 가장 좋은 서비스는? → ②사회에서의 관계를 개선시켜 준다.
4. 다음 중 옳지 않은 것은? → ③많은 도시들이 순찰차의 사용을 추천하고 있다.
5. 만약 당신의 마음속에 "animosity"를 지니고 있다면 당신은 ②적대적인 감정을 지니고 있는 것이다.

45. **정답** 1. ④ 2. ① 3. ②
word beloved : 가장 사랑받는
contemporary : 동시대의, 현대의
extent : 정도 (= degree) / assumption : 가정
divide A into B : A를 B로 구분하다
bosser and bossed : 지배자와 피지배자
efficiency-regime : 효율성을 추구하는 정부
tend to : ~하는 경향이 있다 / immaculate : 청정한
craven : 겁 많은 / fictitious : 가공의
abominable : 혐오스러운
in terms of : ~의 관점에서
by dint of (= by means of = in virtue of) : ~에 의하여
해석 민주주의는 사실상 가장 사랑받는 정부 형태는 아니며, 앞으로도 결코 그렇지 않을 것이다. 민주주의가 현대의 다른 어떤 정부 형태보다 더 싫지 않다는 것뿐이다. 그리고 그 정도 범위 내에서 민주주의는 우리의 지지를 받고 있다. 민주주의는 개인의 중요하고, 문명을 만들기 위해서 모든 유형의 사람들이 다 필요하다는 가정에서 출발한다. 민주주의는 효율성을 추구하는 정부 형태가 그런 경향을 보이듯이 시민을 지배자와 피지배자로 구분하지 않는다. 내가 가장 존중하는 사람은 섬세하고 뭔가 중요한 것을 창조하고 발견하고 싶어 하는 사람들이며, 인생을 권력의 관점에서 보지 않는 사람들이다. 그러한 사람들은 다른 어떤 곳에서보다 민주주의 제도 하에서 더 많은 기회를 얻을 것이다.
해답 1. 사람들은 민주주의가 완전하기 때문이 아니라 다른 정부 형태보다 덜 ④혐오스럽기 때문에 사랑한다.

46. **정답** 1. ④ 2. ② 3. ③ 4. ① 5. ①
word comprehension : 이해력
poor reading : 책을 잘 읽지 못하는 것
some (people) unconsciously : 무의식적으로
get more out of : ~부터 더 많은 것을 얻다
assignment : 과제물

해석 읽는 속도를 두 배로 하면 이해력을 약 8% 정도 증대시킬 수 있다. 읽는 속도가 증대되면 일반적으로 정신도 보다 예리해져서 정신적인 면에서 효율성을 증가시키는 데 도움이 된다. 거의 누구나 책을 더 잘 읽을 수 있도록 훈련받을 수 있는데, 읽는 속도를 두 배 혹은 세 배까지 증가시킬 수 있다. 책을 잘 읽지 못하는 것은 책을 충분히 읽지 않는 결과일 것이다. 그런 사람은 대개 어휘 수가 부족하고, 책 읽는 데 있어서 나쁜 습관도 지니고 있다. 어떤 사람들은 책을 천천히 읽는 사람이 읽은 것으로부터 더 많은 것을 얻을 수 있다고 생각하기 때문에 무의식적으로 변화에 반대한다. 가장 훌륭한 독서가는 보통 어휘가 풍부하며 문장양식에 익숙해 있고, 다양한 인생 경험을 한 사람들인 경향이 있다. 이런 사람들은 내용을 잘 이해하면서 분당 1,800에서 2,400단어라는 빠른 속도로 글을 읽을 수 있다. 분당 10,000단어를 읽어내는 독자는 드물고, 대부분 분당 250단어 정도를 읽는다. 대학생이 과제를 하기 위해서는 분당 600단어 정도는 읽어 낼 수 있어야 한다.

해답 1. 대부분의 사람들은 분당 얼마의 단어를 읽는가?
→ ④250단어
2. 윗글에 의하면 책을 잘 읽지 못하는 이유는?
→ ②어휘 수가 부족해서
3. 윗글에 의하면 훌륭한 독서가는 ③다양한 종류의 경험을 한 경향이 있다.
4. 윗글은 책 읽는 속도의 증대가 ①이해력의 증대를 초래한다고 주장하고 있다.
5. 책을 잘 읽지 못하는 독자의 읽는 속도를 증대시키기 위한 프로그램은 아마 ①어휘력을 포함해야 한다.

47. **정답** 1. ② 2. ① 3. ④ 4. ④ 5. ③
word prior to : ~에 앞서 / a state of rest : 정지 상태
succeed in : ~에 성공하다 / in motion : 움직이는
acceleration : 가속 (도)
deduce : 연역하다, 추론하다
해석 뉴턴 이전에 아리스토텔레스는 물체의 자연 상태는 정지 상태이며 움직이는 물체에 운동을 계속할 수 있도록 힘을 가하지 않으면 그 물체는 정지하게 될 것이라는 이론을 확립하였다. 갈릴레오는 낙하하는 물체의 모습을 정확히 묘사하고, 낙하하는 물체는 그 움직임을 유지하는 데 어떤 힘도 필요하지 않다는 사실을 밝혀내는 데 성공했다. 그는 힘의 효과란 운동을 변화시키는 것이라고 기록하고 있다. 호이겐스는 속도의 변화가 그러한 것처럼 운동 방향의 변화도 가속도를 포함한다는 사실과 나아가서 힘의 작용이 필요하다는 사실을 알아냈다. 케플러는 태양 주변 혹성의 운동을 설명하는 법칙을 추론해 냈다. 뉴턴이 빌려 온 것은 주로 갈릴레오와 케플러의 이론이었다.

48. **정답** 1. ④ 2. ③ 3. ③
word go through : ~을 겪다 (= experience)
assertion : 주장
be true of : ~에 해당되다, ~도 역시 그러하다

patent : 특허를 내다 / berth : 침대
해석 발명은 그 존재에 대한 의심, 중요성에 대한 부정, 마지막으로 그 발명에 대한 영예가 다른 사람에게 돌아가는 세 단계를 거친다고들 한다. 이러한 주장의 세 번째 경우가 사실인지의 얘기 철도 침대차인 "Pullman" 의 발명이다. 사실 첫 침대차는 1838년 필라델피아의 Imlay에 의해 만들어졌다. 1850년 이전에 침대차 비슷한 것이 있다고 광고한 철도회사는 적어도 8군데나 되었다. Pullman의 침대차는 1858년이 되어서야 처음 만들어졌다. Pullman은 1863년에야 접는 2층 침대를 특허 냈다. 그럼에도 불구하고 Pullman이 Imlay보다 훨씬 나은 사업가이자 발명가였던 것 같다.

해답 1. 이 글의 주된 내용은 Pullman의 차가 ④대부분 발명품의 전형적인 기원을 갖고 있다는 것이다.
2. Pullman이 침대차에 한 실질적인 공헌은 특별한 ③침대이다.

49. **정답** 1. ④ 2. ③ 3. ① 4. ② 5. ③
word dream of : ~를 꿈꾸다
considerate : 사려 깊은 cf. considerable : 굉장히 많은
be made up of : ~로 구성되다 (= be composed of, consist of, comprise)
legend : 전설 / Norse : 노르웨이인
Celtic : 켈트인 / exploration : 답사, 탐험
by nature : 본질적으로
해석 사람들은 종종 모든 사람들이 가난하지도 부유하지도 않으며 자기 이외의 사람들을 잘 배려해 주는 그런 완전한 곳에서 사는 꿈을 꾼다. 그러나 그런 곳은 너무도 좋은 곳이어서 실제 존재할 수가 없다. 그런 곳은 어디에도 없다. "유토피아" 라는 단어가 뜻하는 것이 바로 그런 의미이다. 유토피아는 '없는 곳' 이라는 의미를 지닌 그리스어 두 단어로 구성된 곳이다. 이 유토피아라는 단어는 16세기 영국의 작가로서 이상적인 섬나라를 그린 〈유토피아〉라는 책을 1516년에 출판한 토마스 모어경에 의해 처음으로 사용되었다. 토머스 모어의 구상은 고대 그리스 철학자였던 플라톤의 사상에 유래한다. 플라톤의 저작인 〈공화국〉은 완벽한 국가가 어떤 것인가를 그린 책이다. 북 스칸디나비아, 켈트인, 아랍민족들 사이에 전해 오는 초기 시대의 전설도 대서양 어딘가에 '이상향' 이 존재하고 있다고 이야기하고 있다. 그러나 미국인들이 대서양을 탐험하기 시작한 후 사람들은 더 이상 이런 전설들을 믿지 않는다. 그러나 토머스 모어의 시대 이래 작가들이 '이상향' 을 상상해서 그려내는 일이 흔하게 되었다. 오늘날 사람들이 정부나 사회에 어떤 변화를 원할 때, 그들의 생각이 '이상적' 인 것이라고 규정되기도 한다. 이는 그 변화가 효과가 있을지는 모르지만 인간이 본질적으로 분완전하기 때문에 모든 것을 갑자기 완벽하게 만들 수는 없다는 뜻으로 비평가들이 비판하는 데서 비롯된다.

해답 2. 글쓴이에 따르면 유토피아는? → ②사람들의 상상 속에 있다.

3. 토머스 모어의 〈유토피아〉는 ①그보다 앞선 한 철학자의 저작에 근거를 두고 있다.
4. 플라톤의 〈공화국〉은 ②완전한 국가에 대한 플라톤의 이론을 묘사한 것이다.
5. 현대적 의미에서 '이상적'인 것으로 규정된 생각은 ③비실용적인 것으로 여겨진다.

50. **정답** 1. ③ 2. ② 3. ② 4. ① 5. ①
word all the time : 늘, 항상 / mental : 정신적인
relax : (긴장을) 풀게 하다 / executive : 임원, 이사
take it away : 쉬엄쉬엄하다, 휴식을 취하다
frustrate : 좌절시키다
upset : 뒤집어엎다, ~마음을 어지럽게 하다
distressed : 괴로워하는 / high blood pressure : 고혈압 / ulcer : 위궤양 / ailment : 병
해석 우리는 늘 스트레스에 시달린다. 스트레스는 육체적인 면뿐만 아니라 정신적·정서적인 면에서도 생긴다. 스트레스는 개개인에게 특이하고 개별적인 것이다. 그래서 어떤 사람에게는 긴장을 완화시켜 주는 일이 다른 사람에게는 스트레스를 유발할 수 있다. 예를 들어 만약 당신이 늘 일에만 매달려 있기를 좋아하는 바쁜 회사의 임원이라면, 날씨 좋은 날 해변에서 "휴식을 취하는 일"이 실망스럽고 비생산적이고 속상하기까지 하다고 여길 것이다. "아무 일도 하지 않는 것"을 감정적인 면에서 괴로운 것으로 생각하는 것이다. 감정적인 측면의 스트레스가 너무 많아도 고혈압, 위궤양, 심지어는 심장병 같은 병이 생길 수 있다. 일이나 운동 때문에 생기는 육체적인 스트레스가 그런 병을 유발하지는 않는 것 같다. 육체적인 운동은 긴장을 풀어 주고 정신적이고 감정적인 스트레스를 완화시키는 데 도움을 준다는 것이 사실이다.
해답 1. 스트레스는 ③처리할 수 있는 것이다.
2. 윗글에서 언급하지 않은 스트레스의 원인은 ②공부에서 오는 스트레스이다.
3. 감정적 스트레스로 유발된 육체적인 병은 다음 중 ②임신을 제외하고는 전부이다.
4. 윗글에서 언급된 스트레스를 다루는 방법 중 하나인 것은? → ①신체적인 운동
5. 다음 중 윗글의 내용에 일치하지 않는 것은? → ①육체적인 스트레스가 너무 많으면 위궤양이나 심장병이 생긴다.

51. **정답** 1. ④ 2. ④
word passenger : 승객 / get off (내리다) ↔ get on (타다)
해석 어떤 버스 승객이 몇 센트를 아끼려고 어린이의 버스 요금을 지불하지 않고 버스에 서둘러 딸을 태우고 있었다. "얘, 너 몇 살이니?" 운전수가 물었다. "네 살 반이요." 소녀가 답하자, 그는 다시 "언제 5살이 되니?" 하고 물었다. "버스에서 내리자마자요."

52. **정답** 1. ③ 2. ③
word be different from : ~와 다르다
picture phone : 영상 전화
don't have to (= need not) : ~할 필요가 없다
talk to (= speak to, address) : ~에게 말을 걸다

해석 오늘날의 전화는 거의 100년 전 벨이 만들었던 전화와는 매우 다르다. 영상 전화를 이용하면 당신이 통화하는 상대방을 볼 수 있다. 가장 최신형 전화는 건 전화가 통화 중일 때 다시 다이얼을 돌릴 필요가 없다. 회선이 비면 자동적으로 연결되는 것이다. 어떤 전화는 동시에 서너 사람과 통화할 수도 있다.

53. **정답** 1. ④ 2. ③ 3. ② 4. ③ 5. ②
6. ② 7. ④ 8. ① 9. ① 10. ③
word archaeological : 고고학적인 / famine : 기근
shot up to : ~로 치솟다 / predict (= foretell) : 예측하다
expert (전문가) ↔ layman (문외한)
integrated : 통합된 / conception : 임신
measure : 조치 cf. take a measure : ~한 조치를 취하다 / be doomed to : ~할 운명이다
remains : 유적 / overpopulation : 인구 과잉
pose : 자세를 취하다
해석 최고의 역사적 고고학적 증거에 의하면, 지구의 인구가 서기 1세기 말에 존재한 총 2억 5천만에 이르기까지는 약 80만 년에서 1백만 년이 걸린 것으로 추정된다. 그 후 얼마 동안 질병, 기아, 전쟁은 인구의 증가를 년 1% 이하로 낮추었고 그 결과 인구가 5억에 달하기까지는 15세기 이상이 지났다. 그러나 그 후 250년이 지난 1850년에는 세계 인구가 10억으로 치솟았고 오늘날은 30억에 달하고 있다. UN의 조사관들은 오는 35년간 세계 인구는 2배로 증가하여 서기 2000년에는 거의 70억에 달할 것이라고 예측하고 있다. 전문가들은 인구 과잉을 억제하는 가장 효과적인 방법에 대해 질문 받으면, 적어도 3가지 방법이 고려되어야 한다고 답변한다. (1) 저개발 국가에 대한 자원과 식량 공급의 증가, (2) 저개발 국가에 대한 산업화 추진, (3) 임신과 출산의 조절이다. 그러나 전문가들은 제시된 방법들 중 어느 것도 각자로는 절대 효과를 볼 수 없고 모든 것이 통합적인 계획으로 결합되어야 한다는 점을 덧붙인다. 그들을 또한 임신과 출산에 대한 어떤 조정이 없이는 어떠한 다음 방법도 결국 실패하기 마련이라는 점에 동의하고 있다.
해답 1. 서기 1세기 이전 지구의 인구에 대한 우리의 정보는 주로 ④쓰인 기록과 문화유적을 통하여 얻는다.
2. 서기 100년에 지구의 인구는 약 ③2억 5천만 명으로 평가된다.
3. 세계 인구가 ②100년에서 1600년 사이에 두 배가 되었다.
4. 2000년까지, 지구의 인구는 아마도 현 인구수보다 ③40억이 더 많아질 것이다. (힌트) 본문에는 오늘날 인구수는 30억, 2000년에는 거의 70억에 이를 것으로 나타나 있다.
5. 인구 성장은 ②서기 100년에서 1600년까지의 기간에 상당히 제한되었다.
6. "고고학적 증거"를 발견함직한 것은 다음 중 어느 직업인가? → ②탐험가 10. "which overpopulation posses…"라는 표현에서, ③posses는 동사로 사용되었다.

54. **정답** 1. ② 2. ③
   word cite : 인용하다 / square : 네모난 / readily : 기꺼이
          replace A with B (= substitute B for A) : A대신 B
          로 바꾸다
          unfailing : 변함없는 / chimp : (구어) chimpanzee
          think A of B : A를 B로 여기다
   해석 프리맥은 한 실험을 예로 들고 있는데, 그 실험에서 사라 (침팬지의 이름) 에게 실제 사과를 하나 주고, 그 사과의 특징이 되는 상징들-붉은색이거나 초록색, 둥글거나 네모난 모양 등-을 선택하라고 했다. 침팬지는 이것을 쉽게 해냈다. 다음 사과 대신 그 상징인 파란 삼각형을 주고 다시 침팬지에게 그것의 특징이 되는 것들을 골라 오도록 했다. 여전히 변함없는 자신감으로, 그 침팬지는 전혀 사과처럼 생기지도 않은 이 상징 (파란 삼각형) 에다 (사과의 상징과) 동일한 둥글고 빨간 속성을 부여한 것이다. 이는 바로 침팬지가 그 단어를 글자 그대로의 형태 (즉, 파란 삼각형) 가 아닌 그 말이 상징하는 것 (즉, 빨간 사과) 으로 생각하다는 증거인 것이다.

55. **정답** 1. ② 2. ③ 3. ③ 4. ② 5. ②
   word solar energy : 태양 에너지
          alternative source of heat : 대체에너지원
          unavailability : 이용할 수 없음
          conventional fuel : 재래식 연료
          get a sunburn : 일광욕을 하다
          to one's surprise : ~가 놀랍게도
          harness : (자연력을) 이용하다 / switch : 대체하다
   해석 통상적으로 사용해 오던 재래식 연료를 이용할 수 없게 될 것이라는 점이 산업의 큰 문제가 됨에 따라 태양 에너지가 급속히 논리적 면에서 대체 에너지원으로 등장하고 있다. 태양으로부터 에너지를 얻는다는 것은 새로운 생각이 결코 아니다. 매우 놀랍게도 대부분의 사람들은 구름이 낀 날에도 일광욕을 한 경험이 있다. 언제든지 태양 에너지는 존재하고 있는 것이다. 이제 기술이 발전해 태양을 에너지원으로 이용하는 비용이 경제적으로 경쟁할 수 있을 정도로 싸지고 있다. 최종적으로 태양열을 이용한 난방과 냉방이 환경보호적인 측면에서도 매우 바람직하다는 점이 재래식 연료를 태양에너지로 대체해야 한다는 또 다른 이유가 된다.
   해답 2. 윗글에서 "harnessing the sum"의 뜻은? → ③ 태양 에너지를 이용하는 것
          3. 태양으로부터 에너지를 언제든지 얻을 수 있다는 것은 ③햇빛이 구름을 뚫는다는 점을 통하여 물리적으로 증명이 되고 있다.
          4. 태양열이 논리적인 면에서 대체 에너지원이 된다는 것은 ②재래식 연료를 점점 이용할 수 없게 되어 가고 있기 때문이다.
          5. 태양 에너지를 이용하는 또 다른 이점은?
          → ②환경을 오염시키지 않는다.

56. **정답** 1. ① 2. ④ 3. 차별 4. ① 5. 생략
   word passively : 수동적으로 ↔ actively : 능동적으로
          unjust : 정당하지 못한

the oppressed (= oppressed people) : 억압받는 사람들 ↔ the oppressor : 억압하는 사람들
          evil : 사악한 / obligation : 의무 / slumber : 잠자다
          keeper : 파수꾼, 감시자 / injustice : 불의
          segregation : (인종) 차별 / fall asleep : 잠들다
          fail to (do) : ~하지 못하다 (= can't, don't)
          acquiescence : 묵시적 동의
          while often the easier way = though it is often the easier way
          coward : 겁쟁이
   해석 정당하지 못한 제도를 수동적으로 받아들이는 것은 그러한 제도에 협력하는 것이다. 그러므로 억압받는 사람들이 억압하는 사람만큼이나 사악하게 된다. 악에 협력하지 않는 것은 선에 협력하는 것만큼이나 도덕적인 의무이다. 억압받는 사람들이 억압하는 사람들의 양심이 잠자게 결코 허용해서는 안 된다. 종교는 모든 이들에게 자신이 형제의 파수꾼임을 상기시켜 주어야 한다. 불의나 차별을 수동적으로 받아들이는 것은 억압하는 사람에게 그의 행동이 도덕적으로 옳다고 표현한 것이다. 그것은 곧 그의 양심이 잠드는 것을 허용하는 것이다. 그래서 묵시적 동의-설령 그것이 쉬운 방법이 될 때가 많다고 할지라도-는 도덕적인 방법은 못된다. 그것은 비겁한 방법일 뿐이다.

57. **정답** 1. ③ 2. ① 3. ④
   word talkativeness : 수다스러움
          for one's sake : ~을 위하여 / fatal : 치명적인
          B rather than A : A라기보다는 오히려 B이다
   해석 많은 사람들은 말할 소재가 있어서라기보다 단지 말하기를 좋아하기 때문에 말을 한다. 말은 혀의 운동이기 보다 머리의 운동이어야 한다. 말은 단지 혀를 움직이는 데 그쳐서는 안 되며 생각한 것을 전달하는 것이어야 한다. 수다, 즉 말하기가 좋아서 말을 하는 것은 성공하는 데 치명적인 결점이 된다. 사람들이 이야기에 열을 올리다보면 처음 의도했던 것과는 다른 것을 말하게 된다.
   tips 1. not because~but because가 원칙이나, but 이하에 구가 오므로 이유를 나타내는 for가 와야 한다.
          3. 전치사 from의 목적어이며 동사 intend의 목적어이어야 하므로 선행사가 포함된 관계대명사 what이 와야 한다.

58. **정답** 1. ③ 2. ① 3. 생략
   word dictatorship : 독재 / starvation : 기근
          impatient : 참을성이 없는, 조급한 / bulwark : 보루
          sovereign control : 주권 행사
   해석 역사를 통해 볼 때 독재는 강하고 성공한 정부가 아니라 약하고 무기력한 정부로부터 나타나는 것임이 판명된다. 만약 민주적인 방법으로 국민들이 공포와 기근으로부터 자신들을 보호할 수 있을 만큼 강한 정부를 만든다면, 그 민주주의는 성공한 것이다. 그러나 그렇지 못하다면, 국민들은 인내심을 잃게 된다. 그러므로 자유를 지속시킬 수 있는 유일하고도 확실한 보루는 국민의 이익을 보호할 수 있을 정도

의 강력한 정부와 정부에 대해 국민의 주권 행사를
지킬 수 있을 정도로 강력하고 정통한 국민이다.

59. 정답 1. ② 2. ④ 3. ④ 4. ② 5. ② 6. ①
　　word　Much as I liked Antonia
　　　　　= Though I liked Antonia much
　　　　　take a high[superior] tone with : ~에게 큰소리치다
　　　　　resent : 분개하다 / defer to : (남의 의견에) 따르다
　　　　　than : ~이외에 (= except)
　　　　　spade : 삽 / pony : 말
　　해석　나는 안토니아를 무척 좋아했지만 그녀가 이따금 나
　　　　　에게 큰소리치는 것이 싫었다. 그녀는 나보다 네 살
　　　　　더 많아 세상사에 대한 경험도 더 많이 했지만 나는
　　　　　남자이고 그녀는 여자임으로 그녀가 나를 보호하는
　　　　　듯한 태도를 보이는 것이 불쾌했다. 그해 가을이 가
　　　　　기 전 그녀는 나를 동등한 존재로 대접하기 시작했
　　　　　고 교과서 읽는 것 이외의 일에는 내 의견을 따르기
　　　　　시작했다. 어느 날 내가 쉬멜다 집으로 말을 타고 가
　　　　　고 있을 때 안토니아가 삽을 빌리기 위해 러시아 사
　　　　　람인 피터 씨 집으로 걸어가고 있는 것을 보았다. 말
　　　　　에 타라고 제안했더니 그녀는 내 뒤에 올라탔다.

60. 정답 1. ④ 2. ② 3. ① 4. ③ 5. ④ 6. ①
　　word　mounting : 증대하는 / exasperate : 화나게 하다
　　　　　liberal education : 일반교양 교육
　　　　　B.A. degree : 학사 학위 (= Bachelor of Arts)
　　　　　pay envelope : 봉급 봉투 / downright : 노골적인
　　　　　be disappointed in : ~ 에 실망하다
　　　　　economic royalist : 우수 대학의 경제학과 출신자
　　해석　나는 대학 교육을 주제로 한 모든 글을 읽었는데 읽
　　　　　을수록 안달이 났다. 나는 비평가들의 견해에 화가
　　　　　났지만, 일반교양 교육 전문가들의 견해에 더욱 화
　　　　　가 났다. 나는 학사 학위가 봉투에 든 5센트짜리 동
　　　　　전만한 값어치도 없다고 주장하는 부류의 사람들을
　　　　　이해할 수 있다. 그러나 이런 도전을 받아들이고 학
　　　　　위가 결국 금전적 가치를 제공해 준다는 것을 입증
　　　　　하려고 애쓰는 대학인들의 견해에는 너무나 화가 난
　　　　　다. 설사 그가 그 점을 입증한다고 하더라도 나는 그
　　　　　에게 매우 실망할 것이다.나는 대학 교육을 전혀 받
　　　　　지 않았다. 나는 늘 이 점을 후회할 것이다. 그러나
　　　　　만약 하버드대학을 졸업했더라도 지금 금전적으로
　　　　　더 부유해졌을 것이라고 생각하지는 않는다. 나는
　　　　　좋은 대학 경제학과 출신은 아니지만, 지금 잘 해나
　　　　　가고 있기 때문이다.
　　해답　1. →④저자는 대학 학위가 금전적 성공을 보장해
　　　　　　준다는 견해를 갖고 있지 않다.
　　　　　5. →④대학 교육이 금전적인 중요성을 지닌다는 점.

61. 정답 1. ④ 2. ② 3. ④ 4. ① 5. ③
　　word　effect (= produce) : ~을 가져오다
　　　　　dialect : 방언, 사투리
　　　　　those who~ : ~인 사람들
　　해석　사회는 의사소통에 의존한다. 시민들은 서로 이해할
　　　　　수 있어야 한다. 이것은 시민들이 그 나라의 사투리
　　　　　를 즉시 번역해 낼 수 있어야 한다는 것 이상을 의미

한다. 그들은 공동의 문화를 가져야 한다. 그들은 그
것을 이해하는 데 필요한, 그리고 그것을 공유한 사
람들과 의사 소통을 하기 위하여 필요한 지적인 교
육을 받아야 한다.

62. 정답 1. ③ 2. ② 3. ①
　　word　minute : 미세한, 정밀한 / modify : 수정하다
　　　　　mind-picture : 마음속에 그리고 있는 심상
　　해석　역사가들, 정치학자들, 그리고 심지어 사회학자들의
　　　　　정밀한 조사도 낭만적인 남부인들이 마음속에 그리
　　　　　고 있는 심상을 없애거나 완전히 변화시키는 데 성
　　　　　공하지는 못했다.

63. 정답 1. ④ 2. ④
　　word　vast : 거대한
　　　　　each star a sun more or less like our own
　　　　　= and each star is a sun (which is) more or less like
　　　　　　our own
　　　　　more or less : 다소 / the lot : 전체
　　　　　strange though[as] it may be seen
　　　　　= Though it may be seen strange
　　해석　우리는 은하수가 아주 먼 별들의 거대한 따라는 것,
　　　　　그리고 각각의 별은 우리 태양과 다소 비슷한 항성
　　　　　이라는 것을 이제 알고 있다. 은하수의 별들은 대부
　　　　　분이 너무도 멀리 떨어져 있어서 거대한 망원경으로
　　　　　도 셀 수가 없다. 그러나 이상하게 보일지 몰라도 그
　　　　　전체 은하수의 무게를 잴 수 있다.

64. 정답 1. ② 2. ③
　　word　fire = 해고시키다 (= dismiss, expel, discharge)
　　　　　pessimism : 염세주의 ↔ optimism : 낙천주의
　　　　　job or no job : 직장이 있건 없건
　　해석　그날 아침 나는 이 세상이 끝났다고 확신했다. 사장
　　　　　이 나를 해고했고, 젊은 시절의 비관적인 생각 때문
　　　　　에, 나는 다시는 직장을 찾지 못할 것이라는 생각이
　　　　　들었다. 나는 실패자로 낙인 찍혔었다 (나의 나이는
　　　　　19살이었다). 그날 저녁, 뉴욕 필하모니 연주를 듣
　　　　　기 위해 루이스 스타디움에서 친구를 만날 약속을
　　　　　했다. 직장이 있건 없건, 나는 가기로 작정했다.

65. 정답 1. ① 2. ④ 3. ② 4. ③ 5. ① 6~10. 해석 참조
　　word　mature : 성숙하게 하다, 성숙한
　　　　　optimum : 최적의 / efficiency : 유효, 실력
　　　　　foreign tongue : 외국어 ↔ mother tongue : 모국어
　　　　　insight : 통찰력
　　　　　nonlinguistic language : (음성 문자를 쓰지 않는) 전
　　　　　　달 수단
　　　　　statistics : 통계학, 통계
　　　　　indispensible : 없어서는 안 되는
　　　　　be shut off from : ~에서 차단되다
　　　　　conductive : ~에게 도움이 되는
　　해석　영어를 숙달하는 것이 대학에서 해야 할 유일한 일
　　　　　은 아니다. 그러나 (1) 반드시 이 필수적인 기술은 대
　　　　　학교 재학 중 빨리 숙달되어야 하고 졸업할 때면 최
　　　　　고의 실력에 접근해 있어야 한다. 제2외국어 역시 매

우 중요하다. (2) 불어, 러시아어, 중국어 혹은 다른 외국어를 알게 되면 우리 모국어도 훨씬 더 깊게 알게 된다. 더욱 외국문화에 대한 통찰력도 그 문화권에서 사용되는 언어를 알아야만 비로소 가능해진다. 그리고 학생들이 숙달해야 할 말이나 문자를 사용하지 않는 전달 수단이 또 있다. (3) 통계학과 수학은 기술이나 과학의 역할에 분명 필수불가결하다. 그러나 이러한 전달 수단은 사회과학이나 예술을 하는 데도 역시 필요하다. 수학을 무시해도 된다고 생각하는 인문주의자는 정말 잘못 생각하고 있으며 현대사회의 여러 측면과 유리될 것이다. 대학이 보다 높은 수준의 교육을 제공해 줄 수 있는 유일한 곳은 아니다. (4) 어쨌든 대학이 가치를 지니게 되면, 학생들의 높은 수준의 교육은 평생토록 지속적으로 이루어질 것이다. 대학의 중요성은 대학의 체계적인 방식으로 그리고 도움을 주는 방식으로 학생들을 교육과정으로 인도할 수 있다는 점이다. 이것은 다른 무엇보다 개개인이 가진 장점에다 취미를 가지도록 교육시킨다는 것을 뜻한다. (5) 이것이 진정 교육을 계속할 수 있게 해 주는 토대가 된다.

66. **정답** 1. ③ 2. ②
word middle of the roader : 온건 중도주의자
compromise : 타협 (하다) (= meet halfway)
as a result of (= with a consequence of)
: ~의 결과로
해석 온건 중도주의자들은 어떤 다툼에서건 중간 입장을 추구한다. 그들은 어떤 입장이건 타협점을 찾으려하며, 상황이 어떻건 쌍방이 무엇인가를 얻어야 한다고 생각한다. 종종 이들 타협의 결과 어느 쪽도 얻는 것이 없을 때도 있고, 양쪽 모두 잃을 수도 있다.

67. **정답** 1. ③ 2. ④ 3. ①
word convert : 개조하다 / thatched roof : 초가지붕
fairy tale : 동화 / vivid : 생생한
figure : 인물, 모습 / stand out : 두드러지다
be contrast to : ~와 대조를 이루다 / stern : 엄한
disapprove : 탐탁찮아 하다, 반대하다
watchfulness : 경계심 / relax : 느슨한
해석 내가 일곱 살 때 아버지께서 돌아가셨고 어머니께서는 우리들을 스코틀랜드에 계시는 할머니 댁으로 보내셨다. 할머니 댁은 낡은 농가를 개조한 것이었는데, 초가지붕과 한스 앤더슨집처럼 동화 속의 유리창을 지니고 있는 단층 건물이었다. 나에게는 아직 그때의 스코틀랜드 생활을 생생하게 기억시켜 주는 많은 사진들이 있다. 모든 사진에서 할머니의 모습은 주변의 친척 및 아이들과 정반대로 대조를 이루며 눈에 띈다. 할머니는 키가 크고 엄한 표정의 스코틀랜드 여성이셨다. 사진 속의 할머니 표정은 늘 한결같았는데, 그것은 때로는 느슨해 보이지만, 할머니께서 말씀하시던 '바보짓'은 절대 용서하지 않겠다고 말씀하시는 것 같은 일종의 반대하는 경계심 같은 것이 있었다.

68. **정답** 1. 해석 참조 2. respond 3. education

4. Let us cherish this personal element at all costs.
5. 해석 참조
word consist of (= comprise = be composed of = be made up of) : ~로 구성되어 있다
personal tie : 개인적인 유대 / mutual : 상호간의
take the place of : ~에 대신하다
respond to : ~에 반응을 보이다 / chat : 잡담하다
mechanize : 기계화하다
depersonalize : 비인간적으로 하다
deprive A of B : A에게서 B를 빼앗다
ingredient : 성분, 요소
at all costs : 어떤 대가를 치르더라도
take an interest in : ~에 관심을 갖다
해석 대학은 하나의 사회이며, 사회는 개인적 유대로 한데 묶인 사람들로 구성되어 있다. 선생과 학생 사이의 관계는 개인적인 관계이다. 상호간의 이익과 상호간의 도움이 틀림없이 존재한다. (a) 어떤 기계적인 장치도 결코 이러한 개인적인 관계를 대신할 수는 없다. TV 스크린이 우리의 반응에 반응을 보이거나, 우리와 함께 기쁨이나 슬픔을 나누며, 코모도어 룸에서 콜라나 커피를 마시며 우리와 잡담을 나누어 줄 수는 없다. 교육을 기계화시키고 비인간화시키는 것은 교육에서 가장 소중한 요소를 박탈하는 것이다. 우리는 어떠한 대가를 치르더라도 이러한 개인적인 요소를 소중히 간직해야 한다. 다행스럽게도, (e) 밴더빌트는 우리가 서로 알지 못하고 서로에게 관심을 보이지 못할 정도로 크지는 않다. 밴더빌트는 우리가 서로 친구가 되지 못할 정도로 크지는 않다.

69. **정답** 1. × 2. × 3. ○ 4. × 5. ○
word tearful : 눈물어린 / side with : ~편을 들다
albeit : 비록 ~일지라도 (= though)
faintly : 희미하게
breadwinner : 한 집안의 생계를 꾸려나가는 사람
be cut out for : ~에 알맞다 (= be suitable for)
an old maid : 노처녀 / quit (= stop) : 멈추다
transfer : 옮기다, 전학하다
해석 Golda가 자기 반에서 가장 우수한 학생으로 졸업했을 때 그녀의 어머니는 기뻐하였다. 이제 이 소녀는 식료품 가게에서 전적으로 일할 수 있었던 것이다. 심지어 미국에서 마저도 소녀들이 고등학교에 가는 것은 기대되지 않았다. 그러나 Golda는 가고 싶었다. 그래서 얼마간의 눈물 어린 논쟁 끝에 그녀의 부모는 동의해 주었다. 아버지는 한 번 그녀의 편을 들어 주셨는데, 그러나 다소 힘없이 그렇게 해 주셨다. 그는 아마 집안의 생계를 꾸려나가는 사람으로서 사실상 조금 밖에 벌지 못한다는 것 때문에 죄책감을 느끼셨던 것 같다. 그는 현명하고 점잖고 학식 있는 분이셨지만 사업을 하는 데는 어울리지 않는 분이셨다. 그녀는 선생님이 되기로 결심했다. 왜냐하면 그러한 직업이 "지적으로나 사회적으로나 유용" 하기 때문이었다. 그러나 어머니는 결혼한 여자들은 학교에서 가르치는 것이 허용되지 않는다는 것을 알게 되었다. "너 노처녀가 되고 싶어?" 하고 그녀는 Golda에게 소리를 질렀다. "그게 네가 공부하는 이

유야?" 아버지가 이번에는 강력하게 어머니편을 들었다. Golda는 학교를 중퇴하고 자기 또래의 지각 있는 소녀들처럼 돈 벌러 나가든지 직업을 얻는 데 도움이 되는 과목들을 배우기 위해서 실업학교로 전학을 가든지 해야 했다. 누가 알겠는가? 혹 남편도 얻게 될지 … 집을 뛰쳐나와 덴버에 있는 결혼한 언니와 2년을 지낸 후 Golda는 이번 전투에서도 또 승리를 거두었다. 그녀는 고등학교를 마치기 위해 밀워키로 돌아왔다.

70. **정답** 1. ② 2. ② 3. ①
   word No one knows (= God knows = Who knows~?)
      : 아무도 모른다
      grandchildren : 손주
   해석 (a) 기계가 미래의 삶에 어떤 변화를 초래할지 정확하게 아는 사람은 아무도 없다. 그러나 미래의 생활이 현재의 생활과 같지 않을 것이라는 것은 확신할 수 있다. 우리의 생활이 할아버지대의 (b) 생활과 다르듯이 우리 손주들의 생활도 현재의 우리 생활과는 다를 것이다.

71. **정답** 1. ④ 2. ②
   word It is no good[use] -ing : ~해도 아무 소용없다
      fatherland : 조국
      pretend : ~인 체하다 (= make believe)
      be proud of (= take pride in = pride oneself of) : ~을 자랑하다
   해석 이 나라에 살고 있는 우리가 조국을 위대하게 만들기 위해 무언가를 하지 않으면 조국의 위대함을 입으로만 이야기하고 그것에 긍지를 느끼는 척하는 것은 아무 쓸모없는 것이다.

72. **정답** 1. ③ 2. ④ 3. ④ 4. ③
   word make up one's mind : 결심하다
      lest~ (should) : ~할까 봐 걱정하여
      (= for fear of +~ing)
      take one's own life
      (= commit suicide) : 목숨을 끊다
      mean by : ~을 의미하다 / in vain : 헛되이
      be obliged to : ~하지 않으면 아니 되다 (= be compelled to = be forced to = be impelled to)
   해석 어느 날 한 거지가 숙녀를 따라 가며 돈을 달라고 구걸했는데 그녀가 거절했다. 그랬더니 거지는 한숨을 쉬며 하기로 결심했던 것을 해야겠다고 중얼거리며 돌아섰다. 이 말을 듣고 그 숙녀는 그가 목숨을 끊을까 봐 매우 놀랐다. 그래서 그를 다시 불러 1실링을 주고는 무슨 뜻인지 물었다. 그 거지는 돈을 받아 호주머니 속에 넣고는 "부인, 저는 하루 종일 구걸을 했는데 허사였어요. 그래서 만약 부인께서 저에게 이 돈을 주지 않았더라면 일하러 가야만 했을 겁니다." 라고 말했다.
   tips 3. 가정법 과거완료 문장이므로 if절에 had + p.p가 와야 하는데 if가 탈락되어 Had가 문두에 나온 경우이다.
      4. 결과를 두고 봤을 때 그 숙녀가 돈을 주지 않았어야 했다.

73. **정답** 1. ① 2. ④ 3. ② 4. ②
   word the station restaurant : 역 구내음식점
   해석 기차가 어느 작은 역에 멈췄을 때 한 부인이 창문을 열었다. 창 밖에는 한 소년이 있었는데 그 부인이 소년에게 말했다. "나는 빨리 걸을 수 없기 때문에 기차 밖으로 나갈 수가 없어. 그러니 역 구내식당으로 달려가서 아이스크림을 하나 사다 줄래? 네 것도 하나 사고. 여기 20센트 줄게." 소년은 갔다가 기차가 다시 출발하기 몇 초 전에 돌아왔다. 그는 아이스크림을 먹으면서 부인이 있는 창으로 뛰어가서 그녀에게 10센트를 주었다. 그리고는 "식당에 아이스크림이 하나밖에 없더군요." 라고 말했다.
   해답 1. 특정한 시간, 거리, 무게, 금액 표시의 복수형 명사는 단수 취급을 한다. ex) Here is twenty cents.
      3. 그 부인이 소년에게 준 돈은 ②한 사람이 하나씩 두 개의 아이스크림을 사기 위한 것이었다.
      4. 만약 그 부인이 기차에서 내렸더라면 ②그녀는 빨리 걸을 수 없었기 때문에 아마 기차를 놓쳤을 것이다.

74. **정답** 1. ③ 2. ④ 3. ②
   word come [get] to (do) : ~하게 되다
      ready-made : 이미 만들어져 있는
      door step : 문 앞
   해석 오늘날 부모들은 자녀들을 위하여 예전보다 훨씬 더 적은 일을 하게 되었다. 따라서 가정이 작업장의 기능을 더욱 상실하게 된 것이다. 옷은 이미 만들어져 있는 것을 살 수 있고, 세탁물도 세탁소로 보내면 되고, 요리가 되어 있거나, 깡통에 든 음식을 살 수가 있다. 빵도 제과점에서 구워 배달해 주며, 우유도 문 앞까지 배달해 준다. 식사는 레스토랑이나 학교 구내식당에서 먹을 수 있게 되어 있다.

75. **정답** 1. 불필요한 가난
      2. if they made full use of the knowledges and skill of scientists
      3. 질병 (disease)
   word prevail : 널리 퍼지다
      be unaware[ignorant] of : ~을 모르는
      tract : 지역 / abandon : 버리다
      cultivate : 경작하다 / thriving : 번성한
      make use of : 이용하다 / innumerable : 수많은
      suffer from : ~를 겪다
      rules of hygiene : 유전 법칙
      storehouse : 보고, 창고 / waterfall : 폭포
      drudgery : 고역
   해석 대체로 사람들이 가난을 줄일 수 있는 방법을 몰라서 불필요한 가난이 만연해 있는 나라들이 있다. 버려지거나 경작된 적이 없는 방대한 땅이 있는 데 이것이 그들의 과학자들의 지식과 기술을 충분히 활용할 경우 번성하는 사회에 큰 도움을 줄 수 있다. 치료할 수 있는 병, 유전에 대한 간단한 과학적 법칙을 따르기만 하면 결코 걸리지 않을 병에 걸려 고통을 받는 사람이 부지기수다. 바람, 폭포, 태양열과 같은 방대한 자연의 보고가 있는데 과학은 인간의 고

역을 경감시키고 생활 수준을 증대시키기 위하여 이런 자연력을 이용하는 방법을 제시해 줄 수 있을 것이다. 가능성은 엄청나게 크다.

76. **정답** 1. 대학 교육은 전혀 쓸모없다.
2. 대학을 졸업해야 금전적으로 성공할 수 있다.
word come to one's notice : ~의 관심을 끌다
of late : 최근에 (= lately)
impatience : 안달, 짜증 ↔ patience : 인내심
exasperate : 노하게 하다
liberal education : 대학교양교육
B.A. degree : 학사 학위
(= Bachelor of Arts diploma)
pay envelope : 봉급 봉투
to one's sort : ~의 경우에는
downright : 노골적인
cash value : 금전적인 가치
해석 나는 관심을 끄는 주제를 다룬 모든 글을 읽고 있는데 최근에는 글을 읽을수록 더욱 글의 내용에 안달이 난다. 나는 비평가들의 견해에 화가 났는데 대학 교양 교육 전문가들의 견해에 대해서는 더욱 화가 난다. 나는 학사 학위가 봉급 봉투에 든 5센트짜리 동전만한 값어치도 없다고 주장하는 부류의 사람을 이해할 수 있으며, 그런 사람의 경우 대학교육이 쓸모없는 것이라는 주장이 옳을 수 있다고 나는 생각한다. 그러나 이러한 도전을 수용하고 대학 졸업장이 결국 금전적인 성공을 보장해 준다는 점을 입증해 보이려고 애쓰는 대학교수들에 대해서는 정말 분통이 터진다. 그들이 이 점을 입증하는 데 성공한다 할지라도 나는 실망하지 않을 수 없다.

77. **정답** 1. ⓐ 2. ⓒ 3. ⓕ 4. ⓓ 5. ⓔ 6. ⓑ
word grownup : 성인 (= adult)
make a fuss about : ~에 대하여 야단법석을 떨다
puzzle : 수수께끼, 당황시키다
queer : 수상한
bewildering : 당황스러운 / wink at : 눈짓하다
해석 어렸을 때 나는 휴일에 대해서 야단법석을 떨면서도 꿈에 대해서는 조용히 다루는 어른들이 이해가 안됐다. 이 문제는 아직도 여전히 수수께끼이다. 결코 꿈을 꾸지 않는다고 말하거나 이 주제에 대하여 전혀 관심이 없어 보이는 사람들이 나를 당황시킨다. 그들은 산책하러 밖에 나간 적이 없다고 말하는데 이는 더더욱 놀라운 일이다. 꿈은 여러 가지 면에서 이상하고 당혹스럽고 만족스럽지 못하지만 그 나름대로 이점도 있다. 꿈속에는 죽은 이들이 웃으며 대화를 나누고 있다. 과거도 나타나고, 때로는 모든 것이 부서지고 뒤엉켜 있으며, 때로는 데이지처럼 생생하기도 하다. 우리에게 눈짓하는 미래 또한 꿈속에 있다.

78. **정답** 1. duchess
2. if he had le the mouth be the deciding test
3. **해석 참조**
4. a aquiline nose
5. a Roman nose

word chin : 아래턱 / make allowances : 참작하다
snub nose : 짧고 치켜 올라간 코
a Roman nose : 매부리코
해석 웰링턴은 코와 아래턱을 보고 장교를 선발했다고 한다. 웰링턴 공작의 초상화로 판단해 보건대 장교를 뽑을 때 코의 기준은 좀 높았을 것임이 분명하다. 물론 다른 사항도 참작했겠지만, 어쨌든 이런 방법으로 원하는 사람을 뽑아 썼다. 그러나 입을 판단 기준으로 했으면 더 좋았을 것이라고 생각하는 사람도 있을 것이다. 코의 윤곽은 태어날 때 다소 변형될 수도 있기 때문이다. 들창코를 가지고 태어난 어린이는 그가 웰링턴에게 선택될 수 없다는 결정을 그렇게 일찍 내려야 한다는 것을 가혹하게 느낄 수도 있을 것이다. 그리고 매부리코를 가지고 태어났다면 매부리코를 어릴 때 변형시켜 그 코를 가지고도 군대에서 성공할 수 있는 기회를 누리게 될 수 있다. 여러분도 동의하리라 믿지만 이런 것은 너무 불공평하다 할 것이다.

79. **정답** 1. ② 2. ③ 3. ③
word make up : 구성하다 (= compose)
public opinion : 여론 / judgement : 다수의 판단
compensate : 보상하다
해석 여러분의 의견들은 다른 많은 사람들에게 역시 중요하다. 이것은 당신도 대중이라 불리우는 그 집단의 일원이며, 당신의 생각이 여론의 형성에 도움을 주기 때문이다. 어떤 특정 주제에 대한 여론이란 대다수 사람들의 판단 또는 결론인 것이다. 즉 대다수 사람들이 그들 자신의 의견들을 형성했을 때 이루어진 의견인 것이다. 여론은 우리와 같은 민주주의 국가에서 무슨 일을 할 것인가를 결정하는 데 있어서 가장 강력한 영향력을 끼치는 것 중의 하나이다.

80. **정답** 1. 해석 참조 2. increase 3. higher 4. 해석 참조
word stand a good chance of : ~할 충분한 가능성이 있다
lung-cancer : 폐암
male : 남성의 ↔ female : 여성의
diagnose : 진단하다
compare A with B : A와 B를 비교하다
해석 흡연자가 폐암으로 죽을 가능성이 훨씬 높다. 호놀룰루에 있는 하와이대학의 한 보고서는 남성 흡연자가 고지방 음식을 많이 먹게 되면 폐암에 걸릴 확률은 더욱 높아진다는 것을 밝히고 있다. 조사자들은 폐암 진단을 받은 326명과 건강한 사람 965명을 비교했다. 한 사람이 정상적으로 한 달 동안 먹었던 음식을 조사해 봄으로써, 과학자들은 지방질이 많은 음식을 먹은 성인 남자 흡연자가 폐암에 걸릴 확률이 지방질이 낮은 음식을 먹은 성인 남성 흡연자보다 월등히 높다는 사실을 발견했다.

81. **정답** 1. ③ 2. ② 3. ① 4. ③ 5. ①
word if anything : 글쎄 어느 편인가 하면
materialistic : 물질주의적인
put off : 연기하다
dull : (감각이) 둔한

해석 동양과 서양에서의 가치관이 다르다는 것은 간단한 이치이다. 동양 사람들은 서양 사람들보다 인생 그 자체에서 더 많은 것을 얻고 싶어 한다. 글쎄 어느 편인가 하면 동양이 서양보다 훨씬 물질주의적이다. 동양은 역사가 오래되었기 때문에 인생이 얼마나 짧은가를 잘 알고 있다. 인간의 일생이란 금방 지나가 버린다. 그러므로 쾌락을 뒤로 미루어서는 안 된다. 나이가 들면 감각이 둔해지기 때문이다.

82. **정답** 1. ③ 2. ② 3. ②
해석 우리가 중재자가 되는 여러 가지 방법이 있다. 그 하나는 다른 사람들의 견해나 바람을 참고 인정해 주는 것이다. 대부분의 다툼은 논쟁에서 비롯되는데, 사람들의 논쟁 중에 다른 사람이 나타낸 의견에 화를 내게 된다. 우리는 다른 사람이 내세우는 의견이 아무리 어리석어 보일지라도 그가 자신의 의견을 나타낼 수 있도록 허락해 주어야 하고 다른 사람들이 우리처럼 생각하지 않는다고 해서 화를 내서도 안된다.

83. **정답** 1. ⓔ 2. ⓐ 3. ⓒ 4. ⓓ 5. ⓖ
word verbal : 말의 / mighty : 힘이 있는
be true of : ~도 그러하다 (= be applied to)
do without : (= manage without = dispense with)
: ~없이 지내다
immense : 거대한 (= huge)
fail to (do) : ~하지 못하다 (= cannot, do not)
contempt : 경멸 / indifference : 무관심
해석 우리가 살고 있는 시대는 기계의 시대, 과학의 시대, 심지어 핵의 시대라고 불리어 왔다. 또 언어의 시대라고 부른다 해도 타당하다. 왜냐하면 오늘날 언어가 이 세상에서 가장 영향력이 강하면서도 평범한 도구이기 때문이다. 언어의 힘과 대조해 볼 때 전력과 원자력의 힘은 일상생활에서 비교적 중요하지 않다. 이는 물론 다른 시대에도 그러하였다. 문명인이 언어 없이 많은 업적을 이룬 적은 존재해 본 적이 없다. 그러나 문명이 복잡해지면 질수록 문명의 존립이 더욱더 언어의 힘에 의존하게 된다. 오늘날 언어의 힘은 엄청나게 크다. 우리는 언어를 당연시하고 있기 때문에 언어의 힘이 얼마나 엄청난 것인지를 이해하지 못하고 있다. 친숙하게 되면 경멸까지는 아니라 하더라도 무관심하게 되는 것이다. 그러나 잠깐 멈추고 우리가 얼마나 엄청난 언어의 세계에 살고 있는지 생각해 보자. 미래에 있어 매우 중요하다고 느끼는 대학 교육은 거의 전적으로 언어를 통한 경험이라고 해도 과언이 아니다. 우리는 언어로 된 책을 읽고, 강의를 듣고, 인생관을 형성한다.

84. **정답** 1. ④ 2. ① 3. that 4. ③
5. people in the East
word spiritual : 정신적인 ↔ ,material : 물질적인
like : ~처럼 / starve : 굶어죽다 / shelter : 은신처
pay a bill : 비용을 충당하다
distract : (마음, 주의를) 딴 데로 돌리다
take over : 인계 (양도) 하다 / take out : 꺼내다

take on : 떠맡다 / take off : 제거하다
해석 동양은 "정신적"이고 서양은 "물질적"이라고 오랫동안 이야기되어 왔다. 그러나 아무렇게나 이야기하는 것들이 다 그러하듯이 이것은 진실이 아니다. 동양은 정신적인 면에서 서양보다 더하지도 덜하지도 않으며, 서양도 물질적인 면에서 도양보다 더하지도 덜하지도 않은 것이다. 이것은 모든 사람들에게 다 똑같이 이야기될 수 있다. 사람들은 굶기 보다는 음식 먹기를, 집이 없는 것보다 집이 있는 것을, 병에 걸리기 보다는 건강한 것을, 짧게 사는 것보다 오래 살기를, 슬프기보다는 행복한 것을 더 좋아한다. 그렇다면 동양은 정신적이고 서양은 물질적이라는 이 신화 같은 이야기가 도대체 어디서 유래한 것일까? 이는 일종의 사실에 근거를 두고 있는데 이 사실은 다음과 같이 간단한 내용의 것이다. 즉, 동양 사람들은 인생을 즐기기를 좋아한다는 것이다. 그들은 살고, 먹고, 자고, 어린애들과 놀고, 부인이나 가족들과 대화를 나누고 하는 데서 얻는 평범한 즐거움을 누릴 시간이 없을 정도로 열심히 일하지는 않을 것이다. 그들은 하나의 일거리만 가지고도 살아가는 데 필요한 제반 비용을 충당할 수만 있다면 두 가지 일을 떠맡지 않을 것이다. 두 가지 일을 가지게 되면 시간이 없어지고 마음이 분산되기 때문인 것이다.

85. **정답** 1. ④ 2. ① 3. ② 4. from 5. for
6. 해석 참조 7. 영국 연방 8. in 9. for
word migrate : 이주하다 / pest : 해충, 벌레
amount to : ~에 달하다 / natural enemy : 천적
parasite : 기생충 / adapt oneself to : ~에 적응하다
obscure : 숨기다, ~을 어둡게 하다
insecticide : 살충제 / expenditure : 경비
해석 아마 미국은 세계 어느 나라보다 더 많은 피해를 벌레로부터 입고 있을 것이다. 왜냐하면 사람들이 미국으로 이주해 올 때 많은 벌레들이 따라오는데 그들을 잡아먹는 천적은 같이 오지 않기 때문이다. 미국에서는 벌레들만이 망쳐 놓는 자재나 상품이 매년 수백만 달러에 이른다. 농작물에 미치는 손해는 그 이상이 될 것이다. 벌레는 특히 질병을 잘 옮긴다. 집파리는 많은 질병과 기생충을 옮기고, 모기는 말라리아와 로키 산의 진드기 열병을 옮긴다. 벌레는 많은 중요 농작물에도 질병을 옮겨 놓는다. 벌레들은 어떤 종류의 환경에도 잘 적응하고 그들의 크기가 (너무 작기 때문에) 그들의 파괴력이 잘 드러나지 않게 하기 때문에 벌레를 없앤다는 것이 어려운 일이다. 미국은 오랫동안 벌레에 대한 과학적 연구를 진행해 왔다. 프랑스와 이태리는 이 연구의 중요성에 대하여 첨예한 관심을 보여 왔으며, 영국은 영연방 내에서 많은 연구를 진행하고 있다. 미국 내의 거의 모든 해충에 대한 살충제가 개발되어 왔지만 해충 박멸에는 많은 숙련된 인력과 엄청난 비용이 요구된다.
해답 1. 윗글에 의하면 벌레는 ④경작되는 농작물에 큰 피해를 끼친다.
2. 벌레는 ①너무 작기 때문에 박멸하기가 어렵다.

3. 외국에서 온 벌레들은 ②천적이 없이 들어오기 때문에 더 큰 손실을 입힌다.

86. **정답** 1. ② 2. ③ 3. ④ 4. ①
word tribal sense : 부족의식 / expediency : 편의주의
inherent : 고유의, 타고난
for good (= forever, permanently) : 영원히
let alone : ~는 말할 것도 없이
해석 아프리카인들은 시골에서보다 도시에서 훨씬 쉽고, 빠르게 부족의식을 잃어버린다. 그래서 자신들이 새롭고, 훨씬 넓은 범위의 정치 단위인 국가의 일원이 되었다는 것을 깨닫는 기회도 훨씬 더 많다. 이것이 은크루마와 같은 (국가의) 지도자를 마치 부족의 추장처럼 여겨 쉽게 따를 수 있게 해 주지만 이는 어디까지나 편의성의 문제일 뿐이다. (부족이라는) 구제도에는 (국가라는) 신제도가 아직도 지니지 못한 내적인 힘이 있었다. 아프리카인들이 새로운 제도를 완전히 받아들일 수 없게 하는 갈등이 있는데 이것은 새 제도가 구제도를 조금도 고려하지 않고 외부로부터 도입되어 시행되었다는 점을 생각해 보면 그다지 놀라운 일이 아니다. 동시에 구제도는 영원히 사라져 버렸고 도시에서는 구제도를 부끄러운 것으로 여기까지 하기 때문에 이제 더 이상 부족 의식이 도덕적, 정신적 힘이 원천이 되기는커녕 자존심의 원천도 되지 못하고 있다는 점 역시 분명한 것 같다.

87. **정답** 1. ③ 2. ② 3. ④ 4. ① 5. ①
word what do you do for a living? : 직업이 무엇입니까?
for about hundredth time : 약 100번째로
have a trouble (in) ~ing : ~하느라고 애를 먹다
groan : 신음하다
burst into tears : 눈물을 터뜨리다
gratitude : 감사
animated : 활기찬 (= lively)
watch one's language : 말조심하다
해석 지난주 나는 늘 자신을 괴롭혀왔던 경험을 거의 100번째로 했다. 기차를 타고 가면서 옆 사람과 대화를 나누고 있었는데 그가 나의 직업이 무엇인지 물었다. "영어 선생님입니다." 그의 반응이 어떠하였는지 상상하기 어렵습니까? 그는 고개를 숙이고 신음하듯이, "아, 그래요. 말조심해야겠군요." 라고 말하는 것이었다. 경험에 의하면 상대방이 보이는 반응에는 두 가지가 있는데, 첫 번째 경우는 그리 좋지 않은 것이다. "학교 다닐 때 영어를 싫어했답니다. 성적이 제일 나쁜 과목이었죠." 두 번째 경우는-아주 드물어서 그런 응답에 접했을 때 순진한 영어 선생님이면 감사의 눈물을 터뜨리게 할 정도의 것인데-문학과 사상과 미국 언어에 대한 대화이다. 이것은 영어를 who와 whom, lie와 lay의 차이를 분명하게 아는 것 이상의 것으로 여기고 있어서 영어에 대한 변함없는 관심을 보여 주는 그런 대화이다.
해답 5. → ①영어 선생님인 저자는 단어 규칙에 대한 것보다 사상이나 문학에 대한 대화를 나누길 원하고 있다.

88. **정답** 1. ② 2. ① 3. ④ 4. ③ 5. ②
word housekeeper : 가정부 / ladle : 국자
beat time with : ~로 박자를 맞추다
glazed : (눈빛이) 흐릿한 / sphere : 구, 영역
be littered with : ~로 어질러져 있다
on the tip of one's tongue : (말이) 자칫 입에서 나올 뻔하다
dismiss : 해고하다 (= fire, discharge)
pull oneself together : 기운 (침착) 을 되찾다
patch in : 수습하다
해석 부엌의 장면은 충격적인 것이었다. 한쪽 구석에는 겁에 질린 어린 하녀가 서 있었고, 다른 한쪽 구석에는 가정부가 서 있었다. 요리사는 탁자에 앉아 국자를 흔들며 발로 박자를 맞추면서 노래를 부르고 있었다. 그의 눈빛은 희미했고 그의 정신은 어딘가 먼 곳에 가 있었다. 탁자에는 닭 조각으로 어질러져 있었다. 나는 몹시 화가 났다. '나가 버려. 넌 해고야!' 라는 말이 입에서 나올 뻔했다. 그러나 이전에도 몇 번이나 나를 진정시켜 주었던 '이성을 잃으면 자신만 다친다.' 라는 충고가 떠올랐을 때 냉정을 되찾았다. "자, 식사 준비합시다." 라고 내가 말했다. 모든 사람들이 바삐 움직이며 수습하여 곧 저녁 식사가 준비되었다.

89. **정답** 1. two little rivulets 2. our climate
3. Mamie의 코에서 콧물이 흘러내리고 있는 데 대한 혐오감
word rivulet : 개울 / pout : 입을 삐죽 내밀다
sniff : 코를 훌쩍이다 / catarrhal : 카타르성의
repulsion : 격퇴, 혐오감
salty lips : 소금기 있는 입술
해석 그녀는 키스를 받으려고 젖은 얼굴을 들어 올렸다. 나는 키스를 하려는 뜨거운 마음으로 그녀를 내려다보았다. 그러나 그녀의 얼굴을 보았을 때 나는 Mamie의 코에서 두 줄기 콧물이 삐죽 나온 윗입술로 흘러내리고 있는 것을 보았다. 나는 가끔 그녀가 코를 훌쩍일 때마다 혀를 밖으로 쭉 내밀어 위로 올리는 것을 본 적이 있지만 콧물이 흘러내리는 것을 본 적은 없었다. 우리 기후는 점막성 감기를 유발하는 기후이다. 그런데 이번에 이것을 내가 목격한 것이다. 나는 그 이후 어린 나이에도 혐오감을 억누르고 Mamie의 소금기 있는 입술에 키스했다는 사실에 자부심을 느껴 왔다.

90. **정답** 1. jogging 2. ② 3. ② 4. ④ 5. 성공감
word popular : 인기 있는, 유행하는 (= in vogue)
lose weight : 체중을 줄이다
해석 매일 날씨가 어떻든 수많은 사람들이 조깅을 한다. 왜 조깅이 그렇게도 널리 유행하게 되었을까? 대부분 사람들은 조깅이 매우 좋은 운동이라는 말을 듣고서 조깅을 시작한다. 조깅은 심장을 더 튼튼하게 해주고 체중을 줄이는 데 도움을 준다. 조깅은 사람들이 자신에 대해서 더 좋은 기분을 느낄 수 있도록 해 주기도 한다. 42세의 사무실 근로자인 도널드 로빈스는 수년 전 자신이 너무 뚱뚱하다고 생각하여

조깅을 시작했다. 처음에는 오직 100야드 정도 밖에 달릴 수 없었다. 1마일을 달리는 데는 3개월이나 걸렸다. 그러나 2년 후 26마일이 넘는 마라톤 코스를 달렸다. 도널드 로빈스처럼, 조깅을 하는 대다수 사람들은 그들이 조깅에서 성공하면 다른 일에서도 성공할 수 있다고 느끼는데, 이런 감정이 직장에서의 일처리에도 도움을 준다.

91. 정답 1. moment 2. barrier
word first of all : 무엇보다 먼저
be confused with : ~와 혼동되다
explosive : 폭발적인 / collapse : 붕괴
barrier : 장벽 / intimacy : 친밀함
해석 무엇보다 먼저 그것은 사랑에 빠짐, 즉 그 순간까지 낯선 두 사람 사이에 존재하였던 장벽의 갑작스런 붕괴라는 폭발적인 경험과 종종 혼동된다. 그러나 앞서 지적하였던 것처럼, 이런 갑작스런 친밀의 (1)순간은 본질적으로 수명이 짧은 것이다. 낯선 사람이 친밀하게 아는 사람이 된 이후 극복해야 할 (2)장벽이 더 이상 없으며 성취해야 할 갑작스런 친근감도 더 이상 없다.

92. 정답 1.computer 2. most 3. answers
word gather : 모으다 / pour out : 넘쳐흐르다, 퍼붓다
high-powered : 고성능의 / brand : 상표
canned goods : 통조림 상품
flash out : 밝혀 주다
해석 컴퓨터는 정보를 수집할 뿐만 아니라 수집된 속도만큼 빠르게 그것들을 저장하며 필요할 때면 언제든지 그것을 제공해 줄 수 있다. (1) 컴퓨터는 실로 모든-아니 거의 모든-해답을 가진 고성능 기억 장치를 가진 기계이다. 뉴욕과 뉴저지 간의 터널을 지나는데 운전 속도는 어느 정도가 가장 효과적일까? 특정 슈퍼마켓에서 어떤 상표의 통조림 상품이 (2) 가장 대중적일까? 내일 날씨는 어떨까? 컴퓨터는 (3) 해답을 1초도 안 되는 시간 내에 밝혀 준다.

93. 정답 1. ② 2. ④ 3. ① 4. ④ 5. ③
word ride a bicycle : 자전거를 타다
storm break : 폭풍이 불다
to one's relief : ~가 다행스럽게도
solitary : 고독한, 유일한
make a face : 얼굴을 찌푸리다
resign oneself : 단념하다
brand-new : 아주 신품의
jovially : 쾌활하게 (= cheerfully)
해석 내가 새로 산 자전거를 즐겁게 타고 있을 때 하늘이 갑자기 어두워지더니 빗방울이 몇 방울 떨어졌다. 폭풍이 일어나기 전에 집에 도달하지 못할 것이라는 것을 알고 나는 버스를 타기로 결심했다. "요금이 얼마죠?" 내가 운전사에게 물었다. "25센트야." 다행히도 나는 주머니 속에서 단 하나밖에 없는 25센트짜리 주화를 찾아냈다. "자전거를 버스에 실어도 되나요?" "글쎄, 별도로 요금을 내면 되지." 하고 운전사가 말했다. "25센트가 전부인데요." 하고 고백했

다. 그는 큰 천둥 소리가 울렸을 때 얼굴을 찡그렸다. 그래서 나는 단념하고 비를 흠뻑 맞으며 집으로의 긴 여행을 하기로 마음먹었다. 내가 돌아서서 가려고 하는데 "그 자전거 아주 새 것 같구나."라고 운전사가 말했다. "그래요." 나는 대답했다. "그렇다면 그것을 차에 실어라. 6세 이하의 애들은 무료야." 라고 그는 명랑하게 말했다.

해답 1. wage : 급료, 임금
fare : 교통 요금 ex) a bus fare : 버스 요금
cost : 경비, 비용 ex) living cost : 생활비
fee : 각종 수수료 ex) tuition fee : 등록금
price : 물건 값
charge : 부과된 요금 ex) postal charge : 우편 요금
3. clap : 천둥소리, 박수소리, 문 닫는 소리
clang : (쇠붙이, 종소리 등) 쨍그랑
tick : (시계 소리) 똑딱똑딱
4. 운전사는 왜 얼굴을 찡그렸나? → ④굉장한 폭우가 그에게 덮칠까 두려웠기 때문에
5. → ③내 자전거를 버스에 실어 준 것을 보니 운전사가 유머 감각이 있음에 틀림없다.

94. 정답 1. ② 2. ① 3. ④ 4. ③ 5. ②
word afford : ~할 여유가 있는 / insult : 모욕하다
shave : 면도 (하다) / embarrassing : 난처하게 하는
grim : 엄한, 냉혹한 / melancholy : 우울한
take an order : 주문받다 / give an order : 주문하다
해석 늘 시골에 살며 대도시에는 한 번도 가 본 적이 없던 한 가난한 농부가 돈을 많이 벌었다. 그래서 그는 바닷가에 위치한 일류 호텔에서 휴가를 보내기로 작정했다. 그곳에서 첫날 점심시간이 되었을 때 그는 그 호텔 식당에서 식사를 하기로 작정했다. 웨이터장이 그를 테이블로 안내하고 주문을 받고 가 버렸다. 그가 농부를 다시 한 번 쳐다보았을 때, 그는 깜짝 놀랐다. 농부가 냅킨을 자기 목에 둘렀던 것이다. 웨이터장이 이것을 보고 몹시 화가 나서 다른 웨이터에게 그에게 가서 전혀 모욕을 주지는 말되, 이런 고급 호텔에서 그런 짓을 해서는 안 된다고 알려 주라고 했다. 그 웨이터가 농부에게 가서 다정하게 말했다. "안녕하세요. 면도를 해 드릴까요, 아니면 이발을 해 드릴까요?"

95. 정답 1. 해석 참조 2. 대학에 갈 꿈을 포기한 것
3. 해석 참조 4. died 5. ②
word undergo : 겪다 / toward : ~경
only son : 외아들 / take over : 인계받다
before dawn : 동트기 전 / vegetable : 채소
wholesale market : 도매시장
go through : ~을 경험하다 / association : 협회
volunteer : 자발적으로 나서다
emergency : 비상사태 / passed on : 죽다 (= die)
해석 서로 이웃인 두 가게가 비슷한 경험을 했다. 가게 주인인 아버지가 작년 말경 사망하고 (a)그 외아들이 가게를 인수한 것이다. 하나는 이발소이고 또 하나는

피자집이었다. 그리하여 두 아들은 대학에 갈 꿈을
포기했다. 그러나 그들은 (b)그것에 신경 쓰는 것 같
지 않았다. 둘 다 결혼 했고, 새로운 책임감에 가득
차 열심히 아버지의 일을 수행하며 어머니를 돌봐 드
렸다. 이것은 이 두 젊은이들에게 전적으로 새로운
삶을 의미했다. 이발소의 경우 새 주인은 그곳에서
일하는 다른 이발사들과의 관계를 포함하여 경영상
많은 문제점과 이제 익숙해졌다. 피자집 아들의 경우
피자를 만들어 배달하고 고객들과 좋은 관계를 유지
하는 것 외에 중앙 도매시장에서 신선한 고기와 야채
를 사기 위하여 매일 동이 트기 전 일어나는 것을 의
미한다. (c)두 사람 모두 자기 아버지가 수년 동안 겪
어 온 모든 것에 대한 새로운 인식을 갖게 되었다. 두
아버지 다 이웃에게 잘 알려져 있었다. 두 아들은 이
웃에서 자랐다. 주민들은 그들의 학창시절을 기억하
고 있었다. 그들은 인근 청년들의 회합에서 활동적이
었고, 지역 축제에서도 활동적인 역할을 해냈으며,
불이 났을 때와 같은 비상사태에도 자진하여 일을 했
다. 두 아버지는 사망했지만 다행스럽게도 훌륭한 아
들을 둔 것이다. 인생은 계속 이어져 가지만 우리는
우리나라의 미래가 그러한 젊은이들의 손에 있기를
더 바라지, 오토바이나 스포츠카를 타고 소리를 지르
며 돌아다니는 젊은이들이나, 캠퍼스 안팎에서 말썽
을 일으키는 젊은이 손에 있기를 바라지 않는다.

96. **정답** 1. ③ 2. ② 3. ④
　word ocean liner : 기선 / on the move : 움직이고 있는
　　　 day and night : 밤낮 할 것 없이
　　　 around the clock : 24시간 계속하여
　　　 vehicle : 운송 수단 / the Stone Age : 석기시대
　　　 log : 통나무
　해석 자동차, 기차, 비행기, 기선들이 밤낮 할 것 없이 24
　　　 시간 내내 움직이고 있다. 그러나 늘 그러했던 것은
　　　 아니다. 운송 수단도 길도 없었던 시대에도 있었다.
　　　 석기시대에는 사람들이 강물이나 호수를 길로 이용
　　　 했다. 그들은 통나무를 하나, 혹은 몇 개 합쳐서 묶어
　　　 서 타고 다녔다. 통나무가 최초의 운송 수단이었다.

97. **정답** 1. 매우 잘 하는 것은 아니다. 2. birds 3. seen
　word discriminate[distinguish] between A and B
　　　 = discriminate[distinguish, tell, know] A from B
　　　 : A와 B를 구별하다
　　　 protector : 보호자 / persecutor : 학대하는 사람
　　　 at fault : 실수하는
　해석 새들은 종종 보호해 주는 사람과 학대하는 사람을
　　　 구별할 줄 안다. 그러나 매우 잘 하는 건 아니다. 상
　　　 상해 보건대 새들은 단지 사람의 얼굴만을 보지 않
　　　 고 전체 모습을 보는데 옷을 자주 바꿔 입게 되면 새
　　　 들이 알고 신뢰하는 사람과 낯선 사람을 구분하는
　　　 것이 어렵게 된다. 지난번에 검은 옷을 입은 것으로
　　　 보였던 주인이 흰 옷을 입고 밀짚모자를 쓰고 다시
　　　 나타나면 개조차도 실수할 때가 있다.

98. **정답** 1. ① 2. ③ 3. ② 4. ④ 5. ③
　word Dry Goods store : 직물가게, 포목상
　　　 stepfather : 의붓아버지 / odd : 특이한

slight : 하찮은, 호리호리한
overshadow : ~에 그늘지게 하다
stoop : 허리가 굽다 / placid : 잔잔한
exterior (외부의) ↔ interior (내부의)
ferment : 발효, 소동 / be given to : ~에 탐닉하다
go off (= explode) : 폭발하다
go on : 계속 ~하다
　해석 조지 윌러드가 겨우 소년이었을 때 27세의 부인이었
　　　 던 엘리스 힌더만은 평생을 Winesburg에서 살아왔
　　　 다. 그녀는 위니의 직물 가게 점원 노릇을 했으며 두
　　　 번째 남편과 결혼한 어머니와 함께 살았다. 엘리스
　　　 의 의붓아버지는 마차를 끌고 다니며 칠해 주는 페
　　　 인트 공이었고 알코올 중독자였다. 그에 대한 이야
　　　 기는 좀 특이한데 언젠가 하루 정도 이야기할 만한
　　　 거리가 될 것이다. 27세였던 엘리스는 키가 크고
　　　 다소 여위었다. 그녀의 머리는 커서 몸 전체에 그늘
　　　 을 지울 정도였다. 어깨는 좀 꾸부정했고 머리와 눈
　　　 색깔은 갈색이었다. 그녀는 조용했다. 그러나 조용
　　　 해 보이는 외양 뒷면에는 끊임없는 걱정이 소용돌이
　　　 치고 있었다.

99. **정답** 1. unproductive 2. 오염시키다 3. pollution, humans
　word developing country : 개발도상국 / resident : 주민
　　　 pollution : 오염, 공해 / contaminate : 오염시키다
　　　 ecological balance : 생태계적인 균형
　해석 매년 수많은 개발도상국에서는 한때 식량을 생산했
　　　 던 많은 지역들이 완전히 생산력을 상실해 가고 있
　　　 다. 이 지역에 거주하는 굶주린 주민들은 이주를 하
　　　 든 아니면 죽어야만 하는 처지에 놓여 있다. 이 문제
　　　 는 오염에 의해서만 야기된 것은 결코 아니다. 즉, 땅
　　　 은 독성이 있는 화학제품을 사용한 결과에 의해서만
　　　 오염되는 것이 아니다. 오염이 환경을 파괴하는 유
　　　 일한 요소는 아닌 것이다. 환경은 다른 방식으로 한
　　　 지역의 생태적 균형을 교란시키는 인간에 의해서도
　　　 파괴될 수도 있는 것이다. 어떤 지역에서든 자연에
　　　 는 균형이 있다. 자연 체계에 있어 각 부분은 서로 다
　　　 른 부분에 의존한다.

100. **정답** 1. ④ 2. 해석 참조 3. 듣기, 말하기, 읽기, 쓰기 순으
　　　 로 된 과정 4. It is supposed that one has acquired
　　　 a knowledge of reading and writing. 5. ③
　word valid : 타당한 / procedure : 절차, 순서
　　　 mother tongue (= native language) : 모국어
　　　 considerable : 상당한 cf. considerate : 사려 깊은
　　　 facility : 편의, 재능 / document : 문서
　　　 falsely : 잘못하여
　　　 deficiency : 부족, 결함 (= defect)
　　　 exclusively : 배타적으로
　　　 since (= now that) : ~이기 때문에
　해석 과학적으로 황당한 언어 학습과정은 듣기 과정이 먼
　　　 저이고, 말하기는 그 다음이어야 한다. 그리고 난 이
　　　 후 읽기 과정, 마지막으로 쓰기 과정이어야 한다. 먼
　　　 저 듣고 그리고 말하는 것, (3) 즉 이해하거나 말하는
　　　 데 있어 상당한 능력을 획득하고 난 후 비로소 읽고
　　　 쓰는 것을 배우는 것이 어린이들이 모국어를 배우는

과정이다. 그러나 성인들에게 언어를 가르치는 거의 대부분의 전통적인 교육 방법은 이 과정을 완전히 뒤바꾸어 먼저 읽기와 그에 밀접하게 연관된 쓰기를 가르치고, 이에 대한 지식을 상당히 획득했다고 여겨질 때 회화 방식의 수업을 제공한다. 이러한 언어 교수법의 주된 결점은 글로 쓰인 문서와 같은 죽은 형태로만 알려져 있는 그리스어나 라틴어를 가르치던 전통적인 방법에서 유래된 것이다. 고전어가 전적으로 인쇄된 글을 통하여 가르쳐져 왔기 때문에 살아있는 현대어도 같은 방식으로 가르쳐야 한다는 것은 잘못된 가정이었다.

101. **정답** 1. ③ 2. ②③ 3. 해석 참조
word dweller : 거주자 / alleged : (함부로) 주장된, 추정된 / convenience : 편리함 / despite (= with all, for all, in spite of) : ~에도 불구하고 / well-off : 부유한 ↔ badly off : 가난한 / terrific : 대단한, 지독한 / shrewd : 영리한 / wangle a living : 교묘하게 살아 가다
해석 이태리 남부 도시에 사는 사람들은 물론 조금 다른 성격의 사람들이다. 그들은 도시 생활에서 얻어지리라 추정되는 이점과 편리함을 누리고 있지만, 사람들이 붐비는 나폴리 지역의 빈민가를 지나가 보면 농부들의 생활환경이 낙후되어 있다 하더라도 그들이 더 잘 사는구나 하는 생각이 들게 된다. 인구가 많은 이런 남부 도시에서의 생존경쟁은 철저한 것이다. 도시 거주자가 육체적으로는 농부만큼 열심히 일하지 않아도 되겠지만, 교묘히 잘 살아가려면 아무리 하찮은 기회에도 더 재빨리, 더 활발하게 움직여야 한다.

102. **정답** 1. ① 2. ③
word take a pride in (= be proud of = pride oneself on) : ~을 자랑하다 / boast : ~를 뽐내다, 자랑거리
free : 무료의 / public school : 공립학교
해석 국민의 일원으로서 우리 교육제도보다 더 자랑할 수 있는 것이 없다. 모든 소년, 소녀들이 학교 교육을 받을 수 있는 기회를 갖는다는 것이 우리의 자랑거리이며, 이 교육을 무료로 제공하는 것이 국가의 주된 의무라고 우리는 생각한다. 오직 그렇게 함으로써 우리는 보통의 미국인들이 적절한 시민 의식을 갖게 해 줄 수 있다. 미국의 공립학교와 대학이 이런 역할을 잘 수행해 왔다. 이곳에서 가르치는 분들보다 우리 시민들로부터 더 마음에서 우러나는 보다 높은 찬사를 받을 자격이 있는 계층은 없다.

103. **정답** 1. education 2. element 3. personal relation 4. personal element
word consist of (= comprise = be composed of = be made up of) : ~로 구성되다
mutual : 상호간의 / mechanical device : 기계장치
take the place of : ~을 대신하다
chat with : ~와 잡담하다
depersonalize : 비인간화시키다
deprive A of B : A에게서 B를 박탈하다

ingredient : 성분
at all costs : 어떤 대가를 치르더라도
take an interest in : ~에 관심을 가지다
해석 대학은 하나의 공동사회이며 공동사회는 인간적인 유대관계로 묶여 있는 사람들로 구성되어 있다. 교수와 학생과의 관계는 인격적인 것이어서 상호이익과 상호 협력이 있다. 어떠한 기계장치도 이런 인간적인 관계를 대신해 줄 수는 없다. TV 화면이 당신에게 응대를 해 주거나 기쁨이나 슬픔을 같이하고, 클럽 방에서 커피나 콜라를 마시며 잡담을 나누어 줄 수는 없는 것이다. 교육을 기계화해서 인간적인 요소를 빼낸다는 것은 교육에서 가장 소중한 부분을 없애는 것이 된다. 어떤 대가를 치르더라도 이러한 인간적인 요소를 소중히 여겨야 한다. 다행스럽게도 밴더빌트는 그다지 크지 않아서 우리가 서로를 잘알 수 있고, 서로에게 관심을 보일 수 있는 규모이다. 밴더빌트는 규모가 크지 않아 우리는 모두 친구가 될 수 있다.

104. **정답** 1. for 2. 해석 참조
word not so much A as B : A라기 보다는 오히려 B (= B rather than A)
nourishment : 영양 섭취
New Year's Day : 설날
lunar calendar : 음력
해석 중국에서는 일 년 중 어떤 날은 음식을 영양 섭취를 위해서라기보다는 (상징적인) 의미 때문에 먹는 날이 있다. 이것은 특히 음력 정원 초하루인 설날에 그러하다.

105. **정답** 1. important 2. culture (and) intellect
word associate with : ~와 사귀다 / culture : 고양, 문화
atmosphere : 분위기
detachment : 분리, 초연함
ravenously : 게걸스럽게
thenceforth : 그 이후 / folk : 사람들
be superior to : ~보다 우수한 ↔ be inferior to : ~보다 열등한
해석 나는 조용하고 초연한 분위기에서 폭넓은 교양과 높은 이상을 가진 사람과 교제하고 우정을 나눌 수 있는 기회를 갈망했다. 나는 16세 때 일하러 나갔는데 그 나이 때에는 마음껏, 규칙적으로 먹는 것이 중요한 것으로 여겨졌기 때문이다. 아니 실제보다 훨씬 더 중요하게 여겨졌다. 그 이후 나는 학자도 신사도 아닌 사람들과 교류를 가지게 되었다. 여러 해가 지나고 나서야 나는 비로소 나보다 교양이나 지성이 나은 사람들과 가깝게 지낼 수 있는 기회를 가지게 되었다.

106. **정답** 1. for 2. to tell the truth 3. ④ 4. ③ 5. ④
word brilliant : 빛나는 / steep : 가파른
sheer cliff : 가파른 절벽 / vehicle : 차량
open space : 대기 장소 / at intervals : 길 중간에
해석 길이야말로 현대 기술이 이룩한 빛나는 업적이다. 길은 산속으로 수백 마일 이어지는데 산의 가파른 가장

자리 둘레를 뱀처럼 감아 정상까지 올라갔다가, 다시 계곡 너머로 내려온다. 나는 천 피트가 넘는 가파른 절벽에 있는 길의 한 지점을 기억하고 있다. 길의 너비는 단지 차 한 대가 겨우 지날 정도였기 때문에 길 중간에 산 가장자리 쪽으로 대기 장소를 만들어 놓았다. 종종 있는 일이지만 만약 두 대의 차가 마주치게 되면 한 차가 다른 차가 통과하도록 가장 가까운 대기 장소로 후진해야 한다. 날씨가 나쁠 때 차가 무시한 절벽 쪽으로 간다고 생각하면 섬뜩하다. 그러나 운전자들은 별로 개의치 않는다. 사실대로 말하면 큰 사고가 났다는 이야기를 들은 적이 없다.

해답 3. 나쁜 날씨에는 그 길이 무섭다. 왜냐하면 ④대기 장소가 절벽 쪽으로 나 있기 때문이다.
4. 운전자들은 ③걱정하지 않는다.
5. 그 길은 ④정상을 향하여 점차적으로 감고 올라가다가 다시 내려온다.

PART X : 영문 번역

1. word forest : 숲 속 / pick up : 집어 올리다
   raw : 날 것의 / basker : 바구니
   at a time : 한때에
   nothing but : 단지 ~일 따름 (= only)
   vegetable : 야채 / grain : 곡식 / triangle : 삼각형
   fasten : 붙들어 매다, 고정시키다

   해석 깊은 산 속에서 한 사냥꾼이 커다란 날고기 덩어리들을 주워 바구니에 담았다. (A) **한때는 줄곧 몇 날을 그는 고기만 먹었다.** 이제 그는 야채와 곡물이 먹고 싶었다. 그는 바구니를 지어 들고 숲 속 그늘을 지나 숲가로 향해 갔다. (B) **그곳에는 나무들이 함께 붙어 삼각형 모양을 이루고 있었다.** 그곳에서 사냥꾼은 고기 덩어리들을 꺼내 세 그루 나무에 하나씩 붙들어 맸다. 그런 다음 돌아서서 그는 숲 속으로 돌아왔다.

2. word inevitable : 불가피한 / arise : (생각이) 떠오르다
   depreciate : (기차를) 떨어뜨리다
   crumble : 산산이 부서지다

   해석 전반적인 사회체제의 변화는 불가피한데, 이것은 사회 여건이 바뀌어서가 아니라-그것도 한 이유가 되긴 하지만-사람들 스스로가 변하기 때문이다. 우리는 너나 할 것 없이 세월이 흐름에 따라 계속해서 변해간다. 새로운 감정이 마음속에서 일어나고, 낡은 가치관이 퇴조하며, 새로운 가치관이 생겨난다. **우리가 가장 강렬하게 원하고 있다고 생각되었던 것들을 전혀 관심두지 않게 됨을 깨닫게 된다. 우리가 삶의 토대로 삼았던 것들이 부스러져 없어지기도 하는데, 그것은 고통스런 과정이다.**

3. word end : 목표 / devise : 고안하다
   in contrast : 그와는 대조적으로 / realization : 실현
   be concern (ed) with : ~에 관심을 가지고 있다.

   해석 과학자로서는 사실을 발견하고 기술을 발명하며, 수단을 고안해 내는 것이 그의 임무이다. 이와는 대조적으로 **철학자의 임무는 모든 과학적 사실과 기술 지식이 수단으로써 이용되어 실현해야 할 목표들을 인류가 결정하는 데 도움을 주는 것이다.** 왜냐하면 철학은 가치 자체에 관심을 가지며 또한 사물의 현상뿐만 아니라 도덕적인 가치에 대해서도 관심을 가지기 때문이다.

4. word strike : 파업 / papers : 신문
   Public Opinion : 여론
   oppose to (= be opposed to = have an objection to) : ~에 반대하다
   dictation : 명령, 지시
   minority : 소수 ↔ majority : 다수
   toward : ~경, ~무렵 / in favor of : ~을 찬성하다
   a sense of defeat : 패배감
   leader-writer : 신문 편집인

   해석 지난 번 파업이 시작되었을 때 신문들은 여론은 소수 집단의 지시에 반대한다고 발표했다. **파업이 끝날 무렵 신문들은 여론이 어느 편도 패배감을 느끼지 않는 해결책을 강력하게 지지하고 있다고 발표했다. 나는 이 두 발표의 어느 쪽에 대해서도 불평하지 않는다.** 다만, 전에도 항상 그러하였지만, 궁금한 것은 신문 편집인이 여론이 어떠한가를 어떻게 알아내는가라고 하는 것이다.

5. word observance : (규칙, 법률의) 준수 cf. observation : 관찰 / sacrifice : 희생
   commonplace : 평범한 / intercourse : 교제
   make up : 구성하다 (= compose)

   해석 **우리가 우리 자신을 평가하여 문명화되거나 미개하다고 단정하는 것은 도로 규칙의 준수와 같은 사소한 행위에 달려있다. 영웅적 행위나 희생과 같은 위대한 순간은 흔하지 않다. 인생의 대부분을 구성하고 그 인생 여정을 달콤하게 또는 쓰게 하는 것은 바로 일상생활의 작은 습관들인 것이다.**

6. word the U.S. forces cut : 미군 병력의 감축
   enormous : 굉장한 / deficit : 적자
   budget : 예산 / stimulate : 자극하다
   seeing that (= since) : ~이기 때문에 / era : 시대
   collapse : 붕괴

   해석 **미군 병력의 감축은 연방정부 예산의 막대한 적자를 줄이고 경제 회복을 자극하기 위하여 이루어진 것으로** 우리는 이해하고 있다. 유럽 공산주의의 붕괴로 인하여 야기된 전후 냉전 시대에 있어서 현재의 미군을 계속 유지시킨다는 것을 불필요한 것이기 때문이다.

7. word tackle : 해결하다, 극복하다
   in the process of : ~의 과정에서
   industrialization : 산업화 / pollution : 공해
   since (= now that) : ~이기 때문에
   regional : 지역적인 / national boundary : 국경
   해석 산업화의 과정에서 전체 인류가 해결해야 할 가장 중요한 임무는 약화되고 있는 공해로부터 환경을 보존하는 것이다. 공해는 국경을 뛰어 넘어 확산되는 것이라서 환경문제는 각각의 나라에 국한되는 것일 뿐만 아니라 본질적으로 범세계적이고 지역적인 것이기 때문에 국제적인 협조가 이러한 목표에 필수적이다.

8. word As far as ~ be concerned : ~에 관한 한
   pollution : 공해, 오염 / well-being : 복지
   conservation : 보존, 보호
   해석 우리의 환경에 관한 한, 공해는 인간의 건강과 복지에 진정한 위협이 된다. 사실 많은 과학자들은 우리가 곧 우리의 생활 방식을 바꾸지 않는다면, 지구는 언젠가 몹시 오염되어 인간이 더 이상 **지구상에 살아남을 수 없게 될 것이라고 믿고 있다. 우리가 자연 보호에 대해 배운 다음에야 비로소 인류는 안전할 것이다.**

9. word play a part[role] : ~한 역할을 하다
   curse : 저주 / outweigh : ~보다 중요하다
   corrupt : 부패시키다 / instruct : ~를 교육시키다
   put~ to use : ~을 사용하다
   해석 오늘날 텔레비전은 매우 많은 사람들의 삶에 아주 중요한 역할을 하고 있기 때문에 우리는 필수적으로 그것이 과연 축복인지 아니면 저주인지를 결정하려고 노력할 필요가 있다. 분명히 텔레비전은 장점과 단점을 모두 지니고 있다. 하지만, 전자 (장점) 가 후자 (단점) 보다 더 중요한가? 그리고 그것이 우리 자녀들을 타락시키고 있는가 아니면 교육적 가치를 지니고 있는가? **나는 텔레비전 그 자체는 좋지도 나쁘지도 않다는 것을 우리가 깨달아야 한다고 생각한다. 그것의 사회적 가치를 결정하는 것은 그것이 사용되는 방법에 있는 것이다.**

10. word It is true A but B : A인 것이 사실이지만 그러나 B 이다. / menace : 위협하다 (= threaten)
    해석 많은 젊은이들이 자유를 소중히 여기지 않는 것 같아 보이는 것이 사실이지만 우리 중 일부는 여전히 자유가 없으면 인간답게 살 수 없고 따라서 자유가 매우 소중하다고 믿고 있다. **그런데 아마도 지금 자유를 위협하는 세력은 너무나도 강해서 아주 오랫동안 이에 맞서 싸울 수 없을지도 모른다. 그들과 대항하여 싸우기 위해 할 수 있는 모든 것을 다하는 것이 우리의 의무이다.**

11. word of interest : 흥미 있는 (= interesting)
    해석 컴퓨터가 언어에 관한 일을 하는 데 쓰일 수 있다. 영어 문장이 컴퓨터상에서 연구되고 있다. **이런 연구 결과는 다른 나라 선생님들에게 흥미로운 것이 될 것이다.**

12. word similarly : 마찬가지로 / curiosity : 호기심
    be worth ~ing : ~할 만한 가치가 있다
    result from : ~에서 비롯되다 cf. result in : ~를 초래하다 / engage in : ~에 종사하다
    disruption : 붕괴
    cannot A without B : A하기만 하면 반드시 B한다.
    해석 **마찬가지로 오늘날 학자의 호기심을 충족시켜 주는 것이 그로 인해 생길 수 있는 사회의 분열을 야기해도 될 만한 값어치가 있는가라고 하는 것을 판단하는 것은 늘 쉽지 않다.** 학자들은 호기심을 좇다 보면 자주 사회와 싸우게 된다는 점을 배워 왔다.

13. word (A) revolt : 반란 (= rebellion)
    antics : (보통 복수형으로) 기이한 행동
    (B) jack : (무거운 물건을 들어올리는) 잭, 들어 올리다
    해석 (A) 그들은 당시 매스컴의 기이한 행동에 반항하며 성장했다.
    (B) 타이어를 갈아 끼우기 위하여 차를 들어 올려야 한다.

14. word deal with : 다루다 (= treat) / adult : 성인
    instinct : 본능 / stern : 엄격한
    affectionate : 애정이 있는 / put up with : 참다
    strictness : 엄함
    해석 어린아이들을 다루어야 하는 사람은 누구나 지나친 동정심은 잘못된 것이라는 점을 알고 있다. 어린이들은 때로는 조금 엄한 어른들이 그들에게 가장 좋은 사람이라는 것을 쉽게 이해한다. 어린이들이 그들을 사랑하는지 아닌지를 본능적으로 알기 때문이다. **어린이들은 그들에게 애정을 갖고 있다고 느끼고 있는 사람들이 그들이 잘 자라기를 바라는 마음에서 엄격히 대하더라도 잘 참아 낸다.**

15. word A) aspire for (= long for) : ~을 갈망하다
    (B) participate in : ~에 참가하다
    elimination : 제거
    chemical-biological weapon : 생화학 무기
    해석 A) **우리는 핵무기가 없는 평화로운 세계를 갈망한다.**
    (B) **생화학 무기의 완전 제거**를 위한 국제적인 노력에 참여할 것이다.

16. word decade : 10년 / psychologically : 심리학적으로
    face : 직면하다 / abrupt : 갑작스러운
    collision : 충돌
    keep up with : ~에 뒤떨어지지 않다
    incessant : 끊임없는 / acceleration : 가속, 촉진
    concrete : 구체적인
    해석 지금부터 21세기 사이의 짧은 30년 내에 수백만 명의 보통의, 심리학적으로 정상적인 사람들은 미래와의 갑작스러운 충돌에 직면하게 될 것이다. **그들 중 많은 사람은 현재 우리 시대를 특징짓고 있는 끊임없는 변화 요구에 뒤떨어지지 않기가 점점 더 고통스럽다는 것을 알게 될 것이다. 이처럼 변화를 가속화시키는 것은 우리의 개인적인 생활 속에 깊숙이**

파고 들어와 새로운 역할을 해내도록 우리를 떠밀어 내어 새롭고도 몹시 당혹스러운 질병의 위험에 직면하도록 만드는 실질적인 힘이다. 이 새로운 질병을 "미래의 충격" 이라고 지칭할 수 있다.

17. word the other day : 일전에

drop around : 우연히 만나다 / indignant : 격분한

해석 일전에 친구 한 명이 우연히 들러 6개월 전 신문에 **어떤 길을 낼 것이라고 보도했는데 아직 길이 안 났다고 몹시 화를 냈다.**

18. word in the philosophical sense : 철학적 의미에서

compulsion : 강제, 억압

해석 우리는 철학적 관점에서 본 자유는 결코 가질 수 없을 것이라고 믿는다. **왜냐하면 우리는 외적 강제 하에서 뿐만 아니라 내적인 필요에 의하여 행동하기 때문이다.**

19. word according to : ~에 따르면 / precede : 앞서가다

해석 프로이드의 이론과 프로이드보다 수백 년 혹은 수천 년 앞선 저작들이 제시하는 다른 이론들에 따르면, **꿈은 결코 미래에 대한 어떤 것을 나타내지 않는다.**

20. word agent : 대리인, 동인

from one's point of view : ~의 관점에서 볼 때

by reason of : ~ 때문에, ~라는 이유로

해석 우리의 관점에서 볼 때 변화의 파괴의 큰 동인은 사실상 기계였다. 분명 기계는 우리에게 많은 이점을 가져다주었지만, **기계는 오래된 생활방식을 파괴하였고, 또 그 자체가 끊임없이 변화하기 때문에 새로운 것의 성장을 방해하였다.**

21. word (A) wreck : 난파되다, 파손시키다

augment : 증가하다

(B) discard : 저버리다

irrelevant : ~에 관계없는 / profess : 공언하다

(C) faction : 분파, 파벌 / aliment : 자양물

expire : 소멸하다

A is to B what C is to D : A가 B에 대한 관계는 C가 D에 대한 관계와 같다.

해석 (A) 그의 더욱 능동적인 에너지가 그를 파괴시키지는 않는다. **왜냐하면 생물체는 적응을 하게 되고 쇠퇴하는 속도가 빠를수록 그에 상응하여 회복하는 속도도 빨라지기 때문이다.**

(B) 그가 만약 우리가 전통적으로 믿고 있다고 공언한 이상들이 무관하다고 해서 버린다면 그가 어떤 미덕을 지명할 것인가?

(C) 자유가 분파에 대한 관계는 공기가 불에 대한 관계와 같다. 이것 (공기) 은 불이 금방 꺼지지 않게 해주는 자양분인 것이다.

22. word advertising : 광고 (류)

corporate advertising : 기업 광고

availability : 유효성 / uniqueness : 희귀성, 유일성

해석 광고의 가장 기본적인 기능은 광고를 판매 수단으로

활용하는 것이다. 광고의 목적은 특정한 목적에 따라 회사마다 다를 수 있다. 많은 회사들이 제품을 판매하기 위해서 혹은 회사의 이름을 알리고 이미지를 제고하기 위해서 광고를 이용하고 있다. 기업 광고는 회사의 이름과 이미지를 향상시켜 보려는 회사에게 해당된다. 그 목적은 전체로서의 회사를 알리는 것이기 때문에 세세한 사항은 포함시키지 않는다. 반면 특정 제품의 판매를 증대시키기 위해 광고를 할 수도 있다. 이때는 제품의 가격, 사용법, 설명, 유용성, 제품의 특성 등이 강조된다.

23. word save (= except, but) : ~외에

해석 역사란 역사가의 경험이다. 역사는 역사가를 제외한 그 누구에 의해서도 '만들어' 질 수 없다. 역사를 쓰는 것이 역사를 만드는 유일한 방법이다.

24. word be accustomed to : ~에 익숙해지다

take~ for granted : ~를 당연한 것으로 여기다

assume : 가정하다

without hesitation : 주저없이

해석 우리는 진보를 당연시하는 데 익숙해 있다. 즉 지난 수백 년 간 일어났던 변화가 보다 나은 것을 만들어냈다고 주저없이 가정하는 데 우리는 익숙해 있다.

25. word magnitude : 크기, 중요성 / assault : 공격

contamination : 오염 / lethal : 치명적인

for the most part : 대개

irrevocable : 돌이킬 수 없는

initiate : 시작하다

living tissue : 살아 있는 신체 조직

sinister : 해로운

해석 지난 사반세기 동안 이러한 힘은 혼돈스러운 무게로 증가했을 뿐 아니라 그 특징도 변화되었다. 환경에 대해서 인간이 행한 모든 공격 가운데 가장 놀라운 것은 위험하고 심지어 치명적인 물질로 대기, 토양, 강, 바다를 오염시킨 것이다. 대부분의 경우 이러한 공해는 돌이킬 수 없는 것이다. 악의 사슬은 생명을 지탱시켜 주는 세계에서 시작되었을 뿐 아니라 살아 있는 신체 조직에서도 대부분은 돌이킬 수 없는 것이 되었다. 오늘날 이러한 세계적인 환경의 오염을 통하여, 화학 물질은 세계의 바로 그러한 특성-생명의 바로 그러한 특성-을 변화시키는 데 있어서 매우 해롭고 거의 인식되지 못한 방사능의 동반자이다.

26. word name after : ~의 이름을 따라 이름을 짓다

general : 장군

해석 연중 일곱 번째 달인 7월은 줄리어스 시저의 이름을 따서 지어진 것이다. 시저는 유명한 장군이었고 로마의 황제가 되었다. 시저의 시대 이전에는 다른 달력이 사용되었다. 일 년은 1월이 아니라 3월에 시작되었다. 현재의 7월 (July) 은 일곱 번째 달이 아니라 다섯 번째 달이었다. 시저가 이것을 바꿔 놓았다. 그는 새로운 달력을 만들었다. 이것이 오늘날 우리가 쓰는 달력이다. 시저는 7월에 태어났다. 그가 이 달에 July라는 이름을 붙여 새 달력의 일곱 번째 달이되게 하였다.

27. word communicate : 의사소통하다
	approval : 승인
	clap : 손뼉 치다 / thumb : 엄지
	grimace : 얼굴을 찡그리다
	해석 인간은 여러 가지 방법으로 의사소통한다. 그중 하나가 제스처이다. 사람들은 눈을 깜박이거나 박수, 휘파람, 혹은 미소나 웃음으로 찬성을 표시한다. 그들은 엄지손가락을 땅으로 향하게 하거나 혀를 내밀어 붙거나, 손가락으로 코를 잡거나, 혹은 얼굴을 찡그리거나 하여 반감을 표시한다. 손가락질로 방향을 나타내며, 양손을 얼마간 벌려 크기를 나타낸다. 다른 많은 제스처가 있다. 생각을 나타내는 제스처도 있고, 태도나 감정을 나타내는 제스처도 더 있다.

28. word (A) sheer : 단순한 / awhile : 잠시 동안
	(B) look (out) for = search for = in search of : ~를 찾다
	해석 (A) 그러나 여전히 많은 영화들은 순전히 즐거움과 흥분을 제공해 주기 위해서 제작되고 있다. 영화를 보며 우리 자신의 고통을 잊는다. 웃고, 소리 지르며, 잠시 동안 다른 사람의 삶을 사는 것이다.
	(B) 자신에게 의존하는 법을 일찍 배워 두는 것이 중요하다. 왜냐하면 늘 자신을 도와줄 사람을 찾고 있는 그런 사람들에 의하여 이루어진 일이 이 세상에는 거의 없기 때문이다.

29. word (A) like : ~와 같은 / set in : (어둠이) 스며들다
	(B) flesh : 살, 육신 / dwell : 거주하다
	behold : 보다 (= see) / bosom : 가슴
	해석 (A) 사람은 스테인드글라스로 된 유리창과 같다. 햇빛이 비치면 반짝이며 빛나지만 어둠이 찾아들면, 그들의 참된 아름다움은 오로지 내면으로부터의 빛이 있을 때에만 드러나는 법이다.
	(B) 그리하여 말씀이 육신이 되어 우리 가운데 사셨다. 그분은 은총과 진리로 충만하셨다. 우리는 그의 영광, 아버지 하나님의 독생자로서의 영광을 보았다. 그리고 그의 충만함으로 인해 우리 모두는 은총을 충만히 받았다. 율법은 모세를 통해 내려왔고, 은총과 진리는 예수 그리스도를 통해 왔다. 이제껏 아무도 하나님을 보지 못했다. 하나님의 품에 안긴 독생자, 그분은 하나님을 알게 하셨다.

30. word lively : 활기에 찬 (= animated)
	해석 "살아 있다"는 것은 무엇을 의미하는가? 선생님이 그 반 학생들에게 이 질문을 했다. 이 문제에 대한 토론 때문에 학생들은 많은 생각을 하게 되었다. 생명체는 혼자서 움직인다. 동물과 식물은 생명체이다. 학생들은 활발히 토론을 벌였다.

31. word (A) A is one thing, B is another. : A와 B는 전혀 별개의 문제이다.
	keep early hours : 일찍 자고 일찍 일어나다
	few (people) : 거의 없는
	put~ into practice : 실천에 옮기다
	(B) be compared to : ~에 비유되다

last : 지속하다 / get rid of : ~를 제거하다
	해석 (A) 아는 것과 행하는 것은 별개의 문제이다. 일찍 자고 일찍 일어나는 것이 건강에 좋다는 것을 아는 사람은 많지만, 그것을 실천에 옮기는 사람은 거의 없다.
	(B) 책은 이웃에 삶에 비유할 수 있다. 좋은 책은 아무리 오래 있어도 지나치지 않고, 나쁜 책은 아무리 일찍 없애버려도 결코 지나침이 없다.

32. word (A) no doubt : 의심할 나위 없이
	cannibal : 식인종
	feast : 축제를 벌이다
	savage : 야만인
	roast : ~를 굽다
	(B) for all (= with all = in spite of = despite) : ~에도 불구하고
	participant : 참석자 / fiscal deficit : 재정적자
	prescription : 처방, 조치
	해석 (A) 몇 사람의 식인종이 그곳에 있었는데 그들의 손아귀에 들어온 그 불쌍한 죄수들을 죽이고 잔치를 벌였음은 의심할 나위가 없다. 왜냐하면 몇몇 원시 부족들 간에는 전쟁에서 포획한 적들을 죽이고 그 시체를 구워 먹는 일이 종종 관례로 되어왔다는 이야기를 전에 들어본 적이 있기 때문이다. 주위를 둘러보았을 때, 여기저기에 많은 뼈가 흩어져 있는 것을 보았다.
	(B) 그러나 여러 차례의 경고에도 불구하고 대부분의 회담 참석자들은 인도-파키스탄 전쟁이 가까운 장래에는 일어날 것 같지 않다는데 대한 두 가지 이유에 동의하였다. 그 중 하나는 양국 모두 경제적인 문제에 직면해 있다는 것인데, 대규모의 재정적자로 인해 IMF (국제통화기금) 의 가혹한 조치들을 받아들이지 않을 수 없다는 것이다. 실제로 인도는 방위 예산의 9%를 삭감하였다. 파키스탄은 방위비를 비밀로 하고 있지만 군비 축소의 압력을 받고 있는 상황이다.

33. word molecule : 분자
	be composed of (= be made up of = onsist of = comprise) : ~로 구성되다 / poisonous : 해로운
	substance : 물질 / attack : 발명하다
	on the other hand : 한편 / multiply : 증대시키다
	in unlimited quantities : 무한정으로
	해석 유행성감기 바이러스는 수백만 개의 개별적인 원자들로 구성된 단일한 분자이다. 박테리아는 그것들이 발병시키는 유기체 내에 해로운 물질을 분비하는 일종의 식물로 간주될 수 있지만, 바이러스는 유행성감기 바이러스처럼 그 자체가 살아 있는 유기체이다. 그것들은 완전하게 원자구조의 성질을 갖추고 있기 때문에, 우리는 그것들을 일정한 화학 분자로 취급할 수 있을 것이다. 하지만 그 반면에 그것들은 무한정으로 번식할 수 있기 때문에 우리는 그것들을 살아 있는 것으로 간주해야 한다.

34. word (A) eminent : 훌륭한
	do harm[good] : 해[이로움]를 주다

distort : 왜곡시키다

(B) in short : 줄여서 말하자면 / style : 문체

해석 (A) 많은 저명한 역사가들은 그들이 지닌 열정이라
는 왜곡된 매개체를 통하여 사실을 보기 때문에 이
로움보다 해로움을 더 많이 끼쳤다.

(B) 줄여서 말하자면 작가로서 글을 읽을 때는 철저
히, 상상력을 총동원하여, 창의력을 발휘해 가면서
읽어야 한다. 이것은 주제와 문체, 그리고 기술을 따
져보아야 한다는 것을 의미한다.

35. word probably : 아마도 / revolution : 혁명

transition : 변천, 전이 / prelogical : 논리 이전의

benevolent : 자비로운 / apparently : 분명히

manlike : 인간다운 / be capable of : ~할 수 있는

entreaty : 애원, 간청

disembody : (영혼을) 육체에서 분리시키다

since (= now that) : ~이기 때문에

prehistoric : 유사 이전의

survive : ~보다 오래 살다

medicine man : 주술사 / revere : 숭배하다

해석 인류 역사상 최초의 지적 혁명은 아마도 원시 종교의
비논리적인 기반으로부터 자비로운 신의 믿음과 우
주에 대한 철학적 해설에 기초를 둔 종교적 사고 유
형으로의 변천이다. 이러한 변천이 어떻게 성립되었
는지는 아무도 모른다. 명백히 일부 종족들은 인간의
형태를 지닌 초자연적인 존재가 영혼을 육체에서 분
리시키기보다 오히려 그들의 간청을 잘 듣고 답해 줄
수 있음이라는 사고로 발전시켰다. 유사 이전의
인간들은 인간의 정신은 죽은 후 육체에 계속 살아남
는다고 거의 보편적으로 확신하였기 때문에 그리고
주술사들이 폭넓게 숭배 받았기 때문에, 이들 일부
영혼은 산꼭대기나 하늘로 옮겨져서 신들처럼 존경
받았을지 모른다는 사실이 가능한 것 같다.

36. word shine : 빛나게 하다 / overwhelm : 압도하다

stratospheric : 성층권의 cf. stratosphere : 성층권

shield : 방패 / hazard : 위험 / ultraviolet : 자외선의

predict : 예상하다

해석 세계는 이제 위험이 하늘 전체에 미치고 있다는 것
을 알고 있다. 인간 스스로 만든 화학 물질들에 의해
서 지구 성층권의 오존층-태양의 해로운 자외선을
막아주고 있는 방패-은 어떤 과학자가 예상했던 것
보다 훨씬 빠르게 점차 잠식당하고 있다는 증거가
너무나도 명확해지고 있다.

37. word (A) code : 규약, 규범 / detailed : 상세한

trustworthy : 신뢰할 수 있는

self-reliant : 자립적인

(B) primary : 일차적인 / transmission : 전승

surpass : ~을 능가하다

해석 (A) 아버지께서 정하셨던 소년들의 행동규범은 세부
적이고 주문이 벅찬 것들이었다. 사람은 정직해야
하고, 신뢰할 수 있어야 하고 자립적이어야 한다는
것이었다. 그러나 아버지께서 다른 모든 것을 우선
하여 존중하셨던 것은 용기였다고 생각한다.

(B) 문화가 전승되는 주된 경로는 가족이다. 어느 누
구도 어린 시절의 환경에서 획득한 문화의 종류에서
완전히 벗어날 수 없고 또 그 수준을 완전히 능가할
수도 없다.

38. word paramount : 최고의 / objective : 목표

restrain : 억제하다 / impulse : 충동, 자극

minister : 성직자, 이바지하다 / harry : 괴롭히다

exhortation : 장려, 충고 / imitate : 모방하다

해석 사람들은 스스로에게 어떤 하나의 최고 목표를 제시
하고 그것에 도움이 되지 않는 모든 충동들은 억제
한다. 사업가는 부자가 되기를 너무 갈망하여 이 목
적을 위해서는 건강과 자기 자신의 애정도 희생시킨
다. 그리하여 마침내 그가 부자가 되었을 때 자신에
게 남아 있는 것은 다른 사람들에게 자신의 고귀한
본보기를 모방하라고 장려함으로써 그들을 괴롭히
는 것밖에 없다.

39. word sovereign : 독립의 / anticipation : 앞을 내다보는

take the initiative : 주도권을 잡다

bring~ into existence : ~를 창조하다

해석 하나님의 이러한 독립적이고 앞을 내다보는 행위는
여러 면에서 보인다. 하나님은 창조의 주도권을 잡
았다. 그리하여 우주와 그 구성 요소를 창조하였다.
"태초에 하나님께서 하늘과 땅을 창조하셨다."

40. word look back on : 회상하다 / fit : 끼워 넣다

chronology : 연대기 / be apt to : ~하기 쉽다

chaotic : 혼돈의 / proportion : 조화, 비

compensate : 보충하다 / constituent : 구성 요소

consist in : ~에 놓여 있다 (= lie in)

retain : 보유하다

notwithstanding : ~에도 불구하고

해석 우리 자신의 삶을 되돌아볼 때, 모든 사건과 시간적
인 순서를 정확히 짜 맞추기란 어렵다. 만일 우리가
한꺼번에 너무 많은 것을 알아내려고 한다면 그 인
상은 복잡해서 혼란스럽고 무의미해지기 쉽다. 여러
분은 사건들의 조화를 찾아볼 수가 없게 된다. 그리
고 어쩌면 우리의 모든 다양한 삶을 보충해 주는 한
요소가, 스쳐 지나가는 인상들이 다행스럽게도 우리
를 위해 취하게 되는 바로 그 불균형 속에 존재하고
있으며, 그들은 종종 수년간의 경험에도 불구하고
그 불균형을 계속 유지하게 된다.

41. word (A) cone to (one's) sense : 의식을 회복하다

(B) when it comes to : ~에 대해서

second to none : 둘째가라면 서러워할

(C) keep+목적어+from ~ing : 목적어가 ~하는 것을
막다 / expert : 전문가

(D) be caught in a shower : 소나기를 맞다

drench : 흠뻑 젖다

해석 (A) 내가 정신을 차린 것은 다음 날 아침 해가 뜨고
난 뒤였다.

(B) 영어에 있어서는 그가 학급에서 둘째가라면 서
러워할 것이다.

474

(C) 현대는 지식의 양이 너무 방대하기 때문에 하나 혹은 둘 이상의 학문 분야에서 전문가가 되기는 어렵다.

(D) 나는 학교에서 집으로 가는 도중 소나기를 만나 피부가 완전히 비에 젖었다.

42. word joblessness : 실업 / benefit payment : 수당
    equal to : ~와 동일한 / lull : 안심시키다
    dole : 실업 수당 / claimant : 청구자
    suspiciously : 의심스러워하며
    day-care program : 아동을 돌보는 일
    aggravate : 악화시키다
    pregnancy leave : 산후 휴가

해석 그러나 사회주의자들은 딜레마에 직면하였다. 낮은 인플레이션과 확실한 무역 균형이 이루어진 일반적으로 건전한 경제체제 속에서, 그들의 사회정책들이 실업을 조장하게 된 것이다. 예를 들면, 기업체들은 봉급의 40% 이상의 특별 수당을 지불해야 했는데, 이로 인하여 새로운 일자리가 줄어들게 되었다. 일자리를 잃은 불란서 노동자들은 30개월 동안-이는 유럽의 다른 나라보다 더 긴 기간이다-그 전에 받았던 봉급의 60%에 맞먹는 실업 수당을 받았다. 이것이 수천 명을 안심시켜 실업 수당으로 생활을 꾸려나가게 했다. 실업 수당 청구자들의 반 이상이 30개월간의 기간이 끝날 즈음이 되어서야 미심쩍게 일자리를 구하고 있다. 불란서 아동들을 돌봐 주는 프로그램들조차 그런 문제들을 악화시킬지 모른다. 독일에서는 출산 후 출산부들은 다른 사람들에게 일자리는 열어 주면서 전형적으로 몇 년 동안 집에서 쉰다. 그러나 아동을 돌보는 비용이 적은 불란서에서는 많은 출산부들이 6주간의 산후 휴가가 끝나자마자 직장으로 되돌아온다.

43. word turn one's mind to : ~에 신경 쓰다
    wear out : (물건이) 닳아빠지다
    (= no longer usable)
    set to work : 일에 착수하다

해석 그때 나는 지금쯤이면 완전히 닳아 빠져 버렸을 옷에 신경을 써야 했다. 그래서 혼자 힘으로 새 옷을 만들 생각을 했다. 당신에게 얘기했듯이 나는 내가 잡은 짐승들의 껍질을 말려 보관하고 있었는데 이것들이 옷의 재료가 되었다. 내가 처음 만든 것은 큰 털모자였다. 일이 매우 잘되어서 일에 착수하자마자 곧 한 벌의 옷을 만들었다.

44. word distinguish[discriminate] between A and B : A와 B를 구별하다
    i.e. (= id set) : 즉, 다시 말하면 (= that is)
    manifest : 명백한, 표출된 / latent : 잠재성의
    disguise : 변장하다, 가장 / analyst : 분석자
    interpreter : 해설자, 통역관
    in terms of : ~의 견지에서

해석 따라서 표출된 꿈, 즉 경험되고 아마 기록된 것으로서의 꿈과 잠재적인 꿈, 즉 가장된 모습이 제거된 상태로 꿈속에 그대로 표출된 생각과 소망 그리고 열망의 꿈을 구별하는 것이 필요하다. 이러한 견해 하에 정신분석가와 해설가가 할 일이란 잠재적인 꿈의 견지에서 표출된 꿈을 설명하는 것이다.

45. word so far : 지금까지 / empty pleasure : 공허한 쾌락
    sane : 제정신의 / consumption : 소비
    middle class : 중산층

해석 지금까지의 세계 역사에서 단지 소수 엘리트들만이 공허하나 쾌락의 삶을 영위할 수 있었다. 그래도 그들은 그들이 권력을 쥐고 있다는 것과 그 권력을 잃지 않기 위해 그에 걸맞은 생각과 행동을 해야 한다는 점을 알고 있었기 때문에 제정신을 지킬 수가 있었던 게 분명하다. 오늘날 소비라는 공허한 쾌락의 삶을 영위하는 계층은 중산층인데 그들은 정치적, 경제적으로 권력이 없고 개인적 책임감이 약하다. 서양 세계의 대부분은 행복에 관한 소비자 유형의 이점을 잘 알고 있으며 이것으로부터 혜택을 받는 사람들이 증가하며 이것을 원하고 있다.

46. word pollution : 공해 / constituent : 구성
    planetary life : 지구상의 생활 / atmosphere : 대기
    hydrosphere : 수권, 수계 / lithosphere : 암권
    crumble : ~을 산산조각 나게 하다
    millennia : (millenium의 복수) 1천년
    fragile : 깨지기 쉬운
    nextricable : 빠져나올 수 없는
    interweave : 합쳐서 짜다

해석 이러한 비경제의 본질을 이해하기 위해서 넓은 의미에서의 공해의 세 가지 영역 즉-지구상의 생활에 있어 가장 기본적인 구성 요소가 되는-공기, 물, 토양을 조사해 봐야 한다. 공기와 기후를 이루고 있는 대기, 강, 호수, 대양을 이루고 있는 수역, 바위가 수천 년에 걸쳐 부서져 흙이라는 얇고 부서지기 쉬운 외피를 제공해 주는 암계-이 셋은 지구상의 유기체가 지탱할 수 있도록 해 주는 체계 속에서 아주 밀접하게 서로 연관되어 있다.

47. word maturation : 성숙 / benefit : 혜택
    provided that : ~이기만 하다면
    carry on : 계속하다 / exclude : 배제시키다
    comprehensive : 종합적인
    poise : (신체의) 균형, (정신적인) 평온
    enhance : 고양시키다 / obtain : 얻다 (= come by)
    acquaintance : 아는 사람 / mate : 동료, 배우자

해석 이성 간의 데이트는 교육적, 사회적 성숙에서 중요한 역할을 한다. 남녀 아이들 모두 다른 사람들을 제외시키고 계속되지 않는 한 그들은 이러한 체험을 통하여 이득을 얻게 된다. 그의 인격 형성기에 이성적으로 포괄적인 데이트를 경험한 사람은 그의 체험을 넓히고, 인격을 풍부하게 하며, 안정과 균형을 얻고, 다양한 상황 하에서 다른 사람들과의 적응력을 증대시키며, 다른 이성들과의 만남이나 교제에서의 감정적 흥분을 감소시키며, 다른 사람들을 객관적으로 분별 있게 판단하는 능력을 고양시키며, 동년배의 사람들 중에서 그의 명성을 증대시키며, 아마도 배우자를 선택하게 될 수도 있는 더 폭 넓은 친구들을 얻게 되는 경향이 있다.

PART XI : 단어

1. 단어 (동의어 · 반의어)

1. 정답 ③
word abrupt : sudden (뜻밖의), steep (가파른)
quiet : tranquil, serene (조용한)
bold : courageous, daring, gallant, valiant (대담한)

2. 정답 ②
word abbreviate : shorten, abridge, curtail, condense (줄이다) ↔ lengthen
해석 김 교수가 쓴 글을 읽는 것은 쉽지 않다. 왜냐하면 그는 다른 교수들이 보통 줄여 쓰지 않는 단어들을 줄여 쓰기 때문이다.

3. 정답 ②
word abrupt : sudden (뜻밖의) / steep (가파른)
embargo : 수출 금지 / halt : 정지시키다
temporarily : 일시적으로
해석 1807년 제퍼슨이 취한 수출 금지 조치는 갑자기 뉴 잉글랜드 지역의 해상 무역을 정지시켰다.

4. 정답 ③
word abstain : refrain, withhold (삼가다)
해석 내가 사탕 먹는 것을 자제했더라면 썩은 이가 덜 생겼을 것이라고 치과의사가 말하였다.

5. 정답 ③
word absurd : foolish, ridiculous, stupid (불합리한, 어리석은) ↔ sensible, rational abhorrent : 몹시 싫은
prejudiced : 편견을 가진 / absolute : 절대적인
해석 그런 어처구니없는 일을 제안했다니 당신이 참 어리석은 사람이로군.

6. 정답 ①
word abuse : ill-use, misuse, maltreat, reproach, slander (남용하다, 악용하다)
해석 성난 시민들은 힘없는 동물들을 학대하는 것에 항의를 하였다.

7. 정답 ②
word accomplish : achieve, complete, execute, fulfill (다하다, 완성하다)
executive : 이사 / accumulation : 축적
imposition : 부과, 과세
해석 그가 그 회사의 이사였을 때 첫 번째 업적은 보다 나은 작업 여건을 만든 것이었다.

8. 정답 ②
word adept : adroit, deft, dexterous, proficient, skillful (솜씨 좋은)
stratagem : 전략, 계략
timely : 시기적절한
해석 그들은 그것들을 구하기 위한 많은 계략을 구사함에 있어 능숙함을 보여 주었다.

9. 정답 ④
word adult : mature, ripe, grown, full-developed (성숙한)
adolescent : 청년기의
infantile : 유아의
juvenile : 소년 (소녀) 의 (10세 미만의)
해석 성숙한 학생들은 별로 감독을 하지 않아도 된다.

10. 정답 ③
word affluent : rich, opulent, abundant, wealthy (풍부한)
come from : ~출신이다
adjust to : ~에 적응하다
해석 Dick은 풍요로운 사회 출신이기 때문에, 조그마한 시골 마을에 적응하기가 어렵다는 것을 알았다.

11. 정답 ②
word alter : change, modify, vary (변경하다)
fit : ~에 맞게 하다

12. 정답 ④
해석 나의 야망이 나로 하여금 야간대학에 갈 수 있도록 용기를 넣어 주었다.

13. 정답 ③
word ameliorate : improve, better (개량하다)
hasten : 서두르다
macerate : 부드럽게 하다

14. 정답 ①
word anchor : 닻, 고정시키다
inorganic : 무기물의
moisten : 촉촉하게 하다
해석 대부분의 식물은 자신을 흙 속에 고정시키고 물과 무기 화학 물을 흡수하기 위하여 뿌리에 의존한다.

15. 정답 ③
word anonymous : 익명의 / donor : 기증자
reluctant : 싫어하는

16. 정답 ①
word antiquated : old, aged, antique, outworn (오래된)
outward : 외면적인

17. 정답 ①
word apparel : clothing, dress, garb, attire, costume (옷)
shelter : 피난처

18. 정답 ①
word apparent : plain, clear, evident, obvious, conspicuous, manifest (명백한)
complicated (= intricate, completed) : 복잡한

19. 정답 ④
word apt : inclined, disposed, prone, liable, likely (하기 쉬운), appropriate (적당한)
antagonistic : 적대적인 / adept : 정통한

20. **정답** ④
   word argument : dispute, controversy (논쟁)
   해석 경기에서 공정한 태도를 취하기는 어렵다. 그러나
        논쟁에서 공정한 태도를 취하는 것을 더욱 어렵다.

21. **정답** ②
   word arid : dry, desert (마른, 건조한)
        habitat : 거주지, 서식지
   해석 낙타 종류는 대부분 건조한 지역에서 서식하고 있
        음이 발견되고 있다.

22. **정답** ②
   word artisan : craftsman (장인) / novice : 풋내기
        vessel : 그릇 / partisan : 일당

23. **정답** ④
   word assault (= aggression) : 습격
        primitive times : 원시시대

24. **정답** ③
   word assets : 재산
        monies owed (= moneys owed) : 빚진 돈, 대금,
        지불해야 할 금액

25. **정답** ②
   word astrology : 점성술 / astronomy : 천문학
        anthropology : 인류학 / archaeology : 고고학

26. **정답** ③
   word atheism : 무신론 / disorder : 무질서

27. **정답** ③
   word ban : forbid, prohibit, taboo (금하다)
        city council : 시의회
        minor : 미성년자
        recommend : 추천하다
        legalize : 법제화하다
   해석 시의회는 최근 미성년자들에게 어떤 담배이건 판매
        하는 것을 금지시켰다.

28. **정답** ①
   word backbreaking (= strenuous) : 격렬한
        hazardous : 위험한
        pacesetting : 모범적인

29. **정답** ①
   word ban : prohibit, forbid, taboo (금하다)
        call for : 요구하다
   해석 미국 의학협회는 복싱 경기를 금지시킬 것을 요구
        했다.

30. **정답** ④
   word barren : sterile, infertile, unproductive (불모의)
        ↔ fertile (비옥한)
   해석 처음에는 그 땅이 매우 메말라 있었지만, 수년 동
        안의 노력 끝에 마침내 기름진 땅이 되었다.

31. **정답** ①
   word beatific : 축복을 내리는, 행복한
        hesitant : 망설이는

32. **정답** ③
   word benign : kind, humane, compassionate (친절한)
        visual : 눈에 보이는
        popular (= in vogue) : 유행 하는, 인기 있는
        surpassing : 뛰어난

33. **정답** ③
   word bent : taste, tendency, trend, proneness, inclination
        (경향, 기호)
        aptitude : 적성

34. **정답** ②
   word bombastic : 과장된 / solicitous : 걱정하는
        unimpassioned : 냉정한 / rhapsodic : 열광적인
        weightless : 무게가 없는

35. **정답** ③
   word boost : raise, life, elevate, heave, hoist (올리다)
        stabilize : 안정시키다
        necessities of life : 생활필수품
   해석 생활필수품 가격이 지난달 또다시 올랐다.

36. **정답** 용감히 맞서다.
   word brave : courageous, gallant, dauntless, bold,
        daring (용감한)
        lifeboat : 구명정
        towering wave : 매우 높은 파도
        strand : 좌초시키다
   해석 작은 구명정이 매우 높은 파도를 헤치고 나가 좌초
        한 선원들을 구할 수 있을까?

37. **정답** ②
   word cancel : annul, revoke, call off (취소하다)
        call in : 소환하다 (= summon)
        cast off : 던져 버리다
   해석 축구 경기가 폭풍우 때문에 취소되었다.

38. **정답** ②
   word capricious : fickle, whimsical (변덕스러운)
        sheeplike : 양 같은, 온순한
        slippery : 미끄러운

39. **정답** ④
   word careless : heedless, reckless, indiscreet (경솔한)
        fine : 벌금, 벌금형에 처하여
        traffic sign : 교통신호
        jealous : 부러워하는
        vicarious : 대리의
        amicable : 우호적인
   해석 부주의한 운전 때문에 100달러 벌금을 문 뒤, 그는
        좀 더 주의하며 교통신호를 준수하기 시작했다.

40. **정답** ①
   word catastrophe : disaster, mishap, calamity, misfortune (큰 재앙)
   algae : 해조 / fungi : 균류 (버섯, 곰팡이 등)
   phenomenon : 현상 / explosion : 폭발
   해석 자연의 큰 재앙 후에 다시 자라기 시작한 첫 번째 생명체가 해조류나 균류처럼 잎이 없는 식물이었다.

41. **정답** ④
   word census : 인구조사 / opinion poll : 여론조사
   payroll (= pay sheet) : 임금대장, 종업원 명부
   해석 1989년 실시한 인구조사는 약 천만 명이 서울에 살고 있음을 보여 주었다.

42. **정답** ①
   word contain : 내포하다
   center : 중앙 (= core) / fleshy : 살의, 다육질의
   해석 씨앗은 사과나 배와 같은 다육질의 과일 중앙에 들어 있다.

43. **정답** ②
   word charitable : generous, benign, kind (자비로운, 인자한)
   violent : 격렬한 / vicious : 타락한, 악의에 찬

44. **정답** ④
   word chronologically : 연대순으로

45. **정답** ①
   word commence : begin, start, originate (시작하다)
   expel (= turn out) : 내쫓다

46. **정답** ③
   word complex (ed) : complicated, intricate, compound (복잡한)
   compression : 압축, 요약

47. **정답** ④
   word comply (= obey) : 복종하다
   deploy : 전개하다
   deplore : 뉘우치다

48. **정답** ①
   word concede : admit, acknowledge, own, confess (인정하다)

49. **정답** ④
   word confer A on B : A를 B에게 주다
   compromise : 타협하다
   corrupt : 타락하다 / cf) confer with : ~에 동의하다

50. **정답** ①
   word confront : ~에 직면하다
   accuse : ~를 고발하다
   rebuke : ~를 비난하다

51. **정답** ①
   word considerable : 굉장히 많은 cf) considerate : 사려 깊은
   해석 1990년대 초 에는 한국의 성장이 매우 둔화되었다.

52. **정답** ③
   word contrary : opposing, contradictory, inconsistent, paradoxial, opposite (모순되는)
   pertinent : 타당한, 적절한, ~ 에 해당되는 (= proper, relevant)

53. **정답** ③
   word contrary to : ~와 반대되는 / innate : 타고난

54. **정답** ②
   word criterion : standard, rule, measure (표준, 기준)

55. **정답** ①
   word fine art : 미술 (특히 회화, 조각)
   connoisseur : 감정가
   philatelist : 우표 수집가 / prodigious : 거대한
   해석 베이커 교수는 미술품 감정가이다.

56. **정답** ②
   word crude : unrefined, raw (천연 그대로의)
   vehicle : 운송기구, 탈것 / disk : 원반
   해석 초기 탈것의 바퀴는 가공되지 않은 돌 원반으로 만들어졌다

57. **정답** ①
   word cure : remedy (치료하다) / restore : 회복하다

58. **정답** ③
   word degrade : depose, downgrade (격하시키다)
   evaluate : 평가하다
   downhill : 악화, 쇠퇴 / terrain : 지형

59. **정답** ③
   word decade : 10년간 / expand : 팽창하다
   해석 1960년대의 10년간은 경제가 약 2.4배 성장하였다.

60. **정답** ③
   word decent : respectable (훌륭한), refined (세련된)
   impatient : 조바심 나는
   timid : 소심한
   해석 훌륭한 사람이라면 누구나 자기 친구들에게도 감히 말하기 힘든 많은 비밀을 지니고 있다.

61. **정답** ④
   word deception : fraud, deceit (기만, 속임)
   car insurance : 자동차 보험
   perjury : 위증 / treason : 반역
   infidelity : 배신, 불성실
   해석 자동차 보험을 얻는데 속임수를 쓰는 것은 법에 위반된다.

62. **정답** ①
　　word deft : skillful, adroit, adept, proficient, dexterous
　　　　(솜씨 좋은)
　　　　depict : 묘사하다 / superficial : 피상적인
　　　　gaiety : 화려함 / prudent : 신중한
　　해석 노벨상 작가 어니스트 헤밍웨이는 1920년대의 표
　　　　면적으로 드러난 화려함 밑에 깔려 있는 인간의 비
　　　　참함을 멋지게 묘사했다.

63. **정답** ①
　　word denunciation : 공공연한 비난
　　　　condemn : 비난 (책망) 하다

64. **정답** ①
　　word desert : arid, dry (건조한)
　　　　humid : 습기 찬
　　해석 네바다의 거의 절반 지역이 건조한 기후를 갖고
　　　　있다.

65. **정답** ①
　　word destroy : smash, demolish, tear down (파괴하다)
　　　　tear off : 쏜살같이 달려가다
　　　　tear round : 떠들며 다니다
　　해석 그들은 장소에 새로운 건물을 짓기 위해서 낡은 건
　　　　물을 부숴 버렸다.

66. **정답** ④
　　word deter : restrain, hinder, prevent (막다), give up (단
　　　　념시키다)
　　　　retain : 보유하다

67. **정답** ④
　　word discrepancy : difference, inconsistency,
　　　　disagreement (어긋남, 차이)
　　　　reduction : 감소

68. **정답** ③
　　word dissent : differ, disagree (의견을 달리하다)
　　　　harsh : 거친 / hasty : 급히 서두는

69. **정답** ①
　　word diurnal : daily (매일의) / flushing : 수세식의
　　　　two-fold : 이중의

70. **정답** ②
　　word dose : 1회 복용량
　　해석 반드시 적정량을 복용하세요.

71. **정답** 솜털
　　word 수세기 동안 그것의 부드러운 깃털과 솜털은 이용할
　　　　수 있는 것 중 가장 가볍고 효율적인 절연체였다.

72. **정답** ①
　　word drastic : strong (강렬한)
　　　　take a measure : ~한 조치를 취하다

　　해석 정부는 범죄를 막기 위하여 강렬한 조치를 취했다.

73. **정답** ③
　　word ease : 천천히 움직이다 (= move carefully)
　　　　hurry : 서두르다
　　해석 우리는 가시가 있는 덤불을 천천히 뚫고 지나갔다.

74. **정답** ④
　　word eligible : entitle, empower, qualify (자격을 주다)
　　　　manifest : 명백한 / convertible : 전환할 수 있는
　　　　effusive : 넘쳐흐르는
　　해석 투표할 자격이 있는 미국 시민의 숫자가 계속 증가
　　　　하고 있다.

75. **정답** ④
　　word eliminate : exclude, remove, rule out (제거하다)
　　　　make a difference : 차별하다

76. **정답** ④
　　word elimination : 제거
　　　　consist in (= lie in) : ~에 놓여 있다
　　　　nonessential : 비본질적인 / discrimination : 차별

77. **정답** ③
　　word eloquent : persuasive (감명적인 능변인)
　　　　loquacious : talkative (수다스러운)
　　　　colloquial : 구어체의 / fluent : 유창한

78. **정답** ①
　　word embryo : 태아, (식물의) 눈, 싹 / mature : 성숙한
　　해석 성숙한 튤립 꽃봉오리 속에는 식물의 눈이 포함되
　　　　어 있다.

79. **정답** ③
　　word encounter : meet, face (만나다. 부닥치다)
　　　　adopt : 채택하다 / advocate : 옹호하다
　　　　abandon : 포기하다
　　해석 우리는 종종 대학에서 어떤 사람의 견해에 접하게
　　　　된다.

80. **정답** ③
　　word enigma : puzzle, riddle (수수께끼)
　　　　genius : 천재 / saint : 성인

81. **정답** ①
　　word enigma : puzzle, riddle (수수께끼)
　　해석 우주의 불가사의는 인간에게 하나의 수수께끼이다.

82. **정답** ②
　　word entail : involve, include, embrace, contain (포함하다)
　　　　interaction : 상호작용 / advocate : 옹호하다
　　　　exaggerate : 과장하다
　　해석 배우와 청중간의 직접적인 상호 작용을 필연적인 것
　　　　으로 하는 연극이 배우들에게 특별한 어려움을 주는
　　　　것은 아니다

83. 정답 ①
   word equivocal : ambiguous, doubtful, uncertain, vague
       (모호한)
       monotonous : 단조로운
       talkative : 수다스러운

84. 정답 ①
   word eradicate : 근절하다
   해석 소크 백신이 소아마비를 근절하려는 싸움에서 주요
       요소가 되고 있다.

85. 정답 ③
   word essential : indispensable, vital, fundamental, basic
       (본질적인)
       altruist : 박애주의자, 이타주의자
   해석 자신의 이득을 생각하지 않고 남을 도와주는 사람
       은 누구나 본질적으로 박애주의자이다.

86. 정답 ③
   word exact : accurate, correct, precise (정확한)
       consequently : 결국 (= in consequence)
       equitable : 공평한
       exceedingly : 대단히, 몹시

87. 정답 ④
   word exaggerate : overstate (과장하다)
       caricature : 풍자 / verbal : 구두의
       banter : 희롱 / satiric : 풍자적인
   해석 문학에서 풍자는 보통 구두의 과장을 담기 마련인
       데, 작가는 이것을 통하여 우습고 풍자적인 효과를
       얻는다.

88. 정답 ②
   word exhilarating : cheerful, glad (유쾌한)
       consciousness : 의식 / confusing : 혼돈되는
       disorienting : 갈피를 못 잡게 하다
   해석 각성된 의식의 시대에 살아있다는 것을 기분 좋은
       일이지만, 또한 그것은 고통스럽고 혼란스러우며
       갈피를 잡을 수 없는 일이기도 한다.

89. 정답 ③
   word exorbitant : excessive, extreme (과도한, 터무니없는)
       vicious : 악의가 있는   absorbing : 열중케 하는

90. 정답 ②
   word extirpate : eradicate, remove, abolish, annihilate
       (근절시키다)
       favor : 찬성하다 / subdivide : 잘게 나누다

91. 정답 ②
   word evacuate : 피난시키다 / tornado : 회오리바람
       anticipate : 기대하다
   해석 그는 회오리바람이 마을로 다가오고 있는 것을 알
       았을 때 집으로 달려가서 나이 드신 어머니를 즉시
       피난시켰다.

92. 정답 ②
   word feeble : weak, frail (연약한) / pulse : 맥박

93. 정답 ③
   word factor : part (요소, 요인)
   해석 열심히 하는 것이 성공의 중요한 요소이다.

94. 정답 ④
   word colt : 망아지 / belong to ~ : ~에 속하다
       female horse : 암말 (= mare)
   해석 그 작고 붉은 망아지는 저 갈색 암말의 새끼이다.

95. 정답 ②
   word fervent (= ardent) : 열렬한 / strategic : 전략상의
       manipulate : 조정하다

96. 정답 ④
   word sculptor : 조각가 / carve : 조각하다
       figurine (= small statue) : 작은 상 / driftwood : 유
       목

97. 정답 ②
   word firsthand = direct (직접적인) cf. second
       hand = indirect (간접적인)

98. 정답 ③
   word fix : repair, mend (수리하다)

99. 정답 ④
   word flank : side (옆구리)
       fence : 울타리 cf) frank : 솔직한

100. 정답 ③
   word flatter : 매우 칭찬하다, 아첨하다

101. 정답 ①
   word flattery : 아침

102. 정답 ②
   word flaw : defect, shortcoming, imperfect (결점, 흠집) /
       tiny : 작은 / lustrous : 번쩍이는
   해석 흠집이 나 있거나 보석으로서는 너무 작은 다이아몬
       드는 매우 단단한 금속을 자르는 데 사용되고 있다.

103. 정답 ③
   word flaw : defect, shortcoming, fault, blemish (결점)
   해석 어떤 물건에 나타난 몇 가지의 결함은 그것이 수공
       이었음을 보여 주고 있다.

104. 정답 ④
   word flexible (= elastic) : 유연한 / equitable : 동등한
       stiff : 가파른 / rigid : 단단한

105. 정답 ③
   word fluorescent : luminous, luminescent (빛이 나는)
       fungi : 균류 (버섯 등) / aquatic : 수생의

해석 빛이 나는 균류의 종류는 50가지나 넘는다.

106. **정답** ②
word foliage : leaf (나뭇잎) / harvest : 수확, 추수

107. **정답** ④
word follow : ensue, obey (~에 따르다)
emergency : 비상사태

108. **정답** ④
word foremost (= leading) : 으뜸가는
aforementioned : 전술한, 앞에 말한

109. **정답** ②
word fraternal : brotherly (형제의)

110. **정답** ④
word frugality : economy, thrift (절약, 검소)
utility : 유용성

111. **정답** ③
해석 육지에 사는 고래는 종종 다시 깊은 물속으로 다시
들어가 보려고 애쓰지만 아무 소용이 없다.

112. **정답** ④
word furthermore : moreover, in a addition (더더욱)
upset : 전복시키다, 당황하게 하다
해석 더더욱 그의 행동은 교실 전체를 당황하게 만들고
있다고 나는 생각한다.

113. **정답** ④
word guilty : culpable, criminal (죄를 범한)
abet : 선동하다
malignant : 사악한 (↔ benignant)
decrepit : 노쇠한
versatile : 다재다능한
해석 만약 어떤 사람이 죄인을 방조하거나 교사하면, 그
역시 그 범죄를 범한 것으로 간주된다.

114. **정답** ②
word gallant : brave, courageous, daring, valiant (용감한)

115. **정답** ①
word genuine : authentic, real, actual, factual (사실의)
↔ false, counterfeit (허위의)

116. **정답** ③
word germane : relevant, pertinent (~와 밀접한 관계가
있는) ↔ irrelevant
biological : 생물학의
penitent : 참회하는 / gruesome : 으스스한

117. **정답** ①
word grasp : comprehend (이해하다)
compliment : 칭찬 compromise : 타협하다

118. **정답** ③
word havoc : devastation, ruin, destruction (대 파괴)
perspective : 통찰력, 시각, 원근법
valuation : 가치판단 / ordeal : 시련
travail : 수고, 고통 cf) upheaval : 대 변동, 격동
해석 없는 과학, 통찰력과 가치판단이 없는 사실은 결코
대 파괴와 절망으로 부터 우리를 구해 줄 수 없다.

119. **정답** ④
word cf) hallowed : sacred, holy (신성한)
shatter : ~을 산산이 부수다

120. **정답** ②
word handy : convenient (편리한)
constellation : 별자리 / map 지도를 그리다
해석 별자리에 의해별을 무리 짓는 것은 하늘의 지도를
그리는데 있어 편리한 방법이다.

121. **정답** ③
word hang-over : 잔존물 / alliance : 동맹

122. **정답** ③
word haphazardly : randomly, at random (아무렇게나)
precise : 정확한 / linear : 선의
해석 나뭇잎이 나무줄기에 아무렇게나 분포되어 있는 것
이 아니라 최대한의 빛을 받을 수 있게 해 주는 매우
정확한 방식으로 분포되어 있다.

123. **정답** ①
word harry : plunder, loot, sack (약탈하다)
torment, plague, harass (괴롭다)
prey : 먹이로 하다

124. **정답** ③
word hate : detest, abhor, loathe (미워하다)
tug : 잡아당기다
heed : 주의하다 shrug : 어깨를 들썩이다
해석 중서부 지역의 추운 겨울을 싫어했기 때문에 그들
은 Florida로 이사 갔다.

125. **정답** ④
word heredity : genetics (유전적인 특질)
altitude : 고도
해석 동물이나 식물이 얼마나 오랫동안 살 수 있는가 하
는 것은 유전적인 특질과 환경 그리고 우연에 의하
여 좌우되는 것이다.

126. **정답** ③
word hesitant : 망설이는 / incessant : 그침 없는
negligent : 태만한 / reluctant : 싫어하는
exorbitant : (가격, 요구) 터무니없는
해석 그들은 옛 집에 비싼 값에 팔 수가 없기 때문에 이
사하는 것을 망설였다.

127. **정답** ④

word heterogeneous (이질의) ↔ uniform (일률적인)
homogeneous (동질적인)
putrid : 타락한 / simulate : 인체하다

128. **정답** ④
word hiatus : gap (벌어진 틈)
branch : 나뭇가지
gaiety : 유쾌함

129. **정답** ①
word hideous : horrible, frightful, grim (무서운)
ugly (추한) / stormy : 폭풍우의

130. **정답** ③
word hitch : fasten, connect, hook (걸다, 연결하다)
wreck : 난파시키다 / hatch : 부화하다
thatch : 초가지붕
해석 그녀는 그녀의 트레일러를 당신의 차와 연결시키기
를 원한다.

131. **정답** ②
word homogeneous (동질적인) ↔ heterogeneous (이질
적인) / gigantic : 거대한

132. **정답** ②
word hostile : antagonistic, unfriendly (적대적인)
harsh : 엄격한, 거친

133. **정답** ③
word identical : same, exactly, alike : 동일한

134. **정답** ①
word identical : same, exactly alike (동일한)
fool : 놀리다, 속이다
해석 쌍둥이인 파트와 릭은 비슷한 것 같아 보여서 종종
친구들까지도 속는다.

135. **정답** ③
word idle : indolent, lazy, slothful (게으른)
idyll : 전원시 / idol : 우상

136. **정답** ④
word idolize : 우상화하다
해석 맥드웰 만큼 살아생전에 그렇게 우상화된 작곡가는
거의 없었다.

137. **정답** ③
word ignore : overlook, disregard, neglect (무시하다)

138. **정답** ①
word legible (읽을 수 있는) ↔ illegible (읽기 어려운)

139. **정답** ①
word immediately : at once, out of hand, out of control,
in no time (즉시)

right away와 right now도 (즉시) 의 뜻으로 사용되
지만, right now는 현재시제나 미래시제와 함께 쓰
인다.
right down : 노골적으로
해석 오늘 아침 내가 전화를 받았을 때 그녀가 전화를 잘
못 걸었다는 것을 즉시 알았다.

140. **정답** ③
word impartial : unbiased, fair, disinterested, indifferent
(공정한)

141. **정답** ①
word impending (= coming) : 임박한 / lot : 운
explode : 폭발하다

142. **정답** ③
word imperceptible : unnoticeable (알아 볼 수 없는)
greenness : 푸르름
해석 아침과 저녁의 잎이 푸름의 차이는 거의 알아볼 수
없다.

143. **정답** ④
word imprudent (경솔한) ↔ prudent (신중한)
exhaust : 탕진하다
stubborn : 완고한
rotate : 회전하다 / imprecise : 부정확한
해석 오늘날의 기준에서 보면, 옛날의 농부들은 어리석
었다. 왜냐하면 같은 작물을 반복해서 심어 얼마 안
되는 수확하고는 토양의 비옥함을 망쳐 버렸기 때
문이다.

144. **정답** ③
word incessant : uninterrupted, unceasing, ceaseless,
constant, continuous (끊임없는)
illogical : 비논리적인

145. **정답** ①
word incompetent : unable, incapable (무능한)
overthrow : 전복시키다
greedy : 욕심 많은
해석 약하고 무능력한 많은 통치자들이 더 강한 군대에
의해 전복 당했다.

146. **정답** ①
word cf) indolent : idle, lazy, sluggish, inert (게으른)
ook upon A as B : A를 B로 간주하다
arrogance : 오만함
gambling : 도박
suicide : 자살
해석 나는 게으름을 일종의 자살이라고 생각한다.

147. **정답** ③
word industrious : diligent, assiduous, hardworking (부
지런한)
intelligent : 총명한 / cf) industrial : 산업의

148. **정답** ①
　　word inevitable : unavoidable (피할 수 없는)
　　　　influential : 영향력 있는
　　　　fantastic : 환상적인
　　해석 여성을 남성과 함께 우주로 내보내는 것을 피할 수
　　　　없는 일이었다.

149. **정답** ③
　　word initiate (= start) : 시작하다 / infuriate : 격분시키다

150. **정답** ①
　　word inscribe : engrave (글자를 ~에 새기다)

151. **정답** ④
　　word integral (전체적인) ↔ fragmentary (단편적인)
　　　　profane : 세속적인

152. **정답** ③
　　word intermittently : periodically (간헐적으로)
　　　　abundantly : 풍부하게

153. **정답** ②
　　word interviews : 간격, 틈

154. **정답** ③
　　word intrigue : cabal (음모) / conspiracy : 공모, 음모
　　해석 음모 단원들은 그들의 공모가 발각되지 않게 하기
　　　　위해서 비밀리에 만났다.

155. **정답** ②
　　word bring to : ~을 정신 들게 하다
　　　　bring up : (논거 따위를) 내놓다
　　　　bring off : 구출하다 (= rescue)
　　　　bring back : 돌려주다.
　　해석 당신이 내일 모임에서 어떤 문제를 제기할 것입니
　　　　까?

156. **정답** ②
　　word invaluable : priceless, precious (대단히 귀중한)
　　　　distress : 고통 / valueless : 가치 없는
　　해석 그녀의 봉사는 돈 때문에 고통 받고 있는 가난한 사
　　　　람들에게 대단히 귀중한 것이었다.

157. **정답** ④
　　해석 나는 서울에서 어느 날 밤 대단히 귀중한 교훈을 터
　　　　득하였다.

158. **정답** ①
　　word iterate : repeat (반복하다) / shrink : 움츠리다
　　　　divest : 빼앗다 / chide : 꾸짖다.

159. **정답** ②
　　word lure : allure, decoy, attract, tempt, seduce (유혹하
　　　　다), charm (매력을 주다)
　　　　mirage : 신기루, 환상

　　　　metaphysics : 형이상학
　　　　significance : 중요성
　　해석 철학에는 즐거움이 있고, 형이상학의 신기루 속에
　　　　는 매혹이 있다.

160. **정답** ②
　　word jeopardy : risk, danger, peril (위험)

161. **정답** ④
　　word keen : sharp, acute, poignant (날카로운)
　　　　sour : 쓴 / be known to : ~로 알려지다
　　해석 신임 시장은 예리한 유머 감각을 가지고 있는 것으
　　　　로 알려져 있다.

162. **정답** ④
　　word laconic : brief, concise, terce (간결한)
　　　　↔ pompous (화려한)
　　　　radial : 복사형의
　　　　tangible : 만져서 알 수 있는

163. **정답** ④
　　word languid : faint, weak, feeble, listless, exhausted (나
　　　　른한)
　　　　gruff : 우락부락한 / bothersome : 귀찮은 성가신
　　　　selfish : 이기적인

164. **정답** 제휴하다, 연합하다
　　word league : alliance, confederation, union (동맹)
　　　　minority (소수) ↔ majority (다수)
　　　　hold down : 억누르다 (= restrain)
　　　　backward : 낙후된
　　해석 권력을 가진 소수 부유층이 가난한 사람들과 낙후
　　　　된 다수를 억누르기 위해 연합할 것이다.

165. **정답** ①
　　word levy A on B
　　　　(= impose A on B) : A를 B에 부과하다
　　　　correlate : 서로 관련하다
　　해석 브라질 정부는 수입되는 모든 피아노에 일률적으로
　　　　70%의 관세를 부과하고 있다.

166. **정답** ①
　　word liabilities : dents (부채)
　　　　cadaver : 파산, 사람의 시체 cf. liable :
　　　　responsible, answerable, accountable (책임 있는)

167. **정답** ②
　　word lower : reduce, decrease, diminish, lessen (줄이다)
　　　　refine : ~을 정제하다

168. **정답** ④
　　word ludicrous : ridiculous, comical, funny (우스운)
　　　　be forced to (do) : 하지 않으면 아니 되다
　　　　predict : 예상하다 / relatively : 상대적으로
　　　　suspiciously : 의심스럽게도

해석 1989년 한국의 주식 시장이 붕괴되었을 때 많은 주식 소유자들은 그들의 주식을 어처구니없이 낮은 가격에 팔아야만 했다.

169. 정답 ②
   word mortify : humiliate, insult (굴욕감을 주다)
      subdue : restrain (억제하다)
      distress : 고통, 괴롭히다
   해석 선생님은 그런 단순한 질문에도 답변하지 못하여 창피함을 느꼈다.

170. 정답 ①
   word meager : scanty, deficient, insignificant, thin (빈약한)
      dingy : 거무스레한
   해석 그가 제공해 준 식사는 좀 빈약했다.

171. 정답 ②
   word meditate : contemplate, reflect, ponder (숙고하다)
      withdraw : 철수하다

172. 정답 ④
   word medium : means (매개물)
      faction : 당파
      panacea : 만병통치약 (= cure-all)
      charlatan : 허풍선이, 사기꾼

173. 정답 ①
   word meticulous : careful, precise (꼼꼼한)
      awkward : 서투른, 거북한

174. 정답 기뢰, 수뢰
   word mine : 광산, 수뢰, 기뢰
      clear A of B : A에서 B를 치우다 / vessel : 배
   해석 이집트 정부는 수에즈 운하에서 기뢰와 침몰한 배를 치우고 싶어 한다.

175. 정답 ④
   word minuet : 미뉴에트 (춤곡)

176. 정답 ②
   word modification : alteration, change (수정, 변경)

177. 정답 ①
   word moisture : humidity, dampness (습기)
      ↔ dryness (건조함)

178. 정답 ②
   word mold : shape, manufacture, form, make (형성하다, 만들다)

179. 정답 ②
   word momentous : consequent, serious, important (중요한)
      momentary : 일시적인

180. 정답 ④
   word mourn : grieve, lament, deplore, bewail (슬퍼하다)

181. 정답 ②
   word mutiny : revolt, rebellion, uprising, rebel (반항, 반란)
      level off : 수평비행을 하다
      squawk : 큰 소리로 불평하다, 까악 까악 울다

182. 정답 ①
   word nap : 잠깐 눈을 붙이다
      dissent : 의견을 달리하다
      depart : 헤어지다

183. 정답 ①
   word nod : 고개를 끄덕이다
      notify : 통지하다, 신고하다

184. 정답 ①
   word be noted for (= be famous for) : ~로 유명하다

185. 정답 ④
   word onset : start, beginning (시작)
      attack : assault (공격)
      confusion : 혼돈
      fragment : 파편 / delicacy : 섬세함

186. 정답 ③
   word obese : fat, stout (살찐) ↔ lean, khin
   해석 한국에는 20년 전보다 오늘날 뚱뚱한 사람이 훨씬 더 많다.

187. 정답 ②
   word obsolete : antiquated, ancient, archaic (구식의) ↔ novel (신식의, 새로운)
      outworn : 진부한

188. 정답 ①
   word obstinate : stubborn, unyielding, inflexible, headstrong, dogged (완고한)
      cautious : 주의 깊은

189. 정답 ③
   word obsolete : anachronistic, out of times, out of date, behind the times (시대에 뒤떨어진)

190. 정답 ①
   word offend (= displease) : 화나게 하다
      defended : 방어하다

191. 정답 ④
   word ominous : threatening, foreboding (불길한)
      promising : prospective (전도 유명한)

192. 정답 ③
   word optimum : 최적조건
      favorable : 유리한

해석 날씨가 따뜻할 때가 날씨가 추울 때보다 최적의 체온을 유지하는 데 필요한 음식이 양이 줄어든다.

193. 정답 ②
word oriental : eastern (동양의)
↔ occidental : western (서양의)

194. 정답 ①
word originate : start, spring, emanate, initiate (시작하다)

195. 정답 ③
word otherwise : 그렇지 않다면 (= if~not)
operation : 수술
해석 그는 수술을 받아야 한다. 그렇게 하지 않으면 그의 상태는 점점 더 악화될 것이다.

196. 정답 ③
word outrage : anger (화내다)
nsult, abuse, maltreat, injure, offend (해치다)
go ahead : 진행시키다
해석 나는 그녀가 우리와 먼저 의논하지 않고 그녀의 계획을 진행시킨 것을 알고 놀랐고 또 화가 났다.

197. 정답 ④
word outright : frank, candid, outspoken, direct (솔직한)
bewilder : 어리둥절하게 하다
resentful : 분개한

198. 정답 ③
word outspoken : frank, candid (솔직한)
severe : 엄한 / strict : 엄격한

199. 정답 ②
word overrule : reverse (뒤집다, 번복시키다)
inspect : 조사하다

200. 정답 ③
word overwhelming : triumphal (압도적인)

201. 정답 ①
word protract : lengthen, extend, prolong (연장하다)
suffer from : ~을 겪다
from time to time : 이따금 / vitality : 활력
swollen : 부풀어 오른

202. 정답 ③
word rustic : rural (시골의) ↔ urban (도시의)
pasture : 목장
pastille : (원추형의) 향정
pastoral : 전원의

203. 정답 ②
word peculiar : strange, queer, eccentric, unique (색다른)
When it comes to~ : 라는 면에서
heritage : 유산 / phenomenon : 현상

해석 문화적 유산이라는 면에서 보면 재즈는 특이하게 미국적인 현상인 것 같아 보인다.

204. 정답 ④
word penetrate : permeate, pierce (침투하다, 스며들다)
substance : 물질 / identify : 동일시하다

205. 정답 ④
word permanent : lasting, constant, perpetual, everlasting (영구적인)
insure : 보증하다
wanton : 낭비하다
해석 영구적인 세계 평화를 유지하기 위해 모든 노력을 기울이고 있다.

206. 정답 ③

207. 정답 ③
word perpetual : constant, unceasing (끊임없는)
axis : 축
해석 지구가 축을 중심으로 끊임없이 움직이기 때문에 계절의 변화가 생기는 것이다.

208. 정답 ①
word pertinent (= suitable) : 적절한
innumerable : 수없이 많은

209. 정답 ④
word pierce : penetrate (관통하다)
puncture (구멍을 내다)
해석 도널드의 아버지는 그의 아들이 귀에 구멍을 뚫는 것을 허락하지 않았다.

210. 정답 ①
word plausible : probable (그럴듯한)
confident : 확신하는
해석 우리는 무엇 때문에 어떤 답은 그럴 듯해 보이고, 또 어떤 답은 그렇지 않은지 알고 있다.

211. 정답 ③
word plenary : full (충분한)
untrustworthy : 신뢰할 수 없는

212. 정답 ③
word predominant : prevalent, prevalent, prevailing (유력한)
long-sighted : 선견지명이 있는
pre-valent : 만연되어 있는

213. 정답 ①
word prelude : 서곡 / choir : 합창단 / ceremony : 의식
해석 합창단이 그 의식의 서곡으로 노래를 불렀다.

214. 정답 ③
word prescribed : certain (확실한) / vigorous : 힘찬

215. **정답** ①
　　word presume : assume, suppose (가정하다)
　　　　obvious : 명백한

216. **정답** ④
　　word prize : cherish, esteem, value highly
　　　　(소중히 여기다)
　　해석 오늘은 로버트 프로스트를 추모하는 일에 전념함으
　　　　로써 정치인들, 심지어는 시인들마저도 소중히 여기
　　　　는 사색의 기회가 제공되어지고 있다.

217. **정답** ②
　　word prize : cherish, esteem, value highly
　　　　(소중히 여기다)

218. **정답** ④
　　word procrastinate : delay, postpone, defer, adjourn,
　　　　prolong (연기하다)
　　　　insolent : 무례한 / perverse : 심술궂은

219. **정답** ①
　　word prodigal : lavish, extravagant, wasteful (낭비하는)
　　　　↔ abstinent, thrifty, economical, frugal (절약하는)
　　　　gallant : 용감한 / neurotic : 노이로제의

220. **정답** ②
　　word prodigious : huge, colossal, gigantic, tremendous
　　　　(거대한) / slight : 미미한
　　　　tiny : 작은 / moderate : 온건한
　　해석 그는 집에서 만든 빵을 엄청나게 먹어 치웠다.

221. **정답** ②
　　word profound : deep, serious (심원한) / concern : 염려
　　　　with regard to~ : ~에 관하여
　　　　catastrophe : 큰 재앙 / imminent : 절박한
　　　　emergent : 응급의, 긴급한
　　해석 우리는 모두 핵무기가 가져다 줄 커다란 재앙의 위
　　　　험에 관한 그 지도자의 심오한 염려를 나누어 갖고
　　　　있다.

222. **정답** ②
　　word prolific : fruitful, futile, productive (다산의)
　　　　↔ barren, sterile (불모의)
　　　　play a role : ~한 역할을 하다
　　　　evolution : 진화, 발전 / promising : 전도유망한
　　해석 Broadway에서 가장 저작활동이 왕성한 작가의 한
　　　　사람인 리처드 로저스가 미국 음악극장의 발달에 중
　　　　요한 역할을 했다.

223. **정답** ②
　　word proponent : supporter (지지자)
　　　　constituent : 구성요소, 선거구민

224. **정답** ②
　　word punctual : on time (정각에)

in time : sooner or later (조만간에)

225. **정답** ②
　　word pundit : savant (학자, 박식한 사람)

226. **정답** ②
　　word puzzle : bewilder, perplex, confound, confuse
　　　　(당황하게 하다)
　　　　penetrate : 스며들다
　　해석 "사과는 왜 올라가지 않고 떨어지는가?" 많은 어린
　　　　이들이 이 질문을 당혹스런 것으로 생각하고 있다.

227. **정답** ④
　　word ravage : ruin, devastate, destroy, (황폐하게 하다)
　　　　locust : 메뚜기
　　해석 메뚜기 떼들이 농작물을 휩쓸어 버렸다.

228. **정답** ②
　　word ration : apportion, distribute, mete, allot (배급하다)
　　　　petroleum : 석유 / embargo : 수출 금지
　　　　dole : ~을 베풀다 / confiscate : 압수하다
　　해석 최근 석유금수기간 동안 자동차 연료를 배급해야한
　　　　했다.

229. **정답** 추리하다
　　word reason : 추론하다
　　해석 동물이 인간처럼 생각하고 추리하고 기억할 수 있
　　　　을까?

230. **정답** ③
　　word recollect : recall, remember (기억하다)

231. **정답** ②
　　word reconcile : appease, make up (화해하다)
　　　　make off : 도망가다

232. **정답** ③
　　word recover : regain, restore, retrieve, get over (회복
　　　　하다)
　　　　get on : (탈것에) 타다 / get off : ~을 면하다

233. **정답** ④
　　word refuse : decline, reject, rebuff, turn down (거절하
　　　　다)
　　　　turn off : 끄다
　　　　turn in : hand in, submit (제출하다)
　　　　turn against : 거역하다
　　해석 그녀는 함께 저녁 식사하러 나가자는 내 제안을 정
　　　　중하게 거절했다.

234. **정답** ③
　　word reluctant : unwilling, disinclined, loath, averse (싫어
　　　　하는)
　　　　spinach : 시금치 / vegetable : 야채
　　　　imitative : 모방하는 / when (they are) required~

해석 부모가 시금치나 다른 야채를 먹으라고 하면 많은 어린이들은 마지못해서 억지로 그렇게 한다.

235. **정답** ②
word remorse : regret, contrition (뉘우침)
defy : 반항하다

236. **정답** ④
word renowned (= acclaimed) : 유명한, 인정받는
tribe : 종족

237. **정답** ④
word resolve : determine, decide (결심하다)
solve, settle (해결하다)
disintegrate, analyze, separate (분해하다)

238. **정답** ②
word resolve : solve, settle (해결하다)
witness : 목격자 / clue : 단서
consent : 동의하다 / complicated : 복잡한
해석 목격자가 그 신비를 푸는 단서를 제공해 주었다.

239. **정답** 결심, 결단
word resolve : resolution, determination (결심)
inspiration : 자극, 격려
burn victim : 화상을 입은 피해자들
해석 그녀의 의지와 결심은 모든 화상을 입은 피해자들에게 격려가 되었다.

240. **정답** ①
word retard : slow, delay, impede (지연시키다)
humidity : 습기 / evaporation : 증발
perspiration : 땀
해석 지나치게 많은 습기는 몸에서 나는 땀의 증발을 지연시키다.

241. **정답** ③
word reveal : disclose, divulge, unveil (나타내다)
scale : 저울
해석 1985년에 개발된 X선관은 원자 저울 위에 놓여 있는 물체의 구조를 나타내 보여 주었다.

242. **정답** ④
word ruin : decay, downfall, spoil, demolish, destroy, damage (파멸시키다)
Civil war : 미국의 남북전쟁
steam boat : 증기선 / tax : 세금을 부과하다
해석 미국의 남북전쟁 중 미시시피 강 하류의 증기선이 파괴되었다.

243. **정답** ②
word summon : call for bid, convene, convoke (소환하다)
care for : 돌보다
call after : ~의 이름을 따서 부르다

call up : 전화하다
해석 그들은 금년 2월 5일 날짜로 소환되었다.

244. **정답** ②
word sanguine : red (붉은 빛을 띤)
cheerful, buoyant, animated, spirited (쾌활한)
muddy : 진흙의 / stealy : 은밀한

245. **정답** 단련하다, 타이르다.
word repress : 억제하다
해석 그녀는 어려서부터 자신의 감정을 단련하고 억제하는 법을 배웠음이 틀림없다.

246. **정답** 맛을 내다.
word season : 맛을 내다
해석 그들은 고기를 사서 맛을 내고 요리하여 상을 차리는 법을 배웠다.

247. **정답** ②
word sentient : 감각력이 있는
hostile : 적대적인

248. **정답** ④
word serene : calm, tranquil, placid, peaceful, undisturbed (고요한)
obesity : 비만. 비대

249. **정답** ②
word shabby : worn-out, ragged, beggarly, poor (초라한)
old-fashioned : 구식의

250. **정답** ②
word shading : 그늘, 점차적인 변화
shade : hide, screen, conceal, cover (가리다)
subtle : 미묘한

251. **정답** ②
word silly : foolish, stupid, senseless, witless (어리석은)
twofold : 두 배의, 이중의
prudent : 신중한

252. **정답** ④
word simultaneously : concurrently, concomitantly, at once, at the same time (동시에)

253. **정답** ④
word situation : location, position, site, place, spot (장소)
beetle : 딱정벌레
secrete : ~를 분비하다
irritating : 짜증나게 하는
substance : 물질 / gland : 구멍
해석 일부 딱정벌레들은 공격받으면 몸체 앞부분에 위치한 특이한 구멍에서 (상대를) 짜증나게 하는 물질을 분비한다.

254. **정답** ②
   word skim : 대충 훑어보다 / slap : 찰싹 때리다
   Since (= Now that) : ~이기 때문에

255. **정답** ②
   word skinny : thin, slim, slender, lean (가느다란, 마른)
   ↔thick, fat, obese (뚱뚱한)
   talkative : 수다스러운

256. **정답** ④
   word slacken : relax, abate, relieve, mitigate, lessen,
   slow up (완화하다)
   whip : 매질하다 / cool off : 식히다

257. **정답** 늦추다.
   word quantity (양) ↔ quality (질) / sardine : 정어리
   the aging process : 노화
   해석 정어리를 많이 먹음으로써 기억력을 증진시키고 노
   화를 늦출 수 있다.

258. **정답** ③
   word sluggish : inactive, slow, lazy, slothful, indolent,
   inert (느린, 게으른)
   mileage : 마일 수 / acceleration : 가속화
   uneven : 고르지 않은
   해석 디젤 엔진은 뛰어난 주행 거리를 제공해 주지만, 비
   교적 소음이 많고 가속화가 더디다.

259. **정답** ②
   word somnolent : sleepy, drowsy (졸리다)

260. **정답** ②
   word soothe : relieve, allay, mitigate, alleviate, calm (완
   화하다, 달래다)
   해석 그 불행한 아이는 후대하겠다는 약속을 받고 마음
   이 진정되었다.

261. **정답** ①
   word specific : definite (명확한)
   articulate : (발음이) 명확한

262. **정답** ②
   word specious : plausible (그럴듯한)
   suspicious : 의심스러운 / vigorous : 활기찬

263. **정답** ①
   word onlooker : 구경꾼

264. **정답** ③
   word standardized : uniform (표준화된)
   neutralize : 중립화하다 / spare : 절약하다
   해석 표준화된 부품의 도입이 자동차 산업에 상당한 공
   헌을 했다.

265. **정답** ③

266. **정답** ③
   word sublime : noble, lofty, honorable (숭고한)
   quiet : 조용한

267. **정답** ①
   word surprise : astound, astonish, amaze, startle
   (놀라다)
   Since (= Now that) : ~이기 때문에
   poll : 여론조사 / assert : 주장하다
   assuage : 완화시키다
   해석 어느 여론 조사도 승자를 예측하지 못했기 때문에,
   모두 그 선거 결과에 놀랐다.

268. **정답** ②
   word suspend : postpone, delay, defer, put off (연기하다)

269. **정답** ②
   word trivial : trifling, petty, slight, insignificant,
   unimportant, negligible (사소한, 하찮은)
   troublesome : 골치 아픈 / mutual : 상호간의
   complicated (= complex, intricate) : 복잡한
   해석 하찮은 일로 나를 괴롭히지 마라.

270. **정답** ①
   word tantalize : torment, torture, vex (애태우다)
   tease (괴롭히다, 집적거리다)
   confine : 한정하다 / transform : 변형시키다

271. **정답** ①
   word tedious : dull, tiresome, irksome, wearisome,
   boring (지루한)
   unusual : 특이한

272. **정답** ①
   word temporary : transient, transitory (일시적인)
   ↔ permanent, infinite
   fragile : 깨지기 쉬운

273. **정답** ②
   word tenacious (= persistent) : 집요한, 강인한
   tenable : 이치에 맞는
   explosive : 폭발적인
   해석 그는 집요한 성격 때문에 회사에서 최고의 영업사
   원이 되었다.

274. **정답** ②
   word terminate : end, finish, close, complete (끝내다)

275. **정답** ②
   word thrift : frugal, economical, provident (절약하는)

276. **정답** ①
   word thrift : frugal, economical, provident (절약하는)

277. **정답** ②
   word tolerate : endure, bear, stand, withstand, put up
       with (참다)
       put up at : ~에 숙박하다

278. **정답** ④
   word trait : character, feature, characteristic (특성)

279. **정답** ④
   word tranquility : peacefulness, serenity, calmness
       (고요함)
       solidarity : 결속 / equanimity : 평정

280. **정답** ②
   word transform : change, alter, convert, transmute
       (바꾸다)
       divert : distract, amuse, delight (기분전환하다)

281. **정답** ①
   word treat : (음식) 대접하다

282. **정답** ③
   word trepidation : fright, fear, terror, panic (공포, 두려움)
       avarice : 탐욕 / deliver a speech : 연설하다
       dexterity : 교묘한 / fortitude : 인내심

283. **정답** ①
   word triumph : win, succeed, prevail, victory (이기다)
       fault : flaw, shortcoming, defect (결점)

284. **정답** ②
   word trivial : trifling, petty, slight, insignificant,
       unimportant, negligible
       (사소한, 하찮은)

285. **정답** ①
   word ultimate : final, last, extreme (궁극적인),
       fundamental (근본적인) / eternal : 영속적인
       imperishable : 불멸하는 / stern : 엄격한
       sober : 술 취하지 않은
       absolute (절대적인) ↔ relative (상대적인)
   해석 근본적인 실체로서의 진리는 만약 그런 것이 존재
       한다면, 그것은 영속적이며, 불멸하며, 불변성을 지
       난 것임에 틀림없다

286. **정답** ④
   word unanimous : of one's own accord, of one mind
       (만장일치로)

287. **정답** ①
   word uncouth : awkward, clumsy, rude (거친)
       ↔ refined (세련된) /

boor : 거친 사람 / buffoon : 광대
clown : 시골뜨기

288. **정답** ①
   word unfold : expend, reveal, open (펼치다, 드러내다)
   해석 인생 경험에 따르면, 그 책은 그에게 새로운 의미들
       을 보여 줄 것이다.

289. **정답** ①
   word unimportant : trivial, trifling, perry, slight,
       insignificant, negligible (사소한, 하찮은)
       stunt : 위축시키다
       prevalent : 유행하는, 우세한
       trenchant : 날카로운

290. **정답** ①
   word universal : general, entire, ecumenical (보편적인)
       pathetic : 측은한
       irresistible : 견디기 어려운

291. **정답** ②
   word unrest : disorder (불안)
       tranquility : 고요
       hindrance : 장애 방해

292. **정답** ③
   word upbringing : education (양육, 교육)
       reflect : 반영하다

293. **정답** ③
   word upheaval (= violent disturbance) : 격변

294. **정답** ④
   word utterly : completely, entirely, absolutely (전적으로)
       effect : 효과

295. **정답** ④
   word vendor : 판매원
       be engaged in : ~에 종사하다
       operator : 기사
       auditor : 회계 감사관
   해석 판매직에 종사하는 사람은 모두 적절한 자격증을
       소지해야 한다.

296. **정답** ①
   word vanish : disappear, cease, fade, go out of the
       sight (사라지다)

297. **정답** ①
   word vacuous : empty (공허한)
       candid : 솔직한
       superficial : 피상적인
   해석 그 정치인의 공허한 발언이 청중들을 화나게 했다.
       청중들은 내용이 없는 상투적인 말 이상의 것을 기
       대했기 때문이다.

298. **정답** ③
　　word vanity : excessive pride (자만심) fault : 결점
　　해석 자만심 때문에 우리가 자신의 결점을 보지 못한다.

299. **정답** ①
　　word vast : enormous, extensive, immense, huge,
　　　　gigantic, colossal, prodigious (거대한)
　　　　sufficient (충분한) ↔ insufficient, deficient (불충
　　　　분한)

300. **정답** ①
　　word velocity : speed, rapidity, swiftness (속도)
　　　　orbit : 궤도 / diameter : 직경
　　해석 수성의 속도가 지구의 속도보다 훨씬 빠르기 때문에
　　　　지구가 태양을 한 바퀴 도는데 걸리는 시간에 수성
　　　　은 태양 주위를 네 바퀴 이상 돈다.

301. **정답** ③
　　word versatile : 다재다능한 / timid : 소심한
　　　　audacious : 대담한

302. **정답** ②
　　word vogue : fashion, style, mode, popularity (유행)
　　　　current : 최근의 / originate : 유래하다

303. **정답** ③
　　ward want : 원하다, 궁핍해지다
　　　　diminish : 감소시키다 / stagger : 비틀거리다
　　　　collapse : 붕괴하다
　　해석 주로 모피를 지닌 동물의 숫자가 감소하였기 때문에
　　　　1800년대 초 북미 모피 무역도 쇠퇴하기 시작했다.

304. **정답** 물을 주다
　　word justify : 정당화하다 / selfishness : 이기주의
　　　　plunder : ~를 약탈하다 / uproot : ~를 뿌리 채 뽑다
　　해석 세계는 밀림이기 때문에 라는 이유로 이기심을 정당
　　　　화하는 것을 멈추어라. 세상은 마무를 심고 물을 주
　　　　기를 원하느냐, 아니면 약탈하고 뿌리채 뽑아버리느
　　　　냐 에 따 라 정원이 될 수도 있다.

305. **정답** ③
　　word weary : exhausted, tired, wearied (피로한, 싫증난)

306. **정답** ①
　　word well- to-do : well-off, wealthy, rich (부유한)
　　　　neutral : 중립의

307. **정답** ④
　　word whit (= bit) : 조금 / method : 방법

308. **정답** ①
　　word withdraw : retire, retreat, secede, take out (후퇴하
　　　　다, 인출하다)
　　　　take in : 속이다 / put in : 끼워 넣다
　　　　put out : 불을 끄다

309. **정답** ②
　　word wither : fade, shrivel, decay, decline, wilt, languish
　　　　(서들다)
　　　　rot : 썩다 / glisten : 반짝 반짝 빛나다.
　　해석 포도는 포도덩굴에서 시들었다.

2. 단어 빈칸 메우기

1. **정답** ②
　　word rebellion : 반란 / alienation : 불화
　　　　delinquency : 비행 / conflict : 갈등
　　　　impact on : ~에 영향을 미치다
　　해석 아버지가 아들의 프라이버시를 존중하지 않았기 때
　　　　문에 그 소년과 아버지 사이의 불화가 생겨났다.

2. **정답** ③
　　word the plane fare

3. **정답** ④
　　word inheritance : 상속
　　　　compromise (= meet halfway) : 타협하다
　　　　befriend : ~와 친구가 되다
　　　　alienate : 소원해지다, 불화를 빚다
　　해석 상속에 관한 다툼 때문에 형제들이 수년간 소원해
　　　　졌다.

4. **정답** ①
　　word ambiguous : 애매한
　　　　extenuating : 정상을 참작할 수 있는
　　　　detail : 상세히 / 설명하다 / expedient : 합당한
　　해석 그의 애매모호한 지시가 우리를 잘못 인도했다. 우
　　　　리는 두 길 중 어느 길을 택해야 할지 알 수 없었다.

5. **정답** ①
　　word antipathy : aversion, dislike, disgust (반감, 혐오감)
　　　　empathy : 감정이입 / predilection : 편애

6. **정답** ③
　　word applaud : 박수갈채를 보내다
　　　　enthusiastically : 열광적으로
　　　　advertise : 광고하다

7. **정답** ①
　　word appointment : (회합, 방문의) 약속

8. **정답** ①
　　word appreciate : 높이 평가하다, 고맙게 여기다
　　　　denounce : ~를 비난하다
　　　　discredit : ~의 신용을 떨어뜨리다
　　　　disregard : 경시하다 / in general : 일반적으로
　　해석 일부 비평가들이 그 연극을 높이 평가했지만, 일반적
　　　　으로 그들은 그 연극을 무시 해 버리거나 비웃었다.

9. **정답** ①
    word arm with : ~로 무장하다 / shot gun : 엽총
        apprehend : 체포하다 / interfere : 간섭하다
        comprehend : 이해하다 / preoccupy : 선취하다
    해석 경찰이 엽총으로 무장한 중년 남자를 체포했다.

10. **정답** ③
    word valor : 용기 / aptitude : 적성
        have an aptitude for : ~의 소질이 있다

11. **정답** ③
    word archeology : 고고학 / astrology : 점성술
        astronomy : 천문학 / ethics : 윤리학
    해석 하늘에 있는 모든 빛 하나하나가 다 생명체가 살 수
        있는 곳을 나타낸다는 낡은 견해는 현대의 천문학과
        는 아주 맞지 않다.

12. **정답** ①
    word secretary : 비서 / available : 이용할 수 있는
        answerable : 책임 있는

13. **정답** ④
    word ax : 도끼 / trunk : 나물줄기 / quiver : 흔들리다
        shaft : 창의 자루 / blade : (칼) 날, (칼날 같은) 잎
    해석 도끼날이 나무 둥치에 파고들었을 때 나무는 흔들
        렸다.

14. **정답** ①
    word heel : 뒤꿈치 / blister : 물집
        pimple : 여드름, 종기 / cluster : 송이 , 떼
        ripple : 잔물결, 파문

15. **정답** ③
    word empty : void, vacant, blank, unoccupied (빈, 공허한)
        bare : 벌거벗은
    해석 나는 여전히 우유가 좀 있는 줄 알았는데 병은 비
        어 있다.

16. **정답** ④
    word all but : nearly, almost (거의)
    해석 오늘밤 그 책읽기를 끝내려 한다. 왜냐하면 맨 마지
        막과를 거의 다 읽었기 때문이다.

17. **정답** ②
    word be combined in : ~로 결합되어 있다
    해석 근로자들은 더 나은 조건을 요구하는 일로 결합되어
        있다.

18. **정답** ①
    word Memorial Day : 현충일 / observe : 준수하다
        commemoration : 기념
        distribution : 분배 / defiance : 도전
        in commemoration : ~를 기념하여
    해석 현충일은 국가를 위하여 전사한 병사들을 추모하여
        준수되고 있다.

19. **정답** ①
    word compassion : pith, sympathy, mercy (연민, 동정)
        orphan : 고아 / cruelty : 잔인한
      indifference : apathy, unconcern, inattention (무관심)
    해석 고아들에 대한 동정심이 그로 하여금 그들을 돕기
        위한 기금을 내도록 해주었다.

20. **정답** ③
    word a complimentary ticket : 우대권, 초대권
        communicative : 통신의 / commentary : 주석
        compulsory : 강제적인

21. **정답** ④
    word convert A into B : A를 B로 변환시키다
        divert : (기분을) 전환시키다
        lubricate : 기름을 치다
    해석 전기모터는 전기에너지를 기계에너지로 변환시킨다.

22. **정답** ①
    word council : 협의회 / cabinet : 내각
        counsel : 고문
    해석 처리해야 할 사안을 검토해 보기 위해 조직된 모임

23. **정답** ④
    word crash : collision (충돌)

24. **정답** ①
    word damp : moist, humid, wet (습기 있는)
        harsh : 거친 / rusty : 녹이 쓴
        decayed : 부패한

25. **정답** ④
    word decadent : degenerated, deteriorated (타락한, 퇴
    폐적인)
        initiative : 진취성 / vehement : 격렬한

26. **정답** ③
    word definition : 정의

27. **정답** ③
    word incompetent : 무능한 / dogmatic : 독단적인
        punctual : 시간을 지키는 (= on time)

28. **정답** ②
    word effective : 효과적인
        theatrical setting : 무대장치
        reasonable : 합리적인 / respectable : 존경할 만한
    해석 극장의 무대장치가 효과적이기 위해서는 현실과 닮
        아야 한다.

29. **정답** ①
    word emigrant (이민 가는 사람)
        ↔ immigrant (이민 오는 사람)
        native : 원주민 / patriot : 애국자
    해석 다른 나라에 가기 위하여 자신의 나라를 떠나는 사람

30. **정답** ③
　　word ask for : 요구하다
　　　　empty : void, vacant, blank, unoccupied (텅 비어 있는)

31. **정답** ④
　　word enlist : 병적에 편입하다 / term : 학기
　　　　enroll : 등록하다, 입학하다
　　해석 600명 이상의 학생들이 이번 학기 저녁 수업에 등록했다.

32. **정답** ①
　　word enthrall : 매혹시키다 / sheer : 얇은, 순수한
　　　　portrait : 초상화 / depersonalized : 객관화하다
　　해석 미술학도들은 그들 앞에 걸려있는 초상화의 순수한 아름다움에 매료되었다.

33. **정답** ③
　　word erroneous : mistaken, incorrect, false (그릇된)
　　　　everlasting : eternal, perpetual (영원한)
　　해석 옛날에는 많은 사람들이 지구가 평평하다는 잘못된 믿음을 갖고 있었다.

34. **정답** ②
　　word expand : 팽창시키다 / contract : 수축하다
　　　　rot : 부패하다 / rust : 녹슬다
　　해석 열은 금속을 팽창시키지만 냉기는 금속을 수축시킨다.

35. **정답** ①
　　word extinct : quenched, vanished, out of existence (멸종된)
　　　　interior : 내부의 / stark : 굳은, 황량한
　　　　animated : lively, vigorous (활기에 찬)

36. **정답** ①
　　word millenium : 천년의 기간 (= one thousand years)

37. **정답** ②
　　word cheerful : gay, joyful, buoyant, jolly (기분 좋은)
　　　　↔ gloomy : melancholy, despondent, depressed (침울한)
　　　　placid : calm, peaceful, tranquil, serene, quiet, undisturbed (평온한)

38. **정답** ①
　　word handle : 다루다 / fix : 고정시키다, 수리하다
　　해석 그 짐은 너무 무거워서 나이가 든 사람이 취급할 수가 없었다.

39. **정답** ④
　　word heavy traffic : 격심한 교통량

40. **정답** ④
　　word heir : 상속인 / millionaire : 백만장자

descendant : 자손
peer : 동료, 귀족 해석 브라운씨가 죽으면 브라운씨 재산 상속자는 백만장자가 될 것이다.

41. **정답** ④
　　word identify : (신원을) 확인하다
　　해석 많은 비행기들은 제조회사와 모델번호에 의하여 구별된다.

42. **정답** ③
　　word the opening ceremony : 개회식
　　　　protective : 보호하는 / promising : 전도유망한
　　　　impending : 임박한
　　　　upend : 뒤집다, 일으켜 세우다

43. **정답** informal
　　word fundamental : 기본적인
　　　　obtain : 획득하다 (= come by)
　　　　formal (공식적인) ↔ informal (비공식적인)

44. **정답** ③
　　word ngratitude : 배은망덕한
　　　　impunity : 벌 받지 않음

45. **정답** ②
　　word editor : 편집자 / journalist : 언론인, 신문기자
　　　　essayist : 수필가

46. **정답** ①
　　word literal : 문자 그대로의 / colloquial : 구어체의
　　　　distorted : 왜곡된
　　해석 단어의 문자적인 의미란 그 단어의 본래 뜻이다.

47. **정답** ③
　　word malice : malevolence, enmity (악의)
　　　　apparent : 명백한 / competitor : 경쟁자

48. **정답** ④
　　word be interested in : ~에 관심이 있다
　　　　efficiency : 효용
　　　　meet : 충족시키다 (= satisfy) / needs : 욕구
　　해석 우리는 오로지 신발 영업사원이 우리의 욕구를 충족시키는데 효용이 있는지에만 관심이 있다.

49. **정답** ①
　　word misty : 안개 낀 / pursuer : 뒤따르는 사람
　　　　moist : damp, humid (습기 많은)
　　　　mild : 온화한 / messy : 뒤범벅이 된
　　해석 밤에는 안개가 너무나 많이 끼어서 그 도둑은 뒤따르는 사람을 쉽게 피할 수 있었다.

50. **정답** ①
　　word native : inborn, inherent, natural, congenital, innate (타고난)
　　　　foreign : 외국의 / stale : 상한

해석 이것들은 국산 참외가 아니다. 해외에서 들여온 것이다.

51. **정답** objection
    word have no objection to : ~에 반대하지 않다
    (=agree to) cf. have an objection to : object to, be opposed to (~에 반대하다)

52. **정답** objectively
    word go through : 체험하다 (= experience)
    wear spectacles : 안경을 끼다 / taste : 취향
    calling : vocation, occupation, profession (직업)
    prejudice : 편견 / subjectively (주관적으로)
    ↔ objectively (객관적으로)
    해석 우리는 누구나 자신의 취향과 직업과 편견으로 채색된 안경을 끼고서 인생을 살아간다. 우리는 주관적으로 보지 객관적으로 보지 않는다.

53. **정답** ③
    word optimist (낙천주의자) ↔ pessimist (염세주의자)
    chauvinist : 맹목적 애국주의 자
    cf. patriot (ist) : 애국자 / feminist : 여권주의자
    해석 낙천주의자는 모두 것에서 조금이라도 좋은 것을 찾아내려고 애쓴다.

54. **정답** ②
    word victim : 희생자 / ordeal : trial, test (시련)
    plague : 전염병, 재난
    litter : 잡동사니
    해석 살인다가 희생자를 죽이는 것을 목격한 것은 그 어린이에게 끔찍한 체험이었다.

55. **정답** ④
    word urge+목적어+to (do) : ~에게 ~하도록 재촉하다
    pastoral : 목가적인 / patent : 특허의
    penitent : 죄를 뉘우치는
    해석 마하트마 간디는 자기의 추종자들에게 무저항을 추구하도록 강력히 촉구하였는데, 그 이유는 그것이 폭력이나 테러 행위보다 훨씬 효과적이라고 생각했기 때문이다.

56. **정답** ③
    word patience : endurance, perseverance, fortitude (인내심) / prejudice : 편견

57. **정답** ②
    word video signal : 영상신호
    have to do with : ~와 관계가 있다

58. **정답** ④
    word positive : 긍정적인 ↔ negative 부정적인
    conservative : 보수적인

59. **정답** ①
    word immense range of knowledge : 광범위한 지식

60. **정답** ③
    word realize : 깨닫다
    recognize : ~을 인정하다, ~을 알아보다
    해석 그녀는 그 사람에게서 그림에 대한 대단한 재능이 있음을 알았기 때문에 그를 돕기로 결심했다

61. **정답** ①
    word have a reluctance to (do) : ~하기를 싫어하다
    regard A as B : A를 B로 간주하다
    negation : 부정, 취소
    해석 그는 정원사를 도둑으로 간주하기가 아주 싫었다.

62. **정답** ①
    word remark on, talk about : ~에 대하여 언급하다
    notice와 tell은 전치사가 필요 없다

63. **정답** ①
    word repair : fix, mend (수리하다) / decline : 거절하다
    incline : ~하는 경향이 있다
    해석 나는 당신이 나에게 자전거 수리하는 법을 가르쳐 주었으면 합니다.

64. **정답** ①
    word retard : slow, delay, impede (지연시키다)
    rebuke : 비난하다 / retreat : 물러가다
    retain : 보유하다

65. **정답** ③
    word parallel : 평행선 / imitate : 모방하다
    rhyme : 각운, ~과 각운이 맞다
    define : 규정짓다. 'fish' 와 'dish' 는 각운이 맞는 단어의 예이다

66. **정답** ②
    word urban (도시의) ↔ rural, rustic (시골의)
    cosmopolitan : 국제적인
    해석 학교 가는 길이 시골 학생들보다 도시 학생들의 경우 일반적으로 더 짧다.

67. **정답** ④
    해석 폴은 배와 바다를 몹시 좋아하였기 때문에 선원이 되기로 결심했다.

68. **정답** ③
    word trade sanction : 무역제재 / expedient : 편리한

69. **정답** ④
    word undisciplined : untrained (훈련받지 않은)
    self-control : 자제심

70. **정답** ③
    word serenity : calmness, peacefulness, tranquility, undisturbing (고요함) / seraph : 천사
    severance : 절단 / similitude : 유사함
    shatter : 깨지다 / explosion : 폭발

해석 모두 잠든 그 마을의 고요함이 무시무시한 폭발로 인하여 깨졌다.

71. **정답** ③
    word shield : 보호하다, 보호자 / conserve : 보존하다
    spoil : 망쳐 놓다 / absolve : 해제하다
    해석 부모가 그의 자녀들을 모든 위험으로부터 막아 주는 것은 불가능하다.

72. **정답** ②
    word shrewd : acute, keen, sharp (기민한)
    conscientious : 양심적인
    reckless : 분별없는 / moderate : 적당한

73. **정답** ③
    word slander : defame, scandalize, vilify (중상하다)
    dissent : 의견을 달리하다 / apprise : 통고하다
    slake : 갈증을 풀다

74. **정답** ③
    word ludicrous : 우스꽝스러운
    stumble along : 비틀거리며 걸어가다
    해석 하이힐을 신고 비틀거리며 걸어가고 있는 여성을 보는 것보다 더 우스꽝스런 광경이 있겠습니까?

75. **정답** ②
    word suggestive : 암시적인 / suspicious : 의심스러운
    deductive : 연역적인 / disturbing : 방해하는

76. **정답** ①
    word it is~who 강조용법이다 / talking : 이야기
    해석 우리들 대화에서 대부분의 이야기를 한 사람은 바로 Tom이다.

77. **정답** ④
    word knee : 무릎 / cave : 동굴
    enchant : ~를 매혹시키다
    glimmer : 희미하게 빛나다 / tremble : 몸을 떨다
    해석 내가 동굴에 들어갔을 때 무릎이 후둘 거렸다.

78. **정답** ②
    word uphold : ~를 들어 올리다, 지지하다
    upset : 전복시키다 (= overturn)
    upstart : 갑자기 나타나다
    upgrade : 격상시키다
    해석 배 안에서 이리저리 움직이면 배가 뒤집힐 수 있다.

79. **정답** vapor 혹은 steam
    해석 매우 뜨거운 물이 증기라 불리는 기체를 만든다.

80. **정답** wealthy
    word wealthy : rich, affluent, abundant, well-off, well-to-do (부유한)

81. **정답** ③
    word verify : 확인하다 / affirm : 확인하다
    assume : 가정하다

PART XII : 숙어

숙어 동의어

1. **정답** ②
    word be associated with (= be connected with) : ~와 관련된, ~와 관계를 맺고 있는
    law firm : 법률회사
    disappointed : 실망한
    appreciate : 감사히 여기다
    해석 로저씨는 유명한 법률회사와 관계를 맺고 있다.

2. **정답** ④
    word abide by : ~을 지키다
    renege on : 약속을 어기다
    stick to (= adhere to, cling to, hold fast to) : ~를 고수하다

3. **정답** ②
    word account for (= set forth) : 설명하다
    execute : 실행하다 (= carry out)

4. **정답** ④
    word be acquainted with : ~와 친숙한, ~를 잘 아는
    compassion : 동정
    be concerned over[about] : ~에 대해 염려하다
    be concerned with : ~에 관계하다
    inform oneself of : ~에 정통하다

5. **정답** ①
    word all the same (= still, nevertheless, nonetheless) : 그럼에도 불구하고, 여전히
    해석 찬사는 말뿐이긴 하나 그럼에도 불구하고 인정을 뜻한다.

6. **정답** ④
    word as well as : ~뿐만 아니라
    해석 하늘에는 빛을 내는 천체들 뿐 아니라 어두운 것들도 있다.

7. **정답** ③
    word nadir : 천저, 최하점

outbreak (= dawn) : 동틀 무렵
dusk : 해질 무렵 / relapse : 퇴보 (하다)
해석 해질 무렵이면 가로등 불빛이 저절로 켜진다.

8. **정답** ③
word at first hand : 직접적으로 (= directly)
emergence : 출현 / urgently : 다급하게

9. **정답** ①
word at large : 일반적으로, 대개

10. **정답** ④
word go through (= experience) : 겪다
be in labo (u) r : 해산 (분만) 중이다
give birth (= bear, produce) : 아기를 낳다
해석 그녀가 겪고 있는 것은 분만 (해산) 중이라 한다.

11. **정답** ④
word beat about the bush : 요점을 피하다. 넌지시 알아
보다

12. **정답** ③
word break in on : 참견하다, 끼어들다
withdraw from : ~를 철수하다

13. **정답** ③
word break the news : ~에게 (소식을) 알리다

14. **정답** ①
word bring out : 발생하다 (= outbreak, begin)
break off : 꺾다 / break up : 해산하다
break short : 갑자기 그만두다

15. **정답** raised
word bring up : 기르다, 양육하다 (= raise, rear, foster,
educate)
His father died young : = When his father died, he
was young.

16. **정답** ④
word be up to (i) ~에게 달려 있다. ~의 책임이다
ex) It is up to you to do the work.
(ii) ~할 능력이 있다 ex) He is up to the trip
해석 그가 그 여행을 할 수 있는지가 분명하지 않다.

17. **정답** ①
word by no means (= far from + ~ing = on no account
= anything but = not ~at all) 결코 ~이 아닌

18. **정답** ③
word sheer : 단지, 전적인
expert : 전문가 ↔ layman : 문외한
squad : (군대의) 분대 cf. platoon : 소대
manoeuvre (영) = maneuver (미) : 기동훈련, 책략

해석 오직 훈련에 의하여, 그는 분대 전투의 전문가가 되
었다.

19. **정답** ②
word compensate for (= make up for = atone for)
: 보상하다
make the best of : ~을 가장 잘 이용하다

20. **정답** ②
word call off (= cancel) : 취소하다
postpone (= put off) : 연기하다

21. **정답** ④
word carry out : 수행하다 (= execute, perform)
accomplish : 완수하다

22. **정답** ②
word caught on (= become popular) : 인기를 얻다, 유행
하다

23. **정답** ③
word starfish : 불가사리
cling to (= stick to, adhere to, hold fast to) : ~에
달라붙다, ~를 고수하다
suction : 흡입

24. **정답** ③
word come across : 우연히 만나다
second-hand : 중고의
해석 그는 헌책방에서 우연히 아주 신기한 책을 발견했다.

25. **정답** ②
word come down with (= contract) : 병에 걸리다
confide : 신뢰하다
contract : 계약하다 (병에) 걸리다
recite : 암송하다 / flatter : 아첨하다

26. **정답** ④
word come of (= descend from) : ~출신이다
become of : ~이 어떻게 되다
break off : ~갑자기 그만두다
break out : 발발하다 (= outbreak)

27. **정답** ①
word come to the point : 핵심을 찌르다

28. **정답** ③
word come up with (= present, suggest) : 제안하다
act on : ~에 영향을 미치다, ~에 따라 행동하다

29. **정답** ②
word comply with (= conform to, obey) : ~에 따르다
regulation : 규정
vote for : 찬성 투표하다 ↔ vote against : 반대 투
표하다
해석 그 광업회사는 규정에 따랐다.

30. **정답** ③
word comply with (= conform to, obey) : ~에 따르다
agree to : ~에 동의하다

31. **정답** ②
word cope with : ~에 대처하다
해석 그 사람은 자신이 맡은 일의 문제점들을 다룰 수 있는 정도의 충분한 경험은 없다.

32. **정답** ①
word vilify : 중상하다 / skulk : 숨다
recant : 취소하다

33. **정답** ②
word cover a lot of ground : 넓은 범위에 미치다

34. **정답** ①
word be cut out for (= be suitable for, = be suited for) : ~에 적합한

35. **정답** ③
word drop one a line : ~에게 몇 자 적어 보내다, 간단히 연락하다
conduit : 도관, 도랑

36. **정답** ④
word day in and day out : 날이면 날마다 (everyday)
every other day : 하루건너 매일
once in a while : 이따금

37. **정답** ②
word deal with (= cope with = treat) : ~를 처리하다, ~에 대처하다
bring on : 초래하다
해석 미국은 에너지 위기에 의하여 초래된 심각한 문제들을 처리하려고 애쓰고 있다.

38. **정답** ①
word devoid of : ~이 결여된 / maintain : 옹호하다
aviation : 비행 / specifics : 명세

39. **정답** ②
word do away with (= get rid of, abolish, remove, eliminate, exclude) : ~를 제거하다
reverse : 역으로 하다
belittle : ~를 작게 하다, 경시하다

40. **정답** ①
word discard : ~를 버리다
preserve : ~을 보존하다
retain : ~을 보유하다

41. **정답** ①
word draw up (= sign) : ~를 작성하다
look over : ~를 훑어보다

42. **정답** ③
word drop a line : 몇 자 적어 보내다

43. **정답** ④
word drop in : 잠시 들르다

44. **정답** ②
word drop a line : 몇 자 적어 보내다

45. **정답** ④
word be fed up with (= be tired of = be bored with) : ~에 싫증이 나다
grandeur : 웅장함
crush : 분쇄, 혼잡
해석 나는 금지된 도시의 웅장함에 싫증이 났고, 타타르 성밖 중국 도시의 북적거림과 시끄러움에 질색이 되어 버렸다.

46. **정답** ④
word fall back on (= count on = depend on = rely on = hinge on = turn to) : ~ 에 의존하다
refrigerator : 냉장고
second-hand : 중고의
emergency : 비상사태 cf. emergence : 출현

47. **정답** ②
word fall in with (= meet by chance) : 우연히 만나다
be fond of (= have a liking for = like) : 좋아하다

48. **정답** ②
word far be it from me to (do) : ~하려는 생각은 결코 없지만
make a mistake : 실수하다
해석 당신을 바로 잡아 줄 생각 따위는 전혀 없지만, 당신은 심각한 실수를 저지른 것 같습니다.

49. **정답** ①
word be fed up : 싫증나다, 혐오감을 느끼다
ravenous : 몹시 굶주린, 탐욕스러운

50. **정답** ①
word fill out (= complete) : (빈자리를) 메우다, 가입하다
eliminate : 제거하다

51. **정답** ②
word for a song (= for an old song) : 싸구려로

52. **정답** ②
word for good (= forever = permanently) : 영원히

53. **정답** ②
word for the life of me : (부정문에서) 도저히 ~않다, 아무리 노력해도
on one's own : ~의 힘만으로, 자진하여

54. **정답** ②
    word go into : 조사하다 (= investigate), 논하다 (= discuss), 생각하다 (= consider), 종사하다 thoroughly (= thorough and through = completely) : 철저하게
    proceed : 앞으로 나가다

55. **정답** ③
    word sooner or later : 조만간
    gang up on : 집단으로 습격하다, 대항하다
    해석 머지않아 모든 것이 나에게 몰려왔다.

56. **정답** ③
    word get along : 꾸려나가다 (= manage) cf. get along with : ~와 잘 지내다

57. **정답** ①
    word get over (= overcome, recover) : 극복하다
    cancer : 암
    immune from : ~로부터 면제되다

58. **정답** ③
    word in buying~ = when I buy~
    get stuck : 바가지 쓰다

59. **정답** ②
    word get through with : ~를 끝내다 (= finish)

60. **정답** ①
    word get to (= arrive at = reach) : ~에 도달하다
    encounter : 우연히 만나다

61. **정답** ④
    word give one a hand : ~를 도와주다
    fix (= repair, mend) : 수리하다

62. **정답** ③
    word give one a ring (= call one up) : ~에게 전화를 걸다
    call down : 꾸짖다
    ask after : 안부를 묻다

63. **정답** ②
    word give out (= announce) : 발표하다
    emit : (빛, 열을) 방출하다

64. **정답** ③
    word give rise to (= bring about = cause) : 야기시키다
    erase : 지우다

65. **정답** ④
    word give up (= abdicate, surrender, stop) : 포기하다, 굴복하다
    throne : 왕위

66. **정답** ④

67. **정답** ①
    word go through : 겪다 (= experience), 다 써 버리다 (= use up) / go on : 계속하다
    go out for : ~을 요구하여 파업하다

67. **정답** ①
    word give way to (= yield to, succumb to) : ~에 굴복하다
    live up to : ~에 맞추어 살다

68. **정답** ②
    word go through (= experience) : 겪다
    imitation : 모방

69. **정답** ①
    word go with (= match) : ~와 어울리다

70. **정답** ③
    word hold back : 숨기다 (= conceal), 억제하다 (= restrain), 지연시키다 (= retard)
    the accused man : 피고

71. **정답** ②
    word hand down (= bequeath) : 물려주다
    from generation to generation : 대대로
    rebuke (= reprove, reprimand) : 책망하다

72. **정답** ②
    word hard of hearing : 귀가 먼 ex) He is hard of hearing = He has difficulty (in) hearing.

73. **정답** ①
    word hard to believe : 믿기 어려운 (= incredible)
    brutal : 야만적인 (= savage)
    congenial : 동일한 적합한 / invariable : 불변의

74. **정답** ②
    word have the right of way : 길을 앞서가다
    vehicle : 차량 / cut in : 끼어들다
    jam[slam] on the breaks : 강하게 급브레이크를 밟다
    해석 운전을 할 때는 몇 가지 규칙을 따라야 한다. 만약 다른 차가 앞에 끼어들면 갑자기 멈추기 위해 강하게 급브레이크를 밟아야 한다. 어떤 다른 차가 앞서 가려 한다면 양보해주어야 한다.

75. **정답** ②
    word nutrition : 영양 / infancy : 유아기
    adult : 성인 / restore : 회복하다
    해석 유아기 때 영양이 부족하면 성인으로서의 성장이 늦어질 수 있다.

76. **정답** ①
    word hold good : 유효하다

77. **정답** ④
    word hold on : 기다리다

78. 정답 ①
   word hold out : 지탱하다, 버티다 (= resist)
     persist : 고집하다 / desist : 단념하다

79. 정답 ④
   word in retrospect (= looking back) : 돌이켜 보건데
     make a decision : 결정하다
     all things considered : 만사를 고려해 보건데
     in general : 일반적으로

80. 정답 ③
   word immune to (= free from) : ~로부터 면제된, 면역이 된

81. 정답 ②
   word in a coma (= unconscious) : 혼수상태인
     distract " : (주의를) 다른 데로 돌리다
     (= divert, confuse)

82. 정답 ①
   word indulge in : ~에 탐닉하다
     luxury : 사치, 호화스러움 / long for : 갈망하다
   해석 그 노인은 종종 고급 시가를 피우며 즐긴다.

83. 정답 ④
   word in a high spirit (= cheerful) : 명랑한 ↔ out of spirits
     (= depressed) : 침울한

84. 정답 ①
   word in retrospect (= looking back) : 돌이켜 보건데
   해석 돌이켜 보건데 그 전쟁에서 이기려면 이길 수도 있
     었다는 것을 알게 되었다.

85. 정답 ③
   word have insight into : ~에 대한 통찰력을 가지다
     identification : 신분증명 (서)
     hostility : 적개심

86. 정답 ③
   word in terms of (= from the standpoint of) : ~의 견지에서
     on behalf of : ~를 대신하여
     by means of : ~에 의하여
     by way of (= via) : ~를 경유하여
   해석 나는 미국에서 알고 지내던 같은 또래의 아이들이
     라는 관점에서 그를 생각했다.

87. 정답 ③
   word in terms of : ~의 견지에서
     for the sake of (= for one's sake) : ~를 위하여

88. 정답 ①
   word in the end (= in the ultimate = in the long run = in
     the last analysis = after al = at last = at length =
     finally = eventually = ultimately) : 결국

89. 정답 ①

90. 정답 ③
   word in vogue (= popular) : 유행하는
     enthusiastic : 열광적인

91. 정답 ②
   word irrespective of (= regardless of = with no relation
     to = without regard to) : ~에 상관없이

92. 정답 ④
   word behind one's back : ~가 안 보는 데서
   해석 그녀는 자기가 없는 곳에서 이웃 삶들이 자신에 대
     해 말하는 것을 불평해 왔다. 그러나 만약 당신이 나
     에게 묻는다면, 그건 피장파장이다.

93. 정답 ①
   word leave over : ~을 남겨 두다
     spare : ~를 따로 떼어 놓다
   해석 만약 베리가 시간이 나면 나의 불어공부를 도와줄
     것이다.

94. 정답 ③
   word keep [bear] one company : ~와 동행하다
     sympathize with : ~와 공감하다

95. 정답 ②
   word keep up with : ~에 뒤지지 않다, 소식을 알다

96. 정답 ②
   word keep an eye on (= watch) : ~를 감시하다
     look through : ~를 간파하다
     clean out : 다 써버리다 (= ues up), 말끔히 쓸어내다

97. 정답 ④
   word leave off : 그만두다 (= omit)
     application form : 지원서
     curtail (= abbreviate, shorten) : 줄이다
     enlarge : 확대하다 / scribble : 날려서 쓰다

98. 정답 ③
   word lenient (= generous) : 너그러운

99. 정답 ③
   word level up (= enhance) : 향상시키다
     cope with : ~에 대처하다
     renounce : 포기하다, 부인하다

100. 정답 ②
   word perform : 수행하다 / comprehend : 이해하다 (=
     understand, get, grasp, make out, figure out)

101. 정답 ③

word look down on (= despise) : 경멸하다 ↔ look up to
(= respect) : 존경하다

102. **정답** ④
word look forward to (= anticipate, expect) : 기대하다

103. **정답** ②③
word look like (= resemble) : 닮다
reproach (= reprimand) : 꾸짖다
reconcile : 화해하다

104. **정답** ①
word lose one' s temper : 화내다
cf. out of temper : 화가 난

105. **정답** ④
word lose one' s touch : ~와 관계를 끊다

106. **정답** ②
word be lost in (= be absorbed in = be indulged in = be
occupied with) : ~에 몰두하다
go away with : ~을 가지고 달아나다

107. **정답** ④
word make a clean breast of : ~를 몽땅 털어놓고 이야
기하다
confess : 털어놓다
해석 네가 한 짓을 몽땅 털어놓고 이야기하는 것이 좋
겠군.

108. **정답** ②
word make a difference (= matter) : 중요하다

109. **정답** ③
word make believe9 = pretend) : ~인 체하다

110. **정답** ①
word make an effort (= strive) : 노력하다
coerce : 강요하다
falter : 말을 더듬다, 비틀거리다
swerve : 벗어나다

111. **정답** ④
word make out (= figure out = comprehend = get =
grasp = understand) : 이해하다
inherit : 상속하다

112. **정답** ③
word make with : ~을 만들어내다
make over (= hand over) : 양도하다
make believe (= pretend) : ~인 체하다

113. **정답** ④

114. **정답** ②
word make so much of (= respect) : 중시하다, 존중하다

115. **정답** ②
word make the point (= prove) : 입증하다, 잘 납득시키다
sour grapes : (이솝이야기 중에서) '시샘, 허세부리
기' 의 뜻
point out : 지적하다

116. **정답** ②
word make up for (= compensate for = atone for) : 보상
하다
summon (= call in) : 소환하다

117. **정답** ④
word be make up of (= be composed of = consist of =
comprise) : ~로 구성되다
consist in (= lie in) : ~에 놓여있다
consist with : ~와 일치하다
confer with : ~와 협의하다

118. **정답** ②
word make up one' s mind (= decide) : 결심하다

119. **정답** ③
word mix up (= confuse) : 혼동이 된

120. **정답** ①
word move one to : ~를 움직여서 ~하게 만들다
pitiful : 가련한
sigh : 한숨, 한탄
해석 그 가련한 탄식이 우리를 울게 하였다.

121. **정답** ②
word next to (= as good as = almost = nearly) : 거의

122. **정답** ③
word next to none (= second to none = the best) : 최고의

123. **정답** ④
word obliged : 감사하는 (= thankful) cf. be
obliged[compelled, forced, impelled, bound] to
(do) : ~하지 않으면 아니 되다
해석 이웃이 베푼 모든 도움에 대하여 감사한다고 존은
말하였다.

124. **정답** ①
word off and on (= on and off = once in a while = from
time to time = on occasion = (every) now and
then + (every) now and again = occasionally =
sometimes = irregularly) : 이따금, 때때로
imperceptibly : 미세하게
unceasingly : 끊임없이 (= constantly)

125. **정답** ②
word of one' s own accord (= of one' s own will =
spontaneously = voluntarily) : 자발적으로, 저절로

126. 정답 ②
　　word on hand (= available) : 당장 이용할 수 있는, 손 가
　　까이에 있는

127. 정답 ③
　　word on pins and needles : 안달하는, 매우 근심하는
　　sew : 바느질하다

128. 정답 ①
　　word on second thought : 재고해 보니
　　at second hand : 간접적으로
　　by the way : 그런데
　　by no means (= not~by any means) : 결코 ~이 아닌

129. 정답 ①
　　word on the spur of the moment : 즉흥적으로 앞 뒤 가
　　리지 않고

130. 정답 ①
　　word on the way (= about to be born = being pregnant)
　　: 임신중인

131. 정답 ①
　　word be open to (= be subject to = be prone to) : ~받
　　기쉽다, 기꺼이 ~를 받으려 하다

132. 정답 ②
　　word out of order : 고장 난
　　The watch is out of order.
　　= There is something wrong with the watch.

133. 정답 ④
　　word out of place : 부적당한 (= improper, unsuitable)

134. 정답 ②
　　word out of the question (= impossible) : 불가능한
　　cf. out of question (= sure) : 의심할 나위없는

135. 정답 ③
　　word out of work : 실직당한 (= unemployed)
　　well off (부유한) : = well-to-do = wealthy
　　cf. badly-off : 가난한
　　off duty : 비번인 ↔ on duty : 당번인

136. 정답 ③
　　word over and above (= in addition to = besides) : ~에
　　덧붙여서
　　expenditure : 경비
　　board : 식사 (제공), 하숙하다
　　해석 방값과 식사비를 합한 비용이외에 당신이 지출한
　　금액은 얼마입니까?

137. 정답 ④
　　word over and over again : 반복해서 (= repeatedly)

138. 정답 ④
　　word put up with : 참다
　　(=bear = endure = stand = tolerate = withstand)

139. 정답 ①
　　word participate in (= take part in) : ~에 참가하다

140. 정답 ③
　　word pass away : 죽다 (= die), 끝이나다 (= cease)

141. 정답 ④
　　word pass through : 꿰뚫고 통과하다
　　illuminate : 조명하다
　　reiterate : 반복하다
　　deprecate : 반대하다
　　penetrate : 꿰뚫다

142. 정답 ②
　　word pay one's court to : ~의 비위를 맞추다

143. 정답 ②
　　word pick out : 선택하다 (= choose)

144. 정답 ①
　　word picture to oneself : 마음속에 그리다 (= image)

145. 정답 ①
　　word pull one's leg (= tease) : 우롱하다

146. 정답 ①
　　word pull oneself together (= get hold of oneself) : 기운
　　을 되찾다

147. 정답 ②
　　word pull oneself together : 정신 차리다, 기운을 되찾다

148. 정답 ③
　　word pull off (= tear away) : 찢어내다, 떨어져나가다
　　fatally : 치명적으로
　　cripple : 비틀거리다, 불구가 되다
　　rear : 후미의 / cargo : 화물
　　해석 그 비행기는 후미의 화물칸 문이 비행 중 떨어져
　　나갔을 때 치명적으로 비틀거렸다.

149. 정답 ③
　　word pull through (= get over) : 병이 낫다, 뚫고 나가다

150. 정답 ①
　　word put down : 기록하다

151. 정답 ④
　　word put off : 연기하다 (= postpone)
　　withhold : 억제하다 / dispose of : 처분하다

152. 정답 ①

word put up with : 참다
(=bear = endure = stand = tolerate = withstand)
contribute to : ~에 공헌하다

153. 정답 ④
해석 우리는 도시의 매연을 더 이상 견딜 수 없어서 시골로 이사를 했다.

154. 정답 ② Despite of ② → Despite
word regardless of : ~에 상관없이 (= irrespective of = without regard to = with no relation to), ~에도 불구하고 (= in spite of, despite, with all, for all)

155. 정답 ②
word react to (= respond to) : ~에 반응을 보이다
submit (= hand in, turn in) : 제출하다
해석 모든 유기체는 환경의 변화에 반응한다.

156. 정답 ②
word read up on : ~을 읽어두다
take an examination : 시험을 보다

157. 정답 ③
word refrain from : ~를 삼가다, 자제하다

158. 정답 ③
word reside on : ~에 살다
reservation : 보호지역
for the time being : 당분간

159. 정답 ③
word run across (= come across, happen to meet) : 우연히 만나다
talk to (= speak to = address) : ~에게 말을 걸다
trample : 짓밟다

160. 정답 ①
word run out of (= use up) : 다 써버리다
send for : ~을 부르러 보내다
ask for : 요구하다

161. 정답 ④
word run over : 차에 치다
look out (= be careful) : 조심하다

162. 정답 ④
word rule out : 배제하다 (= reject, eliminate)
forestall : ~을 앞지르다

163. 정답 ④
word stand out : 눈이 띄다, 두드러지다 (= outstanding distinguished, noteworthy, prominent)

164. 정답 ③
word second to none : 누구에게도 뒤떨어지지 않는

165. 정답 ③
word see eye to eye with (= agree with) : ~와 의견이 일치하다
hostage : 인질 / scare : 상처

166. 정답 ③
word see into (= look into = search into = inquire into = investigate) : 조사하다
conjecture : ~을 추측하다

167. 정답 ③
word send for : ~를 부르러 보내다
fetch : ~을 데리고 오다

168. 정답 ①
word set up : 계획하다 (= arrange), 세우다 (= erect)
cancel : 취소하다 (= put off)
discard : 포기하다

169. 정답 ②
word shed light on : ~을 밝히다, 설명하다 (= explain)
dissipate : 흩어지게 하다
appall : 공포에 떨다

170. 정답 ②
word abstract : 추상적인
shift into (= convert into) : ~로 전환하다
exaggerate : 과장하다
imitate : 모방하다

171. 정답 ②
word show one's true colors : 진면목을 보여주다

172. 정답 ④
word slip on's mind : 기억에서 사라지다 (= forget)
be supposed to : ~하기로 되어있다

173. 정답 ①
word stand for (= represent) : ~를 나타내다

174. 정답 ②
word stand out : 두드러지다 (= outstanding = distinguished, prominent, noteworthy)

175. 정답 ①
해석 몇 가지 요점이 그의 논법에서 두드러진다.

176. 정답 ②
word stand up for : ~을 옹호하다 (= defend)

177. 정답 ④
word straddle : 양다리 걸치다

178. 정답 ③
word succumb to (= yield to) : ~에 굴복하다

179. **정답** ①
    word take to one's heels : 황급하게 달아나다
        flee : 도망치다

180. **정답** ③
    word take a fancy to (= have a liking for = be fond of =
        like) : ~를 좋아하다
        speak highly of : 극찬하다
        catch sight of : ~를 발견하다
        ↔ lose sight of : 시야에서 놓치다

181. **정답** ③
    word take after : 닮다 (= resemble)

182. **정답** ③
    word humiliate : 굴욕감을 주다
        initiate : 시작하다

183. **정답** ①

184. **정답** ②
    word take down : 기록하다 (= record)

185. **정답** ③
    word take A for B : A를 B로 여기다
        confuse A with B : A를 B와 혼동하다

186. **정답** ①
    word take it : 받아들이다 (= accept), 믿다 (= believe)
        wrecked : 난파된

187. **정답** ④
    word make a decision : 결정하다
        applicant : 지원자
        take~into account : ~를 고려하다 (= consider)
        stabilize : 안정시키다

188. **정답** ①
    word take off : (옷, 신발 등을) 벗다 (= remove), 이륙하
        다 (= depart)
        retain : 보유하다 / entrance : 입구

189. **정답** ①

190. **정답** ③

191. **정답** ③
    word take one's time : 천천히 하다
        come up with : (해결책, 해답을) 찾아내다
        be engaged in : ~에 종사하다
    해석 우리는 해결책을 찾아내는데 서두르지 않았다.

192. **정답** ④
    word take over (= succeed to) : 인계하다

193. **정답** ③
    word think of : ~기억하다 (= remember)

194. **정답** ④
    word throw away : 버리다 (= discard)
        imitate : 모방하다
        extract : 추출해 내다

195. **정답** ①
    word turn down : 거절하다 (= reject)
        put aside : 저축하다 (= save)
        verify : 확증하다

196. **정답** ③
    해석 그 장관은 위원회의 제안을 거부했다.

197. **정답** ②
    해석 그는 5시까지 나타나지 않았다.

198. **정답** ①
    word turn up (= show up = make an appearance =
        appear, arrive, come) : 나타나다
        contemplate : 심사숙고하다

199. **정답** ②

200. **정답** ①
    word without fail (= by all means = for certain = for a
        certainty) : 반드시, 꼭
        be told : 듣다
        cf. be taught : 배우다, be beaten : 맞다, 지다

201. **정답** ③
    word under the weather : 몸 상태가 좋지 않은, 기분이
        언짢은

202. **정답** ①
    word be up for grabs : 누군가 원하는 사람이 획득할 수
        있는

203. **정답** ②
    word (up) in the air : 미정인 (= undecided)
        be set : (계획이) 짜여져 있는

204. **정답** ③
    word be up to something : ~일을 꾸미다

205. **정답** ④
    word virtue and vice : 장점과 결점, 미덕과 악덕
        shortcoming (= fault, flaw, defect) : 결점

1. **정답** ②
   word come up with : ~한 생각을 제안하다 (= propose),
   ~을 따라잡다 / make : 구성하다

2. **정답** matter
   word as a matter of fact (= in point of fact = in fact, in
   reality, in effect, in practice = really, actually) : 사실
   상, 실제로

3. **정답** ①
   word agree with + 사람 : ~에 동의하다
   cf. agree to + 사물

4. **정답** ②
   word at random : 마음대로
   at all events : 어쨌든

5. **정답** ②
   word beside oneself : out of one' s senses, insane,
   demented, mad (제정신이 아닌)

6. **정답** ①
   word call for (= require) : 요구하다

7. **정답** ③
   word call off (= cancel) : 취소하다

8. **정답** ①
   word come by (= obtain) : 획득하다

9. **정답** ④
   word come down with : 병에 걸리다
   come off with : ~을 가지고 가다

10. **정답** ④
    word come to a halt (= come to a stop) : 멈추다
    pass by : 지나가다
    spin : 방적하다 / glimmer : 희미한 빛
    gallop : 질주하다

11. **정답** ②
    word contrary to : ~와 반대로
    away from : ~와 떨어져서

12. **정답** ③
    word cope with : ~에 대처하다
    be a match for : ~의 적수가 되다, ~를 감당할 능
    력이 있는

13. **정답** ③
    word count on (= depend on = rely on = rest on = fall
    back on = hinge on = turn to) : ~에 의존하다

14. **정답** treated
    word deal with (= treat) : 취급하다 cf. deal in : 장사하
    다

15. **정답** ③
    word be different from (= differ from) : ~와 다른

16. **정답** ③
    word give birth to : (아기를) 낳다 (= produce, bear)

17. **정답** ②
    word give up : 굴복하다 (= surrender)

18. **정답** ③
    word give in : 항복하다 (= yield)
    give vent to : ~를 나타내다
    give away : 남에게 주다, 놓치다

19. **정답** ③
    word have no say in : ~에 대하여 발언권이 없다

20. **정답** in
    word in the midst of (= in the middle of)
    : ~의 한가운데에서
    vast : 거대한 / prosperity : 번영

21. **정답** ④
    word keep to oneself : 멀리 떨어져서 홀로 살다

22. **정답** ①
    word let down : 실망시키다

23. **정답** ③
    word lay off : 해고시키다 (= dismiss, fire)

24. **정답** ④
    word look for (= search for = in search of) : ~를 찾다

25. **정답** to
    word look forward to : 기대하다 (= anticipate, expect)

26. **정답** ④
    word make peace with (= make up) : 화해하다

27. **정답** of
    word out of question : 분명한 (= sure)
    cf. out of the question : 불가능한 (= impossible)

28. **정답** ②
    word along with : ~와 더불어
    participate in (= take part in) : ~에 참여하다
    struggle for : ~를 위한 투쟁
    side by side : ~와 나란히

29. **정답** ④
    word pull through (= recover from) : ~를 극복하다

30. **정답** killed

   word put ~to death (= condemn [sentence]~ to death) :
       ~를 사형에 처하다

31. **정답** ④

   word regardless of (= irrespective of = with no relation
       to = without regard to) : ~와 관계없이

32. **정답** ④

   word stand for : ~를 나타내다 (= represent)

33. **정답** started

   word set out : 출발하다 (= start)
       destination : 목적지

실전문제 총정리

부록

시험에 잘 나오는
필수 어휘

A

abbreviate 줄이다
shorten abridge curtail condense
↔ lengthen

abrupt 뜻밖의
sudden

abstain 삼가다
refrain withhold hold back

absurd 불합리한 어리석은
foolish silly ridiculous stupid
↔ sensible rational

abuse 남용하다 악용하다 욕하다
ill-use misuse maltreat reproach(꾸짖다)
slander(비방하다 욕설을 퍼붓다)

accomplish 다하다 완성하다
achieve complete execute fulfill

adept 솜씨 좋은 능숙한
adroit(↔maladroit)
deft dexterous proficient skillful
nimble(재빠른 민활한)
proficient ambidextrous(양손을 잘 쓰는)

adopt 채택하다

adult 성숙한
mature ripe grown full-developed

affluent 풍부한
rich opulent abundant wealthy ample

alter 변경하다
change modify vary

ameliorate 개량하다
improve better

anonymous 익명의
one whose name is not known

antiquated 오래된
old aged antique outworn

apparel 옷
clothing dress garb attire costume

apparent 명백한 외견상의
plain clear evident obvious conspicuous
manifest

apt 하기 쉬운
inclined disposed prone liable likely

적당한 appropriate

aptly 적절히 적합하게
fitting properly appropriately

argument 논쟁
dispute controversy

arid 마른 건조한
dry desert

artisan 장인
craftsman

assult 습격
aggression

assert 재산
property

atheism 무신론

astrology 점성술

astronomy 천문학

anthropology 인류학

archaeology 고고학

acquiescence 묵시적 동의
accepting without protest

administration 행정부
legislature ; 입법부 **judiciary ; 사법부

acme 최고점 정상 정점
↔ nadir ; 최하점

alienable 양도할 수 있는

alleviate 완화하다 경감하다

aging 노화

abate 감소시키다 줄이다
dwindle

abet ~을 부추기다 선동하다 교사하다
aid

abash ~을 부끄럽게 하다 ~을 어쩔 줄 모
르게 하다
humiliate

antinomy 모순 불일치 자가당착
contradiction

abstruse 난해한 심오한

avert 돌리다 피하다 막다
avoid shun

aliment 병 불쾌

apposite 적당한 적절한
appropriate

archives 공문서 기록보관서
public record

acoustic 청각의
auditory

ascribe ~의 탓으로 돌리다

ascent 상승 승진

advisable 권할만한 타당한 현명한

ample 풍부한

attorney 대리인 변호사

analgesic 진통제
anodyne

anthem 성가 찬송가
song
national anthem ; 애국가

artificial 인공의 인조의
synthetic man-made

azure 하늘색의 창공의

adverse 적대의 반대의
negative antagonistic hostile

advocate 옹호하다

altruist 박애주의자 이타주의자

affability 상냥함
pleasantness
ⓐaffable ; 상냥한 친절한(= benign)
↔ surly ; 부루퉁한 뚱한 난폭한

appalling 소름끼치는 섬뜩하게 하는
dreadful

attention 주의 조심
heed

apprehension	이해 (력) 체포 불안 걱정 두려움 (= dread fear)	archipelago	군도 다도해 섬이 많은 바다 group of many islands
applaud	박수갈채하다 성원하다 clap their hands clapping	augment	늘이다 증대시키다 increase
architect	건축가	arbitrary	임의의 재멋대로의 변덕스러운 random whimsical capricious
avid	탐욕한 desirous	abreast	나란히 ~와 병행하여 keep abreast with ; ~와 보조를 맞추어 keep pace with keep up with
awkward	어색한		
alone	홀로 혼자서 by oneself cf) for oneself ; 자기 힘으로	allude (+to)	언급하다 넌지시 비추다 암시하다 mention refer to
assume	떠맡다 take over	autocratic	독재적인 강압적인
ascetic	금욕주의자 고행자 수도자	attest (+to)	~을 입증 (증언) 하다
arbitrary	임의의	acrid	(맛이) 쓴 bitter pungent acerbie
arouse	불러일으키다 유발시키다 provoke		(맛이) 신랄한 trenchant
anemia	빈혈	awhile	잠깐 잠시
accommodation	수용 (= lodgings) 숙박 적응 순응 (= adaptation adjustment)	abrasive	(표면이) 거친 (남과) 마찰을 일으키는 ↔ smooth
acquit	석방하다 무죄로 하다	autonomous	자율적인 독립적인 자치권이 있는 independent
article	기사 논고		
abolition	철폐 폐지 폐기	affectation	~체함 짐짓 꾸밈
aftermath	(전쟁, 재해의) 결과 여파 영향 resulting situation	appraisal	평가 감정 사정
		apathetically	무감동하게 냉담하게 halfheartedly
auspicious	길조의 경사스런	ailment	불쾌 우환 병 disease affliction malady
amity	친선 친목 우호 friendship good will	allegiance	충성 충절 충심 성심 신의 loyalty
assimilate	동화(융화)하다 흡수하다 absorb	apply to	~에 적용하다 for ~에 지원하다
adage	옛날사람의 명언 금언 격언	ascertain	확인하다 ~을 확신 (자신) 하다
ardent	열렬한	appraise	평가하다 estimate
astound	깜짝 놀라게 하다 astonish	annul	무효로 하다 취소하다 conceal
aroma	향기 flavor ; 맛 palate ; 미각	annals	연대기 사료 기록 historical records chronicle
affinity	인척 동족관계 유사 친화력 좋아함 애호 liking fondness attraction predilection	accordingly	따라서 consequently 그러므로 therefore 그에 어울리게 appropriately
apathy	냉담 무관심 ↔ zealot ; 열광자 광신자	afflict	괴롭히다 distress torment affect
advent	출현 도래 arrival	aloft	(아주) 높이 위에 high up
advertize	Vt.~을 광고 (선전) 하다 Vi. 통고 (통지) 하다 알리다 자기선전을 하다 inform	aviation	비행 (술) 항공
		have an ax to grind	딴 속셈 (마음)이 있다 have a selfish ent to gain
amenity	예의 공손함 상냥함		
amenable	순종하는 유순한 복종할 의무가 있는 obedient tractable acquiescent		

B

backbreaking	격렬한 strenuous arduous turbulent violent drastic

Continued from left column:

adversity	불운 불행 역경 재앙
appease	~을 달래다 위로하다 console
altruist	이타주의자
ambivalence	양면가치 반대감정병존 모순 having conflicting values

ban	금하다	prohibit forbid taboo proscribe
barren	불모의	sterile infertile unproductive
beatific	축복을 내리는 행복한	giving bliss
benign	친절한	kind humane compassionate
bent	기호 경향	taste tendency trend proneness inclination
bombastic	과장된	
boost	올리다	raise lift elevate heave hoist exalt
boundless	무한한 한없는	without limits
bulwark	보루 성채 방벽	
banquet	잔치 연회 향연	feast
beset	포위하다 둘러싸다	besiege encompass
beckon	손짓해 부르다	
banner	국기 기	flag colors
blunt	무딘	dull
benefactor	은인 후원자	
belligerent	호전적인 싸움을 좋아하는	quarrelsome
bleak	황폐한 쓸쓸한	desolate bare barren arid
bias	편견	prejudice
bosom	가슴 흉부 유방	
blatantly	심히 눈에 띄는 야한 소란스러운	openly
brochure	소책자 팸플릿	short pamphlet
burrow	피난처	ⓥ굴을 파다 잠복하다
blunder	실수	mistake
banality	진부 평범	↔ freshness
buoyant	경쾌한 낙천적인 쾌활한	cheerful
buoyance	부력 뜨는 성질 쾌활	ⓥbuoy
boon	은혜 혜택 이익	blessing
breakthrough	돌파구 획기적인 전진	most significant advance
boast	자랑하다	
belie	거짓전하다 속이다 중상하다	
brisk	팔팔한 활발한 기운찬 쾌적한 상쾌한	

benevolence	자비심 박애 자선 선행	
bruise	타박상 찰과상 상처 자국	injury scar
band	줄 띠	stripe
blur	희미ㆍ흐릿해지다	indistinct
brine	소금물	= salt water
barrier	장벽 장애물	= obstruction hindrance bar snag
brood	골똘히 생각하다 걱정하다 수심에 잠기다	
blithe	즐거운 유쾌한	
bricker	언쟁하다 말다툼하다	= quarrel
break off	갑자기 중단하다	↪ review (공부를) 다시 하다 복습하다
brush up on	~을 다듬다 다시외다	improve break the news news를 전달하다
break in on	참견하다 끼여들다	= disturb interrupt
break out	발생하다	= out break begin break off 꺾다 break up 해산하다 break short 갑자기 그만두다
boil down to	요컨대 ~이 되다	briefly
out of blue	뜻밖에 불시에 청천벽력과 같은	unexpectedly
a bit	약간 다소	somewhat a little
in behalf of on behalf of	~을 위하여 ~을 대신하여	
blow off	불어서 날아가게 하다	slow out (타이어가) 펑크나다
up	폭파시키다	
blend in with	~와 조화하다	= harmonize

C

cancel	취소하다	annul revoke call off recant
capricious	변덕스러운	fickle whimsical
careless	경솔한	heedless reckless indiscreet
catastrophe	큰 재앙	disaster mishap calamity misfortune
census	인구조사	population count
core	중앙	center

charitable	자비로운 인자한	

charitable 자비로운 인자한
generous benign kind lenient
eleemosynary

chronologically 연대순으로
according to a time sequence

commence 시작하다
begin start originate

complex(ed) 복잡한
complicated intricate compound

comply 복종하다
obey

concede 인정하다
admit acknowledge own confess

confer 物 on 人　~를 ~에게 주다
confer with ~에 동의하다
confront ~에 직면하다
face

considerable 굉장히 많은
considerate 사려 깊은
contrary 모순되는
opposing contradictory inconsistent
paradoxical

criterion 표준 기준
standard rule measure

connoisseur 감정가
crude 천연그대로의
unrefined raw

cure 치료하다
remedy therapy heal

compliment 칭찬
congenial 동일한 적합한
confine 제한하다 한정하다
감금하다 (imprison)
captivity

celebrity 유명인사 명성
fame

condemn 비난하다
countenance 용모 생김새
(얼굴에 나타나는) 표정 안색
face express

connotation 함축 내포
implication

contemplate 심사숙고하다
coalition 합동 연합 연립 제휴
constellation 별자리 성좌
conservation 보수주의
colleague 동료
company associate

contemptuous 모욕적인
scornful

consensus 일치 여론 교감
↔ disharmony

champ 우적우적 씹다
chew noisily

condone 용서하다
pardon excuse

confirmation 확증 확인 증거
proof

concession 양보 허용 면허 특허 구내서점
acknowledgement

catholic 다방면의 광범위한
celestial 하늘의 천체의
centennial 100년제의 100주년의
a 100th anniversary 백년제

conciliatory 타협적인 융화 적인 회유 적인
condescending 겸손한
clarity 명료 명쾌 청명
clown 시골뜨기
cabala 신비철학 신비적 교리
published doctrine

controversial 논쟁의 토론의
debatable

cautious 주의 깊은
coincidence 일치 동시발생
convert 개종하다 전환하다
combative 호전적인
cherish 소중히 하다
conduce 공헌하다
congestion 혼잡 붐빔
교통 혼잡 traffic congestion / jam

contagious 전염성의
infectious

cogent 유력한 사람을 설복시키는
convincing

chicanery 속임수 책략 꾸며 됨
contemporary 현대의 당대의 동시대의
comparison & contrast 비교와 대조
construe 해석하다
interpret

conspicuous 눈에 잘 띄는 똑똑히 보이는
저명한

conscious 의식 있는
chase 추적 추구
pursuit

conjecture 추측 추측하다
guess surmise

comprehensive 포괄적인
(= inclusive) 범위가 넓은 이해하는

complacency 자기만족 안식
satisfaction content

confederation 연합 동맹
certificate 증명서 면허장
crabstick 심술궂은 사람
crave 열망(갈망) 하다
desire yearn for long for

commotion 소동 동요
agitation

contempt 모욕 경멸 치욕
condiment 조미료
seasoning

contemplate 심사숙고하다

chore	허드렛일 지루한 일 잡일
	burden necessary but uninteresting job
concrete	구체적인
	↔ abstract 추상적인
colossal	거대한
	huge
cultivate	경작하다
	raise
component	성분 요소 ~을 구성하다
crucial	중요한
	huge
convict	~의 유죄를 선언하다
congenital	선천적인
	present at birth
conceit	거만 = arrogance
	자부심 (= pride)
clone	복제생물
commencement	졸업식
	graduation ceremony
copious	풍부한 풍족한
	ample abundant plentiful
collusion	공모
	conspiracy complicity
clumsy	솜씨 없는 서투른 어색한
callous	무감각한 굳은 못이 박힌
	insensitive cold-hearted heartless
	unsympathetic indifferent
cite	인용하다
	quote
counterexample	반증 반례
charlatan	협잡꾼 돌팔이의사 (= quack)
commodity(ies)	일용품 필수품 구어체의 담화
	체의 일상회화의
	conversational ↔ literary
concoct	(수표 음료 따위를) 섞어만들다
	(이야기 따위를) 꾸며내다 조작하다
	(계획, 음모 등을) 꾸미다 = devise
conscientiously	양심적으로 성실하게
	diligently
corrupt	부정한 타락한 사악한
curt	무례한
	impolite rude
condescending	겸손한
cargo	적하 뱃짐 화물
	load burden
continent	대륙 육지 자제심이 많은
	극기의 금욕의
chase	뒤쫓다 추적하다 ~을 추구하다
connote	(말이) 언어의 뜻을 갖다
	의미하다 내포하다
	imply
communicable	전할 수 있는 전염성의
	transmittable
coherent	(이야기가) 조리 있는 시종일관한
	logical
cemetery	묘지 공동묘지

chaste	정숙한 순결한
	virtuous modest decent
category	범주 분류
cosmetic	화장품
coarse	거친
	rough harsh
competent	능력 있는 유능한 적격의
	adept
complacent	자기만족의 = self-satisfied
compulsory	의무적인 강제적인
	= mandatory obligation
contention	싸움 논쟁
collaborate	협동하다
	= work together
currency	통화 지폐
	= paper money, bank bill
corporal	육체의 신체의
	= of the human body
caning	매질
custodial	보관의 보호의
collide (with)	~과 충돌하다
	= bump into, crash
call it a day	하루의 일을 마치다 마감하다
	stop
call a person names	~를 욕하다
	abuse
comply with	(규정, 법) 따르다
copy with	대처하다 극복하다
	deal with
per capita	1인당
	per head
count someone in	~를 포함시키다
	include someone
off and cuff	즉석에서 즉흥적인 준비 없이
	without preparation
cut out for	~에 적임자다
	well-suited for naturally suited for
come home to	감동시키다
	사람의 마음에 와 닿다
	deeply impresses
a good command of	자유로이 구사하다
come up with	제안하다
	suggest present

D

degrade	격하시키다
	depose downgrade
decade	10년간
decent	훌륭한 (= respectable) 예의바른
	품위 있는
deception	기만 속임
	fraud deceit cheat
	ⓐ deceptive 속이는, 기만하는 = cheating,
	misleading

denunciation	공공연한 비난 condemn openly	delicate	섬세한 고운 민감한 dainty
destroy	파괴하다 smash demolish tear down	deity	신 god
deter	막다 restrain hinder prevent 단념시키다 give up	deluge	대홍수 호우 범람 overflow flood
		delude	속이다
defect	감지하다, 탐지하다 = uncover	divulge	누설하다 폭로하다 let on
discrepancy	불일치 어긋남 차이 disparity difference inconsistency disagreement inequality	destination	목적지
		depletion	고갈 소모
		distend	넓히다 팽창시키다
diurnal	매일의 daily	dubious	의심스러운 doubtful
drastic	강렬한 strong	deadlock	교착상태 막다름 stalemate dilemma predicament
discrimination	차별	drowsy	졸린
detrimental	해로운 harmful	debut	첫무대 데뷔
		debate	논하다 토론하다
disinclination	싫증 싫음 reluctance	deterioration	저하 가치의 하락 타락 노후화 gradual decline degeneration lapse corruption debasement defilement
dearth 부족	결핍 기근 lack		
detest	싫어하다 abhors	domesticate	길들이다 순화시키다 tame
decimate	많이 감소하다 10분의 1을 제거하다 많은 사람을 죽이다 greatly decrease	deplete	고갈시키다
		disseminate	선전하다 퍼뜨리다 흩뿌리다 disperse
		dissemination	흩뿌림 파종 보급 살포 dispersal
drawback	결점 단점 흠 disadvantage	disposal	처분 처리 양도 cf) at one's disposal 마음대로 쓸 수 있는
distort	왜곡하다 pervert 찡그리다	durable	오래 견디는 튼튼한
defer to	~의견에 따르다 deference : 복종 존경	depict	묘사(서술) 하다 illustrate
dread	두려워하다	dejection	낙담 실망 disappointment
derelict	직무태만의		
damnation	박탈하다 거절하다	detrimental	해로운 harmful
disembarkation	상륙	domain	영토 영역 분야 범위 field area reign realm section
dedication	헌신 봉납 봉헌		
demeanor	태도 품행 행실	derivation	끌러내기 유도 유래 기원 파생어 origin
domestic	가정의 국내의		
dispensary	진료소 병원 clinic	din	소음 떠듦 시끄러운 소리 noise uproar
dwindle	작아지다 쇠하다 감소시키다	disrupt	붕괴시키다 분열시키다 split
divorce	이혼		
digit	손가락 한자리숫자(0~9)	discreet	분별 있는 주의 깊은 신중한 careful
dismissal	해고 해임		
disposition	소질 기질	disavow	부인하다 거부하다
defendant	피고	disparage	헐뜯다 비난(비방) 하다
diploma	학위증	destitute	빈곤한 곤궁한
dissect	해부하다	dearth	부족 결핍 (= lack)
deft	능숙한 skillful	dormant	잠재적인 inactive latent potential

derive	얻다 획득하다 (= get) 기원(유래) 하다(be derived from)	exact	정확한 accurate correct precise
disparage	깔보다 얕보다 헐뜯다 비방하다	equitable	공평한 impartial fair unbiased
dusk	해질무렵 = just before dark	exaggerate	과장하다 overstate
decipher	해독하다, 암호를 풀다, 번역하다 = decord	exhilarating	유쾌한 cheerful glad
discord	불일치, 부조화 = disagreement, disharmony	exorbitant	과도한 터무니없는 excessive extreme
didactic	가르치기 위한, 교훈적인	evacuate	피난시키다 = remove
dribble	똑똑 떨어뜨리다 = trickle	effuse	발산하다 유출하다
dawn	새벽, 여명 = daybreak, first light of day 시작, 기원 = beginning, birth	exonerate	용서하다 무죄로 하다
		equilibrium	균형 평형상태
distract	(주위를) ~에서 흩뜨리다, (딴 곳으로) 돌리다	expound	상세히 설명하다 explain in detail
demography	인구통계학	elucidate	설명하다 밝히다
disconcert	당황케하다 = embarrass, baffle, confuse, puzzle	expository	설명의 해설의
		elapse	(시간이) 경과하다
disparage	깔보다, 얕보다, 헐뜯다, 비판하다 = censure. condemn, reprove, reproach, reprimand	extinct	불이 꺼진 소멸한 멸종한(= die out)
		entrust	맡기다 위임하다
desultory	일관성 없는, 산만한, 주체를 벗어난, 목적 없는 = unmethodical	exclusive	배타적인 독점적인
		expedient	임시방편 수단 편법
deal with	~을 처리하다, ~에 대처하다 = treat, cope with	exploit	공 위업 착취하다 착복하다
dote on	지나치게 귀여워하다 by dint of ~의 힘(덕) 으로 ~에 의해서 cf) dint 힘 폭력	equitation	승마 마술 horsemanship
		epigraph	비문 비명 제명 인용문 inscription
		ethology	원인론 병인학 cause

E

ease	천천히 움직이다 move carefully	emulate	경쟁하다 다투다
		elaborate	정교한 공들인 정성 들여 만들다
ease oneself	안심하다	exquisite	정교한 매우아름다운
eligible	자격을 주다 entitle empower qualify	explicit	명백한 뚜렷한 definite
eliminate	제거하다 exclude remove rule out	eclectic	절충적인 취사선택하는 not choosing
eloquent	감명적인 능변인 persuasive	exalt	높이다 승진시키다
		equator	적도
embryo	태아 (= fetus) (식물의) 눈 싹 a flower bud	entomology	곤충학 study of insects
enigma	수수께끼 puzzle riddle	engross	~에 몰두하다 열중하다
		elegant	우아한 세련된
entail	포함하다 involve include embrace contain	edible	먹을 수 있는 식용에 적합한 ↔ inedible
equivocal	모호한 ambiguous doubtful uncertain vague ambiguity	exotic	이국적 정취가 나는 외래의
		expedient	편리한 convenient
extirpate	근절시키다 eradicate remove abolish annihilate	elusive	포착하기 어려운
		easygoing	태평한 안이한 손쉬운 relaxed
essential	본질적인 indispensible vital fundamental basic	entrepreneur	기업가 사업가

512

encyclopedia	백과사전 전문사전		

encyclopedia 백과사전 전문사전
ecology 칭찬 찬사 찬양
praise

extraneous 본질에서 벗어난 무관한
연고가 없는
irrelevant

evacuate 피난시키다 철수시키다
expire 끝나다 만기가 되다
cease to be effective   be due

enigmatic 불가사의한
mysterious puzzling inexplicable

emancipation (노예) 해방 이탈
exclusively 배타적으로 독립적으로
epitomize 요약하다 발췌하다
expedition 탐험 개발
eccentric 보통과 다른 괴상한 괴짜인
strange odd queer peculiar
bizarre abnormal anomalous

eclipse (해, 달의) 식
solar & lunar

extant 현존하는 잔존하는
surviving existing

expeditious 급속한 신속한
prompt rapid

enticing 유혹적인 매혹적인
ⓥentice = attract

elasticity 신축 탄력성
resilience flexibility

empiric 경험적인
relaying on observation or experiment
not on theory

elicit 끌어내다 유도하다
emissary 사자 연락관 밀사
messenger

extract 뽑다 추출하다
derive pull out

eleemosynary 자비로운, 자비의
= charitable, generous

extol ~를 칭찬하다
epoch 시대 = age, era, period
encompass 에워싸다 = surround
enthrall 매복시키다
exacerbate (병을) 악화시키다
(사람을) 노하게 하다
격분시키다 = aggravate

ethnocentric 민족중심주위의
자기문화중심주위의

eclipse (명성,영광의) 실추, 떨어짐
elude (이름, 기억이) 생각나지않다
even 평활한 규칙적인 한결같은
level, smooth, regular, equal

keep an eye ~을 감시하다
= watch

get even with ~에 보복하다
take revenge on

few and far between 극히 드물게 적은
very few

F

feeble 연약한
weak frail

female horse 암말
mare

fervent 열렬한
ardent

figurine 작은 상
small statue

firsthand 직접적인
direct ↔ secondhand indirect 간접적인

fix 수리하다
repair mend

flank 옆구리
side

frank 솔직한
candid outspoken

flatter 아첨하다 매우칭찬하다
praise too much

flaw 결점
blemish defect fault shortcoming
drawback

flexible 유연한 휘기 쉬운
적응성이 있는 유순한
elastic pliant

fluorescent 빛나는
luminous luminescent

foliage 나뭇잎
leaf

follow ~에 따르다
ensue(잇따라~이 발생하다) obey

foremost 으뜸가는, 맨 먼저의 수위의, 주요한
leading, major, main

fraternal 형제의 우애의
brotherly

frugality 절약 검소
economy thrifty

futilely 헛되이
in vain fruitlessly

furthermore 더더욱
moreover in addition
foolproof = completely safe

facility 쉬움 수월함 편의 편의시설
facile : 손쉬운 용이한

fatal 치명적인 (= lethal)
운명의

faculty 능력 재능 교수진
fury 격노 격분
rage

foul 더러운 부정한(↔ fair)
disgrace(불명예 치욕)

folk 사람들 서민의 일반대중
가족 친척 부족 민족

forfeit 상실하다 몰수되다
frigid 추운 냉담한
fake 가짜 위조품

figment	가공의 일 허구
frustrate	좌절(실망) 시키다 쳐부수다
fallacy	오류
figurative	비유적인
frost	서리
fidelity	충실 충성 성실
fusion	유해 융합 통합 합침 union
fabric	직물 천
forlorn	고독한 버려진 자포자기의 desperate
flint	부싯돌
fraud	사기 기만 deceit
foster	기르다 양육하다 촉진하다 조장하다 promote further encourage
flunk	실패 낙제
failure	실패하다 낙제점을 따다 단념하다 그만두다 give up
feasible	실행할 수 있는 (= practicable) 가능한 (= possible) 적당한 (= suitable) 그럴듯한 (= plausible)
fortitude	용기 불굴의 정신 강한 참을성 인내
formidable	무서운 굉장한 가공할
facet	한 면 국면 양상 aspect phase
felicity	지복 경사 행복 bliss grace
foremost	맨 먼저의 최초의 주요한 principal leading
fallacy	잘못된 생각 (= misbelief) 오류 궤변(sophism)
fragrance	향 냄새 scent perfume
fairly	1) 공평히 완전히 2) 꽤 상당히 적당히 rather considerable respectable
fertility	비록, 다만, 번식력, 생산력 cf) fertility rate 출산율
forestall	(미리) 저지하다, 막다 = prevent, deter
flat	불경기의, 활기없는, 부진한 = inactive
flamboyant	현란한, 화려한 = showy
ask a favor of	~에게 부탁하다
do a favor for	~에게 은혜를 베풀다
fret over	초조하다 안달이 나다 worry about
get to first base	1루에 나가다 조금 진보하다 제 1보를 성취하다 have any success whatsoever

G

guilty	죄를 범한 culpable(culprit: 범법자) criminal ↔ innocent
genuine	사실의 authentic real actual factual ↔ 허위의 false counterfeit
germane	~와 밀접한 관계가 있는 relevant pertinent
grasp	이해하다 comprehend
garment	옷 의복 의상
guise	변장 외관 가면 겉치레 appearance
garner	저축 저장(하다)
genial	따뜻한 다정한 상냥한 cheerful delightful amusing kind amiable affable cordial friendly congenial amicable benign
genteel	상류사회의 좋은 집안에서 자란 품위 있는 well-bred
gifted	재능이 타고난 talented
grumble	불평하다 투덜대다 complain
gregarious	사교적인
grim	엄격한 호된 모진 severe stern
gratuitous	이유 없는 불필요한 정당성이 없는 무료의 무상의
gay	명랑한 쾌활한 활기찬 lively merry vivacious animated 색이 밝은 = bright
glare	섬광 = very harsh light
graze	(가축) 풀을 먹이다 풀을 먹다 = feed
grueling	지치게 하는, 기진맥진하게 하는 = exhauting
gruesome	오싹하는, 소름끼치는 = macabre, appalling
gush-out	솟아나는 뿜어 나오는
go in for	~을 좋아하다
get cold feet	겁먹다 도망칠 자세를 취하다 become timid
go far	대 성공하다
draw a (the) over	용케 꾸미다 속이다 veil
green light	(공식) 허가 permission approval go-ahead

H

havoc   대파괴 대황폐 혼란
devastation ruin destruction disorder
chaos confusion
cf) upheaval : 대변동 격동

hallowed   신성한
sacred holy
↦ 세속의 : profane earthy

handy   편리한
convenient
cf) come in handy : 언젠가는 필요해지다

hang-over   잔존물
surving trace

haphazardly   아무렇게나
randomly at random

harry   약탈하다
plunder loot sack

hate   미워하다
detest abhor loath

heed   주의하다
pay attention to

heredity   유전적 특질
genetics

hesitant   망설이는

heterogeneous   이질의

homogeneous   동질의
same kind

hiatus   벌어진 틈
gap

hideous   무서운
horrible frightful grim
추한 ugly

hitch   걸다 연결하다
fasten connect hook

hatch   부화하다

hostile   적대적인
antagonistic unfriendly

heyday   전성기
golden age

hermitage   은신처 피난처
refuge shelter

humdrum   평범한 단조로운
repetitious

heresy   이단 이교 전제

histrionic   배우의 연기의
theatrical

hefty   무서운 억센

habitat   거주지 서식지
dwelling place

hilarity   환희 유희
↦ 비극 : tragedy

heal   고치다 치료하다

humbug   사기 속임

hoodlum   깡패 건달
gangster hooligan

hoard   저축 저장(하다)
store up

hilarious   명랑한 쾌활한 재미있는

hence   그러므로
as a result

horrendous   무서운 끔직한
terrible

hydrophobia   광견병 공수병

hermit   은둔자 수도자 속세를 떠난 사람

harpoon   작살

hostage   인질

horror   공포 전율 혐오 증오
ⓐhorrible

hollow   속이 빈 공동의
↦ solid

hail   환호하여 맞이하다
인정하다 큰소리로 부르다
acclaim

humanity   인류 인간성 인도
cf) humanities 고전문학 인문과학
liberal studies(일반교양과정)

haughty   오만한 거만한 건방진
arrogant

harsh   호된 거친 사나운 모진 혹독한
severe

hypocrite   위선자

hoop   테
ring

hub 중   심 중추

harness   ~에 마구를 채우다
(자연력을) 동력화하다
이용하다, 조절하다
= control

hIV   인체면역결핍바이러스
human immune-deficiency virus that
cause aids

how goes it ? / not so bad
요즘 형편이 어떻습니까?
잘 되갑니다

hold back   억제하다 자제하다
suppress

hang on   전화를 끊지 않다 (고 기다리다)

hang up   전화를 끊다
방해하다

hit the books   열심히 공부하다
study hard

cool one's heels   (면회, 면담 등을 하려고)
오래 기다리다
= waiting for a long time

I

identical   동일한
same exactly alike congenial

idle   게으른
indolent lazy slothful sluggish inert

idol	우상
idolized	우상화하다
	worship
ignore	무시하다
	overlook disregard neglect
illegible	읽을 수 없는
	↔ legible : 읽을 수 있는
immediately	즉시
	at once in no time right away
	right now (현재 또는 미래시제와 함께)
	cf) right down : 노골적인 (= downright)
impartial	공정한
	unbiased fair disinterested indifferent
impending	임박한
	coming
imperceptible	알아볼 수 없는
	unnoticeable
imprudent	경솔한
	rash ↔ 신중한 : prudent wary
impudent	무례한 건방진
	insolent
incessant	끊임없는
	uninterrupted unceasing ceaseless
	constant continuous
incompetent	무능한
	unable incapable
industrious	부지런한
	diligent assiduous hardworking
inevitable	피할 수 없는
	unavoidable
initiate	시작하다
	start
inscribe	새기다
	engrave
integral	전체적인
	↔ 간헐적인 : periodically on and off
intrigue	음모
	cabal plot scheme
introduce	(논거 따위를) 내놓다
	bring up
invaluable	대단히 귀중한
	priceless precious
iterate	반복하다
	repeat
improvise	즉석에서 해내다 즉흥연주를 하다
	invent without preparation
insert	끼워 넣다 삽입하다
	place put locate
incompatible	양립할 수 없는 모순된
	not in harmony with each other
	exclusive (배타적인 독립적인 ~을 제외하다)
intricate	복잡한
	complicated complex (ed)
induce	꾀다 유도 (유발) 하다
integrity	완전무결 성실 정직 청렴
incentive	자극 동기
irrevocable	취소할 수 없는

inference	추리 추론
immortality	불변 불멸
	ⓐimmortal
intangible	손으로 만질 수 없는 무형의
imperishable	불멸하는
impose	부과하다 강요하다
invalidate	무효화하다
	countervail
impulsive	충동적인
installment	할부 월부
innate	타고난 천성적인
innovation	혁신 쇄신
infuriate	화나게 하다 격분시키다
	angry
impetuous	(바람, 속도) 격렬한 성급한
	충동적인
	(= rash)
impromptu	즉석의 즉흥의
	unrehearsed
insomnia	불면증
	↔ sleep
impetus	힘 추진력 자극
	energy
improvise	즉흥연주를 하다 즉석에서 하다
	invent without preparation
inhale	빨아들이다
	↔ exhale 내뿜다
intrepid	두려움이 없는 대담한 용감한
	fearless
irritable	성급한 성마른 애태우는
	irascible touchy peevish
	petulant grouchy
inept	부적당한 어리석은 서투른
introvert	내성적인 내향적인
	reserve
insolent	거만한 (= arrogant)
	무례한 (= rude impudent)
impede	방해하다
	hinder
intact	본래그대로의 손대지 않은
	완전한 처녀의
intrigue	음모
	conspiracy cabal
incremental	증대 증강 증진
intake	흡입구 (량) 섭취량
intelligible	이해할 수 있는
intellectual	지적인 이지적인
intelligent	지적인 총명한 영리한
	overindulgence 지나친 방임 방종 멋대로 굶
indulge	만족시키다 충족시킨
	(+ in) 빠지다 탐닉하다
implicit	은연중의 함축적인 암시적인
implement	도구 기구 비품 수단 방법
	tool
impoverish	가난하게 하다 곤궁하게 하다

ingredient	성분 원료 재료 구성요소
intrude	간섭하다 말참견하다
	끼어들다 방해하다
	be in the way
irrigate	물을 대다 관개하다
implacable	달래기 어려운 화해할 수 없는
	vindictive
integrity	고결 성실 청결 완전무결
inherent	본래부터 가지고 있는
	고유의 타고난 선천적인
	inborn innate hereditary inherited
	congenital intrinsic
incisive	예리한 예민한 기민한
	shape
ingenious	재능있는, 영리한
	= clever
inquisitive	호기심많은
	= curious
impair	손상시키다, 해치다, 악화시키다
	= weaken, damage
incidence	발생률, 범위, 빈도
	= occurrence
implacable	달래기 어려운, 화해할 수 없는
	용서 없는
informally	비공식적으로
	= unofficially

J

jeopardy	위험
	risk danger peril
jealous 질	투심이 강한
jerk	급격한 움직임
	갑자기 끌기 abruptly pull
juvenile	젊은 어린 소년 (소녀) 의
jurist	법학자 변호사
jubilant	좋아하는 기쁨에 넘치는
judgement	판단 견해
	opinion point of view

K

keen	날카로운
	shape acute poignant
knavery	불법 (부정) 행위
	iniquity
kidnap	유괴하다
kindergarten	유치원
kinetic	운동의 활동력 있는
keep up one's act	눈가림하다
	deceive people

L

lure	유혹하다
	allure decoy attract tempt seduce
laconic	간결한
	brief concise
	↔화려한 : pompous (잘난 체하는 뽐내는)
languid	나른한
	faint feeble listless exhausted
league	동맹
	alliance confederation union
levy	부과하다
	impose (+ on)
liabilities	부채
	debts
liable	책임 있는
	responsible answerable accountable
lower	줄이다
	reduce decrease diminish lessen
ludicrous	우스운
	ridiculous comical funny
labyrinth	미궁 미로
	maze
landscape	풍경 경치
locomotive	기관차
likelihood	가능성
lottery	추첨 복권
leap	뛰다 껑충 뛰다
lateral	측면의 옆의
	sideways
load	지배자 군주
legacy	유산 재산
	property inheritance heritage
lethargic	혼수상태의 무기력한
	활발하지 못한
	sluggish
legendary	전설의 믿기 어려운 터무니없는
loathe	~을 싫어하다 혐오하다
	dislike
linger	지체시키다
	(아쉬운 듯이) 남아 있다
	꾸물거리다
	delay going hesitate
lofty	높은 치솟은
	high
lenient	관대한 너그러운
	다정한 느슨한 가벼운
let up	느슨해지다 그치다 멈추다
by and large	대체로 대개
for the life of me	아무리 노력해도 (…않다)
	try as I may
turn over a new leaf	마음을 돌리다
	새 생활을 하다
	begin a new life

M

mortify 굴욕감을 주다
humiliate insult lose face
억제하다 subdue restrain

meager 빈약한
scanty deficient insignificant thin poor

meditate 숙고하다
contemplate reflect ponder

medium 매개물
means

meticulous 꼼꼼한 신중한
careful precise prudent

modification 수정 변경
alteration change

moisture 습기
humidity dampness
↔ 건조함 : dryness aridity

mold 형성하다 만들다
shape manufacture form make

momentous 중요한
consequent serious important

momentary 일시적인
temporary

mourn 슬퍼하다
grieve lament deplore bewail

munity 반항 반란
revolt uprising rebel

monumental 기념비의 불후의 엄청난
outstanding

meddle 참견하다 간섭하다

mutual 상호의 공동의
reciprocal

mandatory 명령의 강제적인

motto 좌우명 표어

mortician 장의사
undertaker

mushroom 버섯 급속히 생기다

methodize 조직화하다

morale 사기 의욕

mendacious 거짓의 허위의
ⓝme mutter 중얼거림 불평

mock 조롱하다
scorn

menace 위협하다
threat

majesty 장엄 권위 폐하 왕
nobility

modesty 겸손
↔ complacent 자기만족의

miracle 기적

menace 위협하다
threaten

mandate 명령 지시 지령
order

mundane 현세의 속세의 보통의
ordinary

meteorologist 기상학자

millenium 천년 천 년간의

masculine 남성의 남자의 힘센 용감한
↔ feminine

mimic 흉내 내는 모방의 모의의
imitated

mediocre 평범한 보통의

metaphor 은유
cf) simile 직유

mobilize (군대, 함대를) 동원하다
전시체제로 바꾸다

maxim 격언 금언
saying

memento 기념물 추억거리

marvel 놀라운 일 (것, 사람) 경이
wonder prodigy miracle

malevolent 악의 있는 심술궂은
spiteful malign malicious hostile
unfriendly vicious cruel

misdemeanor 경범죄
cf) felony 중죄

face the music (자진하여) 어려움을 받아들이다
당당히 비판하다
가벼운 벌을 받다 = accept punishment

in a muddle 어리둥절한
confused mess

move haven and earth 온갖 일을 다 하다
~하기 위해 전력을 다하다
do everything possible

N

nap 잠깐 눈을 붙이다

novelty 신기함 새로운 것
newness

navigator 항해자
seafarer

nominate 지정하다 임명하다

norm 기준 표준

namely 즉 다시 말하자면

nullify 무효로 하다

nostalgia 향수 향수병
homesickness

nay 부정 반대 아니 아니오 no
↔ yea 긍정 찬성 실로 참으로 indeed

naive 순진한 천진난만한 경험 없는

notion 개념 관념 의견 이해력 의향

nightmare 악몽
bad dream

in round number 대충 어림셈으로 대략
roughly

O

obfuscate	흐리게 하다 obscure
onset	시작 start beginning
	공격 attack assault
obese	살찐
	excessively overweight fat stout
obsolete	구식의 시대에 뒤떨어진
	antiquated ancient
	archaic anachronistic
	out of time out of date
	↔ novel : 신식의 새로운 소설
obstinate	완고한
	stubborn unyielding obdurate inflexible
	dogged
	head-strong
offend	화나게 하다
	displease
outrage	화내다
	anger
ominous	불길한
	threatening foreboding of bad amen
oriental	동양의
	eastern
occidental	서양의
	western
originate	시작하다
	start spring emanate initiate
otherwise	그렇지 않다면
	if ~ not
outright	솔직한
	frank candid outspoken direct
overrule	뒤집다 번복하다
	reverse
overwhelming	압도적인
	triumphal
omnipotent	전능한
overcast	흐린
oblivious	잊은 잊어버리고 있는
overtake	따라잡다 꾸밈
opulent	풍부한
	affluent ample plentiful copious
obedient	복종하는 유순한
ordeal	시련 고된 체험
objective	객관적인
orator	연설자 웅변가
overdue	학수고대하는
obliterate	지우다 말살하다
	erase
oath	맹세 서약 (법정의) 선서
	take (swear/make) an oath 맹세/선서하다
outdo	~보다 낫다 능가하다
	excel
outcome	결과 과정 성과
	result

OECD	경제협력기구
	organization for economic cooperation and
	development
outline	~의 윤곽, 약도를 그리다
	~의 대요를 말하다
	개요를 설명하다
	summarize (요약하여 말하다)
obsolescence	노폐 (화) 노후 (화) 진부화 퇴화
outlying	동떨어진 외진
	remote
ostensible	표면상의 겉치레의
	apparent outward seeming feigned
take an order	주문받다
give an order	주문하다
only a few	불과 소수만
	several

P

proscribe	금지하다
	ban
prescribed	규정된 확실한
	certain
prescribe	규정하다 처방하다
prevalent	널리 보급된 유행하는
	widespread
propriety	예의바른
	decency
premise	전제 주장 근거
	assumption
presume	가정하다
	assume suppose
prowess	용기 용감 무용
proliferate	증식하다 번식하다
prolific	다산의 비옥한
	fertile fruitful productive
	↔ 불모의 : barren sterical bleak
protract	연장 (연기) 하다
	lengthen extend prolong procrastinate
	delay
	postpone defer adjourn
pastoral	전원의
	rustic or rural life
peculiar	색다른
	strange queer eccentric unique
penetrate	침투하다 스며들다
	permeate pierce puncture
permanent	영구적인
	constant lasting perpetual everlasting
	unceasing
pertinent	적절한 (= suitable)
	관계있는 (= related) 딱 들어맞는
plausible	그럴듯한
	reasonable specious
plenary	충분한
	full

predominant	유력한
	prevalent prevailing
prelude	서곡
preliminary	예비의 시초의 서문의
prize	소중히 여기다
	cherish esteem value highly
prodigal	낭비하는
	lavish extravagant wasteful
	↔ 절약하는 : abstinent thrifty economical frugal
prodigious	거대한
	huge colossal gigantic tremendous
profound	심원한
	deep serious
punctual	정각에
	on time
pundit	학자 박식한 사람
	savant
	cf) ⓐ erudite
puzzle	당황하게 하다
	bewilder perplex confound confuse
pressing	절박한 긴급한
	urgent
parliament	국회 의회
predilection	편애 역성
precursor	선배 선임자 선구자
precedent	전례 판례 관례
placid	평온한 침착한
	quiet
parley	토의 회견 회담 (하다)
	discussion
phase	단계 국면 양상
	aspect
progeny	자손
	offspring
propaganda	광고 선전 유언비어
perversion	왜곡
	distortion
plebeian	평민의 시민의 대중의
	folk
predicament	곤경 궁지
proclaim	선언하다 공포하다
	declare
provoke	자극하다 화나게 하다 유발시키다
patent	전매특허 특권
prestige	명성 위신
pupil	학생 제자 미성년자
predator	약탈자 육식동물
paternal	아버지의 세습의
purposefully	고의로
	deliberately
primarily	주로
	principally mainly chiefly
potable	마시기에 적합한
	drinkable
portable	휴대할 수 있는

pause	휴지 중지 중단 한숨돌림
proficient	숙달된 능숙한
	skillful
posthumously	사후의
	after the person has died
plaudit	박수 갈채 칭찬 찬사
peninsula	반도
province	지방 지역
parrot	앵무새
pensive	생각에 잠긴
	thoughtful
provocative	자극적인 ~을 유발시키다
palace	궁전 왕궁
portray	그리다 묘사하다
pace	(생활의) 속도 the pace of life
patron	옹호자 지지자
	advocate
pollinate	수분하다
perch	앉다
	sit
preface	서문
provident	선견지명이 있는 신중한 검소한
	thrifty
painstaking	근면한 성실한 수고
precipitation	투하 낙하 강우량
	rainfall
poll	투표 선거 여론조사
phenomenal	현상의 굉장한 놀라운 불확실한
	불안정한 위태로운
	믿을 수 없는 남에게 의존하는
perfunctory	형식적인 피상적인
postulate	가정하다
	presume
perish	썩어 없어지다 사라지다 썩다
	die
pervade	~에 널리 퍼지다
	고루 미치다 보급하다 스며들다
	ⓐ pervasive
pertinent	타당한 적절한
	proper
prey	먹이 희생
pseudonym	익명 아호
perennial	연중 끊이지 않는
	여러해 계속되는 영원한
	perpetual eternal everlasting endless
	ceaseless permanent
plunder	약탈하다
	despoil loot rob steal
predominant	뛰어난 탁월한 현저한
	눈에 띄는 우세한 압도적인
	overwhelming
polemic	논쟁 논박
penance	참회 회개 속죄 벌
	penalty

pious	경건한 신앙심이 있는
	↔ blasphemous 불경스러운 모독적인
phobia	공포병 (증)
precarious	불확실한
	dubious uncertain ↔ certain
posterity	후손
	descendant
	↔ ancestor forefather
prompt	1) 신속한 기민한
	2) ~을 자극하다 유발하다
	motivate stimulate
philander	(여자를) 희롱하다
	cf) altruist 이타주의자
pristine	원래의 원시적인 초기의
	original primitive
ponder	고려하다 숙고하다
	consider think over
purely	완전히 순전히 순수하게
	exclusively
prerogative	(일반적인) 특권
predatory	약탈의
	plundering robbing
perfume	향기
	scent
pecuniary	금전상의 재정적인
	monetary financial
prune	(가지, 뿌리 등을) 잘라내다
	(불필요한 부분을) 제거하다
	(비용을) 삭감하다 줄이다
	cut back reduce shorten
pass out of existence	소멸하다
	disappear
pull one's leg	~을 속이다 놀리다
	tease
on pins and needless	흠칫하는
	마음을 졸이는
	very anxious
pass up	무시하다 거절하다 간과하다
	reject
to the point	적절한 요령 있는
	relevant
play-wright	극작가
	dramatist

Q

quiver	진동 떨림 흔들리다
	vibrate
queue	열 줄 행렬
quote	인용하다
out of the question	불가능한
	impossible
out of question	의심의 여지가 없는
	unquestionable

to the quick	골수에 사무치게
	가슴 아프게 살아있는 것처럼
	deeply

R

ravage	황폐하게 하다
	ruin devastate destroy
ration	배급하다
	allot apportion distribute meat out
reason	추론하다
recollect	기억하다
	recall remember
reconcile	화해하다
	appease make up
recover	회복하다
	regain restore retrieve get over
refuse	거절하다
	decline reject rebuff turn down
reluctant	싫어하는
	unwilling disinclined loath averse
remorse	뉘우침 후회
	regret contrition
renowned	유명한 인정받는
	acclaimed
	ⓝ renown : 명성 유명
resolve	결심하다 (to do~ on~ing)
	determine decide
	해결하다 solve settle
	용해하다 disintegrate analyze separate
retard	지연시키다
	slow delay impede (방해하다 저해하다)
reveal	나타내다
	disclose divulge unveil
resent	분개하다 화나다
repeal	폐기 철회 취소 (하다)
recess	휴식 휴가 중단하다
renounce	포기하다
	relinquish
repent	후회하다 뉘우치다
	regret
rally	다시 불러 모으다 규합하다
rupture	파괴 결렬 불화
renovate	~을 새롭게 하다 혁신하다
rigid	단단한 엄격한
rage	분노 격노
	fury
resiliency	신축성
revenue	소득 수입 수입원
revolt	반란 반역 폭동 반감
relegate	퇴거하다 추방하다
reckon	세다 계산하다
	calculate
ruthless	무정한 무자비한
	merciless

rescind	철폐 폐지하다 무효로 하다 취소하다 annul
respective	각자의 개개의
respectable	훌륭한 존경할만한
respectful	정중한 경의를 표하는
respecting	전) ~에 관하여
rudiment	기본 기초 초보
rigorous	엄격한 호된 정확한
rash	분별없는 경솔한 성급한 imprudent
recognition	인지 인정 승인
riot	폭동 소동
rear	후방의 뒤 기르다 양육하다
reiterate	반복하다 repeat
refuge	피난 보호 은신처
refugee	피난 자 난민 망명자
reliable	신뢰 (신용) 할 수 있는 의지할 수 있는 틀림없는 trustworthy
respite	연기 휴식 유예 일시적 중지 lull
repel	~을 쫓아 버리다 격퇴하다 repulse drive back
revise	개정 (교정/수정) 하다
relic	유적 유물 잔재 remains remnant
rehabilitate	복원하다 restore improve the condition
reverence	숭배 경의 존경 ↔ disrespect
radical	근본적인 기본적인 급진적인 과격한
reclaim	교정하다 재생하다 개간하다 ⓝ reclamation = recovery
rampant	마구 퍼지는 만연하는 과격한 맹렬한
respiration	호흡 한번 숨 쉼 호흡작용 breathing
residual	나머지의 찌꺼기의 잉여의 ⓝ residue
reciprocal	상호의 mutual
repugnant	비위에 거슬리는 불쾌한 싫은 반항하는
raucous	(목소리가) 귀에 거슬리는 거친 쉰 harsh rough unpleasant
radically	급진적으로 drastically
relent	마음이 느긋해지다 누그러지다 become lenient

resonant	반향 하는 울리는 메아리치는 vibrant echoing
round up	(가축을) 우리에 가두다 (사람을) 체포하다 arrest
at random	닥치는 대로 임의로 목적도 없이 aimlessly
run-down	초라한 황폐한 old and broken shabby

S

sapient	지혜로운 아는 체하는 smart
swerve	벗어나다 이탈하다 커브를 틀다 turns sharply
sip	홀짝이다 한 모금 drink it slowly a little at a time
sporadic	때때로 일어나는 산발적인 occurring at irregular intervals
summon	소환하다 call for bid convene convoke
sanguine	붉은 빛을 띤 red 쾌활한 cheerful buoyant laminated spirited
school	단련하다 타이르다
season	맛을내다 양념하다
sentient	감각력이 있는 capable of feeling
serene	고요한 calm tranquil placid peaceful undisturbed ⓝ serenity = calmness
shabby	초라한 worn-out ragged beggarly poor
shading	그늘 점차적인 변화 small variation
silly	어리석은 foolish stupid senseless witless
simultaneously	동시에 concurrently concomitantly at once at the same time
situation	장소 location position site place spot
secrete	~을 분비하다
secret	비밀의
skim	대충 훑어보다
look at it quick	마른 thin slim slender lean ↔ 뚱뚱한 : thick fat obese
slacken	완화하다 relax abate relieve mitigate lessen slow up alleviate allay assuage soothe
sluggish	느린 게으른 inactive slow lazy slothful indolent inert

somnolent	졸리는 sleepy drowsy			

somnolent   졸리는
     sleepy drowsy

specific   명확한
     definite

specious   그럴듯한
     plausible reasonable

standardize   표준화된
     uniform

stubborn   완고한
     hard to deal with obstinate persistent
     rigid head-strong stiff dogged

sublime   숭고한
     noble lofty honorable

surprise   놀라다
     astound astonish amaze startle

suspend   연기하다
     postpone delay defer put off

susceptible
liable to   민감한 ~에 영향 받기 쉬운
     : ~에 걸리기 쉬운
     cf) liable for : ~에 책임을 저야 할

sack   해고하다
     dismiss

slumber   잠자다

segregation   차별 분리 격리

sovereign control   주권행사

substantiate   구체화하다 열망 우려 걱정
     care

solitude   고독 독거
     seclusion
     ⓐsolitary 고독한 외로운
     lone

stagnant   정체된 불경기의 부진한

segment   단편 부분 분절

sedentary   앉은 채 있는 앉아서 일하는

steer   조정하다

surfeit   과음 과식

speculate   심사숙고하다
     ponder muse brood meditate

scrutiny   정밀조사 감시 감독

stern   엄격한

stunt   위축시키다 발육을 방해하다
     retard delay hinder impede

spook   도깨비 유령

stipend   수당 봉급 급료 장학금
     compensation

sole   오직 하나 독신의
     미혼의 발 (신) 바닥 구두창

steep   터무니없는 지나친
     excessive unreasonable

salvage   구출하다 해난구조
     (침몰선을) 인양하다

summit   정상 꼭대기
     top

strand   좌초시키다

superficial   피상적인 표면적인
     사소한 하찮은
     shallow trivial

supersede   바꾸다 대신하다
     replace

splendid   찬란한 웅대한

sincere   순수한 진지한 성실한

skeptical   의심 많은
     not convinced

status   지위 신분

spontaneously   자발적으로 넘어지다
     비틀거리다 실수하다
     실패하다

solace   위로 위안
     consolation

subsistence   생존 현존 존재 생활

shiver   몸서림 떨림 전율 오싹하게 함
     tremble

split   자르다 쪼개다 찢다 분할하다
     cut

specious   허울 좋은 그럴듯한

senior   연장자 선배

shrewd   약삭빠른 영리한 빈틈없는
     clever astute

sojourn   머무르다 체류하다 살다

stigma   치욕 오명 낙인 불명예
     disgrace

stun   기절시키다

strife   소란 소동 혼란

surpass   능가하다 초월하다
     go beyond outstrip

seclude   분리하다 격리하다
     ⓐsecluded 격리된 은퇴한 인가에서 멀리
     떨어진 외딴 한적한
     remote concealed hidden lonely
     sequestered isolated

submerge   물속에 잠그다 잠기다 잠수하다
     underwater

subtle   미묘한 예민한 날카로운 교활한

shrug   (어깨를) 으쓱하다

strive   (+ to do) 노력하다

sentient   지각력 (감각력) 이 있는
     emotional

scrupulous   빈틈없는 면밀한 양심적인
     신중한 현명한

synchronic   최고의 최상의 가장 중요한

subdue   정복하다

superfluous   여분의 남아도는 불필요한
     redundant needless

suburb   교외 근교

speculate   숙고하다 사색하다 추측하다
     guess

sphere   ①구체 구 구형
     ball
     ②분야 영역
     realm scope field province area
     ③하늘 창공
     sky

sanction	인가 인정 재가 approval endorsement
stenographer	속기사
stationary	움직이지 않는 정지된 변화하지 않는
symmetry	좌우대칭 균형 valance
shun	피하다 avert avoid
salable	팔기에 적합한 수요가 맞는
superstitious	미신적인 미신에 사로잡힌
staunch	신조가 철두철미한 확고부동한 완고한 충실한 튼튼한 견고한 steadfast
spurn	쫓아버리다 내쫓다 퇴짜놓다 경멸하다
scan	~을 자세히 조사하다 세밀히 조사하다 scrutinize examine survey inspect
synthetic	종합적인 합성의
span	한뼘 짧은길이 잠시 잠깐 걸치다 걸리다 cover
slaughter	도살 학살 butcher massacre kill
smudge	더러움 얼룩 (= smear)
sneer	냉소 조소
suffrage	투표 선거권 참정권 찬성투표 동의
spurious	가짜의 위조의
stiff	뻣뻣한 rigid inflexible
stir	~을 휘젓다 감동시키다 지극하다 stimulate motivate prompt
squander	낭비하다 헤프게 쓰다 lavish waste exhaust dissipate
stock	혈통 가계 계보 lineage
soundproof	방음 (의) impermeable to noise
sequence	연속 결과 순서 반복진행 progression
slash	자르다 삭감하다 cut whittle split shear
on the spur of moment	충동적으로 당장의 without previous thought
save one's face	체면을 세우다 avoid losing one's diginity preserve one's dignity
such as it is	별것은 아니지만 poor as it is
stand by	① (말등을) 지키다 remain faithful to

	② 준비하다 ③ 앞에 서있다
stick to one's gun	입장을 고수, 고집하다 물러서지 않다 stand by one's gun serve one's turn (필요, 요구, 목적 에) 충족시키다 소용이 되다 suit one's purpose
make a scene	큰 소동을 피우다 한바탕 소란을 떨다 (심하게) 말다툼 하다 have a violent argument
by the skin of my teeth	겨우 간신히 아슬아슬하게 with the narrowest margin
seek to	~하려고 애쓰다 노력하다 try to endeavor to strive to
stand a chance of	~의 가망 (승산) 이 있다 =have the possiblity of
stack up against	~에 필적하다 compare with
shift into	~로 전환하다 convert into
a rough sketch	개략도 소묘
stand up for	~을 옹호하다 depend
soak up	빨아들이다 흡수하다 absorb
set off	(폭탄을) 폭발시키다 출발하다 trigger

T

tenet	주의 교의 교리 doctrine
thrash	마구 때리다 beat
trash	쓰레기 잡동사니
trivial	사소한 하찮은 trifling petty slight insignificant unimportant negligible
tantalize	애태우다 torment torture vex 괴롭히다 집적거리다 tease
tedious	지루한 dull tiresome irksome wearisome boring
temporary	일시적인 transient transitory
tenacious	집요한 강인한 persistent
terminate	끝내다 end finish close complete
trait	특성 character feature characteristic
tranquility	고요함 peacefulness serenity calmness

transform	바꾸다
	change alter convert transmute
treat	(음식을) 대접하다
trepidation	공포 두려움
	fright fear terror panic
triumph	이기다
	win succeed prevail victory
taciturn	말없는 무뚝뚝한
	silent
	↔ talkative 수다스러운
	loquacious voluble garrulous
trenchant	날카로운
	shape incisive harsh caustic biter
tiffin	점심
taboo	금기
tenant	차용자 소작인
trigger	방아쇠 발사하다
	일으키다 유발하다
	cause
tertiary	제3의
	third
tenable	공격에 견딜 수 있는
	방어할 수 있는
	지지 (변호) 할 수 있는
	= tolerable
travail	산고 진통 고생
tornado	회오리바람 폭풍
tepid	미지근한 열의 없는
	lukewarm warmish
turmoil	투쟁 싸움 다툼
treachery	배반 반역
tentative	시험적인 잠정적인 임시의
	temporary
tacit	무언의 침묵의 묵시적인
	implicit
tidy	말쑥한 말끔히 정돈된
	정연한 청초한
	neat
tyranny	전제정치 폭정 포악 학대
treason	반역 (죄) 모반
thwart	훼방 놓다 방해하다 좌절시키다
	frustrate prevent stop impede obstruct
	hinder hamper stymie
turbulent	몹시 거친 난폭한 소란스런
travail	수고 노고 고통
	toil pain
tantamount	동등한
	equal equivalent
timber	재목 목재
	wood lumber
tryout	시험 검사
	test audition

talk back	말대꾸하다
in token of	~의 표시 (증거) 로 no stock in
	~을 신용치 않다
	믿지 않다 do not believe
on the threshold of	~의 시초에
	at the beginning of
throw away	버리다 없애다
	discard remove eliminate trash abolish
take down	적어두다
	record write down

U

uncomely	아름답지 못한 꼴불견의
	ugly
upgrade	개선 (개량) 하다 품질을 높이다
	improve
ultimate	궁극적인 final last extreme
	근본적인 fundamental
unanimous	만장일치로
	of one's own accord of one mind
uncouth	거친
	awkward clumsy rude
	↔ 세련된 : refined
unfold	펼치다 드러내다
	expend reveal open
universal	보편적인
	general entire ecumenical
unrest	불안
	disorder
upbringing	양육 교육
	education
upheaval	격변
	violent disturbance
utterly	전적으로
	completely entirely absolutely
utter	온전한 철저한 절대적인
	말을 하다 발언하다
underlie	~에 기초가 되다 ~의 아래에 있다
ubiquitous	어디에나 있는
utilitarian	실용적인 공리적인
upright	직립
	vertical
uproar	소란 야단법석 고함 무질서
	tumult commotion shouting yelling
	disorder dishurbance
	confusion chaos
urgent	긴급한 절박한
	pressing
under the weather	몸 상태가 좋지 않은 sick
	↔ above the weather

V

verbatim 축어 적으로 말 그대로
word for word

vender 판매원
be engaged in selling

vanish 사라지다
disappear cease fade
go out of the sight

vacuous 공허한
empty

vanity 자만심
excessive pride

velocity 속도
speed rapidity swiftness

versatile 다재다능한
mand-sides

vogue 유행
fashion style mode popularity

vague 모호한

vest ~ in 주다 수여하다

verify 입증 (확증) 하다

vigil 불침범 철야 밤샘
watch

vulgar 서민의 통속적인 저속한

vehemence 격렬 맹렬 열심 열정
@vehement 열렬한 열광적인

validity 정당한 타당한 유효성

vertical 수직의
perpendicular

verify 입증 (증명) 하다

vulnerable 상처입기 쉬운
공격받기 쉬운 영향 받기 쉬운
susceptible

veterinary 가축병 치료의 수의 (학) 의

vindictive 복수심이 있는
원한을 품은 앙심 깊은

valor 용기 용맹 무용

veteran 노련가 숙련공
old hand skilled worker

vanity 허영 (심) 덧없음 무익한

vicissitude 변화 변천 부침 흥망성쇠
alteration inconstancy instability
uncertainty

vault ①둥근 천장 아치
②뛰다 도약하다
jump over leap spring

vociferous 큰소리로 외치는
시끄러운 떠들썩한
loudly clamorous strident

vessel 용기 그릇 배 도관
boat

W

want 원하다 궁핍해지다
decline

water 물을 주다

weary 피로한 싫증난
exhausted fatigued tired wearied

wary 주의 깊은 세심한
조심하는 신중한
cautious meticulous careful

well-to-do 부유한
well-off wealthy rich

whit 조금
bit

withdraw 후퇴하다 인출하다
retire retreat secede take out

wither 시들다
fade shrivel decay decline wilt languish

warranty 보증 담보 보증서

wholesome 건강에 좋은 건전한

weird 이상한 초자연적인

weep 울다 비탄하다

wicked 사악한 부정의

wager 노름 내기 내기에 건 것 (돈)
내기하는 사람 (경쟁자)
bet

waste one's breath 허튼 소리 하다
speak pointlessly

in the wake of ~의 뒤를 따라 ~에 뒤이어
following

without reserve 거리낌 없이 솔직히
frankly

Y

yet = but

Z

zenith 정점 절정 전성기 천장
(↔ nadir) pinnacle
cf) at the zenith of ~의 절정에 달하여